amilies in Britain

Families in Britain

British Family Research Committee

Foreword by Peter Laslett

Contributions by Jane Aldgate, Roger Ballard, Jocelyn Barrow, Lucy Bonnerjea, Jacqueline Burgoyne, David Clark, Michael Collins, Jack Dominian, Geoffrey Driver, David Eversley, Michael Fogarty, D. Gowler, Brenda Hoggett, Brian Jackson, Daphne Johnson, Bill Jordan, K. Legge, Ruth Lister, Andrew McCulloch, Muriel Nissel, Ann Oakley, Robin Oakley, Roy Parker, Rhona Rapoport, Robert Rapoport, Barbara Rodgers, Nancy Seear, Neil Smelser, Ziona Strelitz, Malcolm Wicks, Peter Willmott, Phyllis Willmott, Harriett Wilson

Routledge & Kegan Paul
London, Boston, Melbourne and Henley

First published in 1982
by Routledge & Kegan Paul plc,
39 Store Street,
London WC1E 7DD,
9 Park Street,
Boston, Mass. 02108, USA,
296 Beaconsfield Parade,
Middle Park,
Melbourne, 3206,
Australia, and
Broadway House,
Newtown Road,
Henley-on-Thames,
Oxon RG9 1EN.
Reprinted in 1983 by
Redwood Burn Ltd, Trowbridge, Wiltshire.

Library of Congress Cataloging in Publication Data
 Main entry under title:

 Families in Britain.

   Bibliography:p.
   Includes index.
   1. Family--Great Britain--History--Addresses, essays,
lectures. 2. Family policy--Great Britain--Addresses,
essays, lectures. 3. Quality of life--Great Britain--
Addresses, essays, lectures. 4. Minorities--Great
Britain--Addresses, essays, lectures. I. British Family
Research Committee.
HQ613.F35 1982   306.8'5'0941   82-7690
  ISBN 0-7100-9236-9   AACR2

Families in Britain

Contents

Preface

The Family Research Committee is a consortium of Institute Directors who have combined forces to stimulate an awareness of issues in the field of family research. For sound policy as well as improved quality of family life, research-based knowledge is essential, and toward this end the Committee has taken two initiatives.

The first was to establish a Study Commission on the Family under the Chairmanship of Sir Campbell Adamson. This is an independent body set up under a grant from The Leverhulme Trust to disseminate information about research on the family and to stimulate media and public discussion of issues.

The second was to assemble this collection of scientific papers under the editorship of Robert Rapoport, Michael Fogarty and Rhona Rapoport.

Many individuals and groups have helped and encouraged us in this effort. Particular thanks are due to the Nuffield Foundation for supporting a workshop conference, and to the Policy Studies Institute for crucial support, both material and moral.

Jack Dominian
Michael Fogarty
John Pinder
Rhona Rapoport
Robert Rapoport
Michael Young

Foreword

Peter Laslett

Families in Britain in the 1980s find themselves in the wake of the following far-reaching changes in the structure of society.   The first is a century-long fall in fertility. This has reduced the number of the average mother's offspring to something below the two and a little more which is required for replacement.   It has also brought about a truly formidable rise in the proportion of the elderly and aged, making the British population one of the oldest which has ever existed.

The second is the ending of a necessary interconnection between regular and habitual sexual pleasure and sexual fulfilment on the one hand, and the responsibilities of procreation on the other hand.   This consequence of highly efficient contraception and its spread throughout the whole population has altered our sexual comportment and the bond between spouses, altered them irreversibly.

The third is the introduction into our society of a substantial number of people not born into 'British' families, though a high proportion was born in Britain.   Many or most of them have been brought up in family systems which are different, some of them very different indeed, from the Christian, predominantly Protestant, monogamous, nuclear model. This had prevailed almost universally in our country until the 1950s and for an unknown number of generations before that, perhaps for as far back as our knowledge is ever likely to go.

In the present winter of 1982 it is tempting to add a fourth fundamental change.   Such is the final cessation of that rapid rise in the national wealth which is associated with successful industrialisation.   This began in Britain 250 years ago and, after notable vicissitudes in the 1920s and 1930s, proceeded during the 1950s and 1960s, during what may now seem to be its final stages, at a particularly rapid pace. By national wealth I intend to convey not only its total sum, but the amount available to each and every family group and individual.

It may turn out to be wrong, of course, to suppose that any of these processes is now at an end.   It could be that the means of subsistence and of self-enhancement available to Britons will begin to go up again later in this decade.   The resources available for redistributions by the State would then increase as well, and it is known that social transfers are easier to institute under such circumstances, likely to diminish when they are absent.   Birth rates could certainly pick up again in Britain, as they did in the 1950s, if not very dramatically.   Immigration might possibly be resumed. Divorce could conceivably begin to fall in its incidence, after the steep and continuous rise of the last twenty years or so.   It is even just imaginable that the secular growth of leisure, and expenditure on leisure, will be interrupted.

It seems to me, nevertheless, that under all possible circumstances it will be the effects on families of the profound and irreversible social changes I have listed which will have to be taken into account.   Each of the studies in the volume analyses one or other aspect of the impact which they have had on the British family, its composition, constitution, behaviour, affective life, socialising and supportive functions.

It has immediately to be added that 'The British Family' is *not* the phrase to use, but a phrase consciously to abandon. For there is now no single British family, but a rich variety of forms, states, traditions, norms and usages, a plurality which it is one of the major objects of this collection to underline.   And this in a country which, as far as we can yet tell, has had until quite recently and over many centuries, a greater homogeneity by region and a greater continuity over time than any other national society, in all matters to do with kinship and family life.   Nevertheless, the historical sociologist feels bound to add that not all the circumstances pointed to as novelties, sometimes as alarming novelties, in this collection are in fact without precedent, or indeed without earlier solutions, in British familial history as it is now becoming known.

It is insisted again and again in these studies, and quite appropriately, that the stereotype of family group consisting of father, mother and at least two residing children, young children, is entirely misleading in contemporary Britain.   A majority of our households now consist in solitaries, people living with persons not their relatives, couples (married or unmarried) without accompanying offspring, or single-parent households.   To these have to be added the even less 'familially' disposed individuals maintained in institutions, a small

but woefully expensive minority. When Britain was still a
pre-industrial society, however, something like 30 to 35 per
cent of all groups were constituted in the same way, and among
the solitaries and the few in institutions, a high proportion
were the old and very old, just as is the case in the 1980s.

Our contributors draw our attention on many occasions, as
indeed they should, to the great and growing number of illegitimate children in Britain and to the very widespread flout-
ing of the 'Christian' marriage rule which forbade sexual
relationship outside marriage. Yet is has recently been
estimated that between 20 and 40 per cent of all first conceptions have always taken place before marriage in England, that
the 'Christian' marriage rules were never obeyed with anything
like universality and that traditional, even respectable
sexual conduct was never quite what the morally minded have
supposed.

This is especially true of that class of personally
upright, socially responsible late Victorians who founded our
tradition of social enquiry. They would, no doubt, have been
surprised to learn that during the early years of Victoria's
reign, regarded by them as it is by us, as the apogee of familial correctness and solidity, the illegitimacy level was
higher than it had been for at least 300 years, indeed the
highest ever recorded until the late twentieth century, and
that this was *not* due to industrialisation or urbanisation. (1)

It is entirely right, therefore, that our book should contain a study written by Neil Smelser on The Victorian Family.
The attitudes and assumptions conveyed by that evocative
phrase decidedly do stand behind the statements made here
about the tendency of British families in the 1980s, even if
they also serve to mask and distort the actual situation in
Victorian times, and to come between ourselves and familial
history in the longer term.

That the longer term, and the wider horizon, are gradually
establishing themselves in studies of this kind is quite evident from the repeated references in what follows to parallel
positions and policies of other nations in Western Europe, and
in high industrial societies everywhere. We should never
forget as we read about ourselves as we are now, that the
German population, east and western, has an age structure
which is even more top-heavy than the British; that Scandinavians have developed a sexual and procreative behaviour far
less 'Christian' than our own; that all economically and
technically advanced countries are under pressure to receive
additions from economically and technically less advanced
countries, with actual and potential familial consequences
similar to those which we experience. The singularity of our

own position in the 1980s is in the extent of recent immigration from cultures and areas so very dissimilar from traditional Britain, and in the severity of the check to the expected growth of economic resources.

The student of social structure over time can only be
uneasy after having committed himself to so abbreviated an
historical analysis. Of course, the huge rise in divorce,
and the increases in illegitimacy and in single-headed households cannot be accounted for by the simple citation of the
separation of sex from procreation. Of course movements in
opinion and conviction have to be taken into account, other
than the virtual disappearance of religious beliefs and practices. The most important is perhaps the movement for
women's liberation.

Of course political ideology and its vicissitudes have to
be allowed for as we contemplate the attitude of scarcity
towards welfare in our present decade in contrast to the attitude of plenty which prevailed from the 1940s to the 1960s.
Here the historian remembers, however, that changes of this
order have certainly happened before. There was the inter-
lude in the late 1800s, for example, when the champions of the
personal dignity of those in need against being treated as
objects of charity, did their best to abolish the perennial
responsibility of the State for the maintenance of the elderly, for the support that is to say of the greater part of the
whole population above 60 years of age. (2) The unintended
and quite inverse outcome was the institution of Old Age Pensions in 1908, and finally the foundation of what we delight
to call the modern British Welfare State.

In spite of all that has been enunciated here in the way of
deep-seated change in fmailial matters during our own life
times, the attitude and expectations of the writers of this
book seem to have a noticeably traditional cast. They remind
me of nothing so much as the on-the-whole kindly, well-dis-
posed neighbours and fellow villagers or townsfolk who took on
themselves the responsibility for running the Old Poor Law,
before the year 1834. Bumbledom, bullying, ignorance of the
outside world, and shortsightedness there were, and meanness
too, though in the 1980s we cannot be so confident that we are
free of meanness either. But what those eighteenth-century
amateurs and officials possessed above all was that, so it
seems to me, the familial expert and the family welfare worker
would most like to possess in our day, really thorough knowledge of the people they were dealing with and what these
people wanted, how they could be helped. And on the standards of their time it could be said they had the wherewithal
to carry out what they knew was necessary.

Not so today. But intimations from the past will not

solve our present predicaments, however significant they may
be to those who recognise that we understand ourselves historically.   'Families in Britain' is about our own decade,
however we may feel that we shall stand in comparison with the
past.

NOTES

1 For these facts about sexual nonconformity, see 'Bastardy
   and its comparative history', 1980, p. 55, etc., and for
   figures making possible comparisons in questions to do
   with family composition, status of household heads, position of the old, the widowed, etc. in traditional England,
   see 'Household and family in past time', 1972, both published by the Cambridge Group for the History of Population and Social Structure.
2 Work of David Thompson, research student with the Cambridge Group.

Part I

International perspectives

Chapter 1

Family policy — international perspectives
Michael Fogarty and Barbara Rodgers

There has been in the last few years, as a Hungarian participant in a recent seminar on families and family policy
said, (1) 'an international contagion of ideas' on family
policy. It is world wide, but in a book about families in
Britain it is best to focus on the experience of countries
with a broader comparable background of European tradition and
industrialisation. In one or two of these countries explicit
family policy goes back to the 1930s, notably in France and
Sweden. A number of countries still have none; among others
Canada, the USA, Israel, Denmark, Ireland and the UK. Since
the Second World War, however, the number of countries with
explicit policies has steadily grown in both Western and Eastern Europe, while in others such as the UK the question of an
explicit family policy has at least been raised.

There are three general reasons for this development. The
first has been practical experience with the development of
social policies in individual fields. Even where these policies were not in the first place geared to the family unit as
such, understanding has grown of the importance of the family
as an intervening variable in applying them.

The family is obviously a demographic unit. It has a spatial dimension, and needs in terms of housing, community
design, transport and communications. It is an economic unit
whose composition and functioning affects the distribution of
incomes, expenditure patterns, the supply of workers to the
labour market and the accumulation and transfer between generations of economic assets such as homes, capital, economic
know-how and networks of contacts for opportunities of employment and enterprise. Unpaid service and mutual aid within
the family constitute a major addition to the real national
income, and often are or may be a substitute for public expenditure. Families are social and psychological units, which
influence their members' personality, impose roles on them,

3

and provide them with more or less free space for social
interaction.   They are cultural and educational units, with
an influence extending across generations.   They are in many
ways political units, power bases from and through which their
members operate, often with a link to their role in holding
and transmitting economic assets, and capable often of standing out against and constituting a challenge to the dominant
ideology of their society.

   To ignore these roles of the family as an intervening variable is likely to mean that social policies will fail to
fulfil their authors' intentions, and not only because of
shortcomings in individual policy fields.   As mediated
through the family, policies are interrelated and may either
reinforce or contradict each other.   They and their impact on
and through families have to be considered comprehensively,
and so there arises the problem of machinery for doing this.

   Secondly, the family itself can no longer be taken for
granted.   It has become characterised by diversity and
change.   The 'traditional' family might once have been
thought of as a black box into which influences could be fed
in the expectation that predictable and fairly uniform reactions would follow, without necessarily understanding the processes through which this came about.   It is an interesting
historical question whether the traditional family ever or
anywhere was quite what tradition made it out to be.   Supposing however that it was, it has now largely gone, and not only
in the regions and districts of most obvious social change.
In Damian Hannan's study of 'Traditional Families?' - the
question mark is significant - in rural Ireland in the 1970s a
main problem was to find regions or families 'traditional' in
the sense described by Arensberg and Kimball only a generation
before. (2)   Family patterns and structures have everywhere
been exploding into a variety of new relationships.   Migration, as Chapters 7 to 9 have illustrated, has imported into
Britain as into other countries patterns and structures from
other societies, often contrasting sharply with native practice as it has recently evolved.   If the effects which follow
policy measures are to be accurately predicted, the changing
contents of the black box now have to be explicitly and systematically examined.

   Thirdly, in one country after another there has emerged a
family lobby, including both people or organisations concerned
for the family and, especially in France and Belgium, organisations *of* families themselves, in effect family trade unions.
Among contributors in the former category have been social
service organisations, women's movements, movements on behalf
of children, and churches and church-related political and
social movements such as the European Christian-Democratic

parties. Social Democratic parties have tended to start from
a concern with general problems such as poverty, and to come
more slowly to concern for the family unit as such, but still
to reach it in the end. In a number of countries individual
writers and research workers have had a significant influence,
for example the Myrdals and their successors in Sweden, or the
role of the Rapoports in originating the Study Commission on
the Family in Britain. Specialised research institutes have
appeared, such as those in Britain represented in the Family
Research Committee. The family lobby has nowhere as yet
acquired the political weight of major interest groups such as
the trade unions. A Polish comment, for example, is that in
that country family research, though influential, still tends
to be isolated from the mainstream of social discussion and to
be 'by women for women'. (3) But in more and more individual
countries, and internationally through the International Union
of Family Organisations or the Committee of Family Organisations in the European Community (COFACE), the family lobby has
today become significant enough for politicians to need to
reckon with it.

These are general factors, whose incidence varies from one
country to another according to historical circumstances,
ideologies and the pressure of current problems. It would be
surprising if Marxists and Christians, liberals and traditionalists, or groups concerned with poverty, with women's and
children's rights, or with the maintenance and development of
national or group cultures approached family policy in the
same way; nor do they. Family policies are like other policies, however, which once started, have a dynamism of their
own. Looking across countries, it is possible to see a range
of common questions and at least some degree of convergence
towards their answers.

POPULATION PLANNING

Population is a continuing theme in family policy in both
Western and Communist countries, but one whose contents have
tended to change and converge. Pure and simple natalism,
such as was characteristic of many of the founders of French
family policy around the time of the First World War, has
tended to give way, even in countries still concerned about a
fall or inadequate growth in their population, to more modest
policies aimed at marginal increments to the 'normal' family -
encouragement for the second and third children needed for replacement - rather than special encouragement for 'large'
families of more than three.

One reason for this is that some developed countries are no

longer in any case as alarmed as in the 1930s and 1940s at the possibility of a declining population. (4)   The same trend shows itself, however, in France, or Israel, or some Communist countries which do still have this concern.   In France, for example, concern about the population flared up at the end of the 1970s, and was focused through a Commission headed by Evelyne Sullerot.   The target for the new policies which emerged remained, however, not 'large' families, but the third child. (5)

Swedish experience illustrates particularly clearly some of the reasons leading to this.   A clearly marked turning point was reached through the work of two successive Population Commissions in 1935 and 1941.   They originated at a time both of concern over a possible fall in the population and of high unemployment, and therefore suggestions that married women should leave the labour market.   'At this juncture', in Alva Myrdal's words,

> Anything could have happened.   The remarkable thing is that, at the crucial moment, the nativity argument was wrested from the hands of the anti-feminists and turned instead into a new and effective instrument harnessed to women's aspirations.   The earlier debate on the married woman's right to work was transformed into a fight for the employed woman's right to marry and have children. (6)

Large families were not to be disfavoured, but family policy must be consistent with women's rights and opportunities, outside as well as in the home, and with the abolition of child poverty and deprivation.   The practical balance sought implied that most women in fact have relatively small families, and that any adjustments in the interest of population growth should be marginal.

A similar balance has tended to emerge in the Communist countries.   Some of these, particularly the Soviet Union and East Germany, experienced massive population deficiencies as a result of war or, in East Germany's case, emigration.   Right across Communist Eastern Europe conditions and policies just after the Second World War put severe pressure on families and led in several countries to what was regarded as a dangerous drop in fertility.   It is, however, a central Marxist principle that neither women nor the family can reach their full potential unless women have a full role outside as well as in the home, and particularly in work.   Measures taken to promote population have never been allowed to interfere with this, and the practical result has been very similar to that in Sweden and other countries of the West.

One problem in all countries has been to establish what effect measures in support of population growth actually have. Evaluation depends on ability to predict what would have

happened in these measures' absence, and on this the present
state of demographic studies is summed up in the sub-title of
a recent British paper on The Certainty of the Uncertain
Future. (7) Experience both in the Communist countries and
in the West suggests one hypothesis applicable to conditions
such as have been emerging in both. In present intermediate
conditions in the developed countries, where women are expected to have a role outside the home, but neither the symmetricality of sex roles nor systems of community care for children
or of provision for home care costs are as yet fully developed, family size tends towards a ceiling; few women are
likely in any case to have more than three children. It is
possible for pressures to build up which will lead to women to
have fewer than this number of children, and in that case
measures to relieve these pressures will let the birthrate
spring back towards the ceiling; Czechoslovakia is an interesting example. (8) At that point, however, there is a kink
in the curve of response, and whether natalist pressures will
persuade any substantial number of women to go beyond the
ceiling becomes problematic.

INDIVIDUAL RIGHTS, EXTERNAL PRESSURES AND FAMILY FUNCTIONING:
THE RE-DEFINITION OF MEN'S AND WOMEN'S ROLES

The time and energy of family members are a limited resource,
which has like any other resource to be economised and used to
the best advantage. It can be under-used: too little use of
and support for extended family networks, under-use of the
capacities of 'traditional' housewives, too little counter-
action to the 'flat tyre' phenomenon in middle-aged marriages, (9) or a tendency, as country studies often comment,
for public policy to drain away from families functions which
they could usefully perform. It can be unevenly and unfairly
used, for example through overload on single parents or on
family members with special responsibilities for the elderly
and disabled. It can also be overloaded and over-used in a
more general way by adding to families' internal activities a
growing range of individual members' outside interests in work
and leisure, in the way illustrated by British studies such as
'Dual Career Families' or 'The Symmetrical Family' (10) and in
Chapter 20. Some families have the health, money and capacity to take the resulting strains, but many do not.
    Imbalances like these could be and were built into tradi-
tional patterns of family living. What is new today, looking
across countries, is the extent to which they arise from the
pursuit of new patterns of living, with immediate short-term
advantage to individual family members, but with less regard

than in the past to their effects on family functioning, and
in particular to the risk that they may result in overload.

The Communist countries of Eastern Europe learnt a particularly sharp lesson about this just after the Second World War.
Their policies at that time were hostile to the family in its
traditional form and role.   They were also characterised by
'economism', that is by a strong accent on production and work
relationships, with very little on what could properly be
called social policy.   The resulting 'propaganda model' of
the family, as summarised for Poland by Kloskowska, (11)
tended to limit the family's role 'chiefly to procreation' and
to lay heavy stress on 'activities outside the family and work
activities on the part of both husband and wife, of parents
and children'.   This model could have damaging effects on
fertility, (12) but also proved to damage more generally families' capacity to meet their members' needs in ways which
public opinion and Communist governments themselves thought
desirable.   By the end of the 1950s a strong reaction against
it developed.   In Poland the new 'propaganda model' laid its
main accent on:

> Expressive and integrative functions, and therefore on the
> role of the family and the socialisation and self-expres-
> sion of individuals.   It rested on the principle of indi-
> vidualisation of inter-personal relationships.   The senti-
> ments of the spouses and of parents and children were
> assigned a high value in it. (13)

In Hungary, Czechoslovakia and East Germany there came to be a
new accent on families' need for psychological space, (14)
'time for free time' and the opportunity to provide care and
warmth, (15) and on the practical value of families for child
care and affective formation. (16)

At the centre of the discussion about functioning and possible overload is the question of family care for children and
the disabled, particularly the former.   Though national policies on child care differ, there is one substantial element of
consensus.   By different routes, both Communist and Western
countries have come to agree that it must include substantial
elements both of community care (over and above basic provision for education) and of care in the family.

Communist countries can still be divided into hard-liners,
such as the Soviet Union and German Democratic Republic, which
start from a strong presumption in favour of community care,
and others such as those just mentioned which lay more stress
on the family's expressive and integrative role.   Both groups
have highly developed systems of care at kindergarten age, but
as regards younger children economics speaks its own language
even to the hard-liners.   Adequate care for children under
three is expensive, and even the GDR has found it advisable to

offer mothers of a second or later child a full year of paid maternity leave. (17)   The soft-line countries go further. Hungary, for example, offers all mothers up to three years' maternity leave, with protection of their job and social security rights, twenty weeks' full pay, and a flat-rate benefit for the rest of the period. (18)

Western countries have tended to come to the same point by the opposite route, starting, except to some extent in Israel, from a presumption in favour of family care.   Over the years there has emerged general acceptance of the value of preschool education and related day care for children aged three or over, on educational grounds as well as to meet the needs of single-parent families and those with parents earning.   In France, Belgium, the Netherlands and Israel enrolment of preschool children aged three to five in pre-school programmes reaches 90 per cent or more.   Provision for children under three has, however, tended to be much more hesitant, and to be geared more to labour market needs and the special needs of the poor and deprived. (19)

Other strands in the discussion are care of the disabled and elderly and, generally, the need for 'time for free time' if the family is to play its part as 'a centre for sentimental relations, sociability, and solidarity' (a French comment), and if its members are to be free to contribute to informal networks of friendship, neighbourhood and mutual aid. (20) What is common to all strands is that, if responsibilities like these are to be met, some member or members of the family must give time and effort to do so.   Whose time and effort is it to be?

Traditionally, the time and effort in question were women's, but women are now claiming equal access to the labour market and other outside interests, and their right to it is increasingly recognised in family and general law.   Some things can be done to relieve the pressures which result. Community care can be extended further, but subject to the economic pressures which have made even the East Germans set limits.   Men can be involved more in their families; but men too, as 'The Symmetrical Family' shows, tend to increase their outside commitments substantially as their education and standard of living rise.   Counselling services can help families to cope more effectively.   Western families have a major advantage compared to the Communist countries in the wider range and better quality and availability of consumer services and domestic equipment in a free market.   But in the end, if pressures build up, something has to give, and in practice, as occupational and earnings statistics and time budgets show, this still tends everywhere to be women's opportunities outside the home.

There are two main policy models for dealing with this situation. One is to accept, explicitly or implicitly, that this is a 'women's question', and to look for a solution by making it easier for mothers who wish to spend more time with their families to do so - by extended maternity leave, for instance, or leave for sickness and other family problems, or part-time work - or for employed women to pay for home help or alternative child care. Israel has a forthright policy on the former lines; no serious challenge to women's traditional role as housewives, nor any major attempt to ensure full equality in employment, but a massive and successful series of measures to enable women to combine work in the labour market and at home. France has come by stages to a more formally neutral policy, intended to offer women an equal choice between caring for their children themselves and working outside. A means-tested 'complément familial' is payable where there is a child under three or else three or more children, and can be used either to enable one parent to stay at home or to pay for child care if both work. In France as in Israel, however, the choice is still usually and primarily one for the wife, and involves no direct pressure to change the husband's role. In practice, if not in theory, the policies of most Communist countries likewise leave the responsibility for reconciling child care with outside roles primarily to women.

Treating the problems of combining domestic and outside roles as a 'women's question' may or may not be acceptable to women. In Israel, for example, it seems to have proved consistent with a high degree of felt equality. Poland still tends to be a country where women's status is seen as different but equal. But certainly this is not the same thing as achieving symmetricality in the family. The second policy model, whose best illustration is Sweden, aims for symmetricality directly.

The keynote of the debate on sex roles which arose in Sweden in the 1960s was rejection of the idea that women have a special home-making role not shared by men. In the words of the Swedish Government's 1968 report to UNESCO on 'The Status of Women in Sweden':

> The goal for a long-range programme of women's rights must be that every individual, regardless of sex, shall have the same opportunities not only for education and employment but also fundamentally the same responsibility for child upbringing and housework. (21)

One practical expression of this, under a law of 1974, is 'parenthood insurance', applicable equally to women and to men. Parents in employment are now entitled to divide as they see fit nine months of child-care leave, during which they receive 90 per cent of their normal earnings, and fifteen

days a year of leave to care for sick children.   They can
also use child-care leave to supplement part-time work.   Only
10 per cent of eligible men used child-care leave in 1976,
though more used leave for sick children.   The principle of
equal opportunity and responsibilities, however, was established by the law of 1974, and progress towards the practical
realisation of equality, or better of symmetricality, is
backed by powerful pressures in politics, the trade union
movement, education and women's movements.   Other practical
inducements remain in discussion, for example a general cut in
working hours either for all workers or for parents with young
children, or provision that part of the months of child leave
may be claimed only by the father.

The Swedish model is far from being fully realised in practice, but raises at the level of principle one of the largest
issues which family policy in other countries has still to
face.   Given that even a formally neutral policy like that of
France, since it leaves families free to arrange their division of labour, still tends in practice to lead to a division
of family responsibilities on relatively traditional lines:
is it, or is it not, right to follow the Swedish example and
force the pace towards full symmetricality?   The drift particularly of Western family policy has been towards recognising a wide range of family patterns as equally acceptable and
a matter for partners' own choice.   Is there, however, in
fact a case for replacing the traditional stereotype of the
family, not with variety, but with a new stereotype, and for
recognising the symmetrical family as *the* pattern for the
future?   Is neutrality enough?

Actually, this is a double issue.   One part of it is about
symmetricality: how desirable is this as a universal pattern?
The other is about the autonomy of families.   However desirable this, or any other, major change in patterns of family
living may be, how far are governments or other wider social
agencies justified in overriding families' own preferences in
the matter, and what degree of pressure are they entitled to
use?   We return to this wider issue below.

EXTENDED NETWORKS - WHOM DOES FAMILY POLICY CONCERN?

When considering families' resources and their use, it is
obviously important to decide who is to be included in the
family; and when considering family policies it is important
to consider their gaps as well as what they currently contain.
One of the curious features of recent discussions of family
policy in Western Europe and North America is that they often
have to be searched with a microscope to discover references

to the problems and possible contributions of post-parental
families, unless as disabled people for which 'the family' may
care, or as a convenient external agency for child care on a
level with child minders or community crèches.   There is a
common turn of phrase which illustrates this.   To quote it in
a French version, a committee of the Commissariat du Plan was
discussing the allocation of social expenditure.   'Have we
not', said one member, 'done enough for the elderly?   Ought
we not to be giving priority to the family?' (22)   Family
policy, as currently understood, focuses overwhelmingly on
families with dependent children.

But should it?   Middle-aged and elderly members of families have problems and potential of their own, arising out of
their marital relationships or from adjustment to new phases
in their life and marriage cycle, and with long-term as well
as immediate consequences;   for instance an impact on their
capacity to manage the transition to retirement. (23)   They
also continue to form part of extended family networks, running to and from the very elderly as well as towards children
and grandchildren, and make a substantial contribution to
them.   Research in a number of countries has shown the continuing strength of these networks and their value for material help, the transmission of values and attitudes, and generally for social relationships within the family.   Grandparents, as one American study points out, can be closer in
some respects to their grandchildren than either are to the
intermediate generation. (24)   An Irish study finds a direct
two-way relationship between the modernisation and economic
strength of farming in what were once the traditional peasant
communities of Connaught and Ulster and the strength of
extended family networks. (25)   Chapters 7 to 9 reinforce
considerations like these from the experience of 'ethnic'
families in Britain.   Extended networks play a large part in
family life in the societies from which Asians, Cypriots and
West Indians have come.   Migration disrupted these networks,
at least temporarily, and life in British conditions has modified them.   They continue however to play an important though
changing part in providing support for wives, a framework for
bringing up children, a positive role for the elderly, a means
of maintaining cultural identity, a refuge against hostile
outside pressures and help in avoiding family disruption or
minimising its effects.   For Asian and Cypriot families, in
particular, the extended family is also an economic asset.

If, however, one asks what thought has been given to all
this in developing family policies in industrialised countries
of the European tradition, the answer is 'very little'.   One
major issue is about the physical linking of extended networks.   'Intimacy, but at a distance', a comment from an

Austrian study, (26) sums up a general view.   Each generation needs its own living space, psychological as well as material, but on terms which encourage a continuing relationship between the generations; and, given the right conditions, the physical distance can be great.   A study of American families which moved to Cape Kennedy in connection with space research programmes shows how extended family networks continued to function in spite of separation by hundreds of miles. (27)   A condition of this, however, was the generous American supply of cheap telephones and road and air transport.   How best, in the less affluent conditions of other countries, can housing, transport and telecommunications policies be managed to achieve comparable or better results?

The shape of extended networks themselves is changing, with both positive and negative results.   As the age of marriage and the size of nuclear families fall and the expectation of life rises, networks become narrower but also deeper.   The four-generation family, including young grandparents who reach that status in their early fifties and while there are still survivors from the previous generation, is in any large numbers a new phenomenon, and one whose implications have still to be fully explored.   There are different styles of grandparenting. (28)   Which of them are appropriate in which cases, bearing in mind that young grandparents themselves, women as well as men, are now likely still to be fully engaged in working life, and that as pension charges and the proportion of the very elderly rise there is an increasingly recognised case for removing conventional retirement limits - as American legislation has already done - and extending working life towards age 70?

The fall in the size of nuclear families means that grandparents' interest is focused on fewer children and grandchildren, and so more intensely on each, and in turn that there are fewer descendants to volunteer for and share the care of the very elderly and disabled of the older generation.   Grandparenting can in any case have its negative side. Polish as well as British studies illustrate the damage which can occur when grandparents become over-involved with their children's and grandchildren's relationships, particularly where this involvement is forced by inadequate alternative provision for child care. (29)   The narrowing and more intensive focusing of extended family networks can increase the risk of damage of this kind, and also that of severe pressure on descendants and their families where only one descendant is available to care for an elderly disabled person.

Both these possibilities raise questions about community care.   Moroney (30) notes for Britain that the proportion of the elderly living in institutions has fallen sharply since

the beginning of the century, and that families show little
sign of unwillingness to take care of their elderly members;
also that there is a risk that in a case like this supply may
create its own demand, and that expansion of community care
may tempt families to give up responsibilities which otherwise
they would readily fulfil.   But how much of this type of responsibility can those family members on whom it falls most
heavily be reasonably expected to stand?   And, if institutionalisation is to be a last resort, is adequate alternative
support being provided direct to families?   As regards both
ascendants and descendants, is there a case for thinking that
the contribution of the young-old to the welfare of other
generations is at present channelled too narrowly through
their immediate family networks?   Should young-old grandparents and other members of the middle generation be encouraged to make more of their contribution through non-family
channels, as 'substitute grandparents' or through other forms
of social service or mutual aid?

The continued effective functioning of extended 'ethnic'
families in Britain is in some ways a special case, interesting, but not necessarily offering much guidance for the
majority of families in the mainstream of native tradition.
The initial poverty and other difficulties of immigrants, the
wish to maintain minority cultural and religious traditions
and the pressure of racialist attitudes in the wider community
have all played their part in it.   There are, however, other
features of 'ethnic' networks which could be cultivated to
more advantage in mainstream families as well.   Some, such as
the role of extended family networks in developing family
businesses or in providing personal and economic support in
times of strain, are more strongly rooted versions of what
happens in mainstream family networks already.   One feature,
however, is especially distinctive.   In the mid-1970s around
9 per cent of all families in Britain with dependent children
were single parent, but among Asian families this proportion
was just 1 per cent.   Though breakdown among Asian families
is increasing, 'unsupported mothers among this group are
extraordinarily rare'. (31)   Where family disruption and
provision for child maintenance are concerned, the negotiating
procedures and sharing of responsibilities in Asian family
networks, as described in Chapter 7, have worked to remarkable
effect: among other things to the advantage of the British
taxpayer by way of reduction in claims for supplementary
benefit and re-housing.

Questions about issues like these are raised here in a very
general form because they have nowhere as yet been as fully
explored as those which follow from the movement for equal
opportunity for women in parental families.   There is an

obvious practical case for concentrating family policy first on parental families, because that is where specifically family issues have become most clearly defined and early action can follow, and incidentally there are legal responsibilities between family members such as arise to only a very limited degree in the extended family; and for leaving the problems of post-parental families to be dealt with in the different, not necessarily or particularly family-centred, context of a category such as 'the elderly'. That is the course which countries generally have followed. In the long run, however, this dichotomy is likely to prove unsatisfactory, for the circles of policy for the elderly and for young-child families overlap. The extended family, including the contribution made by its older members, is highly relevant to the resources and welfare of parental families, and vice versa. The 'family', in its full and natural sense, still has meaning for families at all stages of their life-cycle from formation to dissolution. Couples of any age, whether or not they currently have dependent children, are still families with problems and potential specific to their family relationship, including their own marital relationship as well as their relationships with an extended family. There is a dimension here which family policy needs still to acquire.

THE RIGHT OF THE FAMILY TO AUTONOMY: THE FAMILY AS A POWER BASE

Families, as was said at the beginning of this Chapter, are among other things a power base. In one sense that is a politically neutral comment, and encouragement of the family's autonomy in decision making would be generally accepted as desirable. Families like other social groups grow in responsibility according to the responsibilities which they are expected and enabled to take. To take Moroney's point again, in the grey area where family and community responsibilities overlap a great deal will depend on whether the community encourages and helps families to take their own responsibilities or, instead, offers them convenient ways of shedding them. In the public sphere, it makes a difference whether it is the national tradition, as in Britain or the Netherlands, to leave the promotion of family interests to movements on behalf of families, or, as in France and Belgium, for families to become active participants through associations which they organise themselves.
   But there is also another more controversial issue about the right of families to make their own decisions where these contradict the main ideology of the society in which they

live, and to maintain the continuity of their choices by
transmitting their values, culture and material resources to
the next generation.   Looking again across countries, this
question acquires its sharpest edge in the case of political,
cultural and religious minorities;   historic cases like those
of Poland, Ireland, Quebec, the Jews of the Diaspora, Germany
under the Nazis, the Soviet Union under Stalin, or immigrant
families in any country who seek to preserve their cultural
roots or their traditional practice in matters such as marriage and family formation.   There are minorities within
minorities, such as families which choose English as their
language of education in Quebec or French in Flanders.   The
question of parents' rights to choose the religious and cultural character of their children's education ('Rome on the
rates') has been one of the greatest dividing forces in Western politics.   It is questionable whether one of the two
major forces in European politics, the Christian-Democratic
parties and their related social movements, would have existed
without it.   It can flare up again even, as recently in
Sweden, in cases where it appeared to have been settled. (22)
At a less fundamental but still politically important level,
there are debates such as that in Britain over parents' right
to choose on general educational grounds between State and
independent or comprehensive or selective schools.

There are further issues of this kind over sexual
behaviour and abortion.   There could be another over the
right of families to choose their own division of sex roles,
particularly if policy followed the Swedish line of forcing
the pace towards symmetricality as the norm.

There has also of course long been an issue over the right
of families to transmit economic assets and opportunities to
the next generation.   The trend of policy in Western as well
as Communist countries has been away from the idea, as a
Catholic writer put it a generation ago, that the son of the
head of a business should succeed by right to a top business
position as once, under the feudal system, the son of a general automatically became a general.   What is left of the
older tradition is partly a survival.   It helps to be born a
member of the Soviet elite just as it does to be born a
Kennedy or a member of the British middle class, but these
might be seen as historical survivals which the general policy
aims of the societies in question contradict.   When however
it is a question of interfering with modest inheritance or
with the continuity of family farms, small family businesses,
or even historic homes, pressures from public opinion, on a
variety of economic as well as social grounds, as well as from
those immediately concerned, set limits of principle and practice of which politicians have to take account.   This is even

true to some extent, particularly as regards family farms, of Communist countries. The image of steel magnates with numbered Swiss bank accounts is no longer generally attractive, but at some not very clearly defined point the balance still swings in favour of a degree of continuity of families' economic power.

There are three policy models for dealing with this range of issues, and none of them is easy or uncontroversial. A minimum policy might be to enforce only basic or minimum standards (school attendance, for example, without specifying which type of school) or to intervene only in cases of clear abuse. Just as there was once a school of pure and simple natalists, so there was once a school of pure and simple supporters of the autonomy and continuity of families. In fact they were often the same people, for example the conservatives and traditionalists who played so large a part in the early days of family policy in France. But in its pure and simple form this type of thinking has ceased to be generally accepted in advanced industrial societies. It can place the family itself in a false position by elevating nepotism into a principle and placing family loyalty above wider social obligations. It is no longer generally acceptable to leave the distribution of wealth, incomes and opportunity essentially to the free market, or to abstain from any effort to change the traditional pattern of sex roles. What, in any case, are basic and minimum standards or cases of clear abuse? Was Israel right, in a partly Moslem country, to ban Moslem practice on polygamy, and in some cases divorce, where it conflicts with general Western standards? And what are the conditions in which it is right for children to be compulsorily taken into or retained in care?

One alternative is affirmative action, to help what might be called the victims of family discrimination, those whose family background confers disadvantage or at least no positive advantage. Though more generally acceptable, this can be difficult. Research into transmitted deprivation and policies for correcting it makes this point clear.

Another is negative action to destroy family influence and advantage. Negative action is widely accepted and used, but is controversial even in its milder forms such as taxation of inheritance or pressure for a uniform pattern of schooling. In its stronger forms, as developed at times in the Communist countries, it can damage the functioning of the family itself and its ability to make a social contribution. Even in the Soviet Union, the family farm plot has tended to creep back as a necessity for efficient production. At a more human level, if the family is to be a centre for warmth, intimacy and social relations, what is one to make of the methods of

social control used in the German Democratic Republic in the
light of the comment of an East German couple to one of the
writers that 'the worst thing is that we cannot talk freely to
the children'?

The question of the right balance between autonomy for the
family and social intervention remains open.   Christian-
Democratic and other moderate centre and right-wing movements
tend to be interested in the autonomy and continuity of the
family and its effectiveness as a unit; Social Democrats in
equality and opportunity for individual family members;
strongly ideological regimes, democratic or otherwise, in
causing families to conform to what they see as desirable
norms.   In the words of an official Soviet handbook for
parents: 'Our parents are not without authority either, but
this authority is only a reflection of social authority.   In
our own country the duty of the father towards his children is
a particular form of his duty towards society.' (33)   But
whatever the ideological point of view the question is inescapable.   How far are families to be entitled to choose, live
by and transmit their own values and material resources, and
how far are they to be seen as convenient, or at least un-
avoidable, channels for the application and enforcement of
general social policies?

THE LIMITS OF DISRUPTION

The break-up of families entails social as well as private
costs, for example extra expenditure on housing or social
security: around £1 billion a year, currently, to the British
supplementary benefit system.   It may also entail for the
parties themselves long- and medium-term costs which they may
not fully appreciate at the time.   In the middle term there
are the psychological costs implied in the phrase that 'families need fathers'.   The reconstitution of nuclear families
(Chapter 12) raises a range of problems of its own, not always
well understood either by families themselves or at the level
of research.   'Alternative' families, as Chapter 14 shows
from American and British evidence, tend to be unstable, and
any benefits which they have tend to flow to the adults involved in them rather than to children or to members of the
extended family in its usual wider sense.   In the longer term
the dissolution of a family unit cuts off the prospect of
mutual support by husband and wife in old age and of the development of new extended family networks.   One rather clear
finding of family research is that satisfaction with marital
relations and relationships in the family as a whole tends to
be greater in old age than at younger ages when there are

sharper strains. (34)   On all these counts there is an accepted case for intervention to limit the disruption of families,
but there is still a question about how strong, and in what
form, this intervention is to be.

   The older tradition was that hard cases make bad law, and
that the long-term gains from making family stability the norm
justify bringing strong and often crushing sanctions to bear
on those who depart from it.   The drift of family policy has
now for several decades been away from this, as is shown for
Britain in Chapter 19, and towards an accent on individual
rights and the opportunity to make a new start with a fresh
marriage.   By now, however, it is clear that there is unease
in many countries over the informality and instability of
family relationships which has resulted.   There is among
other things an administrative problem.   As a German paper
comments, 'a grouping whose fundamental relationships, those
between men and women and adults and children, are not somehow
legalised and therefore stably defined is hardly manageable
within formalised administrative procedures.' (35)   But
behind the administrative issue lies the social reality of the
cost of informal and impermanent relationships to adults (old
and young) as well as children, and to society as well as
individuals.

   What does not emerge at all clearly from international comparisons is what precisely can be either effectively or accep-
tably done.   Education and persuasion are clearly acceptable.
One interesting development, for example, is the French concept of 'social centres', financed under a variety of arrangements by the State, family allowance funds, communes and user
groups as well as public authorities involved in their administration, where:

   The users do not have any preconceived idea of their requirements, but they find the entire variety of local services assembled in these centres: home help, pedagogical
   advice, family planning, medical supervision and so
   forth. (36)

That is a way to improve access to services when families need
them.   There is also the question of developing families'
capacity to sort out their problems for themselves - including
the capacity to seek and use advice in good time - as for
example by the educational as distinct from the remedial side
of marriage counselling.   Counsellors of the British Catholic
Marriage Advisory Council were asked to classify and rate for
1973 the relative importance of the problems which they diag-
nosed in remedial counselling.   A factor related to general
ability to face and master family problems of any description
('capacity to cope') was rated as 'central' much more often
than any group of the more specific problems, whether inter-

personal or economic and material, which were the immediate
occasion for counselling. (37)

There is room for dispute over the targets (to say nothing
of the practicalities) even of educational methods.   How far,
for instance, should marriage counselling be concerned with
preserving marriages, and how far with helping couples along a
road which may lead to break-up?   The point where most argument arises, however, is the indefinable one where education
and persuasion become pressure, designed to and perhaps succeeding in overriding the immediate wishes of the couple concerned.

There is one outstanding case, the Soviet Union, of a country which did very effectively put the clock back.   Twenty
years of acute instability after the October Revolution convinced the leaders of the Soviet Union of the need to swing
back from extreme permissiveness to a Victorian emphasis on
stability, duty and discipline, and this was in fact done with
rather remarkable results.   The Maces (38) concluded from
direct study on the ground that Soviet social conditions in
the early 1960s represented an optimum for family life, and
that this was reflected in the actual standard of family relationships.   Bronfenbrenner illustrates the Soviet situation
at that time from a related angle in his comparison of Soviet
and American patterns of education. (39)

The Soviet Union has means of persuasion, and a degree of
readiness to use them, unlikely to be accepted in Western
countries.   These, however, are not the only forms of pressure available.   The experience of Asian families in Britain
shows that even in an open society, and in the case of a
minority community within it, the break-up of families can be
rather effectively counteracted by family negotiations and
social pressures, if this is what opinion in that community
prefers.   Some degree of legal and institutional support is
still useful.   Asians often see in current British practice
in social work and the law a tendency to proceed too directly
to a divorce, instead of negotiating for a continuing viable
relationship - the trend 'from marriage mending to marital
counselling', for example (40) - and unreasonable reluctance
to insist that men shall give priority to their liabilities to
the children of a broken marriage.

The case of Israel, which operates a multiple system of
family laws, Jewish, Moslem, and Christian, suggests a question for other countries.   In today's plural societies, does
legal and institutional support need to be differentiated
according to the terms on which the members of different
groups within a society choose to make their marriage contracts?   Some of the diversity of family patterns in countries such as Britain can be treated as variations within a

common framework.   In other cases, however, it is a matter of distinctive patterns which those who marry and found families within particular ethnic groups, regions, or other groups choose to accept.   British law, as shown in Chapter 21, has tended to withdraw from support for any particular pattern of the family.   Suppose that the law moved back towards more positive support for families and their stability.   Might the time then be in sight when, in plural societies, a common framework based on the lowest common denominator would no longer be enough, and a case for multiple systems of law on marriage and the family and for underwriting a variety of forms of marriage contract could be made?   The answer will of course depend among other things on the answer given to the previous question about the autonomy of families.

It is clear that there is no law of nature which prescribes that countries such as those on which this Chapter focuses should have as many broken and single-parent families as they do.   Nor, where families do break up, does a country like Britain have to make it so easy for fathers to abandon to the taxpayer their debts to the children of the former marriage, or to enter into new commitments before these debts have been accounted for: in a way very different, for example, from what happens in the case of debts from an unsuccessful venture in business.   Do we in these countries, however, know what we want in these respects?   In countries less authoritarian and ideologically committed than the Soviet Union the limits, if any, to be set to informality and instability in family relationships, and the possible ways of enforcing these limits, remain a question without a clear answer.

FAMILY POVERTY AND THE EQUALISATION OF FAMILY BURDENS

Chronologically, concern for family poverty and the equalisation of the standards of living of families with different numbers of dependants became a major policy issue well before, for example, the debate on sex roles.   It is useful, nevertheless, to consider it afterwards, because so many of the issues which it raises are coloured by views on the questions raised in previous sections.

Family support covers an enormous field, including cash provision through money transfers and direct allowances: the impact on families of different patterns of indirect taxation and different methods of providing and charging for services such as housing, health, non-compulsory education and leisure services; and different approaches to the planning of communities, the built environment and pedestrian or wheeled transport; and provision for aid in kind, support services, or re-

payment of the expenses of continuous attendance in the case
of disabled family members.   To illustrate some of the issues
which it raises, however, a useful starting point is OECD's
comprehensive review of cash benefits, tax allowances and tax
credits in its member countries up to 1976 (Tables 1.1-1.8).
It should be noted that the Tables refer only to a single
case, that of an average wage-earner with a particular number
of dependent children.   In other cases the outcomes would be
different.   Among countries with joint taxation of married
couples, for example, the incidence of direct tax on high-
earning couples is more severe in the UK, which has flat-rate
personal allowances, than in countries where allowances are
proportional to income or, as in France and Luxemburg, to the
number of people in the family.

Table 1.2 shows the wide variety of ways in which different
countries arrange for benefits to reach families.   Tax allowances are still the main channel for provision for a second
adult in the family, and cash transfers for children;   in the
latter case the UK has since 1976 ceased to be an exception.
Several countries, including the UK, have been phasing out
child tax allowances in favour of either tax credits or cash
transfers, and there is a general tendency to make more use of
tax credits rather than allowances.

Whatever the channel of delivery, however, what one chiefly
wants to know is the amount and purpose of economic support
for the family, and several general points stand out.

First, as Table 1.1 shows, we are dealing here with substantial sums of money, which make up a significant part of
social and general budgets, at a time when these budgets themselves have been coming under pressure.   There was a very
rapid rise in public expenditure as a percentage of gross
domestic product in a number of the advanced industrial countries between 1965 and 1975 (Table 1.9), and, within this
total, social expenditure increased even faster.   The European Community's second European Social Budget notes that expenditure on health, old age, survivors, unemployment, and
maternity and other family benefits - the figures do not include tax allowances or expenditure on education and housing -
rose in the nine Community countries between 1970 and 1975
from 18.8 per cent to 23.9 per cent of gross domestic product. (41)   By the mid-1970s, however, pressure to limit
further increases became strong, and no further increase was
expected by 1980.   A typical case is that of France, where
the tendency by this time was to shift from fixed benefits and
generous tax allowances towards means-tested benefits, and to
reduce the share of family expenditure in the social budget as
pressure for expenditure on pensions and health
increased. (42)   Economics, and taxpayers' and social

TABLE 1.1   Additional disposable income received by an average
wage-earner (married, wife not working, two children) as per
cent of the disposable income of a single man, 1976

| | Total | of which | |
		Marriage	2 children
Luxemburg	27.6	12.3	15.3
Austria	23.1	2.4	20.7
Belgium	21.1	0.9	20.2
France	20.9	6.3	14.6
Ireland	17.0	6.2	10.8
Germany	16.9	8.5	8.4
Finland	16.7	6.1	10.6
Sweden	16.5	5.5	11.0
Denmark	15.7	9.0	6.7
Netherlands	15.7	3.3	12.4
UK	15.5	5.2	10.3
Norway	14.5	8.1	6.4
Australia	12.9	6.8	6.1
Italy	12.7	5.3	7.4
Canada	11.9	5.7	6.2
USA	11.7	6.2	5.5
Switzerland	10.5	4.4	6.1
New Zealand	9.1	3.0	6.1
Portugal	7.6	-	7.6
Japan	6.2	2.3	3.9
Spain	4.5	1.9	2.6
Turkey	1.8	0.6	1.2
Greece	1.3	0.3	1.0

OECD, 'The Tax/Benefit Position of Selected Income Groups in
OECD Countries', 1978, Table 9.

TABLE 1.2 Tax allowances, credits and cash transfers, as per cent of the gross earnings of an average wage-earner (married, wife not working, two children) in 1976 in respect of marriage and children

	Marriage				Two children				Overall total
	Tax allow-ances	Tax credits	Cash trans-fers	Total	Tax allow-ances	Tax credits	Cash trans-fers	Total	
Luxemburg	7.3	–	–	7.3	5.8	–	6.6	12.4	19.7
Austria	–	1.8	–	1.8	0.4	6.6	8.9	15.9	17.7
Belgium	0.03	0.6	–	0.6	0.1	1.9	13.0	15.0	15.6
France	5.1	–	–	5.1	2.7	–	9.2	11.9	17.0
Ireland	4.4	–	–	4.4	5.4	–	2.1	7.5	11.9
Germany	5.7	–	–	5.7	–	–	5.7	5.7	11.4
Finland	4.0	–	–	4.0	0.8	1.8	4.2	6.8	10.8
Sweden	–	3.4	–	3.4	–	–	6.8	6.8	10.2
Denmark	–	5.0	–	5.0	–	–	4.1	4.1	9.1
Netherlands	2.1	–	–	2.1	1.5	–	6.5	8.0	10.1
UK	3.5	–	–	3.5	4.7	–	2.2*	6.9	10.4
Norway	5.1	–	–	5.1	–	–	4.3	4.3	9.4
Australia	–	5.3	–	5.3	–	–	4.7	4.7	10.0
Italy	– 0.4	1.7	3.2	4.5	– 0.9	0.7	6.4*	6.2	10.7
Canada	4.5	–	–	4.5	0.5	–	4.2*	4.7	9.2
USA	4.8	– 0.2	–	4.6	4.1	– 0.02	–	4.1	8.7
Switzerland	3.4	–	–	3.4	1.3	–	3.6*	4.9	8.3
New Zealand	–	2.2	–	2.2	–	2.2	4.4	6.6	8.8
Portugal	–	–	–	–	–	–	6.7	6.7	6.7
Japan	2.0	–	–	2.0	3.4	–	–	3.4	5.4
Spain	–	–	1.7	1.7	–	–	2.2	2.2	3.9

Turkey	-	0.4	-	0.4	-	0.6	0.2	0.8	1.2
Greece	0.3	-	-	0.3	0.8	-	-	0.8	1.2

* Taxable.

OECD, 'The Tax/Benefit Position of Selected Income Groups in OECD Countries'', 1978, Table 10.

TABLE 1.3   Tax and social security contributions of husbands and earning wives (husband average wage-earner, two children), 1976

	Husband's social security contribution rate (wife not working)		Additional tax and contributions when wife enters employment, as % of wife's earnings when wife earns (as % of husband's wage)	
	Marginal (1)	Overall (2)	33%	66%
Sweden	63	35	27.5	31
Denmark	55	33	38	40
Finland	49	28	26	32
New Zealand	45	24	20	23
Turkey	43	33	28	31
Norway	42	27	29	32 (3)
Netherlands	42	31	33	35
UK	41	26	15	26
Ireland	39	20	41	40
Belgium	37	22	18	27
Australia	35	17	18	23
Germany	34	27	31	34
USA	32	17	27	28 (3)
Canada	30	16	17	17 (3)
Luxemburg	30	16	25	30
Austria	28	14	29	21
Switzerland	27	17	21	27
Italy	23	14	12	14
Japan	21	8	12	14
Greece	17	9	9	10
Spain	16	12	11	8.5
France	16	10	17	19
Portugal	12	12	n.a.	n.a.

1 Proportion of an increase of 10 per cent in gross earnings taken in tax and contributions.
2 Proportion paid on total existing income.
3 Inclusive of tax allowance for child care.

OECD, 'The Tax Benefit/Position of Selected Income Groups in OECD Countries', 1978, Table 10.

TABLE 1.4   Tax and contribution rates - summary from Table 3*

Tax and contributions charged by reference to wife's earnings are:	
Higher than or equal to husband's overall rate and higher than his marginal rate.	Ireland Germany Luxemburg Switzerland France
Higher than his overall rate but lower than his marginal rate.	Denmark Finland Norway Netherlands Beligum Australia USA Canada Austria Japan Greece
Lower than or equal to his overall rate, lower than his marginal rate	Sweden New Zealand Turkey UK Italy Spain

*   Wife assumed to earn 66 per cent of husband's wage.

TABLE 1.5 Income tax systems under compulsory individual taxation in 1976

| | When wife does not work husband gets: | | |
| | | Allowances for: | |
	Basic allowance	Marriage	Children
Australia	Tax rebate	Tax rebate	None
Austria	Fixed allowance plus tax credit of fixed amount	Tax credit	Tax credit
Canada	Fixed allowance	Tax allowances	Tax allowances
Denmark	Fixed allowance plus tax credit	Tax credit (zero rate bracket doubles)	None
Finland	Income related allowance	Tax allowance	Tax credit
Greece	Income related allowance	Tax allowance	Tax allowance
Italy	Tax credit	Tax credit	Tax credit
Japan	Income related allowance	Tax allowance	Tax (4) allowance
Netherlands	Fixed allowance	Tax allowance	Tax allowance
New Zealand	Income related allowance. Tax credit	Income related credit	None (3)
Sweden	Fixed allowance	Tax credit	None
Turkey	Tax credit (5) plus allowances	Tax credit	Tax credit

1 If spouse's income exceeds As 10,000.
2 Wife may renounce option if she pays no income tax.
3 See Section C for full details.
4 Third and subsequent child only.

When the wife works the position is:		
Basic allowance given to working wife	Change in couple's reliefs for:	
	Marriage	Children
As husband	Husband loses	n.a.
As husband	Husband loses (1)	Credit shared (2)
As husband	Gradually loses as income increases	Additional child care allowance (3)
As husband	Husband's losses (3)	n.a.
As husband	Gradually reduced as wife's income increases	Additional allowance
As husband	No change	No change
As husband	Husband loses	Halved
As husband	Husband loses	No change
Smaller than husband's	No change	No change
As husband	Husband loses (3)	n.a.
As husband	Husband loses	Child care allowance
As husband	Husband loses	No change

5   In the form of a fixed deduction, the effect of which is
    similar to a tax credit

OECD, 'The Tax/Benefit Position of Selected Income Groups in
OECD Countries, 1972-6'.

TABLE 1.6   Income tax systems under joint taxation in 1976

| | When wife does not work, couple gets: | | |
| | Basic allowance | Allowance for: | |
		Marriage	Children
Germany (1)	Fixed allowance	Splitting-system and tax allowance (2)	None
Ireland	Fixed allowance	Tax allowance	Tax allowance
Luxemburg	Fixed allowance	Quotient (5)	Quotient (5)
Norway (1)	Income related allowance	Different tax schedules	None (6)
Switzerland (3)	Fixed allowance	Tax allowance	Tax allowance
United Kingdom (1)	Fixed allowance	Tax allowance	Tax allowance
United States (1)	Income related allowance	Different tax schedules, tax allowance and splitting-system	Tax allowance

1 Option exists for separate taxation of spouses - see Section C for details.
2 The splitting system is associated with a doubling of the basic allowance
3 Confederation level only.
4 Husband loses if couple opts for separate taxation.
5 For details, see Section C.
6 At least within age group considered - see Section C.

OECD, 'The Tax/Benefit Position of Selected Income Groups in OECD Countries, 1972-6'.

When wife works, reliefs given to couple change:		
Basic allowance (wife gets)	Relief for marriage	Relief for children
No change	No change	No change
Less than husband	No change	No change
As husband	No change	No change
As husband	No change	Child-care allowance (income-related)
As husband plus add. allowance	No change	No change
As husband	No change (4)	No change
No change	No change	Additional child-care allowance

TABLE 1.7   Income tax systems under family taxation in 1976

| | When wife does not work, couple gets: | | | When wife works, reliefs given to couple change: | | |
| | Basic allowance | Allowance for | | Basic allowance (wife gets) | Relief for marriage | Relief for children |
		Marriage	Children			
Belgium	Inversely related to income (1)	Tax credit (related to tax paid)	Tax credit (related to tax paid)	As husband (2)	No change	No change
France	Income related (3)	Quotient	Quotient	As husband	No change	No change

1 Within minimum and maximum limits, see Section C for details
2 The basic allowance is split between the spouses and the wife gets the same allowance as the husband for professional expenses. Also, above a certain income level, the wife receives an additional allowance of Frs 56,000.
3 This refers to the general deduction equal to 20 per cent of earnings.

OECD, 'The Tax/Benefit Position of selected Income Groups in OECD Countries, 1972-6'.

TABLE 1.8   Summary of cash transfers given for children in 1976

	Paid to	Whether taxable	Change when wife works
Australia	female	no	none
Austria	male	no	none
Belgium	female	no	none
Canada	female	yes	none
Denmark	female	no	none
Finland	female	no	none
France	male	no	partly lost (2)
Germany	guardian	no	none
Greece (3)	male	no	none
Ireland	female	no	none
Italy	male	yes	partly lost
Japan	legal guardian	no	none
Luxembourg	male	no	none
Netherlands	male	no	none
New Zealand	female	no	none
Norway	female	no	none
Portugal	male	no	none
Spain	none	n.a.	n.a.
Sweden	female	no	none
Switzerland	male	yes	none
Turkey	male	no	none
United K.	wife	yes	n.a.
United States	male	no	none

n.a. = not applicable.

2   A separate child care expense cash transfer for low income earners may, at its maximum, equal this one-earner family cash transfer.

3   Unlike other countries, income related (10 per cent of income per child).   It is financed by the employer and included in the employee's wages.

OECD, 'The Tax/Benefit Position of Selected Income Groups in OECD Countries, 1972-6'.

security contributors' reactions, are a hard reality which
everywhere hangs over family support, and, as was noted
earlier in the case of community care for the youngest children in Communist countries, not only in the West.

Secondly, there are wide differences in the provision made
for children and dependent wives, but with some broad trends
emerging.   Wives are still treated essentially as dependants
in countries such as the UK (Table 1.6) which have joint taxation and pay a married man's allowance even where a wife has
her own earnings and is entitled to an allowance against them.
Taxation of wives' earnings itself varies widely (Tables 1.3
and 1.4).   In countries such as Germany, Ireland, France and
Switzerland wives' earnings in the case analysed in the Tables
are taxed at a rate as high as or higher than not merely the
husband's average rate of tax but his marginal rate.   In half
the countries tabulated they are taxed at more than the husband's average rate but less than his marginal rate.   At the
other extreme is an assortment of countries, including Sweden,
New Zealand, and the UK along with Spain, Italy and Turkey,
where wives are taxed lower on both counts.

There are however moves towards standardisation and towards
the definition of wives, not as dependants, but as earners
with responsibilities as parents which they - or their husbands - may at intervals need a compensated break from work to
fulfil.   An increasing number of countries (table 1.5) have
gone over to separate taxation of husbands and wives with
equal and identical allowances.   In one form or another this
also usually implies that both partners' allowances can be
used against the income of one of them if, though only if, one
is not earning enough to use an allowance fully;   as for
example in Australia or New Zealand or as recommended by the
Irish Government's Commission on the Status of Women. (43)

Under the traditional assumption that wives' services were
available free of charge for home duties, no question of
course arose of cash compensation for time spent on the care
of children or the disabled.   As, however, the Swedish Family
Policy Committee was arguing by the 1970s, in the new situation in which wives are no longer normally dependants and the
loss of their earnings means a substantial fall in families'
standard of living, compensation is required;   but economic
pressures, even apart from considerations about the correct
definition of sex roles, require that it be limited to cases
where it is strictly necessary.   What can be and in a growing
number of countries is done is to define limited and special
circumstances in which one or other partner may need to take
time away from employment or to pay for the care of dependants, and to provide for these cases by child-care grants, as
in France or Hungary, or tax allowances, plus protection for

job and social security rights.   The assumption at present is
still usually that the time to be financed is that of the
wife, but at the end of the road is the Swedish idea of
parenthood insurance available to husband and wife alike.
     Tax and social security systems still remain confused over
the question of wives' dependency.   Most European countries
do not treat wives as dependants for the purposes of the husband's unemployment or sickness benefit, but the UK and Ireland still do. (44)   Rules for payment of family allowances
still commonly rest on traditional concepts, occasionally of
the husband as head of the household, more often on that of
the wife's responsibility for housekeeping and child care
(Table 1.8).   Provision for the costs of a wife's disablement
while engaged in household duties is still rare, and there
continues to be confusion over the principles of widows' and
widowers' rights.   The direction of change on wives' dependency is clear, but in detail this is still very much unfini-
shed business.
     Children are a much clearer case in the sense at least that
they are certainly dependants, subject to argument about the
age or stage of education at which dependency ends.   How
much, however, of the costs of children's dependency, or more
precisely of those parts of this cost which are paid by families, is it desirable to replace in the interests of equalis-
ing families' standards of living?
     At the practical level two things are clear.   Firstly,
there are wide differences between countries in the amount of
financial support which they are willing to provide.   In 1976
(Table 1.1) an average wage-earner with two children and his
wife not working benefited in respect of his children by 20
per cent more disposable income than a single man in Austria
or Belgium, by 10-15 per cent more in a number of other countries in north-west Europe, including the UK, by 5 per cent to
8 per cent in Denmark, Switzerland, Portugal, Canada and the
USA, and by very little indeed in Greece, Spain, Turkey, or
Japan.   Secondly, however generous any country's principles
may be, given that cash support for children is the area into
which a very large part of cash expenditure for family policy
falls, the necessities of public finance in practice set a
strong limit.   France has a tradition of high family allowances, and is still among the leaders, but even French allowances still fall far short of what would be needed to allow
families to maintain the same expenditure per equivalent adult
as the number of their children rises. (45)   The case of
Britain is discussed in Chapter 21. (46)   In every country
the cash costs of child care still fall to a substantial
extent on parents' original income, which among other things
strengthens the movement in many countries to make special

provision for single-parent families. If the costs of child
care must in any case be met at least in part by the parents,
the loss of one parent's contribution needs to be made good
even if the remaining parent can earn a full salary or wage.
   Even a stringent economic situation, however, leaves some
room for choice, as was for example illustrated by the increase of over £1 billion (at constant prices) in the British
Exchequer's net contribution to child benefit in the face of
severe economic pressures in 1977-9.   If economic limits were
relaxed, what in principle would countries aim at in the way
of family support, and particularly of support for children?
French experience neatly summarises some of the issues.
After the Second World War its dominant feature was flat-rate
family allowances.   There followed a time when an increasing
proportion of family support came through tax allowances,
which in France are proportional to the number of people in a
family.   Taxable incomes are divided into shares, the 'quotient familial', one for each parent and half for each child,
and the tax rate is calculated on the average income per
share.   The effect of the shift towards tax allowances was
thus to make family support increasingly a matter, not simply
of replacing child costs in some basic sense, but of equalis-
ing the general standards of living of families with and without children within each income group.   'Equal standard of
living for equal work' was one slogan much discussed in Belgium as well as France at that time.   By the 1970s, however,
pressure grew to adopt a third formula of means-tested benefits geared towards the poorest.   As of 1977, about 20
billion francs were reaching families in the form of family
allowances, 12 billion by way of the 'quotient familial', and
9 billion through means-tested allowances. (47)   Given a
degree of choice, towards which of these formulas, or what
combination of them, should policy tend?
   Recent British discussion has turned around the replacement
of tax allowances with flat-rate child allowances or refund-
able tax credits, and around the role of means-tested allowances, including the tax claw-back on flat-rate allowances.
But the principle of 'equal standard of living for equal
work' was earlier discussed at length by the Royal Commission
on the Population on the basis of a proposal by Sir Roy
Harrod. (48)   The Commission rejected the 'quotient familial'
as going too far.   It considered that using income tax to
achieve 'equal standard of living for equal work' would constitute an unjustified redistribution of income from the poor
to the rich, and that income groups as such were not appropriate units for redistribution.   It nevertheless recommended
that tax allowances for children should be a proportion of
income, not a flat rate, and that industrial and professional
bodies should introduce equalisation schemes of their own.

Though the latter as well as the former proposal came to nothing, and the Treasury secured the suppression of the one or two occupational family allowance schemes then existing in the public service, the Royal Commission's proposal for occupational and professional schemes implied a question about the source of funds for family support which other countries' experience shows to remain relevant.   In countries such as Belgium, France, the Netherlands and Italy the main source of funds for cash transfers in support of children is employers' contributions, whereas in Britain, Ireland, Germany and Denmark it is general taxation.   At a time when taxpayers' revolts against increasing public expenditure are widespread, is it entirely an accident that in 1976 cash transfers for a two-child family averaged 9 per cent of the gross earnings of an average wage-earner in the former group of countries, but only $3\frac{1}{2}$ per cent in those which rely on general taxation (Table 1.2)?

Support for the normal living costs of non-earners other than children and wives is probably best thought of as outside the field of family policy, for this type of provision is everywhere made by reference to their status as previous earners or at least potential earners rather than as family dependants.   Repayments of, or aid in kind towards, expenses which would otherwise fall on families in respect of these dependants - for example home help, continuous attendance allowances, or relief to the family through placement in an old people's home or other institution - are on the other hand certainly part of family policy.   So also are subsidies and aid in kind towards the cost of bringing up children (particularly education), housing aid which benefits the family as a whole, and health, environmental and leisure services in so far as they are designed to meet the needs of families as such.   None of these are covered by OECD's Tables, and they will not be gone into in detail here.   But there are two general points to note about them.

Firstly, they all raise questions not only about cost (particularly in the cases of education, housing and health) but about family functioning.   In education, as has been said, the question of families' right to make their own choice on grounds of religion, language, culture, or preference for a particular type of schooling has in many countries been a major political line of division.   There are other questions about how far parents' responsibility to pay for non-compulsory education and for the community care of children, and in the case of children their parental control, should reach;   at one end in the case of third-level students, at the other in that of children at crèche or kindergarten age.   In health services family responsibility is involved in issues about methods of charging, choice of practitioner and the accent to be placed on prevention or on do-it-yourself, about the care of the disabled, or about the involvement of husbands as well as wives in pre- and post-natal education and childbirth.   On none of these issues do international comparisons suggest clear or uniform policy answers; on all of them national practices differ widely.

They differ again on housing.   Should public provision focus on direct allocation of rented housing to families and individuals according to need, and, if so, with what level and type of subsidy?   Means-tested or general?   Close to cost-free, as commonly in Communist countries, or with a high degree of recovery through rents, made up to families by adjustments in cash transfers?   Or should the accent be on owner-occupation, with family responsibility for purchase, sale and upkeep (but does the family for this purpose include the wife?): but also with what degree of family contribution to purchase and what degree of subsidy?   Should it be on co-operative housing, and, if so, family-based or tied to employment?   And how far should housing be designed to support a particular concept of the family, for example the idea of 'service houses' developed in Sweden to support the particular Swedish concept of family functioning and sex roles, by contrast with the British tendency to design houses for families of a relatively traditional kind?   Was Israel right to gear its housing design to the Western emphasis on nuclear families rather than to the accent of people from Asia and Africa on the extended family - a problem which also arises in many parts of Britain? (49)   All these choices have consequences for the functioning of the housing market, but also for family functioning.   The same can of course be said of related decisions about the design of communities and the local environment.

Secondly, when complications and variations like these are added to the variety of practice indicated by OECD's Tables and to the general complexities of family policies within and between countries, as illustrated earlier in this chapter, an obvious question arises about the coherence of family policy. Amid all this variety and complexity, have the practitioners of family policy a coherent picture of what they are doing, and of what the overall results of their policies for families actually are, in terms either of economics alone or of the range of other issues which have been mentioned?

THE COHERENCE OF FAMILY POLICY

Even if consideration is confined to the economic aspects of
family policy, it is clear that a coherent and overall view
even of the relevant facts is often lacking, let alone of
their policy implications. At the level of international
comparisons the OECD Tables, the European Social Budget, or
the Department of Health and Social Security's 'Comparative
Social Security Tables' are useful beginnings, but with present data it is not possible to provide a complete picture of
how the family is faring even in economic terms and within the
European Community. But there is also confusion within individual countries, and not only in Britain. The German Family
Report Commission speaks of the 'accumulation of uncoordinated
financial aids' and the discrepancies and disincentives to
which this leads. (50) Housing policy in France tended over
many years to give least initial support to the poorest in the
oldest and most dilapidated housing, and also a diminishing
incentive, when they did secure moderately satisfactory accommodation, to go on and improve their situation further. (51)
An American study identifies 'at least 268 programmes' which
provide financial assistance or services with a potential
impact on families, as well as 'countless other federal policies' which have substantial impact on families. It adds
that 'much of the data necessary to describe and assess the
impact of policies on families are not available or easily
accessible'. (52)
    Family policy, however, is not only about economics. This
point about coherence is general, and extends across the whole
ground of this Chapter. One of the strongest reasons for
making family policy explicit is that, unless there is a continuing administration and a continuous study programme, even
the material side of family policy is liable to decline into
incoherence; let alone its implications for family functioning or for population. The purpose of the Family Impact Programme at George Washington University, just quoted, is to
find ways and means of attaching a 'family impact statement'
to policy proposals. But it recognises the extent and continuity of the effort which will be needed to achieve this.
In the present underdeveloped state of family policy and its
analysis in the United States it remains 'inappropriate at
this time' for federal, State, or local governments to establish family impact statements as a general procedure. (53)
    The problem of administering family policies, or even sec-
tions of them such as population policy or financial support
and the equalisation of families' standards of living, is that
they cut across normal administrative lines. In all the
countries considered social policies are implemented mainly by

functional departments of government or by functional agencies
providing specific social services such as social security,
housing, education, health, or employment services. In no
country has it proved possible to demarcate an area called
'family policy' which can be put within a ring fence and made
the responsibility of a single Ministry as in a case like that
of education or health. Germany has a Family Ministry, but
it has been graphically described as a 'Ministry of Everything
- or Nothing' whose policies 'hitch-hike' on the back of the
interests of other departments more directly concerned with
individual services. (54) The normal form of co-ordination
in countries which have an explicit family policy is through
a commission or inter-departmental committee, often including
representations from voluntary bodies, trade unions, employers' organisations, or family movements; or, as in
Sweden, through a succession of Royal Commissions.

A crucial factor in this type of co-ordination is relationships not merely within government but between governmental
and non-governmental organisations, and the sensitivity of
both to changes in the family and in society generally. If
co-ordination is to be forceful and effective - something
more than the rhetoric of family policy - experience across
countries shows that it needs to include institutions for this
wider range of discussion, pressure and the mobilisation of
public opinion and action, as well as arrangements for co-
ordination within government itself. A forum is needed to
promote debate and joint action not merely about family issues
in some general sense, but between groups with particular and
special interests in the family; in particular kinds or
functions of families, for example one-parent families or
parent-teacher associations; in individual roles within the
family of men and women, fathers and mothers, or parents and
children; or in collectivist solutions versus family privacy.

A main function of such a forum is to develop a realistic
strategy and set of priorities. It needs to focus the debate
of the whole assembly, or of appropriately constituted committees or working parties, on the most effective means of dealing with particular problems affecting categories of family,
so that realistic proposals for reform can be channelled to
the appropriate point in the government hierarchy. The political effectiveness of proposals will largely depend on how
far they represent, if not the consensus, at any rate the
majority view of the wide spectrum of interests which have
participated in the debate. The more adequately the changing
needs and expectations of families have been researched, and
the more that public interest has been stimulated by wide discussion of problems and proposals, the more likely governments
are to allow themselves to be influenced.

Within the general perspective on family policy which emerges in this way, focus on particular issues is essential for its effective translation into policy and action, and issues have of course to be chosen according to what it is useful to pursue in the circumstances of each time and place.   What was said earlier about the extended and the nuclear family, particularly the family with children, points to one choice of strategy which at present is made almost universally.   The extended family is important, and family policies will be defective so long as this is not taken fully into account. As a matter of immediate practical politics, however, every country in Kamerman and Kahn's international study which can lay claim to an explicit family policy employs at present a definition involving 'at least one adult and one minor child'; (55) even though the parent/child relationship and problems of child rearing are not the primary concerns of many of the organisations which affiliate to family movements and join in debates about family policies.   This accent is found in family lobbies as well as in government agencies. Post-parental families have no lobbies, and lobbies for the elderly tend to be seen as a separate category on their own. In practice nearly all the issues taken up by family lobbies, classified as such, have been concerned with families with children.

To illustrate some typical ways in which family policies are co-ordinated and developed we take four examples; three different national patterns, from the Netherlands, Hungary and France; and international co-operation through the International Union of Family Organisations (IUFO).

THE NETHERLANDS

In everything except the size of the country the Netherlands provides a model particularly useful for comparison with Britain.   It has, like Britain, no tradition of family associations, but has since the Second World War succeeded in bringing together family organisations of all kinds to develop a family perspective over a wide range of social policies and to influence the government to adopt family policies of a more coherent and explicit kind.

The Netherlands Family Council (Nederlands Gezinsraad) was set up in 1947 to provide a national counterpart to IUFO.   It had however a wider membership than the corresponding British committee (later the British Union of Family Organisations - BUFO), which only brought together into a national union those family organisations individually represented on IUFO.   There are forty-five delegates to the General Assembly of the

Netherlands Family Council, coming from organisations as
varied as the Netherlands Roman Catholic Parents Association
and the Council for Marriage and Family of the Dutch Reformed
Church, the Association for the Integration of Homosexuality
and the Foundation for Domestic Science Guidance in Rural
Areas.   A board consisting of fifteen members, plus government advisers from the ministries of Culture, Recreation and
Social Welfare, Economics, Education, Health and Justice, and
the Council's five staff members, meets eight to ten times a
year.   The main sectors of its present work are education,
economics, one-parent families, preparation for marriage and
housing.   A flexible organisation has been found necessary in
order to deal with practical issues as and when they arise:
day-care facilities for children; the reform of taxation and
social security regulations based on family norms which no
longer hold; domestic and consumer information; or the move
in child rearing and education towards more participatory
models.
    Only later, in 1967, did the Netherlands government estab-
lish a General Policy Division within the Ministry of Culture,
Recreation and Social Welfare, to match the wide overall
approach of the Netherlands Family Council.   Its function is
to keep a close watch on changes in marriage and the family
and government reactions to them, in close consultation with
the organisations and ministries concerned.

HUNGARY

It has been shown above how the Eastern European countries
came to face the same problems as in the West of reconciling
individual rights and opportunities with the pursuit through
the family of social objectives and with effective family
functioning, and how the care and warmth of a family and 'time
for free time' were found to be indispensable to many of their
other social objectives.
    Ferge (56) describes how Hungary has comparatively recently
come to use the family as an organising principle in formulating social policies and planning social programmes.   This
change started with the realisation that the long-standing
concern in Hungary with population problems required action
more complex than merely legal reform in areas such as marriage, divorce and abortion under the Family Acts of 1952 and
1974.   Fragmented policies on child allowances, for maternity
and child-care benefits, and the collectivist education of
children had failed to ensure conditions in which normal families could function effectively, or to relieve or prevent the
malfunctioning of problem families.

In Hungary the Ministry of Labour is assigned a leading role in the conception, planning and co-ordination of social policies, and it was this ministry which decided in 1973 to set up a Forum for Family Policy. The Forum is composed of experts working in government bodies (from the Planning Board to the ministries and local councils), in political bodies (the Central Committee of the Hungarian Socialist Party, the trade unions, the National Council of Women), in some of the biggest enterprises, and in research. The Forum functions alternatively as a study group, a discussion group, or a working party. Since 1974 the Ministry of Labour has had to submit regular reports to the Council of Ministers on the actual state of family policy, the main problems to be solved and the proposed solutions. The Ministry is now officially charged with the co-ordination of family policy issues that arise in the activity of national bodies, and has issued directives for family policy work for economic enterprises, co-operatives and local councils. In the latter case it has spelt out in more detail the importance of co-ordinating the many specialised services which work directly with families.

The directives start with a definition of family policy:

By family policy we understand all the planned, intended effects which aim in a complex way at influencing the life conditions and attitudes of families, in order to assure that the functioning of the family will be in harmony with the requirements of socialist development. Family policy expresses, then, a system of interests relating the socialist state and its institutions to the functioning of the family.

This definition shows less respect for the autonomy of the family than would be acceptable in a more pluralist society, and the Family Forum is in no sense part of a voluntary movement with grass roots in local associations. But the debate is not now, if it ever was, about ideologies and theories. As Ferge states, for the time being 'the first goal is to have the family approach accepted and applied in as many areas as possible.' The Forum's reports on 'the actual state of family policy' in the next decade will make interesting reading.

FRANCE

Well before the Second World War France developed both a differentiated family policy and a broadly based and well-articulated family movement. This had its roots in local associations, which greatly increased their political influence by coming together in county ('département') unions and a

national union.   The Union Nationale d'Associations
Familiales (UNAF) brings together the different kinds of
family associations, along with parents' and philanthropic
organisations with special interests such as education, handicapped children or family planning. (57)   These unions
receive considerable financial support from the family allowance funds, and are represented on all national, regional and
local, social and economic planning and advisory bodies.
The debate and practical activities organised by this essentially voluntary movement are taken up by the government.

In 1939 the High Committee on Population, made up of a
small group of MPs and officials, issued a Family Code, which
drew much of its inspiration from a long-standing concern
about the birth rate but also dealt with a whole range of
family problems.   It codified the legislation concerned with
family relationships and child protection, extended family
allowances to the whole population, introduced new family
benefits and tax remissions, and provided other forms of support for families in difficult circumstances, and child protection services where families failed to meet their responsibilities.   The concept was of a family policy primarily concerned with social protection and with the adaptation of collective provision to the changing circumstances of families.
This concept was able to survive the rhetoric ('Travail,
Famille, Patrie') of the Vichy regime.   It already had, and
has continued to have, the support of both the right and the
left wings of political parties, of employers' federations and
trade unions, and of religious and 'lay' associations.

Another report of the High Committee, the Prigent
Report, (58) and other reports submitted to the Planning Commission, have provided the sort of Family Impact Statement
called for in the USA today.   The terms of reference of the
Prigent Report were typically broad and practical: 'To study
family problems, and to suggest to the Government how they
should be solved within the framework of an overall family
policy, taking account of general demographic trends.'   Its
conclusions and recommendations were as much concerned with
the general climate of ideas and the political viability of a
family policy as with specific measures, and led to the
strengthening of the consultative, administrative and representative bodies concerned with every aspect of family welfare.

The debate continues to be fed by a series of authoritative
reports, such as the major studies carried out by the semi-
governmental National Family Allowance Fund (CNAF) and the
Centre for Research and Information on Consumption (CREDOC),
on the living conditions of families (1967) and on the needs
and aspirations of families and young people (1975).   These

were national surveys designed to influence thinking about the objectives of a family policy.   Other reports have been concerned with the means of action: national and local studies of how effectively particular family services, such as daycare or homemaker services, are meeting current needs.   Despite the usual controversies underlying any family policy, the common concern for the well being of the family, and the focus on particular institutions and particular problems, has encouraged the formulation and implementation of genuine family policies over a wide area, though still not the whole, of French social policy.

The results can be seen particularly clearly in the field of social security.   The total sum to be redistributed to families, from a payroll tax on employers and the self-employed with only a minor contribution from general revenues, is decided by the government.   The way in which the Family Fund is to be distributed, however, is largely determined by CNAF, which is now a statutory agency, and the actual operation of the scheme is by local autonomous Caisses d'Allocations Familiales (CAF), run by representatives of employers, employees, the self-employed and family associations.   About 4 per cent of the Family Fund is spent by the local CAFS on additional cash benefits or special services of their own choice.   Involving associations of families and of employers and workers in this way in discussion about the whole system of family income support - how far it should be differentiated according to the number and ages of children, to the weight of family responsibilities at different periods of the family life-cycle, to income, and so on - has proved effective in keeping the government sensitive to families' changing needs and expectations.

Other examples could be quoted from the areas of family law and of social welfare.   The social welfare administration (primarily the Ministry of Health) has a sub-administration of Family and Childhood at national and county levels.   The case of the local social centres which are a long-established feature of the French welfare scene was quoted earlier; they are usually sponsored by the local CAF and family associations.

There are gaps.   The administrations of Population and Immigration, of Social Security and Social Welfare provide an institutional focus for family policies, but in the Ministries of Education and Housing the family perspective is noticeably less evident.   A question also hangs over the role of the government's Consultative Committee for the Family, set up in 1971 to satisfy the family organisations.   It has still to be seen whether it will be as effective in ensuring the implementation of family policy as it has been in formulating it in a more coherent and comprehensive way.

THE INTERNATIONAL UNION OF FAMILY ORGANISATIONS

IUFO was founded in 1947 through French initiative and still has its central office and secretariat in Place St Georges, Paris, the headquarters of UNAF.   From the beginning the French and Belgian member organisations (primarily family associations with and without specific religious affiliations) have provided the strongest element in the organisation.   But over the years it has expanded to include representation from a wider spectrum of organisations for, as well as of, families, and today has 250 member organisations from 53 countries in the five continents.

IUFO aims to bring together both public and private organisations that work for the well being of the family, and to make known to world opinion and to international bodies such as the United Nations Social and Economic Council the family's fundamental needs, rights and requirements.   It has technical commissions on issues such as family housing, marriage and marriage guidance, or education, and study groups on others such as rural families or the development of family movements. It also organises periodic international conferences on broader issues affecting the future of the family.

While IUFO has undoubtedly aided the dissemination of ideas about the objectives and ways of implementing family policies, it is an unwieldy body, and in 1974 its General Council set up a Group of Four to consider how it might increase its efficiency and credibility.   The Group recognised that the movement is insufficiently rooted in national and local unions of the wide range of organisations concerned with one or other aspect of family welfare, and that more use should be made of regional groupings in promoting debate on particular issues. There are already North African and North American regional committees.   A European committee, including a wider range of countries than the Confederation of Family Organisations of the European Community (COFACE) is to be set up.   The Group proposed the creation of a documentation service, with regional groups and accredited national correspondents, to encourage more regular and efficient two-way communication between member organisations, their national and regional committees, and other international organisations such as the World Health Organisation or the International Social Security Association whose areas of work are relevant to family policy. This service has now been set up within IUFO's general secretariat.

THE INTERNATIONAL RESEARCH NETWORK

Finally, a less formal but important development has been the
emergence over recent years of an international research network.   The 'international contagion of ideas' on family
policy has resulted in and been fuelled by the multiplication
of groups and institutes specialising in family research.
The family research network developed in Socialist and Third
World as well as in Western industrial countries, and is
linked by the usual combination of personal contacts, specialist and joint project meetings, and participation in general professional meetings such as those of the International
Sociological Association.   In this as in other fields the
interdependence of research workers has increased rapidly.
A book, and in particular a Chapter, such as this could not
have been written without it.

CONCLUSION: SOME LESSONS FOR BRITAIN

If there is one issue above others which deserves to be highlighted at the end of this review of international experience,
it is the one which has just been considered: that of *the
coherence of family policy and the need for explicit arrangements to ensure it*.

    This is in part a question of capacity to win public sup-
port and to make a well-focused political impact, and on this
there has been a promising advance since the end of the 1970s.
A permanent and effective family lobby in Britain is at last
in sight as a result of the establishment of the unofficial
Study Commission on the Family and of Family Forum.   The Commission is an educational body, promoting public information
and debate on family issues without itself taking sides.
Family Forum, promoted originally by the National Council of
Voluntary Organisations, is an association of most of the main
voluntary associations and pressure groups concerned with the
family.   Its purpose is to influence both public policy and
voluntary action, and - a key point in both its aims and its
methods of working - at local as well as national level.   It
has set out to mobilise a strong local network of organisations concerned with the family, both for action on the spot
and to give its national action depth and the support of wide
consensus.

    There is also, however, a question about the machinery of
government.   Ministries and departments need to be convinced
of the importance of applying a family perspective to the
making and implementation of their specific policies in areas

such as social security, health, education or housing.   Continuing action to ensure the application of this perspective needs to be given an explicit and organised form.   Within each department there needs to be a strong working group or committee, with representatives from relevant statutory and voluntary bodies, and this needs to be supplemented with inter-departmental machinery up to and including Cabinet committee level.   Detailed and accurate family impact statements on the effects of proposed legislation may at first be difficult to achieve, but an early aim might be to introduce a more generalised annual Family Policy Review on the lines of the existing Defence Review.

The experience of countries which have achieved more coherent family policies than Britain underlines the case for government machinery of this kind, and also, as in the case of Hungary, for laying on one department the responsibility for acting as convener and answering for the way in which the machinery of co-ordination functions.   No one department can encompass the whole field of family policy, but a particular department can usefully be given a leading role in ensuring that inter-departmental machinery is initiated, adequately serviced, and effectively functioning.

As regards the subjects of family policy, the field of international experience is too wide to cover in full within the limits of a single chapter.   This Chapter has not for example discussed international experience on some of the classic issues of family law, about separation, divorce, and their legal and financial consequences, or about matrimonial property rights, guardianship, or domicile or the inheritance of nationality;   nor the very large question of the family as educator.   It has touched a number of other issues only incidentally.   The issues of general concern which have in fact been picked out in looking across countries have rather different degrees of immediate importance for Britain.

Population, in the sense of concern over a continuing rise or fall in the population, has in the past been an issue in Britain and could become one again, but currently attracts less attention than the problems caused for planning in education and other public services by the fluctuation of fertility and uncertainty about how it will change in future. It is useful to have been reminded, in case population in the former sense should become an issue again, of the lessons of international experience on the practical possibility and limits of natalist policies, given the social and economic conditions and public attitudes usual today.

The problems of *older families and how best to use the potential of extended families* are important for young families, as well as for the middle-aged and elderly themselves, but Britain as other countries need further study before clear general policies can be expected to emerge. They are likely for the time being, again as in other countries, to be given lower priority than the problems of families with children. The experience of 'ethnic' families in Britain, however, and their lessons about, in particular, the role of the extended family, are a strong reminder of what might be gained by bringing this range of problems more firmly into the scope of family policy. The title of the study by one of the writers on '40 to 60 - How We Waste the Middle-Aged' (59) sums up its findings and carries a warning of its own. The practical lesson of the international review in this Chapter is that a strategic decision to focus family policy in the first place on families with dependent children should not be taken as an excuse for putting off the studies and experiment from which policies to fill these gaps as regards other families and the extended family will emerge in due course.

The problems of *economising family time and of men's and women's roles*, on the other hand, and generally of the distribution of responsibilities within the family and those arising from the *disruption of families*, are immediate and pressing. Where, on these issues, are we in Britain trying to go? Is our target, as in Sweden, full symmetricality, or should we continue to follow a more open and neutral policy even if this amounts in practice, for an indefinite period, to treating the reconciliation of family responsibilities with outside commitments primarily as a 'women's question'? Do we see limits (and if so which?) to the disruption and re-formation of families which has followed from recent social trends? Supposing that we do in principle wish to move towards greater symmetricality or greater family stability, what type and degree of inducement or pressure are we prepared to apply? In the case particularly of stability, what mixture might be required of general measures and of legal or other measures to under-write the marriage contracts and family practice of different ethnic, religious, or other groups within our plural society?

This last group of questions links, of course, with that of *family autonomy*; the degree to which families are or are not left free from pressure in matters such as their division of labour or their practice on sex and abortion, and free to make their own choices about education or the transmission of culture and religion, or to transmit economic resources and power from one generation to another. Freedom of choice for the family has proved in Britain as in other countries to be an issue with sharp teeth, and the tendency of public policy has been where possible to let this sleeping dog lie. It is useful again to be reminded by the experience of other countries that this dog does wake up and bite. The issue of

family autonomy comes up repeatedly, in many forms, and is unlikely to go away.   There are extremes of both intervention
and non-intervention which are clearly unacceptable in developed Western societies.   Where, within these limits, do we in
Britain in fact stand on issues such as educational choice,
the transmission of culture by families of non-UK origin, the
transmission of wealth and economic opportunity, or the idea
of symmetricality as a norm for whose application public
policy should press?

Family poverty and the equalisation of family burdens,
finally, remain as they have been for decades central issues
of public policy.   Analysis of international experience
brings out three main types of consideration.   The first is
the inescapable pressure, in an area like this which involves
heavy expenditure, of competition for funds with other social
and political objectives.   There is always some room for
manoeuvre, but even where ideologies are particularly friendly, as in France in the case of family allowances or in Communist countries in that of community care for the youngest
children, financial considerations often prove in the end to
be decisive: and the more so in the new economic climate of
recent years.   Family support involves a negative as well as
a positive choice.   If more economic support for families is
proposed, what is it proposed shall be cut back to make this
possible?   Or could an alternative source of funds be found
through occupational schemes?

Secondly, there is the variety of objectives and means for
redistributing incomes in favour of those with family responsibilities.   The British tax system, like others, remains
confused over wives' status as dependants or otherwise, but
other countries' experience shows that it does not need to be
as confused as it is.   In Britain as in other countries both
the relief of family (meaning primarily child) poverty and
the equalisation of family burdens at every income level are
recognised as legitimate objectives.   In what order of priority, however, and have we drawn enough on the rich range of
choice of means of pursuing either objective which other
countries' experience offers?   British policy still relies
heavily on a combination of universal, non-taxable, flat-rate
child benefits with supplementary benefits and family income
supplement, which tend in practice to be regarded by governments and beneficiaries alike as a form of public assistance.
Swedish parent insurance, Hungarian child-care allowance, and
the French 'complément familial' and 'quotient familial' are
among the alternatives worth considering.   British housing
and health policies are points on a wide spectrum of alternatives, differing from country to country both in themselves
and in their effect on family functioning.   They cannot all

be right from the latter point of view.   Which are in fact
the most effective?

   Thirdly, and following from this, there is again the question of coherence.   Even a country such as France, which has
been relatively successful in establishing coherent economic
policies for the family, falls down in an area such as housing.   French experience does however show that, even where
family policies lack system and coherence in some fields, a
great deal can be achieved through an approach sector by
sector.   We might well borrow from France the idea of a primary political decision about the total fund to be available
for economic support for families, followed by a more systematic approach to ways of distributing the 'family fund'.   We
do not have to be as incoherent as we are in areas such as the
overlap between direct taxation and the minima guaranteed by
supplementary benefit and family income supplement, or the
anomalies created by different levels of child and other
dependants' benefit according to whether the adults of a
family are on supplementary benefit, on social insrance, or
currently in work.

   International experience shows that family-support policies
interweave and support or contradict one another, and other
economic and social policies, in ways of which few countries -
and certainly not Britain - come near to taking adequate
account.   When to this is added the similar interaction
between other policies for the family and between them and
policies for economic support, the argument returns to the
first point of this conclusion.   If family policy is to be
coherent and to have its optimum effect, it is essential that
there be specific and continuing machinery to keep the impact
of all policies on the family under review and to ensure that
in this respect they form a comprehensive and mutually rein-
forcing whole.   The effort to do this is nowhere entirely
successful.   What international experience suggests is that
it is at least possible to come much closer to success than
has yet been seen in Britain.

TABLE 1.9   Total public expenditure as percentage of gross
domestic product at market prices

	1965	1970	1975	1977
Denmark	31	40	46	46
Germany	37	38	48	47
Netherlands	38	44	55	55 (1976)
Norway	34	43	50	51
Sweden	35	43	52	62
United Kingdom	37	41	50	44
United States	27	32	35	33

Sources: Various national statistics and estimates.
           T. Geiger, 'Welfare and Efficiency', National Plan-
           ning Association, 1978, p. 17

NOTES

1 Quoted in S.B. Kamerman and A.J. Kahn (eds), 'Family
   Policy', Columbia, 1978, p. 15.
2 D. Hannan, 'Traditional Families', Economic and Social
   Research Institute, Dublin, 1977.
3 M. Sokolowska in Kamerman and Kahn, op. cit., p. 268.
4 E.g. on the Netherlands: D. van de Kaa in M. Buxton and
   E.C. Craven (eds), 'Demographic Change and Social Policy
   - The Uncertain Future', Centre for Studies in Social
   Policy (now Policy Studies Institute), p. 65.
5 Note in 'New Society', 3 May 1979, p. 269: and see the
   relevant country chapters in Kamerman and Kahn, op. cit.
6 Quoted by Rita Liljeström in Kamerman and Kahn, op. cit.,
   p. 32.
7 By N.H.W. Davis in Buxton and Craven, op. cit.
8 W. Vergeiner in Kamerman and Kahn, op. cit.; T. Freska,
   Fertility Trends and Policies in Czecho-Slovakia in the
   1970's, 'Population and Development Review', 6.1, March
   1980.
9 As analysed in M.P. Fogarty, '40 to 60', Bedford Square
   Press. 1975, ch. 8.
10 R. and R. Rapoport, 'Dual Career Families', Penguin and
   Harper & Row; M. Young and P. Willmott, 'The Symmetrical
   Family', Routledge & Kegan Paul 1971.
11 Quoted in M.P. Fogarty and R. and R. Rapoport, 'Sex Career
   and Family', Allen & Unwin and Sage, 1971, pp. 48-9.   For

a more recent review see A. Wielowiesky, L'Influence d'un Etat Centralise sur la Politique Familiale Suivant l'Example de la Pologne, 1949-1979, paper to an International Symposium on Family Policy in Europe, Centro Internazional Studi Famiglia, Milan, June 1980.

12   E.g. Vergeiner in Kamerman and Kahn, op. cit.

13   See note 11.

14   Vergeiner in Kamerman and Kahn, op. cit. (on Czechoslovakia).

15   A. Geissler, quoted in Fogarty and Rapoport, op. cit., p. 85.

16   Zsuzsa Ferge (on Hungary) in Kamerman and Kahn, op. cit., p. 73.

17   S.B. Kamerman, Work and Family in Industrialised Societies, Columbia University School of Social Work, cyclostyled, 1978, p. 19.

18   Ibid., pp. 13-14.

19   Ibid., and S.B. Kamerman and A.J. Kahn, Who's Taking Care of our Children?, 'Forum', Special Issue, International Year of the Child, 1979.

20   N. Questiaux and J. Fournier in Kamerman and Kahn, op. cit., p. 129.   Rita Liljeström (Norway) in R.S. Ratner, Report on Wellesley Conference on Equal Pay and Equal Opportunity Policy in the United States, Canada, and Western Europe, Wellesley College, Wellesley, Mass., mimeo, 1979, p. 31.

21   Quoted by R. Liljeström, op. cit., p. 33.

22   Personal communication.

23   Analysed in M.P. Fogarty, '40 to 60', Bedford Square Press, 1975.

24   R. Kalish and A.I. Johnson, Value Similarities and Differences in Three Generations of Women, 'Journal of Marriage and the Family', February 1972.

25   D. Hannan, 'Displacement and Development', Economic and Social Research Institute, Dublin, 1979.

26   L. Rosenmayr, Family Relations of the Elderly, 'Journal of Marriage and the Family', November 1968.

27   F.M. Beradu, Kinship Interactions and Communication Among Space-Age Migrants, 'Journal of Marriage and the Family', August 1967.

28   B. Neugarten and K.K. Weinstein, The Changing American Grandparent, 'Journal of Marriage and the Family', May 1969.

29   M. Ziemska, quoted in Fogarty and Rapoport, op. cit., p. 89.   R. Holman, Unsupported Mothers, 'New Society', 29 October 1970.

30   R.M. Moroney, 'The Family and the State', Longman, 1976, ch. 3.

31 D. Smith, 'Racial Disadvantage in Britain', Penguin, 1977, pp. 49-50.
32 R. Liljeström in Kamerman and Kahn, op. cit., p. 47.
33 U. Bronfenbrenner, 'Two Worlds of Childhood - US and USSR', Allen & Unwin, 1971, p. 3.
34 Data in M.P. Fogarty, '40 to 60', Bedford Square Press, ch. 8.
35 F. Neidhardt in Kamerman and Kahn, op. cit., p. 230.
36 Questiaux and Fournier, op. cit., p. 152.
37 M.P. Fogarty, 'The Catholic Marriage Advisory Council and Its Clients', Centre for Studies in Social Policy (now Policy Studies Institute), 1976.
38 D. and V. Mace, 'The Soviet Family', Hutchinson, 1964.
39 U. Bronfenbrenner, op. cit.
40 'Marriage Matters', Report of a Home Office Working Party on Marriage Guidance, HMSO, 1979, ch. 1.
41 Commission of the European Community, 'Second European Social Budget (1976-80)', 1978.
42 Questiaux and Fournier, op. cit.
43 Report of the Commission on the Status of Women, Stationery Office, Dublin, 1972.
44 Comparative Social Security Tables for Member States of the European Communities, cyclostyled, Department of Health and Social Security, 1978.
45 Questiaux and Fournier, op. cit., p. 167.
46 See also D. Piachaud, 'The Cost of a Child', Child Poverty Action Group, 1979.
47 Ibid., p. 142. For a contemporary comment on the beginning of the shift towards means-testing, see J.J. Dupeyroux, 'Sécurité Sociale', Dalloz, 1971, pp. 502-3; and 'Besoins et Aspirations des Familles et des Jeunes', Etudes CNAF no. 16, 1975.
48 Report of the Royal Commission on the Population, Cmnd 7695, 1949, ch. 17.
49 Smith, op. cit., Table A 10, shows that in the mid-1970s the average number of adults in Asian families was 3.0, compared to a general average of 2.25 for all households in Britain. See also Tables A 58, A 60 and A 61 and pp. 270-2 on density of occupation.
50 Quoted by F. Neidhardt in Kamerman and Kahn, op. cit., p. 236.
51 Questiaux and Fournier, op. cit., p. 156.
52 Interim Report of the Family Impact Seminar, Institute for Educational Leadership, George Washington University, 1978 (cyclostyled), pp. 5, 7.
53 Ibid., p. 9.
54 F. Neidhardt in Kamerman and Kahn, op. cit.
55 Kamerman and Kahn, op. cit., pp. 8-9.

55 Chapter 1

56 Z. Ferge in Kamerman and Kahn, op. cit., pp. 73, 79-80.
57 Robert Talmy, 'Histoire du Mouvement Familial de France',
    Paris, UNCAF, 1963; R. Burnel, La Représentation des
    Intérêts Familiaux en France, paper to the International
    Symposium on Family Policy in Europe, Centro Inter-
    nationale Studi Famiglia, Milan, June 1980.   See also for
    Belgium F. van Mechelen, Non-Governmental Activities:
    Participation in Family Policy, ibid.
58 This report was published in the 'Bulletin Mensuel des
    Caisses d'Allocations Familials', March 1962.
59 M.P. Fogarty, '40 to 60', Bedford Square Press, 1975.

Part II

The British scene in temporal perspective

Chapter 2

The Victorian family

Neil Smelser

The Victorian family was a remarkable institution moulded in a
remarkable era in Britain's history. The period between 1830
and 1870, in which the structure of that family crystal-
lized, (1) was the historical moment of nearly undisputed
economic dominance by Britain, before competition from the
United States and Germany began to ease her from international
leadership. It was the moment of Palmerstonian hegemony in
international affairs. It was the moment in which Britain
escaped the profound revolutionary upheavals of the Continent
and successfully weathered a number of serious episodes of
class conflict and political turmoil. It was, finally, a
moment in which, despite much soul-searching and criticism,
the dominant public attitude toward most British institutions
was one of self-satisfaction and pride. The Victorian family
was one of those institutions, endowed as it was with a time-
less and sacred quality by those who celebrated it.

Even today, more than a century after the Victorian
family's heyday - and when no one would seriously argue that
the family is still essentially Victorian - that family still
persists as a kind of ghostly model. It is both a positive
and a negative model. On the one hand, there lingers an
often unspoken but none the less profound sense that what has
happened to the family in the past century is unfortunate; it
has disintegrated, fallen from grace. And the yardsticks by
which that fall is frequently measured are Victorian stability, solidity and serenity. On the other hand, those reformers who press to liberate us further from the constraints
of the family often find their agenda dictated by a preoccupation with the outstanding features of the Victorian family -
its formality, its repression of sexuality, its sharply drawn
(we would now say sexist) discriminations between the roles of
men and women.

In this Chapter I shall sketch the essentials of the Vic-

torian family, with the hope of providing a comparative and historical base for better comprehending the diverse array of family types portrayed by others in this volume.   Because space is limited, this sketch will have to be an oversimplified composite, concentrating on the central features of family life, only mentioning in passing - and sometimes ignoring altogether - many regional, class and religious variations.

BASIC DISTINCTIONS AND DIMENSIONS

The usual connotation of the term 'the Victorian family' is a specifically middle-class, perhaps even upper-middle-class, one.   That connotation is betrayed even in the few introductory remarks I have made.   But in historical fact there were not one but many types of Victorian family.   One of the major bases of variation, moreover - and certainly major in the minds of the Victorians - was along class lines.   The language of the day often trichotomized class into the aristocratic, middle and working, and endowed each with dominant and perhaps homogeneous characteristics, even though many observers appreciated that the organization of classes was more subtle and complex. (2)
    My own sketch of the Victorian family will be built on the distinction between the middle classes (including mainly professional, business and commercial occupations) and the working classes (defined mainly on the basis of engaging in manual labour for a livelihood).   This distinction, however, is not a clean one, and must be qualified immediately by referring to several other kinds of gradations in Victorian society.   The first is gradations *within* classes.   Certainly high-status professions (legal and medical, for example) distinguished themselves from industrialists, and both groups regarded themselves as different from and superior to shopkeepers and merchants.   Urban working classes differed from agricultural labourers in many respects, and each group manifested variations in skill level, wage level and steadiness of employment. And the really lowest classes - the permanently unemployed and disorganized, the 'lumpen proletariat' - differed so much in life circumstances from other groups in the working classes that they probably should be regarded for many purposes as a separate class.   The second is gradations *between* classes. The upper professional and aristocratic classes blended into one another with respect to education, wealth and lifestyle. Particularly as the century moved along, numerous non-manual but low-salaried service occupations (clerk, shop-assistant, telegrapher, for example) expanded to create a stratum that

overlapped with both the middle and working classes.   The
third type of gradation concerns different degrees of conformity to norms *within* classes.   Middle-class individuals and
families were continuously scrutinized with respect to their
conformity to the norms of gentility in their breeding, cultivation and general demeanour.   And distinctions were frequently made between the respectable (steadily employed,
church-attending, and non-drinking) and non-respectable poor.
These gradations, moreover, made for much greater diversity in
family life than is suggested by a simple division between
middle and working classes.

   Another feature of family life that will command my attention is the connection between family, work and education.
Type of occupation or work determined in large part by the
level of resources a family could command, and therefore the
kind of lifestyle it could sustain.   Moreover, work and
family life were further intertwined by virtue of the fact
that sex was one of the primary bases for determining that
kind of work - or non-work - a person undertook.   Education
was linked with both family and work in various ways.   Level
and type of education were major determinants of future work
and social status.   Education for boys differed from education for girls, and in this way contributed to future differences in sex roles in the family.   And, for the working
classes at least, to work or to go to school constituted
alternative and in many respects competing ways of passing
through childhood and early adolescence.   So intimate are
these various links that this Chapter, while by title about
the family, is really about family, work and education in
Victorian times.

THE MIDDLE-CLASS FAMILY

Work

The aristocratic tradition in Britain included an expectation
that no family member carried on productive work, wealth being
generated by income from land and the family's 'work' being
done by tenants, servants and perhaps family managers.
Family activities were dedicated, rather, to sustaining a
lifestyle of cultivation, entertainment and other leisure
activities.   The middle-class family of the nineteenth century inherited much of this tradition and patterned many of
its own activities after the lifestyle of the aristocracy, but
with respect to work there was a sharp break.   Both the
status and the income of a middle-class family depended on
work.   In many respects the Victorian middle classes were

dominated by the ethic of work and its rewards. (3)   But the remarkable feature of this ethic of work was the degree to which productive work was the preserve of men, and the degree to which women were excluded from it.   One contemporary commentator, J.D. Milne, noted the extremity of this split:

> The time of the other sex (men) is absorbed in business; the day is thrown idle on woman's hand.   The thousand exciting events and under-takings that give eagerness to the attention, and keep on stretch the faculties of man, are reckoned beyond her sphere.   She can take no part, and feel little interest, in public affairs.   The pursuits of men, the movements of industry, the progress of science - in short, the whole ongoings of the outer world, are to her but a phantasmagoria, destitute of reality;   and, indeed from her position, incomprehensible. (Milne, 1857)

A lady 'must be a mere lady and nothing else ... the phrase "working ladies" was, in fact, a contradiction in terms' (Helcombe, 1973).   This split in sex roles was reflected in and buttressed by a legal system that systematically disabled women in the eye of the law, and by an ideology that consigned women to the home and endowed them with the soft domestic virtues.   The Victorian norms governing sex roles provided perhaps the best historical evidence for Engels's assertion that monogamy represents a thoroughgoing economic domination of men over women.

These norms were reflected in historical reality.   In early Victorian Britain virtually no middle-class women were gainfully employed.   For those who were forced to gain a livelihood for themselves - the unmarried - the role of governess was virtually the only available opportunity, and it was low-paid, demeaning and without social respect.   This exclusion from the economic sphere worked special hardship on spinsters - sizeable in number because of the late age at marriage, and because of the high rate of male emigration - and by the 1860s concerned observers were asking 'Why are women redundant?' and 'What shall we do with our old maids?' (Greg, 1869).

Education

The Victorian preoccupations with the hierarchy of classes and the segregation of the sexes were reflected vividly in the middle-class education.   In the higher reaches, families were able to send their sons to non-local boarding schools, which were the most prestigious.   Those with lesser means chose among the complicated array of grammar, proprietary and private schools.   These, too, were graded by curriculum, fees and by the social class of their clientele. Many traditional grammar schools and others aspiring to high status emphasized Greek, Latin and, to a lesser extent, mathematics, subjects which dominated the curricula of the great public schools and the study of which was essential if a boy aspired to attend a university.   Schools of a lesser grade tended to stress 'practical' courses such as accounting, which would destine boys for commercial occupations. (4)

Middle-class parents seemed conscious of the class composition of schools and strove to send their children to schools of appropriate status.   This pattern of choice was reinforced by a graded system of fees, which permitted only families with substantial means to select schools of the higher grade. Commenting on the endowed schools in the West Riding of Yorkshire - not the most class-conscious district in his estimation - J.G. Fitch observed:

> It seems obvious, since fusion of classes is practically
> impossible, and is becoming more and more so, that it is
> the duty of all who are interested in an endowed school, to
> ask themselves once and for all, for what class is it
> designed? and to lay out their plans accordingly.   To say
> that the founder designed it for all classes may be true,
> but it is not relevant.   All classes will not come.   And
> it is found in practice that the one thing which deter-
> mines the class of scholars is the scale of fees.   If
> there are no fees the school is either filled by the very
> poor, or it languishes altogether.   If the fees are fixed
> low, at the rate usually paid in the national school [a
> state-aided religious school for working-class children],
> the school will be attended by children of the national
> school class; and the higher is the scale of fees, the
> higher is the grade of society from which the scholars
> come. (Fitch, 1868)

Boys and girls fared differently in relation to these schools.   Among the upper strata girls were excluded from formal school education altogether.   'There are not Etons for girls in existence,' Emily Davies complained in 1864, and noted that the several hundred ancient grammar schools in England were filled almost entirely by boys (Davies, 1865). Sisters of the boys in schools received their education from governesses for the most part.   Lower in the scale there were some private schools for girls, but the numbers attending were comparatively small.   Furthermore, the content of female education was different, preparing girls with the cultivation and style requisite for a middle-class wife, and minimizing practical studies.

> Society has agreed to set a high value upon a young lady's
> music, dancing, and general air of good breeding, and a

somewhat lower value upon her French and skill in drawing
and fancy work.   These therefore are the arts in which
fathers and mothers desire that their daughters should
excel. (Bryce, 1868)

Family roles

Given the extreme skewing of middle-class economic and educational arrangements, the skewing of family relationships and
activities would seem to follow naturally.   Men, assigned to
the workaday world of business and public affairs, were more
remote from their families than we now feel they are or ought
to be.   Women's place was very much in the home.   They bore
many children - until the beginning of the decline in family
size in the late nineteenth century - and reared them themselves, except in families with a nurse or governess.   Women
were also responsible for the upkeep of the house, whether
directly or through the management of servants.   And the
woman was the specialist in leisure - letter-writing, music,
dancing, sketching, reading magazines, riding and, above all,
entertaining.   Commenting in 1857, Milne said that by virtue
of his involvement in work 'middle-class man ... approaches
more nearly the lot of the labourer,' but woman 'would be an
aristocrat;   must needs spend her time visiting and receiving
visits, or in equally vain makeshifts to kill time' (Milne,
1857).   And everything in the round of family activities
seemed to symbolise status - church attended, circle of
friends, numbers of servants, style of entertainment, even
family vacations - 'the wealthy could travel in puffily up-
holstered first-class carriages, and the less wealthy in a
comfortable second-class;   but there would also be plenty of
accommodation in a third class, even though the sides of the
coaches were open to the weather above shoulder level'
(Dunbar, 1953).
   Since women carried the greatest responsibility for the
family's status-expressing activities, they were probably very
status-conscious as a rule.   After a visit to America in the
1860s, Matthew Arnold mused that American women seemed freer
in their bearing than British women - more natural, more relaxed.   (He was referring mainly to women of the middle
classes in both countries.)   To explain that perceived difference, he turned to the context of social status.   British
middle-class women, he said, could not be free because they
were always haunted by the standards of the class above them
as a model of respectability and propriety - a model that left
them forever self-conscious and constrained, forever preoccupied with doing and saying the right things (Arnold, 1888).

The observation, while no doubt stereotyped, nevertheless suggests subtle differences in the origins of British and American conformism, the British rooted more in class, the American more in the mass.

   Pervading the middle-class Victorian family was the sexual and emotional ethic by which we perhaps know it best; for the immediate and enduring connotations of the word 'Victorian' are those of coolness and distance even in the most intimate relations, correctness in if not prohibition of expression, and disgust with and hostility toward sex, suppressing it officially to minimal gratification in the marital bed. We have little first-hand evidence of the historical realities of the emotional life of middle-class families in Victorian times, but our general knowledge of psychodynamics suggests that the official code of repression could not be completely and effectively superimposed on family members, and that family relations were as a result somewhat stormier than believing Victorians would have wanted them to be. Nevertheless, the Victorian values had their cooling effect, as the novels and the family tracts of the time document, and those values provided ultimately the most direct and compelling evidence for the Freudian insistence on the power of sexual repression in civilized life.

Points of instability and change

One source of instability and change in the middle-class Victorian family was its vulnerability to the stresses of relative economic deprivation. The term 'relative' is critical; in absolute terms the middle classes experienced enormous increases in prosperity in the Victorian era, particularly between 1850 and 1870. But it was this absolute increase in wealth - and, consequently, in resources needed to maintain and even elaborate on an appropriate standard of life - *combined* with the preoccupation with status symbolisation that constituted such a fertile ground for relative deprivation. As families struggled to increase their material possessions, maintain an adequate number of servants, educate their sons properly and relax in proper style, a sense of deprivation was bound to envelop a family, even though it might be wealthy in absolute terms. Also the price of some ingredients of a proper style of life also were to be driven up - the wages of servants, for example, by the increasing demand for them as prosperity continued, and by their decreasing supply, associated with the relative contraction of the agricultural population - always a main source - as well as the increasing opportunities for young women's employment in low-level service

occupations.   J.O. and Olive Banks (1954) have argued that
these kinds of economic pressures, combined with the uncertainties generated by the 'Great Depression' beginning in the
1870s, lay behind the beginnings of the restriction of family
size among the middle classes.

A second point of instability and change lay specifically
in the situation of the middle-class women.   The role of
women in Victorian times constitutes a classic example of the
'emptying-out' of a role.   I have already indicated a number
of ways in which this happened.   From a young age girls were
deprived of formal schooling, especially at the upper ranges
of the class structure, thus excluding them from the most
prized way of spending a childhood and adolescence and preparing them (by neglect) for a relatively empty adult role
with respect to economic and political responsibility.   Marriage, motherhood and domestic responsibility were a middle-
class woman's only valued career.   Yet on this score, too,
signs of emptiness appeared.   Marriage was unavailable to
many, because of the late age of marriage and the ratio of the
sexes.   For those there were few ways of illing a life, since
the exclusion of women from economic and political life was
so nearly complete.   With economic advance and prosperity the
marital role itself was at least partially emptied.   Whatever
residue of productive work (sewing, needlework) might have
remained was rendered archaic and costly by improved productive techniques in industry.   And prosperity enabled increasing numbers of women in the middle classes to turn over domestic chores to servants.   Among the wealthier of those
classes - those who could afford nurses, governesses and
tutors - even the maternal responsibilities of the woman were
eroded.   With increases in the number of servants generally,
women became more nearly managers of and negotiators among
those who actually carried out their traditional responsibilities.

The roots of Victorian middle-class feminism, I would
argue, lie in the social fact that women's roles were becoming
generally more empty, unrewarded and unrewarding.   (This
change, in its turn, was a consequence of the dynamics of
change in the economy and the class system that affected
family and sex roles.)   The most important early preoccupation of reformers in the Victorian period appeared to be on
behalf of those women outside of marriage; marriage itself
and the married life were not so much questioned, but reformers rather wanted to provide educational and occupational
paths of life for those whose lives were emptiest of all.   It
was not long, however, before the feminist impulse generalized, focusing on secondary and higher education for women,
calling for entry into rewarding occupations, protesting

against the degregation of women by divorce laws and laws
affecting prostitutes, and calling for the franchise for
women.   Notable gains were scored with respect to legislative
reforms and educational opportunities, but these must be regarded as minor by contemporary standards.   In addition, the
main augmentation of women's participation in the labour force
occurred in occupations on the border between the middle and
working classes - clerks, shop-assistants, nurses, teachers
and so on.   Furthermore, those advances must be regarded more
as a by-product of the shift of the economy toward service
industries than as a result of any feminist impulse.   Women
scarcely touched professional and business occupations at
higher levels.

THE WORKING-CLASS FAMILY

Work

The Victorian years witnessed the further conquest of the
British economy by mechanized industry, the relative reduction
in the agricultural sector and, later, the vast expansion of
tertiary industries.   These changes were to bring about fundamental changes in the life of the poorer classes with respect to work, education and family.   In one respect, however, continuity with the past is observable in those decades.
That continuity concerns the amount of labour: until the
advent of mass education and effective factory legislation,
all members of the working-class family worked hard to gain
subsistence, much as they had done in the agricultural and
craft past.   What changed so radically, rather, was the
organization of that work, particularly as it affected different family members.
    Work in traditional agricultural and craft (for example,
weaving) families had typically involved the co-operative work
of several family members in a productive economic unit, with
some division of labour and authority along age and sex lines.
The advance of industrial production inevitably - though
irregularly - broke into this family system of labour and
destroyed it, separating the family members and scattering
their labour into different workplaces.   The resulting
pattern of work was a complex one.   The common pattern was
for men to hold a full-time job for wages, except when unemployed, infirm, or aged.   A large number of women were similarly engaged (especially in the textile industries), but
women's work was generally more varied, consisting perhaps of
a wage-paying job supplemented by part-time running of a
household, perhaps domestic work (e.g., clothes-making) sup-

plemented by housework, and perhaps full-time mothering and
household work when children were small.   It was also more
varied over the life-cycle; women moved in, out and around
the labour force as the ages, demands and earning capacities
of their children changed.   Children were put to work as soon
as they could earn as a rule; the main exception to this was
with the best-paid workers, who could afford some education in
lieu of working immediately.   The beginning age of work
varied, being as young as five or six in agricultural districts, where the very young could tend animals and watch for
crows, but almost everywhere it was younger than ten.   Urban
work for children consisted of factory labour, running
errands, petty sales, assistance in domestic industry and,
especially for girls, minding younger siblings to free their
mother's time. (5)   Children worked thus for several years,
contributing to the family purse, then in their teenage years
moved by steps in the direction of residential and economic
independence and the establishment of their own families. (6)

Education

One of the striking features of the development of working-
class education in England and Wales - by contrast with Scotland - was how segregated it was from middle-class education.
British commentators on foreign education, especially American, remarked on this fact repeatedly, and also observed how
appropriate such an arrangement was, given the distinctive
British social class system.   In fact the rightness and the
inevitability of such stratification was not seriously challenged throughout the Victorian years. (7)   Working-class
education was stratified internally as well, with the voluntary but State-supported religious schools (the major type
until very late in the century when State schools came to
dominate) tending to draw from the more 'respectable' poor,
with the destitute receiving no education at all, or placed
separately in ragged or reformatory schools associated with
the workhouse system.
    Another feature of nineteenth-century working-class educa-
tion was the persistence of serious obstacles to its progress.
In the early nineteenth century a significant body of conservative, anti-revolutionary sentiment in the ruling classes
held that education - and ideas in general - for the lower
orders was a source of danger to social order.   As this sentiment gave way to a general conviction that education of the
poor might promote social order, heated debates over what kind
of education that should be continued to rage among the various parties - the Church of England, who claimed a primacy if

not an outright monopoly over education; Nonconformists, who
feared that Church domination; and reformers who advocated
working-class education on more purely utilitarian grounds.
These groups, jealous of their own prerogatives and jurisdictions, constituted effective veto groups against various comprehensive educational schemes which one or another of them
believed would work to their disadvantage.

Another obstacle to educational progress lay in the economic and family circumstances of the working-classes themselves.   Earlier I noted how the working-class family had,
quite early in the Industrial Revolution, already evolved into
a unit whose subsistence called for the participation of multiple wage-earners in the economy.   The fact that this
pattern became established before the advent of mass education
among the poor came to constitute an obstacle to its advance.
When Henry Brougham's Parliamentary Committee surveyed the
curates of every parish in 1818 about the state of education
of the poor, respondent after respondent complained that while
the poor were generally desirous of education, they could not
be expected to take advantage of it in areas (mainly agricultural) and in industries (lace-making and straw-plaiting, for
example) where young children could work and contribute even a
pittance to the family purse.   Such also was the constant
complaint of Her Majesty's Inspectors of Schools in the
decades between 1840 and 1870, and the consistent finding of
the Newcastle Commission in the late 1850s.   Even toward the
end of the nineteenth century, the Booth and Rowntree investigations of poverty turned up much evidence of early withdrawal
of children from school in order to work (e.g. Rowntree,
1901).   Furthermore, when trade was brisk, the schools would
tend to empty as children had greater opportunities to earn,
and in difficult times - as in the Lancashire cotton famine in
the early 1860s - the schools would be positively inundated,
very likely from motives of child-minding rather than those of
educational zeal. (8)   Finally, given the irregular coverage
of the country by the schools, and given the marginal commitment of working-class families to education, many children did
not attend school at all, and reformers complained of urban
gangs of 'street arabs' who they felt constituted a breeding-
ground for crime and a threat to the social order.

As the sexual division of responsibility with respect to
work was less segregated in the working classes than the
middle classes, so was it with respect to working-class education.   Workhouse schools did involve a complete separation of
the sexes.   And while the National Society (the educational
society for the Church of England) preferred separate to mixed
schools, this principle was compromised in small communities
that could support only one school.   The Nonconformists and

the Scots leaned toward mixing the sexes in the same school,
but in all cases boys and girls would separate for part of the
day, with boys continuing their general instruction and girls
receiving instruction in needlework and other domestic subjects, looking forward both to their future domestic responsibilities and to their possible duties as domestic servants.

Family roles

If the middle-class family was vulnerable to conditions of
relative economic deprivation, the nemesis of the working-
class family was absolute deprivation and poverty.   The most
dramatic finding of the surveys of Booth and Rowntree around
the turn of the century was how many people were still below,
at, or near poverty.   Earlier in the century the proportions
would have been higher.   The loss of an adult breadwinner
through death, illness, or unemployment; the loss of a child
or two to school; and the loss of an older child who moved
out and later married - all could make the difference between
economic survival and poverty.   In consequence of this pre-
cariousness, most family expenditures, even for those above
the poverty line, had to be on the necessaries of food, rent
and clothing.   Allowances for drink and tobacco, however,
were frequently made, mainly for the husband.   The mother
tended to be at the centre of income-allocation for the
family.   Sometimes she would receive the entire pay packet
and allocate allowances to husband and older children, and
sometimes the husband would give her a portion of the week's
income for household management, retaining the remainder for
himself. (9)   But in either case the mother was mainly responsible for housekeeping expenditures.

> (The mother) has been the centre because she has been the
> most permanent and most important figure in the family
> life.   The central fact of poor life is the earning of
> money, and some unwritten law forces each boy and girl to
> bring back their wages to the mother.   Her purse or pocket
> is the common fund, and from this she distributes the
> family income.   They are the earners, but she is the
> spender.   Many children bring her an unbroken wage, and
> she allows them six pence back as pocket money.   It is the
> mother who decides the great issues of economy, giving a
> boy some contribution to a suit of new clothes, or finding
> some money for an extra holiday.   She pays the rent and
> faces all visitors at anxious times.   No negotiations with
> the pawnbroker will, as a rule, be conducted by any other
> member of the family. (Paterson, 1911)

As far as the relations of family members with one another

were concerned, work tended to pull them in different directions and apart from one another for nearly six days of the
week.   Even in the remaining leisure time the activities of
husband and wife were segregated, with the husband socializing
separately with mates outside the home (Wright, 1857).

If the Victorian middle-class woman's life could be characterized by an 'emptying-out' of responsibilities, then the
working-class woman's life could be depicted as 'overloaded'.
Responsible often for earning a part of the family's income
in a workplace or at home, responsible for the welfare of a
large family (though often relieved by grandparents, older
siblings, other kin (Anderson, 1971) and the custodial 'dame
schools'), in charge of family budgeting, and generally the
emotional centre of the home, this 'drab and often uncomely
figure' (Paterson, 1911) appears to have moved through much of
her adult life on a day-to-day basis, fighting a battle never
really won, for the economic, social and emotional survival of
her family.

Points of instability and change

In the long run, the precarious and often tragic existence of
the Victorian working-class family has been relieved by the
further economic progress of the nation, improvements in the
distribution of wealth and by the State's assumption of responsibility for the general welfare of its citizens.   More
particularly, however, a number of economic, political and
legal changes began to be observed in the late nineteenth century that began to erode the model sketched in the few fore-
going pages.   Among these changes the following are the most
notable:
1 The decreasing employment of children in factory wage-
   labour, occasioned both by technological changes that rendered them less essential, and by the spread and consolidation of legislation prohibiting or restricting their
   employment.
2 The great increase in occupations in the lower levels of
   the service sector - occupations requiring literacy and
   numeracy, and providing a greater incentive than manual
   work for working-class children to gain those skills
   through primary and perhaps some secondary education.
3 The substantial increase in real wages for the working
   class during the Great Depression, that is, in the 1870s,
   1880s and 1890s.
4 The increased availability of schools after the enabling
   legislation of 1870, and the increasing pressure to attend,
   following legislation of 1876 and 1880, which required it.

5   The emerging political influence of the working classes,
    associated with the extensions of the franchise in the last
    third of the century, as well as the beginnings of greater
    articulation of that influence through a political party.
    The first four trends worked to weaken the need (and oppor-
tunity) for multiple wage-earners, especially children, in the
family, and to shift the complex balance of obstacles, rewards
and coercive pressures away from work and toward schooling for
the young, as well as to ease the constant pressure of
poverty.   The fifth trend provided a political level for continuing and extending the others, and ultimately for extending
State welfare provisions for the poorer classes.

A CONCLUDING REMARK

At the beginning I characterized the Victorian model as a kind
of ghost whose influence we have not really shaken to this
day.   At the end I repeat this observation, hoping that my
sketch of the essentials and the problematics of the Victorian
family has provided some documentation.   Despite repeated
historical assaults, the standards of middle-class Victorian
morality and propriety continue to make their presence felt,
in the form of nostalgia on the part of those who believe our
present family life has corrupted those standards, and in the
form of a guilty conscience on the part of those who believe
we have liberated ourselves from them.   Few regret the passing of the bleakness of the working-class Victorian family,
yet many understandings and traditions of that family persist,
particularly in the role of the mother and in the attitude
that early leaving of school and early work constitutes a kind
of proof of independence and adulthood.
    It is because of the persistence of these standards, more-
over, that many of the contemporary debates over social problems relate to the problematics of the Victorian family.   In
this respect I refer, for example, to the continuing preoccupation with the issue of sexual repressiveness, despite several permissive and pornographic revolutions; the continuing
struggle for economic and political parity on the part of
women, despite several feminist and liberationist revolutions;
and to the continuing concern with the rights of the child,
despite waves of social and legal reform.   Not all of these
problematics were original with the Victorian family; perhaps
some are problematics that are associated with the human condition in general and therefore will be with us indefinitely.
But they were established with such vividness, force and moral
certitude during the Victorian era that they certainly gave
direction to the agenda of the family and its evolution during
the century that followed that era.

NOTES

1 These decades scarcely coincide with Victoria's reign (1837-1901), but are chosen because the main lines of the Victorian family converged and were consolidated in those years; furthermore, it is convenient to demarcate those decades from the later Victorian years, when declining fertility, greater occupational involvement of women, the generalization of restrictions on child labour and the spread of mass primary education generated significant changes in both the middle- and working-class family structure.

2 Hippolyte Taine, for example, noted and reflected on the apparent paradox that the British class system was simultaneously caste-like and open. Taine's 'Notes on England' (translated, with an Introduction by Edward Hyams, London: Thames & Hudson, 1957, pp. 144-5). Taine's visits to England were in 1859, 1862 and 1871.

3 Still the most sensitive characterization of the middle-class Victorian mentality is found in Matthew Arnold's playful but savage descriptions of the Philistines in 'Culture and anarchy: an essay in political and social criticism' (London: Smith, Elder & Co., 1869).

4 For an account of this stratification by type of school and curriculum in Lancashire, see J. Bryce, as reported in 'General Report on the County of Lancashire', in 'Schools inquiry commission', vol. IX, General reports by assistant commissioners. Northern counties (London: HMSO, 1868, pp. 663-9).

5 In their 1863 report on behalf of the Committee of Council on Education, Lord Granville and Robert Lowe explained the smaller numbers of girls than boys in working-class schools by referring to the pattern of girls' assisting mothers with the very young and thus being drawn from school ('Parliamentary papers', 1863, vol. XLVII, p. 8).

6 This sequence is characterized, for Preston, by Michael Anderson in 'Family structure in nineteenth century Lancashire' (Cambridge: The University Press, 1971, pp. 124-35). The best characterization of the differing capacity of the family to generate income over the life-cycle - differing on account of the presence or absence of children, and their ability to earn, as well as the varying ability of the parents to earn, is in B. Seebohm Rowntree, 'Poverty: a study of town life' (London: Macmillan & Co., 1901, pp. 136-8). Rowntree's investigations occurred in a rather later period than the decades of my concern, but some of the general patterns of fluctuation in life earnings no doubt apply earlier as well.

7   Even the three great educational commissions that completed
    their work in the 1850s and 1860s were stratified by class
    – The Newcastle Commission for popular education, The
    Clarendon Commission for upper-class public schools and The
    Taunton Commission for middle-class education.

8   For an account of how brisk trade conditions tended to
    empty pauper schools, see the report in 'Parliamentary
    papers' (1852, vol. XXXIX, p. 56); and for the effect of
    the cotton famine on Lancashire schools, see the report by
    W.J. Kennedy, 'Parliamentary papers' (1863, vol. XLVII,
    pp. 102–3).

9   Laura Oren's characterization of this pattern is based on
    some post-Victorian social surveys as well as earlier mate-
    rials, but undoubtedly has considerable validity for the
    Victorian period generally.   The Welfare of Women in
    Laboring Families: England 1860–1950, in Mary S. Hartman
    and Louis W. Banner, 'Clio's consciousness raised: new
    perspectives on the history of women' (New York: Harper &
    Row, 1974, pp. 226–40).

Chapter 3

Social change and indicators of diversity
David Eversley and Lucy Bonnerjea

HISTORICAL DIVERSITY

We see the family as a social system which has changed continuously over time and which is still changing.   The faster and
the more far-reaching the changes in the organisation of society, the greater the diversity of family forms we seem to encounter.   The family both reflects the changing needs of
society and constitutes one of the most important characteristics affecting any given social structure.   Technical changes
in production and distribution, changes in spatial concepts
due to better means of communication and also the developing
role of the State as the ultimate provider of certain necessary services, have all contributed (Shorter, 1976).
     As this process of change continues, it is not sensible to
look for a single prototype from which to start.   Nevertheless we do well to remember the often quoted Victorian family
(see Chapter 2) because it has played such an important role
in the derivative literature about the modern family: whatever forms the contemporary family takes, it is usually measured as a deviation from this supposed former norm.   It is
clear that by the beginning of Queen Victoria's reign, industrialisation in Britain had been under way for more than a
century.   Urbanisation and the transfer of production to factories were well advanced.   The population was growing fast
and the rural counties began to suffer a net decline by the
end of the nineteenth century losing people both to the cities
and to the colonies overseas.   All these changes affected
family life (Friedlaender and Roshier, 1966).
     We cannot assume that the process of change has been uni-
form over time, or in space.   Side by side, even in the late
nineteenth century, we still had families which were productive units, families consisting of a single male wage-earner
returning each day to his 'nuclear family home', and a large

75

number of one-parent households - either because the father
was dead, or because he had emigrated, travelled seasonally in
search of work, or because he had abandoned his wife and
children.   Fishermen, 'tramping' artisans and building
workers who went to the United States each year to earn large
wages, are well-known variants (Redford, 1926).   At the same
time there were large family-type households, incorporating
not only servants but aged and single relatives (Laslett,
1972).
     In textile areas, most women were working in the mills; in
mining districts few women went out to work.   The novels of
Elizabeth Gaskell or D.H. Lawrence present a picture of as
great diversity as do the census schedules.   This is seen
throughout the literary history of England, as Raymond
Williams (1959, 1961) has shown.   In isolated villages a
medieval system of cultivation survived along with a very
long-established kinship pattern, whilst in cities young women
were already working in offices as 'type-writers'.   In some
areas, most of the inhabitants were, at least as far as we can
guess from the registers, of 'pure' English, Welsh, Scottish,
or Irish stock, but people from all the Celtic areas had long
since migrated south and east in search of work.   Apart from
sporadic Huguenot, Flemish and Jewish migration, industrial
England attracted Germans from the early days of industrialisation, Belgian glass-makers and Italian confectioners.   By
the 1880s, mass migrations of Jews from the eastern parts of
Europe began (Fishman, 1976), and successive waves of immigrants, in search of work or political asylum, or to escape
conscription in their own country, landed in Britain, founded
settlements usually in the poorer parts of the cities and
were eventually assimilated - more or less (Cunningham, 1969).
     So as society evolves, and the family within it, we see a
constantly changing range of types of domestic units.   Both
the median configurations of the family and the variant types
have moved along a spectrum over the years and families in
different localities may not be at the same point at any one
time.   Because changes are so marked a feature of family
life, the process is sometimes wrongly described as the
'break-up' of the family - but statistics for divorce, illegitimacy, one-person working households and old people left to
die alone, provide us with no evidence for this.   Apart from
divorced persons, the other types have always existed in quite
large numbers, though modern methods of household investigation give us more precise measures of many phenomena such as
cohabitation (Leete, 1979 and Dunnell, 1979).
     Because the process of change has accelerated in recent
years (for a variety of reasons ranging from purely technological factors to changing societal perceptions), many

useful categories within nomenclature have become
blurred at the edges. We have fewer urban/rural differentials, and we have a 'suburban' or 'exurban' family which is
similar to that of rapid growth areas (new towns, some regions
like East Anglia), where the nuclear-family type household is
most common. Because more people now retire from work a long
time before infirmity and death,some climatically favoured
areas show a preponderance of pensioner couples and singles
who are physically separated from their offspring (Karn,
1977). In some middle-class households dependent children
never actually live at home from the time they go to prepara-
tory school until they leave university, and are yet members
of, and dependent on, a closely knit family system; in some
working-class communities children start work at the minimum
school-leaving age, continue to live at home until they marry,
but lead much more independent lives than their wealthier contemporaries. Because most women work outside the home, full
time for a part of their lives and part time during the childrearing period, the 'working mother' has become more universal
though still ill-defined (Rapoport and Rapoport, 1978). Some
women have illegitimate children from choice, and some by
chance, and either live alone, or with a man who may or may
not be the father of the child; many have been part of a
consensual union for a long time. American investigators
claim that even now a minority of children live with both
their natural parents (Glick and Norton, 1977).

    Cohabitation before marriage is more frequent. These may
be fashions, possibly responses to changing social and economic conditions, and they can change. But they produce variation. The same is true for ethnic groups we consider, and
there are regional contrasts too. The greater the difference between regions as regards the prospects of the various
types of potential wage-earners, and the more unequal the
supply of housing, the more family types will exist side by
side.

    To paint such a picture of shifting patterns is not to deny
that the family's evolution has been characterised by certain
elements of progression marked by landmarks in our history.
Women in office work began in Victoria's reign and the clerical worker outnumbered the governess/domestic servant by 1911.
The First World War brought many more women into productive
industry outside textile areas where they had been
numerous. The Second World War still further enlarged
women's occupational ranges. Women's mass education began
hesitantly after 1871, accelerated after 1902, and brought
them to universities after the Second World War. However,
they still only form one-third of students enrolled in first
degree courses. Fertility did not decline evenly, there

were sharp reductions in family size after the 'Great Depression' of the 1880s, coincident with the spread of early modes of contraception; the economic disaster of 1929-33 brought fertility to its lowest levels ever, from where it recovered until it declined once more, though at a decreasing pace, between 1964 and 1977.   Legislation to give women equal rights and equal opportunities has been slow to take effect.

The middle classes first accepted family planning late in the nineteenth century and the habit slowly and unevenly spread through all classes.   The average family size falls consistently after 1881.   This average hides the full range of diversity.   However, the smaller the average value, the smaller the range of values on either side.   The declining average means, to a great extent, that there are fewer and fewer families with twice, let alone three times the average number of children.   This is not a case of families converging towards an average size, but one extreme end of the possible spectrum of values being progressively cut.   So on one hand we have less diversity when family size falls, on the other hand the continued existence of, say, families with six or seven children (i.e. three times the national average size) ensures that diversity continues to exist.   In 1900, a family with three times the average number of children would have had fifteen, an even more exceptional figure than six is today.

Ethnic minorities have sometimes been absorbed into the population or even emerged as a part of the highest social strata (Sephardic Jews, Huguenots).   These we say are 'assimilated'.   Others are still culturally distinct but otherwise show behaviour patterns which in many crucial respects (like housing preferences) resemble the host population very closely (old-established Irish, Welsh, Scots migrants, old commonwealth citizens, the professional groups amongst the Afro-Asian immigrants).   Other groups have not made this transition, and do not wish to do so, remaining identifiably separate and sometimes disadvantaged (Poles and Ukrainians displaced by the war, West Indian immigrants, gypsies and other 'travellers') (Adams, Okeley, Morgan and Smith, 1975).

None of these phenomena are new.   What has changed is our perception of the differences as now one, and now another group stands out because of its different norms.   Birth control came later to Catholics and Asian immigrants.   Both communities retain a higher degree of control over their children, or so it is claimed.   Gypsy children are as difficult now as barge-children and tinkers were in the past to bring into a regular educational system.   Strict Moslem wives do not usually work in factories.   Ukrainian children are brought up bi-lingually (but so are many Welsh children).

All these things affect the size, location and lifestyle of the families.

In writing about present-day diversity, therefore, we must take into account that an arbitrary year, or even decade, shows us 'the family' at a point of time in its dynamic evolution.   And we need not assume that this evolution is unidirectional.   When we adopt as our starting point the view that the family changes its form and functions in parallel with the evolution of a society geared to new forms of production and distribution, then we also accept that if there were further drastic changes in the economic environment, the rate and direction of familial changes will be affected.   Whether we think of a world recession, or just energy shortages, or the adoption of microprocessors, we need to see what effect these things have on individuals, groups and areas.   If we postulate that changing attitudes towards cohabitation, illegitimacy, divorce or homosexuality evolve independently of economic changes (perhaps due to better education, or the decline of religion), then we need to see the family also in the context of such an array of possible changes, and words such as 'permissive' and 'adaptive' creep into our vocabulary.

In this study of diversity, we concentrate on the description of changes that have occurred.   It is beyond our scope, here, to explain why functions or values have changed as much as they have, why these changes are not unidirectional, and why they do not affect all groups or areas equally.   At this stage we only seek to record that the family has had many forms in the past (though the censored literature has repressed many of the supposed deviant forms) and certainly has many at the present.   In the following sections we will sketch out a few possible schemata for displaying the array of family forms as they exist today.

REGIONAL INDICATORS

Since the days of Elizabeth Gaskell, England's North and South had been regarded as different countries, the dividing line running somewhere north of the Trent, while Scotland, Wales, let alone Ireland, were always sui generis.   These divisions are now considered to be oversimplified.   We can divide the country much better into types of areas, on a number of admittedly conventional but now much better documented indicators, such as long-term unemployment, sub-standard housing, below-average earnings, industrial disputes, infant mortality, new industrial investment, new house-building, car-ownership and so on (Webber, 1976).

The most favoured of these types of region is what has recently been dubbed the 'sun belt' (Eversley, 1979): a group of counties including the inner south-west region, the south-east region from Hampshire in an arc round north London to Essex, the East Midlands and East Anglia. This group has a characteristic pattern of social indicators favouring for the most part socially valued forms. A high proportion of all households consists of two-parent families (with the exception of those coastal areas which we include under the geriatric belts below). In East Anglia, for example, in 1977, 70 per cent of households were married couple households, while in Greater London it was only 63 per cent. Again in East Anglia, owner-occupation is 56 per cent, while in the North and in Greater London it is 44 per cent. Most married women work, but mostly part time. (In the East Midlands, 57 per cent of married women work, while in the North it is only 49 per cent.) Social Classes I and II are over-represented, the rest under-represented except for the remnants of agricultural workers. In contrast the south west and south east have the lowest percentage of heads of households in manual occupations (35 per cent and 34 per cent). In May 1979, the 'sun belt' voted solidly for the Conservative Party. It has only a quarter of the country's population but a much higher proportion of its university places and airports; and it contains no inner city areas or assisted areas under the regional policy acts.

We are suggesting that this area attracts the family-builders, the upwardly socially mobile, those ambitious for their children, and they will increasingly attract public and private resources to fulfil their ambitions. On the other hand, the area has no room for social elements which do not fit into the production pattern which has been adopted.

The second category may be called the geriatric wards. Originally only stretching along the south coast from Cornwall to Sussex, it is now of some importance in East Anglia, and also occupies the Yorkshire and Northumberland and Lincoln-shire coasts in the east, favoured areas of South Wales and the whole North Wales coast as well as the Lancashire and Cumbrian coasts. These areas will, to an increasing extent, have one- and two-person households, living some distance from their nearest relatives. This pattern may lead to isolation, strain on the local social and health services, and in the long run deterioration of the housing stock through inability to maintain owned properties (Donnison, 1979).

The third group of areas are the older long-term declining industrial areas, largely founded on the older coal fields, iron and steel, ship-building, textile and other industries which had ceased to be competitive by the time of the Barlow

report.   Their population tends to be older, and stable
family type households predominate.   Only textile areas have
above average female activity rates.   The characteristics of
the traditional, patriarchial family structure are still, as
far as one can judge, those observed in the 'Ashton' survey
(Dennis, Henriques and Slaughter, 1956) and by Ferdynand
Zweig (Zweig, 1952).   Family and neighbourhood loyalties are
still strong.   They are identifiable as regions of high
migration, especially of younger people, of continued higher
than average unemployment, of high proportions of men in
social classes IV and V.

The fourth areas are the newly declining industrial areas,
especially of the Midlands.   They are more fragmented and
cannot be so easily pin-pointed.   Because they have always
been areas of high immigration, we would expect to find a
higher proportion of family structures which are different
from the national pattern for industrial areas.   This is confirmed by the National Dwellings and Housing Survey of 1978,
with highly traditional settlements in Black Country towns
like Dudley, and rather fragmented patterns elsewhere.
Women's activity rates were high until recently;   households
were financed by skilled male wage-earners and unskilled or
semi-skilled women assembly line workers.   These areas now
face the prospect of rapid out-migration of young people as
well as unemployment amongst older workers.   In an area
almost entirely consisting of very recent immigrants to the
Midlands, like Coventry, neighbourhood rather than family
provide the frame of reference (as Leo Kuper and Henry Cohen
observed immediately after the war - Kuper and Cohen, 1950).

Fifthly, we have also to single out what remains of truly
rural areas - very few because most non-urban areas now have
such large proportions of commuters, week-enders and retired
people in them that the land-based element is a small minority.   However, there are still some centres of agricultural
production.   In these, the family-based farm still plays a
very large role - increasingly so, as hired agricultural
labour disappears.   So does the family-owned retail business,
the ancillary services for agriculture, or even the small
tourist establishment.   These areas are all too small to
allow identification in any statistical analysis except the
census.   Once again, we have a high proportion of two-parent
families, and of single old people;   few women are gainfully
employed.

The sixth set of areas are the Inner Cities.   They have
received a great deal of attention lately.   Their population
characteristics have recently been assembled by the present
authors (Eversley and Bonnerjea, 1980).   The picture is
familiar as far as it goes.   Apart from indicators of

deprivation, there are a high proportion of immigrants in most of the areas (i.e. 27 per cent in Inner Birmingham, but only 14 per cent in the whole of Birmingham), a large proportion of one-parent households and multi-adult households (11 per cent of households are one-parent households in Inner Newcastle); and a prevalence of poor housing conditions. Many immigrant communities, notably Asian, exhibit a very strong sense of family cohesion. A high proportion of people in these areas have no extended family support systems or only deficient ones. Some are young workers, some are elderly people whose children have migrated to the owner-occupied belts outside the cities, and that large and ill-defined category of single, or family homeless whose numbers are always disputed and who did not appear in any of our statistics. The metropolitan areas contain more than their fair share of long-stay (present or past) psychiatric and geriatric patients, whose future is in doubt: when institutionalised they may be housed in the Green Belt, when discharged, they are returned to the Inner City.

   This typology suggests six main lines of differentiation, based on complex social processes. The 'sun belt' and the geriatric belt seem to be the result of filtering processes: of households headed by two adults and of old people.   In contrast the characteristics of the newly declining industrial areas are based on a more heterogeneous group of families, left over from the social and industrial development of the past.

ETHNIC DIVERSITY

Britain is a multiracial society: there are about three million immigrants and immigrant-descended people, about half of whom are white, from Europe, Ireland and the Old Commonwealth, while the other half are from the New Commonwealth countries of Asia, Africa and the West Indies.   It has already been pointed out that ethnic minorities are concentrated: there are few in the North, in East Anglia and the south east, outside London, and south west.   Greater London, Birmingham and Bradford have relatively high concentrations. In 1977 in Greater London 4 per cent of the population was of West Indian origin and 4 per cent of Asian origin; in Birmingham 5 per cent West Indian, 6 per cent Asian; in Bradford 0.6 per cent West Indian, 8 per cent Asian.

   It is inaccurate to refer to Punjabis, Tamils, Pakistanis and Bangladeshis simply as Asians, since they do not identify with the global terms (Sillitoe, 1979) and their cultural differences are as great as their similarities (Tinker, 1977); nevertheless since this is an over-view chapter, the term

Asian is used to refer to these generalised characteristics, as does Ballard in Chapter 8.

Most of the early Asian arrivals were male workers; women migrated later, and only as dependants of men. By the late 1960s, Indians tended to have balanced sex ratios, were enjoying family life, spending money on consumer goods and developing a community with shops and cinemas, while Pakistani men still out-numbered Pakistani women three to one (Lomas, 1973) and often lived in all-male, overcrowded hostels. By 1971 there was greater balance amongst the Pakistani population. In the field of employment, Asians are most likely to be in manual jobs, and overtime work has become a feature of immigrant life (Desai, 1973). Great prestige is attached to white-collar jobs, and these are sought, through education, for many Asian sons.

Partly due to the relative spatial segregation, and partly due to strong adherence to traditional cultural values, a relatively distinct 'Asian' family type exists. For most Asians marriage continues to be an alliance between families, as much as a union of a man and a woman. It involves both families' reputations and statuses; active involvement in the choice of children's marriage partners is the norm and divorce is rare.

Asian children, like those of other ethnic minorities, tend to be brought up in two cultures: the culture of their parents and the culture of the host community. This usually involves different languages, different food and different values. James (1974) points out, for example, that many Asian families take social behaviour for granted, and what is right and wrong behaviour is not a subject for discussion. Parents may project their ambitions onto their children - fostering anxiety and competitiveness amongst male Asian teenagers about their educational success and/or their employment opportunities. Girls used to be seen as economic liabilities; this has now changed, although they still may be discouraged from further education and jobs which involve contact with the opposite sex. Women, and particularly mothers, are seen as the guardians of values and traditions of the community.

It is important to stress that there is variation within the Asian family 'type'; for example, that Sikhs pride themselves in their freer attitudes to the position of women in society than Moslem tradition does. Nevertheless, Asian families do come close to portraying the 'traditional family' patterns, with extended kinships, multi-generation and family solidarity.

One aspect of Asian family life which has been of some concern amongst the host population has been the high birth

rates of women.   This led to considerable anxiety expressed
in the media and to projections based on faulty methodology.
At least one confusion was due to the substitution of the
birth rate (the number of births per 1,000 Asians) for fertility (the number of births per 1,000 Asian women between the
ages of 15 and 45).   The birth rate was high, and is still
relatively high, because a very high proportion of Asian women
were, and still are, in the most fertile age groups.   There
is evidence of the fertility of those in the main child-bearing groups declining, and the proportion within the fertile
age groups is falling.

The second main ethnic type to be discussed is the West
Indian one.   Again, it is important to remember that the West
Indies consist of several different islands, and the West
Indian family type is merely a model.   West Indians come from
a society with a different family structure.   Marriage is an
event which follows after having achieved a certain standard of
living and having made a home;   it is not a binding contract
taken regardless of a family's circumstances.   Fitzherbert
(1974) argues, 'Today, it is still more important as a statement of economic achievement and class affiliation, than as a
context for a sexual relationship, a shared home, or raising
children.'

In practice this means many women have their first child at
home, enter into a more or less stable union and marry when
economic stability is achieved.   This is shown in the large
number of West Indian births (48 per cent) which are illegitimate, occurring before a marriage ceremony, but not necessarily without a stable partner.   The family size of West Indians
is relatively small and the proportion of births to West
Indian women has fallen considerably.

The absence of a strong patriarchal tradition has certain
implications: for example, responsible stepfatherhood and
declining role segregation.   The main difference from other
family types, and it is an important difference, is the social
context: the economic system combined with racial discrimination confines many West Indians to low status and poorly paid
jobs, and to above average periods of unemployment.   It is
these constraints which contribute to the West Indian pattern,
and it is hardly surprising that the mother's role is the
strongest in the West Indian family system.   However, as
Driver points out in Chapter 9 the 'matrifocal' type of family
(characteristic of Carribean as well as English settings) is
only one variant of the West Indian family, albeit a distinctive one.

Although it is only the Asian and West Indian family types
which have been discussed here in detail, it is important to
note that the Irish, Orthodox Jews, the East Europeans, the

Italians and Greeks all have somewhat different cultural
family types, often with slightly above average number of
children, stable family structure, extended kinship systems
and relative concentration in 'ethnic cities'.   Ethnic diversity is multi-dimensional and has always existed in some form
in Britain.

SOCIAL CLASS DIFFERENCES

The concept of social class can be used to illustrate patterns
of diversity between families, based on occupational grouping.
It is used here as a basis for classifying data, not as a
means of explaining why the diversity exists.   The percentage in each social class (by head of family) is 5 per cent
for Class I, 20 per cent for Class II, 12 per cent for III
non-manual, 38 per cent for III manual, 18 per cent for IV
and 7 per cent for V (Census, 1971).
     Social class differences in the timing of formation of
families are quite large.   Marriage tends to occur earlier in
the manual group (Social Classes III manual, IV and V) than in
the non-manual group (Social Classes I, II and III non-
manual).   In 1971, 77 per cent of married couples where the
wife was under 20 belonged to the manual group, and only 16
per cent were in the non-manual one (7 per cent unclassi-
fied).
     In the age group 20-4, 64 per cent were in the manual
group and 30 per cent in the non-manual.   The non-manual
group also have fewer births at ages under 25 than expected
from the proportion they form of the population of married
women, suggesting a slower pattern of family building than
the manual group.   This is demonstrated in the average age
of mother at first live birth figures: for Social Class I,
the age was 26.3 years, for Social Class V it was 21.9.
These figures show that the differences between Social Classes
in the average age at which women start their families are
considerable.
     With regard to housing, it is the association of the
housing system with the social and economic structure that is
particularly interesting.   In 1977, 56 per cent of dwellings
were owner-occupied, 33 per cent rented from a local authority
and 11 per cent rented privately.   Tenure varies greatly with
socio-economic group: 80 per cent of professional workers
owned their own home, compared with only 20 per cent of unskilled workers.   The former tend to live in environmentally
favoured districts, the latter until recently often in inner
cities with poor housing conditions and lack of amenities.

However, slum clearance in the 1960s and gentrification in the 1970s are both changing the meaning of inner city owner-occupation.   Local authorities have traditionally directed their housing programmes toward specific groups: families, especially large families, with low incomes and local ties.   These are mainly manual workers, and problems include the trapping of families with young children in high rise blocks, and a repair and maintenance system which cannot or will not deal with leaking roofs, dampness and general vandalism.   The privately rented sector has declined: in the 1970s alone it was reduced from 15 per cent in 1971 to 11 per cent in 1977.   (It had been 60 per cent at the end of the war.)   These families frequently live in very low-quality housing and tend to have low incomes.   They are often the more disadvantaged: old people predominate in the unfurnished rented sector, and the unemployed, the unmarried mother and the coloured immigrant compete with the young professionals and students for the furnished sector.   In 1977, 66 per cent of heads of households in unfurnished private accommodation had no educational qualifications and 80 per cent were economically inactive.   While tenure patterns relate to social class and to different family patterns, they are also linked to income, life-cycle and life-chances.

The practical effect of the differences in tenure patterns linked to social class and income is quite important.   Local authorities not only allow the tenancy of a rented house to be passed on from one generation to the next;   but they may give preference in allocating new or vacant dwellings to the children of existing residents.   Therefore, the allocation system reinforces the inherent class bias towards living near one's parents.   For the owner-occupier sector, the opposite may be true: the chances of young people finding somewhere to live close to their parents are small, since they will be looking for smaller, cheaper property, as their parents tend to be at the top of their life-cycle earnings.   Different aspirations and access to the housing market affect the timing of family building: the social class differences in the average age at which women start their families, referred to earlier in the section, may be partially explained by the greater initial expense of owner-occupation, to which the working classes have limited access and lower initial capital resources.

Data on family expenditure show that households where the head is a manual worker spend a higher proportion of their income on food (in 1972:   26 per cent versus 20 per cent) and on alcohol and tobacco (11 per cent versus 5 per cent);   professional and administrative workers spend relatively more on services and household durables.   As a result, mainly of differences in incomes, the possession of a telephone or a car is closely related to social class: 14 per cent of unskilled worker households had a telephone, while 85 per cent of professionals did, and the corresponding figures for cars were 16 per cent and 65 per cent.

Educational attainment is related both to type of school and to the social background of the child's family. Children who leave school early are most likely to come from families with no qualifications and also to leave school without any. Children of the professional classes are more likely to attend independent schools, nursery schools and playgroups. One of the results is shown in the National Child Development Study: 8 per cent of children from Social Class I families in contrast to 48 per cent of children from Social Class V families had poor results on a reading test. One of the factors involved is the home environment: children from unskilled working-class homes were 10 times more likely to live in an overcrowded home than those from professional homes. Also the larger the number of children the less likely the family was to enjoy the sole use of such amenities as a bathroom, indoor toilet and hot water supply.

Overcrowding and a lack of amenities have considerable and measurable effects on educational attainment, social adjustment and health. For example at the age of eleven years, overcrowding is associated with a retardation of about seventeen months in reading age (Pringle, 1974).

Educational attainment affects mobility: on the one hand, children whose education continues longer tend during that period to stay at home or remain in close touch with their parents; though when their education is complete they are more likely to move away. In the unskilled and semi-skilled groups children leave home earlier, but their chances of finding suitable employment nearer home are good (because their skills are less specific). So we would expect a number of patterns to emerge which are connected with class, education and the nature of the local employment market.

Social Class differences within employment are large: one survey of the unemployed in 1974 showed that labourers, who are classified as Social Class V, formed half the sample. The prospects of obtaining a job also vary by occupational group. The 1971 Census showed that the proportion of economically active men out of work increased from 1.4 per cent of Social Class I to 11.8 per cent of Social Class V. Professional and managerial occupations have other advantages too: for example, almost all get paid when sick, as against only 55 per cent of unskilled or semi-skilled manual workers.

Health attributes follow the same pattern: social class differences in mortality rates and morbidity rates persist,

as do infant mortality differences.   For example, the chances
of suffering from some chronic or acute sickness are extremely
high for some categories of people, such as older men in unskilled occupations: in 1972 over 30 per cent of unskilled
manual men aged 45-64 reported limiting long-standing illness;
this percentage rose to 44 per cent for men over 65 who had
been in unskilled occupations.

These differences are, however, primarily relationships
between averages, and the distributions overlap considerably.
But on average, families in Social Class V tend to be formed
earlier, have their first child earlier, have higher infant
mortality rates, less education, more unemployment and more
ill-health.   And in many cases class contrasts have remained
stable over the last decades, despite a welfare state with
some redistributive intent.

DIVERSITY DUE TO WOMEN'S ECONOMIC ACTIVITY RATES AND FAMILY
LIFE CYCLES

One of the most important trends in the employment field has
been the post-war trend of more married women entering the
labour force, in all age groups.   GHS data shows 44 per
cent of all married women worked in 1971, and this rose to 51
per cent in 1977; it is mainly due to the continuing rise in
the proportion of women with dependent children working part
time.   The likelihood of a woman working increases with the
age of her youngest child: 27 per cent of mothers with a
child under five, work, while 60 per cent with a child under
ten, and 72 per cent with a child over ten, do so.

How does this affect the picture of a family?   More wives
and mothers, including non-married ones, are gainfully employed, and are having smaller families.   One result is what
Willmott and Young call the Symmetrical Family: one where
values of loyalty, obligation and deference are replaced by
sharing of earnings and domestic roles.   However, there is a
lot of variation: dual career families (Rapoport and Rapoport, 1976) are perhaps an elite - combining demanding careers
with the sharing of family worlds.   Dual worker families (see
Gowler and Legge, Chapter 6) are more common: the women are
mainly in low-paid, unskilled work, often in factory, domestic
or secretarial jobs.   It is what dual labour market theorists
(Barron and Norris, 1976) call the secondary sector of the
labour market.   Class differences influence work roles, and
the amount of autonomy an individual has: the factory worker
has far less control over his work conditions than the professional.   This is reflected in family life too: there are,
for example, different socialisation patterns for children,

with middle-class parents stressing general principles, rather than obedience to discrete rules (Bernstein and Henderson, 1969).   Race, particularly when combined with class, is another determinant of role expectations and family life-style: American data suggest that lower working-class black males, faced with discrimination and constraints on occupational achievement, often seek to define their male status in terms of sexual or semi-criminal behaviour (Rainwater, 1970). The very poor have again a different kind of family life - one where married women have few rights, and both economic and domestic obligations.   There is little security, and frequent common-law marriages and illegitimacy (Yorburg, 1973).

In addition to these sources of diversity, there is also variation due to stages in the life-cycle.   It was Rowntree who first used the life cycle concept in the context of poverty: the poor moving from poverty to relative prosperity and back to poverty as a result of life-cycle effects on income and on needs.   Today there are other periods of stress, for example, when the two earners become one earner plus child.   As Layard, Piachaud and Steward (1978) have shown, a family with a child under five is likely to suffer from low income and poverty.

Another vulnerable life-cycle stage is just before the eldest child leaves school.   Wynn has commented on the fact that adolescents are more expensive to provide for than adults, yet this is largely unrecognised in our income support system, in contrast to that of Scandinavia, for example. Jackson and Marsden (1962) have attributed to this the pressure on many working-class teenagers to enter the labour force at minimal school-leaving age, without gaining the qualifications appropriate to their abilities.

Cycles of labour force participation are also determined partly by time budgets and partly by local opportunities - which may be seasonal, trade cycle or related to industrial trends;   they are also affected by social provision, i.e. child care, local public transport and family or neighbourhood private mobility.

The position of dependants, the old, the chronically sick and handicapped is much affected by these variations: the women in the centre of the family contrive to perform a supportive role to the members in need, as well as contribute to the family income and continue to take main responsibility for the house, and often the children (Oakley, 1973).   It has not been fully recognised that the 'family' functions of procreation, socialisation and the care of dependants have always been largely the responsibility of the women in the family (Land, 1978).   It is being viewed with some concern that with more women in employment the family is less willing or able to take on these functions.   But the fact that women are not willing or able to exercise former traditional care role in addition to their present ones is not necessarily a prescription for disaster.   There are alternatives constantly being evolved which in fact may suit many people's preferences (Moroney, 1975).

EMERGING FORMS

One type of family, the one-parent family, is on the increase, and is important for social and policy-making reasons.   It was estimated that 750,000 one-parent families existed in Great Britain in 1976 ('Social Trends', 1979) with over one million children.   Of these the majority, 660,000 were lone mothers, and about 90,000 lone fathers.   Of the former 185,000 were separated, 230,000 divorced, 115,000 widowed and 130,000 single.   One-parent families formed about one-tenth of all families with children in 1976.   In 1977, the National Dwelling and Housing Survey found that 6.3 per cent of all households were of the lone parent type: this would imply over a million of such households in England alone (DoE, National Dwelling and Housing Survey, 1978).

The majority of one-parent families result from the break-up of a marriage: two-thirds were estimated to come from separated and divorced families.   In the period 1964 to 1976 there was an upwards trend in divorce rates.   This was partly due to the Divorce Law Reform Act which took effect in 1971, but the increase had begun earlier and has continued. In 1970 the number of divorces was 58,000; by 1976: 127,000. The divorce rate is greatest at ages 25-9, however a recent trend has been the rise in divorce rates among the recently married.   Leete suggests that among members of the 1972 cohort nearly one in five will be divorced after 15 years.

However, the increasing numbers of remarriages suggest that lone parenthood after divorce is often only a transient status.   Leete and Anthony found from a survey (Leete and Anthony, 1979) that in 27 per cent of divorces both partners remarry; in 29 per cent only the man does, and in 23 per cent neither of them do.   They also suggest that remarriage is most likely for those divorcing before the age of 30: 60 per cent, and that it is slightly *more* likely for women with children than without.   The age of the youngest child also seems important - remarriage is more common with children under ten than over.   Burgoyne has pointed out that 'reconstituted' families may also present potential rewards and satisfactions of a type which are absent from more conventional nuclear families.

Another type of one-parent family is the widowed mother,
who has decreased both in absolute numbers and as a proportion
of the total.   It is clear, then, that unmarried mothers are
not the 'typical' one-parent families.   The Finer Report
figures showed them to be 15 per cent of the total, with about
11 per cent of the children in one-parent families.   One way
of estimating families headed by unmarried mothers is with
illegitimacy figures.   However the link is tenuous: many
illegitimate births are to unmarried couples living in stable
unions; many mothers of illegitimate children marry at some
later date; some of the children become adopted and about
120,000 births per year are re-registered as legitimate.   So
while the number of children who are and who remain solely
dependent on their unmarried mothers is only a small proportion of all one-parent families, nevertheless the absolute
number of these families at any one time is considerable.

One-parent status related indicators have been frequently
studied.   In Hunt's (1970) survey for example, while sharing
of households was virtually non-existent among two-parent
families, it occurred to an appreciable extent among single-
parent families, particularly to fatherless ones.   In all the
areas they studied the percentage of non-married mothers whose
education finished at the age of 15 or earlier was higher than
the corresponding percentage of married mothers.   This suggests that many unmarried mothers suffer disadvantage all
round: housing conditions, earning potential as well as
social stigma.   However, within this group there is a minority of middle-class women who are choosing to have children
and to remain unmarried, either living with the father of the
child or having a stable relationship without sharing residence.   Figures on how large this proportion of women is,
are not available.   It is thought to be relatively small,
although possibly on the increase (Dunnell, 1979).

The effect of a lone parent background on children is unclear.   Early studies suggested that children from broken
homes show relatively more evidence of delinquency and psychiatric disturbance.   However more recent work suggests,
where, for example, economic status is controlled for, differences between children from one- and two-parent homes on
variables such as school achievement, social adjustment and
delinquent behaviour, are small or non-existent (Thornes
and Collard, 1979).   It needs also to be emphasised that the
effects of physically intact, but emotionally disturbed familial environment, appear to be equally or even more damaging
for the children than homes in which the marriage has broken
up (Rutter, 1972).   Violence within the family is being increasingly recognised as a problem (Renvoize, 1978).   In
certain cases of violence against wives and children separation of the families seems the preferable solution.

It is the one-parent family, and the reconstituted one, which are the most important emerging forms of family. As suggested, they are complex due both to the diverse causes and the diverse societal reactions. Less significant, in numbers, are other types of families. Communes for example, exist in different forms: self-actualising, activists, therapeutic, religious ones (Rigby, 1974). However, although communal living may conceptually be a positive alternative to the nuclear family, in practice it is often a transitional stage for middle-class individuals after and before being a nuclear family. McCulloch describes the variations and trends in Chapter 16. There are also same-sex unions: this remains an unstudied area and again it is unclear whether numbers have increased or whether it has merely become more acceptable. There are still many problems where children are involved, and these parents often feel themselves stigmatised.

Large families (defined as families with more than five dependent children) are another 'special' group: important not because they are increasing, but because they have special needs. In 1966 there were 250,000 such families with about 1,450,000 children in them; by 1971 only 196,000 such families with just over one million children. There is pressure on the fathers of large families to work long hours, and on mothers to supplement earnings; the latter source of earnings is unreliable due to interruption of childbirth, sickness and accidents, and hence the overall standard of living is frequently low. Land (1969) had indicated the complexities of the picture where the idea of a large family is often romanticised: 40 per cent of large families had incomes below Supplementary Benefit level plus 40 per cent, while another 25 per cent were below the Supplementary Benefit level itself. Families with a handicapped member also have special needs. In 1976 there were 543,000 registered handicapped; Knight (1978) found that only 12 per cent of all identified handicapped people were registered. The large majority of these are living at home, and need special support to enable them to cope with their impairments and to prevent their isolation from society if elderly, and to help them to develop to their full potential if a child.

In this section there has been an emphasis on diversity in relation to needs. The different family forms do not exist in a vacuum, they offer an opportunity for self-development in a variety of ways, if supported. This support needs to match families' diversity.

SOME IMPLICATIONS

The family as a productive unit has dwindled in numbers; the
exceptions here are family-run farms and small-holdings,
retail outlets and catering establishments and it has been
suggested that with the advent of Asian families, in the
cities, the family-staffed shop is on the increase again.

   The family as an economic unit (in the sense of being a
group of people who earn incomes and pool these to finance
common expenditure to a greater or lesser extent) is clearly
changing.   The average number of income earners per household is growing despite the shrinking size of households, and
the ratio of earners to dependants within families is improving all the time, partly because those retired from work increasingly occupy their own dwellings.   These trends imply a
changed set of relationships - not only between spouses, but
also in the role that women play in the wider family and community context.

   Lastly, the family as a caring unit: this is clearly the
most contentious area (Laslett, 1965).   One view seems to be
that the family lost these functions in Britain to some
extent with the 1601 Poor Law, certainly with that of 1834,
and that finally the growth of the Welfare State since the
Lloyd George insurance scheme and the post-Beveridge institutions removed the responsibility of the family to care for
the old, the sick, the out of work, the delinquents, the mentally handicapped, leaving them to concentrate on caring for
children, though even that role was, so it is said, taken
over by schools, professional advisers, the health and social
services and institutional arrangements in those cases where
parents were deemed to have failed.

   However, there is evidence to the contrary: psychological
evidence that stresses the importance of early environmental
events for later development and makes it clear that child
rearing is an important and demanding care function.
Studies on educational attainment also stress that factors in
the home are overwhelmingly more powerful than those of the
neighbourhood and school (Douglas, 1964).   Community care,
which is frequently dependent on family care, is advocated
and has increased for the mentally handicapped.   And most old
people are still the concern of their children despite the
fact that many elderly live separately: in one recent survey
three-quarters of those with surviving children saw one of
them at least once a week (Abrams, 1978).

   The caring function of the family, while difficult to quantify, is nevertheless present in a great variety of ways.
Diversities in families do not lessen the support, they
merely may reflect different means.   For example, while most

English elderly wish to live in their own house as long as possible, many Asians wish to share with their sons and daughters-in-laws.   The other side of the coin is the support offered by society: in relation to the above example, one requirement is the granting of two mortgages to two related, nuclear families for one large house.   The extent to which families can function successfully, depends at least in part on external policies such as incomes, prices, taxation, social security benefits, the availability of housing in relation to incomes, etc.   These social policies function well to the extent that they are adapted to the current and future diversities of family life.

To conclude, the idealised conception of a nuclear conjugal family, with standardised composition and division of labour, is increasingly being questioned (Rapoport, Rapoport and Strelitz, 1977).   At the one extreme there are policy concepts based on the feminist redefinition of marriage as an exploitative relationship in which women exchange free domestic, child care and sexual services in return for upkeep (Garmarnikov, 1978).   At the other extreme, there are policies which attempt to support the model of the family based on rigid sex role conceptions.   Both extremes suggest a pressure to reduce diversity.   Somewhere in between is a more piecemeal pragmatic family policy orientation, concerned primarily with economic questions such as to what extent are expenditures (State education (Plowden, 1967), child benefits (Lister, 1975), or a general maintenance allowance for lone mothers (Finer, 1974)), considered to have a social investment content.   It is this last approach which most needs an awareness of, information on and acceptance of, the wide diversity of family forms.   This may help to create a flexible policy where the diverse roles within the family and the different needs which follow from these, as well as the diverse needs of society at different points in time, are recognised.

Chapter 4

Families and social change since the Second World War[1]

Muriel Nissel

SOCIAL CHANGE AND THE FAMILY CYCLE (2)

Has the family changed since the end of the Second World War?
What have been the social forces affecting it and how has it
interacted with them? The aim of this chapter is to set out
some of the facts about social trends which have affected the
family at four main stages of the life cycle - childhood,
young adult life, middle life and old age.
   Social change has different effects on families and individuals within families at different stages of the life-cycle.
People live their lives in particular ways both because they
belong to a particular age group and because they are part of
a particular generation. To help separate the age effect
from the generation effect this chapter is divided into four
sections related to the family cycle and for each stage a
cohort approach is used to compare family life as it was a
generation ago in the early 1950s with family life today
(1977, this being the latest date for which statistics are
generally available at the time of writing). The broad age
limits selected for the early 1950s (generation I) are: 0 and
under 21, 21 and under 30, 30 and under 60, and 60 and over;
for today (generation II) the limits are slightly different:
0 and under 18, 18 and under 30, 30 and under 65, and 65 and
over. It would be tidier to use the same age limits for both
generations but a child today is no longer thought of in the
same terms as in the 1950s, nor are the elderly; indeed, the
chapter will suggest how these very changes in definition reflect the larger changes. Schematically the presentation is
as shown in Table 4.1.
   Experiences at each stage of the life-cycle are moulded by
the environments of people at that stage. Against each of
the four stages in the two periods we describe not only the
environmental circumstances affecting family life today and in

TABLE 4.1

Life-cycle stage	Age		Birth dates	
	in 1952 Cohort I	in 1977 Cohort II	Cohort I	Cohort II
Childhood	0-21	0-18	1930-51	1959-77
Young adult life	21-30	18-30	1921-30	1947-59
Middle age	30-60	30-65	1891-1921	1912-47
Old age	60 and over	65 and over	Before 1891	Before 1912

the early 1950s, but also the dominating influences relevant to the formative years of the two generations.   Tables 4.2 and 4.4 set out against broad bands of years over the past century approximate figures for some of the main demographic changes.

The first part of the chapter considers the role of children and the effect their increasing importance as individuals has had on other family members.   The second, dealing with young adults, looks closely at the role of women and their greater importance, too, as individuals.   The third, concerned with the 'established' family, suggests how improved living standards have blurred the edges of many class distinctions and have given most families more choice about lifestyles, but it also emphasizes the disparity in living standards arising from such factors as family break-up and from different numbers of earners in the household.   The fourth section, on old age, concentrates on the family issues stemming from the fact that people live longer, belong to smaller families and live further away from one another.   Although the themes are developed in separate sections, they are of course interrelated.   Greater independence of children both affects and is affected by the lifestyle and attitudes of their parents.   Living longer has a significant impact not only on the elderly but on the lives of their families.   The changing role of women has important but different consequences at each stage of the life cycle.

CHILDHOOD

In the first place, what defined a child a generation ago and has that definition changed today?   In the early 1950s the age of majority, which entitled young people to vote or to

marry without their parents' consent, was 21 but it was only
18 for conscription into the Forces.   The minimum school-
leaving age was 15 but young people had to wait till they were
16 before they could obtain National Insurance or National
Assistance in their own right.   Children could be prosecuted
in the criminal courts if they were 8 years old.

In the intervening period, there has been a wide range of
legislation affecting children and young persons.   In 1972
the statutory minimum school-leaving age was raised to 16 and
in 1969 the Children and Young Persons Act for England and
Wales abolished the prosecution of children under 14 and re-
defined the role of the Juvenile Courts.   Of particular significance was the lowering, in 1969, of the age of majority
and the right to vote from 21 to 18.   Not only were young
people legally adults, independent of their parents and individuals in their own right at this younger age, but the change
reflected a variety of social and other factors, such as
earlier maturity, the higher level of education and the
greater economic independence of young people, leading to
their earlier acceptance as adults.   Gradually society's attitudes have been changing and, even before the age of 18, children and young people are now viewed more as individuals making
their own choices and determining their own lives.

A child living a generation ago, here defined as anyone
under the age of 21, would have been born between 1930 and
1951, encompassing the political, social and economic upheaval
characteristic of the war and immediate post-war years.   The
one- or two-child family was increasingly becoming the norm
among the middle classes; to the extent that large families
still prevailed, they were more frequently found amongst
manual workers.   Many children, particularly the older ones,
born in the 1930s and living in the bigger cities, experienced
separation from their homes during the war, either by evacua-
tion or bombing.   Fathers were mobilized into the Forces and
drafted away from home.   Unless their children were small,
mothers too were expected to play a direct part in the war
effort and many children therefore experienced both parents
away from home for much of the day.

People generally experienced the social levelling that war-
time scarcity brought with it.   The war had left its legacy
of destruction and housing was short.   Food was still
rationed until 1951.   There were only about two million private cars and vans licensed and fewer than half a million
television sets.   The National Health Service, the Welfare
State and wider opportunities for further education were in
their infancy.   There remained a belief, fostered by the
organization of the war effort, that governments were powerful
and could transform the lot of the individual.

TABLE 4.2   Demographic influences affecting the life-cycle stages of the two generations alive in 1952 and 1977

Birth years of those at specified life-cycle stages in 1952 and 1977 respectively ('Yesterday')		Population (millions)	
	('Today')		Under 15
1952	1977		
Cohort I	Cohort II		
	1976-9 ⎤	54.4 (1)	21.4 (1)
	1971-5	54.2	23.9
	1966-70 ⊢Childhood		
	1961-5	51.5	23.2
	1956-60 ⎦		
	1951-5 ⎤ Young adult life	49.2	22.4
	1946-50 ⎦		
Childhood ⎯	1941-5 ⎤	46.9	21.0
	1936-40		
	1931-5 ⎦	44.8	24.2
Young adult life ⎯	1926-30 ⎤ Middle life		
	1921-5 ⎦	42.8	27.9
	1916-20 ⎤		
	1911-15 ⎦	40.8	30.8
Middle life ⎯	1906-10 ⎤		
	1901-5 ⊢Old age	37.0	32.5
	1891-1900 ⎦		
	1881-90 ⎤		
Old age ⎯⎯	1871-80		
	1861-70		
	1851-60 ⎦	20.8	35.5

1 1979 (provisional)
2 1856-60: estimate
3 England and Wales
4 Deaths include non-civilians registered in England and Wales during the war years.

Sources: Report of the Population Panel, Cmnd 5258, HMSO 1973.
          Office of Population Censuses and Surveys: various publications

Great Britain					
Age structure (percentages)			Deaths (4)	Live births	Illegitimate as a percentage of live births
15-44	45-59	60 and over			
Beginning of period			('000s) Annual averages		
41.3 (1)	17.7 (1)	19.7 (1)	652	661	9.5
38.7	18.3	18.7	653	761	8.7
			628	910	8.2
39.7	20.1	17.0	617	951	6.7
			588	838	4.9
42.9	19.0	15.7	568	767	4.7
			576	882	5.5
46.9	18.0	14.1	554	761	7.0
			580	696	4.4
46.9	17.4	11.5	550	694	4.7
			543	757	4.8
46.8	15.9	9.4	535	878	4.6
			590	863	5.7
47.9	13.3	8.0	594	987	4.7
			591	1,050	4.4
47.9	12.1	7.4	611	1,071	4.3 3.9 (3)
			636	1,044	4.2 (3)
			598	1,014	4.7 (3)
			594	982	5.0 (3)
			550	862	5.8 (3)
45.9	11.3	7.3	487 (2)		6.5 (3)

To be a child in the later period, here defined as under the age of 18, was to have been born mainly at a time of growing prosperity.   As the practice of efficient contraception spread through all social classes, the two-child family became characteristic of those in both manual and non-manual occupations: today there is thus less dispersion in family size than a generation ago.   There are, however, more young children living with only one parent.   Whereas in 1950 many children had experienced the temporary absence of a father during and immediately after the war and others suffered the loss of a parent through premature death, the experience of many children today, often from a very young age, is of the permanent absence of their natural fathers, through divorce, separation and illegitimacy.   In 1976 the median age of wives at divorce was 33.   Remarriage, which brings with it problems of adjustment to new sets of kin, has become more frequent but often it implies that a child has experienced at least a temporary span of living with a single parent, which can involve intense emotional stress and material deprivation.   The latest figures (using the definition set out in the Finer Report) suggest that in 1978 there were over three-quarters of a million one-parent families (4 per cent of all families) with nearly one and a half million dependent children (11 per cent of all children).   This is an increase in the number of families of about a third within a period of five years.

The stigma of illegitimacy has diminished.   Illegitimate births are now about 10 per cent of all live births, compared with less than 5 per cent in 1951 (see Table 4.2).   Moreover, whereas in the 1950s a girl who became pregnant was likely to be cast out by her family, today she is more likely to be given help either to have an abortion or, if she gives birth, to keep the child rather than to seek to have it adopted.

Changes in attitudes towards marriage and illegitimacy are linked with the growth in what has become known as the 'permissive society' and with the earlier development of sexual activity among young people.   The proportion of girls who marry in their 'teens has been steadily increasing and a survey conducted in 1976 by Karen Dunnell of the Office of Population Censuses and Surveys showed that rather under 1 per cent of 16-17-year-old and 11 per cent of 18-year-old girls were married.   In 1950 it was not very common, even for adults, to use contraceptive devices unless they were married but today, at the age of 16, whether married or not, young people can obtain the 'pill' from their doctors as of right.   Reliable information is hard to come by but statistics from the Brook Advisory Centres for 1978 show that new clients aged under 16 at their London, Birmingham and Avon centres ranged from 3 to 5.5 per cent.   A national survey, carried-out by the

Institute of Social Studies in Medical Care, reported that, in 1978-9, 22 per cent of girls and 31 per cent of boys aged 16 and 67 per cent of girls and 74 per cent of boys aged 19 claimed they were sexually experienced.   This is a major change in sexual behaviour from the society in which teenagers in the early 1950s grew up.

Unlike the early 1950s, children today are accustomed to their mothers working outside the home.   More than half of all married women aged between 16 and 60 now do paid work, compared with about a fifth in 1951, and those with children of school age are more likely to be working than not working. Most mothers, however, work part time rather than full time. This change, which brings with it both advantages and disadvantages to children, has had profound repercussions on family roles and family responsibilities.

TABLE 4.3 Working mothers

	Great Britain percentages				
	1978 Children aged:				
	0-2	3-4	5-9	10-15	All ages
Paid work done by mother					
None	79	69	52	36	51
Part time	16	25	37	42	35
Full time	5	6	11	22	14
Total mothers	100	100	100	100	100

There are now fewer kin to turn to to help families care for children.   Grandmothers may be working and perhaps live a long way away.   Many children of pre-school age may be cared for by a childminder or go to a pre-school play group during the hours when both parents are away from home.   Many of the older ones go to nursery schools or nursery classes in primary schools.   Day nurseries number only 34,000 and are thus for a tiny minority.   Many school-age children may become what are now known as 'latch-key' children.   After school and during the holidays, those with parents out at work have to do a lot of fending for themselves, trying to find whatever fun and mischief they and their friends can together discover.

Primary schools today are larger (about 200 pupils on average), which means farther from home.   As a consequence, children more often have to be accompanied by an adult because

traffic makes it too dangerous to go alone.   Somehow mothers
- or fathers - have to fit this in with their own work commitments and bend family living patterns to fit the demands of
the educational institution.   Secondary schools today are
also much bigger, with at least 1000 pupils.   The increased
size of schools and their greater distance from home, together
with the apprehensiveness many people feel in the face of
school authorities, may mean that parents have less contact
with the school than a generation ago.

Despite a restiveness about the relevance of traditional
education to the demands of adult life, more children do now
go on to higher education.   Although the majority leave
school at the minimum age, about 20 per cent continue in some
form of higher education compared with only 2 per cent in
1950.   And the average school-leaver is a great deal better
qualified on paper than he was in 1950: in England and Wales
at least a half have achieved one 'O' level pass or its equivalent and over 3 per cent have at least one 'A' level pass.

Children are healthier and better housed.   Although the
development of new towns or new estates on the outskirts of
cities was well under way in the early 1950s, the dwellings
in which most families lived were still near the middle of
big cities.   They were usually rented from a private owner
or from the local council and were often in poor condition.
Today children are more likely to grow up in comparatively
well-equipped houses or flats which their parents are buying
by means of a mortgage.   In 1977 8 per cent of families with
children owned their dwellings outright and nearly 50 per
cent were buying them with a mortgage.

Just as the spread of car ownership has affected the physical environment to which children are exposed, it has also
greatly influenced their leisure activities.   Some three-
quarters of households with children now have the use of a
car and increasingly children expect to be ferried to various
activities and to visit friends.   The dangers of traffic
accidents mean that fewer are allowed to ride bicycles and the
decline and high cost of public transport have added to the
difficulties of getting about.   Paradoxically, children have
lost independence to explore whilst at the same time having
their horizons expanded.

The main change in leisure activities between the two generations has been the growth of television.   Compared with
fewer than half a million television licences issued in 1950,
there were 18 million (covering 96 per cent of all households)
in 1978, of which 11 million were for colour television.   In
1978, children (aged 5 and under 16) on average spent 24 hours
per week watching television in winter and 19 hours in summer.
Unlike the 1950s, however, cinemas are much less important,

not just because there are fewer of them and television is a substitute, but because so few films are now granted a 'U' or 'universal', certificate by the Board of Film Censors and so many of them an 'X' or 'adults only', certificate.

The more violent content of the media is also paralleled in the lives of children and young people. Meaningful statistics are difficult to quote because most crimes committed by children are dealt with informally, but rates for the number of juveniles found guilty or cautioned for indictable offences in the 14-17-year-old age group almost trebled between 1958 and 1978: 15 is the peak age for crime amongst boys and 14 amongst girls. Most of the crimes committed are theft or burglary.

One of the most significant changes of the past generation, reflected in advertisements in the media, is the extent to which young people have more money to spend. Not only do most parents have more to give as pocket money, but, for those children who have left school and have been lucky enough to get employment, wages are both absolutely and relatively much greater than they were a generation ago. They are much better off than those continuing in full-time education and there is consequently considerable diversity in living standards between people in their late 'teens. However, in other respects the difference between children and young people is less apparent in that the way they dress and behave is moulded less by their parents' norms and social class and more by their peers and by the media.

How have all these various changes in the lives of individual children over the past generation affected the family? For example, has it been strengthened or weakened by children enjoying better health, longer education, more money, living in newer and better equipped houses often on new estates or in new towns? How has it been affected by more tolerant attitudes towards illegitimate children? Are the material and other advantages of families in which both parents are earning outweighed by the problems many parents face in making alternative provision for the care of their children? How does the growing lack of respect for authority by children affect other family members? Children are quick to sense that the family is no longer the powerful provider, educator and refuge it once was and, though temporarily they depend on it, soon they will be able to shake it off. The changed attitude of children in turn affects the way parents think about the family. Maybe more of them, finding their children unmanageable, escape into employment, careers and a different marriage. However, it is not the purpose of this chapter to develop these theories but to give the statistical background and suggest some of the links between the different stages of the life-cycle.

YOUNG ADULTS

Today young people in general become adults sooner than they
did a generation ago.   In 1950, 90 per cent of children left
school when they were 15 years old and went out to work.   To
this extent they were adults.   But for the most part they
continued to live at home.   If they stayed at school and went
on to further education till they were 21 or more, they still
remained very much part of the family household.   Today,
although children leave school later and more continue in
further education, they move out of the family home
earlier (3) and, if they are students, often maintain themselves during the vacation.   Increased prosperity has also
enabled more young people in employment to move out of the
family home and, if they can find accommodation, set up their
own households at a much younger age.   By the age of 18 they
are young adults.

   One of the most profound changes affecting the two generations of young people has been the changing status of women.
In 1950 the influence of the war had enormously improved their
status but, as men returned from the Forces, it was for the
most part they who were regarded as the heroes and whose jobs
and careers were to be given preference.   In many jobs, for
example, those who had been in the Forces were allowed to
count the whole of their war service towards pensions but
those - mainly women - whose war service was elsewhere were,
at best, only allowed to count half.   It was not until the
late 1940s that the formal bar on the employment of married
women as permanent Civil Servants or as teachers, and the informal bar existing in companies in the private sector, was
lifted.   But it was above all the Social Security Act of
1948, pioneered by Beveridge, which reflected the more traditional attitude towards women and set the seal on the dependent status of married women in particular for the next 30
years.   A man was (and still is) expected to maintain his
wife, and for social security as well as tax purposes she is
regarded as his dependant.

   Up to the stage in her life when she leaves home and takes
a job, a woman has today had to a large extent much the same
opportunities as a man;   thereafter social forces range up
against her.   Moreover, in 1950, the major changes of the
post-war years were yet to come.   It was twenty years before
the most important piece of legislation - the Equal Pay Act -
was passed in 1970, followed, in December 1975, by the setting
up of the Equal Opportunities Commission to enforce the Sex
Discrimination Act.   Other important legislation directly
affecting women has been the Married Women's Property Act
1964, establishing that husband and wife are entitled to share

equally savings from a housekeeping allowance made by the husband to the wife, the Abortion Act of 1967 and the Guardianship Act of 1973 providing equal rights for the parents over guardianship of children.   The Divorce Reform Act of 1969, by accepting irretrievable breakdown of marriage as grounds for divorce, recognized the independent and individual role of both partners in a marriage.

Many legal and administrative anomalies remain.   Social security and tax policy in particular betray an illogical, confused and fumbling approach.   Entrenched attitudes deeply affect the economic and social position of women.   But the possibility of financial independence which women now have, whether they are married or single, with or without children, brings the beginnings of power and more opportunity to participate in society on an equal footing with others.   The life of a young woman today and her role within the family has changed greatly from that of her predecessor a generation ago. Likewise the impact on family life has been substantial. However, although it may seem that the strength of family ties is diminished if wives as well as husbands have more freedom to be independent, to break the marriage bond and to set up house on their own, it does not follow that the family or the quality of family life is harmed thereby.

How does life for young people generally differ from what it was like in the 1950s?   One striking change has been the balance between the sexes.   Whereas today there are 105 men to every 100 women between the ages of 16 and under 30, in the early 1950s the balance was more equal (see Table 4.4).   One likely consequence in the longer term, in sharp contrast to previous generations, is that the proportion of men who will remain permanently single will greatly exceed that of women.

Young people today are more likely to be married today than a generation ago: in 1951 only 82 per cent of women and 75 per cent of men aged 30 were married, compared with 92 and 82 per cent today (Table 4.3).   Although recent trends have begun to change, most people now marry at a younger age, say, $23\frac{1}{2}$ if a man and $21\frac{1}{2}$ if a woman, compared with just over 25 and just over 23 in 1951 (Table 4.3).

There has, however, been a marked change in attitudes towards marriage and sexual relations.   As already indicated in this chapter, sexual intercourse takes place at a much younger age than a generation ago.   It is also far more common before marriage: a survey carried out by OPCS in 1976 indicated that, whereas in 1971-5 three-quarters of women had sexual intercourse with their husbands before marriage, in 1956-60 only one-third did so.   Artificial aids to contraception are readily available to people of all social classes in a way it would have been difficult to imagine in 1950.

TABLE 4.4 Demographic influences affecting the life-cycle stages of the two generations alive in 1952 and 1977

Birth years of those reaching specified life cycle stages in 1952 and 1977 respectively ('Yesterday') 1952 Cohort I	('Today') 1977 Cohort II	Birth rates per 1000 women 15-45 (2)	Expectation of life at birth (1) M	F
	1976-9 ⎤	62	69.7	75.8
	1971-5	73	68.9	75.1
	1966-70 ⊢Childhood	88		
	1961-5	92	67.9	73.8
	1956-60 ⎦	83		
	1951-5 ⎤ Young adult life	74	66.2	71.2
	1946-50 ⎦	82		
Childhood —	1941-5	68		
	1936-40	62		
	1931-5	63	58.4	62.5
Young adult life —	1926-30 ⊢Middle life	70		
	1921-5	82	55.4	59.3
	1916-20	82		
	1911-15	97	51.4	55.2
Middle life —	1906-10	107		
	1901-5 ⊢Old age	114	48.1	51.8
	1891-1900	123		
	1881-90	139		
Old age —	1871-80	154		
	1861-70	152		
	1851-60	146	40	42

1 Beginning of period.
2 Average for period.
3 Aged 15-49.

Source: Office of Population Censuses and Surveys: Various publications.

Great Britain (unless otherwise specified)				
Sex ratio males per 100 females 15-45 (1)	Women aged 30: propor- tion ever married (1) (per cent)	Median age of marriage of spin- sters (2)	Persons divorcing per 1000 married popula- tion (2)	Average size of house- hold (1)
(UK)	(E & W)	(E & W)	(E & W)	
104 p	92	21.5 p	10.4 p	2.8
103	91	21.4	8.5	2.9
	91	21.3	3.9	3.0
101	89	21.4	2.6	3.0
	85	21.8	2.1	
99	82	22.4	2.6	3.2
	77	23.0	3.7	
97	75	22.8	1.0	
	70	24.1	0.6	
91	70	24.3	0.5	3.7
		24.3	0.4	
88		24.3	0.4	4.1
		24.4	0.2	
93		24.5	0.1	4.4
		25.1	0.1	
92		24.9	0.1	4.6
92 (3)				

93 (3)

Younger women are more likely to use the pill as a form of
contraception than older women of an earlier generation: the
OPCS survey showed that over a half of those aged 20-4 used
it, compared with only a tenth of those aged 40-9.

By the time they reach the age of 30 many people will
already have been divorced and may have remarried.   In 1976,
6.8 per cent of men and 9.5 per cent of women who had reached
this age had been divorced, compared with 1.7 per cent and
2.9 per cent in 1956 (Table 4.5).   3.7 per cent of men and
5.3 per cent of women had remarried in 1976, compared with 1.1
per cent and 2.4 per cent in 1956.   Remarriages - for one or
both partners - now amount to about one-third of all marriages, compared with less than one-fifth in 1951.

TABLE 4.5   Proportions (per 1000 of generations who had
divorced by selected ages

Birth generation (1)	England and Wales Age (exact years)			
	25	30	40	50
(a) Males				
1926	3	17	49	93
1936	2	20	100	
1946	8	68		
1952	21			
(b) Females				
1926	9	29	58	95
1936	7	31	103	
1946	20	95		
1952	43			

1   This represents an approximation to the year of birth of
generation.

Source: Richard Leete, op. cit., Table 36.

Those who are 30 today will have had fewer children than if
they had lived a generation ago.   Moreover, whereas average
completed family size used to be inversely related to social
class, today the distribution is more U-shaped, with non-
manual workers in Social Class III having the smallest number
of children.   Although changes in fertility are very difficult to predict, particularly with the increasing number of
second marriages, more couples now do not have children at all
(Figure 4.1).   Although this trend is characteristic of other
highly industrialized countries and reflects many social factors, such as the attraction of higher living standards when

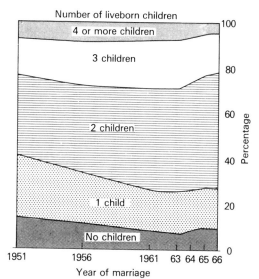

FIGURE 4.1   Family size distributions after 10 years of marriage (for women married at ages of 20-4 and married once only)
Source: 'Social Trends', no. 9, HMSO 1979.

both husband and wife are in employment, in Britain the trend may have been exaggerated by housing problems.   In 1950, scarce though housing still was, privately rented accommodation was available to help young people set up home gradually. Today it is even harder to find and, because it is also very difficult to get on a local authority housing list, many young couples buy a small house or flat with a mortgage granted on the basis of two incomes.   If they have a child, not only is more space needed, but one of them may have to give up full-time employment at least temporarily.   This period after the birth of a first child, when only one income is available and there are three mouths to feed instead of two, may, for many families, be one of near poverty.

Standards of living depend very much on the number of earners in a household and whether or not there are children. Figures published for 1978 (Table 4.6) on incomes at various stages of the family cycle show that the average disposable income of households with two adults and no children and in which the head was aged under 25 was £5,090;   in households with two adults and young children (i.e. youngest under 5) it was only £4,710.   In the first case, 80 per cent of households contained wives working full time and 10 per cent

working part time; in the second case, the rates drop to 20
per cent full time and 20 per cent part time.

Compared with 1950, fewer young adults now go to church or
smoke, but they are more likely to take other drugs and drink
wine, as well as beer and whisky. It is more difficult to
identify occupation or social class from style of dress.
Indeed, up to the age of 30, incomes of manual and non-manual
workers are not very different on average; however, non-manual
workers have better prospects, particularly if they have
obtained a first or postgraduate degree or its equivalent.
Far more have qualifications of some kind than their 1950 predecessors. To some extent thas has meant better jobs because
changes in the occupational structure of the country have resulted in there being more of the better paid professional and
other service industry jobs; but because there are more
people with more qualifications, including women, the scramble
for these jobs is fiercer, particularly during a situation of
high unemployment. Young people are specially disadvantaged
because employers, faced with paying relatively high wages
with high overheads and fairly tough legislation regarding
dismissal, are more likely to play safe and take on people
with experience.

Social change has made class distinctions between young
adults less important over the past generation. It has also
reduced the segregation between the sexes in the way they
live. No longer are they rigidly separated into 'women's
hostels' or 'men's hostel's, but houses and households are
shared in a way it would have been difficult to foresee in
1950. By far the most significant change has been the fact
that women now have a status more nearly equivalent to men.
A young man who has a girlfriend meets her on a more equal
footing and is less likely to have the same feelings of responsibility for her. She is able to keep herself financially
and she has more control over whether or not she has children.
Even if she does have a child there is not the same obligation
to marry. Life for a single parent may be very difficult but
Supplementary Benefit is there as an ultimate safety net
against starvation. These changes in their turn affect young
people's attitudes to employment, both the occupations they
wish to follow and the extent to which they remain committed
to one particular job.

MIDDLE LIFE

Arbitrarily, we can use age 30 as the point of entry to middle
life. The point at which middle life ends and people are
regarded as old rather than middle-aged tends to be somewhat

later today than in 1950, despite the fact that the age for
drawing a National Insurance pension remains at 65 for men and
60 for women.   Those in middle life (i.e. aged 30 and under
60) in the early 1950s were born between 1891 and 1921:   the
period covers the years of economic and political uncertainty
at the end of the last century followed by the 1914-18 war
years and their immediate aftermath.   Although birth rates
were on balance declining, particularly among the middle
classes, they were still high and families were large: nearly
two-thirds of women married around 1860 had five or more
children.   Infant mortality, however, was high, medical knowledge limited and poverty widespread.   Many of those in mid-
life in 1950 thus bore the physical stamp of their birth years
and were less fit at the age of 60 than their counterparts a
generation later.

TABLE 4.6   Distribution of family size in Great Britain

(Births occurring to first marriages)				(%)
Number of children live-born in marriage	Women married in period			
	Mainly around 1860	1900-9	1920-4	1935-9	1955-9 (part estimated)
0	9	10	16	15	9
1	5	14	24	26	18
2	6	18	24	29	34
3	8	16	14	15	20
4	9	12	8	7	(11)
5 or more	63	30	14	8	(8)
	100	100	100	100	100
Average number of children	5.7	3.5	2.4	2.1	(2.4)

Source: Office of Population Censuses and Surveys

   The birth years of this later generation - 1912 to 1947 -
also spanned economic depression and war, but birth rates were
lower and families smaller (less than one-third of women married in the early 1900s had four or more children), living
standards were higher and medical knowledge more highly

developed.   By the time they are 60, people today will thus
tend to be physically fitter than their predecessors and might
be said not to become 'old' till they are 65.

Those in mid-life in the early 1950s were brought up during
a period when class distinctions were sharp and poverty for
many was very severe: when they were young, if they belonged
to the middle class, their families probably had servants,
their mothers did not do paid work and there were relatives
and other children around to help care for them and keep them
company.   Although these conditions no longer prevailed in
1950, the attitudes they shaped were still part of their make-
up.   Today, attitudes amongst those in middle life are different and for the most part it is accepted that families do
not have servants, that rising service costs lead most people
to do a variety of odd jobs around the house, that both
parents probably work, that children go to comprehensive
schools, that the National Health Service is for everybody
and that most families own their own houses, have cars, TV
sets, a five-day working week and four weeks paid holiday.
That important variations remain is evident.   The children of
manual workers are still less likely to aspire to university
and unskilled workers still have a higher chance of being unemployed, of living in over-crowded conditions and of suffering from ill health.   For most immigrants the problems are
magnified.

Standards of living between the two periods have, on
average, risen significantly.   Not only have earnings risen,
but, unlike 1950, most households in this middle stage of the
family cycle now have two earners.   In 1978 half the two-
adult households where the youngest child was five years old
or more included wives who were working part time and at least
20 per cent working full time (Table 4.7).   In contrast to
the relative prosperity of these two-parent families with
children and probably two earners, a growing and already significant number (4 per cent of all families and 11 per cent of
all children under 16) consist of only one parent and, very
often, no earners.   Figures based on the small numbers identified in the Family Expenditure Survey suggest that disposable incomes in 1978 in these latter households amounted to
£2,960 or, on average, more than £2,000 less than those in
two-adult households with children (Table 4.7).

In the later stages of middle life, household incomes can
vary very considerably, depending on whether children remain
in full-time education, take up employment and contribute
their earnings or leave home altogether.   On balance, however, the period is one of comparative prosperity in that the
ratio of earners to spenders is more favourable.   Inheritance
too, for the more fortunate families, starts to play an impor-

tant part as the older generation begins to die.   On the
assumption that the children do not inherit until their mother
dies, the ages at which they can expect to inherit are a function of the mother's age at their birth and of her expectation
of life at that time.   The steadily increasing expectation of
life over the past century and the more recent falls in the
average age at which mothers give birth, reflecting both
earlier marriage and the much smaller time span devoted to
childrearing, have combined to delay the age at which wealth
is passed from one generation to the next.   A woman aged 30
at the beginning of the century could expect to live an additional 37 years, over ten years less than today.   She also
married, on average, nearly three years later and her age at
the birth of her comparatively large number of children would,
on average, have been over 30.   Thus, her children could
expect to inherit when they were in their mid-thirties.
Today the average age at which a woman has children is about
26, an age when she can expect to live almost another 52
years.   The expectation of life of those who own property is
likely to be higher than average but, as they tend to marry
and have children later, the age at which their children
inherit is probably not markedly different from that of other
social classes.

A further effect of the shrinking gap between the generations and the longer expectation of life is that the chance
that those in middle life will have one or more parents living
has become much greater than for previous generations.   Thus,
when their own children become independent, they are more
likely to be called upon to help care for the older generation;   moreover, because of the smaller size of families (a
factor which also affects the numbers who might expect to gain
from inheritance), there are fewer of them to do the caring.

As at other stages of the life-cycle, standards of living
thus depend very much on family circumstances.   In general
and over the period as a whole, real incomes more than
doubled.   According to the reports of the Royal Commission on
the Distribution of Income and Wealth there was a small narrowing of the differential between households in the top and
bottom income groups (both before and after tax) due almost
entirely to a squeezing of the top 5 per cent of households.
Redistribution of income to families with children in the
form of family allowances remained at about 2 per cent of
original gross income: income tax and national insurance
contributions both increased substantially but deductions from
families with children changed in much the same proportion as
from other non-retired households.

Class differences become apparent in the way people spend
their money and there is evidence to suggest that there has

TABLE 4.7 Average incomes, taxes and benefits, 1978 (by life-cycle category of households)

United Kingdom

£ per year

	2 adults, non-retired, no children, head under 25	2 adults, 1-4 children, youngest child under 5	2 adults, 1-4 children, youngest child 5 or more	2 adults non-retired, no children head 45-65	2 adults, retired, no children	1 adult, non-retired, with children
All households Number of households in the sample	117	899	871	771	611	207
Original income	6,130	5,210	6,300	5,810	1,260	2,040
Direct benefits in cash:						
Family allowance/child benefit, Family Income Supplement	–	200	210	–	–	230
Retirement, old age and widows' pensions	20	–	20	70	1,420	110
Sickness, disablement and related pension	30	70	90	120	150	30
Unemployment benefit	40	50	30	20	10	10
Supplementary benefit	20	60	40	30	70	700
Other benefits and grants	–	50	–	–	20	–
Original income *plus* cash benefits	6,240	5,620	6,690	6,050	2,930	3,130
Direct taxes:						
National Insurance	300	220	230	210	–	40
Income tax and surtax	860	700	980	1,030	210	130

Disposable income	5,090	4,710	5,480	4,820	2,720	2,960
Indirect subsidies	50	110	100	120	150	200
Indirect taxes	1,040	940	1,090	970	530	600
Income after all taxes and transfers	4,090	3,880	4,490	3,960	2,340	2,570
Direct benefits in kind:						
Education benefit	—	280	860	10	—	730
National Health Service	210	390	940	260	440	260
Welfare foods	—	30	70	—	—	120
Income after all taxes and benefits	4,300	4,590	5,750	4,220	2,780	3,680
Number of full-time workers per household	1.8	1.2	1.2	1.3	—	0.3
Number of part-time workers per household	0.1	0.2	0.5	0.3	0.1	0.3
Number of persons per household	2.0	3.9	3.9	2.0	2.0	2.9

Source: 'Economic Trends', January 1979, Effect of Taxes and Benefits on Household Income,1977, HMSO.

been a levelling between the two generations.   For example, in the 1950s, many types of goods - refrigerators, washing machines, telephones, cars, television sets - were beyond the reach of most people.   In 1977, of two-adult households with children, about 95 per cent owned refrigerators, 90 per cent a washing machine, almost two-thirds had a telephone, three-quarters had the use of a car and nearly everybody had a tele-vision set.   Housing standards in particular have improved greatly.   Whereas in 1951 central heating was rare, in 1977 nearly two-thirds of two-adult households with children had it.   In 1951, 37.5 per cent of households were without a fixed bath but by 1976 the figure was less than 5 per cent.

The growing similarity in domestic possessions as indicated in the aggregate statistics conceal some very great differ-ences which exist - and may be increasing - between those families where there are two parents, one or both working, and where there is only one parent, and that one possibly not working.   For example, whereas the paragraphs above indicate that, in 1977, nearly all two-parent families owned refrigera-tors and washing machines, almost two-thirds had a telephone and three-quarters a car, the corresponding figures for one-parent families were 83 per cent, 72 per cent, two-fifths and one-quarter.   The sense of relative deprivation was less marked in the 1950s when these possessions were confined to the privileged few.

But incomes and possessions do not in themselves tell us much about the quality of family life.   The care, love and warmth which bind the members of poor families can be as great or greater than the rich.   It is not the level of income but the attitude of mind which has given 'suburbia' a pejorative meaning and leads to a suspicion that the values engendered by the acquisition of and the very goods it possesses may be inimical to vital and creative family living.   Some of these issues are examined more closely in other chapters in this volume.

THE ELDERLY

In 1950 people tended to be regarded as old by the time they were 60.   They had been born before the turn of the century against a background of poverty, hard work and poor housing, when children under 15 made up nearly one-third of the popula-tion and those over 60 only 7.5 per cent (compared with roughly equal proportions of about one-fifth today - see Table 4.1).   Educational levels, and possibly the development of life interests, were lower.   Today old people not only look younger - if only because better dentistry has enabled them to

keep or acquire a full set of teeth and the NHS has also provided them with spectacles and hearing aids - but their health
and expectation of life have increased.   Bronchitis in particular is less likely to afflict them.   In 1951, a man aged
60 could expect a further 14.7 years of life and a woman a
further 18 years.   Today not only do more people survive but
at 60 a man can expect 15.5 more years and a woman 20.1 years:
life expectancy for older women has thus increased more than
for men (Table 4.4).   Moreover, the structure of the population has shifted and there are many more old people: whereas
in 1951 a quarter of the population was over the age of 52,
today it has moved up to over 55.   The age of men who have
retired has moved down quite sharply over the past generation.
In 1951 nearly half of those aged 65-9 were still in employment and one-fifth of those 70 and over: the corresponding
figures today are less than one-third and one-tenth.   The
trends for women, particularly married women, have moved differently: negligible proportions over the age of 60 were employed in 1951 but today over a quarter of those aged 60-4 are
in paid employment.

TABLE 4.8 Economic activity rates (1) 1951, 1971 and 1981

		1951 %	1971 %	1981 (2) %
Males:	60-4	88	87	85
	65-9	48	30	25
	70 or over	20	11	9
Females:	Single:			
	55-9	64	76	n.a.
	60-4	35	33	n.a.
	65 or over	11	8	n.a.
	Married:			
	55-9	16	45	56
	60-4	7	25	32
	65 or over	3	6	8
	Widowed:			
	55-9	39	62	n.a.
	60-4	19	34	n.a.
	65 or over	5	6	n.a.

1 Activity rate = percentage of the population in the age
   group who are gainfully employed.
2 Department of Employment projection.

Source: 'Profiles of the Elderly', vol. 1, Table 8, Age
         Concern 1977.

Both those who were elderly in the early 1950s (born before 1891) and those who are elderly today (born before 1912) have been affected by the high death rates among men during the First World War and by the high emigration rates, particularly of men, during the inter-war years. Those who are nearly 80 or over today show an extremely high imbalance between the sexes, with more than two women to every man.

In 1950 many elderly people lived with their families. Only about 10-15 per cent lived alone. Today far more elderly people live apart from their families. The 1977 General Household Survey showed that, out of an estimated total of nearly 8½ million elderly people over 65, over 30 per cent (2½ million) were living alone, 45 per cent (3¾ million) with a spouse only, and only 25 per cent (2 million) in other types of household; it is further estimated that fewer than 5 per cent live in institutions.

More old people now live alone, partly because their children have moved away from the parental home in search of employment and a more favourable environment, but also because they themselves are likely to be more prosperous. Those who have saved sufficient money and have an occupational pension as well as a social security one may have been able to afford to move away from old housing and local authority rented accommodation in city centres to new, well-equipped houses or flats in a coastal belt or other 'retirement' area. Wherever they live, however, steeply rising fuel costs now make it more difficult for them to keep warm in winter: only about a third of people over retirement age living alone have some form of central heating, compared with half of all households generally.

A generation ago old people relied very little on cars and a great deal on buses, trains and walking to visit friends and relatives. Today, many of those who are able to drive a car find it too expensive to run and the deterioration in public transport services increases their isolation. The use of the telephone is now widespread but fewer than half the people over retirement age have one, and in any case it is not the same as talking to friends and relatives face-to-face. Most old people have television to entertain them, but it may mean that they become still less inclined to make the effort to go out and meet people. Poverty too increases isolation. Although relatively more prosperous than in 1950, the elderly are still poor compared with most other families (Table 4.7). Single women particularly are likely to be poor: in 1976 more than a third were receiving Supplementary Benefit. There are still some wealthy elderly people but they are far less common proportionately than they were a generation ago.

Many of the elderly today, like their counterparts a

generation ago, come from large families.   They themselves,
however, on average had fewer children and, as Mark Abrams has
described in his report on a survey of the elderly carried out
by Age Concern in 1977, those who had the smallest number of
children are more likely to have survived.   In general, as
the elderly grow older and frailer there will be relatively
fewer of the younger generation to help care for them.   Moreover, more of their daughters, as well as their sons, are
likely to be working.   A further problem over the next 20
years is the increasing numbers of very elderly people at a
time when the numbers of younger elderly are declining.   As
they grow older many elderly people cease to have any family
at all.   Their parents, their spouse and siblings are dead.
Even their children, if they had any, may have died or moved
away out of reach.   These are the loneliest of our households.

NOTES

1   The author is particularly indebted to Mr E. Grebenik and
    Miss J. Thompson of the Office of Population Censuses and
    Surveys who not only helped with the statistics but also
    commented at length on the text.
2   The statistics in this chapter generally relate to Great
    Britain.   A variety of sources has been used.   The prin-
    cipal ones are: Central Statistical Office, 'Social
    Trends';   Office of Population Censuses and Surveys,
    'General Household Survey', 'Population Trends', 'Registrar
    General's Statistical Review of England and Wales', 'Birth
    Statistics', 'Marriage and Divorce Statistics', 'Demo-
    graphic Review 1977':   E. Grebenik, 'Family Formation 1976'
    1976':   Karen Dunnell, 'Changing Patterns of Family Forma-
    tion and Dissolution in England and Wales 1964-76':
    Richard Leete;   General Register Office, Scotland, 'Regis-
    trar General's Annual Report';   'Report of the Royal Com-
    mission on Population', Cmnd 7695, HMSO 1949;   'Report of
    the Population Panel', Cmnd 5258, HMSO 1973;   Department
    of Employment, 'Family Expenditure Survey'.

Part III

Quality of life in families

Chapter 5

Conventional families

Ann Oakley

Once upon a time there was a woman who was just like all
women.   And she married a man who was just like all men.
And they had some children who were just like all children.
And it rained all day.

The woman had to skewer up the hole in the kitchen sink,
when it was blocked up.

The man went to the pub every Friday, Saturday and
Sunday.   The other nights he mended his broken bicycle,
did the pool coupons and longed for money and power.

The woman read love stories and longed for things to be
different.

The children fought and yelled and played and had scabs
on their knees.

In the end they all died. (Smart, 1978:89)

DEFINING THE IMAGE

The notion of a 'conventional family' as it is found in
Britain and other industrialised countries today, is one particular cultural interpretation of the 'facts' of sexuality
and reproduction.   It represents these as properly located
within a certain structure, both morally preferable to, and
statistically predominant over, others.   The idea of 'the
family' as used in everyday life has reference to this para-
digm of conventionality: the small nuclear family of two
parents and their dependent children.   Because of the importance of the idea of the conventional family in both the
sociology of marriage and the family and the realities it aims
to depict, this, together with some of its ramifications in
contemporary British culture, is the focus of this chapter.

It is more difficult to say what a conventional family is,
than what it is not.   Many 'deviations' are closely guarded

family secrets because, both in ideology and practice, the
family is a private place, and many conventions sustained in
public are broken in private. Incest, child-battering and
mental illness are extreme examples, but on more mundane
indices such as the distribution of income and housework, many
'conventional' families may maintain arrangements which con-
travene public norms. Thus, husbands may not give their
wives sufficient housekeeping money, or they may be prepared
to do domestic tasks (for example nappy-changing) in private
that they would not happily admit to in public.

Conventional families are nuclear families composed of
legally married couples, voluntarily choosing the parenthood
of one or more (but not too many) children (otherwise they
become another category, 'large families'). Parents and
children reside together as a distinct domestic unit. About
four in ten of all British households are of the nuclear
family type according to 1966 data (General Register Office,
1966:Table 1). This low figure may represent some enforced
attrition of ideals (through for instance, housing problems).
Stacey (1975:110) notes that fewer families conformed to the
ideal pattern in Banbury in 1966 than in 1950. More than
90 per cent of the population get married, around 80 per cent
of adults become parents (Busfield and Paddon, 1977:133), and
88 per cent of families with dependent children are of the
'married couple' type (OPCS Monitor, 29 May 1979, Table 3).
There are grounds for supposing that more people would like to
achieve a conventional family life than actually do so - that
is, as measured in official statistics at any one point in
time. While some 'families' may remain childless or have
only one child, and others have four or more, the average
number of children for women married in 1960-4 is 2.4 (General Household Survey, 1979:Table 2.22), very close to what
has been described (Leach, 1966) as the 'cereal packet' norm.
Most family intentions/fertility surveys find a preferred
mixed-sex pattern of two or three children (Cartwright, 1976;
OPCS, 1978:17-19); according to the Family Formation Survey
(OPCS, 1979:Table 12.3), the ideal family size is 2.4 children
for recent marriage cohorts. Certain other norms of family
life can be derived from official statistics. For example,
the modal age of marriage for women is 21 and for men it is 23
(OPCS, 1979:7): this age difference is in accordance with what
is widely considered 'proper' (Leonard, 1980). It is not
possible to say in how many nuclear family households the
husband-father is employed since employment statistics are not
differentiated by marital status for men, but the General
Household Survey (1979:Table 4.4) shows that 98 per cent of
men aged 25-34 are economically active, compared with 48 per
cent of *married* women in the same age group. The proportion

of mothers who work for pay is lower when the youngest child is under five and highest when he/she is over ten (OPCS, 1978: 20).

Judged by statistical criteria alone, the conventional family is no longer 'normal'. On the contrary, it is not, at any given time, the prevailing social arrangement. Complicating this question of what official statistics mean is the fact that the collection of statistical data is itself an ideological exercise reflecting data-collectors' ideas of normality, which are no less, and probably somewhat more, conventional than those held by the population at large (Oakley and Oakley, 1979).

One way to approach an understanding of the power of the *idea* of conventional family life is to look at families whose normality is threatened by illness, handicap, death or desertion. In a study of the wives of mental patients, one of the most disturbing effects of the diagnosis of mental illness was felt to be that 'The "reputation of the social front" of the family as a congenial, happy group seems shattered' (Yarrow et al., 1955:35). The women in this study were torn between a need for help and support from other people and the belief that only close family members should act as confidants in this way. More recently, Voysey (1975) has spelt out the lessons that may be learnt about the public image-maintenance of family life from a study of twenty-one families with disabled children. By observing the efforts taken by such families to normalise their situation publicly, she concludes that conventional family norms require people to feel that they must (a) provide housing which has the properties of a home, (b) present a front of good health and appearance, (c) allocate time, money and domestic work according to the 'needs' and 'capabilities' of family members, and (d) ensure the socially acceptable behaviour of members outside the home, especially in the case of young children.

Central to the idea of the conventional family is a differentiation by age, occupation and gender between the roles of family members. Parents are responsible for children and not vice versa (until parental old age reverses this pattern). Children go to school and then learn a trade or profession that can make them economically independent. Parents work, but the expectation is that women's work will be in the home and not for pay; men's outside and for pay. Father's involvement with children during out-of-office or out-of-factory hours does not weaken the basic differentiation, and the work of married women which is concentrated in part-time, low-paid and contingent jobs (i.e. jobs which are retained or given up to suit the requirements of the husband's and children's needs) can be seen as an extension of it.

To ask how such ideologies arise is to ask where the image of the conventional family comes from, and why it has taken such a powerful hold on personal relations in twentieth-century Britain.

ORIGINS AND EXPLANATIONS

Before the rise of industrial capitalism, the family was the unit of economic production.   A division of labour by sex (and age) within the family existed;   equal valuation appears to have attached to the roles of both sexes (Scott and Tilly, 1975; Turner, 1971).   Because the family was co-terminous with the world of work, family life and commodity production were synonymous activities.   With the organisation of production in factories under capitalism, two divisions occurred: between the family and work, and between work and personal life.   The first division is the one usually held responsible for the high degree of gender-differentiation of husband-wife roles in the Victorian family, on which modern contemporary family ideals are largely based.   But it is probably the second that was the more determining influence.
    As Zaretsky (1976) has pointed out, the separation of home and work assigned to women a new specialist role as managers and guardians of human relations skills.   This new responsibility for personal relations developed at a time when circumstances facilitated an interpretation of women as more closely tied to the home than men.   These circumstances were the absence of effective fertility control and a safe technology for the artificial feeding of infants, the constriction of employment opportunities with the move towards capital-intensive industry, a masculine hegemony in positions of public power (government, administration, the Church, the legal, medical and academic professions) and the creation of childhood as a legally protected and distinct state. Although some historians (e.g. Anderson, 1971; MacPherson, 1964) have diagnosed the modification of traditional family values with capitalism as one of the replacement of familial by individualistic values, this development is likely to have been more applicable to males than to females, a fact perhaps under-appreciated by male reconstructors of the past.
    During the Victorian era a set of beliefs evolved in which women's domesticity acquired the character of a moral imperative.   Smelser describes the character of these beliefs, and Davidoff, L'Esperance and Newby (1976) indicate that they became crystallised in a form that can be termed as 'mythology' because, as Branca (1975) has observed, the beliefs were always considerably at odds with the realities of

women's lives.   Though espoused mainly by middle-class families, this variance held in both working- and middle-class
contexts.   Nevertheless, this belief system was, and is,
extremely influential in forming images of how conventional
families ought to behave.   Scientific theories of the day reflected, and in their turn legitimated, these beliefs.   'Scientists in areas as diverse as zoology, embryology, physio-
logy, heredity, anthropology and psychology argued that the
pattern of male-female relations that characterised the
English middle classes was natural, inevitable and progressive' (Fee, 1976:180).   Predominant among 'scientific'
theories was that of evolutionism, given new life by Darwin's
'On the Origin of Species', first published in 1859.   Among
the experts most ardently espousing this evolutionary theory
were the 'social' scientists: L.H. Morgan, Auguste Comte,
Herbert Spencer and, in North America, Lester F. Ward and
W.I. Thomas (see Schwendiger and Schwendiger, 1974, especially
Part Ten).   Their general view was that the monogamous family
with patriarchal husband-father at work and submissive-nur-
turant (and nurtured) wife-mother at home was the highest development in a long sequence of family types.   Men had reached
a higher point of evolution than women, whose maturation was
arrested at the level of 'primitives' or children, fitting
them for the performance of the necessary animal function of
reproduction but for little else (Shields, 1975).

RESEARCH ON CONVENTIONAL FAMILIES

In the twentieth century much sociological theory and research
in the area of the family and marriage has continued in the
tradition presuming middle-class conventionality in family
life.   For example, Bott's germinal work in 1956 on families
and their social networks made an important distinction
between joint and segregated marital role relationships.
The typology was based on 'general resemblances' among groups
of families.   Bott says that:
  among the research couples there were some general resemblances in the type of organization characteristically
  followed in a particular type of activity.... Thus in all
  families there was a basic division of labour, by which the
  husband was primarily responsible for supporting the family
  financially and the wife was primarily responsible for
  housework and child-care; each partner made his own differentiated but complementary contribution to the welfare
  of the family as a whole. (Bott, 1971 (revised edn):54)
Bott experienced difficulty in getting the twenty families in
her sample to state the norms of family life to which they

adhered, as they were to a large extent implicit.   They had
to be deduced indirectly from the families' accounts.   Bott
lists (1971:197) as 'norms of common consent' the following:
1 financial independence and a separate dwelling for each
   nuclear family;
2 a basic division of labour by gender with husband-father
   supporting the family financially and wife-mother doing the
   domestic work and childrearing;
3 condemnation of adultery as a serious offence;
4 parental care for children until children are able to look
   after themselves.
Adherence to these norms varied with different social locations.   Bott described two main patterns.   In the first,
husband and wife develop their marriage based on an external
network that is close-knit - i.e. many members know one
another.   Marriage is superimposed on pre-existing close-knit
relationships which merge and continue.   But within the home
there is a separation between the roles of husband and wife.
With the birth of children the wife's external supports are
local and kin-centred;   while the husband's are based on
friends and workmates.   There is a high degree of interconnection between his and her external networks in the sense
that they know one another and feel themselves to be part of
the same community despite the gender segregation.

   The second pattern Bott describes is one of loose-knit networks for each partner existing prior to marriage, and continuing afterwards, so that more of the couple's emotional needs
and energies are directed inwards to the marriage itself.   In
this kind of pattern the couples are more likely to stress
equality and to share interests and activities both in and
outside the home.

   The first of Bott's patterns, that of segregated conjugal
role relationships in combination with close-knit networks,
appears to predominate in settled, working-class communities.
As a theme it has dominated sociological literature on the
family in the post-war period.   An informal 'mother's union'
of mothers and daughters was depicted in Bethnal Green by the
Institute of Community Studies in the 1950s, who drew attention to the symbolic power of motherhood as 'John Bowlby had
done for their psychoanalytically-oriented predecessors, and
concern with the Virgin Mary for their religious ancestors'
(Frankenburg, 1976:43).   'The domestic power of the Mum' is a
chapter in Kerr's 1958 study of a Liverpool slum, 'The People
of Ship Street', and other community studies such as Rees
(1950) in Wales, Humphreys (1966) in Ireland, Stacey (1960) in
Banbury and Dennis et al.(1956) in a Yorkshire mining town, have
described a similar phenomenon to that noted by Young and
Willmott (1957) in Bethnal Green.   In all cases, the point

was made that this structure, which Young and Willmott termed
the Demeter bond, arose partly as a reaction to male solidarity outside the home.   Stacey (1960:124) notes that the
dependent position of women gives them an economic interest in
maintaining relationships with the extended family.   In Wood-
ford, a middle-class dormitory suburb where norms of segregated feminine domesticity persisted but without the close tie-
in to the external system, Young and Willmott (1960) found
less emphasis on the mother-daughter tie and more on the ex-
clusivity of the nuclear family.   It is a theme in much of
the sociological literature that the conventional family form
characterised by rigidly segregated conjugal roles, close-knit
networks and a highly articulated mother-daughter tie, is disappearing.   The disruption of working-class communities and
consequent mobility are seen as combining with improvements in
the status of women to institute the joint-role nuclear family
as the prevailing statistical norm and cultural ideal.
Middle-class families, according to the studies that have been
done of their kinship beliefs and behaviour, show a lot of
variation in this respect (Bell, 1969; Firth et al., 1969;
Rosser and Harris, 1965) though women continue to be what
Firth and his colleagues (1969:139) call 'kin-keepers'.

   In an examination of attitudes to sex and marriage in 1950
and 1969 Gorer found a move amongst younger people away from
an emphasis on the desirability of a double-standard towards
'an ideal of equality, of husband and wife doing everything
together, of minimal separation of interests or pursuits *outside working hours*' (Gorer, 1971), a qualification I have
italicised because of its considerable significance in defining what is meant by equality.

   Young and Willmott (1973) have more recently argued that
the fundamental shift that has occurred in the family is to
organise its functions around its status as a unit of consumption.   This fits with Galbraith's (1973) analysis of
women's 'real work' as housework, servicing and childrearing,
while the 'real work' of men remains outside the domestic
economy.   But the narrow concept of the family as a unit of
consumption obscures the productive character of women's work
within it: the family, as Delphy (1976) and others have
argued, is a system of productive relations.   The idea of
the family as a consumption unit also obscures the force of
women's own socialisation to domesticity which promotes their
identification with, and commitment to the role of housewife
(Oakley, 1974), and is an obstacle to the evolution of more
egalitarian family patterns (Rapoport and Rapoport, 1976).

   It is characteristic of conventional families with segregated conjugal roles, that the belief in housework and child
care as women's work and the belief that only men ought to be

economic providers flourishes more strongly than in joint role families.   There are pronounced social class differences here: working-class couples are more likely to voice a 'traditional' ideology of gender roles and those in the middle class to advocate slightly more flexible arrangements (Hoffman and Nye, 1974; Oakley, 1974 ; Young and Willmott, 1973), though some middle-class groups, for example the managerial families studied by Pahl and Pahl (1971) may practise and preach a highly segregated division of labour by gender.   So strong is the identification of domestic work with femininity that even such variants as dual-career families and alterna-tive families rarely manage to break away completely from the conventional gender pattern (Rapoport and Rapoport, 1976; Abrams and McCulloch, 1976).

Economic pressures may also provide constraints.   Male un-employment or low income may direct wives into an employment role, the taking of which does not necessarily indicate the presence of an egalitarian ideology.   Conventionally, it has been acceptable for a married woman to take a paid job if there are financial problems; so this was a frequent response in early surveys on women's motivation to work (Hunt, 1968). However, the desire for company and the need to get out of the home are now explicitly recognised as motives.

The rise in married women's employment has, however, con-stituted a major development in conventional family life over the last three decades, bringing this family form more into line with its pre-industrial counterpart.   The trend towards more employment among married women is not reflected in a com-mensurate change in male domestic roles, precisely because the sex-role ideology remains conventional.

At every point in the family life-cycle, time-budget studies show that women shoulder the heaviest domestic burden; this is true not only of countries whose official morality is one of conventionality in family life, but of those, such as Scandinavia and the USSR, which espouse more egalitarian ideals (Oakley, 1974:94, 1979; Lapidus, 1977; Sacks, 1977; Robinson, Converse and Szalai, 1972).   A distinction should, however, be made between what people actually believe and what they say they do/believe.   A greater expressed willingness of men to 'help' domestically is widely viewed as accompanying the rise in women's employment.   But the discrepancy remains between the housework husbands report they do and that which their wives agree they do (MGM Marketing Research and Surveys, 1978).

Nevertheless, some families depart from the conventional pattern.   Fogarty et al. (1971) describe the 'new convention-al' pattern as one in which there is some acceptance of male domestic involvement, and the expectation that the wife will

return to work when she can manage it, bearing in mind that
husband's and children's requirements come first.   Of the
domestic tasks assumed by men in more 'joint' conventional
families, playing with children seems to be the most popular
(Oakley, 1979).

Conventional families also have characteristic patterns of
childrearing, though much childrearing is, of course, idio-
syncratic and individual.   This 'patterned variation'
(Rapoport et al., 1977:178) is accompanied by the infiltration
into childrearing theory and practice of 'expert' advice,
though as the Newsons and others show there are social class
variations, another very important development in the evolution of the conventional family form.   Rapoport et al.
(1977:35-6) list ten key conceptions about parenthood which
have dominated this literature.   These include the construction of children's needs as paramount, neglect of which,
especially in the early years, brings irreversible damage;
the dictum that mothering by the biological mother is all-
important whereas fathering is tangential (in the personal
care but not in the economic provider sense);   the notion that
good parenting involves sacrifice.   All these are passed on
from one generation to another and is said to come 'naturally'
- though a certain input of education and information is
necessary (or the experts could be out of business).

THE STRAINS OF BEING CONVENTIONAL

The conventional family may not be normal in a statistical
sense, but as the Skolnicks (1974) note, normality, in the
sense of personal and social desirability is intrinsic to the
imagery of this conventional family type.   In her study of
courtship and marriage among Swansea couples in the late
1960s, Diana Leonard has exposed the 'taken-for-granted'
character of the conventional family as an institution.   Regarding marriage and parenthood as inseparable, inevitable and
desirable, Leonard's informants were able to give very little
in the way of accounts as to *why* they had entered the cere-
monial cycle of courtship and marriage and what the meaning of
its various elements was.   *Whether* to marry and find a family
was not the decision: *who* to marry was.   The taken-for-
grantedness of the desirability of marriage, even its idealisation, may be one factor underlying the rising and earlier
incidence of divorce.   In the 'Family Formation' survey a
tenth of women first married in 1966-70 were separated from
their husbands within five years of marriage, a figure similar
to the proportion separating among women married in 1961-5
after ten years of marriage, and to the proportion separating

after fifteen years' marriage among the cohort married in 1956-60 (OPCS, 1979:87).

Bailyn's study of the marital happiness and career versus family orientations of husbands and wives offers one perspective on the degree to which there is the expectation that adopting the conventional pattern will bring happiness.   But this mode of living is not 'automatically satisfactory' (Bailyn, 1970:105).   Bailyn found that the highest proportion of happy couples were located in the group where the husband's primary orientation was to his family, not his career.   A rigid differentiation of roles, e.g. when the husband was extremely career-oriented, jeopardised the couples' satisfaction, particularly if there was more than one child, even in the conventional family pattern.

Rubin's (1976) study of American working-class women shows that the communication gap between working-class husbands and wives can go along with all the outward appearances of a conventional happy family.   But as these researchers note, beneath the surface there are strains.   Brown and Harris (1978) have shown the chronicity and extent of depression among mothers at home, especially in poor housing conditions. Other expressions of this are dissatisfaction with the work of housewifery, particularly its socially isolated character (Gavron, 1966; Oakley, 1974; Ginsberg, 1976), the heightened vulnerability of married women (as opposed to divorced/widowed women and married men) to mental illness (Gove, 1972; Bernard, 1973), and the disposition of women to be users of psychotropic drugs (Balint et al., 1970; Barrett and Roberts, 1978).   For men, the family as conventionally defined may bring a preponderance of other stress-related illnesses due to the burden they shoulder as family breadwinners.   Heart disease and gastric and duodenal ulcers are characteristic male ailments (Dodge and Martin, 1970; Kasl and French, 1962).

Interpreting these and other studies, it would seem that many women in conventional families might like a little less family-oriented and a little more occupation-oriented life; many men, on the other hand, as Fein (1974) and others have documented, would welcome less pressure to be gainfully and successfully occupied outside the home and would prefer greater involvement in the expressive activities of child-rearing.   They are beginning to suspect the truth of Mead's observation that one reason for women's lesser 'productivity' is not the *burden* of their domestic role but its *rewards*: the fact that 'the baby smiles so much' (Mead, 1975:269).

Conventional families seem to be highly vulnerable to the crises of adolescence and the exit of children from the home. While adolescents are developing their own interests and

searching for meaningful goals to pursue, parents are reviewing their own past lives and revising their own goals; the
two preoccupations, though similar in kind, often have competing consequences.   Women in conventional families are particularly sensitive to the effects of conflict with adolescent children and to the empty nest syndrome, since, if they
have stayed at home and not developed other interests/activi-
ties/roles outside it during the childrearing phase, their
identities are more likely to have remained closely bound up
with motherhood (Rapoport and Rapoport, 1975).

This suggests that this family form is most 'functional'
for the early rearing of children.   The drop in the birth
rate, the earlier age of marriage and increased life expectancy together mean that proportionately more families are at
present in the later stages of development: thus, for
example, in Banbury in 1967, 32 per cent of 'elementary family
domestic groups' were in the 'dispersal' of children stage
compared with 19 per cent in 1950 (Stacey et al., 1975:107).
However, it is not necessarily the case that the childrearing
stage is the most satisfying for husbands and wives: studies
of marital satisfaction tend to find a decrease with parenthood, continuing throughout the dependent child period and
generally being more marked in the case of wives than husbands (Rollins and Feldman, 1970).   While marriage is a
romanticised complex in modern industrialised society, so
also is parenthood (LeMasters, 1957; Rossi, 1968), and the
two realities of marriage and parenthood themselves conflict.

The stage when a couple have been married around twenty
years is likely to see the onset of another responsibility -
that of middle-aged parents for their own ageing parents.
While the care of old people is no longer a key function of
the family in contemporary society, many women find themselves
carrying part of such a responsibility at a time in their
lives when they had been anticipating more freedom (Townsend,
1963, 1968; Bernard, 1975).   Increasing geographical mobility makes fulfilling this obligation much more difficult as
Rosser and Harris (1969:282) note.

To speak of husbands' and wives' worlds as being role differentiated by gender is to gloss over one essential distinction between them in a conventional family situation: the
man has power derived from his economic function which the
woman lacks.   Male power appears to be directly linked to
male income (Blood and Wolfe, 1960; Gillespie, 1971) and to
be heightened when children are young and mothers devoted
full time to their care.   This is reflected in women's lack
of income and also lack of control over their husbands'
income.   The proportion of individuals living in poverty
cannot be gauged from family income alone, since there is a

structured inequality between men and women (O'Donovan, 1978;
Young, 1952).   A rise in male wages is not necessarily accompanied by a rise in women's housekeeping allowances.   A third
of the wives in a London sample surveyed by Syson and Young
for the 'Poverty Report' suffered in this way, which is a salu-
tary reminder 'that mothers and children can be in poverty
while husbands are not' (Young, 1975:15).   Tunstall (1962)
shows in his description of a fishing community how norms
about income distribution within the family become institutionalised in trade union practice;   overtime earnings, not
regarded by the men as part of the wage packet to be shared
with their wives, were a popular item for negotiation.   As
recently as 1970 (and probably still) a significant minority
of wives were kept in ignorance of what their husbands earn
(Gorer, 1971), and British husbands are notably less generous
in this request than others (Feandel, 1975).   Pahl's description of 'A Refuge for Battered Wives' (1978) reports that disputes about money occurred in about a third of the cases, and
illustrates how the alignment of men's greater physical
strength with their monopoly of economic resources can make
victims of women and children when marriages break down.
Going out to work does not automatically solve the problem of
women's dependence on men's economic power, since, as Jephcott
observed in 1962, women's wages (aside from their tendency to
be substantially lower than men's) may be used directly for
household expenditure, enabling husbands to keep their wage
packets for their own use.   It is inaccurate to regard the
system (commonly found in traditional, role-segregated families such as those studied by Kerr (1958) and Humphreys
(1966)) whereby the husband hands over to his wife the whole
of his wage packet, as a strategy for increasing women's
power.   She pays the bills and hands back an allowance to him
for spending money, but under these circumstances money-
management is a 'chore' for the woman, and the basic inequity
of the woman's dependence on a male wage is not mitigated.

SOCIAL CONTROL OF CONVENTIONAL FAMILIES

The conventional model of family life is sought for its positive attractions more than it is avoided for its drawbacks.
Marriage and a conventional family life remain the aspirations
of the majority.   'It is no longer fashionable to predict
that marriage, in any recognisable form, is about to give way
to radically new forms of sexual relationship.   Marriage has
never been more popular, even if it has never been more risky'
comments the recent Home Office Report 'Marriage Matters'
(1979:14).   And, when they say 'marriage', what is generally

meant is conventional marriage.   A survey of Britain's 16-
year-olds published in 1976 revealed a remarkable consensus of
opinion about marriage: only 3 per cent said they did not
wish to marry (Fogelman, 1976).   Longitudinal surveys such
as that of Banbury (Stacey, 1960; Stacey et al., 1975) un-
cover no decline in the popularity of marriage or of the ideal
of a separate marital household supported by the husband.
The gap between end of dependence on the family of origin and
the initiation of a new family of procreation has been tele-
scoped into a brief three years for women and four to five
years for men.   During these years most young people are
actively pursuing the goal of finding someone to marry and
settling down to something like the old-fashioned family roles
(Leonard, 1980).   Indeed, the Finer Report on One-Parent
Families commented that the high percentage of people marrying
is a cause for official concern.   They said that, given what
is known about, for example, the incidence of homosexuality
and chronic ill health in the population, the institution of
marriage must be attracting many people who are unfitted for
it (Finer Report, 1974:para 3.9).

It is ironical that official government reports and committees should express such concern, because the ideology of conventional family life is part of the official morality of government and the State in Britain, and has been since these
bodies were first in a position to act as control agencies.
Wilson (1977) has argued that gender assymetry with women as
dependent, nurturant wives and mothers has been a central
assumption of the welfare state in Britain.   The cohabitation
ruling exemplifies this.   A woman living with a man is not
able to claim supplementary benefit for herself.   The Supplementary Benefits Commission's defence of this ruling is
that it is wrong to treat unmarried people (women) more favourably than married people (women).   The assumption is
clear; that a man should support his wife and the wife should
not be supported by the State if there is a man able to do so
in exchange for her services.   Land (1976, 1978) has demonstrated how this traditional view of women pervades the social
security and income tax systems and re-enforces inegalitarian
family relationships.

This set of official assumptions and policies are, in turn,
buttressed by a set of beliefs - often represented as 'scientific' in character - supporting the notion that normal 'feminine' women *want* the conventional role, and it is only
neurotics and misfits who find disadvantages in it.   Stimson
(1976) has indicated, for example, how women patients are
perceived by GPs as more 'troublesome' than men, particularly
if they deviate from the conventional pattern.   They are seen
as requiring pharmacelogical adjustment to their prescribed

roles.   Looking at the consulting patterns of middle-aged women (a particularly 'troublesome' category) Barrett and Roberts identified a marked tendency for GPs to locate women's complaints in terms of their family functions, while those of men were referred to an occupational context.

> Numerous cases were found ... of a woman performing two jobs (one inside the home and one in paid employment) and suffering from symptoms of stress, anxiety and tiredness. Occasionally a doctor might in such circumstances suggest cautiously that some of the housework could be shared among the family, but this would be rare.   The common response was to advise the woman to give up her job.   Not only might this advice come from the GP, we also found it advocated by the psychiatrists to whom the women had been referred.   Many of the women patients we interviewed had been given, and followed, such advice. (Barrett and Roberts, 1978:44)

Such attitudes are reflected widely in health and welfare provision and in the legal, educational and occupational systems.   It is in this sense, and for this reason, that the conventional model of family life can be seen as linked with the social control of women.   Official reports, consultative documents and White Papers have promoted the conventional vision of the conjugal two-parent unit divided along male-breadwinner, female-housekeeper lines (Court Report, 1976; DHSS, 1977; DHSS, 1976).

As has been noted, there are signs that official stereotypes are being felt to be increasingly archaic and that, in the presence of dissatisfaction with the constraints of the conventional family model, certain groups in the community may be moving towards a more open appraisal of other ways of living - both in and without families.   However, it has to be said that this trend is largely, if not exclusively, confined to the educated middle classes, and more to women than men.   Signs of normative change are not evident throughout the socio-economic spectrum, though there is an increase in variant behavioural patterns - dual workers, single-parent families, etc. - at all levels.   One reason for this is that conventional families are, in an important sense, self-perpetuating.   Conventional gender-assymetrical families promote the development of masculine and feminine personality traits in children and set the pattern for the next generation of parents' commitment to the same model of a division between adult family roles (Chodorow, 1978).   The breaking of this cycle, not necessarily one of deprivation, but certainly one involving a considerable range of problems in today's society, is made more difficult by the devaluation of domestic and childrearing work - its status, skills and achievements -

endemic to the treatment of conventional families and to the ideology of gender that prevails in the industrialised world.

Chapter 6

Dual-worker families

D. Gowler and K. Legge

INTRODUCTION

The stereotype of the post-industrialization British family
(i.e. husband/father as breadwinner, wife as financially
dependent, full-time housewife and mother), except for a short
period in the family cycle, no longer accords with reality.
In most families, for a large portion of this cycle, both
husband *and* wife are likely to be employed outside the
home. (1)   But a statistical trend does not necessarily indicate a well-functioning unit: nor does it follow that social
institutions have adjusted to facilitate its development and
optimal functioning.
   In this chapter we focus on three questions about dual-
worker families:
1 What range of dual-worker family patterns can be identified and what is their distribution in Britain?
2 What are the distinctive characteristics of life within
   such families?
3 What external forces affect the family life of dual-worker
   families, and how are these likely to alter in the near
   future?

DUAL-WORKER FAMILIES: THE EMPLOYMENT PERSPECTIVE

Generally speaking, it is the *wife's* decision to seek (or
remain in) employment that shifts a family into the dual-worker
category. (2)   Before identifying the three major types of
dual-worker family and discussing their characteristic lifestyles, it is therefore worth considering (a) trends in married women's employment patterns and (b) their motivation in
seeking employment, for both factors directly influence (and
are influenced by) their family lifestyles.

Trends in married women's employment patterns

The growth in married women's employment took off in the
1960s (3) and has continued up to the recent recession (when
the unemployment rate for women has risen faster than that for
men).   Thus, while in 1951 married women's overall participation rate stood at 21.7 per cent, and by 1961, at 29.7 per
cent, by 1971 it had leapt to 42.2 per cent and by 1981 (at
the time of writing, 1979), it was projected that it would
have increased to 51.9 per cent, rising to 56.2 per cent by
1991.   A closer examination of Census and General Household
Survey data moreover would suggest the following trends:

(1)   The majority of young married women drop out of all em-
      ployment while their children are of pre-school age.
      However, the minority that does work is growing - rising
      from around 12 per cent in the early 1960s to 26 per
      cent in 1977.

(2)   *Those who remain in employment when their children are
      of pre-school age tend to be either women whose families
      are in economically deprived circumstances (e.g. single
      parents, wives of immigrants and indigenous black
      minorities and other low paid) or women with a high com-
      mitment to work for its own sake (e.g. professionally
      qualified women in 'dual career' families).*   Both sub-
      groups are more likely than the majority of married
      women in employment to work continuously and full time
      (Hunt, 1968; Moss, 1976; Rapoport and Rapoport, 1976).

(3)   *As their children grow older and enter school, married
      women, in increasing numbers, return mainly to part-
      time employment.*   Thus, in 1977, whereas only 19 per
      cent of mothers with a youngest child aged 1 year
      worked, the figure steadily rises with the age of the
      youngest child, viz. 26 per cent age 3, 34 per cent age
      4, 43 per cent age 5, 55 per cent age 10 years (Central
      Policy Review Staff, 1978).   That this work is mainly
      part time is also revealed by GHS data (see, for
      example, GHS, 1976, Table 6.2).   In 1976, for example,
      of the married women in the 25-34 year age range, with
      two dependent children, a mere 9 per cent were in full-
      time employment, while 30 per cent were part-timers; in
      the 35-44 year age range, 21 per cent were in full-time
      employment while 43 per cent were part-timers.

(4)   *A growing minority of women, particularly those with
      only one child, tend to shift from part-time to full-
      time employment as their children become increasingly
      independent.*   (See GHS, 1976, Table 6.2)

(5)   *The larger the family size the less likely it is that
      the mother will return to work.*   For example, in 1971,
      whereas over 50 per cent of married women with two or

less dependent children were employed, only 34 per cent
with four or more had returned to work. However,
whether due to increased inflation or male unemployment,
between 1971-6 the *rate* of increase in participation
rates for women with 3+ children was higher than for
groups with smaller families (Mackie and Pattullo,
1977). *In other words, family size is having a decreasing effect on a wife's ultimate return to work,
although it may delay it.*

(6)   *In areas of traditionally high female employment (e.g.
the north-west) or where the demand for labour is high
(e.g. London and the south-east) participation rates for
married women are above average.* In contrast, in rural
areas, where job opportunities are fewer, the rates tend
to be correspondingly lower (Young and Willmott, 1973;
Moss, 1976).

(7)   Women tend to be employed in the 'feminized' secondary
sector of 'low paid, less secure, less skilled and less
rewarding jobs' (Barron and Norris, 1976; Oakley, 1976;
Mackie and Pattullo, 1977). As a result in many cases
married women tend to have a lower occupational status
than their husbands, and, partly as a result of this and
partly due to part-time working, *to be the secondary
wage earner in the family.* (4) This is particularly
marked in 'dual-worker families' with children, for the
proportion of wives with a 'lower' occupational status
than their husbands rises from 27 per cent at marriage
to 44 per cent for couples with children aged 5 years
(Leete, 1979). This situation both influences (and is
influenced by) a couple's division of tasks (see below).

The decision to work

Evidence would suggest that married women remain in/return to
work for *any or all* of five major reasons - financial; to
gain social contacts; to escape the boredom, frustration,
loneliness and depression of domesticity; to acquire their
'own' personal identity; to acquire or practice a skill to
which they are highly committed and from which they expect
high intrinsic rewards (see Table 6.1). Although research
suggests that financial motivation (5) and desire for social
contact are the most frequently felt and often the strongest
motivators (Yudkin and Holme, 1963; Hunt, 1968; Young and
Willmott, 1973; Hoffman 1974a; Moss et al., 1975) in recent
years issues of personal fulfilment have come increasingly
into prominence (Pahl and Pahl, 1971; Moss et al., 1975;
Oakley, 1976). However the strength of the various

motivators is likely to vary not only with personal or family
circumstances but with stages in the family cycle (e.g. financial motives may loom large with a growing family, social contact and job interest when the family is 'off one's hands'),
and with opportunity (job interest is unlikely to figure prom-
inently if there are no interesting jobs or training opportunities available).   Similarly, a powerful 'personal fulfilment' motive may override difficulties about a husband's negative attitude towards his wife working and shortages of opportunity, whereas in other cases (particularly when the children
are grown up) a low motivation (even a depressed feeling) may
be overridden by the husband and others urging the wife to go
out, and new opportunities being presented, e.g. in the growth
of semi-voluntary organizations with some remuneration.   The
point to be made here is that the nature of the wife's motivation to work is likely to influence significantly (and be influenced by) the family lifestyle.   It is to this major theme
of the chapter that we now turn.

FAMILY LIFE AND RELATIONSHIPS

For the purpose of this chapter we identify three basic types
of dual-worker family.   In order of frequency they are:
  (1) The 'non-career' (6) family (in which both partners are
       employed in a range of semi-skilled or unskilled 'non-
       career' jobs).
  (2) The 'one-career' family (in which one partner, usually
       the husband, has a 'career', while the other has a 'non-
       career' job).
  (3) The 'dual-career' family (in which both partners have
       'careers').
When discussing the everyday life and relationships of these
three types of dual-worker families, (7) one finds oneself
concentrating, perhaps more than in descriptions of 'traditional' family life, on issues surrounding 'sharing' and 'give
and take' between family members.   We shall consider these
issues in three main areas: economic (employment and financial arrangements), technical (household division of labour)
and emotional (interpersonal support, friendships).   These
are analytical distinctions of course, for many family activities (e.g. childrearing, leisure) may involve all three.

Economic

Decisions about career moves appear more likely to involve
joint decision making, than do decisions about non-career jobs
(Pahl and Pahl, 1971; Rapoport and Rapoport, 1976), and for
very practical reasons.   'Career', unlike 'job' moves,

TABLE 6.1 The wife's decision to return to work

Typical motivation for employment	Typical family circumstances	Typical comment	Typical employment pattern
Financial			
1 Necessity	Husband low paid/unemployed/ 'mean' with housekeeping. Large families. (Also single parents, widowed, separated, divorced.)	'I've always worked because I've needed the money, because he spends too much money on drink and therefore I've always had to work to make my own money up ... if I didn't go to work I couldn't afford to dress my children' (Oakley, 1976, p. 150)	Early return to work while children possibly pre-school. More likely to work continuously and full time than any other group except 6. If childminding problems may accept homeworking or shift work.
2 Improve family's standard of living	Children at school.	'My mum worked to buy her own house ... she did night work at London airport, catering for planes so that she didn't have to leave the children. She did it to get out of the prefab; they bought a house, we got out, and then she packed up work' (Oakley, 1976, p. 110).	Part-time job on permanent basis, or when need for major item of expenditure arises. Timing of return to work, its continuity, when and how many hours worked being secondary to domestic considerations. May eventually work full time – or give up work altogether.
Social contacts			
3 As substitute for children's company	Children becoming increasingly independent, possibly leaving home	'You miss your children when they leave home.... You're glad of something to do outside the home.' 'It's another interest. I enjoy meeting the other women at work' (Young and Willmott, 1973, pp. 102-3).	Part-time job after children have entered primary/secondary school or left home. May eventually work full time.

4 To escape from children & boredom & frustration of domesticity into adult company	Wife lonely and depressed at home, possibly does not find day-to-day interaction with young children, nor housework fulfilling. Is 'fed up'.	'The baby screamed all night every night.... It was a tremendous relief when I went back to work' (Rapoport and Rapoport, 1976, p. 166). 'I think I regard my home as a prison. I won't say I dislike (looking after children) but my patience is gradually wearing thin' (Oakley, 1976, p. 143).	Relatively early return to work, probably as soon as children start school. More likely to work full time than 2 or 3 other things being equal, somewhat less likely than 1 or 6.

Personal fulfilment

5 Separate identity	As in 4. Also, as children leave home and wife feels need to establish her own identity.	'I'd rather describe myself as a shrink-wrapper than a housewife' (Oakley, 1976, p. 143). 'I do have this fear of becoming a cabbage' (Pahl and Pahl, 1971).	Timing of return to work and whether to work part time or full time depend on personal circumstances
6 Use of skills	Wife with 'professional' skills/career aspirations.	'(Using skills) is almost like a shot of heroin to a drug addict' (Rapoport and Rapoport, 1976, p. 86).	Early return to work while children possibly pre-school. More likely to work continuously and full time than all other groups except 1.

Sources: Epstein, 1972; Fogarty et al., 1968, 1971; Hoffman, 1974a; Holmström, 1972; Hope et al., 1976; Hunt, 1968; Mackie and Pattullo, 1977; Marsh, 1979; Moss et al., 1975; Oakley, 1976; Rapoport and Rapoport, 1976; Young and Willmott, 1973; Yudkin and Holme, 1963.

frequently involve substantial geographical mobility, with implications for changing houses and schools, and for the partner's employment.   With this in mind, three patterns of decision making about employment tend to appear depending on the nature of the dual-worker family.

In the non-career dual-worker family, there is little evidence of any substantial joint discussion over employment issues per se.   The wife generally takes it for granted that the husband will make his own decisions about what job he does, although there may be some discussion about whether he adopts shiftworking or how much overtime he should do.   Generally speaking, the decisions she makes about her own employment involve more discussion as they may involve negotiating some assistance with domestic/childminding tasks.   However, implicit in any discussions appears to be an unquestioning acceptance that the wife will match her employment to the requirements of her husband, as chief breadwinner, and to the children, as her 'personal' responsibility.

In one-career families the position is somewhat reversed, in that joint discussion is likely to focus on the husband's employment decisions rather than on the wife's (Pahl and Pahl, 1971).   In particular, wives appear to have some say in career decisions when the extrinsic aspects of the husband's move is likely to have important implications for family life (e.g. when the move would be disruptive of the children's education).   But the 'jointness' of this decision making is often more apparent than real, as the underlying structure of employment and male domination tends to bias its outcome in terms of the husband's preferences.   As it is the husband who usually has the highly paid 'career' and the wife the lower paid 'job', it is usually automatically assumed to be 'only right' that the husband's career comes first.   Moreover, if the husband's career move carries with it a larger salary, as is usually the case, one rationale for the wife's need to work is diminished, while many wives have conventionally considered the loss of friendship at work - or for that matter in the neighbourhood - an insufficient, 'selfish' reason for arguing against a move if their husbands were keen. However, this seems to be changing, and the potential negative effects of moving a child from one school to another are now widely appreciated.

In dual-career families, shared decision making about career moves is more likely to be genuine as the decisions one partner makes are recognized to have implications in both domestic *and* employment terms for the other partner.

Scarcity of the 'right' career openings may result in either one partner faced with the possibility of giving up the move and sacrificing a career development opportunity, or the

other of giving up an existing job and its potential for a
less desirable one, or one partner with the decision to com-
mute on a weekly basis with the complications and 'cramming'
this leads to in organizing a satisfactory family and social
life (Farris, 1978; Gowler and Legge, 1979).   As a result of
these dilemmas, many dual-career couples tend to get 'locked'
into one organization or labour market (generally London and
the south-east) sacrificing a degree of individual career development so that there can be a better balance between the
careers of each and between career and family life.   Alternatively, some couples develop rules such as 'your choice this
time', 'mine next', but even this theoretically egalitarian
approach can get undermined by the husband's greater chance of
being offered the posts he applies for (Berger et al., 1978).
This can quickly develop into a vicious circle, for if the
husband's career develops more rapidly than his wife's it
becomes increasingly costly for him to give up salary and
opportunities to forward his wife's career and, hence, the gap
between their career development and the costs in forwarding
hers become even larger.   In these circumstances the wife may
well adopt the non-career wife's position that her husband's
career should come first.

   Patterns of financial decision making also vary in dual-
worker families.   It has been argued that a wife's working,
and hence financial contributions, will automatically give her
more 'say' over family decisions (Bahr, 1974).   But that this
is not invariable (but depends on the couple's level of education and communication) has been demonstrated by useful work
in a male-dominated southern European society (Safilios-
Rothschild and Dijkers, 1978).

   In Britain in working-class (and hence in many non-career)
families, it appears that the wife generally tends to be responsible, if in a constrained fashion, for the family's financial affairs, the husband handing over the bulk of his pay
packet as 'housekeeping' to his wife, who then settles the
regular bills and manages the remaining money (Oakley, 1974).
But difficulties may still arise unless there is some communication about regularly occurring issues such as whether the
sum of money the husband keeps back as pocket money is jointly
agreed upon, whether he is prepared to use cost of living increases to adjust housekeeping in line with inflation and so
on.   Whether such communication is effective, or even exists,
will depend very much upon how egalitarian the marriage
already is.   And this will both influence and be reflected in
the wife's financial motivation in going out to work.   Thus
the wife working for say, a house deposit, is more likely to
enjoy joint financial decision making at home than one who is
working to buy day-to-day necessities because her husband is

'mean' with housekeeping, or personal desired 'hobby' durables which the other partner does not value.

In one-career and dual-career families, financial decision making tends to be shared to a greater extent than in non-career families.   These tend to be the families with joint bank accounts, houses in both partners' names, shared decisions about consumer durables, holidays and leisure (Pahl and Pahl, 1971; Oakley, 1974; Rapoport and Rapoport, 1976). However, in contrast to non-career families, there tends to be a distinction between the financial management of large decisions (e.g., insurance policies, mortgage repayments and other standing orders, major non-routine bills) which tends to be the husband's responsibility and day-to-day budgeting, which tends to be the wife's.   These arrangements are sometimes dealt with in 'explicit contracts'.

This joint pattern of financial decision making is found in middle-class families whether the wife works or not.   But this is not an invariable pattern.   In some middle-class families, whether dual worker or not, the husband's career may take such a degree of precedence over all family activities that a segregated pattern emerges in which the wife manages the family's financial affairs as a support to a largely 'disinterested' husband.   In these families, a 'hidden contract' may exist (Gowler and Legge, 1975, 1978) whereby in return for the wife adapting her job and family life around the demands of her husband's job, she is given the freedom to make virtually unilateral decisions about the family's style of consumption (e.g., choice of house, holidays, furnishings, schools) and its management.   In contrast, in dual-career families where the wife brings more equal financial resources into the family, it is likely that financial decision making will be even more shared than in one-career families, where the husband's greater financial weight may allow him to have the final say (particularly over long-term financial commitments) in spite of joint discussion.

Technical

In the *technical* area of the household division of labour traditional patterns have proved remarkably enduring, in spite of married women's increasing employment outside the home. Firstly, although it would appear from some accounts that employed wives do receive more help in the house from their husbands than do the non-employed (Blood and Wolfe, 1960; Oakley, 1974) others suggest that this is minimal.   For example, in America, Walker and Woods (1976) found that husbands' average time spent on all food preparation increased

from six minutes a day, when their wives were not employed, to
a mighty 12 minutes a day when they were.   Secondly, the
actual amount of help a husband is prepared to give is generally quite small in comparison with the number of tasks required to be done (Boulding, 1976).   This is reflected in
Young and Willmott's data (1973, Ch. 4, Table 14), where married men spent only 9.9 hours per week on household tasks compared with 23.1 hours and 35.3 hours by women employed full-
and part-time respectively.   Thirdly, where it exists, husbandly participation is very much at the level of 'helping
out' rather than assuming complete responsibility for some
traditionally female tasks (Oakley, 1974; Working Family Project, 1978).   Fourthly, when husbands do help out with housework, there appears a general preference for undertaking
rewarding rather than onerous tasks (e.g., playing with children, rather than cleaning or ironing) (Oakley, 1974, Chs 3 and
8).   Indeed, there is some evidence that husbands generally
are more prepared to take over child care than other tasks
(Oakley, 1974, pp. 137-8; also Kharchev and Golod, 1971;
Piotrowski, 1971, for Eastern European parallels). (8)

These comments can be put into sharper focus when considered in relation to different development stages and types of
dual-worker families and to different kinds of employment
patterns.   In most dual-worker families, the husband appears
to give the most and widest ranging help in household tasks
early in marriage, when both partners are working full time
(Bahr, 1974).   This not only reflects their relative employment equality (both have been 'out' all day), but also an
emotional equality and involvement in setting up and 'playing
at house'.   After the birth of children, however, it is probable that the wife will spend some years as a full-time housewife.   It is during this period that the traditional division
of labour tends to reassert itself, partly through the wife's
involvement in motherhood, partly out of convenience ('he
feels I'm at home all day and so I should do it') (Oakley,
1974, p. 158), and partly because most full-time housewives
feel they have to justify their presence at home by performing
the housewife role 'properly', i.e. according to traditional,
generally their mothers', definitions and standards (Oakley,
1974, Chs 6-8).

On the wife's return to work, particularly if pre-school
children are involved, the husband may be the only available,
cheapest or mutually preferred source of child care while she
is working (Working Family Project, 1978; 'Social Trends',
1979, Table 3.5).   In these circumstances, particularly if
the wife's return to work is mutually agreed to be financially
necessary (Pahl and Pahl, 1971) it is likely that the husband
will become involved in child-care activities, if of a relatively passive sort.

Turning to the different types of dual-worker families identified, some variations in their patterns of domestic division of labour can be identified.

Many 'non-career' dual-worker families, having mostly been socialized in working-class culture to believe in a traditional division of labour, tend to revert to this pattern, even when there is an early honeymoon egalitarian phase (Bott, 1957; Oakley, 1974, Tables 8.1 and 8.2). But, generally, speaking, the amount of help a wife can expect to receive on her return to work will depend on such factors as whether her husband approves her motivation in returning to work, whether she is working full- or part time, how old the children are, whether her husband has to work long hours, overtime or shifts. If her husband approves her motivation in returning to work (e.g., they are both saving for the deposit on a house), if she is working full time, if the children are young, and if the husband has some choice in the pattern of hours he works and if her work coincides with his being at home, he is more likely to help in the house and at a wider range of tasks. However, if her husband disapproves her motives in working ('it's only for company and pin money I never see'), if she works part time, if the children are adolescents ('old enough to help their mother') and if her husband works a lot of overtime or is on 'awkward' shifts, she may look in vain for husbandly help. Instead, a common pattern is for such a wife to do housework before and after returning from work while at the same time cajoling some assistance from her children (Powell, 1963; Walker and Woods, 1976).

In one-career families similar conditions are likely to prevail, but with two major differences. Firstly, the husband is more likely to have middle-class orientations and accordingly be more likely to help out in the house. He may have been to university or lived away from home, in conditions of flat-sharing where he is likely to have engaged in such activities as cooking and cleaning, and consequently ceased to regard them as exclusively 'female' (Oakley, 1974, p. 160). However, a second factor may work in the opposite direction. In their survey data, Young and Willmott (1973) found that professional and managerial husbands spent more time per week working and travelling to and from work than any other occupational group - even allowing for manual workers' overtime. In these circumstances a 'career' husband may have limited time, energy and inclination to take responsibility for household tasks (Pahl and Pahl, 1971; Walker and Woods, 1976). Indeed, his wife may well feel obliged to take over even those he recognizes as 'his' - particularly if he is frequently away from home on business trips (Pahl and Pahl, 1971).

In dual-career families, where both partners' career commitment is likely to lead to long hours 'at work', the sheer
overload of work tasks may precipitate a breakdown of the
accomplishment of tasks in the home, particularly if the
family is large, stirring the husband into action.   But as
the Rapoports report (1976, p. 368) even when the husband, as
a matter of principle, intends to share household tasks, the
'cognitive' maps of a husband's role, in which he has been
socialized, are likely to blot out his good intentions.   In
these circumstances, dual-career couples tend to compromise.
Some would appear to let standards of household cleanliness
and cooking fluctuate according to work demands.   But many
seek to maintain standards by buying in domestic helpers -
particularly when the children are young (Rapoport and Rapoport, 1976).   This course of action is facilitated by high
earnings and enables both partners to sidestep the issue of a
fundamental realignment in their division of labour.

In some dual-worker families the desire for a truly egalitarian marriage, with equal sharing and interchangeability in
tasks and responsibilities, has led them to select employment
patterns that will facilitate the achievement of this objective, rather than attempting it within the constraints afforded by traditional employment patterns.   A couple may share
the same job (particularly professional couples) (Arkin and
Dobrofsky, 1978), or each may have a separate part-time job
either in the same or different organizations (Gronseth, 1975,
1978).   Both patterns appear workable, but not without
strains (e.g., financial, the questioning of the worker's -
particularly the professional worker's - commitment to the job
and 'overworking' at a shared job). (9)

Emotional

In the emotional area of family life, a number of issues
emerge.   First, childminding (as distinct from child care
generally), in particular, the issue of who will look after
pre-school children and schoolchildren during holidays, while
their parents are at work, is salient.   For pre-school children the preferred solution seems to be 'leaving the baby with
Granny' (if the grandmother is not herself employed or vehe-
mently disapproving of young mothers working outside the home).
A friend who is not working but has children of the same age
and who is prepared to look after the child 'as one of her
own' for a small sum is another favoured solution (Rapoport et
al., 1977; 'Social Trends 1979', Table 3.5; for American
examples, Emlen and Perry, 1974; Working Family Project,
1978).   With increasing female employment, though, both

grandmothers and childminding friends are harder to come by.
However, there is evidence that many women, particularly in
poorer urban areas, are regarding unofficial childminding as
a form of 'sub rosa' employment.

The more formal alternatives - State or private nursery or
private domestic help - for most dual-worker families are no
real alternative at all.   There are so few (and so unevenly
distributed) State nursery places (Fonda, 1976; Mackie and
Pattullo, 1977), while private nursery places, for many
parents, are prohibitively expensive. Further, the hours
they offer do not always coincide exactly with the 'working'
day.   Au pairs and nannies, the traditional middle-class
solution, are not a widely applicable form of support as few
families have either the funds or accommodation that they
require.

When all these options fail, the couple with pre-school
children are left with several alternatives.   One partner
(invariably the wife) can stay at home until the children are
all at school (and most wives appear to settle for this).
Alternatively both partners can 'work-share' with one partner
always at home providing child care.   The most frequent
pattern is for the wife to adjust her part-time hours to fit
times when her husband is at home (e.g., early morning cleaning, evening or weekend shifts).   Finally the wife can undertake work (i.e. employment) at home.   It is interesting in
this context that in the General Household Survey 1976 over
30 per cent of women respondents with pre-school children
reported that they would return to work earlier than intended
if satisfactory childminding arrangements were available.

There is some evidence that choices between alternative
pre-school child-care arrangements vary significantly according to whether the mother works full- or part-time ('Social
Trends', 1979, Table 3.5).   For example, married mothers
working full time (like single parents) make greater use of
formal child care arrangements than do part-timers (although
both rely chiefly on informal arrangements).   Further, the
type of formal arrangements they choose - mainly nurseries and
childminders - contrast with part-timers' greater reliance
upon play groups.   As for informal arrangements, part-timers
seem able to make far greater use of their husbands than do
full-timers; also they rely to a greater extent than full-
timers on taking the child(ren) with them to work.   It would
appear then that the choice of how many hours (and when) to
work both influences and is influenced by availability and
choice of child-care arrangements.

Once children are at school the problem does not end for
dual-worker families.   Young children often still need to be
collected from school and the school day ends well before the

normal working day.   Then there are problems of care during
illnesses and holidays.   Where the mother does not have a
career these problems are generally tackled through the expedient of part-time working and, if there is no flexibility
at work or help at home, either arranging leave of absence or
taking a temporary break in employment.   Where the family is
widely spaced, older children may help during holidays.   Even
with these expedients some couples, particularly where the
wife works full time, resort to a 'latch-key' pattern.   The
children are given their own house key and left to fend for
themselves, perhaps with a neighbour popping in.   This
pattern, increasing in recent years in urban areas, has become
an emotive one and voluntary groups have been active, particularly in the International Year of the Child, to provide
advice kits for families and neighbours of 'latch-key children' to avoid potentially unhappy consequences of a child
returning to an empty home.

It should be noted that, with all these arrangements, and
in all types of dual-worker family, it is invariably the wife
who is seen as responsible for their organization and who, in
the case of any shortfall, tends to take time off from her
own employment to fill the gap.

There is no evidence that dual-worker families are less
deeply concerned than others with the quality of their child-
care arrangements.   The debates in the 1950s and 1960s on the
effects of maternal deprivation on child development (Bowlby,
1953, 1969) often alleged disastrous consequences of the working mother's 'neglect' of her children.   Although these
theories have been very much revised, and although the available evidence does not confirm the supposed negative consequences of mothers' working per se, many working mothers continue to express anxiety about whether they are doing 'the
right thing' in not being full-time mothers (Hoffman, 1974b;
Oakley, 1976, Ch. 8).

As a result, most seek to compensate for their temporary
absence in a number of ways.   In close knit communities (perhaps more in working-class areas where non-career families
predominate) mothers pride themselves on not leaving their
children with 'strangers' (Oakley, 1976).   They may also
emphasize the material benefits brought to the children by
their working, and often point to their physical appearance
as a sign that they are not neglected.   In many middle-class
(one-career and dual-career) families, while the same considerations weigh, there may be more emphasis on the appropriate-
ness of the substitute care in terms of the child's overall
development (i.e. not just on whether he/she is 'happy', but
on whether he/she is receiving the right stimuli to foster his
psychological and intellectual development).   Their extra

financial resources allow them more options in this area.
For example, parents in dual-career families are able to use
their resources to hire 'daily help' with the cleaning so that
they can set aside time on their return from work for playing
and talking with the children, not to mention joint leisure
activities at the weekend (Pahl and Pahl, 1971; Rapoport and
Rapoport, 1976; Rapoport et al., 1977).

Turning to leisure patterns in dual-worker families, these
have been shown to be linked fairly closely to social class
and family life-cycle stage, irrespective of whether both
partners work or not (Sillitoe, 1969; Young and Willmott,
1973; Rapoport et al., 1975). Dual-worker families, though,
through earning more than their age/stage mates in 'traditional' families, may participate in some more 'up-market' leisure
activities. However, all types of dual-worker families
suffer from a shortage of time. Working wives may feel that
their 'leisure' time from employment is swallowed up by housework (Young and Willmott, 1973, Table 14) - particularly in
situations where their husbands do not help at home and pursue
male-dominated, segregated leisure activities, a pattern more
prevalent in working-class (and hence, non-career) families
than in middle-class (one-career and dual-career) families.
Where there is more domestic work sharing - a pattern more
prevalent in dual-career couples - leisure, especially during
the week, is sacrificed. More frequent and more varied holidays partly compensate, but the problem of achieving an adequate balance between work, family and leisure remains an un-
resolved one (Rapoport et al., 1975).

In attempting to assess the quality of family relationships
in dual-worker families one must bear in mind that there is a
two-way interaction between occupational and domestic forces.
Domestic frustration as well as occupational strains can
affect the quality of family life, and each affects the other.
Research to date seems to indicate that marital happiness
tends to be lower in situations in which the wife feels under
constraint - either to work longer hours, against her wishes,
or where her husband is not practically supportive; or to
remain at home when she feels lonely and wasted. Conversely,
the effects of employment on the marital relationship are
more likely to be positive if the wife's job is one she
enjoys, if the husband's attitude is actively supportive and
if both partners are more highly educated (Nye, 1974).
Bailyn's study of a series of British couples with higher
educational levels indicates that a lower level of marital
satisfaction is associated with one sub-type of the dual-
career pattern, where an 'integrated' wife (i.e. who tries to
integrate a career with family life) is married to a highly
career-oriented husband. Marriages that Bailyn terms

'co-ordinate' (i.e. career-integrated wives married to husbands who, although involved in a career, place primary emphasis on their families) would seem as happy, generally speaking, as conventional families.   Handy (1978) suggests that
two 'thrusters' (couples who place a high value on achievement
and dominance) may be prone to a discontented marriage.   Many
working wives, like husbands under stress of heavy work obligations, indicate that sometimes sheer fatigue makes them
irritable with their families, though they are personally
satisfied with the pattern of work that has been chosen (Nye,
1974; Rapoport and Rapoport, 1976).   This issue, once again,
seems to centre on achieving a balance of commitments.

As the balance between the strains and gains of 'dual working' varies at different stages of the family cycle, so the
quality of family life varies.   The Rapoports (1976) itemize
strains and gains that may be experienced by dual-career
families and suggest that they apply to some degree in dual-
worker families generally.   For example, there are overload
(just too much work, especially for the wife, to cope with),
normative ('Am I doing the right thing working while I've
young children?'),identity ('is it really masculine to be
changing nappies while my wife is working?') and network
dilemmas ('we don't have time to see as much of the parents as
we should').   There are also likely to be conflicts between
home and work expectations (e.g., repeated absenteeism to look
after sick children) and repeated frustrations due to the
barrier of sex role stereotyping at work and home.   On top of
this are the usual problems (e.g., arranging child-care cover
and finding a job with suitable hours).   Against this there
are financial gains for the family as a whole; for the wife,
possibly self-realization and, where both partners work in the
same professional field, support and enhanced career achievement as compared to female contemporaries, not married to a
professional partner (Martin et al., 1975); and a wider range
of potential role models for the children to adopt, along with
opportunities for them to become more independent and self-
reliant.   The strains and gains are weighted differently for
different families and at different stages of their family
life.   The balance struck varies over time.

Most families evolve tension management techniques that
enable them to achieve a balance between the strains and gains
of dual working.   Poloma (1972), for example, has delineated
four techniques of tension management used by wives in dual-
career families: favourable definition of the dual-career
situation, i.e. emphasizing the advantages rather than the
pitfalls of working wives; value clarification, e.g., that in
conflict situations the family demands take precedence; com-
partmentalization; and compromise, e.g., in level of career

aspiration.   However, as the Rapoports (1976) point out,
each family has 'tension lines', points beyond which an individual or couples feel they cannot be pushed.   At some point
this may define the limits to sustaining the pattern at all -
the point beyond which they feel dual working 'is not worth
it' - when the strains seem permanently to outweigh the gains.
Because of the high level of strains entailed, dual-worker
families may be particularly vulnerable to the effects of
extreme family crises, for example, the birth of a handicapped
child, chronic illness, the need to care for elderly relatives
and unemployment.   If such a strain is imposed in addition to
those already arising out of the 'dual-working' situation per
se, the wife may give up work and revert to the traditional
housewife's role.   This is particularly true if the satisfactions and income obtained from the employment are not high.
On the other hand, where commitment to work is high there may
be more attempts at 'finding a way round the problem'.   Continuing work also provides more money to help with the crisis,
e.g., if specialized care is required.
     Paradoxically, some wives prefer to give up or delay return
to employment if their husband becomes unemployed, in spite of
potential financial hardship, rather than 'rub it in' (Hartley, 1978).   *Thus in crisis the dual-worker family is likely
to revert into a traditional family*, rather than adapt in
what would seem objectively to be a more rational manner.   It
will be interesting to see if this is a temporary, transitional response of our times.

RELATIONSHIPS WITH MAJOR INSTITUTIONS

The relationship between dual-worker families and major institutions are constrained by two important factors:
  (1)   Employing organizations operate on the assumption that,
        apart from mutually convenient arrangements such as
        part-time and evening shift working, dual-worker fami-
        lies will accommodate themselves to the organization
        rather than vice versa.
  (2)   Most social institutions operate as though it was ab-
        normal for the wife/mother to work.
Employing organizations tend to operate as though the 'normal'
worker's domestic situation had no implications for his/her
employment relationship at all (other than the need to earn
money for a family).   In so far as a domestic model emerges
at all, it is of the full-time male worker with a home-
centred wife providing the domestic back-up services that
enable him to concentrate fully on a work role without competing demands.   While this 'hidden contract' (Gowler and

Legge, 1975, 1978) generally remains implicit, some organizations, particularly total institutions such as the Church,
military and diplomatic services, go one further and explicitly assume that a wife's time, energy and commitment may be
harnessed in the (often unpaid) service of the organization
(Papenek, 1973; Callan, 1975; Baker, 1976; McCubbin et al.,
1976).

Few organizations recognize the special problems faced by
families with working mothers.   Few provide nurseries
because, as the Institute of Personnel Management (1975:2)
puts it, 'employers do not consider themselves social service
agencies and "are not in the nursery business"'.   Few allow
their employees (either male or female) leave of absence
during school holidays, and such a request on the part of a
father (along with a male request for maternity leave), when
considered at all in Britain, has been thought of as laughable
(George and Wilding, 1972).   Legislation may provide a female
employee with minimal rights vis à vis maternity leave, but
few organizations are prepared to preserve a female employee's
seniority rights during an *extended* break for childrearing,
and few are prepared to look seriously at the career wife's
career-family cycling problems (Rapoport and Rapoport, 1976;
Mackie and Pattullo, 1977).

Still fewer British organizations even consider the possibility of regarding a couple as one employment unit.   Most
large organizations still have nepotism rules which prohibit
a married couple working for the same organization.   And,
where joint appointments are allowed, it is usually assumed
that the wife will be in a subordinate role, that she will
support her husband, who carries responsibility for her as
well as the job.

In terms of public provision, the dual-worker pattern
would be better supported were there:
1 tax allowances recognizing the legitimacy of this option,
   even encouraging it,
2 equal allowances for unemployment and pensions for either
   spouse,
3 nursery school and other pre-school child care provision,
4 child-care arrangements for school holidays.
Though the situation is changing in response to the effects of
pressure groups, the prevailing tax regulations and employment
practices remain a patchwork biased toward the assumption of
the normality of wives' life-long dependency on the provision
made by their husbands (Land, 1976, 1978; Mackie and
Pattullo, 1977).   The economic and policy issues involved
and the challenges confronted are dealt with elsewhere in this
volume.

FUTURE DIRECTIONS

The growth of employment among married women in the last two decades has made the 'dual-worker' family a continuously increasing pattern for many families for an increasing part of the family cycle.   But what is likely to be the future for this family type in the next two decades?

While some factors suggest an increase in this pattern (the conventional wisdom), others point in the opposite direction. The factors which suggest the probability of increase are briefly

1   normalization of the idea,
2   reform of tax and other financial benefits,
3   more flexible employment practices (e.g., job and work sharing, shorter working week) as a response to either labour shortages or unemployment,
4   expanding service sector and new computer based industries containing jobs at which women can excel.

Those which suggest the decrease in the prevalence of the pattern are

1   backlash against 'women's lib' and the increased emphasis on domestic life and care,
2   technological change, *in the short term* (e.g., women's office employment may be hard hit by micro-processors),
3   priority given to youth over women in the event of recession due in part to energy crises and technological change,
4   cuts back in service industries and public sector jobs if the British economy fails to become revitalized.

In other words, the two major uncertainties of the next decades, energy crises and technological change, could work either way.

While we do not feel that the existence, even the wide prevalence of the dual-worker family pattern is at risk, its fate will bear a relationship not only to the well being and satisfaction of specific families but to the larger issues of equality between the sexes. (10)   The development of a wider range of dual-worker family patterns will signify the social acceptance of the idea of equality of opportunity between men and women in a way that no amount of lip-service, or even legislation, can achieve.

NOTES

1   We suggest that families move through several employment phases: the dual-worker phase, both husband and wife working full time (early marriage), single worker phase

(young children), dual-worker phase, various combinations of hours (children at school), multi-worker phase (children working but living at home), single-worker phase (wife retired, children left home).

2   Although this observation is technically accurate, it does have unfortunate sexist overtones. For it implies that husbands/men (other things being equal) do not make an equivalent decision about seeking employment - but that 'going out to work' is automatic and non-problematic for half the human race. It is interesting that there is no discussion in conventional literature of men's 'motivation to go out to work', as there is of women's, only of their motivation to work at particular jobs.

3   Stimulated by a combination of 'pull' (growth in part-time employment opportunities) and 'push' factors (completion of smaller family at an earlier age, increased emphasis on consumption, decrease in time and energy required for housework, due to labour saving devices, etc.).

4   However as Land (1976:119) points out, in 1970 the DHSS 'estimated that the number of poor two-parent families in which the father was in full-time work (poor being defined as having an income at or below the current supplementary benefit scales) would have nearly *trebled* if the father's earnings had not been supplemented by the mother's.

5   The figures here may be influenced by the fact that it may be more acceptable for some wives (and husbands) to state that the motivation to work is financial rather than boredom, personal identity, etc. (equally some wives (and husbands) may prefer to say that the wife works 'for company' rather than for financial reasons!)'

6   While we recognize that 'career' is a highly problematic concept, here we use it simply to designate 'those types of jobs which require a high degree of commitment and which have a continuous developmental character' (Rapoport and Rapoport, 1976:9).

7   It should be noted that whereas excellent empirical studies exist of the dynamics of family life in dual-career families (in particular, Rapoport and Rapoport, 1976) the same cannot be said for the majority of career and one-career dual-worker families. The studies of such families in Britain are far fewer than in America; also they tend to be fragmented and disproportionately survey- and London-based (e.g., Young and Willmott, 1973). Where case studies, necessary for the 'feel' of family life, do exist they tend to be thin and inadequately integrated with existing survey data. Moreover, general studies of family life often fail to indicate not only the nature of a wife's employment but even whether she's

employed at all (e.g., Toomey, 1971).   Hence the following discussion inevitably contains the limitations of the data on which it is based.

8   In fact Walker and Woods found that the time contributed by husbands to household work correlated most strongly with the hours spent on their occupational work.   It should be noted also that their major findings of relevance to dual-worker families was that employed wives spent less time than the non-employed on all household activities, except shopping, in nearly all family size and age of youngest child categories.   Average daily time spent by employed wives on all household work was from 2-$2\frac{1}{2}$ hours less than that of the non-employed at each number of children and from $1\frac{1}{2}$-$2\frac{1}{4}$ hours less at each age of youngest child.

9   It should be borne in mind of course - and for all dual-worker families - that the relationship between patterns of employment and the household division of labour works in *both* directions.   Thus a wife who feels her husband is unlikely to give much assistance in the home, may opt for part-time working and go back 'when the children are old enough to look after themselves a bit', for this very reason.   Equally, a husband's reaction to his wife's motivation to work may have a boomerang effect.   For example, while he may recognize that the family needs the money she feels obliged to earn, he may also feel that this is an implied criticism of his adequacy as a breadwinner and, as a result, seek to assert his masculinity through refusing to touch 'women's work' at home.

10   Joan Aldous, in her edited volume on the dual-earner family (1981), makes the point that the term 'dual earner' has an advantage over the term 'dual worker' in that the latter implies that housework is not 'work'. But, one advantage of the term 'dual-worker' as the more generic concept is that it includes voluntary work.

Chapter 7

Single-parent families

Brian Jackson

'A LOCAL HABITATION AND A NAME'

There is a very difficult but eternally entrancing philosophi-
cal argument which runs like this.   Outside us and inside us
is a kaleidoscope of impressions, experiences, relationships,
objects and subjects.   What, for instance, is the difference
between that 'outside' in the preceding sentence and the consequent 'inside' in the next phrase?   Is it not true that it
is only when we learn to name its elements that we trawl up a
little of this swirl and then can begin to sort, count and
pattern our catch?   Perhaps the act of naming lies near the
heart of social thinking.

   Single-parent families is a name of our time.   Look at
some of the other names of the age which now appear all over
the literature of family policy.   Here is 'child abuse' and
'functionally illiterate';   there is 'autistic' and 'reconstituted family'.   We hear of 'latch-key children' and
'ethnic minorities' and 'childminders'.   Or 'word blindness'
and 'numeracy';   as we once discovered 'teenage peer groups'
and 'juvenile delinquency'.   Each generation and each culture
names its social phenomena, and having named them, then begins
to knit thought around them.

   There are two initial points that we should make, and then
try to push aside so far as we can.   The first is that such
social phenomena existed even before they were named.   The
word 'childminder' has not appeared in any major dictionary by
1965.   Yet in 1865 it is clearly a part of normal British
life as we can see from Charles Dickens's 'Our Mutual Friend'.
'Child abuse' was demonstrably vaster a century ago, and still
is so in most other cultures today - but it was only when it
became *small* enough for us to be individually shocked by it,
that we could move away from the more general Victorian idea
of 'cruelty to children' and rename it in a way which permits

us to measure, analyse and seek for its end.   'Adult illit-
eracy' has *never* been less in Great Britain, and only some
fifteen of the world's *industrial* nations have squeezed it so
small.   Yet it is the very success in *reducing* it, that gives
us the sense - after a century of state education - of utter
disappointment that we have not banished the beast forever.
Out of that comes the new phrase.

The second point to resist is the negative origin of such
terminology.   Because some 'latch-key' children are poorly
cared for does not mean that all are - or that most are.   If
we are to report the social patterns truthfully and not (dare
a social scientist still say it) as items in the propaganda
for a better world, then we might see also the 'latch-key
child' as lucky to have a latch-key in the first place;   and
sometimes too as an example of future rhythms of family life
in which the child (and the parent) has an extra degree of
freedom.

This 'naming of parts' in our social thinking is a prelude
we often pass too lightly over.   I find it extremely difficult to think dispassionately about single-parent families.
Firstly, because they are a *naming* in our own time and culture, though their invisible history may stretch back to the
origins of man.   Secondly, because the word is embedded in
the language of social pathology, and it may be that many
single-parent families are like Sunday's child 'happy, blithe,
bonny and gay';   and at least as well placed on any emotional,
psychological, or social dimension as if they were couples
with children.   Clearly, the single-parent family is not in
itself 'a problem', though it may frequently be under more
than ordinary pressures and placed in a social landscape which
is less than usually hospitable.   Thirdly, and this is the
most unfashionable of the thoughts in this modest paper,
should we only see such families as ones needing and lacking
the just resources that the commonwealth could provide?   As a
citizen, I certainly think that we should;   and I trust the
data I bring supports that.   But as social scientists we have
to try to see phenomena and patterns as they are, perhaps
slightly distanced, and that may sometimes lead to other kinds
of logic.   It is a difficult, and not always popular patrol-
ling of possible intellectual boundaries.   Nevertheless,
these are the terms in which this chapter is presented.

DID THEY HAVE SINGLE-PARENT FAMILIES IN THE PAST?

Peter Laslett remarks how in reading history it takes a distinct effort of mind to think of 'nearly half of the whole
community living in a state of semi-obliteration'.

Single-parent families are one group who hardly appear in the
historical records, yet it becomes reasonable to suggest that
they have been around in large numbers for a long time.   Now
that we are more sure of the presence of the nuclear family as
far back as the seventeenth century,   it is less easy to
assume that the single parent was easily or always absorbed
into the network of extended kin.   Not all the causes of
single parenthood today were there in time past, but some of
them were.   There was the death of man in war and fighting,
though almost the only poignant record we have of the mother's
plight is that left in ballad and folksong.   There was unmarried pregnancy, there was desertion - perhaps men being
press-ganged or taking the King's shilling.   There was migration, first to the New World, then to Australia and lastly to
Africa.   And there was that persistent difference between
male and female mortality, which even today we do not wholly
understand.

    Quite apart from single parenthood, almost one-third of
Victorian women had to remain spinsters because of the bias
against men in the mortality rate, and because of the new
opportunities that a naval Empire offered.   The effects
of this on our culture, on legislation and economic allotment
to all those outside the 'complete' family, on the self-image
of women, men and children were colossal.   They could be
positive (as the line of single women novelists from Jane
Austen to Emily Brontë demonstrates), but they could be very
negative indeed.   What we might note at this point in our
analysis is how fiercely this helps form our own consciousness
today - within which notions like the single-parent family are
enfolded - and how dramatic has been the change of sensibil-
ity.

    That change of sensibility has some clear determinants.
They do not account for all (and for the moment I leave
slogans aside: 'a family has a right to ...'; 'in the best
world the woman should have ...'), but here is a powerful
back-light on why we now accept 'single-parent families' as a
serious constituent in the social scene.   The first, and historically underdiscussed reason, was the relatively sudden and
vast emigration of males in Victoria's expanding Empire.   For
fifty years it was - for some men - like the exploding uni-
verse.   So the century began with the mother and child open
to the risk of losing the father.   That became certain with
the re-entry into all Europe - after a long time - of major
and mortal war whose effects shuddered along future generations.   Almost a million such young men from Britain died
between 1914 and 1918.   The consequences for other nations
were as savage.   In Britain by 1901 there were already only
962 bachelors to each 1,000 spinsters.   By 1921, there were
894.   That created quite a different social world.

Next one has to remember that the phenomenon of the one-parent family is essentially defined by the existence and dominance of the two-parent family - or at least by that ideal.   This is not the place to discuss that ideology of family structure; but the evidence is that marriage became increasingly popular in Victorian and post-Victorian times. By 1950 something like seventy-five more women in each thousand had married before they were fifty.

This heightening of the norm first of all sharpened the silhouette of those left out (and again literature leaves us the crispest record of the mother all alone); but it also provided the background of fact, of expectation and of the dream ideal against which the rise of the modern one-parent family was sensed.

And though that rise can only be understood, I would suggest, against something like the change sketched here, nevertheless it had its own forces.   One change generated or challenged another.   The age of marriage dropped.   At the middle of this century the number of teenage brides almost doubled, and certainly did so amongst *poorer* groups.   The reasons are no doubt complex, and without wishing to claim that this is the whole truth, we might note both the *evidence* for this (allowing for economic pressures) and the *concept* (allowing for inner forces now demanding certain family ideals).   This in itself meant that married life (especially in less affluent groups) would be *extended*.   Add to this an increasing expectancy of life, and we begin to see the structural inevitability of the one-parent family.   Some men, some women, simply would not tolerate this new length of relationship.   In this situation (apart from many other reasons) there was certain to be a pressure for and a welcome given to better contraception. And that could not but help towards the parent taking more control of their individual and now-longer married life - rather than disappearing within older kinship and religious patterns.   After this comes the slackening of divorce procedures (though I follow only one thread of logic, one must remember there are many more in the weave); and by the last quarter of this century, the single-parent family - as we see and feel it - is really a new fact, a new concept: but one we are searching to fit into our older habits of thought, former patterns of expenditure, our sluggish systems of law, and our tolerance of multiplicity.   The one-parent family is no longer a stranger in this human encampment.   And the idea of marriage and nurturing a child as but an episode in a longer life is now conceivable, and sometimes welcome.   Few of our ancestors saw their place in the human condition, or that of their children, quite like *that*.

As we see then, the concepts of the one-parent family - and

the reasons for its existence - shift, diverge, multiply,
clash.   The basic argument of this chapter is that we have to
stand back and see more than the static image of a deserted
mother with young children, living in poorer circumstances
than most in society.   That dimension is well and powerfully
documented;   but what I want to suggest here is the
dynamic and many-faceted nature of the one-parent family as we
travel through remembered into future stretches of history
which we or our children shall experience.

   I should therefore like to propose nine forms of such experience.   These are not strictly typologies, nor yet exhaustive.   But they may help develop the basic argument.

A SHIFTING EXPERIENCE

Perhaps the law which has had the most dramatic effect on
single-parent families in current times is the Divorce Reform
Act of 1969.   Within three years, the number of divorces
doubled.   Of course there was already a steamhead of desperate and unhappy situations there, which may account for the
burst.   But the trend continues.   If we examine it more
closely, we see that in at least a half of the marriages there
was *no* child anyway - a factor often overlooked in propaganda
discussions.   Examined even more closely, childless couples
became actually a small proportion of all divorces after the
Act.   So we can then quite clearly see that, when we have
subtracted the childless marriages, the new - or rather discovered urgency for divorce - came much more strongly from
couples with fresh, young children.   In over 90 per cent of
situations, there were less than three dependent children.

   That should prompt more thought than it yet has.   We can
see some of the bare demographic and economic bones behind it
(earlier marriage and a teenage sense of relative affluence).
We may speculate at the poor provision for future parenthood
in our education system;   or at the bright, desirable family
norms (clean, happy baby;   sparkling house) projected through
the media.   But the very essence is that couples are having
one child or two children together - and then, very much at a
young age - breaking up.

   The shock of this can be enormous, especially within a
society which has not yet adjusted itself to the *continuing*
phenomenon of the one-parent family.   Neither laws, customs,
money nor institutions match the need of the one-parent
family.   Hence those daily stories of single-parent families
expected to buy school uniforms or school meals that - quite
suddenly - they can no longer afford.   Or the eternal vigi-
lantes within the salaried state service, checking if a parent
has a lover - who could be an alternative economic provider.

But now one has to turn this data on its head, and see it as moving film and not a stuck-down snapshot.   Up to two-thirds of divorced people marry again.   The numbers are rather higher for men than for women; or to put it in a slightly different way, the number and age of her dependent children (we will look at him later) noticeably but not radi-cally reduces the fact of a second marriage.   The reconstitu-ted family follows the single-parent family as the normal course of events.

What we might elicit from this is that the one-parent family is not one brick in the edifice of society.   It is part of our current and foreseeable process of living together, of breaking up and rebuilding.   It is *far* more ordinary than the statistics usually suggest, since people are continually moving in and out of it in very large numbers, or know if vicariously through kinship, friendship, neighbour-hood.   There is the shock of happening, a passage marked for most by material and emotional deprivation and challenge, but for most too there is the creation of another two-parent group.

This is not so for everyone (and that is where the keenest loneliness and severest, long-lasting poverty usually lies).   Nor, as we saw earlier, does every one-parent family formally come into being by divorce.   Death still takes its toll of parents of all ages and babies are still born to single mothers.

Nevertheless, it is as a flowing part of our social experi-ence, that we should see the one-parent family, and not as a kind of category, a parking bay.   It is experienced as a passage by most of those involved and they are both larger than they seem at first glance and steadily growing.

HEADED BY A WOMAN

The one-parent family is largely part of a woman's experience.   So far as we can pierce the mists, this has always been so in our society.   Today that is overwhelmingly the situation.   But whether, in this curious conflict of rights and roles, it may be the same tomorrow, is altogether more dubious.

Just under 90 per cent of such families are headed by a woman.   There are signs that this might be decreasing a little, as more fathers retain the child or win custody.   But clearly it is not going to change so rapidly as to alter this fundamental fact.   We should therefore consider what effect this can have as dispassionately as one can.

First of all, it has an implicit strength.   Women have a much stronger tradition and present experience in nurturing, picking up loose ends, coping.   One can see this by comparing families headed by a woman with those headed by a single man. Both adults may have a sense of loss, of unfairness.   Both may have material difficulties and feel their situation is unjust.   Both may feel imprisoned within the one-parent family and feel their own chances of personal self-development or leisure are stunted.   But normally a clear difference between them is that the woman is much more familiar with the micro-worlds around the child - shopping, cooking and feeding; health, doctors and clinics; nappies, washing, ironing, clothes; and most of all the rate of a child's development, the plateaux, recessions, tantrums, spurts.   I don't want to overestimate this, because many first-time mothers, for instance, have never handled either a nappy or - in any intimate sense - a baby.   Nevertheless, the single-parent father is usually having to acquire all this knowledge, *as well* as meeting the other, common pressures.

Secondly, this huge preponderance of one-parent families led by a woman has an equally clear weakness.   That could be called the *dependency relationship*.   It takes several shapes, of which I'll note three.

Of these, the most obvious is economic dependence on the male.   And though some such women are financially self-sufficient, or accustomed to earning sufficient to support a family, that is not the usual situation.   A family headed by a woman will normally not only experience a sudden drop in direct income, but then may (through letters, meetings, telephone calls, courts, orders) be committed to the pursuit of a substantial portion of the father's income.   This is part of the economic nature and the psychological feel of such a family.

The next clearest side of that dependency relationship is with the state.   For the many historical and cultural reasons that we need not set out here, the modern state still treats the mother alone (as it treats many other groups) as a dependant.   The attitude is expressed in law, custom or bureaucratic procedure.   The single-parent woman, when she cries for help, is essentially as an informal ward of the state. This can sometimes be to her clear advantage, as in certain disputes with the father.   But as an *experience* it certainly means state patronage in modern styles, and an atmosphere in which help is a *gift* of the community rather than a basic citizen's *right*.

And then there is a dependency relationship to paid work. For the reasons previously set out, most one-parent families must at least seek to supplement their income.   Neither a male-headed nor a female-headed family is in a strong position here.   In broad terms, the woman is less educated, less skilled in the tasks that provide money.   This works uncomfortably against her; and the nature of part-time, odd-hours, casual employment is such that this is the kind of low-cost, intermittent labour that is sought.   Even with very sophisticated skills (typing at home, writing novels, childminding, making clothes, offering a consultancy) it is still extremely hard for the individual (and impossible for the group) to escape once again from dependency.   In all these examples, the mother is very rarely indeed in control.

Lastly, there is the central relationship on which we have all too little research: the parent and the child. There may be differences between male- and female-headed households and we really have little more than common sense, some rapportage and intelligent speculation from which to work.   But the often enclosed and frequently intense relationship with the child can create a psychological dependency as powerful as the economic forces and social procedures pressing in on the family.   The world shrinks in, and a sometimes obsessive concern with the child which may certainly thwart the parents' own expansion, commonly gives rise to fears about the child's sexual growth; and as teenage approaches, may sharpen the child's assertion of independence and identity.

This shuttering-in of the family has one common pattern for a mother: but a markedly different, if equally testing one for a father.

HEADED BY A MAN

In the most important document in this field - the 'Report of the Committee on One-Parent Families' (the 'Finer Report') - households headed by the lone father are negatively described as motherless families.   That Report drew on the 1971 Census which suggested that some 100,000 fathers were single parents solely responsible for the rearing of 160,000 children. This (leaving aside widowers and widows) is less than a quarter of the households headed by a woman.   But it is hardly insignificant; and its structures and pressures can be quite distinct, and should be explored.

I would select four elements which are worth at least preliminary analysis.   To begin with, the man expects to be in the world of public work.   Even if unemployed, the norm is always work - work denied, work sought, work avoided, work lost.   Habituated and trained to be a hunter in the economic jungle, the man faces a quite new dilemma if he is to be a single parent.   Next, he very commonly does not have the micro-skills.   There are some splendid examples to contradict this, but the breadth of evidence is overwhelming - men neither inherit nor invisibly acquire the habits of nurturing a small child.   As a dual parent that may be a delight, but as a single man it all has to be learned.

And yet if we fuse these two together, a third element of experience emerges.   Male parenthood is seldom residual nor a matter of custom; it is usually an act of will.   It is a counter-swirl in the patterns of society and an utterly different experience.

Lastly, it is an act which has met considerable opposition. In the early stages of organisations representing single-parent families men were actually denied admission.   The grounds for this were never really clear; it was more a sense, baffled and defensive, that the single-parent family was about mother and child.   The law too was loath to change. And it was not until late in 1979 that male single parents were allowed to claim social benefits on equal terms to women. More generally, the man may have to cope with an atmosphere in which his decision and his lifestyle are sensed as odd and peculiar.   Every man is familiar with the back bar jokes here; and yet single-parent fathers could be amongst the unwitting and often unlucky heralds of a new sense of future parenthood.

PROSPEROUS FAMILIES

The popular image of the one-parent family is of need and relative deprivation.   There is no doubting this major truth; yet if we take an overall look, it is striking that single-parenthood affects all social classes.   So that if we look at the pyramid, there is certainly a considerable if minority group who have relatively high income and assets.   The proportion of one-parent families in the more prosperous groups is only 1 per cent different from those in the poorest ones.   We know nothing at all about this reach of experience, and it is rarely recorded in the literature.   Novel and film are a better source than social science.

FAMILIES UNDER STRESS THROUGH TIME

A quite different dimension essential to understanding the one-parent family is that of stress.   This is universal, whether families are rich or poor; headed by a man, a woman, a teenager; bereaved by death or broken up by desertion, separation and divorce, or never married at all.   Perhaps one could say that having children commonly involves stress

anyway. Certainly some evidence does suggest that up to a
third of mothers, especially in poorer groups, soon experience not the joy of babyhood but what health visitors commonly
term 'the birth of the blues'.

However that is, the first years of being a parent in such
a family are usually emotionally severe. There may be the
long grief after death, the violent forces of guilt or recrim-
ination after a break-up. Either way, the nurturing of the
child can be extra hard as one tries to create tender spaces
in which to care for it, and yet needs adult privacy to cry or
swear at life.

It is likely to be harder yet. Since most families, as we
have seen, are headed by a woman, then there is the common
effect of losing the man's income. Even if you are reasonably well off, the shock of a drop in living standards is very
keen. If you are not well off, you are conscious of having
tumbled back into society's survival threshold (or the cellars
underneath). At the same time may come a loss of esteem, as
all one's emotional and economic vulnerability is exposed.
So many personal accounts of life in the one-parent family
touch on this. It may fade within years, or may be very
long lasting indeed and require a powerful counter-statement
of dignity. Cyril Smith, the Liberal Member of Parliament,
records his later reaction to growing up illegitimate in
a single-parent family. He had become Mayor of Rochdale in
Lancashire, but had not forgotten the lone family experience:
'I was conscious of it, yes, and quite deliberately avoided
it. It was for that same reason I didn't make her Mayoress
straight off. I made the excuse that I didn't want her to
have all the pressure and strain, but really I didn't want her
to be embarrassed, because when you're made Mayor, they say
who your father is and all that. Then when I was sure it was
all right I made her Mayoress. I made her Mayoress for her
sake, to show that a woman could get over her early problems,
and a bit to cock a snook at the system.'

Such turbulent and difficult feelings, as we see from all
autobiographical accounts, are only too likely to spill over
into the child's early experience. And yet oddly that may
happen less than it could in a two-parent family facing immi-
nent break-up or perpetual stress. Again we are driven back
to family memoirs, personal records of living through the experience of single parenthood. Most of these tell the
adult's story, few tell that of the child. Nevertheless, the
adult memory is one of taking *more* care of the child, of
creating sheltered moments in life, of new intimacy, of thinking about the child in fresh and caring ways.

We should not conclude this analysis of obvious and many-
sided stress without recognising - that from the point of view

of the child - the experience of being brought up by a lone parent can include sensations of relief, of simplicity; and an experience of personal, top-quality attention which may otherwise not have been their lot.

TEENAGE LOVERS

In England and Wales in 1901, only 1.6 per cent of men married before the age of twenty. By 1971 it had risen to 10.2 per cent, and the number of young women marrying had increased to 31.1 per cent - and even a little higher in Scotland. From being a marginal happening, teenage marriage now involved one man in ten and a *third* of all women. This trend is very much stronger in poorer or less-skilled groups. Over 40 per cent of women marrying a man under twenty take a husband who does unskilled manual work; only 4 per cent marry one on the self-employed professional ladder.

A very large number of such marriages do not last very long long. For teenagers the peak year for a break-up is the fourth, but over one in ten have already ended before then. The great majority of such couples have already borne a child or children.

There are also couples who have children outside marriage. The trends here are very puzzling, and clearly increasing. In 1964 the Registrar-General observed that 'extra-marital conception is not specifically a teenage problem; the probability that an unmarried woman will conceive in the course of a year is one in thirty-four if she is under twenty. It rises to a peak of one in fifteen if she is 20-24, falls to one in twenty if she is 25-29 and to one in forty-five if she is 30-39'. Perhaps over 60,000 children will be born illegitimate in any one year, but only a small proportion will remain in one-parent and usually teenage families. The others may be born into stable unions, to mothers who soon marry, or are adopted. Some 9 per cent of births in Britain are to unmarried mothers compared to over 14 per cent in the USA.

Single parents who are still teenagers are a very distinct group. As we see, there is no doubt that they have grown considerably. The marriages are often fragile, and the great majority of children born within wedlock. We do not know exactly why this has come about, but it is clearly an unhappy trend. It may be that the glamourisation of marriage has encouraged it, and the lack of realistic preparation for adult life within schools may have also counted. Behind all lies the breakdown of older sexual taboos, the mass use of contraception and unforseen results.

However that is, two types of loners ask for special concern. One is the schoolgirl mother. In Britain if she is under 16 she receives no financial help from the state. That seems harsh and yet it could be wise. The family has to cope, to face the future realities and almost always decides in favour of adoption. The second is illegitimate birth, particularly to a teenage girl. Such babies are half as likely again to die within one year of birth as legitimate children and twice as likely to die within the first week. There is a common myth that teenage mothers bear babies easily and healthily. In reality, the girl who has such a child very often has it in poor circumstances, with meagre preparation. The baby may frequently have a low birthweight, and be extremely vulnerable to secondary infection.

In either of these situations the experience of being a lone teenage parent may be brief; though one should not the increasing resistance to immediate adoption - a resistance often encouraged for the best of reasons and with the worst of results.

Nevertheless, though this kind of single parent is now so large, it can fairly be said that it is, for most, only one passage in life. If decent care can be taken of the living child the parent can move on to a different world. Behind many happy families today lies the healed wound of such a teenage experience. It would heal the quicker if there were more effective policies and more caring attitudes to those entrapped within it.

FAMILIES WITH ETHNIC MINORITIES

We have looked at the single-parent family along social class dimensions; in terms of gender and income and age. And along emotional dimensions too.

But quite a different viewpoint can be pointed up if we consider such families within their culture. Whether there is 'a culture of the poor' or a sense of 'working-class community', are more general notions, too large to be explored here. But we can at least look at the dramatic differences within all developed societies if we compare the family within ethnic minorities. Such minorities are of course universal: Fiji tries to balance a triad - Polynesians, Indians and Chinese. The Soviet Union has a thousand such permutations. But within the more prosperous nations the ethnic minority takes on a different social timbre. They are the 'gastarbeiter' of West Germany, the Polish vote in the USA, the North Africans within metropolitan France. And in Britain, I would like to take three examples of such immigrant working groups.

The first is the Asian community, most of which was now born in Britain.   Within it, the single-parent family exists but compared to the host population it is a rarity.   When it does occur, perhaps through bereavement, there is rapid re-marriage (especially for a man) or the family is absorbed into the larger kinship system.   This has strengths and flexibili-ties which most of the rest of Britain does not possess. Perhaps that is symbolised by the fact that in Bengali there are 53 different terms for a relative.   In English we operate from a basic dozen.

A second instance would be the Chinese community.   Whereas Asian communities congregate together and relatives are near at hand, the Chinese minority has the opposite characteristic. Outside the small chinatowns of London and Liverpool the normal Chinese family is a tight, in-turning unit.   It is based on the restaurant and takeaway food trade and moves geographically to wherever there is a gap in the market.   So we find them in Peebles or Penzance, often miles away from relatives and from anyone who speaks their language or shares their culture.   Those closest to them are often their busi-ness rivals, and warily regarded as such.   In this situation, Chinese colleagues point out, with pride, that the one-parent family only seldom exists and they look with horror at our acceptance of marital breakdown as they do at our disrespect for old people.   On the other hand, I have often felt that the appearance of the one-parent family in such a community would be a positive gain in human freedom, especially for the woman tied inextricably to an unhappy and claustrophobic relationship.

My third contrasting minority would be the West Indian. Here the proportion of single parents is much above the aver-age.   It is often this (as well as the type of accommodation) which is reflected in the different proportion of single parents in different social service authority areas.   In London, Lambeth has 17.4 per cent and Hammersmith 18.8 per cent, whereas the figure drops to 6.1 per cent in Bexley and 5.5 per cent in Havering.

The reason for the large incidence in the West Indian com-munity is not marriage break-up as in the host community.   It is late marriage.   Many West Indian women bear and bring up their young children with no stable support from a man.   They are three times as likely to have to go out to work, and much more likely to use the poorest day-care facilities.   An esti-mated 50,000 small West Indians are with unregistered child-minders and this may have a link with their relatively poor start at school, and the disproportionate number allocated to special schools.

Some argue that the frequent failure of the man to take on

family responsibilities at this stage is a relic of slave culture, when men were devalued inside the family and often separated from it.   However that may be, and I am not wholly
convinced, it means that many West Indian children spend their
early years in single-parent families, struggling under very
harsh circumstances.   Marriage comes later and the rest of
childhood may be within a two-parent family, but one of which
the mother is very much the centre.

Looking forward it seems likely that this minority at least
will move towards the norms of the host community, lowering
its birthrate and increasing the popularity of marriage.   But
the economic circumstances of single-parent families within
it, with the massive dependence on low-paid unskilled work by
women, are likely to continue to be difficult to improve,
short of effective shifts of wealth in society.

FAMILIES IN POVERTY

A one-parent family has five main sources of income: earnings, maintenance, supplementary benefit, widows' benefits or
the conversion of existing assets such as savings, property,
belongings and all around the kitchen sink.   The last source
is very small.   In 1972, only 13 per cent of single parents
drawing social security had any capital assets, and only 2
per cent had sufficient for them to be taken into account
when calculating their entitlement.   This is largely to
be explained by the youth of so many one-parent families:
they have had little time to build up assets; and there is
this huge preponderance of women, who have restricted access
and minor control over whatever previous income there ever
was.

Similarly we can, to an extent, remove widows' allowances
from the argument.   Far fewer of them depend on supplementary
benefit or are on the margins of poverty.   This may be
because they are older, have returned to employment after
childrearing years and even may be receiving payment from a
working son or daughter.   But there is a more fundamental
explanation.   State support for widows was built into the
very fabric of the welfare state.   Support for one-parent
families was not.   Public opinion understood the clear-cut
needs of widowhood; clear lines were drawn and allowances
increased in time.   There is no such simplicity in public
understanding, nor in legal inheritance nor in bureaucratic
procedure so far as the single-parent family is concerned.
They have lived in a twilight area where their income has been
affected by divorce laws, separation orders and by the long
shadow of the Elizabethan Poor Law as it lay across the

various regulations for national assistance and then supplementary benefit.   Sir William Beveridge in 'Social Insurance and Allied Services' struggled for a formula to include the special needs of one-parent families in the document which led the way to the post-war welfare state.   It was only a very small part of the Report: nevertheless there was there the suggestion for a 'separation benefit'.   It got nowhere, and there was general reluctance to become involved in the difficult questions of illegitimacy, marriage breakdown and divorce.   As a consequence, unmarried mothers, divorced, deserted, or separated wives were left entirely out of the new policy which shapes today's world.   That is one major origin of their *recurring* poverty today.

Consequently many mothers alone must depend on earning (which is extremely difficult and sometimes undesirable when you have young children to rear).   Or they must look to maintenance from the father (and this clumsy and often unfair transaction can be irregular, or non-existent - especially in poorer circumstances).   Or they must turn to the state. That is what they do.

But with the state they are locked in an annual series of hope and disappointment as budgets come and go.   Of course there have been improvements such as the introduction since 1971 of the Family Income Supplement, the later arrival of Child Benefit, of the extra 'Child Benefit Increase' which is a small but distinct supplement for most single parents.

Yet none of these regular devices alter - *or can alter* - the poverty trap for a third or so of lone mothers, and a scatter of fathers.   This occurs whatever party is in power. 1979 was a characteristic election year.   The outgoing Labour government was well aware of poverty amongst some single parents, and had not succeeded in doing very much about it. The opposition were clear-cut in their pledges and putative policies 'Our tax system must be more family-oriented', 'We must concentrate relief where there are dependent children. The next Conservative government will give it top priority.'

Having won the election, the new government fulfilled its pledge by quickly raising single parents' tax allowance by £380.   This gave 400,000 one-parent families who pay standard tax a gain of £1.78 a week.   By the time this came into action (and as often the Treasury delayed that date for some months) inflation and other budgetary changes had reduced the practical value to 26p - the price of a pair of shoelaces. There was no rise in Child Benefit, but one of 50p in the Child Benefit Increase.   By the end of the year in which this was first paid, inflation had overtaken it completely - and more so.   The single-parent family slid backwards.

This is not at all to make a party political point.

Something like this - good intentions, an extra increase - has taken place ever since 1945.   And it is perennially unsuccessful.   It must be so, until single parents are given basic rights in the way that Beveridge suggested them for other groups in society such as the sick or the widowed.

It is difficult to estimate the scale of poverty here, but also important neither to exaggerate nor understate it. Other groups are more at risk than single-parent families. Peter Townsend looked at thirteen social minorities and tried to rank them by using a number of indices.   This is always a difficult task;   and some belong to several minorities at once.   But of the thirteen very vulnerable groups (which ranged from the disabled, through large families, to immigrants from Ireland, the Caribbean or Asia) single-parent families came about half way.

We may dispute for a long time what 'relative deprivation' means in modern Britain, but the Finer Report suggested that between 1969 and 1971, some 45 per cent of such families were either receiving supplementary benefit (the state's definition of need) or were within a couple of pounds of that standard. The poorest of all are clearly separated women who have several children to bring up.   They are also the least likely to remarry.

What this means for both parent and child is an episodic life in which there never is any guarantee that it will get better.   It means poor housing, sharing bedrooms, basic food, worries over fuel and other bills, no holidays.   On one sample 75 per cent of children under 14 never had a birthday party.   It is surely intolerable.

But it is also unchangeable unless one-parent families are brought into the very fabric of state's support, and not merely attended to on the margins.   Budgetary tinkering leads nowhere.   What is needed at the heart is generous allowance for all who are tending children.   This is the seedcorn of the future, and no distinction needs to be made between one parent and any other kind of family.   It needs to be a right, as pensions are, whatever one's circumstances may be.   It can be funded through graded taxation in the normal way, and - though there are other unfairnesses to be dealt with - this would basically unlock the poverty trap for single parents. There are necessary supplementary reforms;   but this should be a major item on the 'Agenda for the Second Welfare State'.

CONCLUSION

The one-parent family may have been with us for a very long time, but like America, it was discovered relatively recently

and the date is a matter of dispute.   It was a marginal, and
then abandoned concern in the report which shaped the welfare
state.   British government does not begin to collect statistics under this head until 1967.   Yet the naming of it as a
social phenomenon has enlarged our knowledge, mildly increased
our action and generally created a characteristically misleading stereotype.   We do not agree how many single-parent families there are; but it seems likely that by 1970 there were
over 500,000 and by 1980, over 800,000.   These difficulties
in counting are not camouflage but dilemmas in definition.
How long or formally does a family have to be split up in
order to qualify?   Should we include the 14,000 wives of
prisoners, who are effectively living the single-parent life?
Should we include grandparents or others who are bringing up a
child by themselves?   Personally I feel we should, and that
regulations should be altered to recognise this, and that the
higher rather than the lower estimates are nearer the truth.

But perhaps all those are the wrong numbers to consider
anyway.   There are always going to be more one-parent *children* than one-parent *families*.   Over 50 per cent have one
child, around 30 per cent have two, 12 per cent have three and
6 per cent have four or more.   That means we are discussing,
in Britain, a million and a half of today's children and
tomorrow's adults.   Perhaps a little too much of the literature has concentrated on the adult, and not quite enough on
the child.

At any one time, seven out of eight of those adults is a
woman.   The tendency is for it to be a young woman with
weaker education, poorer earning power and less personal
financial assets.   This is the expressway into the poverty
trap which subsequently catches at least four out of ten.

We know remarkably little about the future trends of the
one-parent family.   We are in the doubtful position of long-
range weather forecasters: there are some indicators, but not
enough to give full confidence in such a complex estimate of
probability.   But behind us we can see the trends of the
century - the fall in adult mortality, except for the vast
toll of war; the lowering in the age of marriage; the shifts
in migration; the improvement in contraception; and the increasing legal and social acceptance of separation and
divorce.

In this chapter we have tried to see the single-parent
family in a fresh and not always a problematical way.   It is
not a static fact, but a passing experience for far larger
numbers of parents and of children than we have so far calculated.   For most it leads to re-marriage, reconstituted families, new and stable unions which may offer much more than the
old.   'Til death do us part' was perhaps (and only perhaps)

the best formula in societies where marriage came later, where the sex balance was different and where life was shorter.   We have moved into a society where one facet is the early trial marriage, then dissolution and then a permanent second union. If we take the immediate, and crisis view, this can be extremely troubling (especially if we consider the needlessly born child).   But if we stand further back and review the life pattern as a whole it is by no means certain that the one-parent family, as a transitory state, represents some kind of breakdown in society, or a dimunition of the sum of human happiness.   Nor can it be taken as a token of that.

The evidence does not suggest that the experience of lone parenthood is a permanent disadvantage.   Indeed the surveys here are quite contradictory;   and all turns out to depend on the values and the angle of approach that has been taken, rather than on the data in itself.   Looking back one now sees so clearly the concern with the 'broken home' which dominated post-war thinking and which represented a kind of religious or at least tribal shock.   To some at least of the individuals concerned, it may have represented a kind of jail-break, a bid for freedom.

To extend this theme, we have at least seen signs that single parenthood *can* not only be an escape over the wall, but an active choice.   That is particularly clear with some fathers, but it is also there in the many, brief autobiographical accounts by mothers.

None of this is to deny the loneliness and pain that is so often involved ('Sunday afternoons were the worst.   Everyone was off enjoying themselves, but what could I do with the kids?   I came to *dread* Sunday afternoons').   Nor is it to overlook the variety of lifestyles.   And above all, not to put aside the needless and ever-repeating poverty trap which always catches such a proportion and some for ever.

But looking at the family in Britain, past, present and future, we have to break up the stereotype of *the single-parent family*.   Taking class, age, economic, gender, cultural and time perspectives (if but briefly) we have seen how it is not one of the *problems* of modern society, but one of its varied phenomena.   And one which has strength and hope as well as vulnerability and despair.

Social attitudes, laws and procedures (like social sciences) always lag behind social reality.   Perhaps we have to learn to reconsider a society in which early death has been vastly reduced, but in which marital relationships change far more than in the past.   I don't see this as a film-star recipe for endless, brief marriages or a licence for teenage promiscuity.   Humankind cannot take too much of that.   Nor can children, nor can the common purse.

But old stigmata, old law, old procedures, old allocations of wealth must change; as early adult death and child illegitimacy, with their ancient history, also disappear.   The one-parent family is part of us now and tomorrow.   As they have to live with us, we too have to learn to live with them, with ourselves.

Chapter 8

South Asian families

Roger Ballard

INTRODUCTION

The presentation of a brief and generalized account of the
major features of family organization in South Asian settlements in Britain poses many problems. Although lifestyles
within such groups may seem quite distinctive to outsiders,
there is a great deal of internal differentiation. Migrants
have come from different parts of the sub-continent, and they
and their children have adopted a range of strategic responses
to their new social and economic environment. Yet despite
these diversities, it is possible to identify a number of
underlying structural continuities which run across the whole
population category. The central aim of this chapter is to
establish and illuminate the basic patterns and principles of
family organization which are characteristic of virtually
every community of Indian, Pakistani and Bangladeshi origin
in Britain.

  The South Asian population of Britain currently numbers
rather more than a million people, about half of whom were
locally born. Mass migration from the sub-continent began in
the 1950s when the country was suffering from an acute shortage of labour, and although the entry of adult males is now
tightly restricted, some men who have long been resident in
Britain have still not yet brought their wives and children to
join them. Thus while some families have long been reunited,
others are still in the midst of reconstituting themselves.
Demographically the South Asian population of Britain still
remains unbalanced. It contains a disproportionately large
number of women of child-bearing age, and a correspondingly
small number of elderly people.

  Most migrants were of small or middle peasant background,
and have come in large numbers from a few compact areas,
notably in Punjab (somewhere in the order of three-quarters

come from this region), Gujerat and Bengal.   The majority of
East African Asians have similar origins.   In the course of
settlement in Britain aggregations based upon commonalities of
religion, area of origin, caste and most especially kinship
have grown up, and the greater part of most migrants' domestic
and social interactions are now conducted within arenas
ordered in these terms.   Thus although the South Asian population in any particular city may be large, internally significant communal aggregations often include no more than 100
families.   A substantial number of studies of such communities are now available, all of which indicate the great significance of kinship loyalties both during migration and in the
subsequent processes of communal and ethnic consolidation. (1)
None, however, examines the content of family organization in
any detail, so this chapter can thus be seen as an attempt to
remedy that deficiency.

Yet before doing so some fundamental problems of definition
and vocabulary must be disposed of.   It is striking, for
instance, that whenever the structure of such families is
being publicly discussed, the qualifiers 'joint' or 'extended'
are invariably employed.   Yet what precisely do these terms
mean?   Very often their use indicates nothing more than that,
from the speaker's perspective, South Asians keep in touch
with a wider range of relatives than he would expect to do
himself.   If we are to achieve any analytical clarity, our
terminology must be much more precise.   Even the concept of
family is problematic in a similar way.   In common English
speech, its meaning can range over the members of a household
(that is those who live together under the same roof), those
who feel strong bonds of obligation to one another by virtue
of close kinship (even if they do not live together), those who
claim descent from a common ancestor (for instance 'of good
family') and finally all those with whom a person can trace a
relationship, whether by blood or marriage (as in 'a family
gathering').   Each of these levels of meaning is of significance in understanding South Asian kinship, but nothing but
confusion arises if they are not distinguished.

The problem of just what should be identified as constituting a family can be illustrated by considering the disjunc-
tions which often arise during the process of migration.   The
most concrete kinship aggregations that can be observed in
Britain are households, that is groups of people who live
together and who make common domestic arrangements amongst
themselves.   Yet among South Asians the members of such
households often regard these arrangements as a matter of temporary convenience.   From their perspective the network of
obligations and expectations between those who would have
lived together had they still been resident in their villages

of origin may be of far greater significance.   Thus an empir-
ically observable household in Britain may often be no more
than a local facet of a much wider network of familial relationships which bind together similar households scattered
around the world.   It is these networks of binding relationships which are very often the most appropriate focus for an
analysis of the family.

AN IDEAL MODEL OF THE SOUTH ASIAN FAMILY

The essential logic of South Asian migrants' families can best
be understood by tracing them back to their historical and
geographical roots, and the most convenient way of doing this
is by setting out a model of the way they were 'traditionally'
organized. (2)   It should be emphasized, however, that this
ideal model is no more than a convenient fiction, which can be
used as a kind of template against which to set currently
observable behaviour.   It is not, nor is it intended to be,
either an indicator of the statistical average or an accurate
representation of the way in which families were actually
organized in the past.
    The basic pattern of family membership was very clear cut:
it consisted of a man, his sons and grandsons, together with
their wives and unmarried daughters (see Figure 8.1).   Only

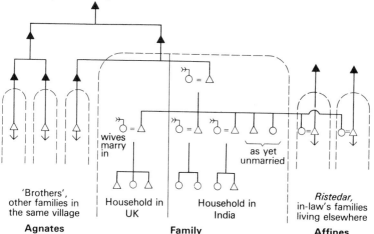

FIGURE 8.1   An outline representation of South Asian family
membership and the relationship between familial, agnatic, and
affinal kinship

sons had full rights of inheritance and so remained family
members all their lives.   At marriage daughters left their
natal home and became members of their husbands' family.   The
family was both a corporate and a multi-functional group.
Not only did its members hold land, or a business, or a right
to perform some craft skill in common, but they lived and
worked co-operatively together, sharing agricultural, domestic
and other productive tasks among themselves.   Ideologically
it was assumed that obligation to the group would always be
put before personal self-interest.   Individual freedom was
not regarded as being of great significance, for family members' social reality was seen as arising much more from their
mutual interrelationships than from the intrinsic qualities of
their individual personalities.   As a corporate group the
family had an essentially permanent existence over time.   It
was not necessarily dependent for its continuity on the maintenance of a relationship between any particular married
couple.   Rather, long-term stability was most crucially
guaranteed by the birth of sons, whose eventual marriage
would sustain the group for a further generation.   In sharp
contrast to English families in both modern and historical
times, in the South Asian context it has never been assumed
that sons should establish independent households of their
own at marriage.

The underlying structure of the family is most clearly
highlighted by a consideration of the distribution of property
rights among its members.   Ownership of the patrimony was
formally vested in the eldest male member, who was expected to
manage the family's affairs to the benefit of all.   Inheritance of property - most especially of the land which is so
crucial in any peasant society - was effectively restricted to
the patriarch's sons.   Daughters and grand-daughters were entitled to a dowry (usually jewellery, clothing and household
utensils) at marriage, when they were transferred irrevocably
to their husband's families.   Since sons could only gain
access to land, and indeed most other occupations, through the
family, they normally stayed at home with their father.   Only
after his death could brothers claim separate shares in their
inheritance, and so establish separate families of their own.
Although the ideal has long been that a man's sons should continue to live together co-operatively after their father's
death, with the elder brother becoming the patriarch, in practice it seems that most families whose livelihood was drawn
solely from peasant cultivation have always divided their land
in such circumstances. (3)   But this does not imply that at
partition each brother went off as an individual, rather it
was a process whereby one corporate family split along well-
established lines into a number of smaller but structurally
identical groups.

Relationships within each family were ordered in terms of an ideal of unrestricted interpersonal reciprocity, quite accurately summed up by the dictum, 'from each according to his ability, to each according to his needs'.   Yet it was far from being an egalitarian group, for each member was regarded as having a distinct but complementary role to play.   All relationships were intrinsically hierarchical, as between the sexes, as between the generations, and as between older and younger in the same generation.   Superordinates were expected to support and care for their subordinates, while subordinates were expected to respect and obey their superordinates.   It was upon the maintenance of these asymmetric reciprocities that the unity and continuity of the family depended.

STRUCTURE AND PROCESS

As stressed at the outset, this model only provides a sketch of the basic moral and legal parameters within which real families operate, and should not be taken as a statistical norm.   For instance, although the ideal presumption has always been that families should be large multigenerational groups, most families were not so constituted, even in the 'traditional' past.   When many mothers died in childbirth, many children failed to survive infancy and few adults reached old age, it was statistically impossible for more than a minority of families to approximate the ideal.   It is only recent advances in standards of public health which have made it more widely attainable.

Similarly it is vital that the content of interpersonal relationships within the family should be approached from a dynamic perspective.   Although constructed around an ideology of co-operation and harmony, South Asian families are not therefore marked by a complete absence of conflict and tension between their members.   On the contrary every participant in every family is constantly engaged in securing his or her own interests, and consequently in limiting and curbing the advances of others.   It is of course impossible to give an exhasutive account of all the manoeuvres which may take place, so all that will be attempted here is to set out some illustrative generalizations about the kinds of processes which can be observed in virtually all South Asian families.

Let us begin by considering the relationship between father and son, between whom a degree of tension is unexceptional, and explosive conflicts are by no means uncommon.   These may be contained by using a variety of strategies, but amongst the most common is for the father to give his son largely autonomous responsibility for some aspect of the family's affairs.

Tension may similarly be eased if a son goes to work abroad for a few years, though when he finally returns with his savings to add to the family's resources, conflict may recur in an even more acute form.   As a result of his financial contribution a son may expect to have more influence within the family, but his father may still be reluctant to cede much power.   Yet eventually all fathers age, and as their physical strength wanes, so does their ability to dominate their sons. In the long run patriarchs have little alternative but to retire gradually from everyday management of their families' affairs.   Those who are wise do so gracefully, retaining only symbolic authority, though reassured by the formal respect which their sons are usually prepared to offer.   Sons know that it is only through their fathers that they can gain access to land and retain their good name in the community, while fathers are well aware that it is sons alone who can provide security in their old age.   There are often disagreements about what the precise content of their relationship should be at any particular point in time, yet both sides are normally very conscious that a mutually satisfactory arrangement *must* be achieved.   All other outcomes spell disaster for them both.

THE POSITION OF WOMEN

The adoption of a similar perspective also helps to illuminate the position of women, for their formal subordination to men does not indicate that they are necessarily devoid of power. On the contrary the very separation of women from men by the conventions of <u>purdah</u>, together with their control of the domestic economy, means that they operate in a partially autonomous world from which it is possible to bargain both individually and collectively with men.   Although outcomes necessarily vary, husbands cannot afford to ignore the interests and concerns of their wives.   Few heads of households - and no wise ones - make any important decisions without conferring extensively with every member of their families, women as well as men.

   In considering the status of women the distribution of power amongst women themselves must also be considered, not least because they spend so much of their time apart from men. A newly married bride is always amongst the weakest members of the family.   After an initial honeymoon period when she is on display, she is constantly at the beck and call of her mother-in-law, whose jealousy she must be careful not to arouse as she seeks to establish a relationship with her husband.   In the early days of marriage husband and wife see relatively

little of one another, except at night, and are not expected
to show any overt affection for one another.   Only after the
birth of children does a woman's place within the family, and
her relationship with her husband, become really secure.
Sons bring long-term continuity, and ensure that a woman will
one day become a mother-in-law herself.   It is then that she
will be able to order the household to her own satisfaction,
to have a more openly affectionate relationship with her husband, as well as having sons and daughters-in-law whom she can
expect to carry out her wishes.

Such a brief outline inevitably obscures the setbacks that
invariably occur in a woman's hoped-for passage to a position
of influence in her husband's family.   She may fail to have
children, her husband may fall out with his brothers or his
parents and take it out on her, or she may find herself in
intense competition with her sisters-in-law.   As such events
occur women (and men) constantly manoeuvre in order to advance
their interests, and to counter the activities of others.
There is no space here to discuss the strategies adopted, but
they include passive non-cooperation, forming alliances with
others, acting (or threatening to act) in such a way that the
family's honour might be endangered, and dropping barbed comments about discrepancies between formal ideals and actual
behaviour.   Such tactics provide a very effective means
whereby those with little authority can embarass and constrain
those who are behaving in an overbearing way.   Once such a
perspective is adopted it soon becomes apparent that despite
the institutionalized hierarchy within the family, formal subordinates are by no means necessarily in a position of unmiti-
gated oppression.   What ultimately counts is the skill with
which each individual is able to deploy whatever bargaining
strength he or she can muster. (4)

HONOUR AND SHAME

The complexity of the question of the asymmetry of the sexes
is nowhere better illustrated than in the concepts of honour,
izzat, and shame, sharm.   In its narrower sense izzat
is a matter of male pride.   Honourable men, as in many Mediterranean cultures, are expected to present an image of fear-
lessness and independence to the outside world, and at the
same time to keep close control over the female members of
their families.   For a woman to challenge her husband's or
her father's authority in public shamefully punctures his
honour.   To sustain male izzat wives, sisters and daughters must be seen to behave with seemly modesty, secluding
themselves from the world of men.   The ideas of honour and

shame thus reinforce the formal hierarchy of relationships
within the family.

   But honour accrues to the family as a group, and not just
to individual males within it, the advancement of their corporate _izzat_ is one of the most important goals which South
Asian families set themselves.   The maintenance of _izzat_
depends both upon the family's wealth and its members' conformity with ideal norms of behaviour; but it is advanced most
effectively by arranging prestigious matches for the family's
daughters, and by outshining its rivals in the gift exchanges
which take place at such events.   Yet it is striking that
women play at least as great a role as men in the promotion of
the family's honour.   It is they who make and record all the
decisions about gift giving.   Very often they also handle all
the private negotiations which precede their husbands' formal
public confirmation of their daughters' marriages. (5)   In
the vigorous pursuit of an idea which intrinsically subordinates them, women gain influence not just over other women,
but over men.   But all would be lost if any public acknowledgment were to be made that this was indeed the case.

STRUCTURES OF EXTRA-FAMILIAL KINSHIP

Although our central concern here is with processes internal
to the family, kinship relationships established between families must also be examined.   Limitations of space mean that
the discussion must be extremely compressed, but readers
should at least be aware of the way in which the ideology of
kinship may be utilized in the construction of wider social
institutions.   Although there is widespread local variation,
most North Indian peasant farming families are aggregated into
   corporate patrilineal descent groups.   The ancestor of each
such local group, it is usually claimed, founded the village in
which all his descendants now live.   Such clan-brotherhoods
(variously _biraderi_, _bhaichara_, _khandan_) are internally divided
into sections and sub-sections in a segmentary fashion, and
relationships between them are ordered in terms of a calculus
of kinship and descent.   Families with a common ancestor are
expected to abandon their internal disputes to act as political
allies should any one of their number come into conflict with a
more distantly related fellow villager.   Such segmentary line-
age systems, of which the family is the basic constituent unit,
provides the framework for the structure of the village and
its politics in most parts of Northern India. (6)

   The idea of brotherhood on which these systems are based
both unites and divides, for while common descent implies
special loyalties, it also generates competition.   This is

latent between real brothers, but much more overt between
families and groups of families which split apart in the past.
The proximity of each family's land holdings provides ample
opportunities for boundary disputes, while competition for
izzat ensures that everyone takes elaborate steps that they
are not outshone, most especially by their close 'brothers'.
Yet despite their constant competition the fact that
'brothers' are neighbours gives them good reason to make
common cause against more distant kin.   Segmentary lineages
are thus built up on the basis of a nesting pattern of opposi-
tions and alliances between agnatically defined groups.
Relationships between classificatory brothers' families
(serike in Punjabi) are ordered in terms of reciprocity, but
this is not of the unrestricted kind expected within the
family.   Amongst serike co-operation is tempered by a
strongly competitive edge.
   In contrast to these ties of agnatic kinship, affinal relationships are established with families from which wives have
been taken, or to which daughters have been given in marriage.
Such kin are known categorically as ristedar.   Amongst
Hindus and Sikhs, at least, marriage within one's own clan is
forbidden, (7) although it must take place within the caste.
The effect of this rule of exogamy is that at marriage women
always leave their villages of origin and take up residence
elsewhere.   It also gives rise to a web of affinal relationships between families living in different villages.   If
agnatic ties are characterized by proximity and competition,
affinal ties are, at least initially, formal and hierarchical.
In many areas the bride's family treats the groom's with great
respect, such that they may even refuse all proffered hospitality, feeling it more appropriate to give rather than to
take.   However, the bride's brother is expected to take a
close interest in his sister's welfare, and to establish a
close and affectionate relationship with her children.   It is
above all from one's mama, mother's brother, that disinterested backing and support can be expected in times of personal
difficulty.
   While Hindu and Sikh marriage rules have the effect of
strictly differentiating between affines and agnates, in most
Moslem groups there is a preference for marriage between close
kin, so that agnatic and affinal ties become closely intertwined with one another.   Moslems nevertheless still sustain
the conceptual distinction between the two kinds of kinship.
   While it is clear that kinship does not cease at the boundary of the family, it is worth emphasizing that its quality
does change sharply at this point.   Familial ties are, or at
least should be, unrestricted and open-ended.   They are
founded on a sense of commonwealth amongst participants, so

that no overt calculation of an individual's contribution to, or benefit from, the whole should ever be made.   Kinship which is less comprehensive than this is extra-familial. Thus two brothers who quarrel and split apart are described, pejoratively, as acting like serike.   They have ceased to belong to a single family. (8)

THE FAMILY IN THE PROCESS OF MIGRATION

South Asian families have undergone a sea-change as some or all of their members have uprooted themselves to settle in crowded industrial cities over 5,000 miles away.   Yet it should not be assumed that such upheavals have either under- mined or stood in contradiction to family unity.   On the con- trary migration has taken place within the context of familial obligations and has if anything strengthened rather than weakened them.

Early migrants to Britain were typically drawn from peasant families with limited land-holdings, but a multiplicity of sons.   Ten acres might be a fair-sized holding for one man, but split among three or four sons it would leave them all relatively poor.   In such circumstances one or more sons might be sent abroad, primarily to restore and advance the family's collective fortunes.   Overseas earnings could be used to redeem mortgaged land as well as to buy more, to pro- vide sisters with dowries, to build new houses and to purchase agricultural implements.   More recently the migratory process has tended to fuel itself.   As increasing numbers of families sent sons abroad, all except the very richest have felt the need to send someone too, in order to participate in this new- found source of wealth.   Not to do so might imperil their own izzat. (9)

On arrival in Britain few migrants expected their sojourn to last long, but most have stayed for much longer than they intended.   High incomes always tempted them to stay on and save a little more, added to which migrants soon began to find themselves caught up in networks of obligation within the ethnic colonies which they rapidly established.   As these social arenas began to take on a life of their own, so migrants began to consider bringing their wives and children to join them.   But they did not do so without considerable misgivings, for from their perspective British society seemed materially attractive but morally bankrupt.   Above all the ideas of honour and family loyalty by which they set such store seemed to be almost entirely absent.   Few migrants wished their families to be affected by British cultural stan- dards.

Nevertheless as ethnic colonies grew in size and sophistication, so did migrants' confidence that they could safely reconstitute their families despite the alien surroundings. Such decisions were taken at different speeds in different groups, but by now virtually all South Asians have set about calling their wives and children to join them. Once they arrived, migrants' lifestyles in Britain began to be transformed.

In the pioneering days when saving was the overriding goal, a group of men would often rent a large delapidated house, share household tasks and expenses between themselves, and maximize their savings by living in squalid conditions. With the arrival of women and children there was a move to smaller, sounder houses and an improvement in living standards. Households were still usually made up of several married couples, and very often several lodgers as well. Sharing made good economic sense. It lessened the cost of housing and made it easier to acquire expensive but prestigious consumer goods such as television sets, hi-fis, cars and washing machines. But as time has passed so residential units have come to have a more conventional membership in sub-continental terms. In the early days all-male households often incorporated unrelated men, who treated each other as if they were brothers. However in the longer term co-operative domestic arrangements have generally only been sustained by those connected by prior ties of familial kinship. More distantly connected agnatic and affinal kin often lived co-operatively together for a while soon after their arrival, but such households have invariably proved unstable.

Most migrants have made great efforts to sustain the unity of their families, both because this proved an excellent way of coping with their economic circumstances, and also because this was perceived as a most effective bastion against the corrosive influence of British culture. By now many migrants have gone on to assume that any deviation from the ideal norms must necessarily be the first step on the slippery slope towards wholesale Anglicization. The slightest lapse thus seems to indicate total disloyalty. Such growing conservatism should not, however, be seen simply as a negative reaction to British ways. As settlements grew in size, so each ethnic colony has become an arena for status competition in its own right. Families have begun to outbid each other in the scale and style of their performance of traditional rituals, just as they did back home. _Izzat_ is at stake, and it has become imperative for every family to participate in the game of status competition if they do not wish to fall behind. The consequent necessity for every family member to maintain an impeccable and honourable reputation is a thoroughgoing constraint on everyone's behaviour. (10)

CONTINUITY AND CHANGE

Although most migrants are strongly conservative in their
attitudes and convinced that they have maintained traditional
patterns in their entirety, it should not be assumed that no
change has taken place in their behaviour.   Family organization, like everything else, has been radically affected by the
new context in which it is set.   However, the widely expected
assimilation of English cultural patterns has not occurred;
instead South Asians in Britain, in parallel with many other
minorities, are autonomously evolving their own distinctive
lifestyles.   It is these changes that we must now consider.
    Major changes have arisen as a result of families' removal
from a world of subsistence agriculture, and their entry into
an urban wage-based economy.   The household has generally
ceased to be the focus of production, for most adults now
leave home everyday to earn wages.   At least half of all
South Asian women in Britain go out to work, and many of the
remainder earn money at home, usually by sewing up clothes as
outworkers.   The widespread availability of wage work has
significantly changed the balance of power within the family,
so that wives are no longer so economically dependent on their
husbands, nor sons on their fathers.   Even so these developments have brought their own disadvantages.   Just as in
English families women often have to do their wage work in
addition to their regular domestic tasks, while the fact that
the household has ceased to be the focus of production makes
it a lonelier place for those, such as women caring for infant
children, who spend much of their time there.   For the same
reason elderly people may find that with no buffaloes to milk,
no cotton to spin, and with their grandchildren learning unfamiliar skills in a foreign language at school, their lives
seem largely stripped of meaning and purpose.
    The size and qualify of housing in Britain has also had
its effects on migrants' families.   The large Victorian
terraces which were often occupied at the outset may have been
of a sufficient size to accommodate large families, but they
are generally located in unsalubrious areas.   There has been
a general tendency to seek to move up-market - though different groups have moved at widely varying speeds - but in general it is true to say that better housing tends to be smaller.
Faced with the fact the most recently constructed houses in
Britain have been designed for occupation by small families,
a number of solutions have been adopted.   Some migrants continue to live in large Victorian houses, despite their un-
attractive location.   Others have bought adjoining houses,
both terraced and semi-detached, and knocked through a con-
necting door.   Yet more live in very overcrowded conditions

in houses which they acknowledge are too small.   But a much
larger number have now accepted that in Britain there is
little alternative but to split the family into several domestic groups.   Today the majority of South Asians in Britain
live in conjugal households which contain only a single married couple. (11)   Yet when members of a single family live
in the same city, they almost invariably buy closely adjacent
houses, and can constantly be found visiting each other,
eating and taking their leisure wherever seems most convenient.   Many families have made a virtue of this partial separation.   They believe that it can reduce the impact of
internal rivalries, while still allowing the maintenance of
extensive co-operation.   Moving slightly apart in domestic
terms is often the best means of ensuring the smooth operation
of wider familial reciprocities.

   For whatever reason it occurs the trend towards conjugal
households means that women often find themselves in sole
charge of their own domestic establishment a good deal earlier
than might have occurred in a rural context.   Her independence is thus enhanced, and her relationship with her husband
is usually closer.   Yet precisely because the other women in
the family are at a distance, she may find herself saddled
with unexpectedly heavy responsibilities, and very often in a
strange environment as well.   Greater independence may bring
isolation of a kind that was never known at home.   Not only
were most village households larger, busier and more multi-
functional, but moving between them was very easy, for it was
a short step over the roof-tops to a neighbour's courtyard.
In Britain, however, a woman must go 'outside', and traverse
an unknown and alien world before she can meet her friends.
It is not surprising that many women feel isolated, even if
most spend much more time in each others' company than do most
of their English neighbours.

   Such feelings of isolation tend to lessen the longer women
have lived in Britain, and hence the more they have been able
to set up their own networks of communication and support.
The speed with which these networks grow depends on a wide
range of factors, including the size and scatter of the community, the way in which the rules of purdah are interpreted
in their own particular group, and the number of kinswomen
living in any particular locality.   Women rely on these networks in times of marital stress and their absence may set
them at a grave disadvantage.

CONFLICT IN MARRIAGE

Divorce is infrequent in most parts of the Indian sub-continent. Since marriages are invariably arranged, (12) it is
the responsibility of those who brought the couple together to
do all that they can to ensure that their relationship is a
happy one. Marital conflict is thus by no means the concern
of the two spouses alone. If a husband feels that his wife's
behaviour is unsatisfactory then he may complain to her
family, and similarly a woman expects her father and brother
to put pressure (ultimately by threatening violence) on her
husband and his family should she feel herself mistreated.
Divorce is seen as a last resort, to be adopted only when
other remedies fail. For a woman remarriage is not an
attractive proposition. It spells dishonour, both for herself and her family, and she is unlikely to be able to obtain
a well endowed groom.

When marital relationships show signs of strain in Britain,
strategies similar to those employed in the sub-continent are
usually brought into play. They are, however, rather less
likely to be effective, especially when there are no other
women in the household from whom a maltreated wife can seek
assistance, and when her male kinsmen live too far away to be
of much immediate help. Sanctions are certainly sometimes
effectively imposed, but not without some danger. Should a
group of loyal brothers be observed chastizing an errant husband by a passing policeman, they are likely to be charged
with assault. South Asian women in Britain thus tend to be
rather more exposed in situations of marital conflict than
they would have been at home.

To put some flesh on bare bones, let us take a case which,
if not typical (there is no such thing), is at least representative. Nur Mohammed has been working in Britain for 15
years, but only brought his wife and daughters to join him
three years ago. He still sends money back home to his
father and younger brother, as he always has, but is finding
it increasingly costly to support his wife and children in
Britain. He works twelve-hour night shifts in a textile
mill, as he always has, but recently he has been reduced from
six to five nights. One night less is a relief, for it
enables him to see much more of his family, but it also means
that his income has been significantly cut at a time when his
responsibilities have never been heavier. He is worried that
he might lose another night too, and then he really would be
in financial difficulties.

Since her arrival in Britain his wife Mumtaz has had
another daughter, but since its birth she has done nothing but
complain to Nur Mohammed. The child is ill, she doesn't know

how to take it to the doctor. She doesn't think the doctor
is any good. She is lonely. She is tired. She misses
everyone back home. He is absent from home for too long
every night, leaving her frightened that the house will be
broken into. She believes he has been visiting English
prostitutes - that is why he has no money. In the end it is
all too much for Nur Mohammed: he explodes, and beats her.
In his eyes it is quite justified. Does she think he *likes*
working so many hours every night? In any case she has not
borne him a son, and she is now no longer young. Does she
not know how much he spent on bringing her to England? Perhaps he would do much better to take another younger wife,
whose parents would certainly give a large dowry for the
privilege of marrying their daughter to a husband working in
England. A new wife might at least have the capacity to
bear him a son.

RENEGOTIATING RELATIONSHIPS

Where a family is under external stress, those of its members
with the least effective bargaining power (usually, though
certainly not inevitably, a woman) often have to bear the
brunt of the difficulties. Situations of this kind can and
do lead to great distress and very often to violence, especially in the absence of a mediator. If a woman like Mumtaz
has no local support, and no kin to whom to flee she may well
end up on the doorstep of her local police station or in the
casualty department of the hospital, with very severe bruising
and her marriage apparently in tatters.
    It is easy for doctors, solicitors, policemen and social
workers who become involved in such cases to misinterpret what
is at stake, because of their unfamiliarity with the cultural
context. (13)   They often assume that arranged marriages are
necessarily problematic, that independence and personal freedom are goals to which everyone will unreservedly aspire, and
that a woman's departure from home, especially in the context
of a violent assault, necessarily means that her conjugal
relationship has irretrievably broken down. Given this
perspective the most appropriate course seems to be to obtain
a legal separation and then a divorce, and to assist such
women to establish independent households of their own. In
some cases this may indeed be the only available solution, but
is it *necessarily* the case that this will be so?
    Let us take the case of Nur Mohammed and his wife as an
example. Their problems obviously arise primarily from the
pressures under which they find themselves, and from Mumtaz's
inability to put sufficient pressure on her husband to take

her concerns seriously enough.   Back home the traditional solution in the face of extreme marital difficulties was for a woman to return to her natal home, _peke_, and to refuse to return until her husband promised to treat her more considerately.   To retrieve his wife a husband would then have to run the gauntlet not only of his wife's father and brothers, but also of her assembled female kin.   Their scabrous comments on his character and behaviour were a very considerable deterrent.   But Mumtaz's _peke_ live 5,000 miles away.   They can be of little immediate help to her.

Yet what other alternatives are available?   Despite its apparent attractiveness to outsiders, divorce is likely to redouble Mumtaz's difficulties.   If she were to leave, she would play straight into Nur Mohammed's hands.   After a short interval he might obtain a new, hopefully more compliant and more fertile wife from Pakistan.   But where would a woman like Mumtaz live?   If she were to live close to other South Asians she would be likely to be branded as shameless, and to be pestered by men who believed that she was now a 'free' woman.   She is also likely to live in fear that her husband and his kinsmen will seek to steal her children away from her. Perhaps they will not bother since they are girls: they would certainly do all they could to reclaim a son.   Yet if she were to move away into the outside English world even greater difficulties would ensue.   She would almost certainly have to cut her links with her own kin and indeed with the whole of the cultural system in which she had grown up.   She would face isolation in an alien world, and she and her children would be in considerable danger not just of racist abuse, but of physical assault.

Given the enormous difficulties and disadvantages that permanent departure from the family almost invariably entails, it is obviously worthwhile making every possible effort in identifying and achieving an internal renegotiation of relationships.   Indeed, in the case of conjugal breakdowns in Asian families the most useful assistance that an outsider can render lies in seeking to reinforce a woman's bargaining power.   To assume at the outset that relationships have irretrievably broken down may well be to sell the pass before the battle has even begun.

Though in some cases things may have gone so far that no reconciliation is possible, it seems that for the overwhelming majority of women a temporary departure from home provides a means of drawing public attention to her plight.   It may thus be a convenient tactical move whereby a husband can be backed into a corner, and more satisfactory terms for their relationship thrashed out.   But while such renegotiation is going on it is vital that a woman should sustain an unimpeachably

honourable reputation.   It is quite clear that in Mumtaz's
case the worst possible result would be for Nur Mohammed to
successfully label her as a shameless whore, so giving him a
legitimate excuse to obtain another wife from home.

It seems likely that apparently disastrous breakdowns in
inter-personal relationships within South Asian families in
Britain are much more susceptible to resolution than many outside observers commonly suppose.   Most cases are much more
complex than the example cited here and the scapegoats are
certainly not always married women, though they usually are.
Elderly parents, weak and vacillating husbands and confused
adolescents may also find themselves in impossible positions,
and seek help from outside.   However daunting the task may
initially seem, it is always worth seeking to renegotiate
relationships rather than acting on the assumption that they
have irretrievably broken down.   Success can often be
achieved, especially if the kind of support which the victim
would otherwise have received from kinsmen can either be
mobilized or replicated. (14)

THE SECOND GENERATION

Until recently it was widely assumed (at least amongst the
English majority) that South Asian migrants' tight knit families would soon be undermined by the changes amongst their
British-born children.   Contact with the ethnic majority, it
was thought, would soon precipitate thoroughgoing Anglicization.   Personal freedom would inevitably seem more attractive
than the restrictions of traditional family obligations.
However, ethnographic observation, as opposed to a priori
ethnocentric speculation, is now beginning to reveal a very
different picture. (15)

Children of South Asian origin in Britain are certainly
exposed to, and participate in, two very different cultural
worlds.   At home parents expect conformity to the norms of
co-operation, respect and familial loyalty.   Most take great
care to instill these values into their children, and to stres
stress the superiority of their own cultural traditions as
opposed to those of the English.   At school, however, children are exposed to a wholly contrary set of values and expectations.   South Asian lifestyles are generally not admired,
and individual self-determination is both encouraged and presented as the most appropriate moral foundation for personal
action.

As a result of the very fundamental contradictions between
these two worlds, many young Asians feel themselves to be
faced with acute dilemmas as to how they should organize their

lives.   However, most have long since learned to cope with
these contradictions by switching their modes of behaviour
depending on the context in which they find themselves.   It
is often forgotten that just as one can be bilingual, so one
can be multi-cultural.   In other words a person can acquire
the skill to act and react appropriately in a range of different cultural settings.   Provided that the arenas within which
a person participates can be kept apart no problems need
arise.   In fact it is clear that most young Asians are very
skilled at doing just this, as well as playing both sides
against the middle.

Even so acute problems often do arise when Asian adolescents are in the midst of establishing themselves as beings
independent of their parents.   But in any society teenagers'
rebellious attitudes - very often expressed as a threat to
leave home and never return - provide a very poor guide to
their likely future behaviour as adults.   In fact it is
striking that the overwhelming majority of young Asians return
to the family fold (if they ever left) in their late teens and
early twenties.   Although they may continue to present themselves in a very 'English' way at work, most choose to organize their domestic and personal lives on the basis of strong
continuity with the established values of the communities into
which they were born.   Although they may eventually adopt
considerably modified versions of their parents' lifestyles,
their behaviour generally remains quite distinct from that of
their 'English' peers. (16)

Such cultural and ethnic distinctiveness is being sustained for a variety of reasons.   Most parents put a great
deal of effort into ensuring that they transmit the basic
tenets of family morality to their children.   The need to put
group loyalty before self-interest is constantly stressed,
above all because this creates warmer, more secure and more
human relationships than anything available in the outside
world.   In cases of possible deviance parents also emphasize
- sometimes to the point of blackmail - the extent to which
they would be personally distressed, and the loss of izzat
that the family would suffer if any one of their children
should depart too seriously from established norms.   While
the English world certainly offers the attractions of personal
freedom, of having one's hair cut and of wearing jeans, many
young people are sceptical as to whether these could possibly
recompense the loss of familial security.   They are also far
more aware than their parents of their ultimate unacceptabil-
ity in majority circles because of the colour of their skins.
Despite parents' constant worries that their children might
slip away and 'become English', most young people have long
since decided that a strategy of comprehensive assimilation is
futile. (17)

Yet this does not mean that they are no different from
their parents.   They are in fact generating a range of new
lifestyles as they seek to reform, modify and rework their
parents' cultural heritage, such that many long-established
conventions are now the subject of close critical scrutiny.
While most young people are still usually prepared to pay
formal respect to their elders, they also insist on playing a
much more active part in decision making.   Husbands and wives
expect to have closer and more autonomous relationships, and
young people are demanding that they should be consulted more
fully before the arrangement of their marriages.   Although
everyone accepts that familial loyalties should be sustained,
the value of participation in more far-flung networks of
extrafamilial kinship is looked upon with increasing scepticism, especially since they tend to generate a suffocating
traffic of gossip and scandal.

The distinction between agnatic and affinal kin is also
beginning to wane in significance, especially since the
patterns and landownership and village residence from which
these distinctions sprang are of much less importance in
Britain.

In the great majority of families change is taking place
relatively smoothly, following well-worn tracks of bargaining
and negotiation.   Yet it would be facile to assert that this
is always the case.   Things may go wrong, and sometimes dis-
astrously so.   Parents may be so strict in their attitudes,
and so unbending in their exercise of authority that their
children explode under the constraints put upon them.
Others may be so tied up in making a success of a fledgling
business, or so hard pressed to meet their financial obligations both in Britain and at home that they fail to pay enough
attention to their children, letting them run wild.   Children
may successfully conceal a good deal from their parents, but
the scandalous exposure of a secret romance can easily force
the most tolerant parents into hasty and ill-advised action.
Parents from rural backgrounds, even with the best of intentions, may find it exceedingly difficult to make adequate
decisions about their children's marriages.   Some parents are
frankly bewildered by their children's behaviour and attitudes, and assume that all change necessarily indicates a
weakening of loyalty to the family.   As a result they may so
pester their children about their alleged Anglicization that
their concern becomes a self-fulfilling prophecy.

Nevertheless in only a small minority of cases have such
difficulties led to cataclysmic breakdowns.   Despite the
apparent rigidity of their formal structure most South Asian
families have shown considerable flexibility in practice.   To
those within them the benefits of membership invariably seem
to outweigh the inevitable costs.

SOURCES OF UNITY IN URBAN ENVIRONMENTS

Perhaps the clearest examples of the benefits of family membership, and of the utilization of familial loyalties as a
resource, can be found in the innumerable small businesses
which have been established by South Asians in Britain.
Typically these are corner shops, restaurants, market stalls
and small clothing workshops, all of which require only a
limited initial investment of cash, and depend for their success upon a massive input of labour.   In so far as they
depend upon long hours of work, long-term forward planning
and close co-operation between a small number of people, they
are founded on skills which are nothing new to peasant far-
mers.   It is thus small wonder that South Asians (along with
members of almost every other migrant group of peasant
origins) have set up so many businesses, at least some of
which have now grown quite large.   There is nothing like
participation in a profitable enterprise to hold a family
together.
    Although only a minority of South Asian families in Britain
are ordered around such enterprises, the cohesion of all
arises in a similar way.   Many families are now best understood as miniature multi-national corporations, each of which
includes a number of partially autonomous sub-divisions drawn
together by their mutual interdependence.   Each branch can
offer access to resources which the others value, while the
very diversity of members' activities provides an excellent
insurance against misfortune.
    Let us consider what might currently be regarded as the
ideal disposition for four brothers in a Punjabi peasant
family.   The family's base and ultimate security lies in its
land, which can best be safeguarded by ensuring that one
brother remains at home to cultivate it.   Yet successful
cultivation depends upon a secure supply of electricity, fer-
tilizer and diesel oil.   This and much else can be obtained
by placing another brother in local government service.   If
the remaining two brothers go to work abroad, one in the Gulf
States, the other in Britain, further advantages accrue.
Those abroad can generate a considerable cash income, and have
access to consumer products such as tape-recorders, televi-
sions and cars, which are scarce and expensive in Punjab.
They can also provide access to well-paid jobs, to advanced
educational facilities and to advantageous marriages for the
next generation.   Finally the very diversity of the family's
activities means that should the going get tough for any particular branch, personnel and resources can be redeployed.
The greater the diversity of activities, the greater are the
advantages that accrue from maintaining links of reciprocity.

Yet families organized on this basis are clearly institutions of a rather different kind from those set out in the ideal model with which we began.   Land may continue to be of symbolic importance, but it is no longer the main source of subsistence.   Some families, especially those which settled in East Africa, have now gone 'off-shore', and no longer even maintain a foothold in the sub-continent.   Common residence in a single household has ceased to be the norm and a series of more clearly conjugal units have been established.   An aged patriarch, if he survives, will certainly be treated with great respect, but his power is likely to be minimal.   In families of the kind just described elderly parents are likely to spend most of their time rotating between their children's various households.   Nevertheless it should be clear that there is still a remarkable degree of continuity in the basic principles of family organization, even if the way in which they are worked out in practice has changed a great deal.

SOURCES OF DISUNITY

Despite the highly successful adaptation to new opportunities achieved by many South Asian families, it would be idle to ignore the forces working in the opposite direction, and the fact that some families, perhaps an increasing number, will succumb to these pressures.   South Asian migrants came to Britain to take jobs in labour intensive under-capitalized industries such as iron foundries and textiles.   In the current technological revolution it is precisely jobs in these industries which are disappearing.   By the early 1980s there will be large-scale structural unemployment in Britain, and many of the unskilled jobs traditionally performed by migrant labour will simply no longer exist.   South Asian families and especially those whose members have more recently come to Britain will thus stand disproportionately exposed.
As presaged in the case of Nur Mohammed and his wife, economic recession, and above all unemployment will put enormous strain on relationships within the family.   Although reciprocity may provide a cushion against adversity, there is a limit to the fatigue it can absorb.   Moreover, in the sub-continent itself it is families with at least minimal resources which have most effectively sustained their unity.   If family members are in such desperate straights that they have nothing left over to offer each other, reciprocity itself disintegrates.
It is too early yet to know just where breakdowns will occur in the face of unemployment, but a number of points of tension can certainly be identified.   Many migrants have

particularly heavy responsibilities, for they may also be
helping to support the remainder of their family back home in
Pakistan or Bangladesh.   Will they halt their remittances?
And since they came to Britain to work, will they go home when
work disappears?   They will certainly be tempted to do so and
may even be encouraged in this direction by formal government
policy.   Yet a migrant who does return in such circumstances
may not be accorded the honour to which he aspires and his
children may see little future in what is to them a foreign
country.

To all this must be added the implications of increasingly
stringent immigration controls, which have themselves been
precipitated by popular demands from the majority population,
whose members are also fearful of the implications of recession.   All families which have gone multi-national stand in
grave danger of having their members arbitrarily separated as
a result of vagaries in the operation of immigration legislation.   Sensible planning is often difficult since the rules
are frequently revised, and informal obstacles (such as excessively detailed scrutiny of applications stemming from the
sub-continent combined with an insufficiency of officials to
process them) can make a nonsense of formal legal rights.
Families which get trapped in this legal and administrative
maze - and there are many - may find that it is the Immigration Department of the Home Office which represents the
greatest obstacle to their consolidation.

CONCLUSION

Although it has not been possible to pay much attention to the
question, there are great variations both within and between
different South Asian communities in Britain.   In some, such
as families whose members have only recently arrived from the
remoter parts of Mirpur or Sylhet, strict adherence to the
rules of purdah may be the unquestioned norm.   In others,
such as Gujerati Vohra families whose members have long been
resident in East Africa and most have professional occupations, daughters may even be allowed out unchaperoned once
parents have carefully vetted their boyfriends. (18)   There
are also major variations in personality and style between
families; some parents are strict and others more lax, some
skilled at holding their families together, while others are
much less successful.   Finally it is clear that there are
major variations in the economic success which different families have achieved, and that the divergencies between them
will become more striking as the recession deepens, and there
is less and less of a demand for unskilled labour.

Yet despite these major variations it is still useful - at least for the purposes of an introductory discussion - to regard all South Asian families in Britain as being organized along similar principles.   Although migration and relocation in urban industrial Britain has certainly precipitated change, it has not resulted in breakdown.   On the contrary co-opera- tion and corporate loyalty has generally been sustained. Such continuities would seem to stand in contradiction to much established sociological theory - and indeed to popular pre- supposition - but they should not really be regarded as any- thing very novel.   Essentially similar developments have occurred in families of the same origins whose members have moved to urban areas in the sub-continent, (19) and indeed amongst peasant migrants almost everywhere.

Of course there have been changes, such that expectations about roles and relationships are being revised, often in quite fundamental ways.   But these developments have by no means necessarily led to an erosion of family loyalties and reciprocities.   Although the proponents of 'modern' philoso- phies of freedom and self-determination have often expected that tradition would crumble in the face of 'progress', most members of most South Asian families are very sceptical about the benefits to be gained from the wholesale adoption of such ideas.   They perceive that complete personal freedom can eliminate the advantages to be gained from familial recipro- city.   Indeed there is good reason to suppose that if any- thing which may undermine Asian family unity, it is not such ideological influences, but the corrosive effects of poverty and unemployment.   But even so it seems likely that those who are so economically disadvantaged will develop their own distinctive lifestyles, rather than merge into the generality of those in the same structural position as themselves.

Development and change in migrants' families has thus been much less straightforward than many ethnocentric commentators had expected.   South Asians of all kinds in Britain have ex- perienced, and are still experiencing, massive changes in their social, economic and moral environment, but they have made the best of the uncertain world into which they have been plunged by the adaptive utilization of their kinship resour- ces.   They are likely to continue to do so, in their various ways, for the forseeable future.

NOTES

1 Ethnographic descriptions of various aspects of life
   within a range of South Asian communities in Britain can
   be found in the work of Anwar, the Ballards, Dahya,

James, Jeffery, Saifullah-Khan, Sharma, Taylor and Wilson.
The arguments presented in this chapter are based partly
on these sources, supplemented by information directly
acquired during the course of the author's ethnographic
fieldwork.   This was carried out mainly in Leeds and
mostly with Sikhs between 1971 and 1979, though at varying
levels of intensity during that period.

2 Perhaps the best acccunt of 'traditional' family structure
can be found in Madan (1965).   Although this book is
about the Pandits of Kashmir (few of whom have migrated to
Britain) peasant families throughout Northern India are
ordered along essentially similar lines.   The best sources on family organization in areas from which migrants
have come to Britain are Eglar (1960) for Pakistani
Punjab, Kessinger (1975) for Indian Punjab and Pocock
(1972) for Gujerat.

3 See for example Kessinger (1975:187) and Madan (1965:165).

4 Such processes are graphically illustrated by Jhabvala
(1955, 1956) in her novels about Punjabi family life in
Delhi.   In the same vein Rogers (1975) argues that
peasant women generally can often use informal strategies
to acquire considerable power over men, despite their
apparent subordination to them in public.

5 Such processes are very clearly described by Jhabvala
(1955, 1956).   In her discussion of Vartan bhanji
Eglar (1960) makes much the same point.

6 More detailed accounts of extra-familial kinship, and of
the form and structural significance of unilineal descent
groups in Northern India, can be found in Alavi (1972),
Barth (1959), Kessinger (1975) and Pocock (1972).

7 Marriage is also very often forbidden with members of the
spouse's mothers', fathers' mothers', and mothers'
mothers' clans as well.   Moreover, if a girl has been
given to another family, then in that generation additional brides may be sent there, but none may be taken back.
The effect of these rules is to ensure that every family
has a very wide spread of affinal kin.

8 Dry academic prose is not the best vehicle for representing the vigour, vitality and complexity of family life in
South Asia.   Jhabvala's novels have already been referred
to, but readers insterested in getting a feel for the
quality of rural life in 'traditional' India can do no
better than to turn to Waris Shah's rendition of the Punjabi folk epic Hir Ranjah   In it can be found vivid
accounts of family and clanship, of friendly alliances and
vicious feuds, and of uproarious celebrations and jealous
double-crossing, all in the context of a moving tale of
romantic love.

9   The best detailed account of a village from which large
    numbers of people have emigrated is Kessinger (1975).
10 An overview of the development of South Asian colonies in
    Britain can be found in Ballard and Ballard (1977).
    Saifullah-Khan (1976b) shows how many Mirpuri women's
    lives may become more constrained by the rules of purdah
    due to their families' changing status in Britain.
11 There are however considerable variations both by region
    and by precise communal affiliation.   Hence households in
    London seem to be larger than in Leeds, due primarily to
    higher housing costs in the south.   Within Leeds Sikhs
    have moved much more rapidly towards residence in smaller
    conjugal households than have the Moslems.   Household
    size and composition is also affected by the stage in
    their developmental cycle which families have reached.
    As yet there are few elderly South Asians in Britain, but
    those that have come have invariably taken up residence in
    one or other of their children's households or circulate
    between them.   As the number of elderly people who have
    long been resident in Britain grows, there is every like-
    lihood that they too will be reincorporated into their
    children's households.
12 A detailed discussion of arranged marriages can be found
    in Ballard (1978).
13 Examples and analyses of such misunderstandings can be
    found in C. Ballard (1979) and in Ahmed (1978).
14 The importance of using culturally appropriate strategies
    in dealing with cases of interpersonal conflict in South
    Asian families is only just coming to be more widely rec-
    ognized (see R. Ballard, 1979).   Some specialist case-
    workers have now been appointed in a number of different
    cities, and although a wide range of strategies is being
    tried out, those of the kind outlined here seem often to
    be the most successful.
        It is striking that most English social workers, soli-
    citors and other professionals who may become involved in
    cases of matrimonial breakdown rarely consider renegotia-
    tions as a serious possibility.   Indeed some are even
    hostile to doing so.   One reason why this may be so
    emerges very clearly from Hoggett's chapter (21) in this
    volume.   Despite widespread formal commitment to the
    value of family unity, contemporary English law is much
    more concerned with allocating rights and responsibilities
    subsequent to marital breakdown than with enabling plain-
    tiffs to seek restitution within the context of an ongoing
    relationship.   Many of the 'old-fashioned' remedies
    which have now been abandoned might be much more relevant
    to many South Asian families in Britain.

15   Ethnographic accounts of the lifestyles adopted by the
     children of South Asian migrants to Britain can be found
     in C. Ballard (1978, 1979), Brah (1979), Crishna (1975),
     Taylor (1976) and Wilson (1978), while Dhondy (1976,
     1978), through the medium of his short stories, is emerg-
     ing as quite as subtle a chronicler of the British scene
     as Jhabvala is of Delhi.   Meanwhile Shamsher (1972) pro-
     vides many poignant insights into the pleasures and heart-
     aches of Jat Sikh workers and their families in Britain.
16   These processes are examined in detail in C. Ballard
     (1978, 1979) and Brah (1979).   On the face of it Wilson
     (1978) predicts much more revolutionary breakdowns in
     family organization, but her opinions seem often to stand
     in contradiction to her informants' views, especially as
     reported in Chapter 6 of her book.
17   Brah (1979) makes this very clear.
18   A feeling for the extent of such variation can be gained
     by comparing Saifullah-Khan's descriptions of Mirpuri
     women in Bradford with that of Westwood and Hoffman (1979)
     who write about East African Gujarati women in Leicester.
19   In her study of urban families in Meerut, Vatuk (1972:
     200) concludes:

> Although the middle-class urban neighbourhood in India
> has become the setting for considerable social change,
> urbanization has not had a radical impact on the family
> or kinship system.   The degree of social stability is
> as noteworthy as that of change.   The urbanite still
> operates within a familiar social framework, and voices
> familiar values, although he is becoming gradually
> aware that his behaviour, or at least that of his
> neighbours, is gradually beginning to deviate from
> those values.

Although the changes described in this chapter are the
outcome of residence in a specifically British context,
there is a strong case for arguing that they are better
understood as being primarily the consequence of a move
from a rural to an urban environment, rather than from
East to West.

Chapter 9

West Indian families: an anthropological perspective

Geoffrey Driver

For English readers we should begin by referring to relevant studies carried out in recent years as part of the attempt by anthropologists and others to document and explain the range of family forms and household structures prevalent among Afro-Caribbean and Afro-American populations. The focus of much research and discussion has centred on the weakness of conjugal ties and the greater reliance put upon consanguineal relationships - particularly involving maternal kin - in an unusually large number of families. The incidence of this phenomenon has been noted in rural and urban contexts throughout the Caribbean as well as on the adjacent mainland of North and South America among families of predominantly African descent, whose ancestors had been brought to the New World as slaves.

The explanations of the evidence have tended to emphasize two elements. Firstly, the historical influence of slavery which, it has been argued, weakened conjugal bonds but laid greater stress on the relations between women and their children. Secondly, the effect of an economic system in which men have little chance of stable and regular employment has meant they have for generations been unable to offer adequate economic and social support to their conjugal partners and offspring. Beyond these more specific explanations there is also the nature of Creole culture to be reckoned with. It has been noted that the plural, social context of the Caribbean is an ethos in which internal variation and change rather than structural uniformity characterize cultural forms and processes.

The majority of writers who have dealt with the experience of West Indian migrants in Britain apparently disregarded such cultural issues in their assessments. For the most part the newcomers were expected to embrace the norm of English 'nuclear family' life. With two or three major exceptions,

notably Fitzherbert (1967) and Patterson (1965), writers have
given little attention to differences in family and household
social structure among the 'immigrants' from the Caribbean.
Many were preoccupied by macro-structural issues, e.g. Rex and
Moore (1967), and felt that in any case social and economic
conditions were so different from those of Jamaica and Trinidad as to make family forms and household structures unimportant.   Hence no great attention was paid to the work of Simey
(1947), Matthews (1953), Henriques (1953), Clarke (1957), R.T.
Smith (1957), Blake (1961) and others.   They also tended to
ignore studies of Black families in the Southern and Northern
United States.   Particularly during the 1960s, American
interest was generated in the kinds of family organization of
urban Blacks, as is shown variously by the work of Rainwater
(1966), Liebow (1967), Stack (1970), Lander (1971), Aschenbrenner (1975) and others.   Their research led to debate on
such specialist concepts as 'matrifocality' as writers such as
Gonzalez (1965) engaged in the effort to comprehend the elements of family structure in populations associated with the
Caribbean and slavery.
    In the following paragraphs we shall consider in some
detail the way this sort of analysis links up with the situation of West Indian families in Britain today.
    According to the 1971 Census statistics, roughly 300,000
(or 0.5 per cent) of UK residents were born in the West
Indies.   Estimates now put the size of the West Indian minority here, including those born in Britain of West Indian
parents, at more than 500,000.   That would suggest that in
1980 it could be assumed that there are somewhere about
150,000 West Indian family households in the United Kingdom.
Roughly half these families originated in Jamaica (mostly the
rural areas) with others coming from Trinidad, Guyana,
Barbados and St Kitts, etc.
    There can be no doubt that the family systems out of which
many of the West Indian migrants came were by no means so
homogenously structured as those to which the majority population in Britain were most accustomed.   In Jamaica and elsewhere, the 'nuclear family' (or 'Christian marriage') form of
household organization, while it may have been sought after as
an ideal, was only to be realized among the small part of the
population with the economic means and social status to
achieve it.   For the rest, other means of carrying on relations between the sexes in order to create another generation
had to be devised.   The nature and extent of the alternatives
to 'Christian marriages' are hard to estimate, though in the
Jamaican case there are few signs of disagreement with the
general practice set out by Henriques (1953).   He claimed
that only 25 per cent of Jamaican domestic groups were based

on legal monogamous marriage, with another 25 per cent on
common-law (or consensual) unions, while 50 per cent were
female-dominated households of one sort or another.   In many
of the latter, either a grandmother or some female relative,
perhaps mother's sister, takes over the role of father and
usurps the function of mother (who may have other social activities to perform either inside or outside the household).
In other of these female domestic groups the mother herself is
compelled, as in single-parent families elsewhere, to be head
of the household and to fulfil all parental functions.
   Perhaps the most classical accounts of these female-dominated types of domestic group are the mother-centred household
described by R.T. Smith (1956) and the maternal kin household
(or 'grandmother family') as presented by Clarke (1957).
Smith studied cohabiting couples in Georgetown, Guyana, and
concluded that where unemployment made it impossible for men
to carry out the providing function associated with being husband and father, women took a more central role in the economic and social subsistence of the family.   According to
Smith's simple explanatory model, societal conditions create
the conditions for 'male marginality' and 'matrifocality'
within the family households which he studied.   In this sense
he perhaps too simplistically lumps all his observed non-
nuclear family arrangements, generated through adverse socio-
economic conditions, into a single strand of development.
   Clarke on the other hand suggests that in her three Jamaican rural communities that it is necessary to consider carefully the detail of local status structures and availability
of resources which affect individuals differentiated by sex,
age, wealth, social respectability, marital and familial
status.   She shows how different forms of marital relationship complement and contribute to the stability of different
domestic arrangements and how in turn these predominant forms
of household and family organization correspond with the
character of the rural communities in which they are set.
Hence in a very poor community, Clarke notes the prevalence of
lifelong consensual relationships and patriarchal family
organization.   In another different but equally well-integra-
ted community, marriage was seen as part of the local class
structure and was reinforced by strong social sanctions.
Meanwhile, the conglomerate population of a sugar estate
demonstrated, according to Clarke, no adult male patterns of
conjugal or paternal responsibility.
   While Clarke's analysis of marital role relations and
domestic group organization appears more subtle and sensitive,
it would be hard to discern its immediate implications for
West Indian migrant workers' families in a whole series of
life-situations, even within one island or area, let alone

across the range of West Indian island/territory backgrounds.
Nevertheless, Clarke's analysis alerts us to looking carefully
at specific characteristics of domestic group life and suggests that Smith's simple model of analysis needs to be carried further where possible.

The relative rarity of 'Christian marriage' family households amid the social and economic conditions found in Jamaica
and other parts of the Caribbean, and the interconnectedness
of arrangements whereby mother and children live with the
maternal grandmother, mother lives with her man on a temporary
'trial' basis, or enters into a stable but not legally recognized marital arrangement with a man and is able to build up a
home with him and her (if not his) children, must even today
be part of the experience of the majority of West Indians now
living in Britain.   Given their upbringing in such a context,
one in which they themselves would consider it normal for few
children other than those from Christian family homes to pass
their entire childhood in the same household (though within
the same extended kin structure), sons might be expected to
find it hard, despite what they took to be majority pressures
to conform, to embrace the role structure of the nuclear
family household.

The fact that few researchers or professional practitioners
too stock of this situation, for whatever reason, has possibly
given rise to unwarranted assumptions about the incidence of
functionally 'non-nuclear' family households which were then
taken to indicate 'deprivation', 'family instability' among
West Indians in Britain.   Certainly few have been able to see'
that those West Indian extended family households, generally
composed of an assortment of maternal kin - uncles, aunts and
cousins and especially grandmother - offer a framework of
family security which a child's parents are unable to offer
it.   By and large observers have failed to recognize the
possibility that it is the very unavailability of these maternal kin to support the mother in the task of childrearing that
creates problems for her and the children, which may have been
and may continue to be the case despite the availability here
of resources from Britain's welfare state (though the latter
is of course geared to the norms of the majority so far as the
economic and social structure of young families is concerned).

Given the likelihood that many West Indian adults, seeking
to establish themselves and their children in Britain, could
not rely on the kin from whom they had become separated
through migration, and given also the majority convention of
legal monogamous marriage, it is of course likely that many of
the men and women adopted that convention - back home, with
other social conditions and family resources, they might well
have acted differently.   It is impossible twenty years later

to get any clear idea of the extent to which some of the men,
who had been the first to arrive in Britain, found themselves
in a new role as the principal source of the domestic group's
income, and as the legally recognized owners or occupants of
the houses in which the women and their children came to live.
In these circumstances, the apparent dependence of the women
on their partners for shelter and support was, similarly,
something which many of them had not been brought up to expect
in their Caribbean homelands.

The fact that in many cases the men ceased to be the source
of a stable and adequate income for their wives and children,
due to some extent to the economic changes which took place in
British industry in the late 1960s and 1970s, may well have
given rise to post-migration forms of functional 'matrifocality' and 'male marginality'.   At the same time these developments could well be cloaked under externally conventional
patterns of nuclear family life, maintained particularly by
the exigencies and benefits of the welfare state and the lack
of access by the mother to her kin.   It is obvious that no
general statistics would show up, particularly among the so-
called 'first generation' of West Indian family-settlers,
these developments.   It is possible, however, that with a
second generation of West Indian mothers now producing their
offspring, together with the possible availability of kin-
support, in the prevalently adverse employment conditions suffered particularly by West Indian men in Britain, that externally apparent diverse family forms will, as in the West
Indies, reassert themselves among the minority population
settled in English cities.

Returning to Henriques's typology of marital forms in
Jamaica (Henriques, 1953), it is clear that it cannot be
directly superimposed on the West Indian population in the
United Kingdom.   While the minority is likely to have
retained elements of those forms, it would appear likely too
that they have been modified to cope with new situations in
Britain in the places where the so-called 'immigrants' have
been engaged in reorganizing their lives for almost a generation.

Unfortunately little research has gone on during that
period into the specific ways in which West Indian domestic
kin groups are evolving.   Even less has there been any systematic surveying of domestic kin groups in the West Indian
minority population as a whole during this period, though perhaps historical records (from health visitors' reports, etc.)
could offer some clues as to the ways in which West Indian
family organization was developing in the 1950s and 1960s.

Whatever the difficulties in making retrospective enquiries, it is at least becoming clear that we are now likely to

find a distinctive range of family and household arrangements in areas where West Indians have settled in Britain. There has always been a certain awareness among professionals, such as teachers, medical practitioners, social workers and the like, that the minority's patterns of childrearing, sex-roles, peer-group formation, etc. differed from those of the majority. Possibly because of the prevalence of assimilationist philosophies and polices of integration, such differences were not studied sufficiently vigorously. At least there is now an increasing awareness that the understanding of these differences cannot any longer be deferred.

When one looks at the sorts of family household organization which had been found by the writer in West Indian settlements up to the mid-1970s, it is clear that the domestic groups observed were for the most part two-generational and composed of the original migrants and their offspring (with children of all ages up to their late teens living at home). Only in exceptional cases had the migrants brought their parents to join them in Britain.

Analysis of a dozen such domestic kin groups, on which the writer collected detailed information, suggests two broad types of organization. In one, the nuclear family type, responsibilities for domestic arrangements, childrearing, etc. are seen as the mutual responsibility of a married couple. In the other, which is usually but not necessarily associated with the lack of stable employment on the part of the husband, there appears to be little reliance placed on the conjugal relationship as a basis of responsibility for family affairs. In such a situation, the woman is effectively left to run the home, bring up the children and provide a source of income. One such woman called this kind of arrangement 'English marriage' - although the name clearly belies the strongly West Indian implications of both male marginality and female centrality, a kin structure based on consanguineal rather than conjugal ties. For convenience, this is labelled as the mother-centred family. The two types are taken here to symbolize the two ends of a continuum between which other family patterns are ranged.

The question about West Indian 'English marriage' is of course the extent to which it differs from similar patterns among English majority families (i.e. where women take major responsibility for running the home). Research here would need to take stock of those indications of role-relationships which emphasize blood ties with maternal kin as the direction in which the women in question can be expected to seek help. The fact that the close female kin of these women were often separated as a result of migration, since they often followed their men to different overseas destinations instead of

remaining close to the maternal home, obviously suggests such
indications were relatively few in the period immediately
after migration to Britain.   Conversely the possibility of
supportive ties being built up through the men needs to be
studied to see to what extent these sisters-in-law could and
would help one another (e.g. help being offered by and given
to the wives of a woman's husband's brothers).   Since men
came in such clusters (e.g. brother and close friends - often
referred to as 'brother-friends'), there is a high incidence
of such families living very close to one another in a number
of West Indian settlements in Britain.   The implications of
such a finding would be significant if found on any large
scale since it would suggest a corporate responsibility among
paternal kin which is not found frequently in West Indian
family households except in the case of what Henriques calls
the 'Christian marriage' type of family.
    Unfortunately any survey of the kind which Henriques car-
ried out into domestic social structures in Jamaica has not
been done among West Indian families settled in Britain.
What we have instead is simply a few descriptions of distinctive forms of social organization noted by such writers as
Patterson (1965), Fitzherbert (1967) and Foner (1979) and
presented in the course of their accounts of the experiences
of particular West Indian families in London.   To take their
approach a small step further, the writer here proposes to
offer descriptions of two different family households.   The
two types which they represent can be detected in the functional analysis of their role-structures.   The approach is no
more than exemplary at this stage (although subsequent
research has borne out the pattern in other family studies
more recently) and cannot take proper account of the extended
kin involved, to whom the researcher has no direct access.
    The accounts of two families, belonging to a boy and a girl
attending a West Midlands secondary school, are inevitably
brief.   The family histories of Alric Campbell and Erica
Spencer which follow are representative basic categories of
family organization to which reference has been made, one consanguineal and the other conjugal.   It is hoped they can
highlight structural patterns and stress points which are
readily apparent to and directly experienced by those involved
in the households concerned.

THE CAMPBELLS

Alric Campbell was the eldest son of Gilmour Campbell and
Paulette Lindsay of Hanover Parish, Jamaica.   In the late
1950s Gilmour and two of his brothers came to Britain to get

work.   After an initial period of shared bachelor accommodation these men were able to set up separate homes for their
families to join them.   Paulette, by now Mrs Campbell, having
left her mother's home initially got a job in a factory to
augment their income.   The arrival of more children subsequently meant her contribution was curtailed.   Nevertheless
sufficient money was available to bring over the elder children (two boys, one of whom was Alric) in 1963 to join three
others born in the UK by that date.   A further three children
were born after that date - altogether making a very crowded
household for the Campbells in their Victorian terrace house.

Further problems arose for the Campbells when Gilmour's job
was lost due to recession.   After 1970 he took little interest in work, Paulette, virtually without help in looking after
the children, was obliged at the same time to go back to work,
relying on whatever help she could get in the form of childminders and nurseries to look after the younger children,
though rarely able to rely on her unemployed husband or elder
sons to care for them on a day-to-day basis - nor was she able
to call upon the wives of her husband's two brothers, who
lived close by;   these women, in any case facing similar problems, were so remote that at fourteen Alric did not know their
names.   By contrast, Alric knew all his mother's siblings,
despite the fact that all lived far away - in Canada, Jamaica
and southern England.   He also remembered fondly his grandmother, who had been responsible for his upbringing until the
age of six when he came to Britain.   The sense of binding
loyalties and affection which Alric showed to his mother's
side of the family was not present to the same extent towards
his father's kin, despite the fact that several of the latter
did not live so far afield.   It could only be assumed that
had they lived in the same area as Paulette and her children,
they would have provided much more economic and social support than she was able to obtain locally from her husband, his
brothers and their wives.   As it was, Paulette's own kin, the
Lindsays, were scattered widely, leaving her mother, Dorothy
Lindsay, almost isolated from both children and grandchildren
(this despite the fact that, in bringing up Alric and his
brother, it was clearly demonstrated that she regarded rearing
of her daughter's offspring as an important part of her role).

The question which arises from this outline of domestic and
kin arrangements before, during and since migration must be to
ask in which direction lies stability - or at least minimum
strain and maximum use of available resources for family
household group survival.   Put in other words, what complex
structures of role-relations optimizes available and co-opera-
ting family personnel resources, both externally to provide
income and internally to manage a growing and developing
household?

The chart of Alric's household and extended kin portrays clearly the isolation of his mother from her supportive kin, i.e. her mother, sisters and brothers.   It also indicates by implication the role being forced upon her of housekeeper and childrearer to her husband and children while at the same time being the family's only source of earned income.   The result is for her a position of both personal stress and of increased social power while her husband is unable to act as provider and does not take on a larger domestic or social role.   Their situation is one in which, despite the superficial appearance of a nuclear family system, Paulette is carrying out virtually singlehanded the major functions of the head of the Campbell household.   Perhaps because of the immediate requirements of finding a home at the time of family migration, Gilmour acquired certain formal and legal responsibilities which are normal to a husband in English society, e.g. rent-book holder, but it does appear that in day-to-day terms Paulette has been the executor of such formal responsibilities.   To what extent this will continue to be the case with the Campbells and other families like them is a moot question.   It will depend on both the perceived social pressures and the practical advantages and disadvantages of 'English marriage' to women who, unlike Paulette, may in the succeeding generation not be so far isolated at the time of childrearing from their maternal kin.   In the meantime the isolation and stress they have had to cope with has undoubtedly been considerable.   The positive outcomes for them may be, as Foner (1979) has suggested, a life in which they find more fulfilment in terms of work outside the home than would have been the case in the West Indies, and in which their domestic and social status is continuously being enhanced by virtue of the dependence of other members of the domestic kin-group upon them.

There is, of course, the further case of the role of the other spouse in this kind of domestic group.   Gilmour Campbell is clearly the incumbent of a role which makes his status and importance to the other members of his domestic kin group increasingly marginal as time elapses.   What causes this is apparently his restricted value as a provider and his inability or unwillingness to adopt a more active role in childrearing and household management.   The outcome may be expected to involve a decreasing claim on the loyalties and responsibilities of other members of the group, his wife and children, towards him despite the fact that they live under the roof for which in the UK he is legally responsible.   At the same time Gilmour is getting older and less able to compete as a youthful member of any male peer group (see Wilson, 1969) so that his credibility at home and his reputation with his friends may be expected increasingly to be threatened.   In his, and

other cases like his, as old age approaches he can only hope
to become dependent on those around him.   This must have some
implications in terms of his own psychological development,
and for the relationship he has with his wife given her isolation from those maternal relatives who would naturally give
her support in childrearing and in providing a home.   In turn
the norms of this home situation may be expected to mould the
expectations which their children are likely to have of home
and married life and to create in their turn as adulthood
comes along.

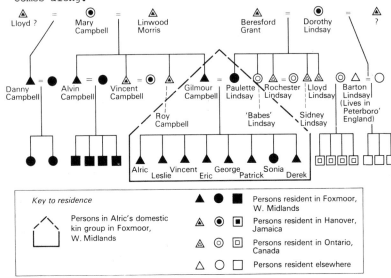

FIGURE 9.1 Household and extended kin of Alric Campbell

THE SPENCERS

Erica Spencer was the eldest daughter of a couple from St
Kitts who married and came to England in 1957.   Ernest and
Esmeralda had six children, all born and raised in Foxmoor,
part of a West Midlands city where a large number of West
Indians have settled.   Before leaving St Kitts, Ernest had
been a clerical assistant working for the government.   He
hoped to get a similar job in Britain but found he needed to
earn more money than such employment offered and so took
manual work.   More recently he had had to quit work completely as major health problms due to a heart ailment over-
took him.   At the time when the research report was compiled
Ernest was in his early 40s, an unhappy man, in poor health

and largely restricted to his house.   His wife Esmeralda re-
fused to allow this gloom to overtake her.   She spent a great
deal of energy and imagination on her family and home life,
obtaining the active and willing co-operation of Ernest as far
as he was able to run the home.   Both of them were concerned
that the children got a good start in life and that they took
all the opportunities which came their way.   Esmeralda saw
her place primarily as within the home and had never taken
employment in order to supplement the family's money despite a
limited income based largely on social security allowances.

Despite the increasingly difficult conditions at home,
Ernest and Esmeralda clearly retained a view of their roles in
which he was the family breadwinner and as such was head of
the household, while she took the role of household manager
and childrearer.   Interestingly enough, several of Esmeralda's sisters and brothers, though scattered, lived in Britain.
She kept in touch with them and they visited one another, yet
without developing any maternal kin ties which would imply
limited dependence upon Ernest's role as head of his family
and its chief provider (despite his long period of illness).
The attached chart (Figure 9.2) of Erica's extended kin and
household group shows that Esmeralda's sisters were sufficiently established to 'share' their mother between them.
Since Mary Williams had come to join them in Britain she had
not established an independent home of her own.   Each of the
sisters lived in a separate household and beyond the possibility of having holidays in each other's homes, made little
effort to consolidate into any kind of 'grandmother family'.
Two of the sisters who were unmarried and both of whom were
nurses in Britain (Rhona and Rosanna) maintained their own
separate homes.   It was in one of these that their mother,
Mary Williams, was more or less a permanent lodger.

In the extended kin of Esmeralda Spencer (née Williams) as
well as in her own domestic situation, there is a regular
preference for 'nuclear' family domestic arrangements.   Roles
are understood and arranged accordingly both within households
and between the extended kin.   Reciprocity of 'Christian
marriage' arrangements in this way were found to characterize
the extended kin systems reported for the three other pupils
along with Erica who also had 'Christian marriage' home backgrounds.

The psychological strain in the Spencer household clearly
centred on Ernest who due to ill health was clearly unable to
do all that was expected of him in the life of his family.
However it was also clear that his role as head of the family
was not threatened.   In fact there is little sign in the case
of the Spencers of any departure, despite obvious economic and
social pressures to the contrary, from the role-structure on

which conjugally based nuclear families would seem normally to function.

As well as the case of Ernest, it is also clear that Esmeralda was under considerable physical and emotional strain in the sense that she had the most to do in keeping the family going under testing circumstances presented by Ernest's illness. This does not however appear to have affected role expectations within this kind of domestic social structure or with respect to wider kin roles. The tendency here is not yet towards role redefinition and there is no sign of reorientation of this family role-system to one in which the role and status of a man as head of household is reduced because of an inability to fulfil the role of provider.

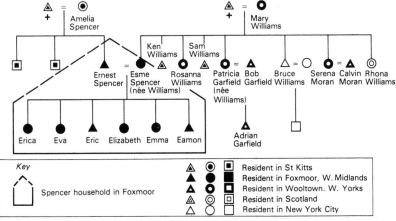

FIGURE 9.2   Household and extended kin of Erica Spencer

DISCUSSION

The comparison and contrast of the two West Indian families focuses on two features. Firstly, it is apparent that in one there is evidence of a mother-centred family type of domestic kin structure and in the other there is virtually none. Alric was brought up for the first six or seven years of his life by his mother's mother in Jamaica. As for his parents, Gilmour had clearly been socialized to take a very limited view of his role responsibilities as a husband and father, and Paulette, for her part, seemed not really to expect Gilmour to act in any other way. Her actions in taking virtually full responsibility for the home seems indicative of the underlying and possibly resurgent role-structure of such households. The principal inhibiting factor, and one which must continue to impose a strain on women in a similar position to Paulette, is the absence of the grandmother figure, either because she is still resident overseas, or because she has no independent household readily accessible to her daughters and their children in this country, or because she is obliged to work for her living in the UK and therefore is not free to take on the full range of functions which have so frequently become associated with her status in Caribbean family social structure.

The Spencers, by contrast, showed no strong tendency, despite particular strains induced in the household close kin group by Ernest's illness, to consider a reformulation of roles.   The rights and responsibilities of the extended kin on Esmeralda's side were not apparently open to such remodelling.   Nor was any effort apparently made to negotiate any reworking of roles which may evolve from social experience in Britain.

It seems from the Spencer's case that the conjugally based West Indian family system in Britain, ostensibly a 'Christian marriage', of itself may be less prone to change.   It is also possible that shared (rather than conflicting) economic and social interests between husband and wife provide important reasons for the stability of 'Christian marriage'.   However, some of those interests may not exist in the overcrowded and depressed conditions in which many West Indians live in Britain, and may therefore engender changes in West Indian 'Christian marriage' family structure as a result.   The extent to which the very architecture and location of the houses in which these family groups live and will live, together with the social status of the member of the domestic group who owns or rents such properties, is something which is bound to influence the situation but about which any specific comment seems impossible at present.

The two families appear to represent two stable types of domestic kin organization.   Both result from socializing influences in the predominantly rural environment of the Caribbean.   These two general types, which are the writer's own examples from his ethnography of what appear to be opposite orientations in family life, may well be undergoing modifications in the urban conditions of the United Kingdom where the West Indian minority settlements are to be found.   The principal evidence of those modifications is already being provided by the new generations of children born to West Indian families in this country as they mature and create their own extended kin networks and domestic groups.   Modification and adaptation at this complex level in which agreements and understandings about rights and responsibilities are evolved and negotiated between many people take place in response to new social pressures and different social conditions.   Creole culture generally is a prime example of this process.

The pressures of modification and adaptation at the individual level can be seen in the case of Paulette.   There can be little doubt of the effect of migration on her relationship with her immediate kin.   Responsibilities which would not necessarily have been hers had not only been forced upon her, but rights had also been denied - though certain other opportunities available through the social services of the welfare state had also been provided.   It is as we are able to observe the range of choices which the family and social structure presents to her daughter (and others like her) that we shall hope to identify the new family forms which may evolve from social experience in Britain.   Of course their immediate physical and social conditions are part of the experience which is taken into account as these families seek to organize themselves, with hope as well as uncertainty in the minds of their members.   Whether such conditions will be part of the reason for such changes, if they are likely to take place, remains to be seen.

The two descriptions do not of themselves offer sufficient information on the extended families' system of rights and responsibilities, since so little access was available to their members.   There will of course be new possibilities of observing these ties with the maturation of a generation of children raised in Britain and yet aware of the reciprocal responsibilities which are taken for granted in their families.

CONCLUSION

By presenting these two exemplary families the writer has tried to give a broad picture of the structural antecedents, present and likely future developments of domestic close-kin groups within Britain's West Indian minority population. These two cases cannot represent the entire range of West Indian domestic social structures, but it is hoped that in broad measure this is the case, as a useful step towards an understanding of orientation and adaptation process to which many West Indian families now settled in Britain have been subjected.

The Campbells and the Spencers throw into contrasting relief each others' survival strategies.   Both families are poor yet each has its distinctive view of what has to be the basis of secure role relationships and family survival.   From that springs a different use of relations with other members of the wider kinship network.

For their part, the Spencers showed no indication even
under pressure that any of the necessary renegotiation with
members of Esmeralda's scattered kin which would be necessary
to form a working basis for a 'grandmother family' type of
home was even about to take place.   Their case, with its un-
doubted hardship due to Ernest's illness, indicates no clear
shift from the husband-wife conjugal relationship as the
structural basis for domestic family organization.   In marked
contrast, the Campbells represent a family form which conform
much less to 'nuclear family' patterns.   Even so there are
underlying signs elsewhere in the minority culture that this
type of adaptive structure continues to be a vital one.   The
writer's earlier study (Driver, 1977) asserts the priority
accorded to girls over boys with regard to educational resources and encouragement on the part of many West Indian parents.
The level of educational achievement which so many of the
girls attain is so consistently superior to the boys in question that one is led to assume that many West Indian girls
and women in Britain are unlikely to seek a dependence-rela-
tionship with a West Indian husband as provider during the
period of childrearing if other accepted and possibly more
functional structural arrangements along the lines of the
'grandmother family' are available to them.   Modifications of
longstanding patterns there may well be, but it will be interesting to see whether many contract a similar kind of 'English
marriage' in the way their mothers did in the aftermath of
migration to Britain.   Wider field evidence seems to suggest
new developments of the 'grandmother family' among West Indian
households a generation after they arrived here.   To what
extent it is right to label these new developments as 'mother-
centred' family households is open to debate.

We need much more field information to understand developments in the domestic kin and extended kin relations of West
Indians in Britain.   There can be little doubt that such
developments while they take into account the physical and
socio-economic realities which many of these people suffer,
reflects the positive and real choices which are made to individuals and groups to use the cultural resources at their disposal.   The picture is a dynamic one and worthy of further
study, and not only - or even primarily - in the framework of
economic and racial deprivation, as so much of the productive
earlier work of Rex (1967) and Smith (1976) in the UK, and
Moynihan (1965) and Lewis (1968) in the USA.   As Roger
Ballard and I have argued elsewhere (1977) West Indians and
other ethnic minority groups are capable of marshalling cultural resources to cope with and often overcome formidable
economic obstacles - and these resources are largely generated
and organized within the medium of close, family or family-
type relationships.

Chapter 10

West Indian families: an insider's perspective[1]

Jocelyn Barrow

An earlier writer who attempted an 'insider's' perspective on West Indian family life was so struck by the shattering effect of the slavery experience that she argued that 'for two centuries the institution we consider most fundamental to human society was forgotten' (Fitzherbert, 1976).

We can see now that family life has been damaged during slavery, but not entirely forgotten as new patterns emerged. The resilience of West Indian families in coping with problems of survival both in the West Indies and in Britain are now more understood than previously, as Geoffrey Driver has shown. However, given the great gaps in our knowledge and at the same time the interest that this group holds for contemporary society, we can try to sketch in some of the processes of their adaptation in Britain - on an impressionistic basis, as a 'participant observer', pending the accumulation of more detailed anthropological and sociological studies.

The West Indian studies have provided something of a framework which can serve as a point of departure. There have been two generations of studies now, using different terminology but coming to rather similar formulations. Beginning in the 1940s with the study by Simey (1947) and following up with the studies by Matthews (1953) and Henriques (1953) certain patterns were described which seemed to be common to the islands generally, and to provide a structure which was more meaningful than the grinding poverty and want described by a despairing V.S. Naipaul who wrote in 'The Middle Passage':

> Every day I saw the same things - unemployment, ugliness, over-population, race - and every day I heard the same circular arguments.... They were the accumulated pressures of the slave society, the colonial society, the underdeveloped, overpopulated, agricultural country;

The generation of researchers which followed in the 1950s, Smith (1957) and Clarke (1957) for example, though changing

their language and adding some dynamic interpretations, essentially agreed with the earlier typology of West Indian families. There were three types (2) mainly observed with the
second being by far the largest:

(1) *The conventional nuclear family household*, based, essentially, on the model of the Victorian family as described by Smelser. In earlier social research, and still
today amongst many West Indians, it is termed 'Christian
marriage', and is more to be found amongst the economically better-off and/or the more religious members of
the community.

(2) *The common-law family household*, in which couples live
together without formal marriage, and care for children
who may or may not be theirs biologically. This form
of family life was termed, in earlier studies, 'faithful
concubinage'; or, by Henriques, the legal bond. In
its more transient forms, it has been termed the 'companionate' union, by Simey.

(3) *The mother household*, in which a woman - mother or
grandmother of the children - is not only an influential
figure in decision making and home management (as she is
in the other types of household as well), but where she
is the sole stable household head.

In the West Indies the conventional nuclear family type is
generally associated with adequate resources ranging from the
ownership of land, professional status and steady employment.
Marriage tends to take place in the early twenties and
although more women in this category are now working the husband assumes financial responsibility for the household. In
the common law union similar arrangements of responsibility as
in the nuclear family type obtain; the differences, however,
are that the households tend to be set up at a much earlier
age and the partners are generally from the lower socio-economic groups. In the mother households, where mothers, grandmothers or older female siblings are the stable figures, resources tend to be even more limited and housing and social
conditions tend to be poor; the responsibility for their survival rests solely with the female members of the household
who are employed.

Each of these types of household is understandable both in
terms of the history of the West Indian Blacks, and in terms
of the current environmental pressures and constraints. The
mother-household can cope with the care of children born into
or left within it because of the supports in the largely rural
West Indian environment. And she has a heritage of having
been supported in child care from the slavery days when one of
the few forms of viable family life was when a slave-master
had children by his household slave.

Geoffrey Driver has described two sub-types of the conventional nuclear family; one, the Spencers, fits more closely to the Victorian model and is called 'Christian marriage'; and the other, the Campbells, resembles that form in structure, but is more 'matrifocal' in actual functioning.

MIGRATION TO BRITAIN

The pattern of migration to Britain in the 1950s and early 1960s was made up of three main groups: (1) the male head of the conventional nuclear family or of a common-law union, who came and worked, maintaining responsibility for his wife and children 'back home' in the islands. Subsequently they would join him in Britain as conditions warranted or he might return. The main distinguishing characteristic is that the family unit was, in the minds of all concerned, a cohesive and binding unit. (2) The unmarried man or woman who had children in the West Indies, whom they acknowledged but had no established household. In this case they often left their children behind with grandmother. Subsequently when they established a new household here, they tended to send for their children. (3) Single men and women who had left no dependent children behind; these, however, were in the minority.

There were two major interrelated factors which influenced the migration of West Indians to Britain, the first was the Second World War and the second was the acute unemployment in the Caribbean. In the early stages of the Second World War, large numbers of young men and women from the West Indies came to Britain to join the armed forces, especially the Army and the Royal Air Force. Many of these who for a variety of reasons did not qualify for the Services worked in munition factories. In 1945 at the end of the war, the servicemen returned to the West Indies but found there even greater unemployment than before.

Some demobilised servicemen and a few others chartered the steamer 'Empire Windrush' in 1946 and returned to Britain. The American McClaren Act limited the migration of West Indians to the United States, and at the same time some British service industries, e.g. London Transport, began active recruitment campaigns in the West Indies. All these factors added to the numbers migrating to Britain.

Although economic pressures in the West Indies was the major motivating factor for migration there were other factors which were also relevant. People in the West Indies were brought up with an image of Britain as the 'mother-country', and therefore that they belonged there. This feeling of

belonging to the 'mother-country' had been created in the days
of slavery, but even more after Emancipation in the education,
the laws, the language and the whole cultural ethos in the
former British colonies.   Above all, the example set by the
colonial administrators and the plantation owners was a key
element.

Both sets of feelings - economic pressures and a sense of
belonging were brought from the West Indies in the mass migration.   West Indians came to Britain in search of jobs and
better educational opportunities for their children.   Most of
the newcomers found jobs in the service industries and at the
dirty end of manufacturing industries.   The housing accommodation available to them was poor and inadequate and this led
to West Indians living together in close proximity in overcrowded conditions in the decaying centres of our large towns
and cities.

But a less expected aspect of life was the hostility of the
environment and the unwelcoming attitudes of the people,mani-
festing itself in prejudice and discrimination.   This forced
the West Indian community, by no means a homogeneous group, to
look inwards and to use the internal structures of West Indian
family patterns as their means of survival.   At the same time
they were anxious to conform to the outward pattern of English
family life.   This situation placed stress on the male-female
relationships, even in the 'nuclear family' of Christian marriage.   A major disadvantage which the immigrant West Indian
experienced was the lack of the wider network of kinship
(especially the kinship of the mother) and to substitute for
this new types of arrangements and institutions were created.
The childminding arrangements and casual fostering of children
are examples.

READAPTATIONS OF FAMILY TYPES

In the early days of migration from the West Indies, individuals from three types of households already mentioned settled in the decaying centres of inner city areas.   They
tended to occupy single rooms in large multi-occupied Victorian houses sharing kitchens and bathrooms;   the tendency was
for a man, woman and children to occupy the same room.   In
cases where the West Indians had been actively recruited by a
service industry they were provided with accommodation as described above very near their place of work.   Thus West
Indians can be found around the major bus termini in the
Greater London area;   these areas 'of first settlement'
attracted the friends and relatives of those already living
there.

There was a time lapse of about five years for the men from
the conventional nuclear family type before their wives and
children joined them in this country.   They tended to buy
small terraced houses without the usual modern conveniences in
the small back streets of the areas in which they were already
living.   The wives, because of the economic burden of the
mortgage, were forced to go out to work;   invariably both
parents worked on a shift system so that one parent was available to look after the children.   Frequently both parents
would work as much overtime as was available to them.   Men
and women from the other two types of households lived on
their own when they first arrived, but within the first couple
of years had set up some kind of household arrangement with a
West Indian partner.   These varied from visiting relationships to stable common-law unions.   Those who prospered economically followed the familiar pattern of movement toward the
suburbs.

Throughout, the economic and social problems have been
bothersome.   Of the many problems associated with this, I
shall concentrate on one - the childrearing patterns, with
particular emphasis to the management of adolescent problems.

CHILDREARING PATTERNS AND PRACTICES

Parents were themselves unaware of the numerous adjustments
that had to be made to live in Britain.   These adjustments
included working very long hours, tedious and boring routines;
in a hostile climate both environmentally and physically, with
very little religious support (except for the small Black-led
churches) and above all no family and kinship network.   In
these circumstances parents were unable to help their newly
arrived children from the West Indies to cope with the adjustments necessary for living in a complex sophisticated metropolitan society.

The childrearing practices used in the West Indies were
applied in Britain without recognition that these practices
could disadvantage their children.   As in the West Indies
mothers took the major responsibility for the rearing of
children in all the family types.   When they worked, informal
supports of a familiar and trusted kind were readily at hand.
In Britain, when West Indian mothers are forced by economic
pressures to go out to work, no such support system is available for looking after their children.   Hence the use of
childminders by large numbers of these mothers often without
the necessary screening and monitoring of the care being provided.

At every level of the society in the West Indies parents

are accustomed to having somebody else help them look after their children.   This help takes different forms in the different family types - from paid help in the conventional nuclear family to grandmothers, aunts, older siblings and even neighbours in the other two groups.   The care of these children provided by kinfolk is as good as that provided by their mothers.   There are many advantages of childrearing in the West Indies that are taken for granted and parents are unaware of the emotional and intellectual benefits these provide for their children.

In the Caribbean children spend most of their time playing outside the house with mud, sand, water, and climbing trees and playing with animals.   Even the grinding poverty of the area provides these young children with an advantage: since parents are too poor to buy toys children are forced to use the odds and ends found in the 'backyard' resulting in a lot of creative and imaginative play.   This play provides them with intellectually stimulating experiences.   The play with sand and water or mud develops their manipulative skills and physical co-ordination in readiness for school.   In keeping with the oral tradition of the West Indies - part of our African heritage - there are always two or three older women talking to the young children, telling them stories, teaching them and answering their questions.   This provides them with a rich language development.   As the children are generally in groups of eight to ten there is good peer group socialisation as well as good adult child relationships.   No one in the Caribbean recognises these advantages.   The people see themselves as poor, that they lack money to buy toys and books and that they lack enough space in which to live; the warmth and enormous love and care with which they surround the children are taken for granted.

In Britain because of the shortage of pre-school facilities very few West Indians are able to get places for their children.   They therefore choose as an alternative childminders and in many cases this is where their difficulties and problems with their adolescent children begin.   Most parents are content with West Indian childminders without establishing the living conditions of the home because their Caribbean experience leads them to expect that their children will be well looked after.   But in Brixton, Deptford, Leeds, Birmingham many West Indian children are being reared in poor and inadequate housing where it is impossible for the childminder to provide sand trays and water troughs, toys or books.   And where the economic and social pressures also prevent the childminder from spending time talking to, playing with, or telling stories to her young charges.   It is also outside her cultural experience to use the media, both radio and television's children's programmes, to stimulate and entertain the children in her care.

The result is poor manipulative skill and physical co-ordination and language development as well as very little peer group socialisation or adult-child socialisation.

This type of early childhood rearing, which results from West Indian parents' lack of knowledge about the educative value of play, and the importance of stimulating early childhood experiences, tends to put many West Indian children at a disadvantage when they enter the Infant School. The children may be physically well cared for, well fed and clean, but their emotional and intellectual development is not as well catered for as if they were growing up in the natural environment of the Caribbean.

The contrast between the environment of the childminder or parents' home and that of the nursery or infant classroom is so great that very many West Indian infants are unable to cope, but more importantly the teachers are unable to cope with them. The language of the classroom and the teacher is bewildering, the variety of choice and stimulation is overwhelming. The result of this conflict is that children tend either to withdraw or, because they are confused, become overactive. Most teachers are also confused and bewildered, because they are not equipped either by their training or experience to cater for these new demands. One of the most crucial areas of infant education is at risk - the teaching of reading. Teachers tend to find it very difficult to know what to do with these children. Their training has not given them the skills to carry on language development and pre-reading activities with children with poor and limited vocabularies. The nonacquisition of reading is linked with classroom problems and other forms of attention-seeking behaviour, which teachers tend to interpret as a form of sub-normality. The educational psychological services are called in, and using instruments which do not diagnose the roots of the problem, label the children as ESN (educationally sub-normal).

So far I have looked at the educational aspects of early childhood, but what of the home? Parents are anxious for their children to do well at school, and tend to become disturbed about their children's lack of progress at school and their behaviour. Like the teachers, the parents are unaware of the causes of the problems and in any case lack the skills or resources to offer solutions. A further element, adding to the parents' confusion and frustration, is the lack of accustomed networks of support that exist in the Caribbean. They do not know where to turn for help and advice.

The parents blame the children's laziness or playfulness and the lack of discipline (corporal punishment is what is generally meant) in the school.   Parents find it difficult to visit the school and even when they do, the discussion/talk with the teachers are often not helpful.   Parents often come away from the encounter even more confused and frustrated. The parents' experience of the education system in the West Indies or even in the UK does not equip them to question the teachers or the social worker or the psychologist and to have a meaningful discussion.   They are therefore unable to help their children because, without their traditional sources of help and advice they need guidance themselves.

The traditional support system consists of the family, the loosely knit extended family, which tends to be extremely supportive, or kinship group and the church.   I have already described how the family support system works so I shall now look at the role of the church.   Religion is important throughout the whole society in the West Indies not just in terms of faith and belief, but also because of the provision of education and social welfare.   As in Victorian England, church going conferred respectability, but with the development at the turn of the century of the small Black-led churches, an additional significant benefit was the economic and social development work carried out within these church communities.

In Britain, because of the pattern of immigration, there is no extended family support network.   Even where there are other members of the family living in the neighbourhood, the pressures of living in a metropolitan society seems to prevent them from functioning as a supportive network.   There are, however, some exceptions, especially among the small Black-led churches and some of the parents' groups and other organisations.

The educational difficulties experienced by West Indian children in the infant school carry on into the junior school and create new anxieties for theparents.   The nine-year-old children who have not learnt to read begin to recognise that they are malfunctioning in the classroom and begin to compensate for this in their behaviour.   They need to have the respect and appreciation of their peer group, so if they are not good at class work, they will be the clowns, or fighters or begin to excel at some form of physical activity.   However, in spite of this apparent adjustment to this situation in the classroom they are beginning to develop a poor self-image. The poor self-concept is frequently reinforced by the expectations of the teacher, and in racial hostility in the larger society.   While the children are having these experiences in the schools and the neighbourhood, the parents are frequently too busy working and coping to recognise their children's difficulties.

Poor parent/child relationship and the lack of communication leads into an adolescence of non-involvement with parents.   West Indian adolescents, like adolescents anywhere in the world, have the same need of acceptance by their peer group, role models in society with which to identify, and above all opportunities for success.   In Britain the reality for very many West Indian adolescents does not meet any of these needs.   In the first place his junior school experiences have created poor self-concept and the school curriculum and materials only help to reinforce this.   At this stage teacher expectation is not the only major outside influence. The adolescents have reached the developmental stage, at which they are very sensitive to the hostility projected by society towards them.   In their search for models from within their own community, on which to pattern themselves, they become extremely frustrated and angry because they find so few.   This frustration leads to a crisis of identity and the search for self-image and self-concept intensifies.

These West Indian adolescents reject their parents' strong work ethic and their parents' value system.   They question in their own aggressive and non-verbal way why their parents are so hard working, law abiding, and are so acquiescent to the prejudice and discrimination they suffer.

This alienation from both parents and society is demonstrated in a variety of ways, by different groups of adolescents. Non-communication with adult society whether it be parents, teachers, or youth workers, contributes to what often becomes a vicious cycle.   This gap in communication gives rise to a feeling among many adolescents that adults are not concerned or interested in their welfare or success.   Many adolescents interpret their parents strong work ethic as another form of slavery and reject it out of hand.   In addition there is the confusion caused by the conflict between home and school in the ways in which discipline and authority is exercised;   and the adolescents accuse both parents and teachers of not understanding and above all of not caring.   On the adult side, the feeling is that the young people are lazy, work-shy, or gone bad.

There are indications that British born West Indian adolescents who were sent back to the West Indies by parents for their secondary education when they return are confident and self-assured and seem to have nothing of the identity crisis of their British educated peer group.   This is the result of living in a country where they see Black people filling all the major roles from prime minister to teacher;   and thus they have many role models to emulate.

Underachievement in schools, racism and the economic pressures in inner city areas lead to a disproportionately high

rate of unemployment among West Indian adolescents.   The
further disillusionment which unemployment or very poor unemployment prospects create for the West Indian adolescent lead
to further conflict with parents often resulting in homelessness for the adolescent.   The dependence on peer group for
help and understanding at this time increases, and the 'gang'
becomes the main point of reference and guidance.   The very
nature of this type of situation makes the West Indian adolescent vulnerable to conflict with the police and drug pushers.
This leads to even further alienation and non-acceptance by
parents.   It also has another damaging effect, a type of
self-fulfilling prophecy that makes younger West Indians begin
to believe that this is the inevitable destiny for them and
they begin to opt out at an even earlier age.   This seems to
be truer for young boys than for young girls.   Therefore
West Indian adolescents have to develop techniques for survival in this hostile environment, and in response to racism
have begun to choose alternative lifestyles.

Of course these problems do not apply to all West Indian
youths and their families.   Ken Pryce in his study of the
West Indian community in the St Pauls area of Bristol described six adolescent lifestyles - 'hustlers, teeny boppers,
proletarian respectables, saints, mainliners and inbetween-
ers'.   There is not enough space in this chapter for a description of each of these lifestyles so I shall use the two
broader groupings, namely: 'the stable law-abiding orientation' and 'expressive-disreputable orientation'.   The former
tend to work, the latter to 'hustle'.

In their efforts to establish an identity adolescents from
both these major orientations may appear similar in terms of
external behaviour, patterns of speech, music, dance styles
and dress.   These elements are part of a new cultural tradition, and has meaning to young Blacks in the British context.
But there are differences underneath these behaviour patterns
ranging from the Rastafarians at one extreme to the punk
rockers at the other with the mainliners somewhere in the
centre.

The Rastafarian cult is a male-dominated social structure
as opposed to the matrifocal structure of most of West Indian
society and this may well be one of the main psychological
reasons why so many young adolescent males choose to follow
it, in their attempt to escape from the dominance of mother
and other women folk.   It may also provide them with a frame-
within which they can come to terms with and match white male
prejudice at work, at school and in society generally, especially those who openly advocate racial hatred.   Some of those
who remain outside the Rastafarian cult may develop a strong
sub-culture based on the Black English Reggae and other forms

of Black music and Black dance styles (all of which have their roots in the Rastafarian cult).   These elements provide self-esteem and identity without the anti-white elements being so strong.

Because in the Caribbean coping with adolescence is generally shared by more than one generation, parents do not always recognise that their adolescents have one foot in childhood and the other in the adult world, and in the case of the West Indian adolescent in Britain there is the additional dimension of being halfway between the society of the island their parents come from and that specific segment and sub-culture of British society where they are growing up.

Related to this is the new problem of involvement with the police and the courts.   Most Caribbean-born adults go to great lengths to avoid involvement with the police.   It is therefore a cause of great anxiety when their adolescents are picked up for 'causing an obstruction', 'loitering', 'SUS' and 'stop and search'.   Parents are genuinely perplexed and confused as they do not understand how many of their natural cultural patterns of behaviour are considered to be 'crimes' in Britain.   There is in the West Indies a strong 'open-air culture' both in the streets and 'backayard'. (3)   Loud music, loud talking, getting together to share news and gossip, just 'lining' (standing and observing the activities and people of the area) are all offences in Britain.

For climatic reasons an open-air lifestyle is not feasible in Britain.   But, paradoxically, the social environment in which most West Indians live forces them into the streets. Poor housing conditions, unemployment and the silent hostility in many of the traditional meeting places, i.e. pubs and social clubs, leave adolescents and many male adults with no alternative meeting place but the 'street'.

Increasing conflict between Black adolescents and the police frighten most West Indian parents to such an extent that many of them do not want their children to be on the streets at all, but especially at night.   But within the home there is considerable stress, as discussed above.   This sometimes leads to a breakdown in relationships, with the adolescent storming out with varying degrees of parental participation.   The resulting 'homelessness' of the adolescents makes them even more vulnerable to conflict with the police and leads to ever greater alienation not only from parents, but also from other caring or concerned West Indian adults.   This further increased the dependence of West Indian adolescents on their peer group and within that context to develop a lifestyle that shields and protects, while being impenetrable to authority figures - parents, teachers, youth workers and the police.   The statutory agencies which offer help and guidance

to West Indian parents when their adolescents are involved
with the police, or are experiencing other difficulties, tend
to lack the expertise and knowledge to cope with the specific
problems of West Indian youth.   Parents feel a great sense of
helplessness in these situations, and because they don't know
where to turn for help, often appear to be indifferent and un-
caring, though this is usually far from true.

The picture painted so far may be thought to be particularly gloomy and depressing, but there are many hopeful and encouraging signs developing in the West Indian community during
the past few years.   Many of these initiatives have been
sparked off by particular educational issues, such as the
parents and community groups that developed to cope with the
ESN problem in the late 1960s.   Some of these organisations
disbanded after the specific issues had been satisfactorily
aired, others widened their activities and promoted various
self-help projects including pre-school play groups, drop-in
and community centres, hostels for the homeless and unemployed, supplementary schools and summer projects.   A few are
developing in new directions and accepting the challenges.
There is the project in South London, inspired, organised and
run by a mother of three, who has both fostered and adopted
other children into her own home.   She has recently worked
with her community to raise more than £50,000 to help rebuild
the centre which was deliberately destroyed by fire.   In
North London there is a project which works at keeping families in difficulties together.   This work entails helping
both parents and adolescents to verbalise the difficulties
they are facing first separately, then as a family group and
supporting them through the early tentative stages of a reconciliation.   Most of this painstaking and delicate family
casework is undertaken by volunteers, many of them from the
small Black-led churches.   An unusual feature of this project
is that it is willing to share not only its specialised knowledge of West Indian family life but also the techniques it
employs in this work, with social workers, probation officers,
teachers and the police, as it regards helping to train the
professionals an essential element of its contribution to
society.

As in other sub-groups, there are many Black parents who
use the knowledge they gained from coping with their children's problems to helping other parents in similar circumstances.   This informal support system flourishes where there
are neighbourhood and community facilities.

The humour and laughter so characteristic of the people of
Caribbean origin helps to enliven local community life, i.e.
in Brixton market on a Saturday where West Indians can be
heard laughing and joking not only with members of their own
community but with Whites also.

Furthermore, and this is a development in which many Black youths participate, there is the Nottinghill Gate Carnival. This is a transfer of Caribbean street culture to London in which Whites as well as Blacks share.   A small section of the Caribbean population gives pleasure and enjoyment to about half a million Black and White people who for two days in the summer abandon some of their inhibitions and enjoy the pulsating rhythms of the Calypso and steel band.

In conclusion, my feelings as an insider in West Indian life suggest that just as during slavery patterns of family life and support systems emerged to enable the survival of the group, so too, out of the British experience of hardship and discrimination will come new patterns of family lifestyles which will have positive value, both for West Indians and for their neighbours.

NOTES

1   This chapter is part of a research thesis at the University of London, Institute of Education, and is based on a mixture of research and voluntary work in a West Indian community, as well as living within it as a member of the community.

2   In the West Indies, the general distribution of the different family types is divided roughly into thirds.   The conventional nuclear family of legal marriage represents a third.   Another third is made up of the faithful common-law union and the companionate union.   (Companionate unions are like faithful common-law unions but tend to be of limited duration whereas most faithful common-law unions result in marriage - usually in the couples' middle age.)   The other third is made up of matrifocal households or those dominated by women.   Within the matrifocals there are a variety of types from the extra-residential that has some stability and where the man may accept paternal responsibility right through to casual mating or even promiscuity resulting in children.   There are, however, exceptions to this distribution in some territories such as Trinidad and Guyana, with their Asian populations resulting in a higher incidence of conventional nuclear family of legal marriage type.

3   'Backayard' means the large communal space or yard shared by a number of families and where a great deal of social life takes place.

Chapter 11

Cypriot families[1]
Robin Oakley

INTRODUCTION

The presence of a Cypriot minority in Britain is a product of
the large-scale movement of population from the economically
underdeveloped countries of the Commonwealth that took place
during the first two decades following the 1939-45 war
(Oakley, 1971, Part I).   Cyprus itself remained almost wholly
given over to peasant agriculture until the 1950s, when
British military construction programmes generated an increase
in social and economic change on the island, indirectly fostering the high levels of emigration that followed.   In
Britain, Cypriots are fewer in number than the Asian or West
Indian minorities considered as wholes, but constitute the
largest of the 'non-coloured' minorities deriving from the so-
called New Commonwealth.   At the present time there are in
the region of 140,000 Cypriots living in Britain, a figure
which includes the British-born children of immigrant parents.
Like Asians and West Indians, though, their apparent unity
lies more in the eyes of the British (and in the political
constructions of British history) than it does in their own,
for quite apart from several rather small minorities (such as
Armenians), Cypriots in Britain (as in Cyprus) divide in a
ratio of approximately four to one into populations of Greek
and Turkish ethnicity respectively.
   On Cyprus itself the differentiation between Greeks and
Turks has a long history.   The primary differences lie in
religion and language, and the significance of these became
enhanced by a nationalistic identification on the part of the
respective groups with Greek and Turkish peoples generally.
From the dawn of its recorded history the island has had a
predominantly Greek population, but it has had many overlords,
and it was during the period of Ottoman rule that many Turks
settled on the island.   Under the British rule that followed

(from 1878), Greek and Turk continued to live adjacently and often work together, but the rarity (for religious reasons) of intermarriage and the persistence of separate educational systems ensured that the ethnic division remained uncompromised, although for a long while stable.   However, with the prospect of Independence from British rule (in 1960) and the subsequent reality of an imposed and unworkable Constitution, fears and tensions arose between Greeks and Turks which developed in due course into overt hostility and violence, leading eventually to the war of 1974-5 and the present division of the island between the two ethnic groups who hold one another in extensive mistrust.

Greek and Turkish Cypriots in Britain therefore share the same geographical and economic background, though distinguish themselves sharply in terms of ethnic and national identification.   Cultural values differ far less than the latter might imply, and do so chiefly in so far as they emanate from religion.   In family life in particular the differences between the two groups arise mainly in the spheres of inheritance and marriage, though also in a variety of more superficial cultural manifestations.   For this reason, I concentrate in this chapter on one ethnic group in particular, the larger Greek-Cypriot group, noting briefly some of the different characteristics of Turkish-Cypriot family life where appropriate.   It should be pointed out, however, that despite these differences of culture and of national sentiment, relations between Greek and Turkish Cypriots in London have generally remained co-operative and friendly, insulated as they have been from the immediacy of the tensions of the last few decades on the island itself (Ladbury, 1977).   Even when the 1974-5 war threatened this relationship through its impact on property interests and the welfare of kinsmen (several thousands of whom as refugees have been accommodated by relatives established in Britain) pragmatic - and in some cases ideological - motives sufficed to maintain the working relationship between the two communities.

To this ethnic division must be added a further source of cultural diversity among Cypriots in Britain - that due to length of settlement and generational differences.   These different dimensions will be explored in the subsequent sections.   However, it must be pointed out that, as yet, the amount of research that has been carried out among Cypriots in Britain is very limited (Constantinides, 1977;   George and Millerson, 1967;   Ladbury, 1977, 1979;   Oakley, 1970, 1971, 1979), and none has yet been undertaken with the specific aim of measuring and explaining patterns of continuity and change in family life.   The present article therefore draws on such research on Greek and Turkish lifestyles as has been carried

out, not only in Britain but also in Cyprus (especially
Peristiany, 1955a, 1968;   Loizos, 1975) and elsewhere (espec-
ially Campbell, 1964;   Du Boulay, 1974;   Friedl, 1962;
Stirling, 1965) and in parts draws directly on my own first
hand knowledge of the experiences of the Cypriot minority in
Britain.

HISTORICAL

The history of the Cypriot settlement in Britain begins in the
aftermath of the 1914-18 war, when small numbers of young
Greek men began to venture further abroad than the neighbouring Mediterranean countries that had been the traditional
destinations of emigrants from the island (Oakley, MS.).   The
accessibility of Britain (as compared with Australia and South
America), and the success of pioneer migrants in finding
employment in the kitchens of large London hotels, led in due
course to an increase in the number of migrants, especially
during the later 1930s, to the extent that by the outbreak of
war in 1939 it was estimated that around 8,000 Cypriots had
settled in London.   This initial phase of Cypriot settlement
in Britain appears to have been entirely Greek in composition.
Moreover, it did not extend outside London, where it was
highly concentrated in and around the main hotel area of
London's West End, in particular around the Soho area.   Here
Cypriots found both work and lodgings, and passed their
leisure hours in the various Greek-run cafes that began to
grow up in the vicinity.   The great majority of the settlers
at this stage were men, and the number of Cypriot wives and
children were at this time few.   Many of the men were still
young and as yet unprepared for marriage, but among the
earlier settlers a substantial proportion had married English
(or sometimes Irish or Scottish) wives.   In this early phase
of settlement therefore, it could not be said that any traditional pattern of Greek Cypriot family and community life had
yet reestablished itself in Britain to any degree.
    The 1939-45 war had two major effects on the development of
Cypriot settlement in Britain.   In the first place, it
created new opportunities for Greek Cypriots already settled
in London, many of whom grasped openings left by Italians in
the catering industry, both in hotel work and in the restaurant trade.   This improved living standards and economic
security among the settlers, but more importantly it created
in turn the prospect of further employment openings for future
immigrants, these now being increasingly at the disposal of
members of the ethnic colony itself.   That is to say, it laid
the foundations of the specific ethnic economy of Cypriots in

Britain, based largely on small family-run establishments in
the services sector - an economy well suited to expansion by
means of a cycle of hard work, thrift and reinvestment leading
to the multiplication and/or diversification of small units
rather than (with few exceptions) to large enterprise as such.

The second effect of the war was to open up the horizons of
those back in Cyprus.   In part this occurred through the war
experiences of Cypriots in the Allied Forces, but more fundamental changes took place as the Colonial administration began
a programme of economic, social and military development on
the island, particularly following the outbreak of war in
Palestine and the consequent shifts of power within the Middle
East.   However, the demand for employment and for a higher
standard of living was far from satisfied by the new job
opportunities created.   Both men and women began in steadily
increasing numbers to emigrate to Britain to take up employment.   In doing so, the great majority followed lines of kinship and patronage (Oakley, 1979), not merely because of their
own preference, but also because the issue of travel documents
to a prospective emigrant required official sponsorship by
someone already resident and established in Britain.   Likewise, where dependants were to be left behind in Cyprus, the
Cyprus Welfare Department required that adequate provision
were made for their support until the family could be reunited.   Indeed in the majority of cases, families either
travelled as a unit, or if the father/husband travelled ahead,
he did so only by a few months in order to make arrangements
for his employment and for satisfactory accommodation for his
family.   Traditional values therefore strongly shaped the
pattern of post-war Cypriot migration, providing for the
maintenance of family units and of kinship ties, and also for
a relatively balanced sex ratio among the settlers, which in
turn ensured a ready supply of marriage partners from within
the ethnic community itself.   In these ways, therefore, the
first generation of settlers has succeeded in transplanting to
Britain their traditional patterns of family life through the
process of 'sponsored' chain migration, adapting and redeploy-
ing these so as to exploit the new economic opportunities
available to them in the urban setting.

During this second stage of the migration the number of
migrants increased steadily up until 1962 when Cypriot
migrants became subject to immigration control in the form of
the first Commonwealth Immigrants Act.   Successive further
restrictions then sharply reduced the number of Cypriots
entering Britain, and by 1966 it could be said that the migration, as a social *movement*, was at an end.   It has been estimated that a total of 75,000 Cypriots had emigrated to Britain
during the twenty-odd years since the end of the war.   Yet if

the history of the migration as such had ended, that of the
Cypriot minority within Britain was entering a new phase.
Children born to marriages among the earlier of the post-war
migrants were now in their teens, and experiencing the often
contradictory pressures of Cypriot home and English school.
For this second generation, that is of young people who had
passed all their formative years in Britain, the traditional
values have not passed unquestioned: alternative standards
of conduct and models of the family, learnt in school or from
the mass media, are perceived and in varying degree adopted by
young Cypriots today.   In the absence of research, it is not
possible yet to delineate at all precisely the emerging
patterns of family life among this group; there appears to be
some degree of variability in their response to the experience
of being between two cultures, though their commitment to the
core values of Cypriot culture and to a Cypriot identity
appears widespread and relatively firm.

SETTLEMENT PATTERNS

Some three-quarters of the 140,000 Cypriots in Britain are
resident in the Greater London area, a pattern of concentration initiated by the original settlers and maintained across
subsequent decades (George and Millerson, 1967; Oakley, 1970,
1971: Part II, in preparation).   Within London, however, a
substantial change in residential patterns has taken place.
Post-war settlers were obliged to seek accommodation outside
the focal pre-war area of Soho, and found cheap yet accessible
housing in the adjacent areas to the north in Camden Town and
Islington.   In Camden Town in 1948 the first Greek Cypriot
church in London was opened, and nearby there grew up a
variety of cafes, groceries and other retail shops to serve
the consumer needs of the settlers.   Employment was still
chiefly found in the West End, mainly either in the catering
industry or in the tailoring and dress-making workshops with
their long history of dependence on low-waged immigrant
labour.   Within this localised area, therefore, there became
established a well-defined colony of Cypriot immigrants whose
sense of ethnic unity was now sustained by the re-creation of a
variety of traditional institutions and the provision of
ethnic-style services.   Immigrant families became able to
meet their various needs largely within the confines of their
own ethnic, and above all linguistic community.
    In the subsequent decades there have been pressures towards
both continuity and change.   For some Cypriots, economic success brought the opportunity to realise higher housing and
general living standards.   Their movement outside the central

settlement area expressed symbolically their achievement of a
new status within the community.   There began, therefore, a
shift in settlement patterns which took many families further
northwards into suburban areas (chiefly Haringey) which were
still accessible to the main centres of Cypriot activity in
London.   This dispersion, and hence separation from the
localised community pattern of the early settlers, was comple-
mented none the less by a persistence of the latter due to
continuing immigration of Cypriots through the 1950s and early
1960s.   Islington soon became the principal 'reception' area
for new arrivals, and Turkish Cypriots who now joined the
migration in numbers equivalent to their proportion in the
overall Cyprus population (approximately one-fifth) increasingly settled here and in neighbouring Hackney and Stoke
Newington.   In these areas, despite the degree of immigrant
mobility *through* them, the pattern of life remained relatively
constant.   The poorer families, in low-standard multi-occupied rented housing, not uncommonly shared their homes on a
temporary basis with one or more relatives, either out of economic necessity or to tide over the newly arrived immigrant,
thus producing an untraditional 'extended family' household
pattern.   Since the mid-1960s, however, the inflow of new
immigrants has almost ceased, and this source of continuity in
Cypriot lifestyles has been removed.   The composition of
Cypriot residential and therefore family patterns has
thus in an overall sense been more liable to change during the
last decade.   This has been far less for Turkish Cypriots who
have tended to remain in their areas of primary settlement.
    The economic basis for these residential patterns lies pri-
marily in the exploitation by Cypriots of opportunities in the
services sector of the modern urban economy.   From their
initial involvement as kitchen-hands and waiters in the catering trade, many have moved both outwards and upwards in the
occupational system.   In the first place there has taken
place a steadily increasing diversification in the occupations
pursued by Cypriots, although these have continued to remain
highly concentrated in the service industries.   Cafe and
restaurant work, hairdressing, shoemending, tailoring and
dressmaking are among the more common occupations, though
Cypriots have also moved in small numbers into a much wider
range of service occupations, especially in the retail sphere,
in fact wherever an opportunity seems to have arisen to meet
the specific need for services within the ethnic community.
Tailoring and dressmaking, however, have developed more as
manufacturing businesses in which the various stages of production call for specialist workers to perform in workshop
settings, though some types of work can be done on a putting-
out basis on sewing machines in the home.   Dressmaking along

one or other of these lines has been the occupation of the
great majority of women immigrants in employment. Work at
home has been particularly popular among those with young
families, but women in this situation often experience extreme
isolation and monotony, whereas those in workshops secure contact and solidarity with other women which may otherwise be
lacking in their relatively secluded domestic lives.

On this economic and residential basis, Cypriot settlers
have been able to recreate adaptations of their traditional
social institutions in the British context. At the primary
group level, family and kinship ties, reconstituted through
the chain migration process, have been sustained and utilised
in work relationships and family businesses, and in the frequent contacts and visits which are possible in the context of
a localised settlement pattern. So far as secondary associations are concerned, a variety of forms of association have
been established, from the more informal encounters of the
local shopping centre, cafes and village-clubs, through to the
more formal organisation of churches, political associations,
women's philanthropical groups, evening and weekend schools,
and so on. Such institutions provide for participation by
Cypriots in activities on a community-wide scale (particularly
among Greeks, whereas among Turkish Cypriots such institutions
are less developed), and although the degree of participation
in them by individuals varies greatly, they contribute strongly to both the sense and the actuality of social cohesion
among Cypriots in Britain. On the other hand, it may well be
questioned whether it is appropriate to speak of ethnic 'communities' in this context, even among the more organised Greek
Cypriots where divisions, especially that between the Orthodox
Church and its supporters and the Communist political clubs
and their associated groups, are marked and faction-like. It
is also important, of course, to bear in mind that some
Cypriots are dispersed in parts of London quite distant from
the main settlement area, and also that some 30,000 or more
Cypriots reside in altogether different parts of the country.
However, in the major provincial towns and cities where Greek
Cypriot settlement has taken place (such as Manchester,
Birmingham, Cardiff and Leeds) a similar pattern of settlement
has grown up, often more centrally organised around the local
Greek Orthodox parish church with perhaps a stronger claim to
the designation 'community'.

The specific effect of this recreation of community-wide
patterns of association on family patterns is more difficult
to gauge. In the first place, the division between Church
and Communist factions among Greek-Cypriots provides for two
alternative conceptions of family life - a strictly traditional model, and one subject to definite modernising influences,

particularly towards greater liberalisation of relations between husband and wife in accordance with conventional socialist philosophy. Furthermore, it should be noted that Greek Orthodoxy as such does not in general provide overt direction as to the conduct of family life (in contrast to the Islamic teachings followed by Turkish Cypriots), and the Church's influence apart from its role in *sanctifying* marriage and its associated obligations (i.e. no divorce, abortion or contraception), is principally one of exercising a general conservatism as regards lifestyles among its practitioners. Both agencies therefore possess the capacity to accommodate themselves to change, although their basic dispositions on the issue are fundamentally opposed. This is often evident from the Greek Cypriot press, within which it is in the left-wing weekly 'To Vima' that one may find a far fuller coverage and freer discussion of the issues currently facing parents in Greek Cypriot immigrant families. The obvious degree of parental concern about such issues draws attention to the pressures for change that are being exercised on children of Cypriot parents from outside their community, principally through the educational system. Cypriot parents attempt to counteract these pressures, not merely in their direct up-bringing of their children, but also by participating in the wider activities already mentioned 'en famille', by regular visiting of family and friends, and by involving their children in Cypriot youth activities and weekend or evening schools. Although many of the latter groups are very active, there is no doubt that they cater for only a minority of Cypriot children. Any persistence of Cypriot ethnicity across the generations is likely to be more due to the personal bonds created within the family than to the efficacy of community-based institutions, and it is to consideration of these that I now turn.

FAMILY PATTERNS

The traditional pattern of Greek Cypriot (and indeed all Greek) family life is one in which the nuclear or conjugal unit of parents and children forms a very close-knit and exclusive primary group, patriarchal in structure, and sharing a strong sense of interpersonal loyalty and of joint responsibility for the honour and reputation of the whole. The family in this sense is the basic unit of traditional Greek Cypriot society; moreover, in spite of the existence of villages and wider forms of association, it would be true to say that only the family provides an enduring and truly solidary social context for the individual. The degree of exclusiveness and mutual opposition between families is such that Cypriot villages are more arenas for competition than in themselves cohesive units: families, though attached to the land through inheritance and interlinked among themselves through ties of kinship and marriage, are constantly striving to maintain and improve their standing and reputation, and to defend their honour against slights and misfortune. Family loyalty is the paramount virtue, while a family divided against itself evokes the kind of horror so well expressed in the ancient Greek tragedies. Only one's immediate family can one trust in matters of importance, and it is to them that one turns in time of trouble. Beyond the scope of one's near kinsmen, the world is an alien one, uncertain and threatening, and it is characteristically Greek to regard life as a challenge and an adventure, to be met boldly in the manner of the heroes of classical Greek literature. In this 'struggle' (a word often used by Greeks in this context) each family must remain united and upright, and must acquit itself as honourably as fate will allow.

The immediate family therefore traditionally aims to be self-reliant in everything. Each family farms its land, runs its household, travels, celebrates and generally faces the world as a single unit. Every member is expected to contribute his or her appropriate share in promoting the welfare and reputation of the group. None the less, just as the bonds within the family are close ones, so the ties with parents and siblings remain still strong when a child marries and sets up a new family on its own. Such ties, and hence those with cousins and other second-degree relatives also, are the ones on which a Greek can call in time of need, although as already emphasised, they are not ones which can or should be unequivocally relied on.

Within the family, there is a general division of labour between husband and wife. The husband would traditionally manage the family farm or other business, although a wife would also participate in farm labour, undertaking specific kinds of activity; she, on the other hand, would have the domestic side of family life as her exclusive responsibility. A husband is expected to be authoritarian and the source of family discipline: the wife, though she in turn expects obedience from her children, is seen as the provider of emotional warmth and security. In all the external dealings of the family, it is the husband who acts as its representative and protagonist, whereas the wife's place traditionally is strictly in and around the home.

This division of family roles is a direct manifestation of a fundamental feature of traditional Greek thought (which is mirrored also in certain religious conceptions). The two sexes are conceived of as essentially different in their nature and temperament. They are thought of as opposed, and yet as also complementary to each other. It is only in family life, in the privacy of the home, that this interdependence of the sexes is realised, and even here there is very strict demarcation of roles. Otherwise, in public life, the two tend to avoid each other, each having its separate sphere of activities. When they do come together in public, each group will keep as much apart as possible, the most obvious example of this being in church, where traditionally men stood (or sat) on one side, and women on the other. Among Cypriots in Britain, however, this practice is no longer followed.

The traditional ideal of masculinity is the active man, worldly and adventurous, strong and unflinching, free from the constraints of dependence on others, always loyal to his family. As in individual he is inspired by his sense of 'philotimo'. This word lacks any direct equivalent in English, though a literal translation would be 'love of honour'. The term denotes a kind of self-esteem, and it is often (rather misleadingly) compared with the English notion of 'pride'. True 'philotimo', however, lacks the elements of arrogance, of self-satisfaction and of passivity, that give the English notion its adverse connotation. Greeks tend to conceive of 'philotimo' as a sort of metaphysical entity, which transcends the crudeness of the physical body. It is in a sense a Greek's self-image, his own internalised version of what the ideal man should be.

The Greek conception of feminine character is closely bound up with notions about female sexuality. Women should be passive in temperament and should be submissive in their relations with men. Within the family, therefore, the wife comes wholly under the authority of her husband and her loyalty to him is complete. Outside the family, the woman lacks any clear-cut role, for in traditional Greek society public life is almost exclusively a male affair. Because of her sex and temperament, a woman abroad is regarded as a woman in moral danger, a prey to philandering males. Whether or not there is real danger is not necessarily to the point. For in a society where the moral reputation of each family counts for so much and where chastity is regarded as absolutely essential in a bride, even the merest suspicion of a lapse can still be severely damaging. Women should therefore be secluded from public life and in the company of men they should display the utmost modesty. This is especially important with adolescent and marriageable girls, whose words, looks, deportment and dress should all be unquestionably virtuous and who should never be allowed out unchaperoned. Departure from these ideals brings shame not only on the girl, but also on her whole family.

On the positive side, both as daughter and as wife, a
female is expected to display qualities of diligence and
industry in all that she does.   To say of a bride-to-be that
she is 'diligent' is high praise: her diligence and her
chastity are two sides of the same coin, the twin traditional
ideals personified.   Once married, she is expected to move on
directly to the very purpose of her existence - childbearing
and motherhood.   All her training in early life has led up to
this.   It is as a mother that she will be judged by others,
particularly by her husband, and it is as a mother that she
will be loved and remembered by her children.   To her sons
she feels especially close, since any honour and success they
win in life will be a testimony to the high quality of their
upbringing, and it will be to them that she will look for love
and support in her old age.   As she grows older, too, it will
be particularly through her sons that a woman may be able to
exercise influence on wider family matters, though in fact
despite the strongly patriarchal ideology, there are within
the family system a variety of ways in which women can exercise power informally over their men (cf. Friedl, 1967).

None the less, the value placed on cohesiveness and family
honour in Greek culture necessitates that disputes and problems arising in the family are at best suppressed, or at least
resolved within the group before any public awareness of them
becomes possible.   A mother's tact and skill, and the
father's authority and decisiveness should be the normal agencies for dealing with such matters.   Disputes, however, are
often accompanied by a strong and immediate outburst of felt
emotion, producing a sharp family row among all those present,
though one which through the immediate release of tension
commonly moves to a rapid, if not permanent, resolution.
Over serious issues, physical violence is often resorted to,
both in disciplining children, and by husbands against wives;
indeed, generally, since anger is expressed so directly, the
threat of violence is always present.   Misfortune, on the
other hand, such as in health or other personal matters,
elicits a different response.   Although there may appear to
be some reluctance to recognise a threatening problem when it
arises, as soon as its potential seriousness is appreciated,
a concerted effort will be made by the group to tackle it,
though as far as possible still from within.   Such an attempt
will continue until the strain on the family becomes intolerable, and even then it may only be the unintended signs of
stress noticed by outsiders that leads to any intervention.
For the family itself, to seek or accept outside help is
tantamount to a recognition of failure, and even with such
evident misfortunes as a child's disability, the sense of
self-blame on the part of a mother may be acute and quite

sufficient to bring on psychiatric symptoms such as those of
depression.   The strongly familistic ethic of Greek Cypriots
may therefore sustain a marked appearance of order and self-
discipline but the cost borne in terms of strain on the individual personality may often be considerable.

The above outline of the organisation, values and individual experience in Greek Cypriot families holds true in its
essentials for Turkish Cypriots also, although the cultural
expression of ideas is obviously very different.   Among
Turkish Cypriots perhaps less emphasis is placed on nuclear
family exclusiveness and, at least ideally, more on kinship
ties outside the family, particularly agnatic ones (in contrast to the bilateral character of Greek kinship).   Yet, in
practice, household composition among Turks is little different from that among Greeks.   In general, both Turks and
Greeks participate in a wider syndrome of cultural values and
social structure that characterises much of the Mediterranean
littoral, throughout which life in predominantly peasant farming communities is structured by the complementary sex-linked
personal ideals of 'honour' and 'shame', though apparent in a
variety of cultural manifestations (see especially Campbell,
1964; Davis, 1977; Peristiany, 1965b; Pitt-Rivers, 1961,
1963).

As 'core' values of the traditional culture, in the migrant
situation they may none the less be expected to be tenacious
and to survive numerous changes in the more superficial
aspects of Cypriot lifestyles.   The recreation of so many
traditional institutions and patterns of economic and social
organisation among Cypriot immigrants in Britain has allowed
many aspects of this traditional pattern of family life to
persist with little change.   Among the first-generation
migrants, however, two particular factors have introduced
change, both primarily affecting the position of women rather
than of men.   In the first place, the relative dispersal of
Cypriot households and their physical isolation (behind closed
doors in an inhospitable climate) have created a degree of
social isolation for women (especially mothers) at home that
contrasts sharply with the physical openness and outdoor character of life in Cyprus, with its opportunities for women to
meet collectively.   The modern urban role of the husband,
employed long hours outside the home, exacerbates this change
in women's situation.   Furthermore, the isolation has been
the more stressful as mothers alone have been obliged to cope
with the difficulties of bringing up children influenced by a
different and often poorly understood culture.   On the other
hand, Cypriot women migrants have had the usually novel opportunity of earning wages of their own through employment in the
clothing industry.   Although for many the wages may be low,

and entail long hours of work often at home rather than in
company at a workshop, this acquisition of income might be
expected to alter significantly the relationship and status of
Cypriot wives with regard to their husbands.   It appears,
though, that such wages, while often saved, none the less are
regarded as part of the collective family wealth, so that even
where the wives themselves have responsibility for managing
family expenditure, the decisions as to allocation and use are
made primarily by the husband.   With daughters' earnings on
the other hand, the position is often different.   This raises
the question of changes taking place among the second generation, which I shall discuss in the following section.

FAMILY CYCLE

Traditionally in Cyprus, the child's position in the family is
as one of a team.   Each is expected to pull his or her weight
in whatever tasks are allotted.   Children are subject to firm
parental discipline, and among themselves, elder brother is
responsible for younger, and brothers for sisters generally.
There is none of the child-centredness common in British or
American families, although Greeks greatly love children and
count childlessness a grievous misfortune.   Boys on the whole
are preferred to girls, and this is in accordance with the
emphasis placed in general on masculinity in Greek society.
Sons symbolise family vigour and will transmit the family name
to the next generation; sons, too, are traditionally considered greater economic assets than daughters, since they can
assist with the heavy work on the farm.   Daughters will drain
the family capital by requiring dowries on marriage, and will
then be 'lost', as it were, to another group.
   Only in the stage of infancy is the child an independent
focus of attention.   As a babe-in-arms, the whole family will
minister to its needs, and as a toddler it still receives a
great deal of notice.   As it moves into the third and fourth
years, though, the indulgence declines, and a process of
disciplining and toughening-up get under way.   In the subsequent pre-school years this becomes more systematic, for, by
now, children are expected to have some 'sense' of their own,
to be able to identify authority, and to have acquired some
notion of right and wrong.   Children of this age are required
to run errands and undertake other small tasks; they are
therefore expected to respond to commands, and their parents
start to use rewards, threats and even physical coercion.
Response to commands is by no means always immediate and
parents are often slow to follow up the initial order.   Young
children are commonly somewhat lax in their reactions, though

they soon learn to tell when a voice conveys urgency and conviction.   A certain amount of stubbornness, particularly in
boys, may even be admired, provided it is not overdone, for it
indicates the presence of the masculine virtues of strength
and independence.

The beginning of school introduces a new phase in the
child's life, principally because it now becomes for the first
time an independent representative of its family in the outside world.   Even before it feels any responsibility towards
itself, the child is made to feel a wider responsibility
towards its family, particularly so far as its school performance is concerned.   School, though, does not absolve the
child from duties at home, and from this age onwards boys and
girls increasingly begin to model their behaviour on that of
adults of their sex.

As they approach puberty children would traditionally come
to regard themselves as junior adults.   In many ways their
parents would treat them as such.   In normal family discussions, for instance, though no child, however young, would be
excluded from listening, the young adolescent would be entitled to a say: any opinion would always be considered
(though not of course necessarily accepted) by his elders.
At this age too, brothers and sisters tend to draw apart from
each other a little: a boy finds another as friend and com-
panion, while his sister withdraws more into the family
circle, her company mainly limited to that of female cousins.

Marriage remains well beyond the male horizon for a number
of years to come.   The period of the late teens and early
twenties is traditionally regarded as the best part of a
Greek's life.   Fully a man, yet untrammelled by the responsibilities of married life, he is free to indulge himself and
to seek adventure.   A girl, however, will begin to think
seriously about marriage from soon after the middle of her
teens;   for her this is an event of much greater importance
than it is for her brother.   For both, though, marriage is
the final step into full adult status.   The sense of self-
reliance and of personal responsibility which parents instil
in their children from the early teens is really part of a
long apprenticeship for adulthood, not to be mistaken for
adult status itself.   For, until their marriage, children
tend to remain both economically and psychologically dependent
on their parents in a number of ways.   Traditionally, the
community at large would never grant them recognition as full
members until they had families of their own.   Only recently,
during the post-war period, has there developed in Cyprus a
consciousness of youth as an autonomous group, separate from
and opposed to that of adults.

The two most important features of traditional Greek

Cypriot marriage are firstly, that marriages are arranged
between families, and secondly, that the bride must bring with
her a dowry to help set up the new family unit.   Love in a
marriage is considered desirable, though not by any means
necessary: more important is the financial side of the
matter, and the fact that the match must do justice to the
pair in terms of the standing of their families within the
community or neighbourhood.   Traditionally in the villages
the dowry was paid in kind, comprising sheep, land, household
linens and various other goods: as a whole these would constitute the daughter's share of the patrimony.   More recently
it has become common for the bride's parents to provide a
house for the couple.   On the other hand, the dowry requirement has clashed to some extent with the demand for secondary
and vocational education for girls, since the provision of
school fees for a child is normally regarded as the delivery
of its share of the inheritance.   To some extent, though, the
system is self-compensating, since in the eyes of a groom and
his family, education in a bride (like beauty and good character) may be a partial substitute for wealth.   The engagement
traditionally lasted for two to three years, being formalised
with a religious ceremony which in turn was the culmination of
a series of delicate negotiations between the families concerned.   These would normally have been conducted (and indeed
initiated) by a professional matchmaker.   The young people
themselves would be aware of the proceedings and would be consulted regularly: parents might exert pressure, but would
never force their children into a marriage against their will.
    Although the children on marriage would normally leave
home, the position of the elderly traditionally remains secure
with regard to economic and social support.   The father would
continue to farm either alone or in co-operation with one or
more of his sons, and the elderly couple remain, if mainly in
a titular sense only, as now more joint heads of the family.
It is particularly their presence and influence that sustains
a continued sense of an 'extended family' wider than that of
their children's own households, and it is the visiting and
co-operation in connection with the grandparents that makes
the wider unit a reality.   On their eventual death the bond
is broken, and although in sentiment the tie between siblings
is strong, the competing interests of their spouses, new
affines and young children now render the tie one which can no
longer command primary consideration.
    Turkish Cypriot families, again, demonstrate broadly simi-
lar patterns to those described for Greeks.   In Turkish families, the authority of the husband/father is traditionally
greater, and is more likely to sustain a patrilineal three-
generation household.   Solidarity among wider kin is greater,

and is enhanced by the preference for close cousin marriage
(on the father's side) which is prohibited for Greeks by the
Orthodox Church.

A variety of factors in the British context are operating
so as to produce changes in this traditional cycle, and these
include not only economic factors, but also demographic
changes, and above all the influence of formal British schooling in the socialisation of the child.   School is indeed the
main arena within which the tension between relations with
parents and with the wider society are worked out.   The degree
of impact of schooling and other agencies of British cultural
influence clearly depends on a number of further factors,
which include age of entry into school (in the case of child
immigrants), school composition and presence of older siblings, quite apart from the parents' own approach to child
upbringing.   Studies of friendship patterns at school have
shown clearly the predilection for fellow-Cypriot companions
within the school, particularly at the important developmental
stage around puberty and the early teens.   Data on intermarriage patterns also suggest that outward signs of accultura-
tion to British lifestyles do not indicate dissociation from
ethnic identification so much as variation within it.
Although the parental arrangement of marriages takes account
of (but is not initiated by) the child's wishes, most children
are willing to abide by the traditional format of marriage
procedures.   Parents in turn find themselves obliged to recognise the independence of mind of their British-schooled
children, and perhaps more importantly their degree of economic independence.

None the less, during the teenage period in particular,
relations between parents and children may be especially
strained, as parents strive to insist upon traditional standards of conduct which their offspring see as over-restrictive
and archaic by the standards of their British peers.   Whereas
boys to some extent escape this control in view of the traditional license for young men to display their independence,
girls on the other hand have become more sharply subject to
the exercise of parental authority.   This conflict over what
is appropriate behaviour for a teenage daughter is the major
point of tension within the Cypriot family in Britain, and has
led to much bitterness and resentment on either side, in the
more extreme cases culminating in violence and children leaving home.   On the other hand, perplexed Cypriot parents have
not uncommonly found that the rebellious teenager tends to
return to the ethnic fold as the years move on and the prospect of marriage comes to the fore.

Further changes in the family cycle among Cypriots in
London are evident from a recent study (Constantinides, 1979)

of a small sample of Greek Cypriot marriages.   Particularly
striking here was the fall in the birthrate.   As compared
with the large families traditionally common in Cyprus, the
young couples in Britain had only between one and three children, and generally saw three as the maximum family size desirable.   Nevertheless, the idea of marriage as 'for children'
rather than 'for love' (on the English model) remained strongly adhered to, and great importance was attached to the early
production of strong healthy infants.   None the less, despite
the official teachings of the Orthodox Church, couples were
willing to practise various methods of contraception, and also
abortion, where this was felt to be in the family interest.
The change in family-building patterns, however, clearly
permits a less onerous and enduring phase of childrearing for
Cypriot mothers, and in general it is noticeable that young
Cypriot men show willingness to help domestically (especially
in the care of very young children) where their own fathers
played virtually no part at all.   Here the English role
models may help to give legitimacy to essentially pragmatic
considerations, where in terms of traditional values such participation in the roles of the other sex is seen as 'shame-
ful'.

A final area of change is that of the position of the
elderly in relation to family and community.   Here it is only
recently that numbers have become at all significant.   Most
adult migrants were in their twenties and thirties, and where
elderly persons migrated, it was generally where a widowed
parent in isolation was brought over to be cared for by an
already settled married child.   The absence of a senior
generation among the settlers has no doubt contributed to a
loosening of bonds between siblings and cousins, and although
a new elderly stratum is now emerging, their lack of control
over major resources needed or desired by their children will
further weaken the traditional extended family ties.   Moreover, their very commitment to and idealisation of traditional
Cypriot culture already sets them apart from their more
British-culture oriented children, and can only increasingly
do so as the family cycle moves into its next generational
phase.   With on average fewer of their siblings among the
emigrants, and themselves with fewer children than their
parents' generation, they are tending to suffer a degree of
social isolation as well, which is further compounded by the
residential dispersal of Cypriots in London.   Their difficulties are ones that the ethnic community and outside agencies
have only recently begun to appreciate.

CONCLUSION

The migration and associated urbanisation of Cypriot families
has had a far less disruptive effect than among many other
migrant groups in the modern world, for three main reasons:
the strength of family ties, including in the migration process itself; the strength of ethnic identification; and the
pattern of economic opportunities created in British cities,
which have served as the basis for the recreation of a relatively self-sufficient ethnic community organised in terms of
traditional values and institutions.   In these circumstances,
given the separation of work from home, the novel physical
environment and the partial loss of traditional networks of
kin and affines, it is remarkable how little has been the
degree of cultural change necessary for the establishment of a
satisfactory 'accommodation' of Cypriots to the new British
context.   To speak of 'assimilation', however, would be to
jump well ahead of present trends, which reveal change in the
more superficial aspects of culture (including language)
rather than in core values and ideals.   Given first the homogeneity of the host culture, and second that of the settlers
and their continuity in social organisation, a rapid diversification of family lifestyles seems unlikely.   The Greek
experience in America, where almost complete assimilation has
occurred over three generations (Kourvetaris, 1978), for these
reasons should not necessarily be regarded as predictive of
the London Cypriots.   Furthermore, by contrast with, for
example, the earlier Jewish immigrants to Britain, with whom
in cultural terms the Cypriots have a certain amount in
common, such sources of diversity are largely absent.   Jews
were already differentiated by regional origin and religious
practice on arrival, and an element of contradiction (absent
among Cypriots) between strict religious teaching and successful adaptation to economic advancement has further helped to
produce the variety of lifestyles that characterise Anglo-
Jewry today.   For Cypriots, the rewards of the pursuit of
wealth are in no way necessarily incompatible with traditional
values and ideals; in so far as success can be measured in
purely material terms, its translation into social prestige is
achieved by emphasising family and general ethnic values
rather than disregarding or challenging them.   Such diversity
as does exist within the community tends merely to reflect
degrees of poverty/wealth and socio-economic status rather
than any more radical division, though the contrast between
those who have immigrated and those for whom Britain has been
their only home becomes increasingly evident.   A further
source of diversity will of course continue to be that between
Greeks and Turks, the latter being generally more traditional-

istic in their value orientation, not merely as regards family and religion, but also as regards educational and economic aspirations.   The degree of change involved in what on the surface appears as 'assimilation' may not be as great as might be supposed.   Shorn of its specific cultural symbolism and linguistic medium, Cypriot familism is not in principle at variance with the traditional family ideals of British culture generally.   In terms of its future development, it may perhaps best be viewed as in many respects lying at the Victorian-style patriarchal end of a continuum that encompasses both recent historical and contemporary variants of family life in modern Britain.

NOTE

1   I wish to thank Dr Pamela Constantinides and Dr Sarah Ladbury for helpful comments on a draft of this paper.

Chapter 12

Families in poverty
Harriett Wilson

To have to include a chapter on families in poverty in a book
which concerns itself with the diversity of family life in
Britain is an admission of communal failure to solve the problem of the distribution of wealth.   In the immediate post-war
period Britain enjoyed continuous economic growth, low unemployment, and fast rising real standards of living.   With
this went the foundation of a social security system and a
health service which promised the abolition of poverty.
These hopes were never met.   There is considerable inequality
in the distribution of resources, and the provisions made for
the support of those who are out of work, sick, disabled, or
elderly is inadequate.   Not only are insurance benefits
pegged beneath the 'poverty line', but in addition they are
underpinned by a means-tested system of supplementary benefits
which may lead to the 'poverty trap' - each additional pound
earned may cost the same or more in loss of means-tested benefits and in marginal taxes.   Moreover, low earnings, coupled
with inadequate child benefit, result in a considerable number
of families being in poverty in spite of full-time employment
of the head of the household.   The more recent economic stag-
nation, rapid inflation and fast rising unemployment provide
a backcloth to a bleak prognosis for families in poverty.

DEFINITIONS AND MEASUREMENT

Definitions of poverty have historically been expressed in
terms of a level of minimum needs.   These were gradually
widened to include a measure of relative deprivation in an era
of rising standards of living.   Rowntree's original poverty
line of 1901 was defined as an income that meets basic needs,
not including such things as a newspaper, fares to work, a
contribution to sickness and burial funds, or even a glass of

beer.   In the 1930s Rowntree defined poverty anew and allowed
for these and other customary items of expenditure.   Rowntree's rather austere poverty line formed the basis of the
provisions made after the war in the form of national assistance (now renamed supplementary benefit) for those among the
population who have no income and no resources, or whose
income is beneath the poverty line.   Persons dependent on
insurance benefits are entitled to supplement these on a
means-tested basis to a level considered by parliament to be
required for subsistence.   The supplementary benefit rate is
kept more or less in step with the cost of living index.
It covers essential expenditure but does not allow for the
purchase of major items, as for instance a winter coat, or
blankets, or the expenditure incurred in special diets
ordered by a doctor.   For such items an application for a
special grant is required which may or may not be given.
Persons who are no longer required to register for work and
who have drawn supplementary benefit for one year are
entitled to the long-term rate which is a little more
generous.   But these provisions are what parliament has
enacted in its wisdom over the post-war years, and there
is no guarantee that, meagre though they are, they will be
maintained or improved in a period of economic stagna-
tion.
    For convenience most investigators of the incidence and
distribution of poverty choose the long-term supplementary
benefit rate to express the deficiency of incomes of individual families.   This is done not because it is considered to
be an adequate standard but because it is the only measuring
device which is readily available.   By this standard it is
estimated that in 1977 just under four million families in
Britain had incomes either below or at SB level.   There were
just under one and a half million children in these families.
Taking all families in poverty and on the margins of poverty
(i.e. with incomes up to 40 per cent above SB) the total
number is estimated to be over seven and a half million, or
30 per cent of all families in Britain.   There are just over
three and a half million dependent children in these families,
more than a quarter of all dependent children in Britain
(Family Expenditure Survey, Hansard, 23 October 1979 and 24
October 1979).
    The distribution of persons and families in various circum-
stances is shown in Table 12.1, which shows families and individuals as (1) living below and not receiving supplementary
benefit, (2) as normally on SB, and (3) as living on incomes
within 20 per cent above the basic SB scale rate.   The total
number of persons living at or below the SB rate is over six
million (6,180,000);   and including those living on incomes

TABLE 12.1 Families and persons with low net resources: December 1977

Families and persons (thousands)	(1) Below SB and not receiving it		(2) Normally on SB		(3) Above SB (within 20%)	
	Fams	Persons	Fams	Persons	Fams	Persons
Under pension age:						
Married couples with children	160	670	150	700	360	1,520
Single parents with children	40*	110	320	900	50*	180
Married couples with no children	50*	90	80	160	80	160
Single persons with no children	390	390	390	390	180	180
Over pension age:						
Married couples	130	260	290	580	510	1,020
Single persons	490	500	1,410	1,410	830	830
All families	1,260	2,020	2,650	4,160	2,010	3,890

Source: Central Statistical Office, 'Social Trends', 10, 1980.

* Subject to considerable sampling error.

within 20 per cent above SB, the total number of persons is over ten million (10,070,000).

Old people are the group most prone to be in poverty, especially if the head of the household has no occupational pension.   Layard et al. (1978) showed that the risk of poverty is also high in single-parent families, in families where the man is disabled, and in families where neither the husband nor the wife had been working for most of the year. Fifty per cent of households where the man is disabled are in poverty;   and in families with three or more children, where the father had worked for less than 40 weeks in the year, very nearly three-quarters are in poverty.   In these families poverty would be even greater if the mother did not work.

DEPRIVATION AND LIFE CHANCES

A standard very different from the above defines poverty in terms of relative deprivation: 'Individuals, families, and groups in the population can be said to be in poverty when they lack the resources to obtain the types of diet, partici- pate in the activities and have the living conditions and amenities which are customary, or at least widely encouraged or approved, in the societies to which they belong' (Townsend, 1979a:31).   Townsend's study is based on a representative national sample survey in which data on wealth, living condi- tions, income, work and use of the social services were col- lected.   The evidence of various types of deprivation sug- gests that government estimates of poverty tend to be inaccu- rate because the poor in surveys like the Family Expenditure Survey are underrepresented.   Townsend measured deprivation by a standard of income below which people reported that they experienced various forms of deprivation; the threshold was at levels higher than the prevailing SB standard, especially for households with children and households with disabled people. The following adaptations to poverty provide examples of vari- ous types of deprivation: a retirement pensioner living alone did not have a summer holiday, seldom goes out, has meat not more than three times a week, and goes to bed at 8.30 in the winter to save fuel.   At Christmas she spent nothing on presents (Townsend, 1979a:311).   A young family with three children, father disabled, rely on secondhand clothing from jumble sales, have no shoes for rainy weather, do not go out in the evenings, and go to bed early to save fuel.   For breakfast the mother cooks porridge for the children but she and her husband have nothing.   They are used to days without a cooked meal, and they have little fresh meat (Townsend, 1979a:308-9).   On a deprivation standard of this kind

Townsend estimated the percentage of households in poverty to be one-quarter.

Townsend found the risk of being in poverty to be highly correlated with occupational class.   While none of the families of professional and managerial occupations was in poverty, the percentage of unskilled manual workers with three or more children was 64 on the SB poverty standard, and 93 per cent on the 'relative deprivation' standard.   The risks are also associated with dependency: the retired, the unemployed, the disabled.   In other words, the families typically affected by chronic conditions of poverty are in marginal societal positions.

The non-skilled worker is particularly at risk of experiencing spells of poverty.   Giddens (1973) talks about a 'dual labour market' which is a rapidly developing feature of Western economies and which results in a vicious circle of underprivilege for those without skills.   There is a 'primary market' catering for skilled workers and for others capable of negotiating long-term contracts collectively, and a 'secondary market' catering for those unable to enter the primary market. 'A primary market is one in which available occupations manifest the characteristics traditionally associated with white-collar jobs: a high and stable or progressive level of economic returns, security of employment, and some chances of career mobility.   A secondary market is one in which these conditions are absent' (Giddens, 1973:219).   Studies of the unemployed (Sinfield, 1970;   Daniel, 1974) and of deprivation in work (Wedderburn, 1974) have shown that the lower paid, largely non-skilled sector do not have the advantages of stable earnings, an incremental wages structure, security of employment, adequate insurance cover against sickness, or chances of career advancement.   Life chances of this sector are determined by very limited job opportunities and by a significantly greater risk of unemployment, sickness, or disability than the rest of the population.

From this follows that an assessment of the risk of poverty must take into account earnings' patterns in the life-cycle of families as well as opportunities for savings and investment, provisions for retirement, expectations of inheritance, appreciation of household and other property, employers' fringe benefits and access to credit or mortgage facilities. Runciman (1974) suggests that a new classification of households might be not in terms of occupation, but in terms of the potential for formation of assets, and that there appear to be four such groups: 'those for whom the net accumulation of assets is easy;   those for whom it's not easy, but they manage it;   those for whom it's not easy, and they don't manage it; and those for whom only a windfall will make it possible'

(Runciman, 1974:97).   Recent investigations of the distribution of wealth in Britain show a very slow shift in the decade
up to 1977, a period when total wealth rose by more than 300
per cent.   The wealthiest 10 per cent of the population still
owned 61.1 per cent in 1977, a drop of 7.6 per cent, and the
bottom 50 per cent of the population owned 5 per cent of
wealth, a rise of 1.5 per cent during the last ten years
('Social Trends', 10, 1979).

THE PERCEPTION OF POVERTY

The European Anti-Poverty Programme included a special survey
which was carried out in each of the EEC member States in
1976 to ascertain opinions and attitudes in relation to
poverty and the poor.   The survey found that within each
member country 'value systems' seemed to constitute a powerful
filter which affect the perception of poverty and the attribu-
tion of poverty to individual fault or social injustice.   In
Britain the blame is more often laid on individual laziness
and unwillingness to work.   In contrast, in France and in
Italy poverty was more often seen as a result of the injus-
tices of society.   An overall 54 per cent of those interviewed thought that the public authorities were not doing all
they should do for the poor, but 20 per cent of those interviewed in Britain considered they were doing too much (Commission of the European Communities, 1977).
    The way in which poverty is perceived is governed by basic
assumptions about the nature and organisation of society and
the role of individuals in society.   One such assumption is
that we live in a society with largely shared values that are
functionally related to its economic and social structure, as
argued by Parsons (1961).   These values are largely concerned
with the problems of social order.   On the level of the individual, character traits that are commonly appreciated include
ambition, the will to work hard, and the will to defer pleasures, to do one's duty, and to learn to carry responsibility.
This ethic emphasises conformity and stresses personality
development.   Adherents of this viewpoint place much importance on the socialisation process of early childhood which
facilitates the internalisation of these values.   The poor
and other disadvantaged groups are seen as deviants who lack
the ability to function as independent self-supporting members
of society.   Explanations of their state vary, but three main
approaches are discernible.   There are, first, explanations
in terms of a pathology.   This school of thought tends to
stress genetic aspects of the personality and emphasises sub-
normality, mental illness and heritability (see for instance

Tonge, James and Hillam, 1975).   A second school of thought
stresses cultural aspects of personality development and explains low status in terms of 'cultural deprivation', a
deficit in child development that needs to be filled by 'compensatory' education (see for instance Ferguson and Williams,
1969).   A third, less coherent, variety of thought is the
traditional one underlying Victorian poor law provisions, and
is expressed in terms of a 'social problem group, the source
from which the majority of criminals and paupers, unemploy-
ables, and defectives of all kinds are recruited' (Caradoc
Jones, 1945).   Persons of low status are not so much deprived
as depraved and are in need of stricter discipline and more
effective societal systems of control.   This view has largely
found expression in the literature concerned with problems of
public health (see for instance Wright and Lunn, 1971).

An alternative basic assumption questions the validity of
the organic society of shared values and postulates instead an
intricate pattern of possibly overlapping sub-cultural systems
within a larger society, with more or less sharp boundaries
defining their own sets of values.   Rex (1961) describes this
approach in terms of a 'conflict model'.   Sub-cultures often
historically precede a mainstream culture, as for instance the
various regional sub-cultures in Britain, or those introduced
by immigrant groups;   others arise in response to demands
within society, as for instance the post-war youth culture.
Whether a person's life is governed primarily by sub-cultural
values, or which aspects of his life are subject to them,
depends on a person's sense of identity.   In contrast to the
Parsonian metaphysics of order and hierarchy the conflict
model emphasises liberty and equality and diversity.   The
absence of material wealth and low occupational status are
explained not in terms of individual failure in a society
offering equal chances to all, but in terms of class barriers
which account for persisting inequalities.   The Nuffield
Social Mobility Survey (Goldthorpe, 1980) provides empirical
evidence that in post-war Britain those born into families of
non-skilled manual workers are more than three times less
likely to end up in administrative and professional occupations than are those born into these classes.   About 30 per
cent of the non-skilled manual sector experience intergenerational stability.   This core group, one must assume, are
caught in the poverty trap not just materially, but in the
full sense of the concept including lack of social competence,
narrow visions and a deep-seated feeling of failure and hope-
lessness.   In this view, what needs exploration is not the
personality characteristics of those in poverty but the social
mechanisms which distribute privileged positions in childhood
very unequally, and which do not question the personality

characteristics of those who enjoy these positions.   The
biographies of wealthy persons provide data which have not
been scrutinised to the same extent that the case records of
poor people have been; as an example here is an extract from
one of them:

> My parents belonged to a section of society known as 'the
> idle rich', and although, in that golden age, many people
> were richer, there can have been few who were idler.   They
> took no part in public affairs, did not read the news-
> papers, and were almost entirely without the old upper-
> class feeling of responsibility for their tenants.... My
> father had been put into the family firm and, at the age
> of twenty-two, was made a director.   He used to tell me
> with deep emotion that for two years he worked.   The ex-
> perience made an indelible impression on him.   An histor-
> ian of the family firm found no evidence of this.   On the
> contrary, he discovered that after two years young K.M.
> Clark was told by the Board that he must choose between
> sport and business.   He chose sport. (Kenneth Clark, 1974)

The following account provides a suitable 'Gegenstueck':

> My father had a small, shy talent which was crushed by the
> circumstances of his upbringing and working life.   He was
> a brainy boy, and recalled often with wry pride that he
> used to get nine out of nine on his school reports, three
> for reading, three for writing, and three for arithmetic.
> ... Unfortunately, when my father was only five his father
> died, and left my grandmother to bring up a large family as
> best she could.   There was no possibility of my father
> sitting the scholarship.... The acute consciousness of a
> wasted life, the bruising and blunting of a shy personality
> by the rough world of the mill, became the more unbearable
> to my father as he never got away from that world or even
> that particular mill.   Not altogether joking, he would say
> for the shocked amusement of the rest of the family, 'If
> Ah'd known then what Ah know now, Ah'd have thrown meself
> in t'cut' (canal). (Dennis Marsden, 1968)

THE SYNDROME OF POVERTY

In am empirical study of families in poverty (Wilson and
Herbert, 1978) the problem of stress and how parents adapt
were discussed in interview.   Stress in the milieu of poverty
is all-pervading in the sense that there is a chronic condition of being in want of something that is needed or desired,
and quite often this is an essential article, something that
people are expected to have and the absence of which marks
them as deficient.   Parents found this particularly upsetting

when it concerned their children.   Often money could not be
spared for the children to take part in woodwork or domestic
science lessons, or to go on excursions.   Parents gave
accounts of the difficulties they encountered in fitting the
children out for school.   For families whose income is at or
near supplementary benefit level there is no money to spare
for sports kits, or for a change of shoes.   Since 1944 local
education authorities have had powers to give grants for
school clothing, but in recent years drastic cutbacks have
been made.   The Child Poverty Action Group found that many
authorities now provide no grants, even for children at the
official poverty level, while the grants paid by other authorities do not meet the full costs incurred in obtaining a
school uniform (Tunnard, 1979).   An example of public attitudes towards children who do not wear the required clothing
at school is provided in a survey of schools serving a large
area of inner London (Rutter, 1979).   The objective was to
measure the impact that schools make on the development of
children in terms of behaviour in school, attendance, examination success, employment and delinquency.   Of these five
measures the behaviour rating scale is of interest in the context of this discussion.   The scale was made up of 25 items
of which three were about school clothing.   There was one
direct question: 'How many times have you not worn school
uniform last week?', and two observational items to record
(a) those not wearing uniform during the administration of
questionnaires, and (b) those wearing anoraks or overcoats in
the classroom.   Poverty thus counts towards 'misbehaviour' in
school.   The reactions of teaching staff towards children
without uniform are not recorded, nor are their comments on
the inclusion of three such items in schools that serve many
disadvantaged families.

Family activities in conditions of poverty are severely
curtailed.   Holidays with overnight stay away from home,
outings to theatres or places of interest, or sports activities are too costly and often families feel embarrassed to
take the children out because of an acute shortage of decent
clothing.   Parents may not be able to afford simple materials
for the pursuit of hobbies.   The children consequently have a
narrow range of activities and social experiences compared
with less disadvantaged children (Wilson and Herbert, 1978).

But prolonged poverty means more than that.   The accumulation of unpaid bills may have severe consequences, such as the
cutting off of electricity or gas supplies, or eviction for
rent arrears.   Major purchases are usually financed by means
of a loan from a 'club' that advances money at high interest
rates, thus adding to the cost of articles.   These experiences are described by Hoggart (1957) as 'a life of tightness

and contriving' that in his childhood had brought about 'a
feeling of sick envy of those who could pay their bills cheer-
fully', a life lived week by week in the knowledge that there
is little one can do about it except keep one's dignity.

Beyond these shared experiences of want many families in
chronic conditions of poverty have to adapt to additional
stresses, such as prolonged unemployment, or the presence of a
handicapped child demanding much attention from an already
overburdened mother, or chronic illness or disability of
either or both parents.   The correlation of social class and
rates of psychiatric disturbance has been recorded for some
time;   recent work by George Brown and others has established
the importance of severe life events and major long-term difficulties in the aetiology of depression among working-class
women (Brown, 1978).

Stress and nervous conditions can be caused by poor housing
conditions.   Houses which are damp, inadequately heated and
lack sufficient ventilation are detrimental to health.   In a
survey of a large number of children, reported by the Chief
Medical Officer, DES (HMSO, 1972) a social class gradient was
found in the frequency of chronic cough, history of bronchitis
and diseases of ears and nose.   The risks to health are manifold.   The poor physical development of disadvantaged children has been recorded in the course of a longitudinal study of
a cohort of children born in 1958 (Wedge et al., 1973).
Among eleven-year-olds there was a greater prevalence of infections generally and of respiratory infections in particular, accounting for significant differences in absence from
school.   A marked hearing loss was found four times more frequently among these children than among the rest.   The Court
Report (1976) provides an overall picture of the impact of
poverty on child health;   low income, bad housing and inadequate child health services combine to place children at
greater risk of ill-health, handicap and death.   Perinatal
and infant mortality, despite improvements overall, has remained at twice the rate among unskilled families than it is
in administrative and professional classes.   The Report expresses 'profound anxiety about the present stage of child
health in this country, about the shortcomings of the services
and those working in them, and about the prospects for new
generations if they are to grow up in the same deprived physical and emotional circumstances as many children contend
with.'

The evidence of multiple deprivation, affecting at the most
austere level some 10 per cent, and including those living on
the margins of poverty affecting one-fifth to one-quarter of
the population, gives reason to doubt the effectiveness of any
of the welfare measures which were adopted in the post-war era

of economic growth.   In fact, the rise in the number of
retirement pensioners, in the number of disabled persons and
in the number of long-term unemployed is constantly increasing
that sector of the population who are outside the labour
market and are dependent on social security.   By the end of
the century this number could well consist of a third of the
population.   The Beveridge philosophy, which inspired British
welfare legislation, assumed that Britain would maintain full
employment and a growth economy, and that the small minority
of those who were dependent on State support could be financed
by self-insurance and by taxing the better-off.   Experience
has shown that the measures advocated by Beveridge are not
effective.   'Poverty is a fraction of riches', says Townsend,
'poverty is the creation of resource distribution.   We cannot
understand or defeat it except in the context of present inequalities in the distribution of wealth and resources'
(Townsend, 1979b).   It is in this context that the lives of
poor families have to be seen in a collection of essays that
explore the diversity of family life.

Chapter 13

Families in divorce
Jack Dominian

HISTORICAL INTRODUCTION

Marital breakdown and divorce were handled for centuries by
the ecclesiastical courts and until 1857 marriages could be
set aside only by a combination of their approval and an Act
of Parliament. The number of divorces were of the order of
two to three each year and this privilege belonged to men of
standing whose wives committed adultery. The Matrimonial
Causes Act of 1857 brought divorce into the hands of the
secular law. The grounds for divorce remained similar but
showed a bias against women. Thus a man could obtain a
divorce on the grounds of the matrimonial offence of adultery
of his wife, but the wife had to show, in addition to her
husband's adultery, further aggravating offence on his part.
In 1923 this inequality was removed and women were permitted
to seek divorce on the same grounds as men.

The major law changes on divorce took place in 1937 and
1969. In 1937 a new law was introduced, still retaining the
concept of matrimonial offence which now consisted of adultery, desertion for 3 years, cruelty, and after 5 years of
admission to a mental hospital for mental illness. Furthermore, divorce was - and still is - not available during the
first three years of marriage except for grave reasons of
hardship or depravity. In 1969 the Divorce Reform Act was
passed, making the sole ground of divorce the irretrievable
breakdown of marriage. The grounds, however, on which this
conclusion is reached are predominantly the familiar matrimonial offences which are:

1 adultery which the petitioner finds it intolerable to live
  with;
2 that the behaviour of the spouse is intolerable and the
  petitioner cannot live with this;
3 that their spouse has deserted them for at least two
  years;

263

4 that the spouses have lived apart for at least two years
   and the respondent consents;

5 that the spouses have lived apart for five years, when
   divorce is obtainable despite the opposition of the respondent.

This Act came into operation in 1971 and in many ways has
transformed the divorce scene in that anyone who really wants
a divorce can have it by using the provisions of the Act.   An
account of the background of this Act is available (Lee,
1974).

   In addition to the changes in the law, there has also been
financial support to litigants through the Legal Aid and
Advice Act of 1949, with financial revisions in 1960 and 1970
for inflation.   Recent changes in the Legal Aid Scheme do not
provide for divorce but financial assistance is still available for legal advice on the distribution of property, custody
and care of children and if the divorce is defended.   Divorce
has increased substantially in the last 20 years and one
explanation offered for this has been the increased financial
assistance available.   This view has been opposed by Chester
(1972) who states - 'The most plausible explanation of the
divorce figures for the past two decades is that they reveal a
decline from the post-war numbers, followed by a rapid and
equally continuing rise which is related to social and cultural changes much more fundamental than amendments to the terms
of a somewhat limited welfare scheme.'

DEMOGRAPHIC DATA

Rise in divorce

The factors that contribute to the incidence of divorce are
the size of the population, the percentage ever married and
the absolute change in the number divorced.

   The size of the population of England and Wales was some 32
millions in 1901 and is about 49 millions at present.   During
the last two decades the population has increased by some 3
millions, not sufficient in itself to account for the large
increase in divorce ('Population Trends', 1979).

   As far as marriage is concerned the annual total of first
marriages for both parties has naturally risen with the growth
of population from about 253,000 in Great Britain at the
beginning of this century to some 357,000 in 1971 but this
increase reflects also a growing propensity to marry.   The
percentage of ever married shows that by the age of 49 the
ever married were consistently 90 per cent for men and 93 per
cent for women in 1974.   It is worth noting, however, that

1971 was the peak year for first marriages which have been declining in numbers since then.   A further examination of the fall in first marriages indicates that this is due to a decline in marriage rates of people aged 25 or under and particularly of teenagers.   This drop in teenage marriages is significant, not only because youthful marriages are prone to dissolution, but also because youthful marriages – accompanied by premarital pregnancy – are particularly vulnerable to marital breakdown.

   There are several ways of showing the increase in divorce. Divorce can be calculated in terms of absolute petitions or divorce numbers, divorce rate per 1,000 married population, or the rate per 1,000 women who were ever married.   In this chapter I will confine myself to the first designation because petitions in particular show the range of marital disruption even better than divorce figures.

TABLE 13.1 Petitions and divorces for dissolution and annulment of marriage for selected dates for England and Wales

Year	Petitions	Divorces
1911	902	650
1921	2,848	2,733
1931	4,784	4,013
1941	8,305	6,368
1947	48,500	60,254
1951	38,382	28,767
1961	31,905	25,394
1971	110,900	74,400
1972	110,700	119,000
1973	115,500	106,000
1974	131,700	113,500
1975	140,100	120,500
1976	146,400	126,700
1977	170,000	120,000

Source: Registrar General

Table 13.1 confirms the great increase in petitions and divorce which began from about 1961, following the reduction

of the post-war bulge.   This increase is absolute and cannot
be accounted for by an increase in population, marriages or
longevity in life expectation.   A significant cultural
phenomenon has emerged which is also present in other European
countries (Chester, 1977) and in the USA (Glick and Norton,
1973).

Persons involved

The number of men, women and children involved in divorce
every year is approximately the couple and on an average two
children.   A more accurate estimation is given for the year
1973 ('Population Trends', 3, 1976).

TABLE 13.2   Percentage distribution of couples who were
divorced in 1973 by number of children

Age of wife at marriage	No. of children	Duration of marriage in years (all durations)
All ages	0	25
	1	24
	2	27
	3	13
	4+	11
Total divorce in thousands	106.0	

An approximate calculation from Table 13.2 shows that the
number of adults and children involved in 1973 was about
373,000.
   A further picture of the number of single-parent families
emerges from another study which shows that by 1976 there were
750,000 one-parent families involving 1.25 million children
('Population Trends', 13, 1978).

Remarriage

The high number of divorced is accompanied by an equivalent
increase in second marriages.   The increase in remarriage is
indicated by the fact that in 1965 11 per cent of the 370,000
in that year involved a divorced person.   This increased to
22 per cent in 1972 and had become 1 in 4 marriages by 1974.

TABLE 13.3   Remarriages: numbers in thousands

Year	Men	Women
1951	23.1	21.1
1961	18.8	18.0
1971	42.5	39.6

The swelling of the total number of marriages by second marriage is an ever-increasing phenomenon and will continue to be
so whilst divorce continues at the high peaks it has attained.
The peak rate of remarriage for both divorced males and
females occurs in the age group 25-9.   At every age the remarriage rate for divorced persons exceeds that of the widowed
and that of males of either status exceeds that of females
('Population Trends', 3, 1976).   At present it is calculated
that, if remarriage rates were to remain at current levels,
one in five of men and women born around 1950 will have
entered a second marriage by the age of 50.

Duration of marriage and divorce

The data available for the duration of marriage prior to
divorce have normally been calculated on the length of marriage to divorce.   This is known as the de jure duration.
However, couples often split up some time before they obtain a
divorce and thus the de facto duration of marriage is a much
more accurate description of the duration of marriage.   This
fact has been brought out by Chester (1971) and Thornes and
Collard (1979).   Thus Chester found that 38 per cent of
divorcees had ceased to cohabit by their fifth year but only
16 per cent had divorced during that time and Thornes and
Collard found that 34 per cent of their divorcees had separated by their fifth anniversary and only 11 per cent had
obtained a divorce.   These facts have to be taken into
account when the natural history of marital breakdown is
examined.
   By emphasising the de facto duration of marriage we get a
better idea of the duration of marriage.   It can be seen from
Table 13.4 that breakdown occurs throughout marriage but there
is a high incidence in the first five years and another peak
late in marriage.   If we combine the figures for the first
ten years, some 60 per cent occurs during the early years
which makes this phase of marriage particularly vulnerable.
What is the length of time between the facto and the jure

TABLE 13.4   Year in marriage when final separation occurred

		% of 520 divorced men and women	
By	1st anniversary	5	
	2nd "	7	
	3rd "	8	34%
	4th "	6	
	5th "	8	
	6th "	6	
	7th "	5	
	8th "	7	26%
	9th "	4	
	10th "	4	
	11th "	6	
	12th "	3	
	13th "	2	19%
	14th "	4	
	15th "	4	

Source: Thornes and Collard, 1979.

duration? Chester (1971) and Thornes and Collard (1979)
noticed respectively a duration of 4.6 and 5.2 years and
McGregor found a mean delay of five years from magistrates
court to divorce (McGregor et al., 1970).   This interval and
any further period prior to the formation of further relationship is important from the health and psychological point of
view because the separated spouses experience considerable
stress (Dominian, 1979).

Recognition of marital problems

One more demographic point worth considering is the recognition of marital problems by gender.   Which of the two spouses
begins to sense dissatisfaction and feels that there is something wrong?   The evidence is fairly unequivocal that it is
the wife who is first alerted to the problem.   In a study of
recognition of marital problems of 520 divorcees by the first
anniversary of marriage, 44 per cent of wives as compared with
23 per cent of men had recognised there was a marital problem
and, indeed, by the third anniversary 69 per cent of wives had
reached this conclusion compared to 46 per cent of husbands
(Thornes and Collard, 1979).   The research evidence in fact
generally supports the notion that marriage tends to satisfy
far more the physical and emotional needs of men than of women

and that the latter have to make greater adjustments than their husbands (Gurin et al., 1960).

Conclusion on demographic data

The demographic data indicate that divorce in England and Wales has rapidly increased in the last twenty years, affecting couples at all stages of their marriage but with a pre-dilection for the early years and a smaller peak in the last phase of marriage.   Clearly different factors are operating for marital breakdown in the various phases of marriage and the next section will examine these.

LIFE-CYCLE OF MARRIAGE AND DIVORCE

The concept of life-cycle

The description of marriage is often limited by referring to it as an institution which is described in static and demographic terms.   Couples who remain married on average some fifty years do not experience it in this way.   Marriage is far from a static entity as the couples progress from being a dyad, to having their children, who in turn attend school and grow up, depart and leave the couple in the original dyadic structure.   Each phase of marriage has its own unique charac-ter which is experienced with rich variations by individual couples.   Social scientists have been trying to capture and describe this unfolding process in a life-cycle.
    In a classical life-cycle description proposed by Duval (1977) of the USA an eight-stage process has been proposed. Stage 1 describes the couple without children; stage 2 from the birth of the oldest child to 30 months; stage 3 covers the phase of the first child from 30 months to 6 years; stage 4 studies families with schoolchildren with the oldest child between 6 and 13; stage 5 the oldest child is now between 13 and 20; stage 6 the family has young adults; stage 7 con-cerned with middle-aged parents (empty nest to retirement) and the final stage 8 covers the period of retirement to the death of one partner.
    In this paper a shorter version proposed by the author will be used (Dominian, 1979).   This is a three-phase cycle with each phase being examined for the prominent social, physical, emotional, intellectual and value systems.   The three phases include phase 1 as the first five years which approximate from the mean age of marriage (25.1 for men and 22.8 for women) to the late twenties or early thirties, a second phase from 30 to 50 and a third phase from 50 to the death of one spouse.

Phase 1: first 5 years of marriage

Social factors

1 Age at marriage   The relationship between age at marriage and outcome has been studied extensively and the results have been repeatedly the same.   Youthful marriages are risky propositions ('Population Trends', 1976; Thornes and Collard, 1979; Glick, 1957).   The situation is summed up in 'Population Trends' thus:

> There is a very much enhanced risk of divorce at any given duration if the bride is under 20 at marriage.   For example, 9% of all marriages contracted in 1963 had ended in divorce by 11 years of marriage duration; but where the bride was under the age of 20 years at marriage, 16% had ended in divorce at the same marriage duration, compared with only 8% where the bride was aged 20-24 at marriage. The much higher risk of divorce of younger brides is enhanced still further if the groom is also under age 20 at marriage.

Two qualifications need mentioning as far as youthful marriages are concerned.   The first is that this age group contains an excess of premarital pregnancies and also couples from social class V and both factors are known to increase the risk of divorce.   Of course, not all youthful marriages break down and those that survive have support from parents, usually good housing from the beginning of marriage and their personalities are able to endure stress better than those who succumb to the vortex of disadvantage which this age group experiences.

2 Premarital pregnancy   The presence of premarital pregnancy enhances the possibility of divorce.   Work over several decades by Christensen (1963) has confirmed this finding which has been subsequently found in other studies ('Population trends', 1976; Thornes and Collard, 1979).   In England and Wales the proportion of brides who were pregnant on their wedding day increased from the mid-1950s until 1967 when 22 per cent of all spinster brides - but 38 per cent of those aged under 20 - had a birth that was premaritally conceived. But since 1967 there has been a sustained reduction in the number and proportion of brides who were pregnant at marriage and in 1973 only 16 per cent had a birth that was premaritally conceived.   The decline of premarital pregnancy was particularly evident for brides 18-22 with little change for those aged 16 and 17.   The fall of premarital pregnancy may be associated with the Family Reform Act which permitted earlier marriage, the availability of contraception or abortion.

There are several reasons why premarital pregnancy may

affect the marriage adversely.   Such a couple may not be
ready for marriage, may not be particularly attached to their
spouse if the conception was an 'accident' and the couple may
lack accommodation, adequate financial resources and kinship
support.   Another factor is that the presence of the baby
prevents the formation of a strong bond between spouses whose
attention is diverted to the needs of the child (Pohlman,
1969).

As with the factor of age, not all premaritally conceived
pregnancies end in divorce and there is evidence that those
whose marriage continues had longer courtships, less parental
opposition, less premarital problems and less post puerperal
depression (Thornes and Collard, 1979).   But, independent of
the outcome, all those with premarital pregnancies tended to
share a higher sexual activity within marriage, premaritally
and extramaritally, to have less religious affiliation, to be
working class and not to have had a selective education.

3 Housing   Most couples would like to start with accommodation of their own where they can have the privacy and comfort
to establish their new style of life.   Research evidence
(Thornes and Collard, 1979) shows that a divorce group were
more likely than a continuously married one to share their
housing and to be in conflict with the shared party by the end
of the first year of marriage.   Furthermore, the divorced
moved from one accommodation to another far more frequently
than the continuously married.   These changes were not
planned but often forced by circumstances which led to hap-
hazard and impulsive change.   Such changes mean that the
couple had frequently to interrupt their contact with neighbours and friends and start afresh, which is stressful.

4 Social class and education level   Repeated studies in the
USA have shown an inverse relationship between social class
and divorce;   that is to say the lower the social class the
higher is the risk of divorce.   The same applies to education
level (Glick and Norton, 1971).   In England and Wales an
early study by Rowntree and Carrier (1958) showed no such
inverse relation.   A more recent study has generally confirmed the absence of this inverse relationship but it was noted
that social class V had the greatest propensity to divorce,
followed by social class III non-manuals (Gibson, 1974).
Gibson's findings have been confirmed in the study by Thornes
and Collard (1979).   But what are the reasons for this finding?   Social class V has in fact a loading of divorce-prone
partners through a number of social reasons, such as age at
marriage, premarital pregnancy, housing difficulties and other
adverse factors.   Social class II non-manual have other problems.   They are particularly vulnerable to the fact that
their social position is not safely entrenched in either the

lower or the upper socio-economic groups.   In a sense they are a social class in transition without clear support from either the social class above or below them.   In particular, if the husband has done well at work and is moving upwards in the social scale, this may result in the seeking of new friends and a different style of life with which his spouse may not be comfortable.   The ensuing tensions may contribute to the alienation of the couple as they move into different social worlds.

Education level, which seems to play an important role in the US with the same inverse findings, is not found in England and Wales.

5 *Religion*   Marriages of mixed religious faith are more prone to divorce in the US (Landis, 1962).   The absence of any religion in either couple was found to be associated with marriage vulnerability (Landis, 1963), a finding which has also been confirmed in the UK (Thornes and Collard, 1979).

As might be expected, regular church attendance is associated with greater marriage stability, a finding in the US and in this country (Goode, 1956; Thornes and Collard, 1979). These findings are explainable on the grounds that both the Christian and Jewish denominations lay great emphasis on indissolubility and thus, the more committed is the adherence to one of these faiths, the greater is the barrier to divorce. But, since the secularisation of society is proceeding at an accelerated rate, it is possible that these findings will assume lesser importance in the future.   But, when husband and wife are deeply involved in their faith, then - depending on the denomination - there may be conflict over contraception, abortion, sterilisation, religious education of children and the value orientation of the couple.

Other social factors

The factors mentioned above have been measured and assessed over several decades and a certain clear picture has emerged from these variables.   There are other factors, however, which are not easily measurable and reliance is placed on observation of repeated patterns.   These factors include separation from parents, agreement on financial matters and the distribution of household duties, the handling of premarital friendships or the arrangement of leisure and work.

1 *Separation from parents*   In Western culture marriage means the transfer of centrality from parents to spouse.   The majority achieve just that.   There is, however, a small number of marriages in which the parents remain the central focus of one or other spouse.   Whenever they need to discuss

anything of importance, to seek advice, to initiate something important, it is mother or father who is consulted and not the spouse.   Naturally this creates jealousy and anger in the bypassed spouse.   When trouble escalates as the spouse complains of being ignored, there may be an impulsive departure by the parent-orientated spouse who returns to their childhood home.   The bond between child and parent is stronger than that with the spouse and the consequences are that parents or in-laws continue to rule the lives of the newly married.   The traditional jokes about mothers-in-law have a certain validity in practice.

A particular form of complexity is met when both spouses are trying to emancipate from their parents but do not find each other strong enough to take the place of their parent. The spouses are eager to sever their connection but they do not find their partner reliable or strong enough to become a substitute security.   Both partners have much greater needs than they have available resources of emotional stability and the marriage may founder on the continuing of the parental attachment.

2 *Financial arrangements*   In the presence of severe marital conflict the question of money often arises.   The wife complains that her husband is stingy or financially irresponsible and the husband retaliates that his wife is a poor housekeeper or is unduly indulgent with her personal appearance.   The wife in turn may complain that her husband drinks, gambles or cannot cope with money.   Bills are left unsettled, threats to cut off various supplies recur at monotonously close intervals. Money has a reality of its own; it is needed for material survival.   But gradually it also assumes a symbolic significance of affection.   'If you loved me you would not be stingy.'   Or 'I would not always have to ask first', or 'You would not complain that I am extravagant.'   But, although money has a significance of its own in these two ways, it may also be used as a conflict to hide deeper personal conflicts within the marriage.   Occasionally a wife has to take charge of all bill paying because her husband cannot cope.   She does this which gives her a degree of security but she resents her husband's incompetence and her image of him turns gradually into one of less trust, respect or admiration.

At the beginning of marriage the wife is usually working and the husband's financial irresponsibility may be rectified by her earnings.   But when she becomes pregnant and may have to withdraw from the world of work temporarily, then the marriage with unsatisfactory financial arrangements takes a turn for the worse.   Occasionally, however, the recognition of the utter dependence of wife and child on the husband acts as a sobering experience which makes him become more responsible financially.

3 The distribution of household chores   Marriage is in the
midst of fundamental changes which include a greater sharing
of household tasks by both spouses.   Both are encouraged to
run the house.   How this can be done in a marriage where both
spouses have a career has been described by the Rapoports
(1971).   This is an example of effective co-operation.   At
the other end of the scale, a husband promises to help and
fails to do so.   When his wife is working and has also the
whole responsibility for the house, she begins to get excessively tired and starts complaining.   The complaint extends
to the fact that the husband continues to go out and pursue
his bachelor leisures without assisting at home or his assistance is more in the nature of a hindrance.   There are other
men who promised to help during courtship without genuinely
realising what this implies and, after marriage, revert to the
traditional husband and wife roles.

Another common complaint is that of the husband promising
to fix some part of the house which needs repair and either
not doing it or starting it and never finishing.   If the
kitchen is the area involved, the wife feels particularly
upset and complains.

4 Friends   Every couple come to marriage with their own set
of friends.   Some of these will be assimilated and become
friends of both;   others will remain friends of the individual
spouse and others will be dropped.   Difficulties begin when a
particular friend assumes such significance that the spouse
feels jealous or threatened.   If this friend had an affair
with the spouse, the jealousy may be increased.   There is a
particular syndrome when a husband or wife feels so insecure
that they continue to question their partner about previous
friendships and affairs.   This questioning can extend repeatedly into the early hours of the morning when the drowsy and
fatigued spouse is questioned for the umpteenth time of what
his/her love making was like with the person concerned and how
it compared with their present intercourse.   Such persistent
jealous questioning can be the beginning of the end of a marriage as the jealous partner tries to catch out their spouse
over details and is never satisfied with the answers.

Another problem with friends may arise when one spouse has
no friends and the other has several.   The isolated spouse
relies on their mate's social world and such dependence may be
coupled with jealousy, rudeness and rejection of the circle of
friends, leaving the wife isolated and restricted to her
partner's company.

5 Leisure   The balance between sharing leisure and doing
things alone needs to be worked out by every couple.   The
time spent by the husband alone in the pub or playing games
has to be balanced by the activities of the wife who plays

sport, visits her friends or relatives.   Going out together
visiting, to the cinema, theatre, pub, etc. is a shared
activity which will occupy increasingly the time of the
couple.   Difficulties arise when one spouse resents allowing
their partner any time on their own or are not inclined to do
anything together.   The spouse may feel watched and imprisoned as their leisure activities are curtailed and disap-
proved.   Hasty courtships which do not give the couple a
chance to know each other may lead to marriages where little
of mutual interest is shared.

Another complaint is that the husband returns home, has his
meal and is glued to the TV without wanting communication or
any desire to listen to his wife.

6 Work   The pattern for most husbands is to continue their
work after marriage.   Increasingly that applies to the wives
as well.   Some 70 per cent of married women are working in
their first year of marriage and this percentage drops during
this phase of marriage so that, by the fifth year of marriage,
some 30 per cent are working ('Population Trends', 2, 1975).
The drop in percentage is related to the timing of the first
baby.   Recently childbearing has been deferred in the early
years of marriage and so both spouses remain economically
active.

Work, however, not only provides financial independence
for the wife; it also gives her access to friends at work
and is a powerful source of her identity.   When she ceases to
work she may find being alone with a young child a very trying
period.   Reference will be made again to this transition.

The feature that stands out for the working wife is her
degree of tiredness if her husband does not help in the house.
Tiredness leads to irritability, loss of sexual interest and
frequent arguments which are one cluster of problems in this
pattern of marriage.

Physical factors

The principal element in the physical life of the couple is
the success of their sexual life.   However, before this is
described there is an infrequent pattern which is worth mentioning.   This is the pattern when one spouse falls seriously
ill immediately after marriage and spends long periods in
hospital before sexual intercourse is established.   Common
conditions for this may be acute rheumatoid arthritis, tuber-
culosis, ulcerative colitis, psychiatric and other rare illnesses.   The concern of the husband is with the health of his
wife and sexual needs are suppressed.   If a number of months
or years pass prior to initiation of intercourse, this may in

fact be impossible.   In these rare instances marital breakdown may ensue.

Sexual satisfaction and a good marriage often go together.
It is possible to dissociate the two but this is rare,
although good marriages without sex do exist.   In a study in
the USA of 100,000 women, 84 per cent of the wives who said
they were 'mostly happy' described the sexual side of their
marriage as good/very good.   Conversely, the majority (53 per
cent) of the wives who reported a poor sexual relationship in
the marriage were mostly unhappy (Levin and Levin, 1978).

In a study in Britain 520 divorced men and women claimed an
initial sexual satisfaction of 79 per cent and 570 continued
married men and women of 88 per cent, the divorced women
showed a higher percentage (24 per cent) of dissatisfaction
than divorced men (15 per cent) (Thornes and Collard, 1979).
Thus some 12-20 per cent of spouses experience difficulties in
their early years of marriage with the divorced showing a
higher incidence.   What are these difficulties?

These difficulties include first of all the factors of communication and shared responsibility.   Sometimes couples fail
to tell each other what pleases them and how they want their
spouse to make love to them.   They may be shy, unaware of
what they want and an unsatisfactory pattern of intercourse is
established from the very start.   A husband may lack sensitivity, variation;   may be convinced he is pleasing his wife
when this is not the case and the wife may be afraid to voice
criticism in case she hurts her husband.   He may make love to
her under the influence of drink, without the sort of hygiene
she expects from him, be rough, inattentive or lacking in preliminary affection.   Another problem is the couple who are
both sensitive, cannot accept personal responsibility over any
of their actions and accuse each other that the sexual difficulty is entirely the other's fault.

Other reasons are related to sexual dysfunction.   The dysfunction that may be encountered immediately is that of non-
consummation (Friedman, 1962).   Non-consummation is often
present when a wife is unduly sensitive of vaginal penetration
through fear or immaturity and her husband is too gentle or
unwilling to hurt her.   After a few failed attempts the
couple give up and the subject is not referred to again until
there is pressure to have children.

A low sexual desire on the part of either partner, but particularly the husband, may mean intercourse every four to
eight weeks which very soon becomes a tension focus between
the couple (Jehu, 1979).   Other problems include persistent
impotence or premature ejaculation on the part of the husband
or vaginismus, anorgasmia - and possibly dyspareumia - on the
part of the wife.   All these topics are extensively treated

in modern studies which are focusing on such problems in particular after the pioneering work of Masters and Johnson
(1970).

All these difficulties may appear early in the marriage and
some such as loss of libido, impotence, premature ejaculation
and vaginismus or anorgasmia, at a later stage.   Increasingly, however, as personal expectations of fulfilment rise, such
failures - which in the past were tolerated - are accepted
less nowadays.

Finally, one or more affairs early in marriage may be tolerated but may also spell the end of the marriage, depending on
the sensitivity of the partner.

Emotional factors

The emotional conflicts early in marriage which lead to marital breakdown are related to the ability to demonstrate affection and to receive it, to a sensitive awareness of mutual
needs and to personality disturbances of such a degree that
the spouse finds it impossible to live with.   Often when a
marriage falls apart in the first five years of marriage a
detailed history will reveal the presence of one or both partners who are extremely vulnerable.   Their vulnerability may
be due to a deprived childhood or to an excess of anxiety in
their make up.   These are men and women who find a close relationship difficult and expect love, affection, understanding, to a considerable degree.   They have little capacity for
disappointment and their trust and hope vanish quickly.   When
they encounter a spouse who lacks sensitivity, is undemonstra-
tive, drinks too much, gives too little to the partner,
gambles seriously, has a low threshold to frustration, loses
their temper rapidly and then withdraws for long periods, then
the presence of one or more features erodes the hope of the
partner very quickly.   Often such vulnerable personalities
attract each other and they compound their disappointment.

Another pattern of emotional difficulties in this phase is
the marriage of a man who unconsciously projects maternal expectations on his wife and behaves as a dependent child or a
wife who treats her husband as a father figure.   Indeed, the
projection may not be as clear as this and the spouse projects
on the partner the characteristics of desired qualities in
either parent or seeks features that were missing in childhood.   Sometimes spouses marry someone similar to an imagin-
ary or dominant parent and they find in practice that their
spouse refuses to act this role but wants to be treated as
themselves.

When two very deprived persons marry they want a lot of

love from each other which may not be available, but an even
more complicated situation arises when one of them tries to
love the other and finds that their spouse cannot accept love
but are extra sensitive to any rebuff, criticism or rejection
which they seize on at once and both exaggerate and enlarge
the hurt.

These combinations of emotional conflicts are finally completed by the failure of one spouse or both to appreciate what
their partner needs.   Whether the need is sexual, emotional,
social or intellectual, if the spouse cannot comprehend or
respond, there soon arrives the moment when their needy partner will despair and give up.

As with the sexual life, emotional fulfilment has become a
normal expectation for more and more couples and emotional
conflict is a big contributor to marital breakdown and
divorce.

Intellectual and value system

Usually couples will select one another from similar backgrounds and therefore will share a high proportion of similar
values and intelligence.   However a hasty courtship, a marriage that is opposed by the parents and is entered into in
defiance of their strictures or one in which a spouse, usually
the husband, marries below his own social level, may lead to
situations where the couple share very little apart from their
sexual life.   If their leisure, circle of friends, interests,
opinions and values are vastly different, the marriage is unlikely to survive.   It must be stressed, however, that such
mixed marriages in education, religion and background form a
small contribution to the overall number of divorces.

Children

The advent of the first child is of the greatest significance
in marriage.   It changes the couple from a twosome to a
threesome, from wife to mother, husband to father, often withdraws the mother from work with all the consequences of loss
of economic independence and self-esteem and it introduces a
great deal more fatigue for both parents but particularly the
mother.   A couple may face problems about the care of the
child when there is conflict about upbringing but, increasingly nowadays, both parents play an active and positive role in
the care of their child.

Tiredness, irritability and temporary loss of sexual
activity is a triad that most young parents will experience to

a certain degree, coupled with a diminution of time for each
other and opportunities to go out together which in turn
depends on the availability of reliable baby sitters.

One feature stands out in relation to childbearing and marital breakdown.   A small percentage of women get a prolonged
period of post puerperal depression.   Many mothers get temporarily depressed, the so-called maternal blues that may last
from a few hours to a few days (Pitt, 1973).   It is the
former that contributes to divorce.   These are the mothers
who remain depressed, tired, irritable, lose their sexual
desire and are often in a hostile and angry mood.   They
remain tense and agitated, lose their concern for their
appearance and drag themselves around from month to month.
The condition may last from several months to several years
and acts in the most destructive manner to the marriage.
Only in the presence of a very patient and loving husband can
this personality change in the wife be tolerated for long
periods.

The cause for this condition is unknown and there are dia-
metrically different views from social explanations, regarding
the isolation and absence of male support, in working-class
women with a loss of mother under the age of eleven (Brown and
Harris, 1978) to organic causes such as hormonal imbalance.

The postpuerperal period has other social factors which
affect the wife.   Often she stops working and this leads to a
loss of economic independence, the reward of doing something
creative and the companionship of colleagues.   For some
women the availability of reliable baby minders, creches and
pre-school nursery classes becomes essential in order to facilitate a return to work.   An early return to work is essential
for some women and is one of the many topics examined on the
subject of parenting by the Rapoports (1977).

Thus the post puerperal syndromes which are so intimately
related to marital outcome are the result of complex social
and psychological factors which impinge on both parents but
particularly on the young mother.

Second phase: 30-50

This is a long phase which covers the growth of the children,
changes in the work of the husband and wife with accompanying
moves to new houses and parts of the country.   At the very
centre of this phase is to be found social and emotional
change.   As the couples pass through their thirties and forties, they emerge as more clearly differentiated persons with
needs, attitudes and feelings which may be radically different
from those with which they entered marriage.   These changes

are either adapted to or produce irreconcilable conflict leading to marital breakdown and divorce.

Social factors

The important social changes which are to be found in all
social groups - but more commonly in the upper socio-economic
groups - are an upward mobility as a result of successful
work.   The risk here is that the husband will move to a different cultural milieu which may be unsuitable for his wife
and thus there is a clash between his new circle of friends
and interests and hers.   If she is a shy, rather withdrawn
woman, she may find the new world of her husband threatening
and distasteful.   She may attack him for his newly found
friends and interests maintaining that he is attempting to mix
in a society beyond his normal background.   He in turn will
accuse her of jealousy and envy.   In this way the couple may
become alienated.
    A little later on, in the middle forties, a different
social picture may arise from the work position of the husband.   If he is in a professional or managerial post he may
find that he has reached the limits of his promotion and cannot go any further.   His self-esteem may suffer a blow which
reverberates in his relationship with his wife.   It is her
turn now to be supportive and encouraging.   This may coincide
with the period when other strains are emerging.   The children are now adolescent and working out their autonomy with a
necessary defiance towards parents.   The grandparents are
ageing and one may die necessitating more attention being paid
to the surviving spouse who may even have to be accommodated
in the home.   One by one the children will depart and get
married leaving the parents alone to adapt afresh to a one-to-
one situation.   All these social upheavals may influence the
marriage but usually are not responsible for its rupture.
    This is also the time when wives will return to work in
large numbers.   It is vital for the husband to play his part,
helping in the house if the wife is not to be confronted with
work outside the home, housekeeping and caring for the children.   These are the circumstances when some wives begin to
feel that the only role they play in the life of their husband
is to be an efficient economic and housekeeping unit.   This
feeling of not being loved or appreciated other than for being
a skivvy is a constant criticism of women who feel unapprecia-
ted.

Physical factors

This phase is not marked for any particular emergence of new
sexual difficulties.   What often happens is that the difficulties of the first phase continue and after some years
either spouse who was hoping for an improvement begins to
realise that none will be forthcoming.   An awareness emerges
that the sexual life is poor.   Sometimes it takes a long time
for one spouse to appreciate that the problem is not necessarily theirs, although they thought all along that they were
responsible for the poor performance.   A brief affair or even
a single act of intercourse may show them what is possible
under different circumstances.

The single most important new phenomenon has already been
mentioned; namely a prolonged post puerperal syndrome which
makes sex virtually non existent.   If there is continuous
absence of sex, this is the phase when its impact impinges
seriously on the marriage.

During these two decades there should normally be little
sexual dysfunction.   There are, however, certain difficulties
such as gradual male impotence, loss of sexual desire or premature ejaculation which affect a small percentage of husbands
who are no longer able to meet the needs of their wives.   If
intercourse is important to her, then the marriage may be in
jeopardy (Jehu, 1979).

Emotional factors

Emotional and psychological changes are common during these
years.   There is a movement of autonomy from dependence, a
differentiation and clarification of the identity so that the
spouse knows more clearly who they are, what is their potential and what they want to do with their life.   In most
couples this emergence of self or self-actualisation is a symmetrical, parallel event.   Sometimes, however, one partner
emerges from dependence to independence and the spouse cannot
accept the change.   Thus a wife who starts her married life
very dependent on her husband, following his initiative, meeting his friends, going where he wants, complying with his way
of seeing life, may gradually begin to change.   She may find
that she wants her own circle of friends, to have her own car
or at least learn how to drive, take decisions in conjunction
with her husband, have her own opinions which are listened to
and so on.   Most husbands will welcome these changes but
there are a few who find the loss of absolute control intolerable and thus put obstacles in the way of their wife's development.   This in turn makes the wife feel crushed, her

emerging personality destroyed and her life gradually annihilated.   She will become angry and there will be arguments. The arguments will turn into fights and she will withdraw sexually.   This will accelerate the alienation and finally she will discover another man who behaves towards her as she wants to be treated.

The growth of independence from dependence is proceeding concurrently with a development of a balance between togetherness and distance in the relationship.   Most couples find the right mixture of being together, doing things as a couple or family and also being on their own and doing things by themselves or with a friend.   Some couples do not find this balance and the problem emerges during these years.   One spouse feels trapped by the other whose needs of closeness are suffocating.   This spouse will be described as possessive or jealous and their partner will feel that no part of their life belongs to them.   This pattern is very destructive to marriage and the trapped person escapes when the opportunity arises.   Alternatively, of course, there is the spouse who is never home or when there either reads the paper or watches TV, but shows little affection or participation in the life of the family.

The conflict arising out of any of these patterns may be accentuated by alcohol or physical violence and a vicious circle established which leads to divorce.

Intellectual and value systems

Change certainly affects these two parameters.   The emergence of an awareness of one's abilities may lead a spouse to change jobs, pursue further education and slowly reverse the intellectual status in the couple.   There may be changes in ideologies and values from material to spiritual concern, from a life of hard work and success-chasing to one of pursuing aesthetic and other goals.   There may be a clash of the educational and discipline ideals of the parents towards their children.   These changes by themselves will not damage a marriage irretrievably but, if they are accompanied by other conflicts, the couple begin to realise that they share very little.

Third phase: 50 to death of one spouse

The third phase of marriage covers the period when the children have left home and the couple return to a dyad which negotiates some twenty to twenty-five years of marriage.   The early period of this phase will still see divorces but the numbers get less as the couple enter into their retirement phase.

Social factors

The process of self-actualisation and differentiation of self with its social upheaval may be present in this late period for some people.   These are men and women who have matured late and their social life expresses the upheaval that is usually seen in the previous decade.   In particular there is a period covering the middle forties to the middle fifties when husbands in particular may begin a second journey of occupation.   Having completed one successful career, they start a completely different one, often turning to social, community or pastoral work.   This may create an upheaval which is intolerable to the wife.

   This change of course affects the few.   Many more are now caught up in early retirement or redundancy, leaving them unemployed at a critical period of their life.   Continuous unemployment is corrosive to marriage.   It undermines the confidence and self-esteem of the man who, feeling a failure, may become irritable or withdrawn leaving the initiative to his wife who often remains employed.   The sense of failure or not being wanted may penetrate the intimate aspect of the life of the couple and the husband withdraws sexually or turns to drink for solace.   He feels his authority is reduced in the household and time hangs heavily on his hands.   If the wife is supportive, the difficulties are reduced;   if she is critical and hostile, the man may run away from an intolerable situation.

   For the vast majority of couples, this is a phase where they see their children marry and they become grandparents and thus assume a new role in their life.   This new role is coupled with an increasing responsibility for their own parents who are frail, may become chronically sick and needing care.   The needs of the parents of the spouses may be a source of friction but is rarely a serious one leading to divorce.

Physical factors

The very beginning of this phase often coincides with the menopause.   Many myths are associated with the menopause; for example that it causes diminution in sexual interest or other sexual dysfunctions.   In fact a small percentage of women - of the order of 10 per cent - get menopausal symptoms which are severe enough to need medical attention.   During this period sex suffers but for the majority of women the menopause does not produce any interruption in sexual activity.   The woman who uses the menopause as an excuse to avoid or cease having sex is in fact often rationalising her distaste for intercourse which was present long before the menopause started.

In fact it is the man who begins to experience increasing difficulties sexually during this phase.   Secondary impotence was shown by Kinsey (1948) to be associated with age.   Every subsequent study has confirmed this finding and increasingly in this phase men will lose their libido and erectile power. The loss is slow and sexual intercourse continues for the majority of couples in their sixties and seventies.

Extramarital relations occur at all stages of marriage but show a certain peak in the forties and fifties as both spouses may experience certain doubts about their sexual identity and seek reassurance and confirmation elsewhere.   Whilst in earlier phases extramarital relations may be threatening and damaging to the marriage, affairs later in marriage are particularly threatening to the wife who feels increasingly at a disadvantage to compete with a younger woman.   Such extramarital affairs may produce an upheaval and really disrupt a marriage in this phase.

Emotional factors

Perhaps the commonest reason for divorce in this phase is the departure of the children.   A couple may have lived together for twenty years or more.   They have slept and eaten under the same roof.   The departure of the children means more time together to do and enjoy all the things they could not do hitherto.   For some, instead of finding a new intimacy, they discover to their horror that with the departure of the children they look at one another and they see a stranger.   They had not realised that in fact they had lived through their children and they themselves had not established any intimate, genuine relationship.   They have nothing in common except their memories of bringing up their children and that is not enough to sustain them in this extended period of marriage. Separation and divorce are not infrequent.

Intellectual and value systems

As already indicated, the middle forties and this phase can be a time of change of direction from emphasis on success and material gain to service for others. The views of one partner may clash violently with those of the other. A husband may want to go on working and accumulating money whilst his wife wants a simpler life and emphasis on more time together. A husband may want to give up his lucrative post and change into an infinitely less remunerative work of service which his wife may not wish to follow.

Statistically husbands die earlier than wives and there are many more widows in this phase of marriage than widowers. The widow has her grief reaction which may be short or prolonged and then she gradually adapts to a new life. The widower often faces a much more difficult situation with the loss of his wife on whom he may have been far more dependent.

SUMMARY OF CONTEMPORARY DIVORCE

Statistics show a continuously rising figure for divorce in this country and indeed throughout Western society. Statistics, however, hide the variety of reasons for marital breakdown and divorce. As indicated in this paper, divorce occurs throughout the marriage cycle with a large peak at the beginning and a smaller one later on in marriage. However necessary divorce may be, it is a phenomenon which is costly to the State which has to support the wife and children who are financially in need and there is a good deal of suffering for the spouses and children involved. Prevention is one remedy within a framework that always permits those who want to divorce to be able to do so. If prevention is to be taken seriously, if indeed marriage is to be taken seriously, then the variety of situations that lead to marital stress have to be understood and society has to provide the education and training so that both couples and agencies of help know much more clearly the crisis points.

Chapter 14

Reconstituted families

Jacqueline Burgoyne and David Clark

In recent years academic social scientists, lawyers and social commentators have begun to discuss the distinctive features and potential problems of step-relationships in a way which suggests, at first glance, that family reconstitution through the remarriage of one or both partners is a quite new and potentially hazardous solution to the problem of single parenthood. However it is clear, both from historical data on the family and the strength and persistence of the negative stereotypes attached to step-parents, particularly step-mothers, that family reconstitution has a much longer history.

Social commentators on the family have frequently been criticised by historians for their tendency to refer back to a 'golden age' in which family life was entirely free from the change, conflict and strain, which are frequently ascribed to the contemporary family. Two historians of family life in Britain, Laslett and Stone, suggest that, in the seventeenth and eighteenth centuries, the period immediately before the Industrial Revolution, children were as likely to lose a parent during childhood as they are today and that, in addition, remarriage and step-parenthood were also very common. Reviewing a variety of evidence collected by his Cambridge research group, Laslett suggests that, whilst it was relatively uncommon for children to lose both parents, about 20 per cent of all children lost one parent before they themselves grew up. From the Cambridge study of nineteen English communities in the period between 1599 and 1811, they estimate that about 20 per cent of these orphans, defined by Laslett as children who have lost one or both parents, lived with a step-parent, most frequently a stepfather (Laslett, 1977:166). Stone draws similar conclusions and, whilst he recognises the difficulties of obtaining and interpreting this type of historical data, claims that 'what can be said with some confidence, however, is that unions including widows or widowers

with stepchildren of their own or families which included
orphaned or abandoned nephews or nieces were far from rare.
Perhaps a quarter of all families were of this hybrid character' (Stone, 1977:58). Laslett points to some of the differences between the experiences of these children and that of
comparable children in the twentieth century:

> It seems very likely ... that the child of peasant parents
> was brought up with a bevy of other children, caressed and
> attended to by a knot of other mothers and other adults
> too, ... rather than being nurtured in the privacy of the
> cottage, shack or the boarded-off rooms which the family
> inhabited. A little boy or girl with such a plurality of
> parental figures would seem likely to have felt the depri-
> vation and sudden change rather less keenly than the one
> who, like the children of the supposedly isolated cell of
> the late twentieth century conjugal family, had been exclu-
> sively tied to two parents, and especially the mother.
> (Laslett, 1977:166)

As Laslett admits, generalisations about the isolation of the
contemporary conjugal family are frequently oversimplified.
However, although it is possible to find a variety of communities and sub-cultures in which the responsibilities of childrearing are shared more widely, it is probably true that the
great majority of children in Britain grow up in family units
where the degree of isolation from other obviously involved
parental figures ensures, as Mead has suggested of the USA,
that, 'each American child learns early, and in terror, that
his whole security depends on that single set of parents who,
more often than not, are arguing furiously in the next room
over some detail in their lives' (Mead, 1971:113).

Another important factor which distinguishes the child who
is deprived of a parent in the late twentieth century from his
earlier counterpart is that the loss is now much more likely
to be the result of marital separation or divorce rather than
from the death of a parent. This difference is critical to
our understanding of the changing character of family reconstitution. The marked improvement in life expectancy which
eventually followed industrialisation, together with the trend
towards earlier marriage, has resulted in marriages of much
longer duration in the late nineteenth and twentieth centuries, a tendency which has only been halted as divorce has
become more common. However, it cannot be inferred from the
low divorce rates in Britain in the period up to the Second
World War that all children, particularly those from working-
class families, necessarily lived with both parents throughout
their childhood, because of the evidence of marital breakdown
provided by the large number of legal separation orders made
in magistrates' courts. As the Finer Committee reported, 'In

the early years of this century magistrates were hearing more than 15,000 applications for orders, most of which can be reckoned to represent marriage breakdowns' (DHSS, 1974:para. 3.36; also McGregor et al., 1970; Gibson, 1974). It was impossible to estimate how many of these separated spouses entered into new de facto partnerships, but one of the pressing arguments put forward by those who advocated the reform of the divorce legislation which was eventually embodied in the Divorce Reform Act 1969 was that couples in these stable unions should have the opportunity to acquire legal status. Trends in divorce and remarriage in the years immediately following the implementation of the 1969 Act demonstrate that large numbers of older couples did avail themselves of this opportunity.

Most commentators on divorce trends since the Second World War agree that, although levels of divorce have been affected by legislative and administrative changes which have made divorce 'easier', and which have thus drawn on a backlog of previously broken marriages, there has also been an underlying upward movement which began before the implementation of the Divorce Reform Act 1969. Leete concludes, 'this substantial rise [in divorce] has affected every marriage cohort at each length of marriage, although the level of divorce is highest for those who marry youngest' (Leete, 1979:5). Increasingly high divorce rates are matched by high rates of remarriage, especially amongst those whose first marriage and subsequent divorce occur at an early age. Using recent registration statistics, Leete concludes, 'considerably more than one-third of people now divorcing will ultimately remarry (although) remarriage rates tend to decline as the time of divorce recedes' (Leete, 1979:6). As Table 14.1 demonstrates only some remarriages creates tep-relationships, but it is clear from a number of interrelated trends that an increasing number of children acquire a step-parent as a result of their custodial parent's remarriage. In the first place, we know that since 1971 the number of children involved in divorce has risen sharply, keeping pace with the general rise in divorce. Secondly, the majority of these children stay with their mother after their parents split up. Eekelaar and Clive's study shows that about three-quarters of the children involved in divorce petitions were living with their mothers at the time of the divorce hearing and 'overwhelmingly the petitioners sought the court's approval for the continuation of the existing arrangements.' Indeed, even where custody was contested, the courts still tended to favour maintaining existing arrangements so that children remained where they had been since their parents split up (Eekelaar and Clive, 1977:8, 31). Thirdly, younger divorced women are more likely to remarry

TABLE 14.1

		Without children	With illegitimate child(ren)	Without children	With child(ren)	Without child(ren)	Non-custodial parent	Custodial parent
Bachelors		╲	3	╲	11	╲	╲	21
Widowers	Without children	╲	4	╲	12	╲	╲	22
	With child(ren)	1	5 Stepsibling family	9	13 Stepsibling family	17	19	23 Stepsibling family
Divorced men	Without children	╲	6	╲	14	╲	╲	24
	Non-custodial parent	╲	7	╲	15	╲	╲	25
	Custodial parent	2	8 Stepsibling family	10	16 Stepsibling family	18	20	26 Stepsibling family

than their older sisters. Whilst this group of younger divorcees will include women who have not yet started a family, it is also true that it is women who marry early who are most likely to be pregnant at the time of their marriage or to start a family in the very first years of their marriage. Thus increased rates of remarriage for younger divorced women in recent years suggest that step-relationships within families are becoming increasingly common. Unpublished data from the 1976 OPCS Family Formation Survey indicate that in 1976 about 7 per cent of all children under seventeen were stepchildren. (1)

Yet such figures tell us little about the actual experiences of those living in stepfamilies. It is helpful to consider the issues facing the remarrying in two ways. On the one hand their dominant concern is undoubtedly practical and material; in this sense reconstituting family life is about concrete matters like housing and income along with the more specific problems posed by maintenance, custody and access arrangements and parenting someone else's children. On the other hand they face a different set of problems of a more subjective kind, which for the individuals concerned are often less clearly perceived and only weakly articulated. These are to do with how men and women make sense of the process of family reconstitution, how they give accounts of what has happened to them and how they accommodate actual marital and familial experience to their existing expectations. Indeed, the ways in which expectations are altered by marital breakdown and the decision to remarry are important aspects of subsequent stepfamily life. It is clear that the warp and woof of everyday life in stepfamilies differs from that of unbroken families not merely because of external constraints which frustrate the efforts of those who may seek, as some do, to recast their family lives in the mould of the nuclear family, but that family norms themselves may also be markedly altered, tempered to fit the limits of the new situation and fabricated anew from the post-marital residue of family beliefs and sentiments. Thus, in referring to the process of family reconstitution, we are speaking of both a practice and a theory in which the material base and the normative superstructure of remarried family life act upon each other to produce a distinct family form.

STEPFAMILY LIFE-CYCLE

In the Sheffield study we found that stepfamily life-cycles could be divided into three types, determined principally by the position of the children in the family (Burgoyne and

Clark, forthcoming). A first group, drawn from those remarriages where the wife is still young enough to have children,
is made up of those who choose to have a child or children of
their own within the stepfamily. A second group consists of
those who choose to have no more children despite their second
marriage. The third group is made up of those older remarrying parents whose age prevents them from having to think about
having children. Consequently, assumptions about the centrality of childbearing and rearing to family life are immediately complicated for remarrying parents, who may, for
example, make a distinction between the related tasks of step-
and natural parenthood. The differing meanings attached to
these roles, along with their associated practical difficulties are, of course, frequently cited as the most typical
problems associated with life in stepfamilies (see, e.g.
Bowerman and Irish, 1962; Fast and Cain, 1960; Maddox, 1975;
Thomson, 1967).

Within the first group, many men and women will have
already had children in their previous marriage and may have
come to consider their childbearing days over and their families complete. A second marriage may, however, typically
create new expectations, notably a desire consciously to rebuild family life, frequently finding their most overt expression in the decision to have another child. For couples in
the Sheffield study (2) two kinds of meaning were attached to
this decision. In the first instance, having a child was
seen, as in most first marriages, as an expression of the love
relationship between husband and wife. In addition, within a
remarriage such children are often viewed as conferring positive benefits on family life; here the typical metaphors por-
tray the child in terms of the 'bond', 'seal' or 'unity' which
he or she brought to the stepfamily. Couples who each have
custody of children from a previous marriage, i.e. stepsibling
families (Table 14.1, particularly types 1, 8, 13, 16, 23 and
26) felt the need for such a child more acutely in so far that
it would serve to direct attention away from stepsibling
rivalry and conflict through the provision of a common focus
of love and affection. Parents, and especially fathers, also
found, perhaps contrary to their earlier fears, that renewed
satisfaction was brought through 'having a baby in the house
again'.

Within the second group, certain men and women may be
characterised, as some of the Sheffield sample were, by a
reluctance to 'go through the nappy stage again', feeling
that, whether or not the particular stepfamily which they had
created by their remarriage actually contained their own
children, it was nevertheless a *complete* family and, as such,
set limits on the size, if not the nature and the quality of

subsequent family life.   Having experienced children in a
previous marriage, they were no longer on the agenda when they
remarried.   Others, however, are unable to have further
children perhaps despite their wishes, because of an earlier
sterilisation.   Thus remarriage may either reinforce decisions about fertility made earlier in life, or may in fact
precipitate new problems when an earlier and sometimes irre-
vocable, decision is reassessed in the light of subsequent
events and a new relationship. (3)   This led one couple in
our study to seek a reversal of an earlier operation in the
belief that even a slender hope of conception was better than
none at all.   Naturally the problem is most acute where a
bachelor or spinster marries a partner who, having had children by a previous marriage, has also undergone sterilisation.
Here we can see how the satisfactions derived from having
children, as opposed to merely parenting them, are invested
with overriding importance.   For whilst the previously unmarried step-parent *does* have children to care and be responsible
for, to whit a ready-made family, paradoxically the problems
arising from this may also engender a desire to have a child
of one's own.   For, not only can the ready-made family present a range of difficulties associated with parenting someone else's children, often without the benefits of any previous experience, but also becoming a parent in such a situation can serve to highlight a step-parent's absence from the
stepchildren's earlier development.   Since a common theme in
both professional and folk ideologies of parenting is the
parental satisfactions which derive from observing the gradual
unfolding of a child's personality and practical accomplish-
ments, some of the step-parents felt a sense of relative
deprivation vis-à-vis the natural parent they had replaced.
Here the actual experiences of step-parents were markedly at
variance with those idealised expectations of parenthood
generated solely with reference to the unbroken nuclear
family.
     For the third group, remarrying men and women beyond the
age of further childbearing, children may play a less central
part in their vision of subsequent family life.   Such couples
in the Sheffield study saw custody and day-to-day care of
children merely as a short-term aspect of remarriage and
looked forward to the departure of teenagers from the home
with some satisfaction.   Such older couples had more limited
horizons and expectations for the future and began to antici-
pate a time when they could be together, free from the responsibilities and constraints of dependent children.   However
the relatively short period spent together as a stepfamily was
frequently a troubled one, because of the often problematic
relationship between teenage children and their step-parents.

Here the classic problems of adolescence are often compounded by step-relationships in which legitimate authority, mutual trust and recognised family routines have not been fully worked out. Moreover, the difficulties encountered by step-parents tended to be amplified by the interpretations which they themselves placed upon them, as they regarded many of the general and universal difficulties encountered by parents with adolescent children as specific consequences of their earlier divorce and remarriage. Sometimes the guilt and uncertainty engendered by such interpretations, in turn, diminished their confidence as parents during this period. Children may, likewise, feel a sense of exclusion in observing the commitment expressed by their parents to new partners, as recognition of the sexuality of older parents is also difficult to come to terms with, especially during the period of courtship which preceded cohabitation or remarriage. Despite its relatively curtailed nature, this form of stepfamily life-cycle may, in certain cases, prove the most difficult.

These distinctive stepfamily life-cycles also have important consequences for the identity of family members as well as for the family as a whole. There is a sense in which every family has a collective identity which is shared by all its members. Most commonly this manifests itself in those public settings where an individual's family identity takes precedence over, for example, identity as a work-mate, friend or client. It is in this sense that when we refer to 'the Browns' we are not merely referring to that group of individuals linked together by dint of consanguinity but are, in fact, conjuring up a set of referents which socially locate and depict the family. The strength in detail of the mental picture which we thus create is to some extent dependent on the degree of visibility of the family in question. In general those families which are the most visible in our society are those which, for whatever reason, have been designated deviant in some way or other. Stepfamilies may fall into this category, precisely because of the untypical morphology of the stepfamily life-cycle. In this respect perhaps the most obvious difference, when compared with the idealised image of the unbroken nuclear family, is that stepfamily life-cycles lack a *planned* quality. In stepsibling families, for example, all of the children may be clustered in a very narrow age range or, by contrast, separated by an unusually large number of years. Such features draw attention to the unplanned nature of the stepfamily when compared with its unbroken counterpart, in which family planning represents much more than merely contraception, signifying in addition, family building as a life project. Discrepancies of this sort are often further reinforced by differences in surname, which, once again, may serve to single the family out for unwelcome scrutiny when engaged in some public encounter such as a visit to a doctor, dentist or school. It is this sense of discrepancy and asymmetry which forms the starting point for any understanding of family reconstitution as a process.

THE PROCESS OF RECONSTITUTION

The central task confronting those who remarry may be depicted as one of emotional and material reconstruction in the light of an existing heritage whose often conflicting parts may continue to affect decisions and family organisation long after an earlier marriage has been formally ended in the courts. Accordingly, the expectations and aspirations of couples in the Sheffield study were themselves tailored to fit pre-given contingencies imposed by post-divorce arrangements. In turn, these constraints interacted with perceived changes in self resulting from the experiences of marital breakdown, so second marriages were entered into with a re-ordered set of priorities. Typically, this sort of self-evaluation and reassessment stemmed from a desire to make sense of past events. This is frequently a dominant theme in second courtship where new partners seek to give one another some meaningful account of their experience of marital breakdown. Indeed, our study suggests that during their periods of courtship men and women spend considerable amounts of time talking over their earlier lives, frequently rationalising past and present in terms of one another (see Burgoyne and Clark, 1979). This often meant a conscious renunciation of an earlier personality or behavioural trait such as selfishness, jealousy or heavy drinking, by which the process of mutual confession proves to be a cathartic experience which, in turn, provides the basis for personal reconstruction. This 'courtship as confessional' can, of course, also be partly attributed to the loss of confidence and sense of guilt which frequently attends the break-up of a marriage. When new partners systematically work through past events they are reconstructing personal biographies (4) which they feel are internally consistent and which, above all, form a manageable basis from which to initiate or develop new relationships.
     Many who remarry appear to meet a new partner soon after, if not before, the break-up of an earlier marriage and may already have a fairly clear notion of the type of relationship they are looking for. Moreover, sensitised by earlier mistakes and pitfalls, they seek to guide future actions accordingly. Few, it would appear, regard remarriage in the manner of Dr Johnson as a 'triumph of hope over experience', but feel

instead capable of utilising their experience in order to construct relationships in a more instrumental manner.   Despite
this increased clarity of expectations we must avoid imputing
an over-rationalised view of the decision to remarry.   For
many of the working-class couples in the Sheffield study the
coincidence of certain material and emotional needs with the
apparent means for fulfilling them, precipitated, often quite
quickly, the decision to cohabit or marry.   Accordingly, when
the remarried give some sort of public account, such as in a
sociological research interview, of meeting a new partner and
deciding to marry again, the language which they employ is
often curiously pragmatic in tone and essentially devoid of
the culturally prevalent ideologies of romantic love.
Instead they emphasise such matters as the importance of housing, income and travelling costs as deciding factors.   Thus
two single parents may readily see the practical and financial
benefits which might derive from cohabitation and ultimately
marriage, before they are fully committed to each other at an
emotional level.   The decision may also be crystallised when
parents introduce a new partner to their children.   For all
concerned this can be a difficult encounter, which is frequently invested with almost prophetic significance.   Indeed
some of the parents we studied, on the basis of one or two
often carefully engineered meetings, felt capable of judging
whether or not the two parties have 'taken' to one another and
if indeed, in the long term, they might 'make a go of it'.
Introducing potential sets of stepsiblings can present similar
problems in a context where parental anxiety can easily lead
to unwarranted assumptions about the possible compatability of
different children.

   Reminders of earlier marriages may also contribute to the
process of reconstitution.   These often appear as direct comparisons between first and second partners.   Indeed, for many
this lies at the heart of any rationalisation of marriage
breakdown; to have 'chosen the wrong person' is often the
least problematic public explanation which an individual can
give to friends, relatives or neighbours.   Yet this may be
qualified by more explicit references to perceived changes in
self and a sense of increased maturity, along with an altered
view of marriage itself.   Typical comparisons between first
and second marriages may thus refer to both changes in the
domestic division of labour, financial arrangements and attitudes towards bringing up children as well as to personal
growth and development.   Not surprisingly the remarried are
capable of effecting post hoc rationalisations which underline
and confirm the belief that 'everything has turned out for the
good', so that their accounts frequently seek to give a gloss
of stability to recently created family units, even where

these have come into existence after a relatively short period
of marital breakdown, second courtship and cohabitation.
Indeed many may feel, though it is harder to acknowledge, a
sense of urgency about settling down with a new partner,
especially those who return to live with parents after their
first marriage has ended.   For many working-class men and
women in this position a second marriage may be the only
acceptable means of asserting individuality and independence.
However, those who enter second partnerships and begin to make
a home for the children of one or both partners find that they
carry into their new relationship a material, economic and
legal inheritance which affects their everyday life and which,
over a long period of time, continues to remind them that they
remain in certain respects at least different from 'ordinary'
families.

THE ECONOMIC AND LEGAL CONTEXT OF REMARRIAGE

Duncan and Morgan's longitudinal survey of the economic circumstances of 5,000 American families demonstrates how, in
every income group, remarriage helps to reverse the loss in
real income which results from widowhood, separation or
divorce (Duncan and Morgan, 1976).   This improvement in economic circumstances following remarriage is obviously more
marked for women than for men and these economic advantages
will include not only the direct savings which derive from
merging two household units but also the more indirect advantages of sharing the multitude of tasks and responsibilities
which are part of any domestic economy.   Yet these economic
gains may also have social and personal costs.   Although cohabitation, 'living together', is becoming increasingly common
and is felt to be more widely accepted, in some local or occupational communities it may still have costs in the form of
some loss of respectability.   For the reasons we have discussed above many couples start to live together within a very
short time of the breakdown of their first marriage and before
the legal formalities surrounding their divorce have been completed.   Some couples in the Sheffield study saw this period
of cohabitation as a 'trial' marriage, uncertain whether they
wished to marry again when their first had failed so recently.
Others saw cohabitation as a preferred alternative to formal
marriage and regard themselves as pioneers of an alternative
lifestyle and type of commitment.   However, a third group of
couples were very clear that they wished to marry immediately
they are free to do so and found the period of waiting one of
considerable strain and uncertainty.   Their guilt about the
failure of their first marriage and their violation of

previously held norms about extramarital intercourse was,
therefore, echoed for them in the ambiguity which surrounded
their status as a cohabiting couple with children.   Research
carried out in 1973 by Elston, Fuller and Murch showed that
many petitioners, even when their divorce petitions were undefended, were very anxious both about their appearance in
court and the way in which any outstanding issues related to
property or custody of children would be resolved (Elston,
Fuller and Murch, 1975).   Although as a consequence of the
Matrimonial Causes Rules 1975, undefended divorce has become
an 'essentially administrative process' (Eekelaar, 1978:144)
where parties do not even have to appear, our own evidence indicates that anxiety and uncertainty persist.   Whilst some
couples did not attach much significance to their impending
divorce proceedings, others did not feel free to resume a new
life until their divorce was made absolute, and consequently
felt rather unhappy about the partnership they had already
entered into.   Many couples, describing the arrangements and
events surrounding their divorce, admitted that they did not
really understand what the legal provisions actually meant nor
what was being done on their behalf by the various legal personnel involved.   For many women reliant on social security
when their marriage breaks down, their first contact with the
court is an application for a separation order in a magistrates' court, 'largely associated in the public mind with
criminal law' (Eekelaar, 1978:201), thus compounding the sense
of guilt and disrepute which is then transferred to the
divorce proceedings themselves.
    Although the majority of divorce petitions are now undefen-
ded, the continued coverage of a small minority of contested
divorce or custody cases in the media helps to reinforce the
stigma still experienced by many divorced people.   If they
have already begun a new relationship, its early stages may be
marked by personal disappointment about the failure of their
first marriage, expressions of informal disapproval from
neighbours, friends and kin.   These feelings are, in turn,
exacerbated by their perceptions of how they are viewed and
treated by members of the legal and social work professions
whom they encounter.   It is unfortunate that such perceptions
and experiences bear little relationship to the kinds of
ideals embodied in recent divorce law reform (see Eekelaar,
1978:ch. 7).
    Similarly, unresolved disputes with an ex-partner may con-
tinue to play their part in the everyday conversation and
mythology of their new life for many years to come, structuring both its material conditions and the couple's explanations
of any difficulties they may face.   The financial settlement
made at the time of divorce continues to affect any subsequent

marriage in a number of ways.   In recent divorce practice, if
a wife retains, or is given, custody of her children, then her
husband will be expected to enable her to remain in the matrimonial home while the children grow up.   Council tenancies
may be changed into the wife's name, and, if it is possible,
husbands who owned their own homes will be expected to provide
sufficient maintenance to allow their wives to take on mortgage payments for the matrimonial home (see Barrington Baker,
1977).   Thus, many remarried couples begin their life
together in the wife's former home, which may be a source of
difficulty for both partners.   The wife must live with her
memories and also with worries about neighbourhood gossip,
while her new partner is also likely to find it difficult to
settle down in a home which is not 'his' in the sense that he
was not instrumental in either choosing, decorating or fur-
nishing it.   For many of the families in the Sheffield study
part of the settling down process included a move to a new
area, where they felt they could 'start afresh'.   In a new
neighbourhood, free to create a new identity and reputation as
a family, many felt able to create and enjoy domestic life in
the new home they had built up together.

   Maintenance payments also provide a continuing financial
link with ex-partners.   Although any maintenance payable to a
wife ceases if she remarries, this is not true of payments in
respect of children. (5)   It is impossible to estimate what
proportion of divorced fathers continue to pay maintenance and
for how long payments continue.   There is evidence to suggest
that payment is linked to the exercise of rights of access, so
that as the children get older and visiting may become more
difficult, fathers' payments may gradually cease. (6)
Middle-class fathers are probably more likely to continue to
pay, both because they find it easier to find an identity and
role as a non-custodial parent and, therefore, to continue to
have contact with their children and also because, as Eekelaar
points out, they continue to enjoy tax relief on their maintenance payments (Eekelaar, 1978:170f).   If maintenance is
still being paid domestic finances are complicated by such
payments so that the actual sums of money involved, the decision to return to court to get an order varied, and the regu-
larity with which payments arrive all provide constant reminders of the past.   Where both partners are divorced the
family balance sheet may include both income from and payments
to their respective ex-partners (see Figure 14.1).

   Eekelaar and Clive's study shows that only a relatively
small proportion of non-custodial fathers continue to visit
their children regularly (Eekelaar and Clive, 1977) and many
of the fathers in the Sheffield study described how they
gradually lost contact with their children from their first

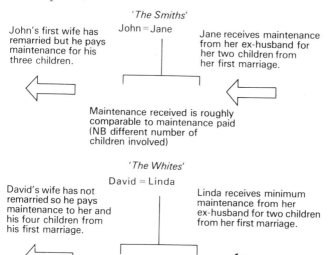

FIGURE 14.1   Maintenance payments

marriage.   One of the main reasons for a father's failure to
retain contact with his children is probably uncertainty about
his role as non-custodial father, especially where he has, in
effect, been replaced by a stepfather.   There is considerable
evidence that the obligations and responsibilities of fatherhood are very diffusely defined in our own society;   mothers
are felt to be mainly responsible for the welfare and public
behaviour of children; (7)   fatherless families are expected
to manage on their own, albeit in reduced circumstances,
although we do not have similar expectations of motherless
families (see George and Wilding, 1972);   fathers continue to
play little or no part in the care of babies or toddlers in
many families. (8)   The obligations of fatherhood are most
clearly articulated in terms of being a good provider, ensuring economic security for the mother who takes direct responsibility for the care of his children.   The ambiguity of the
non-custodial parent's role is further illustrated when we
consider access visits themselves.   If the children are still
very small their father will usually have to see them at home
unless he meets them at their grandparents' or other relatives' house.   Once they are older they may resent the way
their father's regular visits interfere with their own weekend
plans.   In addition non-custodial fathers often continue to
feel uncomfortable about their visits to their children which
may involve contact with their ex-wives.   In our society

there are few norms structuring the post-divorce relationships
of either married partners or other kin; we are generally
surprised if ex-partners continue to get on well together and,
as Mead has suggested, 'among the older generation there is
some feeling that any contact between divorced people smacks
of incest; once divorced, they have been declared by law to
be sexually inaccessible to one another' (Mead, 1971:121).
Therefore, even if divorced parents consciously desire to continue to exercise a shared responsibility for the care of
their children there are important informal pressures tending
to undermine this intention especially where one or both of
them has remarried.

Although there is insufficient data to draw very definite
conclusions, it does seem from the limited evidence available
that many non-custodial fathers lose contact with their children from their first marriage and may eventually become stepfathers to someone else's children. Consequently the
Houghton Committee's comments and recommendations on step-
parent adoption, emphasising the desirability of a continuing
relationship between children and their non-custodial father,
conflict sharply with the experience of many remarried parents
and fit in with the lifestyle of only a minority of step-
parents (Masson and Burgoyne, 1979).

CONCLUSION

In this chapter we have attempted to outline some of the main
demographic trends affecting remarriage and to consider the
structural context within which such remarriages take place,
but we have also tried to explore some of the most important
ways in which the process of family reconstitution affects
individuals; in particular, we have been concerned with how
they themselves make sense of this increasingly common experience. We have tried to suggest that it is still often the
case that stepfamilies are reconstituted according to a normative blueprint which is based on the unbroken nuclear family.
Those who marry again are, therefore, heavily reliant on criteria of success, failure and adequacy which are drawn from
'normal' family life. Consequently evaluations of stepfamily
life are typically made according to criteria of 'ordinari-
ness'. However it is clear that stepfamilies differ in the
extent to which they consciously attempt to 'pass' as an unbroken nuclear family by, for example, taking a new job and
moving to a new area. Naturally this may seem to be the most
obvious strategy; it brings about the normalisation of family
life and, in the case of young adults with small children
where divorce and custody are uncontested, this may well prove

to be both practical and expedient.   However this may be impossible for other families.   Where legal aspects of custody, access and maintenance arrangements are disputed and where older children and non-custodial parents are in regular contact, then the stepfamily is less likely to succeed in attempts at normalisation.   For these families two possible strategies are available.   Some may, out of a sense of guilt, propriety or confusion, choose to fly in the face of the structural factors which make their existence as a stepfamily both visible and incontravertible.   The pursuit of the goal of normal family life is inevitably frustrated, as subjective ideals clash continually with external and material constraints.   Others, to the extent that they recognise the nature of these problems, may reject, either explicitly or implicitly, such a course.   Members of these families, sensitised by media coverage of trends in divorce and remarriage, see themselves as pioneers of an alternative lifestyle. Having accepted their situation, they formulate an ideology and practice to match it.   In marked contrast to some of the literature which emphasises the negative aspects of step-relationships, they are clear that their way of life may also represent a source of potential rewards and satisfactions of a type absent from more conventional nuclear families.   Typically these step-parents emphasise the material and social benefits which stepsiblings derive from one another's presence in the family, the value and importance of additional parental figures, and the fulfilment which results from reconstituting a single family from its disparate elements.

NOTES

1 Karen Dunnell, Office of Population, Census and Surveys (private communication).   In the USA, recent calculations suggest that in 1977 13 per cent of all children under eighteen were living in families in which one of the two parents was not the biological parent (Visher and Visher, 1979:xviii).
2 The Sheffield study refers to a small-scale study of a group of forty families undertaken between 1977 and 1979 by the present authors (see Burgoyne and Clark, forthcoming).
3 Claire Raynor, the advice columnist of 'The Sun' receives a large number of letters from men and women who wish to have sterilisations reversed when they enter into new partnership (private communication).
4 The idea of constructing and reconstructing personal biographies is suggested by Berger (1966) and Goffman (1968

and 1968a).   Examples of how this is done by separating
couples may be found in Weiss (1975).

5   Fathers no longer have to pay maintenance for their children if they give their consent to their adoption by their
mother and new stepfather, thus relinquishing their parental rights.   However following the recommendations of the
Houghton Committee (1972), contemporary legal practice in
relation to step-parent adoption is changing (see Masson
and Burgoyne, 1979).

6   See Eekelaar and Clive (1977).   Preliminary data from the
DHSS Monitor of the Children Act, 1975, Stepparent Adoption Study, currently being carried out by Masson and
Norbury suggest that about half of the adopting step-
parents in this sample had never received maintenance,
whilst a quarter had initially received it but payments
became increasingly irregular, finally ceasing before the
application to adopt the children was made.

7   See, for example, the Newsons' comment:
   even in this age of vastly increased involvement of
   fathers ... mothers remain more vulnerable to social
   criticism.   This is because of social expectations;
   in the end, criticism of the upbringing of a young
   child is still primarily aimed at the mothers.
   Fathers are not expected to take public responsibility
   for either the behaviour or the appearance of very
   young children, and blame will be transferred to the
   mother even where father has voluntarily accepted the
   major involvement. (Newson, 1972:30)

8   See, for example, Oakley (1979:211).   In her sample, 'a
third of the ... fathers saw their five month old babies
for less than an hour a day'.

Chapter 15

Foster and adoptive families
Jane Aldgate

PART I: FOSTER FAMILIES

Historical background

> What happens is this: children are boarded out in the
> country one, perhaps two, rarely more than three in a
> family; they acquire the habits and feelings among whom
> they are brought up; they see the struggles of the family
> to maintain their independence: they see the kind of feel-
> ing that is entertained in reference to paupers, they
> acquire a sort of domestic attachment to the father and
> mother, or to the old woman with whom they are boarding and
> they are well educated, and ultimately they melt into the
> population, so you cannot find a trace of them, and they
> are not distinguishable from the people who have been
> brought up in independence. (Report to Select Committee on
> the Poor Law, Sir John McNeil, 1869; cited in Ferguson,
> 1966:10)

The social policy of boarding out children deprived of their
own families originated in the seventeenth century under the
auspices of the Poor Laws.   Its long history has left a
legacy of recurrent themes.   Successful citizenship is related to the experiences of childhood.   The institution of the
conventional family is the traditional way to deal with children and within this model, parents have responsibility for
their upbringing.   If parents fail in their duty towards
their children, are they the casualties or the deviants of
society and should they be helped or blamed?   Similarly,
should children be rescued from their parents and given a
clean break and fresh start or should society try to retain
for a child his biological blood ties and provide him with
supplementary care from time to time which complements the
lifestyle of his own family?

303

Up until the end of the nineteenth century, as Sir John
McNeil's quotation demonstrates, the emphasis was very much on
'rescue' but throughout this century and especially with the
coming of the Welfare State, the balance has shifted towards a
policy of using fostering as a supplementary social service.
In spite of this, the confusion and ambivalence towards families who use public care remains.

Foster care as we know it today developed after the formation of Children Departments in 1948.   During the early
1950s, it was characterised by the provision of short-stay
foster homes where the emphasis was on minimising the ill
effects of a family crisis by placing children with families
which were similar to their own.   To this end there was a
development of fostering families who were also relatives of
children.   By the early 1960s, research studies indicated a
high failure rate and the unsuitability of foster care for all
children.

> There was a growing realization that foster care was not a
> simple system where by a substitute could be provided for
> the parent-child relationship.   There was also a growth of
> practice wisdom and skill which was built on an apprecia-
> tion of the complex dynamics of the inter-relationships
> between a child, his family and his foster home. (DHSS,
> 1976:13)

The increasing emphasis on the service elements of foster home
care led to a tightening up of selection and recruitment of
suitable foster parents.   This was paralleled by the increasing emphasis on social work to prevent children coming into
care.

In the post-Seebohm mid-1970s, there was a renewed interest
in foster families which reflected the philosophy of finding
community-based solutions for families with social problems.
The Department of Health and Social Security thought fostering
of sufficient importance to merit a working party which produced the 'Guide to Fostering Practice' in 1976.

Numbers

Official statistics of fostering provide only a general summary of its use.   Although there is some distinction between
long- and short-stay foster homes, there is no indication of
the range of fostering provision nor the length of time which
children actually remain in care.   In 1977, 24,000 children
in the care of local authorities in England and Wales were in
foster homes.   It is estimated that 11,000 were more than likely
to be in private foster homes.   On average, about four out of
ten children in the care of local authorities live with foster

families rather than in children's homes.   As Packman (1968)
has illustrated, local authorities have always varied in their
provision of foster homes.   A review of the current variations reports a wide range from 22 per cent in two London
boroughs, 54 per cent in Sheffield and 60 per cent in Devon
(Prosser, 1978).

Definitions of fostering

The Association of British Adoption and Fostering Agencies
(1979) defines fostering as 'a way of providing family life
for children who, for various reasons, cannot live with their
own parents whether for a short or long time' (p. 1).   The
essential difference between foster families and those described so far in previous chapters is that the fostering role
is superimposed on another family system.   Foster families
may be at the same time conventional families, dual-worker
families or one-parent families.   They may also be of differing ethnic groups.   Families may take on the fostering role
at any stage of their life-cycle and therefore it is possible
to find foster parents who have young children of their own;
older couples with grown-up families and childless couples.
The psycho-social life of foster families operates at two
levels.   There is the original family, with its kinship
system, roles and expectations.   Then there is the foster
family which is a complex system consisting of the foster
child, the foster parents and its social network, which will
include the child's own parents and the agency which placed
him.
  Fostering can be said to be a generic term.   The 'DHSS
Guide to Fostering Practice' (1976) believes that fostering:
  is not in itself a single identifiable method of care.
  It offers a range of placements which have in common only
  the fact that they provide care in a family setting.
  There are even more types of foster homes than there are of
  residential homes.   Each family is unique and each has
  different qualities to offer the child who comes into its
  care.   Successful fostering depends upon the matching of
  child and foster family, (pp. 6-7)

The legal framework

All foster placements are governed by children's legislation.
Some parents make private arrangements for their children to
be looked after by foster parents.   These homes are subject
to approval and some supervision by the local authority.

Other children are in the care of local authorities or voluntary child care agencies.   These homes are governed by the
1955 Boarding Out Regulations (England and Wales) which provide details on their selection and supervision.   The local
authority has a duty to visit the home and report on its suitability.   It must also keep records of foster children,
ensure they have medical examinations and make statutory
visits at fairly frequent intervals.   The foster parents have
to sign an undertaking to provide proper care for the child
and must allow the local authority to visit or remove the
child at will and notify any change of address.   A crucial
element in the success of fostering in Britain today is the
relationship between the foster family and the social worker.

The circumstances under which children come into the care
of the local authority vary and account for the range of
foster homes that are needed.   The child in care may be any
age from a few days old to adolescence.   Some children are in
care at the request of their parents; some may have been
deserted by them.   Others may have been committed to care by
the court following the separation or divorce of their parents
or because they have been found to be in need of care and control; for example, those who have committed offences or who
have been seriously neglected or placed at risk by their
parents.   One sub-group of foster children are those of mixed
race or from minority racial groups (Rowe and Lambert, 1973).

Foster family life-cycles

There are two ways of studying the life-cycle of foster families.   The first is from the child's standpoint, examining
the type and duration of foster home care experienced.   The
second is from the standpoint of the foster parents, in their
family life-cycle.

Social workers accept the importance of the idea that each
foster home placement should be planned and of limited duration.   To aid planning, there is a statutory review system.

The 1955 Boarding Out Regulations divide foster homes into
short term (under eight weeks) and long term (over eight
weeks).

Short-term homes are used in many different ways.   Among
the most common are the care of children during parental illness, mother's confinement or family crisis; pre-adoption
care; holiday homes for handicapped children or those attending special school; part-time care for one-parent families;
foster homes used for assessment.

The time span of long-term foster homes may vary from a few
months to several years.   As with short-term placements, it

is considered best that they should be of determinate length. Children come to these foster families because of long-term illness in their own parents, family breakdown caused by marital difficulties, homelessness or family relationship problems.   Recently, a special range of medium length placements has been developed for children and adolescents with special behaviour problems.   They have a carefully considered time span and the emphasis is on foster parents providing therapeutic family experience.

There seems to be considerable discrepancy between theory and practice in relation to the characteristic time span of foster placements.   The theory assumes that most placements are of medium length and planned to span specific life crises in the child's family of origin; but recent research evidence suggests that children may spend a great part of their lives in foster care.   Shaw and Lebens (1976) and Rowe and Lambert (1973) both found that at least 70 per cent of foster children were placed early in their lives and were expected to remain in care until their eighteenth birthday.   Looking at factors influencing children's length of stay in care, Aldgate (1976) found that the chances of rehabilitation for children diminished rapidly after the first two years in care.

One of the problems arising from the indeterminate nature of active (as distinct from theoretical) time spans of placement has been the role confusion experienced by foster parents.   The foster family tends to de-emphasise its fostering role and to absorb the child into its own family group. This becomes problematic when the fostering phase in the child's life-cycle is terminated.

The family becomes quasi-adoptive.   The foster child may even use the name of the foster family indicating his assumed status.   But, while the 'permanent' foster home is a contradiction in terms, and cannot offer legal security, in some situations permanent foster families may be 'the best achievable rather than the most desirable solution' (Association of British Adoption and Fostering Agencies, 1975:5).

Motives for fostering and life-cycles within the foster family

Becoming a foster family results from the interaction of two main factors: the characteristics of families who put themselves forward for selection and the selection criteria used by social workers.   These two factors interact in that social workers' selection criteria adapt to some extent to available resources.   Social work literature has provided guidelines for social workers on the areas they should investigate in foster home assessment (Wolins, 1963; Pugh, 1968; Kline and

Overstreet, 1972), but George (1970) found that in practice, social workers tend to rely on impressions and occasional discussions and observations rather than on an objective system analysis of factors indicated by foster care literature. On the family side research indicates that many foster parents have in common certain social and psychological characteristics and are motivated by unmet needs.

This unmet need may reflect, in part, a strong self-concept as parents, free energy to reach beyond the boundaries of the biological family in a giving relationship with children in the biological line different from their own, and belief in a value system which includes sharing and giving to the full extent of one's capacity. (Kline and Overstreet, 1972:241)

Foster parents tend to come from groups in which there is a norm of large families (Babcock, 1965; Wakeford, 1963). Wakeford believes that by fostering such families attempt to assimilate the size of their family to their own conceptions of the ideal family.

Several studies over a period of years have noted a predominance of older foster parents (Gray and Parr, 1957; Jaffe, 1965; Adamson, 1973). Many families in this category have older children who have reached adulthood or are living away from home. It may well be that this group have a strong desire to extend the active parenting phase of their own family life-cycle. Some foster parents wish to relive their own parenting experiences with a particular age range, for example, young babies.

Studies frequently report that the skilled working classes are over-represented among foster parents (Trasler, 1960; Parker, 1966; George, 1970). It is difficult to know whether this represents the type of family which offers itself for fostering or whether it is a reflection of social workers' choice of a family which is socially near that of the foster child. There are probably mixtures and combinations in different settings.

Compensation for unmet needs may motivate many foster parents. But it would seem that this in itself is less crucial in assessing a family's potential for successful fostering than whether the needs are found in emotionally mature individuals (Kline and Overstreet, 1972). Maturity involves the capacity for giving and receiving, adaptability, reality testing and learning, and ego identity and ego integrity. While in its most idealised form the maturity model provides an impossible set of standards, it seems clear that marked immaturity is potentially damaging.

Trasler (1960) found that placements failed when the foster family could not accept the child's individuality and his

relationship with his family of origin.   He related this
failure to the foster family's unreal expectations of the
child or to the internal demands deriving from inter-family
relationships which took precedence over the needs of the
child.   Jenkins (1965) and Fanshel (1966) found foster home
placements least satisfactory where foster parents had a
strong need to make reparation for bad childhood experiences.
Placements were most satisfactory where foster parents displayed 'an open expression of affection' towards children and
felt that the placement brought their family size up to the
norm.

There have been no profiles of day-to-day lives of foster
families in the same way there have been kinship studies of
conventional families.   What can be gleaned from the very
scanty work in this area (Fanshel, 1966; George, 1970), is
that foster parents tend to adopt traditional division of
labour by gender.   Fanshel found that 'for the women, direct
contact with the child loomed high as satisfaction; for the
men, the desire to serve a worthy cause and to provide a
masculine model for the foster child appeared to be the most
prominent themes' (Fanshel, 1966:48).   Traditionally, the
boarding out allowance or fostering salary has been paid to
the foster mother.   One can only speculate that this is in
recognition of the fact that the main burden of the fostering
task falls upon her.   The 'own children' of the foster
parents have been ignored in available research reports, as
have the external social relations of foster families.   The
main concentration has been on psychological problems arising
from conflicting role expectations in the relationships
between the foster child, his natural parents, foster parents
and social workers.

Characteristic issues in long-term fostering

The problematic issues emerge most sharply in long-term placements and centre on the viability of *shared parenting*, which
is the key concept guiding modern foster care.   Kellmer-
Pringle (1975) describes problematic characteristics of long-
term foster placements:

    There is much more uncertainty and impermanence than in
    adoption; and the involvement is closer, more personal and
    intimate than in residential care.   Some of the complexity
    arises from the rather ill-defined roles of, and relation-
    ships between, all concerned: the child who is being
    placed; his parents; his foster parents; and the placing
    agency's caseworker.   Furthermore, the assumptions, expec-
    tations and needs of each are widely different. (pp. 140-1)

The core element lies in the concept of shared parenting. Problems arise in sharing parental involvements as between biological parents and others who accept parenting responsibility. This problem is not exclusive to foster care. Similar problems are found in other family types, including reconstituted and alternative families, where parenting extends beyond the biological parents.

The responsibility for the child is shared between parents, foster parents and the placing agency. Ideally in foster care, the aim should be to maintain the child in as close a relationship to his natural parents as possible while avoiding excessive conflict. The actual role that foster parents develop varies, partly in relation to which aspects of the parenting role are still being exercised by the natural parents and which are being undertaken by the agency.

Holman (1975) has classified foster parents as falling into two broad types: 'inclusive' or 'exclusive'. The exclusive model of fostering 'may be so termed in that it attempts to contain the foster child within the foster family while excluding other connections' (p. 8). Foster parents regard children as part of their own family and wish eventually to adopt them. Confirmation of a desire to adopt comes from several research studies (Holman, 1973; Adamson, 1973; George, 1970; Aldgate, 1977). Another feature of this model of fostering is the exclusion of natural parents reported by several studies. George (1970) found that two-thirds of foster parents thought their foster children should be more attached to them than to their natural parents. Visits from natural parents were accepted grudgingly. The Barnsley study (1975) reported a more hostile attitude towards natural parents. Aldgate (1977) found that over 50 per cent of foster parents thought that there should be no contact between the child and his parents. Consistently, foster parents wished to see the relationship with social workers as one of friend rather than that of colleague or employer-employee, thereby denying that social workers have the power to remove the child. Attitudes towards social work visits are ambivalent with workers being seen 'as pleasant and supportive, but, in the end, rather peripheral' (Shaw and Lebens, 1976:27). Above all, in the exclusive model, the emphasis is on continuity and commitment. By contrast, the inclusive model is based on the readiness to draw the various components into the fostering situation. Foster parents can offer love without having to regard themselves as the real parents ... natural parents are regarded more positively with the greater willingness that children should possess full knowledge about them. The social workers are also included ... with the inclusive concept, emphasis is placed

on the children's needs to obtain a true sense of their
present identity and the past history within a framework of
affection. (Holman, 1975:10-11)

Only a minority of long-term foster homes could be described as inclusive although undoubtedly a great many successful
short-stay placements come into this category.   Fostering
research has found consistently that long-term foster parents
wish to see themselves as the child's parents.   This is consistent with foster parents' unmet need to augment their
family size.   Effective foster parents, like parents generally, base their expectations on common sense and their own
life experiences (Adamson, 1973).   As Shaw and Lebens (1976)
conclude 'in general, foster parents are, in their own eyes,
engaged in the task of bringing up children as they would a
child of their own (precisely as the Boarding Out Agreement
demands!) without reference to anyone else' (p. 26).

Foster children

There are two crucial issues for children who live with foster
parents: the development of a clear identity and the need for
a sense of belonging.   The need for a clear self-image is not
exclusive to foster children and is shared by others who live
with families where one or both biological parents are absent.
The importance of self-knowledge is described by Cowan and
Stout (1939).

It is possible that clear and unbroken tread of memory extending from the present into early childhood and even
vicariously into the experiences of past generations
through remembered tales of the reminiscences of parents
and grandparents may constitute for an adult an important
component of the complex emotional pattern carried over
from day to day and known in its dependable entirety as
emotional security. (p. 338)

Research by Weinstein (1960) and Thorpe (1974) has indicated that foster children who identify with their natural
parents have a higher average emotional well-being rating than
those who identify with foster parents or have mixed identification.   A foster child's self-image is helped most if he has
regular contact with his natural parents (Weinstein, 1960;
Holman, 1966).   Holman found the less contact a foster child
had with his parents, the less chance he had of knowing the
truth about his relationship with them;   the more chance of
ill health;   the more the retardation in developmental stages;
and the more the trend towards poor educational achievements
in writing, arithmetic and reading.   These findings led
Holman to the conclusion that an 'inclusive' model of

fostering is more likely to promote a child's well being.
Parker (1966) would dispute this, maintaining that some of the
most successful foster placements in his study were those
termed semi-adoptive, with no contact with natural parents.
The benefit of parental visits in all circumstances has also
been questioned by Shaw and Lebens (1976) and Tizard (1974).
It would appear likely that the studies report different sorts
of parental situations, but further research will be required
to make the necessary discriminations.

Although the value of parental visiting is in dispute,
there is unanimous agreement, both in foster care and adoption
literature, that children need knowledge of their origins.
In the foster home, 'children must feel free to ask questions
themselves about their situation as well as to express their
feelings without fear of rejection' (DHSS, 1976:117).   Whatever the reason for admission to care, children in foster
homes may feel that they have been rejected by their parents
and some may fear a second rejection unless they appease their
foster parents.   If foster parents compare natural parents
with themselves unfavourably, children may be frightened of
talking about their families of origin for fear of invoking
disapproval.   Many foster parents assume that because foster
children do not talk about their natural parents, they have
forgotten them (Aldgate, 1977).   Thorpe (1974) found great
concern expressed by foster children for their natural parents
and shared the conclusion of Kline and Overstreet (1972) that
'the absent parent continues to hold an important part in the
child's inner life' (p. 151).

The second issue facing children who live in foster families is the impermanence of the placement.   The open-ended
long-term placement is condemned by Goldstein, Freud and
Solnit (1973) as one of the major causes of foster home breakdown.   Bryce and Ehlert (1971) summarise the view held by
many researchers into child development.   'It is our conviction that no child can grow emotionally while in limbo, never
really belonging to anyone except on a temporary and ill-
defined or partial basis.   To grow, the child needs at least
a promise of permanency in relationships and some continuity
of environment' (p. 451).   What has been emphasised is the
importance to the child not only that an an adult be constantly *there*, but that he is important to that adult.   This is
what brings trust and confidence and the potential for making
good relationships in adulthood.

Natural parents

The role of the natural parents in fostering has much in
common with the role of absent parents in one-parent and reconstituted families.   The major issue centres on the maintenance of contact between the child and his natural parents.
In foster parenting this is crucial as the goal is to return
the child to the natural parents.   The maintenance of frequent and regular contact between parents and foster child is
a primary factor in influencing the return of foster children
to their own parents (Fanshel, 1976; Aldgate, 1976).   Allowances must be made for a child's time scale and developmental
changes.   It is extremely painful for a natural parent to
face the fact that a very young child may quickly transfer his
primary allegiance to his foster parents.

This continuity of contact and of attachments is more to be
found in short-term fostering situations.   Research shows
children in long-term foster care are found to receive few
visits from their natural parents (Aldgate, 1977; George,
1970; Thorpe, 1974; Adamson, 1973; Rowe and Lambert, 1973).
It is tempting to suggest that parents who manage to reunite
their families are those who have most interest in their
children anyway.   In reality it seems the situation is far
more complex.   Contact between parents and children in foster
care may be affected by the actual reasons for care, parents'
reaction to separation from their children, the age of the
child at separation, the attitude of children and foster
parents towards the parents, the distance between the foster
home and the parental home and the encouragement to maintain
contact given by social workers (Aldgate, 1977).

Stevenson (1968:13) has drawn attention to the fact that
even 'perfectly normal parents' feel an acute sense of failure
when their children are received into public care because of
the value placed on successful childrearing.   Prior to separation, natural parents are often living in financially dependent and materially deprived circumstances which leaves them
devoid of energy and initiative (Mapstone, 1969; Thorpe,
1974; Aldgate, 1977).   On separation, they experience acute
filial deprivation which can be emotionally paralysing
(Jenkins and Norman, 1972; Aldgate, 1977).   With these emotional handicaps, natural parents often find foster parents
very threatening.   They represent the worthy and more affluent citizens that they themselves are not.   Foster parents
are viewed as unequal rivals who would undoubtedly win any
contest for children's affections.   Even if parents resolve
their separation anxiety, they have to acknowledge that in
handing over their children to foster parents, they automatically forfeit the right to day-to-day decision making.

Shared parenting is mutually embarassing.   The foster parents
have an unclear role when the parents of children they are
looking after come to visit them.   The natural parents, too,
have an unclear role when they visit their children in someone else's home.   There are no precedents for appropriate
behaviour in normal social interchange.   The descriptions of
visits by two natural mothers summarise the problem:

'You feel like you're intruding as if you don't belong
there and your bairns don't belong to you.   They are very
welcoming and all that but all the time they are watching
you.'

'I never know what to say when I go there.   You're expected to sit down and talk to the bairns.   I can't talk to
them.   I talk to Mrs. Anderson instead.' (Aldgate, 1977:
446)

Feeling uncertain of their role, it is easy to see how
natural parents may be persuaded by foster parents to withdraw
from the placement, particularly if their visits seem upsetting to the children.   Alternatively, they may turn to the
only weapon they have left - verbal or physical aggression.
This is likely to upset foster parents, and possibly can set
up a spiral of mutual hostility leading to termination of all
contact.

Even with the best will in the world, shared parenting is
equally hard to achieve in practice from the foster parents'
point of view.   There are many ways in which parents can
cause trouble.   They can leave children distressed after
visits and, even if the theory of normal separation reactions
is understood, this is a very different matter from coping
with the reality.   Parents may promise to visit and then never
turn up or undermine the equilibrium of the foster home by
inciting children to take sides.   Desperate to win their
children's affections, they may arrive with extravagant
presents or sweets which foster parents feel are totally inappropriate.   Above all, the presence of natural parents
reminds foster parents of the impermanence of their relationship with the child.

Parental visiting is at once the most important and most
complex issue in fostering.   It relates directly to the
emotional well being of the foster child and the inclusiveness
or exclusiveness of the role taken by the foster parents.
The life span of the foster placement is a crucial element.
Initially it may be acceptable for all to adhere to the inclusive model of fostering.   But even if natural parents visit
weekly, there will be a shift in responsibility over time
resulting in a transfer of primary parenting to foster
parents.   Rowe (1977) believes that this presents a dilemma,
and a crucial question is whether there can be a successful

mixture of the inclusive and exclusive roles for long-term foster care. Elements of both seem to be needed if the concept of shared parenting is to work in reality.

The responsibility for role clarity in fostering lies with the agency (Kline and Overstreet, 1972) and the pattern for interaction is set early in the placement (Pugh, 1968). But research indicates that social workers are confused and ambivalent about their own relationships and expectations in fostering. They shy away from the difficulties through not visiting foster homes (George, 1970; Aldgate, 1977), they collude with foster parents in their desire to become natural or adoptive parents (George, 1970) and they deny the child the right of access to knowledge about his natural family (Thorpe, 1974; Aldgate, 1977). Although parental contact is applauded in theory, in practice social workers adopt a passive attitude and do little to help natural parents to overcome the very real problems they face in maintaining contact with foster children (George, 1970; Thorpe, 1974; Aldgate, 1977).

In theory, social workers should be able to resolve their difficulties. They are trained to deal with complex emotional problems. They have a clear responsibility to act as coordinators for all the services the foster child needs (DHSS, 1976). Above all, the law demands that they consider the long-term interests of children in their care (Children Act 1975, Section 59). Rowe (1977) believes that the discrepancy between theory and practice results from 'uncertainty about long-term goals linked with discomfort over the inadequacies of past and present services to parents, doubts about priorities and a general unwillingness to provoke difficulties or rock the boat' (p. 19).

Outcome of foster care

The viability of foster families can be considered in relation to the outcome. There are three ways in which outcome has been measured: the maintenance of continuous care by the foster family, the emotional adjustment of the foster child and the subsequent adjustment of the foster child in adult life.

With all the confusion surrounding long-term fostering, it is hardly surprising that researchers report a high incidence of breakdown in the continuity of foster care - a widely reported figure is around 50 per cent (Trasler, 1960; Parker, 1966; George, 1970). Parker (1966) developed a useful prediction table of factors influencing successful fostering to aid social workers, but George (1970) found that in practice there was little use of research findings.

It seems that long-term foster care is more likely to succeed if foster mothers are older (Trasler, 1960; Parker, 1966; George, 1970) and have older children who are not in competition with foster children or no children at all.   At least one year's experience of fostering before a long-term placement is made increases the chance of success.   The younger a child, the more likely he is to succeed in the placement.   A long period of institutional care before fostering is a negative factor but a short period in residential care giving time for assessment and preparation can help the placement to succeed.

The second evaluation of foster families comes from looking at the adjustment of foster children.   Prosser (1978) reports 'there is substantial evidence that children in foster care are maladjusted but little is known about whether this disturbance is caused by the fact of foster care per se' (p. 15). Holman (1973) reports that aggression, anxiety and difficulty in making relationships are the problem areas.   Whether this type of behaviour is brought into the foster home or stimulated by it, it is clear that each successive rejection by foster parents increases a child's difficulties of being successfully re-fostered.   Success in long-term fostering is dependent on the careful matching of the needs of the child and his foster family.

The third way of evaluating foster families is to look at the effects of fostering in later life.   There have been few studies in this area and results are mixed.   Ferguson (1976) claimed that children who had been in foster homes did better in adult life than those who had been in residential care. The relationship of foster children with their foster parents continued into adult life in nearly one-third of the sample. Meir (1962) found that in comparison with the general population, a sample of former foster children exhibited a higher incidence of marital breakdown and, among women, there was a significantly larger number of illegitimate children, still births and miscarriages that did not seem to be related to economic circumstances.   Socially and economically, nearly the whole group were adequate but tended to underestimate their social effectiveness.   On balance they were more successful than their biological parents.   Current research by Triseliotis (1978) comparing the outcome of adoptive, foster and residential homes reports favourably on the adult adjustment of foster children.

PART II: ADOPTIVE FAMILIES

The characteristic impermanence of the foster family and its
concomitant problems lends itself to comparison with the permanence offered by adoptive families. This section is by no
means comprehensive but it points to some of the major issues
in adoption and compare this family type with foster families.

Legal framework

Adoption in its present form has been a legal process since
the first Adoption Act of 1926. Current adoptions are governed by the 1958 Adoption Act as amended by the 1975 Children
Act. Because adoption is final in the sense that it places a
parent and child in the legal relationship that they would
enjoy had the child been born to the parent in marriage, the
law has sought to balance the interests of all parties concerned - the child, natural and adoptive parents. Although
grounds do exist for dispensing with natural parents' consent,
it is generally assumed that parental agreement to adoption is
an important part of the whole process. As Rowe points out
(1976:1) 'The balance has shifted from time to time with increasing attention being given to the child's need.' The
1975 Children Act Section 3 demands that first consideration
be given to the long-term welfare of the children who have
been adopted.
    Children may be adopted by relatives or non-relatives.
There are certain qualifications governing the suitability of
potential adopters in both these circumstances.
    Adoption may be arranged through an agency or placements
may be made direct by the natural parents or through third
parties. The 1975 Children Act seeks to abolish third-party
placements, an amendment founded on the belief of practitioners that some adopters in these cases may not be suitable.
Agency placements offer the safeguard in that there is a
thorough scrutiny of the potential adopters, while the law
demands in all cases that there be medical examinations for
adopters. In direct placements there is no scrutiny of what
an agency might consider to be good parenting qualities. On
the other hand, in a direct placement the natural parents may
choose the family in which their child will grow up. In all
cases, the law demands that before a court hearing an independent report is submitted by a guardian ad litem who has to
confirm that parental agreement was given freely and that the
adoption will be in the child's best interest. The court
hearing itself may take place at either a magistrates court or
a county court.

Agency adoption has for a long time been associated with voluntary agencies - some national like Barnardo's, some offering an independent service in one particular area, like, for example Family Care in Edinburgh or the Independent Adoption Society in London and others which are linked to churches and serve particular dioceses.   Before the 1975 Children Act some local authorities also acted as adoption agencies. Although not implemented yet, part of the 1975 Act seeks to ensure that adoptive services are extended in all local authorities as one alternative of a range of child care options available to children who come into the care of the local authority.

Numbers

Recent statistics suggest that about half a million children have been adopted over the last 50 years.   In 1968 27,000 orders were granted but numbers have declined since then. In 1975 there were 22,000 adoption orders made (Rowe, 1976:1). Rowe believes that this figure represents the change whereby the number of children who have been adopted by people unrelated to them has dropped considerably but the number adopted within their own families has gone up.   During the mid 1970s this was shown by an increase in the number of illegitimate and legitimate children being adopted by their mothers and their stepfathers.   Considerable concern was expressed about the latter resulting in changes in the law.   The 1975 Children Act emphasises that for legitimate children custody orders should be sought rather than adoption by step-parents in order to preserve some relationship with a child's absent biological parent.   (It is also proposed that custodianship under this Act will perform a similar function for the fathers of illegitimate children.)   Recent case law has suggested that this section of the Act is being put into effect with the result that step-parent adoptions for legitimate children are on the decline.   There is also no doubt that numbers of illegitimate children being placed for adoption has declined.   Rowe (1976: 1) suggests a drop of over 40 per cent in the number of illegitimate babies being placed by adoption agencies in the mid-1970s.   Although a minority of small babies are still being adopted the emphasis has shifted very much towards the adoption of older children with special needs.   In 1978 there were 12,121 adoption orders registered for England and Wales, the lowest annual number in the post-war period.   Of the total number of children adopted in this year, 45 per cent were under five years old, 33 per cent were aged five to nine and 22 per cent were 10 or over.   Such a change has brought a new role for adoptive parents. Adopting a baby is very different from absorbing into the family a seven-year old who is handicapped and of different racial origin. Carriline and Sawbridge (1975) give examples of successful homefinding of mixed race or handicapped children who traditionally were considered hard to place. Although more recently James (Triseliotis, 1980:178) reports on the success of programmes for the adoption of older children. She concludes (p. 195) 'It is now clear that children previously considered unadopt-able can be adopted, that there are people willing to be parents to such children and prepared to work hard to build a family in this different way.' Among these hard-to-place children are those who have been foster children or who have been in long-term residential care. Rowe and Lambert (1973) drew attention to the diminished chances of rehabilitation for many children in long-term foster care and argued strongly for adoption as a permanent and better alternative. The 1975 Children Act has reflected the importance of permanence and a sense of belonging by sanctioning the application for adoption from adults with whom children deprived of their natural parents have spent at least five years. The Association of British Adoption and Fostering Agencies (1976) puts the case for adoption: 'the vital ingredients for adoption success seem to be security, commitment and clarity about the parent-ing role. Adoptors definitely see themselves as parents whereas foster parents often wonder what their relationship is supposed to be.'

The optimism about adoptive families as a viable alterna-tive to long-term foster families is supported by research evidence. Citing several studies, Kellmer-Pringle (1975) believes that adoption is 'one of the soundest most lasting and incidentally cheapest ways of meeting the needs of certain children who are socially deprived and in need of a normal home life' (p. 146). She also records that early stresses and disadvantages can be overcome by the favourable environ-ment of a permanent family. Research from Kadushin (1970) and Jaffee and Fanshel reports favourably on the successful adoption of older children. This contrasts with the adverse findings of a high breakdown rate in the placement of some older foster children (Parker, 1966; George, 1970). In Jaffee and Fanshel's study (1970) neither the age of placement nor the number of changes prior to adoption had any signifi-cant affect on adjustment.

In spite of its apparent success rate, adoption is not without its problems. As in foster care, one of the main issues is the child's search for identity. An important piece of work in this area is that by Triseliotis (1973) who interviewed adoptive adults in search of their origins. He

identified three areas of need in the adoptive child: 'The
developing child's need for a warm, caring and secure family
life; the adoptee's vulnerability to experiences of loss rejection or abandonment; and the adoptive person's need to
know as much as possible about the circumstances of their
adoption and about the geneological background in order to
integrate these facts into their developing personality'
(p. 1).

Another problem of adopters is coming to terms with their
infertility. Pre-adopters may need considerable skilled
counselling in coming to terms with their childlessness; they
may also need to think about their attitude towards illegitimacy. Rowe (1977) argues that adopters should also have to
prepare themselves for parenthood.

The adopters' acceptance of infertility and illegitimacy
are vitally important but they are unsufficient without the
ability to accept the full role of parents. Only when
they can do this are adopters free to allow their child to
be curious and to explore his biological origins because
his interests no longer threaten the reality of their life
together as a family. Some adopters never achieve this
completely and for others it may come only gradually and
in response to the child's complete acceptance of them as
parents. Agencies may do much to help or hinder the process by their placing methods and by the timing and manner
of giving background information about the child's natural
parents.

The successful outcome of adoption depends upon the handling of these major areas. Triseliotis (1973) believes that
the issues specific to adoptive families require attention at
each different stage of the family cycle. The support from
outside which is available to foster families should be equally accessible to adoptive families, and there is a need for
adoption agencies to see their work as part of an ongoing process rather than a once and for all activity.

CONCLUSION

In this chapter I have attempted to outline the main factors
which distinguish the foster family from other family types.
Foster families are characterised by their complexity and are
vulnerable to failure. The major issues result from confusion about roles and relationships. These relate to the concept of shared parenting and the peculiar domination of this
family type by a major institution.

Over the next decade, the character of foster families may
change. Parker (1978) believes there will be a decline in

the numbers of foster parents coming forward.   The indications are that this will not be matched by a decline in the
demand for foster homes.   The types of children coming into
public care are changing.   They are often older and need more
specialist placements.   One-parent families have always been
a high-risk group who have needed public care for their children (Packman, 1966; Mapstone, 1969; Adlgate, 1977).   The
continuing growth of the one-parent family may lead to a great
demand for specialist part-time relief foster care.   The formation of the National Foster Care Association reflects the
concern that foster parents have expressed about their lack of
rights and the unsatisfactory nature of an open-minded, long-
term placement.   It may be therefore that foster care develops inttwo directions.   On the one hand, the caretaking
aspect of the foster family's role will be played up with more
so-called 'professional' placements where the foster families
take on the role of 'foster care workers' (George, 1970:79-81)
and are paid a salary for meeting the needs of a child who has
specific problems.   These placements will invariably be time-
limited.   There have already been several successful schemes
of this type for adolescents and handicapped children.   If
more develop, some foster families may change their role to
that of the dual-worker family where the foster father continues his traditional employment but the foster mother
becomes a full employee of the social services department and
receives training.

   Alongside the professionalisation of time-limited placements, there may be a revaluation of the use of long-term
foster homes.   Already, the transition from foster to adoptive family after five years must become a reality.   The 1975
Children Act also proposes a new form of guardianship or custodianship for which long-term foster families will be eligible.   Custodians would not be supervised by social workers,
thus altering the balance of power between carers and the
local authority.   It would also bring some measure of privacy
which at present has been denied the supervised foster family.
Under custodianship access from natural parents would still be
allowed and in certain circumstances custodianships could be
revoked.   It remains to be seen whether this new semi-adoptive care will help resolve the issues of impermanence and
shared parenting which are characteristic of foster family
care.

Chapter 16

Alternative households
Andrew McCulloch

This chapter is principally about those contemporary groups
known as communes: that is intimate domestic groups who aim
to, or if it is not the primary intention, in fact do,
restructure normal domestic and kin relations in a collective
setting. (1)

It is in order to disentangle ideology from the actuality
of domestic arrangements that the central concept of this
chapter is not that of the family - a notoriously slippery
notion - but that of the household. It is certainly a recognised position in anthropology to regard the household as a
more theoretically significant concept than that of the
family. Goody, for instance, argued that the family is a
static concept whereas that of the household is a dynamic one
(Goody, 1958). Sociologists, in contrast, use the concept of
the family more widely, orientated as they are for the most
part to functional analysis of relations amongst the various
social institutions. And they use the family concept dynami-
cally, in the developmental framework of the family life-
cycle.

A paradoxical reason for the persistent interest in the
sociology of the family stems from the rise of the women's
movement. Women's studies have tended to be Marxist-orienta-
ted, and in the study of sexual divisions and domestic labour
they have tended to displace and supersede the study of the
family; but through their polemical attack on the nuclear
family these writers have served to maintain the concept of
the family, albeit as their target. The emphasis on sex as
the most powerful division in society supports the focus on
the study of family life, even though, as in Christine
Delphy's work, the family is portrayed stereotypically in
negative terms, as patriarchy. To the extent that feminist
writers focus on the goal of creating a 'political economy of
women' (as does for instance, Maxine Molyneux) then the family

is explicitly dismissed as the central object of analysis.   A
position somewhat between these two is taken in the work of
Mary McIntosh.   For her the family is prior to the capitalist
mode of production and has proved obdurate and persistent,
though inadequate for the reproduction of the working class as
a whole.

Nevertheless in this type of analysis, it is not really the
family that is brought sharply into focus, but the household
system, the sexual division of labour, the forms of social
reproduction, the capitalist labour process, the class structures and so on.   Particular types of household are the complex loci of these various structures, including the 'ideology
of the family', which is one of the ways in which the household systems we have are maintained.

In the tradition of British sociology the biases induced by
social class have sometimes been muffled.   In such studies as
Young and Willmott's 'Family and Kinship in East London'
(1957) and the line of middle-class studies beginning with
Colin Bell's Middle-Class Families' (1968) and continuing
through the Rapoport's 'Dual-Career Families' (1971) and Young
and Willmott's 'The Symmetrical Family' (1975), there has been
a certain evolutionary optimism which anticipates that the
middle-class family household will be first to breach new
developments.   This view of the cultural leadership of the
middle class is shared by many who live in communes, which are
themselves overwhelmingly middle class in social composition.

The position taken in this chapter is that what is happening in the middle class does not tell us anything very much
about 'the family' in general, or households in general, or
the directions in which they are both evolving.   Similarly,
we would argue that middle-class communes are not an unequivocally progressive social form.   They are characteristic of
the capitalist society within which they have arisen, with all
the contradictions that that implies.   If communal or collective forms of household arise elsewhere than in the middle
class in a society trisected by sex, race and class they can
be expected to be different in structure and significance.

In the USA there are varying estimates for the number of
communes.   For instance, the Constantines estimated from 1970
US Census material that 8 per cent of all marriages were experimental: 'we can refer with some certainty not to scattered thousands, but possibly to millions whose marriages and
family living style depart dramatically from traditional concepts of these institutions in America' (Constantine and Constantine, 1976:6).   Judson Jerome had on file in 1973 definite information about 1,000 communes and estimated that there
were 5,000 public communes and an additional 20,000 private
ones in the USA (Jerome, 1975:18-19).   Most of these were

rural rather than urban.   As a consequence the literature on
American communes has been enormous, although unfortunately,
with naturally a few exceptions, hardly rich and varied.   In
Britain the scale of experimentation has been much smaller and
so has the size of the literature.   In making any comparisons, however, it is well to bear in mind that the definition
of a commune has tended to be much broader in the USA than
here.   In the USA conditions are more appropriate to the existence of large rural collectivities, who do not necessarily
share a common household, but who have some form of collective
life and as a result call themselves a commune.   In Britain
the term commune has tended to be reserved by actual practitioners, and by those studying them, for those groups who
share some or all of the facets of a common household.

No attempt is made in any official British survey or census
to identify such communal groups and therefore all the information we have about their incidence and prevalence is extremely imprecise.

There are only, to my knowledge, three relatively serious
published sets of studies of those communes in Britain which
attempt to create kin-linked households on a different foundation from conventional family households: Andrew Rigby's
'Alternative Realities' (1974a) and 'Communes in Britain'
(1974b), Clem Gorman's 'People Together' (1975) and the study
Philip Abrams and I wrote, 'Communes' Sociology and Society'
(1976).   There is in addition Richard Mills's 'Young Outsiders' (1973) which examines extremely transient or work-
based hippy communal groups.   Finally, there is R.M. Lee's
splendid thesis, 'Communes as Alternative Families' (1979).
It is either nervously conceded, proudly proclaimed, or, as
in our case, smugly revealed, by these studies (as in the
American studies) that these new forms of household are all
decidedly middle class in orientation and social composition.
In the groups we visited we encountered people who were
antique restorers, dentists, journalists, architects,
painters, potters, weavers, builders, photographers, book-
sellers, secretaries, students and, overwhelmingly, teachers,
from primary school to university level.

These middle-class alternative households take many forms
but the ideological hallmark of their collective project is
the attempt to create a form of intimate existence characterised by openness, and non-exclusive attachments.   This
struggle systematically to open up the domestic and intimate
relations of the normal kin-based nuclear household is pre-
mised on the belief that what is chiefly at fault with the
conventional family household is that it is excessively closed
and rigid.   Furthermore, this isolation is a threat to the
very integrity and expression of the self.   This picture,
however, requires some qualification as I shall show later.

Those interested in communal living have complained about how conventionally loving in essence meant owning, about the irksomeness of normal female-male roles, and reflected bitterly upon the 'isolated, narrow-minded, egotistical' nuclear family forms which 'restrict human potential, freeze relationships, stunt the exploratory and innovating side of our consciousness and cause manifold frustration' (Abrams and McCulloch, 1976:124-5).

In principle this objective of 'non-possessive attachments' and a determined self-conscious effort to construct caring and loving relationships between adults and between parents and children rooted in an ideal of relational openness is admirable, brave and hazardous.   Many, but by no means all, of the problems of alternative households spring from this aim, and it is the main reason we should have some regard for them. This objective of free and sincere caring and loving can be realised in many different forms: a wide range of intentional or developmental communes, and group or 'multilateral' and open marriage.   Such a continuum slides into the partner swapping repellantly known as 'swinging' and into that constant shadow of the bourgeois marriage, the affair.   Indeed some couples have actually travelled up this road of increasing openness to reach communal living.

It might therefore be reasonably supposed that the forms of these alternatives to monogamous marriage and the conventional family household are related to the perceived failures of these institutions.   Indeed, they are, but the relationships between the perceived failures, the level and development of the critique and the forms in which they are embodied are not unmediated nor simple.   On the one hand, ideology cannot be directly and immediately lived, particularly if it derives its force from a reaction against marriage and 'family' rather than towards a positive institutional commitment.   On the other, the power of ideology, undeveloped through ideological beliefs are in British communes, has certain effects, and the strains consequent upon specific beliefs cannot be escaped. But whatever the quality and content of the ideological structure, two key problems of the 'factual' order obdurately remain: the care of children and the sexual division of labour.

The clandestine affair, an old-established institution amongst the middle classes, and 'swinging' or 'wife-swapping' as it was once revealingly known in the Sunday papers, are both essentially private and supplementary to the conventional forms.   It is almost impossible to say anything of worth about 'swinging'.   Most of the literature is exhortation; there is no published empirical research on it in this country, and little in the USA.   In Britain there do exist rather shabby magazines advertising contacts for 'swingers' but it is impossible to say how widespread the activity is or pronounce upon its consequences for marriage and the children.   There does appear to exist what we might call open and closed 'swinging'.   Swinging is open when the marital partners share a wide variety of other sets of partners, and closed when the 'swopping' takes place only between firmly established friends of long duration.   This latter form leads analytically and sometimes actually, into an alternative form of household. Danfield and Gordon report that there are two kinds of swingers: recreational and utopian, and this perhaps also coincides with a class difference.   The latter believe that swinging will lead to sexual liberalisation and possibly social liberalisation.   All believe that 'the damaging aspect in extramarital sex is the lying and the cheating, and if this is removed extramarital sex is beneficial to the marital bond' (Danfield and Gordon, 1971:473).

Affairs exist at all because there is a conflict between the relatively permanent responsibilities of children and household and the normally less permanent phenomenon of romantic love.   The more marriage is viewed as a rational conditional liaison for the purposes of personal development and enjoyment the more corrosive this is of marital stability, which itself may partly be a condition of that development and enjoyment.   The affair offers one resolution of this dilemma.

The pressures for clandestinity are (a) fear of loss of the valued relationship of a marital partner or partners; (b) possible adverse effects on children;   (c) pressure of public opinion and, most especially close relatives and (d) material costs such as possible loss of a house to live in, perhaps a job, and the ensuing need to support dependants of a broken relationship.

An open marriage is one which recognises that the affair is a natural concomitant of marriage and freely acknowledges this.   The sexual activities of the partners outside the marital bond become part of their everyday existence together. Its most celebrated advocates are the O'Neills in the book entitled 'Open Marriage' (1973).   In it they press the opportunities for personal development that such a marriage opens up.   The paradox, as the O'Neills make clear, is that to engage in such a marriage the participants have to have strong identities, i.e. to be already personally developed.

In considering relations between the sexes within communal collective settings we shall have to bear these points in mind.   Alternative family households attempt, in some sense, to mitigate these strains and problems.   The opportunities for 'affairs' within communal households, for example, are increased, particularly for women.   Nevertheless, many of the strains persist.

In Britain there are few collective attempts to supersede or replace the conventional household system and most do not last very long.   The Commune Movement was established in October 1968 and in 1971 their Directory listed forty-five enterprises in Britain.   Four could not be called collective or communal and three of the remaining had already collapsed at the time of printing, leaving thirty-eight groups of which a significant proportion (seven) were religious groups, either Christian or Buddhist.

Rigby estimated that in 1972 there were probably 100 communes altogether, counting those not affiliated to the Commune Movement and those that avoided publicity.   Rigby himself had direct knowledge of about fifty communes and Gorman claims the same number.   Their pages are studded with accounts of communes that folded during the course of their research, sometimes before they even had time to visit them.   Our study lasted five years and we had knowledge, of varying quality, of about sixty-seven groups.   Only about six groups persisted through that period and five now remain.   The one that disappeared had fair claim to be one of the longest lived and most firmly entrenched of any secular 'family' commune in Britain.   Communes are now much less evangelistic than they were and much more committed to their privacy.   This withdrawal and increase in caution has not led to them becoming more widespread.   My impression is that there are probably now no more than fifty groups in Britain, although there are considerable grounds for being more optimistic about the chances of the long-term survival of what appear to be now much more modest experiments.

It is not a simple matter to judge what counts as success in these precarious exercises in new forms of solidarity. After a long argument, taking into account an ideology which aimed to balance conditional mutual affirmation and rational self-realisation, we came to the conclusion that 'a commune is a success in so far as its members seem able to negotiate their way towards a society of equals - and to do so without sacrificing their individuality in the process' (Abrams and McCulloch, 1976:161).   Unfortunately such a utopian definition of success - the pursuit of a form of solidarity which is not experienced as externally induced - is rarely if ever realised.   In our study of communes we implicitly and explicitly came to a number of more specific interrelated criteria: the extent of sustained mutual attentiveness or reciprocated caring, the longevity of the group, the emotional security of any children of the group and the quality of the sexual division of labour.

Until this point we have used the term communal in its generic sense to mean all experimental household groups which

practise an ideology of sharing.   Within this large category
two distinctive types have emerged and been described analytically by Ron Lee (1979).   Lee has reserved the term 'communal' for those households in which each individual shares
with all other individuals.   In contrast, 'collective' households retain the nuclear family as the basic unit, with each
family sharing the resources with all other families.   The
distinction is relatively easy to make analytically, if not in
practice.   This is because alternative family households
appear to be in a process of constantly exploring modes of
relating which lie between these modes.   For Rigby and Gorman
a significant act in making a commune was calling yourself
one.   We ourselves at first took this position but eventually
created an ideal-type definition of a communal household, part
of which reads as follows:

> The most complete (communal household) would be one in
> which the group shared a single dwelling or tightly inte-
> grated cluster of dwellings and the basic services within
> it.   All areas of activity would be common and so would
> property.   The group would earn its living together and
> divide all that it earned equally, and all surplus would be
> available to all members.   The group would constitute the
> the circle of best friends for all its members, and the
> functions of the family would be concentrated within it;
> the depth and range of emotional interaction between the
> members would be great.   Stable couples would not be rec-
> ognised, and many different lines of relationship would be
> possible.   Children would be regarded as the children of
> the group as a whole, and everyone, including the children
> themselves from an early age, would have an equal say in
> their upbringing.... Decision making would be achieved
> through universal participation and assent.   Leadership
> would be an irrelevance. (Abrams and McCulloch, 1976:38-9)

No one has come across any groups who could live up to such
high expectations, but it is clear from the work of Rigby,
Gorman and ourselves that this was an ideal that many communal
households would recognise and see themselves as struggling
towards.   The essential movements are an attempt to disperse
the intimacy and caring of the conventional family household
throughout the communal group coupled with the enclosure of
all important affectionate and emotional relationships within
it (see Figure 16.1).   By contrast a collective household is
segmental in structure, composed of separate nuclear family
households who share many facilities and activities but not
all.   Friendship is communal but intimacy is private.   In a
communal household the negotiation with the group is consensual, informal and on an individual basis; in a collective
household it is formal, tends towards the contractual and is

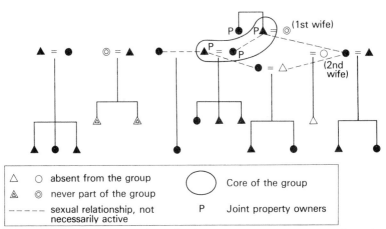

FIGURE 16.1 Relationships within a communal household (based
loosely on an actual group) (1)

1 It is not possible to clearly separate the generations but
   in the diagram the higher up the page the greater the age.

on a family household basis.   Income and property is a collective household are not shared, and the separate nuclear
family household retains its conventional structure, with
children as subordinate and the responsibility for their care
and control firmly with their parents.   There are strains
within both these ideal forms which draw the one towards the
other.

   The more intense and intimate the relationships within a
group, the smaller it tends to be.   The amount of 'relationship work' becomes too great.   Group or multi-lateral marriage, i.e. a commitment to loving, sexual relationships
throughout the group, which obviously defines part of the
extreme end of the spectrum of communal household, has few
overt proponents who are practitioners in this country.
Rigby found no one to defend group marriage.   Gorman reports
that the Ramsgate community - his only example - broke down
into couples after arguments over the rights of refusal to
sexual access.   In our only example the men felt unable to
comply and eventually all left.   Perhaps these groups were
already too large.   Ramey's (1977:23) finding in the USA was
that the triad was the most common and stable form (i.e.
everyone of the three relating to everyone else).   The Constantines, however, in their study found that two couples were
most usual (Constantine and Constantine, 1973).   It is not
surprising that the main difficulties that the Constantines's
group encountered were personal friction, communication

problems and jealousy.   Small size entails emotional compression, at the same time as promising depth in the relationships.

Larger groups defuse this emotionally explosive situation, but equally court the danger of the obvious crystallisation of an explicit social structure, and, if they become too large, the diminution of intimacy.   It is perhaps for these reasons that the most communal households range between five and twenty-five adults.   The most fascinating illustration of this was a group which we studied and which started life as a large family collective household and moved towards a communal household.   It was unable to manage this move with the size and composition of membership it had, and divided internally into three cells - two communal and one collective household. The more vibrant communal household then gradually absorbed the other.

Collective households can sustain a much larger number of members and it also appears a wider age range.   Old Hall, a collective household, contains thirty-five adults from their middle twenties to sixty years of age and twenty-five children.   Given the nature of their enterprise the members of a collective household are resigned to a certain level of bureaucracy and Old Hall, for instance, has an elaborate system of committees and meetings.   Nevertheless, there has to be total consensus on important decisions (see Lee, 1979).

In a communal household the larger the size the more explicit is a distinction which all studies note in one form or another: be it recognised as leadership, more extravagantly as charisma, or like us, as a distinction between core and fringe, there is an acknowledgment that some are more central to the communal project than others: 'to the observer it often appears that a crude distinction can be made in the membership between the founders, appointed leaders, or spokesmen of the group and the "joiner" or rank and file members' (Rigby, 1974a:40).

The core and fringe exist in a symbiotic relationship: each is necessary for the continued existence of the other. The composition of the core and fringe is not immutable and the changes reflect and determine the group's progress towards either a communal or a collective household, or dissolution. The distinction is at its most stark in religious projects. In communal households the quest for self-realisation within, and identity with, the communal experiment is more strenuous than in collective households, although in the latter it is still present.   The consequences are that this violation of the belief in equality has deeper and wider effects in a communal household.   The irritation and disappointment of members of the fringe, if unable to win their way into the core,

leads to a high turnover. And it is the changing quality of
the relations between the core and fringe which lie at the
heart of the slumps and booms in morale in communal groups
which Gorman describes.

It is, of course, obvious that pair-bonding has a much
higher salience and is much more clearly defined in collective
than in communal households. There is a remarkable disparity
between the intentions of those living in communal households
and their actual practice in this respect. Judson Jerome
asserts that the tendency is for couples to disappear, and
many would agree with this but 'in practice most British communal projects are really collections of couples living
together' (Gorman, 1975:124). The real difference is that in
communal households, as opposed to collective households, particular couples have a less stable existence. In one communal household they compared their life together with 'a series
of shipboard romances'.

The commonplace nature of stable pair-bonding helps dis-
guise sexism and the exploitation of women. In places where
pair-bonding is more fluid, the taken-for-granted nature of
sexism is more likely to be unmasked. Strangely, Rigby has
little to say about sexism in British groups, although he is
driven to presume, by American evidence, that it must exist.
Gorman is much more definite: 'attempting to maintain some
sexist attitudes in an otherwise communal situation, has been
shown by the bitter experience of many British projects to be
disastrous for communal spirit' (Gorman, 1976:35).

Contemporary British and American studies show a common
theme in their analysis of communes' attempts to rework the
goals of nuclear family households in collectivist terms.
The goals are perceived to be self-realisation or personal
identity. Every book on communal and collective households
bursts with quotations in which those living in collective or
communal household groups, or wanting to, plead for somewhere
where they can be themselves. The 'conventional family
household' at the very least is seen as not satisfying this
desire, as we saw earlier.

> I have been searching for a long time for an alternative
> ... in which I could use my talents for the good of others,
> and not have a great deal of pressure put upon me, espec-
> ially by people in authority, to actively participate in a
> way of life that is totally opposed to all the good things
> in people and which does not allow me to reach my true
> potential as a human being. My earnest desire in life,
> and which provides the key to my whole personality growth,
> is to be given the full opportunity to love and be loved,
> and if communal life gives me this opportunity I will be
> eternally grateful. (Abrams and McCulloch, 1976:116)

There are no grounds for simply equating the quest for
self-realisation with selfishness.   This particular quotation
illustrates a widespread understanding that the search for
self-realisation can be a social enterprise.   Self-realisation as a social and mutual enterprise requires the readiness
of all to throw themselves into the process of mutual development.   If some invest themselves deeply in a particular
interpretation of the goals or methods of the group, others
tend to experience it as alien.

In principle, there is an antinomy between self-realisation
and possessive individualism.   The self cannot be simultaneously perceived as a possession which can only be realised
detached from social relations and also as a social product.
The quest for it to be both creates a dilemma.   There are two
ways out of this principled dilemma of freedom or structure.
One is to accept, albeit reluctantly, that a clear social
structure is necessary in order to serve the personal trans-
cendance.   At Findhorn, the large collective in the north
east of Scotland, this resolution is expressed in religious
terms.   There is an explicit definition of roles and use of
rituals.   In more secular communities the instruments of
structure are less readily available, but many do come to
introduce it in the interests of organisation.

The other avenue is via the creation of a precious private
sphere apparently detached from wider social relations in
which the feeling of self-realisation can be made operative in
a small-scale practical way.   This is done in a number of
ways.   One way relates to money.   There is a need to generate fairly large sums of capital to begin such ventures.
This affects the process of selection.   It is possible to
join communes without much capital (there are some who make
capital available altruistically to communes in which they do
not live - so that others who have less can benefit).   But
there is a tendency to require capital (which gives communes
a middle-class bias) and within communes for those with more
money invested to enjoy privileges.

Economic pressures are also generated by the fact that most
communes are unable in practice to achieve their ideal of
self-sufficiency - e.g. through subsistence farming or craft-
work.   This also militates toward differentials, with the
more affluent members feeling less pressure to work.

A hazard which is widely appreciated as a potential consequence of these differentials is that of crystallised inequalities in the division of labour within the commune.   In our
study of communes we were impressed with how people *so* ideal-
istic about equality and sharing could endure *such* inequalities.   The key to understanding the discrepancy seems to lie
in the feeling that it is fluid and negotiable, not a fixed
and inevitable reproduction of the outside divisions.

One basis for sustaining this sense of a negotiable division of household labour is economic.   By detaching ownership of the household from individuals and vesting it in a corporate body, the division of labour can be more open to negotiation than in the conventional family household.   Furthermore, for such negotiations to avoid adverse results, there is a channelling of communal income toward those making a primarily domestic contribution - alleviating one of the sore points of conventional 'captive', 'exploited' housewives.   In addition, many communes press their more affluent members to lower their personal aspirations and to pool their property.   Normally communards contribute towards a household fund.   As there are considerable economies of scale resulting from communal living, some of this pooling is beneficial to the donor as well as the others, but there is no doubt about the large element of risk.

In collective households no one expects, or risks, so much. Every family household has to risk a certain amount of capital in buying in, but there is no income sharing, little voluntary asceticism, and few elements of inter-unit division of labour. Collective solidarity is limited and briskly practical.   The goal is to avoid the segmented character of urban living while retaining the full autonomy of the nuclear family household. The anomalies of wage or salary labour are recognised reluctantly as necessary and to be compensated for in the co-operative form of domestic existence they have adopted (Lee, 1979).

Aside from economic investment, communal households rely on emotional investment, and here too there are contrasts between the two types.   In collective households there is far less of a core commitment for others to appropriate.   The ditches separating the private and the collective are more deeply dug. The ditches stipulate in advance the condition under which the collective project was entered into and circumscribe any future variation.   In collective households the relationships of parents to each other and to their children are not put so seriously into question as in communal households.   The children are children of a particular nuclear household, and not of the group as a whole.   At Findhorn, a very large religious collective household, formally organised day-care arrangements are made for children, but this is not usual. In principle, any loosening of the principle of private ownership is largely adventitious: it is to realise the potential of what each family has rather than to change its nature, that they choose collective households.

It is a significant difference in more than one way, between collective and communal households, that in collective households a major point of discussion and unease is the extent to which adults can discipline and control children other than their own. In communal households there is a sustained effort to open up the relationships of adults to each other and to their children and within those relationships to realise the values of mutuality and equality. The hope is that the children belong to the group as a whole. It has proved easier to realise these values in the relationships of the parents to each other than in the relationships of parents to children. The status of children in communal groups tends to be deeply problematic. The rhetoric is often that 'many communal projects are started because of children, whether to give them a better life or because of the economic strains they create for single parents in cities' (Gorman, 1975:125). Furthermore, there is overwhelming agreement about what communal living can achieve for children: greater variety of role models, more companions, a mature emotional security and above all freedom from an exaggerated emotional dependence upon the parents - language which springs from the belief in adult self-realisation. It is argued that all mothers and fathers are not necessarily cut out to be good parents and the collective setting provides help and support for such a burdensome role. The reality tends to be somewhat different and is well conveyed by the offhanded way children are mentioned, for instance, by the Constantines. In their study of group marriages they found that the principle reasons for joining were 'greater companionship, sexual and intellectual variety, and personal growth, along with creating a better child-rearing environment for children' (Constantine and Constantine, 1976). In one American 'commune' studied by Berger (Berger et al., 1972) the children themselves formed a separate colony, joining it at the age of four years old. In British communal households we often saw displayed to us the benefits that a large group of children together bring in terms of their own happiness and enjoyment and in the impressive, solicitous care that the older gave towards the younger. But if one or both of the parents leave the children must leave with them. The children then may become very lonely, bereft of their former peers and by adults 'viewed as intrinsically worthy of love and respect *but not necessarily of attention*' (Berger, 1972: 287).

And, if in collective households there is a reticence about instructing the children of others, in communal households there is the danger of a multiplicity of adult rule-enforcers overwhelming the children (see Kanter et al., 1975:449). It would appear that this is no accident and can be reasonably viewed as one adaptation to the growing power of children and young adults within family households in Western capitalist societies.

The commitment on the part of the adults towards a lack of

deliberate internal structure in a communal household means
that the relationships that do emerge in some senses appear
'natural'.   What they are, of course, is the result of wider
social determinations penetrating largely unfiltered into the
communal household.   Thus, all the studies both here and in
America unequivocally report that mothering is a burden less
easily escaped than fathering.   The reasons for this are that
the outside world, especially if the child is at school,
demands that the child knows who it is - in other words, who
is its parent.   The child is given to understand that it requires someone in this social role to achieve any well being
or self-respect.   And it is mothers rather than fathers who
step into this breach.

Indeed it is quite often the case that the domestic structure of a communal household rests upon a woman who is prepared to act as a mother to the whole commune.   In our study
we found that the gains made by women in communal households
are only through the co-operation of the women within their
feminine roles as wives and mothers, and this does not often
entail a shift of power from men to women.   The status and
power of men, given them by the wider social structure, and
within the group, the subscription to the values of equality
openness, freedom, conditionality of relationships and so
forth, can leave women with children more exposed to the
prospect of being deserted by their men than before.   However, whilst the beliefs of communal households condone the
ending of dead relationships they also provide a supportive
atmosphere when breakdown does occur and if, as is often the
case, the father leaves.   No woman has been thrown out of a
commune because 'her' man has left, but one group who had too
frequently experienced this pattern of male desertion began to
regret the emotional costs involved for the group.

In one instance we came across where the women did actively
challenge the power of men, the men first withdrew emotionally
and then left.   More generally we found 'what is tantamount
to a conspiracy to enlarge the value and meaningfulness of
conventional women's roles on the basis of more or less elaborate or symbolic concessions to participation by men and the
guarantee that women's work will in the end be performed by
women' (Abrams and McCulloch, 1976:144).   None of the other
published studies give any real reason to dispute that gener-
alisation.

The largest group who seek membership are female single
parents, and most groups are wary of the costs entailed in
taking on someone with probably few funds, requiring emotional
support and quite possibly so consumed by their childrearing
role as to be able to give little to the communal venture.
Although it has been frequently suggested that all-female

communes should be formed for single parents, we found none.
In collective households single female parents have to meet
strictly financial criteria, so most are excluded on those
grounds.   If they do, however, become a single parent whilst
living in a communal or collective household then the impressive support they receive demonstrates the potentialities of
communal living.   For the elderly, the bereaved, widows and
the otherwise unattached, communal and collective households
can provide generous levels of support.   But these groups
only exceptionally seek to draw in such people so as to apply
their relationship capacities upon them.   And, the closer a
group moves towards the communal rather than the collective
form, with a few exceptions, the increasingly intolerant they
appear to be of age.

Communal households very rarely sustain intergenerational
solidarity.   This is for two main reasons.   Communes have
appeared no more capable of resolving the ambiguous status of
adolescent children - as person or as possession - than have
ordinary households.   The problems may even be increased:
for example, at what age does a child become a sexual participant in the group and what are the consequences of this?
Communal households are not well geared to provide a stable
childrearing structure because of their emphasis on instrumental and/or hedonistic groupings within one generation.   The
group of adults is the decisive point of reference, and intergenerational relationships and child care are secondary.
Children have no special rights or status.   In order to find
themselves the children must leave.

In theory this is less true of collective households.
There are several instances of parents and grown-up children
with their own families becoming new units in collective
households.   But as with communal households, very few of
children born in a collective household remain.

It is often argued that one of the major reasons for the
evanescence of collective and particularly communal households
is the hostility of the outside world (Kanter, 1973).   Paradoxically, this is argued most strongly with reference to
North America where there are both more communal ventures and
much more violent hostility.   In Britain there is less evidence of either.   'Hippy' communes have attracted considerable hostility, it is true, but the projects I have been discussing have suffered little harassment from neighbours or
the forces of the State.   They do not 'squat' and illegal
drug taking is prohibited or very discreetly practised.

There are regulations relating to the sharing of mortgages,
council grants for property renovation, and safety which may
be said to penalise them, but little else.

Ten years ago it would not have appeared sensible to make a

strong distinction between communal and collective households, because there were so few instances of the latter.   Now, if anything, the tide appears to be flowing in their favour, particularly amongst middle-class families.   Their method of alleviating the economic and social stresses of urban family household living may well become attractive to wider sections of the population.

NOTE

1 I have learnt from the work of Ron Lee and his thesis distinguishing between collective and communal households (Ron M. Lee, Communes as Alternative families, MPhil thesis, 1979, North East London Polytechnic).   This chapter is written as an extended commentary upon an earlier brief draft written by the late Philip Abrams to whom this chapter is dedicated.   The argument is, however, rather different in many places.

Chapter 17

Children and family diversity

Phyllis and Peter Willmott

Young children, more than anyone else, live in the world of the family, and changes in its patterns have a major impact on them. The main purpose of this chapter, building on earlier work (Willmott and Willmott, 1978; Willmott and Mayne, 1980) is to make some assessment of the effects of current trends.

We begin with the demographic background, picking up from the earlier chapters by Muriel Nissel and by David Eversley and Lucy Bonnerjea. We then review such evidence as there is on the likely effects of different kinds of family experience upon children. We go on to draw upon a small study of a particular centre for children from one-parent families, which serves to illustrate one particular change in family patterns - increasingly common - which can have profound consequences for children.

CHANGES IN FAMILY STRUCTURE

Since we are drawing comparisons with families in the past, we need to say something, if only briefly, about what 'past' we are comparing with. In one sense, like Muriel Nissel in Chapter 4, we are looking back to the characteristic family of the 1950s. In another sense the comparison is with a longer established style of family life. We have in mind here the concept of the 'marching column' (Young and Willmott, 1973), the argument being that at any point in history people and families span a range of lifestyles - some traditional, some contemporary and some already anticipating the future. In terms of this model, it can be argued that a certain style of family life - based on 'companionate marriage', contraception, smaller families and single-family homes - began to develop among the professional middle classes (Banks, 1954) and subsequently spread to embrace the majority of the population.

A lower middle-class and working-class version was emerging in
the new semi-detached housing that sprang up in the London
suburbs of the 1930s (Willmott, 1979), but it did not achieve
dominance until the relative prosperity of the 1950s.

Among families with young children, the stereotype and the
norm then largely coincided.   Typical 'Happy Families' consisted of a husband-cum-'daddy' who went out to work, a wife-
cum-'mummy' who stayed at home, and two children (the offspring of daddy and mummy), all living as one household in a
semi-detached house or a flat.

This had always been an oversimplification; many more families than was commonly recognised failed to fit the idealised
model.   As at any stage in history (including of course the
present), there were sub-cultural variations according to
region, social class and ethnic origin.   But in recent years
such uniformity as there was in the 1950s has given way to
much greater variety.   As Rapoport et al. (1977) point out, a
number of changes have widened the gap between myth and
reality.   They quote an estimate made by Cogswell and Sussman
(1972), based on USA census data for 1970, which suggested
that at that time only 30 per cent of families with children
were of the standard kind - with two parents of whom only one
was working.   It has not been possible to make exactly comparable calculations for Britain, but available statistics
indicate that in Britain, too, they are now a minority.

There have been various strands in the processes of family
change.   One is the growing propensity of marriages to end in
divorce, described by David Eversley and Lucy Bonnerjea in
Chapter 3.   This increase in divorce is common to most Western countries, although the rates differ.   France and Belgium, for instance, have lower rates than Britain; Sweden,
Denmark and the USA have higher.   Projections for the USA in
particular suggest that, if recent trends continue, about 40
per cent of current marriages will end in divorce.   So if
Britain were to follow and the trend were to accelerate, the
current estimate of one divorce in every five marriages could
by the end of the century easily become as high as one in
every two.   This demographic change matters to the children
because a growing proportion of divorces - in Britain now
three-quarters - are between couples who have dependent children.

While more people are ending marriages, fewer are embarking
on brand-new ones.   The number of first marriages has steadily fallen during recent years and, associated with this, the
trend towards early marriage, evident since 1945, was reversed
in the 1970s.   It now looks as if marriage is a less popular
institution among the young than it used to be, a change which
would be consistent with the current more permissive and more
open attitude to sexual relationships.

Although the trend to younger average age of marriage has ceased and shown signs of turning, the age at which people begin sexual relations continues to fall.   In recent years sexuality, childbearing and marriage have become less closely related than in the past.   Evidence for the 1976 OPCS Family Formation Survey shows that growing proportions of couples live together before, and outside, marriage. (Leete, 1979)

Leete also shows that the proportion of women who, on first marriage, had previously lived with their husband increased more than threefold between the last half of the 1960s and the first half of the 1970s.   Evidence that the current pattern is chosen rather than the result of chance is given by the trend in illegitimate births.   Over the period from 1971 to 1976 the percentage of premaritally conceived births fell while the percentage of illegitimate births rose, with more and more illegitimate births being registered by both parents rather than, as in the past, by the mother alone.

The picture is further complicated by the changes in remarriage among divorcees;   the number of remarriages has increased as that of first marriages has declined, accounting for nearly a third of all marriages in 1977.   About three-quarters of divorcees remarry and about two-thirds of these have dependent children.

These various changes explain the increase in one-parent families, also noticed in Chapter 3 and discussed more fully by Brian Jackson in Chapter 7.   If amongst some sections of society marriage amongst the young becomes less common whilst amongst others divorce and remarriage remain the pattern (or even increase), it seems inevitable that a growing proportion of children must, at some stage, have just one parent.   One in nine of all families with dependent children now has only one parent.   Of course such families do not all continue indefinitely in their one-parent status.   At any one point in time most one-parent families are at the stage when the mother is between one marriage and the next (Leete, 1978).   Thus more and more young children now start off in a two-parent home, experience the break-up of their natal family followed by a period in a one-parent home and later a two-parent family, with a stepfather or stepmother.   Similarly, there are more fatherless families than in the past which stay that way, either from choice or perforce.

As other chapters show, there are many other possible variations from the old 'standard family', though each applies only to a tiny minority.   There are one-parent families, about a sixth of the total, where the father is the lone parent.   There are West Indian and other families in which the child's own 'natural' father is the first among many

'fathers' who appear on the domestic scene.   There are families into which children are fostered (a growing proportion)
or adopted (a falling proportion, because of the decline in
illegitimacy and the increase in single mothers keeping their
babies).   There are extended family households.   There are,
finally, a small number of children who grow up in communes
and similar experimental groups.   Cogswell and Sussman
(1972), estimated that communal living arrangements accounted
for 6 per cent of all families with children in the USA in
1970.   Again, comparable figures are not available for
Britain, but as Andrew McCulloch notes in Chapter 16, it is
likely that the proportion is lower.

OTHER CHANGES IN SOCIETY

Even taken together, these various minorities are at present
still the exception rather than the rule.   Relatively few
children (about one in ten) are born outside marriage.   Most
families contain two parents.   Most couples do not divorce
and most of those who do, as we have said, later remarry.
But even among the majority of families who marry and whose
first marriage remains intact, the pattern of life has greatly
changed in other ways likely to affect the family and therefore the children.
    For one thing, as contraception has spread 'downwards'
through the class structure, family size has fallen, not so
much since the 1950s but over a longer span, so that more
children today than, say, a half century ago have only one
sibling or none.   Household size has likewise dropped, not
only for this reason but also because fewer households now
share a dwelling than did so at any date in the past.   Housing is also more spacious and better equipped, though a larger
proportion of families live in council flats where they lack
'private open space' for children's play (Ward, 1979), and a
minority of families are 'trapped' in poor housing, lacking
access to anything better (Shankland et al., 1977).
    At another level, there have been changes in the attitudes
of parents to their children - now more permissive and 'democratic' - and of children to parents - less repressed and less
deferential, reflecting a general weakening of respect for
authority.   It is of course extraordinarily difficult to
begin to assess the multifold effects of such changes as
these.
    We can, however, say something about one of the biggest
changes of all.   The world of work has pulled more and more
wives out of the home.   In spite of the economy's ills, the
proportion of married women at work has gone on increasing.

The percentage of married women who were economically active
was 22 per cent in 1951, 42 per cent in 1971 and 48 per cent
in 1975.   Over the same 24-year period, the proportion of men
who were economically active fell from 88 per cent to 81 per
cent (Central Statistical Office, 1979).   In this sense, the
family has become more 'symmetrical' (Young and Willmott,
1973).   The causes are many.   One is the financial advantage.   Virtually all families benefit when mothers go out to
work and, among the poorest, working wives keep many above the
poverty line who would otherwise sink below it (Shankland et
al., 1977).   Other explanations include feminist aspirations,
the crumbling of male resistance, the introduction of anti-
discriminatory legislation and changes in the economy and the
occupational structure.   Whatever the reasons, the change has
meant different things to different families.   Most mothers,
in single- or two-parent homes, still stay at home until their
youngest child goes to nursery or primary school.   Bone
(1977) found in her study of the need for preschool day care
that only 12 per cent of children under one year had a working
mother, rising to 37 per cent of those aged four.   Of those
who did work, most worked part time.   Not only is part-time
work preferred by many mothers when the children are young and
also at later ages, it is clear that most mothers still rele-
gate their paid job to a secondary role (Young and Willmott,
1973).   Among the others, some have, not just a job, but a
'career' and a 'dual-career family' (Rapoport and Rapoport,
1976).

    Thus, in comparison with the past, there is now a much
wider range of family settings in which children grow up.
There are, however, some general features which are important
from the viewpoint of children.   They can be summed up as
follows.   More children than in the past (even the recent
past) are likely to see a dissolution of the relationship
between their natural parents (who may or may not be formally
married).   More are likely to experience changes in the
'parental' setting of family life; and more are likely at
some stage to have a 'parent' who is not their natural father
or mother, such as a step-parent, a foster mother or a house
mother (for children who go into care), or the transitory
partner of their own mother or father.   Children in all families (that is, whether with one or two parents) are more
likely than in the past to have parents going out of the home
to work; in consequence children, especially those of school
age, are likely to get less sustained attention from their
mother in particular and to spend more time with their peers.
During their preschool years, more are likely - particularly
in one-parent families - to have some experience of day care.
Those of school age are more likely to be at school all day,

having no contact with their home and parents during the day,
and more likely to be at home without parental care during
school holidays or after school hours.

EVIDENCE FROM RESEARCH

What is the impact of all this on the children?   There are
two separate questions.   One is about the effects on the
children while they are children: do the changed family patterns we have described make them less happy, more anxious,
distressed?   The second is about the longer term consequences: are the children likely to grow up into different kinds
of adult from those who experienced the conventional childhood
of the past, and if so how are they likely to differ?   A
number of recent reviews throw light on these issues.   Examples are Hoffman (1974); Rutter and Madge (1976); Clarke
and Clarke (1976); Pilling and Pringle (1978); Tizard
(1979).   Also relevant are the main British longitudinal
studies, reported for example in Douglas (1964) and Davie et
al. (1972).
   Essentially, the questions are about the short- and long-
term effects of 'broken homes' and mothers working.   In 1977
over a million children in Britain were living at home with
only one parent (One-Parent Families, 1979), and there were
perhaps as many more who had been part of one-parent families
but were now again in a rebuilt two-parent home.   In the same
year over 100,000 children, almost 12,000 under the age of
five, were in care; of these at least a half were from one-
parent families (although one-parent families made up only 11
per cent of all families with dependent children).   Children
in care from one-parent families had, moreover, been in care
longer than others.   Whether or not being 'in care' is in the
long term 'damaging' there can be no doubt that, during their
formative years, the children experience a very different
style of life from that in the 'family-and-home' setting, however much that varies in its turn.   Crucial factors influencing its effects are the length of time spent in care, the
number of occasions a child moves in and out of care, and the
quality and stability of the 'substitute parenting' available.
There is a long history of research on children who have been
in care to suggest that such experiences can be damaging.
'Prolonged institutionalisation during the early years of life
leaves children very vulnerable to later stress', wrote
Pringle (1977), adding 'there is no new evidence that contradicts this conclusion.'   Some such children have been encouraged to express their own feelings about their disrupted or
deprived family life.   Again, whether or not lasting damage

results, the experience for most children hurts, as was illustrated by such remarks as these (Page and Clark, 1977):
    'There are times when I feel like lashing out at someone -
    even my best mate - just because I miss a family atmosphere
    - and the feeling that someone really cares for me and
    loves me.'
    'It's the coming and going that hurts.   The first time you
    move to another place it hurts bad so you build up a shell
    but one day the shell cracks.'
    Although there is some evidence that difficulties in child-
hood and later in life are associated with the experience of
growing up in a 'broken home' - or of 'family separation', as
Rutter and Madge more accurately describe it - the picture is
a complicated one.   It seems that there is no strong association between family separation in childhood and mental retardation or educational failure, but the longitudinal study by
Davie et al. (1972) suggested that children not living with
both of their natural parents showed less skill at reading
when aged seven.   Reading ability, however, is also associated with occupational status, and the study found that, when
family background was controlled by occupational status,
family separation appeared to have a deleterious effect upon
reading among children from middle-class and skilled working-
class backgrounds but not among those from low-skilled working-class homes.   Almost all the other evidence suggests
little or no association between family separation and educational performance.
    Other research suggests that psychological disorders and
anti-social behaviour such as delinquency may be associated
with growing up in a 'broken home'.   Because such disorders
are more common among people whose childhood home was broken
by divorce or separation rather than by the death of a parent,
together with other evidence about the relationships between
parents in homes that are not broken, it has been suggested
that it is the discord and stress that give rise to these
outcomes.   Other factors, such as social class and economic
status, are also relevant.
    In any event, it seems that family separation, as well as
causing some distress and unhappiness during childhood, may
have some effect on educational performance and upon adjustment in later life.   But it has to be borne in mind that even
the studies that show some variation in behaviour according to
parental context deal only in relatively small differences in
percentages.
    Much of the research is marred by the fact that it has used
very simple definitions of family separation, relying upon
evidence about one point in time (asking, for example, whether
current one-parent status is associated with educational

disadvantage) or ignoring the duration of family separation and examining whether children with any experience of it have been affected. What is more, studies have seldom taken systematic account of the consequences of parental discord inside marriages which have remained intact; such research as there has been, as already noted, suggests that this may be as important as the fact of separation.

We conclude that, although research suggests that there is probably a somewhat greater propensity to difficulties among people whose childhood was affected by parental separation, most children are probably more resilient than it has been fashionable to admit. Whatever their experience in childhood, history suggests that most will come through relatively unscathed; if this were not so, the huge brutalised underclass described by Mayhew and Booth would still be conspicuously present. Of course, if children suffer continual or recurrent physical injury, or emotional, material, educational or other deprivation, any damage is more likely to be severe and long lasting.

CHILDREN OF WORKING MOTHERS

A number of studies have addressed themselves to the question of the effect of mother's employment on development in childhood and subsequently. Some research suggests that there is a retardation, though a small one, in some aspects of educational performance. But the evidence as a whole contradicts the stereotyped beliefs about the effects of mothers working. Pilling and Pringle (1978) reviewed the literature on the effects of maternal employment during a child's preschool years and concluded:

> Whether the mother works or not in the pre-school years does not affect the child's emotional or social adjustment, either at this stage (Nye et al., 1963) or subsequently, in the early primary years (at the age of seven - Davie et al., 1973), at pre-adolescence or adolescence (Burchimal, 1963).... There is no evidence that children in this age range suffer adverse consequences from substitute care for the full working day, apart from a very slight educational retardation.

For under fives Tizard (1979) reached similar conclusions: 'for what they are worth, the findings are, consistently, that no striking long-term consequences emerge.' Not surprisingly, research on the effects of mothers working when the children are older comes to much the same conclusions. Likewise, Rutter and Madge (1976) show that neither delinquency nor psychiatric disorder in adulthood are associated with maternal employment in childhood.

These largely negative findings about the effects on children of maternal employment and of day care are only part of the story.   In the first place, it would be wrong to draw the conclusion that the alternative arrangements made by parents for the care of their children are unimportant.   Most of the reviews point out the contribution that can be made by good child-care arrangements.   Other research has pointed to the bad effects, at least in the short term, of inadequate arrangements.   Pollak (1972) showed the retarding effects, particularly among West Indian families, of poor and frequently changed childminding arrangements on some under fives. For older children, the relative neglect implied in the phrase 'latch-key children' is a commonly expressed concern. Simpson (1978) has estimated that 225,000 children aged five to ten in Britain are left alone after school hours and 300,000 during school holidays.   For good or bad, the child with working parent(s) lives in a substantially different daily environment from that of the child in one of the supposed standard forms.   Being brought up in a day nursery, even one run along 'family group' lines, is not the same as being at home alone or with one, or at most two, other children with mother for most of the day.   Similarly, the life of the school-age child who goes home at midday for lunch differs from that of the child who spends all day at school.   And the child who goes home after school to an empty house is living differently, and experiencing differently, from the child whose mother is there to greet - or to grumble at - him or her on arrival.   Certainly, most parents recognise this and respond to what they regard as their child's interests - staying at home, adapting their working hours and doing their best to make alternative arrangements during their absence.

So a child's experience and his or her response to it depend greatly on the details of what happens.   'For children of all ages the effects of day care will depend upon its duration, its quality, the quality of the home, and the child's biological make-up and experience' (Tizard, 1979).   Pilling and Pringle (1978) note that 'if the child is provided with stable, good-quality care and is able to develop secure attachments to one or two adults there are unlikely to be direct adverse effects on his development'.   Little, in fact, is known about how many people a young child can tolerate without disturbance.   It is well known that a hazard of most day-care services is a rapid turnover of staff caring for children.   Continuity of adult care, it has recently been suggested, may be more important than the numbers of adults concerned (Smith, 1979).

There are other important influences as well.   Hoffman (1974), drawing mainly on American research, adds:

The data, on the whole, suggest that the working mother who obtains personal satisfactions from employment, does not have excessive guilt, and has adequate household arrangements, is likely to perform as well as the non-working mother or better; and the mother's emotional state is an important mediating variable.

Related to this is the point made by Rapoport and Rapoport (1976) that parents vary in the efforts they make to compensate for the absence of one or other of them, and that 'dual-career' couples in particular devote a good deal of attention and energy to trying to ensure that the arrangements for their children are satisfactory.

One of the limitations of so much of the research, that of the Rapoports apart, is that it operates on the assumption that the only issue is the consequences of *mothers* working. Although it still remains more usual for mothers to regard child care as their preserve, along with housekeeping, cooking and other traditionally female tasks, more and more couples see the problem as one to be solved by both of them.   The message of Levine (1976), summed up in his title 'Who Will Raise the Children? New Options for Fathers and Mothers', almost certainly indicates another direction in which family patterns are changing.   To the extent to which this happens, some of the stresses that might result from maternal (and paternal) employment might be more easily resolved in the coming decades.

Some research is revealing about the influence of childhood experience upon character, suggesting that there may be beneficial consequences for children in less traditional arrangements.   Pilling and Pringle refer to a number of studies which show that children receiving what they call 'substitute care' are more often 'outgoing, superficially self-confident, and more resistant to discipline', while maternal care children are 'more obedient and conforming, but also more timid and anxious'.   Hoffman's review (1974) made the same point:

Daughters of working mothers compared positively with daughters of non-working mothers, particularly with respect to independence ... working mothers seem to stress independence training more than non-working mothers and give their children more household responsibilities. Both these patterns have been linked to independence, achievement and responsibility in children.

We return to these points later in the chapter.

How, then, should we sum up the conclusions from research about the consequences of the growth of maternal employment and the increase in family separation?   The evidence suggests that mothers working as well as fathers, although undoubtedly affecting their style of family life, is unlikely to seriously deprive children or, if the arrangements are handled sensibly, have any deleterious effect. Nor does it seem as if the experience of being a child of working parents (in contrast to going into care) is necessarily distressing or disturbing. These experiences can indeed, as we have illustrated, have some positive advantages for children; they certainly can have for parents, particularly mothers, who might otherwise feel 'trapped' (Gavron, 1976) or suffer from depression (Brown et al., 1975) - conditions which themselves would have 'spill-over' effects on the children.

Even without the trauma of going into care, family separation is a rather different matter from having both parents working. It seems likely that children find the experience of family break-up and its immediate aftermath emotionally distressing, possibly predisposing them to long-term emotional, psychiatric and behavioural devaince. The point made by Rutter and Madge, amongst others, must of course be borne in mind: parental stress can also be disturbing when it occurs inside a marriage that remains formally intact. What is more, there can be negative effects on children even of what would be thought of as 'normal' family life. Nevertheless, it seems reasonable to assume that a growing proportion of children are being - and will be - disturbed by changes in the relationship between their natural parents. There must have been in the past a sizeable proportion of marriages which, though not particularly 'happy', ticked over in the sense that they provided a moderately settled milieu from the point of view of the children, and that changing attitudes, reinforced by legislation, are leading to more emotional upsets in the lives of more children.

CHILDREN'S VIEWPOINT

What is lacking in virtually all the research drawn on so far is any picture of how the new forms of family living seem to the children themselves. This is not surprising, since it is more difficult to do research with children than about them. The comments given earlier by children in care are one exception, an attempt to give children some opportunity to voice their opinions. But it was not research-based.

Recent work from the National Children's Bureau offers some information from 16-year-olds who at any stage during the National Child Development Study had been living with only one parent. They were asked to complete a questionnaire about their experience of family separation. The main aim of the research was 'to find out if children in one-parent families as a group showed any more evidence of discouragement in their

feelings about family life than children in unbroken families'
(Essen and Lambert, 1977).   The results suggested that 'the
young people's view of their relationship with their natural
parents did not differ very much between one and two-parent
families.'   The authors, however, also drew attention to the
conclusion drawn by Ferri (1976) on the basis of her analysis
of the essays of 11-year-old children asked to imagine their
lives at the age of 25.   Ferri found that fewer fatherless
children imagined they would marry or have children than those
with both parents.   There seemed to be a similar, if slight,
tendency in the 16-year-olds' group, but Essen and Lambert
took the view that, since only a small proportion expressed
unwillingness to marry, this 'would seem to be a positive indication that although their experiences of family life had
been unusual their expressed attitudes towards future family
life were not greatly affected by these experiences of living
in a one-parent family.'

Such insights are valuable, but they are of course based
largely on the one hand on hindsight and on the other on the
future aspirations of the children studied.   Nobody, so far
as we know, has asked younger children themselves about their
feelings at the time.   This applies not only to children of
single parents but those whose parents have divorced and remarried, and those from two-parent families where both parents
are working.   There are three questions that need to be
answered for contemporary children in different kinds of
family setting.   Firstly, are they 'happy'?   Secondly (in
comparison with the traditional 'ideal family'), are they enjoying an emotionally richer or poorer childhood?   Thirdly,
are they likely to suffer any long-term effects and, in particular, damage?   The third question has received some attention from researchers, and there is some information to which
we have referred earlier.   The first and second questions
remain unexplored.

THE GINGERBREAD STUDY

In search of some insights into what the experience of parental separation, and the subsequent complex changes in relationships, mean to children at the time we can draw upon a
small case study we carried out in co-operation with Gingerbread Playschool in Croydon, London.   This is one of seven
family day-centre projects, all very different, funded by the
EEC and the Home Office Voluntary Service Unit under the European Anti-Poverty Programme.   In a capacious Victorian house
it provides after-school and holiday care for children, aged
five to eleven, from one-parent families.   The study, in

spring 1979, covered the 120 children, from 82 one-parent families, on the roll.   The great majority of the children - over four-fifths - were living with a divorced or separated parent.   Few of the families were ones where the parents were single and fewer still widowed.   Most of the parents were mothers; just over one in ten of the children were living with lone fathers.   All were also, as a condition of being at Gingerbread Playschool, the children of a working parent.

The main aim of the study was to learn more about what growing up in a one-parent family meant to the children and to see how far a scheme like Gingerbread Playschool could help them.   In fact, as we later realised, most of the families using Gingerbread Playschool were not typical one-parent families.   They were, as a whole, the more fortunate (or more competent) who with the help of Gingerbread had been able to mitigate the grosser effects of bringing up children alone. In one respect they may have been better off than many two-parent families with both parents working, in that their children had a reliable and stimulating place to go to after school and in school holidays.

Since it is widely assumed that it is better for children to grow up in a happy, secure home - and this is usually assumed to mean a home where there are two parents - other important questions are, firstly, how much contact if any these children had with the parent who had gone and, secondly, what family structure operated in place of the traditional one?

Most of the Gingerbread Playschool children were living with a single adult, most commonly their mother.   The average number of children in the family was 1.3, so that few children had a circle of siblings.   Beyond the home, the extended family did not seem to play a very important part in helping with the care of children after school or in holidays, except among those families where the parent was widowed.

Excluding the children of unmarried mothers and of widows or widowers, about half had no contact at all with the other parent or saw them only seldom.   About a quarter saw them occasionally or irregularly, and the remaining quarter had regular contact, usually weekly.   It seems as if such contact may be important.   One five-year-old, 18 months after her parents divorced remarked, 'So when am I going to see my Dad again, then?'   From a comparison of the two extreme categories - the nine divorced and separated parents whose children had no contact and the nine whose children had regular weekly contact, it seemed as if the former included more children assessed by Gingerbread staff as under stress.   It would be rash to assume from this that it was necessarily the non-contact with the other parent that caused the strain; in general, these seemed to be the families which had exceptional difficulties before the marriage breakdown, the effects of which may have continued afterwards. The children assessed as under stress included an eight-year-old boy whose mother had left him as a baby, even though at the time she was breast-feeding him. The child had recently remarked to a member of the staff: 'I am very slow. I am slow because I am sad.' (It is irrelevant whether the child's logic was correct; what cannot be ignored is his sadness.)

Other children judged by the staff as under stress included the following:

One little boy, aged eight, came to Gingerbread from a children's home. His parent is concerned about him, but the child is insecure over whether he is wanted. He is a year and a half behind with school work. No contact with other parent.

A little girl, aged six, has a strong 'bossy' elder brother who has no apparent difficulties. The staff reported, however, that they found the girl 'very, very quiet, and has unexpected reactions. Her behaviour takes you unawares. We told her off once and found her climbing out of the window.' The brother and sister visited their father 'regularly' but never went together.

Despite this sadder side of the story of children's lives in one-parent families, the general picture from the Gingerbread study was far from gloomy. We tried to make some assessment, on the basis of the subjective impressions of staff, whether children were, in general, 'secure' or 'insecure'. For just over a third we could not clearly decide, having insufficient information from the staff to attempt such an assessment. For between a quarter and a half of all the children no sign of stress seemed apparent to the staff. Staff comments on these children included the following:

'Bouncy, happy outgoing child.'
'Sunny, extrovert child.'
'Very happy children.'
'Delightful children; well adjusted and amuse themselves.'
'A wise little old man. Everybody adores him.'
'Calm little boy, very intelligent and self-sufficient.'
'Delightful child. Lots of love from Mum.'
'Child seems fine, despite father's intrusions into life.'
'Nice kids. A very close family.'
'Bright, lively little boy despite impoverished home life and constant state of aggro over maintenance.'

Children from such families are of course in no sense representative of all children from contemporary homes, but one-parent families illustrate in an extreme form something of the changeability - and in particular the decline in parental presence - characteristic of parent-child relationships in many contemporary families.

The evidence from Gingerbread Playschool shows that children can indeed come through such changes wholly or relatively unscathed, and if they are fortunate even enriched.   We cannot conclude from this that there is no cause for concern - or that increasing child benefits or setting up Gingerbread Playschools is all that is needed to come to terms with new family patterns and needs (desirable as both these policies may be).   Family breakdown does cause unhappiness and insecurity for the child in the best of circumstances, but particularly where it is associated with other disadvantages - low occupational status, low income, limited education, poor housing, bad health.   There is a sizeable minority of such disadvantaged families and, since they tend to be larger, proportionately more children in them.   We need to be particularly concerned about these children because there are no ready solutions to ease things for them.

GAINS AND LOSSES

The family, increasingly diverse as to form, provides in consequence less permanent a setting than it used to, for parents and children alike.   A currently two-parent family may next year have only one parent, and a year or so later a different pair of partners.   A mother who has given up working outside the home may then resume, then give up once more.   Children may enter and leave local authority care, or may change foster parents.   Au pairs may come and go.

To say that this amounts to greater 'instability' for the children may, by the use of such a pejorative term, seem to prejudge the issue.   We have no desire to do so.   But the terminology, whether pejorative or not, does suggest the likely negative consequences for children.

Whatever the judgment about long-term effects, there is no doubt about the upset for children caused at the time by the rupture of a social unit as small and delicate as a family, by the quarrel or the sexual adventure that ends in separation, the sudden loss of a father who has deserted or, less dramatically, by the daily departure of a mother who has gone back to a career in teaching or taken a part-time job at the electronics factory.   The children are unsettled, to a greater or lesser extent.   We have, of course, noted that they can also suffer in homes where bitter and antipathetic parents struggle on (in both senses) 'for the sake of the children'.   And they may suffer in a different way if their mother martyrs herself, a 'captive wife', sometimes through lack of opportunity to work but often again supposedly in the children's interests (Gavron, 1966).   But our own judgment would be that more children are hurt at the time by family separation than by family adhesion, more by parents leaving the home temporarily or permanently than by their staying in it.

The negative side is even more emphasised as soon as one brings social class into the equation.   The new impermanence is easier to handle in families with ample financial resources, just as a working mother who is relatively well-off can more readily compensate for her absence from home (although, paradoxically, it is less of an economic necessity).   One of the reasons one-parent families and working mothers have a bad press is that they are more often thought of as having failed to provide the perfect family environment for their children. Certainly working-class one-parent families are not only more numerous, they are also less able than others to cope economically (not surprisingly) and more likely to end up with their children in care.   It seems probable that children from such homes might be those who suffer more emotionally too. 'Latch-key' children of working mothers may also lose out in some ill-defined ways, such as going to school without breakfast or coming home to the unstimulating environment of a cold and empty house.

Against these negative aspects, there are some developments that may give grounds for optimism.   As we have said, children are resilient; they are also adaptable.   In any case it can be argued that some children from standard two-parent, two-child families are themselves deprived by the very narrowness of their lives, and are held back by an over-protectiveness unequalled in any other period of human history.   It could also be argued that few children of the kind who have gone through Gingerbread Playschool suffer the 'severe weaning' from home, as Geoffrey Gorer described it to us, that some middle-class children traditionally underwent when sent off to private schools.

The 'age of family diversity' offers some possibilities of strengthening rather than weakening both society and families. One likely result, as children who have gone through this mill themselves reach parenthood, is a growth in sympathy towards one-parent families and to a greater variety of family patterns.   Prejudice will surely diminish as the recognition grows that one-parent status can - and increasingly often does - happen to many families and that many family forms are possible.   This awareness should lead not only to more effective demands for help to meet the special needs of some families but also to an appreciation of the needs which are common to all (for example, for such services as the Gingerbread centre).   Specialist self-help organisations, like

Gingerbread itself and 'Families Need Fathers', are evolving to help compensate for the losses that have resulted.   There has, furthermore, been a welcome new recognition of the rights of children and of their special needs in the changed circumstances;   the group calling itself 'The Voice for the Child in Care' provides one example.

Another positive development is the growing relaxation over sexual roles, something that is almost certainly being encouraged by - as well as partly resulting from - changes in the family.   This will probably mean further changes in the attitudes of both sexes (but more significantly of girls) towards education and the need for a career.   Today's children will have observed new sexual roles - fathers as housekeepers, mothers as breadwinners - and any experience of hardship will have highlighted the fact that families can survive better, at least economically, if parents are able to command better jobs.   Furthermore, most of us try to correct as adults, and particularly as parents, what we felt was wrong in our own upbringing.   It seems probably therefore that children who have experienced family separation will want to minimise its negative consequences when they in turn become parents.   It does not follow that they will necessarily wish to return to the closed, traditional, two-parent family.

So we would conclude, on balance, that the present picture is by no means cause for despair.   What seems to be happening is that the family is being remodelled, partly in order to compromise with the two-parent ideal.   The tie between spouses may indeed be weaker.   We are almost certainly witnessing the end of the era of lifetime 'romantic love' matches, for so long a part of Western culture.   In compensation, the vertical ties between ascendants and descendants (grandparents, parents and children), which seemed to be weaker in recent years, may now be strengthening again.   (It is surely no coincidence that the recent Domestic Proceedings and Magistrates' Courts Act gives a new right of access by grandparents to both legitimate and illegitimate grandchildren.)   Alongside these changes, a new form of 'extended family' is developing, in which step-relationships play a bigger role (partly replacing the former predominance of siblings and cousins, uncles and aunts).

If, as we suggest, the family is redefining its relationships, the current changes can be seen as one more stage in its evolution, aiming not at its destruction but at its continuing survival.   The family may be adapting to a new and perhaps, for our times, more suitable form and one in which children, in time and given the will, do not inevitably have to lose more than they gain.

Part IV

Policy issues

Chapter 18

Family and social policy: an overview

Roy Parker

It is plain that the identification and analysis of 'family policy' presents a difficult and tantalising task. Indeed, my colleague Hilary Land and I recently concluded that Britain had never had any explicit family policies, although we hastened to add that there were policies which *affected* families and which certainly embodied powerful assumptions *about* families (Land and Parker, 1978). There are good reasons to explain why 'the family' is significantly absent from the language of our social legislation. Most of these reasons are of a political nature.

1 THE POLITICAL BACKGROUND

Kinship systems meet a wide variety of social needs. Were there to be a substantial decline in the capacity or willingness of people to observe the usual expectations of kinship, then the State would be faced with major repercussions. Needs which had been met by families would have to be met in other ways, or measures would have to be taken to force families to reassume or discharge those responsibilities which they had abandoned. Indeed, precedents for this already exist; for example, in the treatment of financially liable relatives. Whatever the actual response to any significant retreat from kinship might be, political and economic stability are assumed to be threatened in the process.

It is this prospect which confronts the State with the problem of how to support families sufficiently to ensure their widespread continuity without, at the same time, seeming to encourage the weakening of the very responsibilities which it seeks to consolidate. Of course, different governments will assess the likelihoods involved differently; yet the underlying assumption seems to remain. If the balance between doing too little and too much is *wrong*, then the institution of the family is liable to be tipped into a dangerous state of instability.   Facts and beliefs about *trends* in family life influence the degree of concern with which such a possibility is viewed.

Hence, when the State assumes all or part of certain responsibilities which the family carries, or might be thought capable of carrying, the ostensible reasons for doing so have also to indicate that there are well-designated limits.   This message is signalled in several ways.   Help may be provided for families on the understanding that they are (or can be) classified as in some way special or deviant.   That being so, others are not encouraged to identify themselves with these special predicaments.   Where services *are* more general - for example, education or health care - the case for the State's involvement is couched in terms of their being outside the competence of families;   that is, families are not *expected* to do these things.   Yet other services may be characterised as mainly fulfilling purposes other than the support or replacement of a family contribution;   for instance, the alleviation of poverty, the provision of housing, or the protection of children.   They can then be portrayed as only *incidentally* family policies.   Last, the State may choose to implement policies connected with the family through quasi-governmental agencies or voluntary organisations, thus indicating that there is no presumption of an extended role for the State in that particular sphere.

It is not only in the provision of direct social services that the problem of political legitimisation arises.   Where the State is involved in the regulation of behaviour or transactions within families, it is liable to be charged with trespassing upon cherished areas of privacy.   Since the typically rather private nature of contemporary family life serves important social and economic ends it may prove politically costly to disturb them.

Other unwelcome political problems face the State should it adopt clear and unambiguous family policies.   In particular, such a course of action involves the definition of what actually constitutes a family.   The broadest definition would be in terms of kinship, but even this may fail to take account of households living like families but without kinship connections.   Unless drawn as widely as this, however, definition only becomes possible by excluding certain groups or relationships.   Since that is likely to have redistributive implications, some will see themselves as potential losers.   How politically important their anxiety is will depend, amongst other things, upon their number;   that is, upon the prevailing demographic structure.   The history of the Seebohm Committee

(1968) demonstrates how difficult it can be for a government to contemplate, say, an essentially child-centred 'family service' in a country with one of the oldest populations in Europe (Hall, 1977). (1)

Even when families *are* defined in a limited fashion for policy purposes, they can rarely be treated in practice as un-differentiated units.   There are conflicting and competitive interests *within* families which are likely to be exposed once policy becomes more specific.   The child benefit fiasco illustrates the kinds of political repercussions likely to arise when the interests of one spouse (the wife) are considered by powerful interest groups (the trade unions) to be pursued at the expense of the other (the husband).

Viewed more broadly, it is important to recognise that a 'family policy', rather than a policy for *homeless* families or *disadvantaged* families, implies general application.   Yet the more general the application the greater the likelihood of controversy about what that policy (or policies) should be. It is politically much less hazardous for a government to adopt family policies which are implicit, fragmented or disguised as the incidental effects of other initiatives. It is difficult enough for a government to manage issues of parenthood, marriage, birth control, child poverty or divorce, let alone an amalgamation which a truly comprehensive and explicit family policy would require.

Of course, some symbolic initiatives which extol the virtues of the family in a general kind of way may win a good measure of support and consensus.   But once the slogan has to be replaced by the detailed specification needed for *implementation*, then that general support is wont to evaporate.

None of this is to say that States cannot, or will not, construct explicit and general family policies;   only that in this country the political costs of so doing (in terms of the loss of support or the erosion of political capital) are likely to be high.   If family policies are desired, then it will make good political sense to make them implicit, to camouflage them as something else, or avoid comprehensive reforms in favour of those which are piece-meal.   Likewise, those who seek the development of policies to assist and promote the family may find that the direct route is not necessarily the easiest.   For reasons like these the analysis of family policy demands a somewhat tangential approach.

These conclusions may be illustrated by exploring four different kinds of questions about the family and social policy:

1 What use is made of the family as an administrative category in the social services?

2 What uses are made of the family as a model in the organisation of services?

3 What underlying assumptions about families are embodied in different policies?
4 Are there policy areas which affect families, or family life, but which remain largely unexamined from a family perspective?

2 THE FAMILY AS ADMINISTRATIVE CATEGORY

The administration of the social services relies upon systems or principles of allocation. Services are rarely universal in the sense that they are available to all indiscriminately. Various conditions of eligibility are imposed which concentrate resources by *excluding* certain claims. The rules of eligibility may be based upon the condition of each individual (for example, in assessing the need for medical treatment) or rest upon the simpler fact of their membership of a specified social category (for instance, being of school age, unemployed, over sixty-five, or a parent).

Such allocative systems are, of course, more than administrative conveniences. They incorporate many of the complex assumptions about the purposes of policies, as well as indicating preferred priorities. If, then, we would judge the place of the family in social policy, the pattern and frequency of certain classifications offers one means to that end. Plainly, however, *the family* is not used as an administrative category. Indeed, there is no obvious way in which, without further qualification, that would be possible. Nevertheless, there are examples where the specification of certain *kinds* of families serves that purpose, as well as instances where individual eligibility for a particular service depends upon membership of a family.

Families with dependent children provide the most plentiful examples of eligibility resting upon family structure. The family income supplement is only available to families with one or more dependent children, although they must also meet the requirement that the head of the family is in full-time, low-paid work. A widowed mother's allowance is paid as long as the widow has a child under sixteen living with her, or under nineteen if in full-time education. The degree of kinship is widened in, say, the case of the invalid care allowance, but the benefit is still limited to those who are looking after a severely disabled *relative*.

In instances like these benefits are restricted to particular kinds of families. The presumption is that they have special claims upon assistance which do not apply to all families. Other social policies are not so closely circumscribed but do accord *priority* to certain kinds of families. In the

housing field, for example, local authority building programmes have concentrated for long periods on supplying dwellings of a size to suit the family with two or three children,
and the allocation of council houses has similarly given preference to applicants with children. In the calculation of
most means-tested benefits or charges the composition of the
family (or household) affects the level of award or liability,
albeit that there is little consistency between one scheme and
another. Indeed, it might well be argued that one of the
principal changes which has brought issues of family structure
into the social policy arena has been the proliferation of
means tests.

The additional benefits which accrue to families of certain
kinds should not obscure the fact that, almost without exception, they are granted to specific individuals within those
families; for example, child benefit, rent allowances, or
council house tenure. Other members may enjoy the benefits
so provided, but the family as a whole is *not* the formal
recipient. This begs many questions about the actual distribution of benefits (and costs) *within* families: questions
about their micro-economies, pecking orders and patterns of
power.

In a similar vein it should be remembered that membership
of families may actually *weaken* claims upon certain social
services. There was, of course, the infamous household means
test of the 1930s, but contemporary examples are not hard to
find. There is now convincing evidence that the practice of
not supplying certain services (like a home help) where female
kin are on hand is widespread (see, e.g., Moroney, 1976;
Hunt, 1971; Harris, 1968; Rees, 1976). Over and above
that, preliminary evidence also suggests that when, for
example, old people move in with their offspring services
which they previously received are withdrawn. (2) That confirms the familiar picture which shows that, in the case of
the elderly at least, *less* social service help is allocated to
those who live with their children than to those who do not,
even though they may be in greater need (Hunt, 1978).

This raises the interesting question of the use of 'living
alone' as an administrative category. In deciding upon priorities in the allocation of community services to the elderly
the fact that they live alone is a convenient and apparently
legitimate criterion. The absence of proximate family
becomes the qualifying condition. That, of course, serves to
highlight the crucial distinction between policies which are
aimed at *supplementing* family resources and those which offer
substitution. In terms of political legitimisation and economy the latter are more readily defensible but lead to an
emphasis upon their residual nature. Such an emphasis may

then place an unreasonable burden upon families who are not prepared to accept, or who are not yet considered to need, substitutes.

A truly family orientation in the social services would devote as much priority to supporting what is being done in and by families as upon coming to their rescue when they break up, become overwhelmed, or no longer exist.

This brief review of the family as an administrative category points to a number of tentative conclusions. *Firstly*, social policies take explicit account of families only in as much as they belong to other social categories as well. Typically, families with *children* are such a sub-group.   That being so, it is perhaps more realistic to think of policies towards children or towards parenthood. *Secondly*, policies which superficially might be regarded as general family policies actually discriminate between different kinds of families.   In that process some are excluded.   The criterion for the provision of a service is, therefore, less a matter of family or non-family policy than of which family *type* is the target.   Of course, some policies pay no explicit attention to any family type even though they may, as I hope to show later, have consequences for families. *Thirdly*, the close definition of family composition in eligibility categories may become a cause of inflexibility.   There are relationships (and numbers seen to be growing) which are not based upon kinship; 'family' categories are not, therefore, easily applicable.   'Household', 'parenthood', or 'dependant' may offer much more scope for the adjustment of services to 'unconventional' living arrangements.   Of course, the fact that unadjustable categories are employed will confirm a policy preference for conventional arrangements.

These possible conclusions apart, the closer inspection and analysis of administrative categories does seem to offer a way of unravelling the many strands in the tangle of social policy purposes, priorities and presumptions, particularly with respect to the family.

3   THE FAMILY AS A POLICY MODEL

The relationship between family and social policy is generally approached in terms of the influence of policies upon families.   It is less common to trace the connection in the opposite direction; that is, to consider the influence of images of the family upon policy.   Several examples can be drawn from the child care field.   In the 1950s and early 1960s the organisation of facilities for children in the care of local authorities was much influenced by the desire to create family-like provision.   One way in which this found expression was in the importance attached to family group homes often ordinary houses on residential estates staffed by a couple but where the man followed his normal occupation.   The aim was to establish a setting which resembled the ordinary family as closely as possible.   It was felt that this would be a superior form of care to that offered in larger and more traditional children's homes.   However, insufficient attention was paid to the many ways in which such a group inevitably differed from an ordinary family: the housemother and father did not fulfil the normal roles of natural parents; children came and went and, of course, the children's own parents were often involved.   These complications were recognised in due course and it was realised that a family setting could rarely be recreated in these circumstances.   None the less, the family as a model for the way in which services like these should be designed did exert a considerable influence.

A second and similar policy emphasis is to be found in the enormous impetus imparted to foster care at about the same time.   Comparable difficulties were faced - not least those which sprang from the fact that foster parents were asked specifically to bring up foster children as their own but were not accorded full responsibility, and were also exhorted to collaborate in the eventual restoration of the child to his own family.   Despite such daunting problems, foster care remains the preferred way of looking after deprived children, although the foster home is less often regarded as a family replica.

The image of the family has influenced child-care policy and practice in other ways too.   In day nurseries, for instance, young children are cared for in small groups often called families or family groups, despite the many obvious ways in which they differ from ordinary families.   What is important in cases like these seems to be the prescriptive message about styles of relationship which the language of 'the family' conveys.

It is not only in the child-care field that family reference points like these are employed.   Old people's homes, or homes for the handicapped, are 'better' when they are able to create a 'family-like' atmosphere.   To the extent that that suggests informal relationships and familiar furnishings it must surely be commended; but such language may yet again fail to acknowledge the ways in which these settings are fundamentally different from the family lives formerly experienced by the residents.   More important, perhaps, it may discourage the staff concerned from working out the most appropriate modes of care from a careful analysis of the particular characteristics and opportunities of residential homes.

Other images of the family are to be found amidst the terminology of the social services, tending to imply how they should be delivered or organised. There are, for example, family practitioner services in the National Health Service based, presumably, upon the idea of the family doctor. That particular usage is so familiar that one may fail to consider the case against different family members having the same GP. Where there is a risk of child abuse, for instance, it may be highly desirable for one doctor to attend the child and another the parents.

The example of the family practitioner draws attention to the part which the family plays in theories of social pathology. Family relationships, particularly parent-child relationships, have provided explanations for behaviour in other settings - from juvenile delinquency to educational performance and from mental illness to infirmity in old age. In their turn such theories come to influence the shape of social policy remedies.

Theories of this kind have encouraged important shifts towards considering and treating individuals in their social settings. At the same time, of course, the dominance of the family perspective has tended to divert attention away from other powerful social influences upon individual behaviour. Our systems of juvenile justice acknowledge family influences but less often recognise (and incorporate in their procedures) the influence of peers: most juvenile offenders commit their offences in *groups* (see. e.g., Priestley et al., 1977). In the educational system achievement may be as much influenced by informal peer groups as by family background or teacher diligence. Indeed, in some countries such as the USSR, peer groups are regarded and *used* as a valuable means for the instillation of values and the promotion of competitive achievements (see, e.g., Bronfenbreuner, 1974).

In short, different social theories tend to encourage different social policy emphases; and theories about the family are no exception. The interesting questions concern the relative explanatory weight attached to the family in *general*, and then what kinds of theories about the nature of that influence find favour in the political arenas.

4 ASSUMPTIONS ABOUT THE FAMILY

Many social policies which do not immediately appear to be 'family policies' nevertheless embody assumptions about the nature of families and thereby influence what families are expected to be. In particular, there are assumptions about roles and relationships within families.

One such dominating assumption concerns the social and economic dependence of wives upon their husbands. This remains a prominent feature of our social security and taxation systems, as does the distinction between married couples and those who live together but are not married. Note, for example, the conditions for the payment of widow's allowances. The assumption of female dependence is closely related to a view of women's employment as a marginal and an optional condition, despite the fact that some two-thirds of married women are now in paid work (albeit many on a part-time basis) and that a significant number of households is entirely or largely dependent upon women's earnings (Land, 1976; Hamill, 1978). Married women cannot draw the invalid care allowance for looking after sick or elderly relations, on the grounds that they would not generally work and thus do not forego wages in undertaking the care of these dependent relatives. A constant attendance allowance is not available for children under the age of three, the assumption being that all children under three require (their mother's) constant attention anyway. Yet about a third of mothers with children below this age do work, either from choice or from necessity (Bone, 1977).

Our social security system contains and is fashioned by an identifiable set of embedded presumptions about the proper division of labour between the sexes and about the kinds of obligations each has to the other. It

does not recognise that most married couples share the economic support of their families and that some may wish to share responsibilities for domestic work: breadwinners are male. Only women care for children, the sick and the old, and if they have paid employment this must take second place to their domestic duties. (Land and Parker, 1978:341)

Similar views can be detected in the taxation system, especially through provisions whereby various allowances can be set against income. The married man's allowance is perhaps the single clearest (and certainly the most expensive) example. A set of social and fiscal policies which incorporated *different* assumptions about family relationships would lend its support and encouragement to different patterns of family life.

The point may be further illustrated by considering what kinds of assumptions are to be found in social policies about the relationship between parents and children. They are to be found at all the ages and stages. In the case of young children, some of the most powerful assumptions have concerned the unique nature of the bond between mother and child. There are other less explicit assumptions which operate at other ages and in other matters. Take, for example, money. An adolescent's income is virtually disregarded in most means-tested assessments to which his parents are subject. One must suppose that this is in order to be consistent with the treatment of children's income for purposes of parental taxation.   Whereas the taxation system 'recognises the family as an entity by aggregating the members' incomes and attributing them to the head of the household' (MacDonald, 1976), that principle seems not to be extended from wives to children. As Richard Titmuss pointed out some years ago, the failure to take account of children's incomes, especially investment income, may well distort the statistics of income distribution, with greater underestimation occurring amongst the wealthier groups (Titmuss, 1962).   Furthermore, as he was at pains to emphasise, 'it becomes ... necessary to examine the ways in which income and wealth may be split, rearranged and reallocated over time between family members and relatives by means of gifts, "one-man company incorporation", transfers, family settlements, discretionary trusts and other manipulative acts' (Titmuss, 1962:23).   The burden of his argument is, of course, that at the very least policy and law *permit* families to protect and increase their resources over time through the institution of the family.   In this there is a convergence of family and *class* influences which benefits richer families rather than families in general.   The assumption that children have no incomes, or that they are negligible, favours those in particular whose families are able to make arrangements for their children to receive investment income which is not subject to 'family aggregation' for tax purposes.

This example serves to indicate the kinds of assumptions about the family as an economic unit which are made in social policy.   It also highlights the fact that notions about how the *majority* of families operate may actually benefit the 'non-conformists' rather than penalise them.   A third issue is also illustrated - namely, the importance of time and the family cycle.   Policies which are based upon conceptions of families at one stage of their lives may have a quite different impact on other families who are at other stages and, of course, upon the same family in ten or twenty years' time. Local authority housing policies are a case in point.   The allocation of a dwelling of a particular size to a family of matching size ignores the possibility of further births and, given low rates of mobility, takes no account of the prospect of under-occupation when the 'family' is eventually reduced to an elderly woman living alone.   Muriel Nissel, in writing about the effects of taxes and benefits on families, was led to conclude that 'Government departments tend not to think in family cycle terms.   Until they do, and until they organise their information systems to enable them to do so, any attempt to develop explicit and rational family policies will be thwarted' (Nissel, 1978:3).

The last formal obligation of a parent to an 'adult' child is exacted in the requirement that a grant for higher education be determined with reference to parental income.   In some ways that marks an age and stage boundary in family policies. Nevertheless, assumptions about the obligations of parent and child to each other continue to influence policies beyond this point, albeit in a more implicit fashion.   When it comes to caring for the severely handicapped child, for example, parental responsibilities are expected to continue.   Indeed, it is not seen as especially remarkable for a parent who has reached the age of retirement still to be providing extensive care for an adult son or daughter now in their forties.   Relief and help are provided by statutory and voluntary services but there is an underlying presumption that, until matters reach crisis point, such assistance will supplement parental care rather than replace it (Moroney, 1976).

When parents become old and infirm, as I have already indicated, social services are liable to be withheld on the assumption that their offspring, usually daughters, will supply routine daily care.   It is interesting to see that this view also extends to daughters-in-law and that they *do* help considerably in these ways (Hunt, 1978).   Whether help will be provided (or be expected to be provided) as readily by stepchildren remains to be seen as those who divorced and remarried in increasing numbers during the last decade or so begin to reach old age. (3)   In this respect, of course, there are areas of policy and personal relationships where it remains unclear what either the explicit or implicit assumptions are or, indeed, whether any exist at all.

What is clear, however, is that the significant changes which have been occurring in the demographic structure of this country, and which will continue for some time, make us one of the   oldest   populations in the world.   The preocccupation in social policy with families as if they only comprised couples with dependent children will have to be enlarged to incorporate at least a three-generation definition of 'the family'. When the growing number of elderly is placed alongside the rising proportion of women in paid employment, we find ourselves, with a few other countries like East Germany, in a position where the traditional source of care for the growing population of the elderly is likely to be increasingly *less* readily available to give that help.

In some ways we have reached a turning-point in the thinking needed about relations between the dependent elderly and their kin.   Looking back, there was a period when the popular view was that many families no longer offered them the care that had formerly been provided.   Then a variety of studies, starting with Townsend's 'Family Life of Old People' (1957), made it clear that kin, especially female kin, were giving immense amounts of assistance and support to elderly relatives as well as to the handicapped, chronically sick and dying (e.g. Mills, 1962; Cartwright et al., 1973; Meades, 1972; also Moroney, 1976). We could all relax. Now, however, two additional factors emerge to complicate the issue yet again.

Firstly, there is the question of whether kin are willing and able to provide such help and at what level it is reasonable to expect them to do so. That arises in large part from the recognition that these responsibilities are carried disproportionately by women. The period of childbearing and childrearing has been shortened, but the growing number of dependent elderly confront more women with the prospect of a second, and often lengthy, phase of tending, frequently at a point when they are re-established in the labour force. The policy presumption seems to be that they will be prepared to shoulder this extension and enlargement of their 'two roles': they may not be.

The second matter which now complicates the question of the role of the family in the care of elderly kin is clearly set out in a recent publication by Age Concern. 'For well over one-third of all elderly people', the report concludes, 'it is certainly not a fact that family members are available who can fill the role of unpaid nurses and home helper.' Thus, as they go on to argue, attention needs to be shifted 'to discover what are the social conditions most likely to produce what might be called "*pseudo-family*" relationships' (Abrams, 1980:60). Whether such an initiative could still march under the banner of 'family policy' is hard to say, but it does indicate the constraints which might be imposed upon new thinking by a narrow and rather tightly defined family perspective.

The various examples offered in this section indicate that there is a web of assumptions, both explicit and implicit, about the family and about what the family should be. These influence social policies. In their turn these policies go some way to shaping family life, and certainly they can stamp the hallmark of approval upon particular roles and relationships within families, especially those concerning the sexes and the generations.

5   UNEXAMINED PERSPECTIVES

The connections between family and social policy tend to be sought in certain spheres rather than in others. A fuller appreciation of the present position and future prospects may be obtained from examining some of the less obvious ways in

which policies impinge upon family life.   In particular, to
see what disruptive, and therefore adverse, effects might
exist.

The educational system is not generally viewed from this
perspective.   Yet compulsory education exerts a profound and
wideranging influence upon the day-to-day life of families
with children.

> It can provide respite for mothers as well as for their
> children; it enables mothers to take paid work outside the
> home for limited periods without anxiety about their off-
> spring; [but it also] sets the need for certain routines
> and then, in the holidays, requires substantial readjust-
> ments to be made.   It makes regular and irregular calls
> upon a mother's purse as well as stretching her patience in
> battles about the 'right' clothes or actual attendance.
> (Parker, 1980:33)

In these senses the organisation of schools imposes both
opportunities and constraints on the way families live
together and how the problems which arise can be dealt with.
After a sleepless night with a young baby, the mother (or
father)*has* to be ready next morning to take her five- or six-
year-old offspring to school on time.   Requirements like
these do not affect all families equally: the single-parent
family or the larger family may be especially disrupted by
school routines.

The effect upon family life of the way in which outside
institutions are organised is now more readily acknowledged in
the case of work; but there is still much that could be
achieved through more flexible hours, work sharing, better
holidays and leave being available to both men and women to
care for sick relatives.   Likewise, low rates of basic pay
which oblige people to work long periods of overtime may have
a multiplicity of adverse effects upon family life.   Taken
together, therefore, the twin sets of requirements imposed by
school and work hold families with children in the grip of externally contrived routines which are not of their choosing.

Paradoxically, the social services *in general* may have an
adverse effect upon some families even when the benefits are
welcome.   This may even be the case where services are regarded as progressive and of a good quality, for then demanding standards are set to which, in different ways, the consumers also have to subscribe.   This, in its turn, may create
anxiety and even guilt in those who feel unable to live up to
what is expected.   In this context there are often only
mildly disguised models of what, for example, the 'good
parent' or the 'good home' is thought to be.   Take the case
of the apparently progressive move to allow the unrestricted
visiting of young patients in hospital.   The mother with

several children may face difficult problems in taking advantage of this arrangement and yet feel that there is an expectation that she should visit the child in hospital, not only frequently but for extended periods. If she works and has no car and no telephone, arrangements to do so may be particularly complicated.

This is *not* an argument for reactionary or poor quality social services but it is an example (and there are many others) of the way in which their organisation can establish norms and expectations about the styles and degrees of commitment of family members to each other. If these are based on images of family life and access to resources which are not shared by large sections of the population, then the ensuing stresses and strains imposed may well have adverse effects, in particular, I would suggest, upon working-class mothers.

My purpose in raising these issues is to suggest that we will understand the interaction of social policies and families better if, as well as noting the positive effects, we also consider the ill effects. In doing that we will rarely draw the conclusion that there are adverse effects on *all* families, only on some. In the same vein, it is unlikely that *all* members of a family will experience the negative consequences of social policies. By adding to questions about whether policies aid families others which ask whether they create extra burdens, the redistributional effects of policies will be kept clearly in sight: redistributional consequences which:

1 differentiate between one *kind* of family and another, by composition, class or age;

2 distinguish between different *members* of families, by gender and generation; and

3 note the differences between kinship groups and groups *not* based upon kinship.

If such crucial questions are to become a meaningful part of the approach to family policy in the future, then much more detailed and accurate knowledge is called for about the realities of family life in at least three major areas. We need to know how different kinds of families operate as economic units, both as regards the present distribution of income and wealth and its movement between generations. We also need to have a much better understanding of the means whereby families arrange for the care of dependants of all ages. Finally, we need accurate information about the changes which occur within families at different stages of their evolution. This is not only a question of taking more account of family cycles but also of the ways in which family units are reconstituted at *particular* points of change, such as births and deaths or divorce and remarriage.

A more careful analysis of the relationship between family and social policy which is based upon improved information of this kind will allow us to replace the slogans and catch-phrases about family policy with detailed, explicit and well-grounded proposals. Whether that is actually realised will depend, I suspect, upon whether the political reasons for not doing so continue to have the same force.

NOTES

1 For comparative material see United Nations (1979). From Table 7 it can be seen that the German Democratic Republic, Sweden and the UK have the highest proportion of population over 75 (between 5.5 and 5.75 per cent).
2 From work currently being completed by my colleague Michael Power at the University of Bristol.
3 Currently, nearly a third of all marriages are second marriages, in the sense that one or other partner has been married before ('Social Trends, 1980', no. 10, 1979).

Chapter 19

Families and educational institutions
Daphne Johnson

Because of the compulsory nature of a substantial part of education, families with children inevitably become involved with educational institutions of one kind or another. Earlier chapters demonstrate that whatever the aspect or mode of family life under discussion, the question of education is always relevant. This chapter draws on recent research to illuminate and illustrate some of the many interconnections between families and schools.

During five years of continuous qualitative research in and around nine comprehensive schools in outer London, the author and other members of a research team based at Brunel University have studied the experiences of and relationships between teachers, parents and pupils. (1) The research material drawn on here is chiefly from home interviews with parents of pupils at three of the schools studied.

FAMILIES AND COMPULSORY EDUCATION

Four assumptions about family structures and practice appear to be implicit in mainstream school provision: that the school-age child has the status of dependent minor; that the parent has prime responsibility for the child; that the school-age years of childhood and adolescence ante-date the young person's participation in either economic or sexual activity; and that family residence and membership are stable during the school-age years.

Perhaps the principal assumption underlying mainstream education is that the school-age child is a dependent minor who can be contained, directed and benefited, whether he will or no. Childhood as a minority status is a subject in its own right, and will not be enlarged on here. But *pupil*hood as a minority status is central to our whole discussion in that it

draws families and schools inexorably together into some combination of responsibility for the child, during the school-
age years.

Although the demarcations of responsibility may be differently drawn between different families and different
schools, (2) the emphasis placed by our society on private
citizenship rather than State collectivity makes it inevitable
that primary responsibility for the school-age minor rests
with the family. Consequent assumptions about the role of
the parent are of great importance in understanding the relationship between family and school. The parent is the adult
chiefly responsible for the whereabouts, conduct and conformity of the school-age child to the law of the land. (3)
Whole sectors of law and social policy delineate and reinforce
that responsibility. But parental responsibility must co-
exist, and may conflict, with other adult roles about which
there may also be policy or legislation.

The role of employee is perhaps the adult role most likely
to impinge on parental responsibility, especially parental
responsibility at the margin between home and school (see
Chapter 6). The values to which many teachers and educational administrators subscribe about the pre-eminence of the
parental, and especially the maternal, role over other legitimate adult roles are often clearly demonstrated in school procedures.

Our research in comprehensive schools indicated that a
telephone number enabling prompt contact during day-time hours
is one of the few pieces of information which parents are systematically requested to supply to the school. Several
teachers commented that one of the most effective ways of involving parents in disciplinary problems with their child at
school was to ring them up at work, or require them to take
time off work to come to the school to discuss their child's
misdemeanours. And a number of mothers found education welfare officers and teachers ready to imply that one parent
should remain at home during school hours in case the child
truanted from school. Employment of the mother outside the
home was often defined not only as facilitating the non-atten-
dance of pupils, but as positively encouraging it.

Given the psychological, social and financial pressures on
all adults to enter and sustain paid employment (reinforced by
legislation prohibiting sexual discrimination in such matters)
it is perhaps surprising that schools are not organised to
take account of parents being at work, and that teachers are
prepared to express resentment if parents are not always on
call. Certainly from the parents' own point of view, our
research confirmed that the childminding aspects of publicly
provided education are an important element in family organisation and budgeting. (4)

Another assumption, implicit in educational provision, is
that the school-age years are a preliminary stage in life,
which fitly precede and antedate the pupils' own participation
in the workforce and also in sexual partnership, marriage and
childbearing.

The idea that school-age young people are unfitted or un-
ready for sexual activity and sexual responsibilities is, with
the progressive raising of the school-leaving age, increasingly called into question.   The fact that the school-leaving
age and the age of consent at present coincide seems fortui-
tous rather than inevitable.   The twentieth century trend
towards earlier puberty might support the case for lowering
the age of consent, but in fact this has remained at 16 years
since 1885.   By contrast, the school-leaving age was not
raised to 16 until 1972.

Whatever the legalities, it is manifestly not the case that
secondary school pupils are unequal to sexual activity.
Nevertheless in Britain arrangements for the counselling and
continuing education of the sexually active pupil or the
school-age parent are responsive and ad hoc rather than systematic and active, whereas in the USA the counselling and
education of pregnant schoolgirls and school-age mothers,
especially among the Black population, is in some States an
accepted part of mainstream educational provision.

Given the moral debate and strong conflict of values which
accompany any initiatives in the field of sex education and
counselling, it is perhaps not surprising that the assumption
continues to prevail that sexual activity will not begin until
schooldays are over, any exceptions being regarded as cases
for treatment rather than as pointers to policy formulation.

An allied assumption, part and parcel of the view of school
years as a preliminary stage, is that economic activity will
also not begin until schooldays are over.   Here educational
policy is more forthright, and backed by specific legislation,
which seems, however, to be more honoured in the breach than
the observance.

The *legitimate* employment of children in the use of skills
intrinsic to their youth and fostered by their formal education does not appear to have attracted the attention of students of the sociology of occupations or indeed the sociology
of education.   The field of enquiry would probably have to be
limited to Cathedral choir schools and some few branches of
the performing arts, but might provide useful insights into
the effect on families of school relationships when schooling
is officially concurrent with employment rather than preceed-
ing it.

For many families, however, the jobs held down by their
school-age children are a matter to be concealed from the

school rather than discussed as part of the child's educational experience during the growing years.   Yet recent research
(5) indicates that for many young people under school-
leaving age, their part-time work is an important part of
their life outside the school.   The protective legislation
which sets limits and conditions for the employment of schoolchildren is fairly easily evaded by consenting employers and
employees, and the education welfare service whose task it is
to monitor school-age employment has other more pressing functions to perform.

One other assumption about family practice implicit in educational policy remains to be discussed before turning to the
implications of present-day family diversity for educational
policy in all its forms.

Devolving control of the delivery and administration of
compulsory education to local government assumes, among other
things, that family residence and membership are sufficiently
stable to enable children to follow through the eleven years
of compulsory education in one local education authority.
The conflicts between this assumption and some aspects of
housing and employment policy and family practice are too evident to need outlining.   It can be noted, however, that local
variation in educational provision seems on the increase with
differing ages of transfer to secondary school brought about
by the introduction of middle schools in some areas.   The
currently equivocal attitude of central government towards the
reorganisation of secondary education on comprehensive lines
will also facilitate and perpetuate local variation.

Within individual schools, arrangements for meeting the
social and affective needs of pupils are also based on expectations of through-school continuity, with pastoral systems
aiming to build up knowledge of the child by continuous association with particular members of staff, such as the form
tutor who in theory sees the child through at least three
years of his school life.   In recent years teacher mobility
and promotion have been chiefly responsible for discontinuities in teacher/pupil pastoral association.   But in the
coming years of contraction of the education system due to
falling rolls, the mobility of pupils and their families,
drawn to new housing developments or relocated employment
opportunities, may become more salient.

Compulsory general education, first of an elementary nature
and more recently through to the secondary stage, has undoubtedly played a part in shaping the structure, process and
values of family life in Britain.   The family life which fits
most easily into mainstream educational provision is child-
centred, with traditional sex-role division between mother and
father, providing full financial support and sheltered

surveillance of all offspring throughout the school-age years, with long-term stability of residence and family constitution. Such historical knowledge as we have of unexceptional families (see, e.g., Shorter, 1977) indicates that these characteristics were not typical of pre-twentieth-century family life.   By the late twentieth century, however, the schools can count on the co-operation, or resignation, of the majority of families concerning the constraints placed on family practice by compulsory education.   A great many families do allow their residence, employment, holidays and other leisure activities to be strongly influenced by considerations of their children's schooling.   These constraints weigh less heavily on some families than on others.   The new alliances and manifestations of family diversity discussed in this book may be less congruent with mainstream educational provision than is the case for conventional family structures. (6)

THE IMPLICATIONS OF FAMILY DIVERSITY FOR EDUCATIONAL POLICY AND PROVISION

Mainstream schooling, as at present provided, envisages a client group of conventional families.   Manifestations of family diversity may therefore confront the educational system with new burdens and complexities, but may also offer new resources and potential for partnership between home and school. Taking first the more positive approach, it can be postulated that the resources made available as a part of family diversity include the wider range of work experience and skills of dual worker as opposed to single breadwinner families, the examples of resourcefulness and independence provided by lone parents, the similar resourcefulness and initiative of immigrant families as well as their cultural heritage, with its potential to enrich the host culture, the availability of adult members of shift-working families to visit the school during day-time hours, and the possibility that reconstituted families muster additional adults who, together with the child's natural parents, can offer interest and support during the child's school years.

   This is the rosy side of the picture, and one which it is important not to overlook lest family diversity should automatically be equated with child deprivation.   This is in danger of becoming the case for one-parent families.   Some children in every generation including many who are notably successful in later life, have been brought up in one-parent families, because of the death or departure of father or mother.   In recent years, perhaps because of the moral judgments surrounding divorce, now the most frequent cause of lone

parenthood, the one-parent family is readily defined as the
harbinger of disadvantage and deviance.   Yet the effective
lone parent may well have qualities and devise family practice
which get the children off to a good start in life and enable
them to make the most of their educational opportunities.
   Some of the most obvious difficulties which family diversity may present to the educational system are strictly practical ones.   The working hours and holidays of dual-worker
families will almost certainly not match school hours and
holidays.   If the school pupil, as a dependent minor, is
meant to be passed from care of family to care of school and
back again without any break in surveillance, either school
hours or parents' employment hours need to be flexible.
Dual-worker families where one parent is a teacher or ancil-
liary worker at the child's school are not faced with this
problem, but this dovetailing of work and family responsibilities is not possible for many parents.   Working mothers
interviewed in our research often worked part time while their
older children were still in primary school, so as to be at
home when school ended.   Later in the family cycle, children
now at secondary school took over responsibility for younger
brothers and sisters enabling the mother's return to full-time
work.   However, the time gap between the end of the primary
and the secondary school day was a problem.
   Other dual-worker families with young children managed by
alternating their working hours, the mother doing early morning cleaning or an evening shift, while the father worked a
more conventional day.   Some instances of job sharing between
husband and wife have been reported, though none came up in
our research.   This practice has more potential for couples
with trained professional skills than for the semi-skilled or
unskilled manual workers chiefly encountered in our outer
London study.   In any case job sharing which, of course,
brings in only one whole income, is more likely to be adopted
by parents who are anxious to share baby care and economic
activity rather than as a means of bridging the gap between
school hours and normal working hours.
   John and Elizabeth Newsom, in 'Seven Years Old in the Home
Environment' (1976) report a number of family arrangements for
keeping tabs on children between the end of school and the end
of the parents' working day.   These were all ad hoc individual arrangements.   Although creches for preschool children
may be matched to the hours of parents' employment, we know of
no primary school which doubles as a creche, retaining the
school-age child on the premises for a couple of hours after
school, until the parents leave work.   Some youth centres are
however now providing 'latch-key' clubs for children to come
to straight from school.   Very few schools, by contrast, have

after-school clubs of a general social nature, or where food
can be obtained.

School organisation does not at present seem to have the
flexibility of some other organisations to adapt to changing
family needs. (7)   There is little provision, for example,
for homework to be completed after school on school premises,
delaying the return home.   The unionised demarcation practices of teachers with regard to working hours, which regularly call into question the acceptability even of lunchtime
duties or after-school meetings of staff, make it unlikely
that the duration of the teacher's spell *in loco parentis* can
be adjusted to match with parental employment.

One of the schools studied in our research did, however,
offer what was known as a 'Third Session' in the early evening.   This arrangement was in fact a range of early evening
classes, beginning at 4.15, including sporting and craft
activities, for which both pupils and adults might enrol, and
for which teachers were separately paid.   Many of the main
teaching staff taught on Third Session which was held on three
evenings a week, but some teachers were recruited from elsewhere.

It is not our contention that the latch-key child of secondary school age is necessarily a neglected child (Johnson,
1977).   This stereotypification is as insensitive as that of
the one-parent family as an agent of child deprivation.   But
although the adolescent may be well able to look after himself
for an hour or two after school, if his temporary responsibility extends to the surveillance of younger family members,
this may be a matter of some concern for parents.   For dual-
worker and one-parent families it is undoubtedly more difficult to match school hours and working hours, and they are
more likely than conventional families to make use of after
school and school holiday care for their children, whether by
school, youth and community or voluntary sector provision.

Apart from any mismatch between the hours when parents and
teachers can take responsibility for the surveillance of the
child, the question of parents actually visiting the school is
probably more difficult for dual-worker or lone parents to
arrange than for conventional families.   Shift-working
parents may however be at a positive advantage.

At one period during the research contact with outer
London comprehensive schools, one school put on a joint staff/
pupils/parents play.   The producer planned to hold rehearsals
at 4.00 pm for staff and pupils and at 6.00 pm for parents.
However, he found that the parents who offered to participate
could also manage rehearsals at 4.00 pm, chiefly because they
were on shift work.   This was one instance where shift working facilitated home-school co-operation.   And home

interviews with parents indicated that shift working sometimes
made it possible for parents to accept day-time invitations to
visit schools, and to some extent made it easier for parents
to spend time with their children if they were away from
school or in the holidays. (8)

Not all invitations to parents to visit the school are for
social or recreational occasions.   The extent to which secondary school teachers look to the parents of troublesome children to come to the school as part of disciplinary procedures
may be unknown to the parents whose children are unobtrusive
pupils.   School policy rarely allows for teachers to call on
parents at home but it is common practice to ask parents to
come to the school to discuss their child's misbehaviour
during school hours.   The use of temporary suspension of the
pupil, as a cooling-off period for teacher and child, is also
a common practice.   The period of suspension is usually
phrased in the letter to parents 'until such time as you can
accompany your child to school to discuss the matter'.   Head
teachers comment that this ploy rarely fails to bring about a
speedy parental visit, usually within twenty-four hours, as
the parents are anxious to hand the child back to the responsibility of the school.   The question of whether parents
should be drawn in to the disciplinary handling of children at
secondary school is not being debated here. (9)   Our point is
that family diversity, compared with conventional family
structure, may require parents to give higher priority to
attendance at their place of work than to home-school co-operation of this kind.

The custodial and disciplinary functions of the school are
pro-parental functions which have some counterpart in family
arrangements, even if there is little congruence between the
way these functions are performed in school and home.   The
teaching function of the school is more specialised and professional, with less potential to involve pupils' families in
activities of partnership.   Nevertheless, it is educational
practice to keep parents informed about their children's progress in school, and to consult parents, however nominally,
about their wishes at certain turning points in the child's
school career.   Examples are the time of transfer from primary to secondary school, when optional subjects are selected
within the secondary school curriculum, the stage of entry
for public examinations and when decisions have to be taken
about post-compulsory schooling, further or higher education,
or entering employment.   On all these occasions, parents are
given the opportunity to express their views and preferences,
even if the invitation to do so is somewhat perfunctory, and
the degree of influence available to parents far from
clear. (10)   Parents are also quite likely to be asked to

endorse school policy on homework, religious teaching and sex education. Moreover, from the time the child first starts school, school reports begin to flow home on a regular basis, usually with the invitation to come to the school to discuss the child's school work. What are the implications of family diversity for all these consultative procedures?

Family structure was not a criterion for the selection of parents interviewed during our research. For the most part, the families encountered were conventional in structure, but a minority were one-parent or reconstituted families. However the family was constituted, it was usually the case that *someone* at home read the child's report with interest and at least occasionally went to parents' evenings at the school to talk with teachers. Although the intensity and frequency of school contact varied considerably between families, this was not noticeably related to family structure. A number of wives in conventional families said they did not go to the secondary school to talk to teachers unless their husbands were free to accompany them. But some lone mothers had found the courage to do so. 'I'm on thorns all the time, but I go', said one such mother.

A more important criterion than family structure in influencing the response of parents to consultative enquiries by the school seemed to be their appraisal of the child's own capacity to make judgments, and their confidence in the teachers. At least during the secondary school years parents felt pupils and teachers should decide together on choices the outcome of which would involve them closely. School procedures tacitly reinforce that view by using the pupil as intermediary in consultative enquiries. Many parents were well aware that their children filtered, suppressed or delayed the delivery of co-respondence from the school, if they preferred to keep their parents' involvement with the school to a minimum. However, the procedures which schools presently adopt about consulting parents do presuppose that families are of one mind about what their child's school experience should be – whether they believe in letting well alone, with minimum intervention, or have clear-cut views about the desirable choices and outcomes of particular educational turning points.

Fathers and mothers in conventional families whom we interviewed were not always of one mind about educational matters but were usually in process of negotiating a compromise, or else had settled for the mother's views taking precedence during the primary school years, with the father having greater influence during the secondary school stage. Divided or reconstituted families can presumably achieve similar compromises, once the family restructuring has been established. The time of greatest difficulty, from the school's point of

view, is the period of family dispute or disengagement when
the question of access to and influence over the children or
a disintegrating union is heatedly at issue.   Our research
encountered examples of parents using the school as a venue to
make contact with the children they no longer lived with,
causing teachers some concern as to the responsibilities of
their own role *in loco parentis*.   For one couple, deeply
estranged, but still sharing a home, the research approach
itself, requesting an interview to elicit the parents' views
on their children's secondary school experience, was a temporary focus of controversy.   Appointments for the interview
were repeatedly made and cancelled by one or another partner,
and the eventual interview with the mother only, although the
father was in the house, laid great stress on how the father's
activity and attitudes were counterproductive to the mother's
aims in the upbringing of the children.   At times like these,
the best policy for the school is probably to abandon attempts
to consult with parents and to concentrate on providing a
stable and ordered, if part-time environment, for the children
who must live with dissension at home.   However, it was our
experience that secondary school teachers were not usually
aware of family crises or even separations, unless remarriage
entailed a new surname for parental contact on the school
record.

In considering the implications which family diversity may
have for home and school co-operation, we have so far examined
practical issues of gaps in custodial provision as between
home and school and intra-familial issues of appropriate
parental response to consultative overtures from the school.
But family diversity can have implications for the educational
system which are less domestic.   The presence in Britain of
ethnic minority families entails the management of access to
educational institutions by newly arriving families, and the
continuing recognition of possible cultural discontinuities as
between school and home.

Any discussion of ethnic diversity in our population which
lumps all non-indigenous families together is bound to under-
rate complexity through over-generalisation.   For our purposes we will leave aside the Jewish, Irish, Polish and other
European families who have, over the years, brought their expectations and influence to bear on public education in the
UK.   We will focus instead on the Asian and West Indian families whose children are now at school here. (11)   Some of
these children shared the family experience of emigration.
Others were born here, but are the first generation to pass
through British schools.   Two outcomes of their presence will
be discussed here.

Those families who arrive with children already of school

age are, in the first instance, the concern of the education office rather than the school.   The immigrant family (12) taking up residence in a local authority area could be seen as a special case of the acceptance onto roll procedure laid down for families migrating from another part of the country. Important differences are, however, evident.   Immigration patterns are such that an area which receives any ethnic minority families is likely to receive many within a relatively short period of time.   The education office may have to cope, within two or three school years, with the allocation of an influx of families with children of both primary and secondary school age.   Moreover, these families may be experiencing language difficulties and culture shock.

For indigenous families, association with the educational system is mediated through a series of particular institutions - the schools attended.   For the majority of such families, the only time of unattachment is the summer holidays between primary and secondary school.   We have discussed elsewhere the difficulties which many families encounter in tackling the impersonal and bureaucratic office rather than the recognisable if formidable school, if they are dissatisfied about the arrangements made for their child's secondary education (see Johnson and Ransom, 1980).   However, the relationship of direct dealing between education office and parent, though often uneasy, is usually short lived.   Once the child has become a pupil at the new school, the educational forces with which the family has to deal are once again personified in teachers with a professional duty towards the child rather than officials whose primary duty is to make administrative arrangements for the delivery of professional services by others.

The characteristics and style of negotiation between immigrant families of Asian or West Indian origin and education department officials have not been systematically researched. But if the relationship between indigenous families and the office is uneasy, it seems likely that negotiations between office and parent have considerably more potential for friction where ethnic minority families are concerned.   Difficulties are likely to be most acute where newly arrived families are moderately numerous but not such as to justify the appointment of liaison officers with special responsibility for the induction of such families to the ramifications of the education system.   Observation suggests that the clerical workers, education welfare officers and immigrant parents who in most education authorities have to deal together, are experiencing some difficulty in coming to terms with one another.

While the arrival of immigrant families presents education

departments with one kind of challenge, the presence of pupils from ethnic minority groups on the roll faces the school itself with another kind of problem. Should the school celebrate or ignore cultural diversity? The melting pot theory of gradual racial assimilation seems to advocate the latter alternative, but increasing experience of the education and employment difficulties faced by immigrants from the West Indies is leading to the recognition that cultural differences do not just go away (Milner, 1975). For British-born children of ethnic minority families the problems of participation in systems evolved with the indigenous population in mind may in fact be exacerbated by intergenerational value conflicts. The generation which made the decision to emigrate has made an investment of confidence and energy which it is constrained to back by continuing efforts towards satisfactory co-existence with the host society. The generation born here but finding itself disadvantaged by racial discrimination and cultural dissonance is likely to be at odds with schools and the employment system and also with their parents whose cultural identity has not been tested in British classrooms.

Inevitably this discussion of families and educational institutions has dwelt chiefly on families with children, and on primary and secondary schools. (13) These are the most salient educational encounters which families make *as* families, whether conventional or diverse.

The formulation of family policy, however, to which this book hopes to contribute, should not confine itself to the interests of families with dependent children. Family life goes on despite a series of status passages and the need and capacity for education is not confined to a particular age group. In the concluding paragraphs of this chapter we reflect on the educational experience and opportunities of older family members.

Although education is often philosophically defined as a lifelong experience, educational institutions are almost exclusively for young clients. For most people in Britain (14) the exposure to formal education is a once-for-all package, co-terminous with the years of compulsory schooling. Because of large-scale reorganisation of secondary education and the raising of the school-leaving age during the 1970s, an inequality of educational opportunity now exists between the present younger generation and their parents and grandparents at least as great as that which previously existed within the age cohort whose secondary education was provided in the schools of the 'tripartite' era. (15)

Intergenerational disparity between exposure to formal education can best be described in percentages. At least 80 per cent of those now over forty-five had only an elementary

education and left school at fourteen.   Perhaps 70 per cent
of those aged between twenty and forty-five left school at
fifteen years of age.   They spent the years from eleven to
fifteen in secondary schools offering restricted curricula
closely tied to the particular aims of the three types of secondary school.   (Our discussion here is limited to those of
the population who received their education in the public
sector.   Changes have also taken place in private sector provision and, to some extent, in the constitution of the private
sector of education's client group.)

For the present generation of secondary school pupils and
their parents, intergenerational disparity of educational
opportunity presents some problems which influence the course
of the relationship between home and school (see Johnson
and Ransom, 1980).   But the restricted educational
experience of those now over thirty-five is not important
solely in terms of how it affects their perspectives on the
schooling of their children.   Consideration should also be
given to the life space and lifestyle of those who never have
been parents or for whom the role of parent is no longer central.   Life expectancy is now greater, the childrearing years
are abbreviated and employment opportunities are shifting and
shrinking.   As the falling birth rate decimates school rolls,
the greatest scope for educational institutions lies in the
field of adult and continuing education.   The implications
for institutional change of such a switch in client group
would be far greater than any of those stimulated by the patterns of family diversity discussed in this book.

NOTES

1   The author is convenor of the Educational Studies Unit,
   Brunel University.   She is greatly indebted to Maurice
   Kogan, Director of the Unit, for his helpful elucidation
   of many of the issues explored during the Unit's research,
   and further reflected on here.
      Between 1974 and 1980 the Educational Studies Unit
   carried out two consecutive studies, which are briefly
   described below.
   (a)   'Schools, Parents and Social Services' project, DES
   funded from 1974-7.   A study of four comprehensive
   schools and a number of social agencies in two outer
   London boroughs, also 109 home interviews with parents of
   children attending the schools.   See D. Johnson et al.,
   1980;   also Johnson and Ransom, 1980, and D. Johnson and
   E. Ransom, 'Family and School', forthcoming.

(b) 'Disaffected Pupils' project, DES funded 1977-80. A
study of problem pupils in six outer London comprehensive
schools.   See C. Bird et al., 1981.

2 Residential schools or denominational schools, for example, by definition embrace a wider sphere of responsibility than day schools or secular schools.   And the expectations of immigrant families about the home/school
contract may differ from those of indigenous families.

3 In most cases the natural parent retains this responsibility, but it may pass to step- or foster parent, or other
legal guardian.   In certain circumstances a Social Services Department may be the surrogate parent.

4 One working mother commented that on a school day she had
to give her son 15 pence (the cost of a school dinner).
If he had a day off school for any reason while she was at
work, it meant an outlay of at least one pound (parent
interview, 1976).   More typically, however, parents commented on the custodial rather than the economic aspects
of school containment of their children while they were at
work.

5 'Disaffected Pupils Project', see note 1.

6 By 'family diversity' in this chapter we encompass dual-
worker, shift-working, one-parent, reconstituted and
ethnic minority families.   By residual definition, 'conventional' families are indigenous, and comprise two
parents (one of whom is the chief breadwinner working
'social hours') with children who are the product of a
long-term marital relationship.   Oakley, in Chapter 5,
points out that conventional families are often defined by
the exclusion of 'exceptions'.

7 Nevertheless, it should be recognised that Youth and Community provision comes within the orbit of the education
departments of local authorities, so the educational
system if not the school itself is in some cases meeting
family needs.

8 This point should not be overplayed, however, since in
many ways shift working drastically reduces opportunities
for family togetherness during evening or weekend hours.

9 In fact the majority of parents interviewed during our
research in 1976/7 thought it reasonable that they should
be so involved, although for many of them the question was
thus far hypothetical.

10 The most noticeable turning point, for most children, is
the transfer to secondary school.   We have discussed
parents' perspectives on transfer procedure and practice
elsewhere (see 'Family and School', forthcoming).   The
subject is an important one so far as home/school relationships are concerned, but space will not permit enlarg-
ing on it here.

11   The author shares the reservations of Eversley and Bonner-
     jea (Chapter 3) about the use of the blanket terms 'Asian'
     and 'West Indian'.   They are however useful terms in
     general discussion.

12   The term 'immigrant' seems to be acquiring derogatory
     overtones.   It is used here in its strictly technical
     sense.

13   Nursery schools and other forms of preschool education are
     not discussed in this chapter.   References to this stage
     of education are however to be found in other chapters,
     notably Chapter 6.

14   This situation is not of course exclusive to Britain.
     Our discussion here is in fact chiefly stimulated by
     debate of similar issues of educational demography cur-
     rently taking place in Sweden.

15   From 1944 onwards, public sector secondary education was
     provided in secondary modern, technical or grammar
     schools.   By 1979, the great majority of the secondary
     school population were attending comprehensive schools.

Chapter 20

Families and employment
Nancy Seear

In all countries, before the onset of industrialisation, economic activity was dominated by agriculture, in which a high
percentage of the population were employed.   Different
patterns of agricultural organisation developed in different
countries and in different stages of evolution, but typically
agriculture has always been a form of family enterprise, with
women and children, as well as men, making an obvious economic
contribution to the maintenance of the family.   No doubt some
differentiation of function existed, as in medieval British
agriculture, where as Ivy Pinchbeck (1930) has pointed out,
the farmer's wife ran the dairy industry from the cow to the
customer.   Such differentiation did not, however, mean that
women were confined to the least arduous work.   As Evelyn
Sullerot (1968) has shown, women in many countries not infrequently performed some of the physically most demanding agricultural tasks.
   Nor was this activity confined to the production of food.
In medieval and early modern times, with few opportunities for
sub-division of labour and for trade, many of the necessities
of life were made at home.   In both manor house and cottage
the various essential stages in the preparation of food and
clothing were undertaken by the women of the family, helped by
their children.
   Throughout the period of the cottage industries women
worked in their homes as spinners, while Defoe's famous
passage in his diary in 1724 comments on the work done by
children: 'all employed, from the youngest to the oldest,
scarcely any thing above four years' old but its hands were
sufficient for its own support' (Defoe, 1927).   For better or
worse, in farm or cottage, the family worked as a unit.
   Industrialisation brought changes in the structure of economic activity and in the economic role of women, though the
nature of the changes varied in different parts of the

country.   In textiles women and children moved from cottage employment to the newly established factories, continuing their economic function and maintaining their position as earners and contributors to the family income.   Elsewhere, however, as the factory system developed, work was removed from home to factory, while many women remained at home, with a more restricted domestic role.   Where women were not employed in factories they not infrequently added to the family income by taking in 'out-work'.   This might, for example, be sub-contracted production jobs from a neighbouring factory, or dressmaking or laundry for a private household.   For many women 'out-work' was the only practical way of earning money while coping with domestic duties, it was also a primary source of sweated employment.

Important though factory employment became in the nineteenth century and has remained in the twentieth, it has never entirely dominated the world of work.   The small business and the self-employed man engaged in crafts and the simpler type of manufacturing, in repair work, in selling, in catering, in the provision on a small scale of a wide range of goods and services, have been part of the economic fabric from medieval times and have persisted to the present day.   In such activities wives have frequently played a part.   In some they have been named the proprietors.   Elsewhere their role has been less well defined, but not necessarily for that reason less significant.

It is important also to recall a characteristic of nineteenth-century social life which has had a marked impact on the employment opportunities of certain categories of women. In the prosperous middle classes it became a mark of affluence and success for a wife to have no apparent economic function and to be kept entirely by her husband.   Such wives lived in varying degrees of comfort, sometimes in splendour, but at the price of total dependence.

The contribution of children to the family income, important in both the pre-industrial period and in the early days of the industrialisation of the textile industry gradually diminished as consecutive Factories Acts raised the age at which children could be employed in factories, and Education Acts required full-time attendance at school.   Exclusion from factories did not, however, mean that all earning by children ceased, as they continued to be employed on odd jobs before and after school and during the school holidays.

The First World War saw a big influx of married women into paid employment and into jobs where previously they had not been countenanced.   But after the war they withdrew again to the home with the result that in the 1921 census only 8.9 per cent of married women were economically active.   At this

date, in most if not all British families, there was a clear
differentiation of role behaviour between husband and wife.
The husband was the money earner, carrying on his work outside
the home.   The wife had a varying degree of responsibility
for spending the money earned, though not infrequently she did
not know the extent of her husband's income and the amount of
money at her disposal was totally determined by him.   Her
primary task was the bearing and rearing of children and the
maintenance and comfort of the home.

The changes of the last half century have been dramatic,
both within the family and in the relations between the family
and the labour market.   As in so many other aspects of
women's altered way of life, the newly acquired control over
fertility is probably the root cause of these remarkable
changes.   Never before in human history has it been possible
for the vast majority of women to decide how many children
they will bear and when they will bear them.   As a consequence, the number of live births per 1,000 women aged 15-44
has dropped from 154.0 in 1871-5 to 52.7 in 1977 and childbearing has been restricted to the earlier years of married
life.   Before assuming that this automatically means far
greater freedom for mothers, other changes in the pattern of
the family have to be taken into account.   In most, though
not all, parts of the UK, the extended family has virtually
disappeared.   In many areas it is rare for relations to be
near at hand to give the kind of assistance with children and
in emergencies that has always been the norm in small, static
communities.   This can severely limit the wife's freedom of
action, even in very small families.   One other characteristic of the small family can also have an important bearing on
the employment position of the members of the family.   The
second half of the twentieth century has seen a marked increase in the proportion in the population of the very old.
People live longer, but many, in old age, need help.   The
social services have not been able to provide all the help
required, nor is this the kind of help that many old people
seek.   In earlier generations the grandmother in the household was often of great assistance to the mother, and her
period of physical incapacity was short.   Grandparents do, of
course, still sometimes live with the families of sons or
daughters.   But less and less do three generations easily
share the same home.   The need to care for frail, old
parents, whether or not they live with the family which
undertakes the caring, adds considerably to the demands on the
time and energy of the carer.

Important as are these constraints on the freedom of action
of the modern family, they have not prevented dramatic changes
in the position of married women in the labour market.

Between 1921 and 1975, the activity rates of married women have risen from 8.97 per cent to 47.90 per cent (HMSO, 1980) and many married women today expect to spend only a small number of years totally outside the labour market.   Some combine family and employment responsibilities without any cessation of paid work.

The Second World War led to a mass entry of married women into paid employment.   After the war many returned to full-time domestic life, but over the post-war decades the upward trend in activity rates has been maintained.   In the 1950s and 1960s full employment meant that all over the country jobs were available, often unskilled jobs, but jobs none the less. Moreover, throughout this time in most parts of the country there were chronic shortages of labour in traditional women's jobs, such as nursing and secretarial work and in many forms of manual work.   Faced with persistent vacancies employers were prepared to grant concessions to attract female labour and it became common for wives to be able to obtain part-time employment.   In the absence of all but the most scanty provision for child-care services part-time work was, to many women, very attractive.   Meanwhile, the rising level of expectations characteristic of the post-Second World War period made the second pay packet more and more indispensable.   In the period 1951-60 there were 6,970,000 owner-occupied dwellings.   By 1978 the figure had risen to 11,390,000.   Car ownership rose from 57 cars per 1,000 of the population in 1953 to 260 per 1,000 in 1977.   Holidays taken by residents in Great Britain rose from 27,000,000 in 1951 to 48,000,000 in 1978.   Of these 9,000,000 were holidays abroad in 1978 compared with only 2,000,000 in 1951 (ibid.).   For such goodies appetite grows with eating, but in many cases, without the second pay packet, one or more of them would disappear.

But rising expectations were by no means the sole reason for the rise in the employment of women with family responsibilities.   Changes in attitudes and in the social controls which in the past held ill-matched marriage partners together, combined with the greater social acceptance of the unmarried woman with a child, have led to the emergence of a significant number of women who are heads of households and also breadwinners.   For them the money earned in employment is often the means to an improved standard only in the sense that it is an improvement on social security payments.   In a smaller number of cases, married women in two-parent families are the main breadwinners because of the incapacity of the husband, or as a matter of choice between the marriage partners.

Surveys enquiring into the reasons why wives work usually, if not always, show the need for money as the main cause. Other motives are, however, of importance.   The small family, which has made the return to work easier, has also, for many women, made work a necessary substitute for the continuing demands of the large family of earlier generations.   If the last child enters school when the mother is thirty-five her need can be acute to find an outlet for energy and a role to fill the gap as domestic demands contract.

These changes taken together mean that over the last half century there has been a relatively steady increase in the supply of women seeking employment in the labour market. Different approaches to employment are to be found in the different categories of women who together constitute this female labour supply.   The attitude of the woman head of a household with heavy financial responsibilities differs from that of the highly qualified wife in the two-parent family, aware both of her own capacity and potential earning power and of the responsibilities and pleasures of family life as she perceives them.   Different again is the outlook of the woman with little, if any, specialised training, but with a strongly felt need to contribute to the family budget and to find a place for herself in the world of work as well as within her own family circle.   In the last two decades to these groups must also be added the wife in the immigrant family settled in this country but with a valued cultural background which influences her whole approach to paid employment.

To what sort of a labour market do these women come?   How well or ill is it suited to their needs?   How, if at all, can it be adapted to provide a better fit between the desires of the woman applicant and of her family and the requirements of the employing organisations and the economic purposes they serve?

The characteristics of available employment are the product of the technical and economic requirements of the employing organisation.   Conditions force continuous process industries and hospitals to work by night as well as by day.   Fruit picking and processing have peak periods, with a good deal of overtime, followed by slack periods or even the total disappearance of the job.   Postmen begin very early in the morning.   There are many variations.   But for all that there is a widely understood concept of a 'normal' working day, when work begins somewhere between 7 am and 8 am and finishes between 5 and 6 pm for five days a week, with weekly hours of work between around forty or forty-two hours, plus perhaps two or three hours' overtime.   Office hours are shorter, but are within the same overall pattern.   The work itself is broken down into conventional categories: Managerial, Professional, Technical, Administrative, Clerical, Distribution, Skilled, Semi-skilled and Unskilled Manual.

In the great majority of families in the past the husband

and father slotted into these traditional working hours, in
whatever category he was employed, leaving home quite early in
the morning, and returning in time for a meal with his wife,
but not always his children, at the end of the day.   The
whole pattern of normal working has grown up to suit the needs
of the organisation and the way of life of a male head of
house supported by a wife who maintains the home and looks
after the children.   Into this established way of working and
living has come the working wife, the dual-career family.   Up
to now, to an overwhelming extent, the wife has had to fit
herself into the established programme, adjusting her behaviour to meet both the demands of domestic life and the traditional expectations of employing organisations.

In many cases it has not been an easy accommodation.   How
has it been done and at what cost?   What future adaptation of
the traditional pattern might be made to produce a better fit
for both families and employing organisations?

Employing organisations, confronted with married women
applicants, have responded in a number of fairly predictable
ways.   Until the Second World War, aside from textile areas,
the vast majority of employers, including the civil service,
disposed of the problem by banning the employment of married
women altogether.   They would not engage married women, and
single women already in employment were required to leave on
marriage.   Manpower shortages and the crisis mentality of
the war years destroyed this simple solution of the problem of
the employment of married women.   But, though by 1945 married
women had established a place for themselves in the labour
market, it was expected that in normal circumstances they
would conform to the conventional pattern of work and would
accept the limitations laid on the employment of all women,
married or single - limitations which tended to confine their
employment to the traditional women's professions, to clerical
work and retail distribution and to a narrow range of manual
jobs mainly in semi-skilled and unskilled grades.

They were not, however, permitted to conform in all respects, even if they wished to do so.   Protective legislation,
originating in the first half of the nineteenth century,
limited by law the hours women might work, excluding them
altogether from night work.   Defended on the ground that for
health reasons women stood in special need of such protection
these laws curtailed women's job choice and sometimes excluded
them from better paid work.   It was always possible, however,
for employers to apply to the Factory Inspectorate for exemp-
tion from the operation of these laws, and in recent years an
increasing number of such exemptions have been granted.
These limited modifications apart, it can be said that the
working wife entering the labour market had no option but to

accept traditional patterns of working life.   For her this
frequently meant working at hours which meshed ill with her
domestic duties in a job with poor pay and poor prospects.

Changes in this traditional pattern have taken place when
labour shortages have given working wives some individual bargaining power.   War-time periods and very full employment in
the post-war period saw the widespread introduction of part-
time jobs.   Many different patterns emerged.   The morning
shift and the afternoon shift, covering between them the whole
of the normal working day, were common; and the evening shift
became well established in parts of the country.   There were
also many other variations arranged between employer and employed for mutual convenience.   These included 9.30 am to
4 pm; 11 am to 3.30 pm in department stores; Saturday only,
and even a fortnight on and a fortnight off.

Part-time employment has been seen by some people as the
obvious solution to the problems of the working wife and
mother, and there is no doubt that there has been a widespread
and persistent demand for such work.   It has, however,
serious disadvantages.   With very few exceptions part-time
workers are women.   In 1977 40.4 per cent of all women in
employment were working part time, compared with 2.1 per cent
of all men.   Part-time jobs are to be found almost entirely
in work that requires little skill and has poor pay and prospects.   Trade unions find part-time members difficult to
organise, and, as recent Industrial Tribunal cases have shown,
part-time workers are sometimes paid a lower hourly rate than
full-time workers, solely because they work part time.   Part-
time work is essentially a method by which wives adapt to the
traditional system of work.   If, however, there is to be a
serious attempt to enable the father instead of the mother to
take the major responsibility for child care, consideration
should be given to finding ways of operating a far wider range
of jobs on a part-time basis, including higher paid jobs.

The key question, however is: 'In what way can the traditional system be adapted to fit the labour force of today and
especially the varying and various patterns of the family
today?'

There can be no doubt that the optimum solution is one that
is seen to be advantageous to both the family and the employer.   Such a happy solution is, no doubt, hard to achieve,
but if an arrangement is to endure it needs to be accepted by
all those who have to make it work.   The best changes are,
therefore, those which offer advantages to all parties.   The
primary task of employing organisations is, after all, the
fulfilment of the purposes for which it was established, not
the provision of employment opportunities to meet family
needs.   The first responsibility of a hospital remains the

care of patients and of the electricity industry the continual
provision of electrical power.   The primary aim of the family
is to maximise its satisfactions and to meet its obligations
in a variety of different ways.   Sadly, there is no divine
law which ensures that the action needed to achieve these
various aims will be identical.   And it has to be remembered
that if the employing organisation is run less efficiently to
meet the desires and convenience of the family, someone has to
pick up the tab.   In the very long run it will probably be
the members of the family, but the chance they will see it
that way is about nil.   The objective must be, so far as possible, to meet the needs of all concerned, and where this
cannot be done, to arrive at a compromise solution which gets
as near as possible to this optimum.

In attempting to identify the steps to be taken to this end
several general points can perhaps usefully be established.

1   Employment practices based on a different kind of labour
    force may well not be the most efficient in the new cir-
    cumstances and should be reviewed with the changes of per-
    sonnel in mind.

2   The emergence on to the labour market of large numbers of
    women who in previous generations would not have been
    available for work offers the possibility of improving
    standards which it would be unwise to ignore.   The con-
    centration of women in low-level jobs can only meant that
    a number of them are wastefully utilised.

3   The situation of the family is not uniform and is not
    static.   The variations between families in terms of
    desires and capacities are great.   The variations in
    terms of desires and capacities of any one family through-
    out its lifetime are probably just as great.   What is a
    good 'fit' for one family, is a poor fit for another, and
    a poor fit for the same family at a different stage of its
    existence.

From an examination of the implications of these statements, it may be possible to derive policies appropriate for
the economy and for the families of today and tomorrow.

1   Organisations need to look at their employment practices to see if changes could be made which would both increase their own effectiveness and meet the employment needs
of families.   A simple example is the departmental store
which made a careful study of the work loading in its departments and found that in the interests of its own efficiency it
ought to employ people on a variety of different shifts during
the day, on different days of the week, and at different times
of the year.   This matched the employment needs of many women
who were seeking work during the limited, but domestically
convenient, hours proposed.   Technical change in general and

micro-processing in particular invite similar mutually satisfactory innovations.   There can be little doubt that in the
future an increasing number of paid jobs can be carried out
in the home.   For both men and women this would solve many
domestic problems.   It would at the same time cut down on the
employer's costly requirements for space and office upkeep.

2 Companies need also to challenge many established practices to see if in fact they deter applicants from joining the
company or cause existing employees to leave.   An example
here is the mobility rule in many banks and insurance companies.   The commitment to mobility is certainly a deterrent to
many women.   Often too, with established homes and children
in local schools, men find it cuts across important family
needs.   If the organisation is depriving itself of good-
quality staff, may this not be too high a price to pay for a
commitment to mobility?   Can not the purpose of the mobility
requirement be achieved in some other way?

3 The maintenance of rigid hours of employment for both
men and women is another aspect of traditional practice that
may well cost more than it is worth.   The introduction of
flexi-time in a number of organisations would have been un-
thinkable twenty-five years ago.   Of course, such schemes
have their limitations, but it is at least worthwhile to
attempt to estimate whether the benefits exceed the costs.

If employing organisations need to challenge their conventional approaches, so do individuals and the general public.
Shift work has a bad name, but highly paid short shifts worked
in high value-added industries may prove to have an unexpected
attraction.   The 'evening shift' in manufacturing industry
did not normally offer either high pay or prestigious work,
but all over the country firms advertising such shifts were
inundated with applications.   As mother left home for work
after a hard day with a young family, father took over her
domestic responsibilities.   The arrangement apparently had
considerable appeal.   In organisations as diverse as the BBC
and hospitals work all round the clock has long been accepted.
The Equal Opportunities Commission reporting on the Health and
Safety Regulations and on the case for demanding special limitations on women's hours of work found examples where families
regarded shift working as the preferred pattern.   In capital
intensive industry the high level of plant utilisation made
possible by continuous process working can in favourable circumstances enable the enterprise to pay comparatively high
wages for short, if unconventional, hours of work.   It is not
too fanciful to contemplate six-hour shifts, or, eventually,
even shorter spells of work.   Where a husband and wife are
both employed on this basis, one or other could always be in
the home, and there would also be substantial periods when

both were in the house together.   Over ten years ago a
Swedish petro-chemical company was employing women on shifts
all round the clock, with a total working week of approximately 30 hours.   According to both the management and the woman
shop steward, the arrangement worked well (Seear, 1971).   It
is important not to confuse the *opportunity* to work shifts wi
with the *obligation* to work shifts.

The fact that family needs change markedly over time suggests that policies based on continuity of service and seniority call for scrutiny.   While compulsory mobility can run
directly counter to the needs of the family, the ability to
change jobs when it suits them, at different stages in the
career of both husband and wife, is essential.

If the optimum arrangements are to be made for both family
and employer, it has to be possible for a wife to pursue her
career while a husband spends more time in the home.   This
calls for paternity leave as well as maternity leave and seniority rules and pension provisions will also need adjustment.
At the present time most men would consider that a couple of
years taken off work would have a permanently detrimental
effect on their careers.   The fact that a woman's career is
already regularly affected in this way is not a sound argument
for extending the practice to men.   The answer for both is a
more critical look at the alleged need for continuity.

Another essential element in the creation of greater flexibility within the family and the labour market is the availability of training and re-training.   A good deal has already
been done to make training available to people of all ages, to
help women to re-enter the labour market after a period at
home and to enable both men and women to switch careers in
mid-stream.   We need to look much more seriously at the proposal that everyone should be allowed a given number of years
of post-school training and education to be taken as and when
their circumstances and needs make it appropriate.   Widespread discussions on worksharing are already taking place and
entrenched attitudes are being taken up.   It seems only sensible to give priority to forms of worksharing where men and
women temporarily removed from the labour market are able to
use the leisure gained to their own and ultimately society's
benefit by acquiring the skills and knowledge needed for new
and expanding jobs.

The adjustments this implies in the universities and col-
leges and in Open University type courses are vast, but flexibility in educational training opportunities is an essential
element in any attempt to serve the best interests of both the
family and the economy.   Such extended training opportunities
are also essential if women are to make the kind of contribution of which many are capable.   The customary exclusion of

women from many skilled and responsible jobs deprives the
economy of manpower resources in areas where they are badly
needed, as the present shortage of skilled and technically
qualified personnel demonstrates.   The same tradition limits
the return to the woman and the family in terms both of financial reward and of the satisfaction and interest to be derived
from more skilled and responsible work.   The main thrust of
equal opportunities legislation is intended to change traditional patterns.   Section 47 of the Sex Discrimination Act
1975, which permits reverse discrimination to provide training
for either sex markedly under-represented in any occupation
was designed to correct this position.   It has scarcely been
used and pressure should be brought to bear on Industrial
Training Boards and on employers to take action to redress the
balance.

The importance of training and re-training can hardly be
over-stressed.   At the same time it is equally important to
take steps to see that during the time that either the father
or the mother is primarily involved in bringing up the family,
every effort is made to ensure that professional knowledge and
skill is kept up to date.   The scheme under which women doctors have been paid an allowance while at home to encourage
them to undertake a small number of clinics and to attend a
minimum number of conferences in order to keep in touch with
professional work could be copied and extended far more
widely.   Such schemes would not only reduce the amount of
money and effort required when fathers or mothers decided to
return to full-time employment.   It would also help to prevent the development of the feeling of loss of confidence said
to be widely experienced by those who have had a long spell at
home, out of the labour market.   There can be no doubt that
this loss of confidence makes the whole process of re-entry
difficult and painful, creating a barrier which some women
never surmount.

The types of employment so far discussed depend in the main
on the existence of large- or medium-sized employers of
labour, prepared or required to adjust traditional practices
to meet changing conditions.

But such enterprises are not the only element in the economy or the only source of livelihood.   From the earliest times
self-employment or work for very small employers have provided
many families with their main or only source of income.   In
very recent years it has been realised in the UK that this
section has been unduly neglected and steps are being taken to
revive this type of enterprise for sound economic reasons.
The flexibility of concerns of this type make them specially
suitable for the employment of family units.   'Living over
the shop' no doubt has its disadvantages, but, together with

the small family farm, it probably remains the best-known way
by which a family can earn a living, with the different members of the family making a contribution in the way that suits
them best, while keeping an eye on the youngsters, and if
necessary grandfather as well.   Women have shown great entre-
preneurial flair in the development of small businesses, and
the satisfaction of family needs is yet another good reason
for their active encouragement.

Of course, there is no doubt that the position of the
family in relation to employment would be greatly eased by
better child-care arrangements.   The Equal Opportunities Commission has reported that in 1973 child-care provision from
all sources covered 29 per cent of the age group 0-5, mostly
on a part-time basis.   Full-time provision was available for
only 0.7 per cent.

As to provision for the child of school age, the Commission
wrote in 1978: 'We would calculate that over half a million
school age children are left unsupervised for at least part of
the day outside school time, that one million mothers of
school age children want after-school care and that one and a
half million mothers want school holiday provision for their
children' (EOC, 1978).   Some of the demand might be reduced
if more flexible working arrangements were introduced, but it
will remain large.   Many other countries make more ample provision than the UK, but nowhere is the demand fully met.
Many families find that, over time, it pays them to make a
substantial contribution to the cost of such provision, a contribution which has to be seen in relation to the woman who
makes the choice to forego the opportunity to earn money and
to look after her own children.

Because the needs of families differ so greatly and because
in any one family needs change as the years pass, there can
never be any simple optimal solution to the relationship
between the family and the labour market.   The keys are
flexibility and a wide variety choice between differing types
of employment.   Policy should, therefore, focus on the removal of obstacles to flexibility and the provision of the
maximum amount of choice.

Chapter 21

Families and the law

Brenda Hoggett

Family law in England and Wales, (1) as elsewhere in the Western industrialised world, is completing a transition from its
traditional role to an entirely different task.   In the old,
the constitution of the family unit and the legal relationships of its members with one another and with the outside
world, were strictly defined and controlled.   In the new, an
almost infinite variety of family arrangements is accommodated, but should they fail to provide adequately for the needs
of family members, the law increasingly intervenes to attempt
protection, support and adjustment. (2)   'The change is characterised by progressive withdrawal of legal regulation of
marriage formation, dissolution and the conduct of married
life, on the one hand, and by increased regulation of the economic and child-related consequences of formal or informal
cohabitation on the other' (Glendon, 1977:1).

THE OLD ROLE

At the beginning of the nineteenth century, the only legal
structure available for the organisation of family life was
'Christian' marriage. (3)   This was both a contract and a status,
founded on three basic premises which have not yet been entirely
abandoned.   Firstly, 'whereas the parties to a commercial agreement may make such terms as they think fit ... the spouses'
mutual rights and duties are very largely fixed by law and not
by agreement.' Secondly, 'unlike a commercial contract, which
cannot affect the legal position of anyone who is not a party
to it, marriage may also affect the rights and duties of third
persons.' Thirdly, 'until about ten years ago extra-marital
cohabitation gave neither party any rights over and above those
possessed by other persons living together who were not married
to each other' (Bromley, 1981:17, 649).   Effective sanctions

against fornication had, however, been abandoned in the seventeenth century. (4)

The rights and duties fixed by the law were the product of two separate jurisdictions whose objectives were not entirely harmonious.   The secular authorities, represented by the King's courts and later also by parliament, were originally concerned with the family as dynasty, as a device for the accumulation, control and orderly devolution of property and its accompanying status.   They devised the proprietary and contractual consequences of marriage and the means of identifying the heir.   They were not concerned with the personal relationships and conduct of family members.   The Church, however, was interested in establishing the Christian concept of marriage as the 'voluntary union for life of one man with one woman to the exclusion of all others'. (5)   It was able to do this because of the willingness of the medieval secular courts to accept, in almost all cases, the Church's judgment as to the existence and validity of any particular marriage (see Jackson, 1969; also Glendon, 1977:ch. 7, n. 3).   By this means, the stability of marriage was established as a value as important as the stability and continuity of the family group.   But the former could readily pose a threat to the latter.   A man might be tied for life to a barren or unfaithful wife, who endangered the succession, or trapped into a clandestine and unsuitable union through the lax attitude of the Church to formalities.   Some intervention by the secular authorities to remedy these problems was found necessary before the nineteenth century.

Despite these tensions, the terms of the marital package deal of approximately 1800 were both strict and coherent. Secular law was, in 1765, summed up thus: 'By marriage, the husband and wife are one person in law; that is, the very being or legal existence of the woman is suspended during the marriage, or at least is consolidated into that of the husband'. (6)   This maxim was not a rule, but it served to explain, and occasionally to produce, a series of rules governing the status of married women.   Essentially, these denied her control over any property, including the rewards of her own labour; consequentially, she was denied both contractual capacity and independent standing in civil litigation; her husband was enabled to use self-help to enforce her duty to live and have sexual intercourse with him; and litigation between them was impossible, even to enforce his admitted obligation to maintain her: 'they can claim a kind of sacred protection behind the door of the family home which, generally speaking, the civil law cannot penetrate' (Evershed, 1957:xv).

Ecclesiastical law did not discriminate between husband and wife and allowed some litigation between them (Helmholz, 1962).

The decree of restitution of conjugal rights was devised as a remedy for desertion, to enforce the duty to live together. But it was recognised that in cases of severe hardship, adultery or 'saevitia' (Biggs, 1962), relief from that duty should be granted.   Thus developed the concept that matrimonial relief of any sort - from the obligation to live together or from financial need resulting from separation - depended upon a contractual analogy.   Breach by one party of the fundamental marital obligations of cohabitation, fidelity or minimal conjugal kindness entitled the innocent party to a remedy. That concept was in accordance with secular requirements principally in relation to wifely adultery, which basis was adopted when parliament devised a procedure for the dissolution of the marriage bond. (7)

The third main feature of the marital relationship was entirely dictated by secular requirements.   The law was scarcely concerned with the welfare and upbringing of young children, but rather with the identification of heirs and the control of their property if orphaned at an early age.   There was a strong presumption that any child born to married woman was her husband's child.   Respect for the ties of blood made it necessary to combine that presumption with a strong obligation of wifely fidelity.   The husband's effective control over his family was eventually translated into a series of defined paternal rights over his children's upbringing. These included the right to appoint a guardian to stand in his shoes should he die before they reached the age of majority. The courts were prepared to enforce these rights against the child, the mother and the outside world.   Only occasionally were they able to hold that the father had so grossly endangered his children's welfare as to forfeit his rights.   Only then did the court have power to grant custody or even access to anyone else, including the mother (Pettitt, 1957:n. 13). While the innocent wife had an inalienable, although often unenforceable right to be maintained, she might be deprived of her children even if the separation had been brought about by her husband's breach of matrimonial duty.

Clearly this package was developed by and for a limited section of society.   That section was also best able to avoid its excesses - through marriage settlements enabling property to be limited to the separate use of a married woman and then either to descend to her children or revert to her own family, (8) through litigation in the ecclesiastical courts for a decree of divorce a mensa et thoro, through formal deeds of separation (Wilson v Wilson (1848) 1 H.L. Cas. 538), and even through the parliamentary procedure for complete divorce. (9)   The extent to which the Poor Law imposed similar rules at the opposite end of the social scale differed

largely in accordance with the cost to public funds. (10)
But all sections were theoretically bound by the same rigid
structure, much of which was no longer consistent either with
the economic realities of industrialisation or with changing
social values.   Prominent amongst the latter was what has
been described as the growth of 'sentiment' in family life.
Family members might no longer be expected to subordinate
their own wishes and feelings to a higher duty to their family
group and its future, but they might be expected to enter a
state of domestic bliss, characterised by love and duty
towards both spouse and minor children (Shorter, 1976; Stone,
1977).   It cannot be a coincidence that the first statutory
step into the transitional phase enhanced the claims of
motherhood.   In 1839 parliament began the process which cul-
minated in the equality of maternal and paternal rights over
legitimate children (11) and the development of the para-
mountcy of the child's welfare in the resolution of their competing claims.

TRANSITION

Therein lay the disharmony which characterised the transitional stage.   The long retreat of the State from the regulation
of married life began with what seemed at the time the obvious
steps, the progressive removal of the disabilities of married
women (Mill, 1869:ch. 2).   From one person embodied in the
husband the couple became, not a partnership in which each
enjoyed reciprocal rights and duties, but two separate individuals.   Step by step, but mainly in 1882, wives acquired
proprietary and contractual capacity. (12)   Individual bar-
gains and litigation between them became possible at the same
time, but litigation in tort had to wait until 1962 (Law
Reform (Husband and Wife) Act 1962).   Husbands lost their coercive powers in 1891. (13)   The obligation to live together
became completely unenforceable on 1 January 1971 and had in
practice been so for years. (14)   The only exception to this
trend away from automatic consequences in marriage was the
development of rights of occupation in the matrimonial home,
culminating in the Matrimonial Homes Act 1967.   But the
courts' powers to regulate that occupation (15) seem more
often to be used to enable couples to separate than to oblige
them to stay together. (16)   Claims against third parties
who interfere between husband and wife also became impossible
on 1 January 1971 (Law Reform (Miscellaneous Provisions) Act
1970, ss. 4 and 5).   And with the recent extension in remedies for domestic violence, (17) the 'sacred protection behind
the door of the family home' has virtually disappeared.

Yet throughout this period, the stability of the conjugal family was highly valued. Some saw the equalisation in status between husband and wife as gravely prejudicial to that stability: 'such tendencies would appear to lead to the result that husband and wife in law and in form would become ... partners in the firm of marriage. If such were the end, then clearly Lord Penzance's definition of marriage [the voluntary union for life] would cease to have significance and the family could no longer survive as the essential unit of society' (Evershed, 1957:xvi). Such pessimism was presumably based upon the inherent instability of a democracy of two. Alternatively, it may have been thought that, if it is impossible to devise a legal system which keeps both spouses at home, it is better to have one firmly tied down while placing so few constraints upon the other that he may never be tempted to leave.

Despite creeping equality between the sexes, therefore, throughout most of the transitional period the restriction of matrimonial relief to the innocent victims of breach of the matrimonial obligations was strenuously defended. It was assumed that the restriction in itself was capable of keeping marriages together and further that to do so was a protection for the more vulnerable members of the family (see, e.g. Report of the Royal Commission on Marriage and Divorce 1951-1955; cf. Rheinstein, 1972). In practice, there was little evidence that restrictive divorce laws had any effect upon marital stability. But it was clear that the combination of such an approach to matrimonial relief with the concept of separate property did little to provide for the economic needs of those more vulnerable members. This ignored what was then thought to be the 'natural' inequality (Kahn-Freund, 1955) in the respective roles of the sexes. The breadwinning spouse was very much better equipped to acquire and keep separate property than was the home-maker. Yet the law did not make them 'partners in the firm of marriage' in any economic sense. There had been a great improvement in the remedies available for the enforcement of family support obligations, (18) but these were still firmly based in the old concepts of maintenance or 'endowment'. The wife might now have a little money of her own and contribute to the acquisition of some of the family's assets. Others might be deliberately given to or shared with her by her husband. The courts became astute to adapt legal concepts in order to recognise her contributions to the extent that this was in money or money's worth. But housekeeping, childbearing and child care were never defined as 'money's worth'. The major part of the family's resources would still belong to the breadwinner. Out of this, he was expected to house, feed and clothe his dependants. The

wife had an inalienable right to that provision.   The husband
could not expect to be relieved of it even if she chose to go
out to work (Attwood v Attwood [1968] p. 591), or if they were
divorced, (19) or if she remarried a poorer man. (20)   But a
husband could not be expected to waste his resources on maintaining two separate establishments unless he had agreed to do
so.   It followed that if the wife were in some measure to
blame for the separation, her entitlement to support might be
reduced or even extinguished. (21)   Thus the retention of the
doctrine of the matrimonial offence, thought so essential to
the preservation of marriage and the protection of dependants,
in practice denied support to a needy dependant whose conduct
might have played a relatively small part in the marital disagreement.

THE NEW ROLE

The contradictions of the transitional phase - between the
notional equality but the practical inequality of the separate
property system, between abandoning the enforceable union
while clinging to the matrimonial offence, between the logic
of that concept and concern for the economically dependent -
these have all been resolved.   Any attempt to regulate the
conduct of married life or to provide a legal 'buttress' to
its stability has been abandoned. (22)   On the other hand,
there has been considerable movement towards the concept of
partnership 'in the firm of marriage'.   The medium for both
developments has been the introduction of readily accessible
'no-fault' divorce accompanied by extensive discretionary
powers of adjustment. (23)
     At the beginning of 1971 irretrievable breakdown of mar-
riage became the sole ground for divorce. (24)   That this
spelt 'no-fault' divorce was not immediately apparent, for
breakdown must be proved by one of five facts.   Three of
these closely resemble the old breaches of matrimonial
duty, (25) divorce by consent requires at least two years'
separation, and non-consensual, non-fault divorce at least
five. (26)   Problems may still be encountered by couples
wishing to resolve the affairs of an obviously broken marriage
as soon as possible but without committing perjury and by
those who effectively require their spouse's co-operation
before separation is feasible.   But the courts have usually
done their best to provide a solution.   Two of the apparently
fault-based facts, which permit divorce without lengthy separation, have been so interpreted that no meaningful attempt
to allocate blame need be involved. (27)   Separation may
exist under the same roof. (28)   If a separation fact is

admitted, the courts will not investigate a fault-based one
(Grenfell v Grenfell [1978] Fam. 128).   Undefended suits,
already the vast majority, are positively encouraged rather
than frowned upon as potentially collusive.   There are frequent judicial assertions that the allocation of matrimonial
blame is harmful, impossible and irrelevant to the issues of
prime importance, such as housing, finance and the care of
children.   If this be so, it is no longer possible to define
matrimonial rights and duties.   The rights are unenforceable
and breach of the duties leads to no practically significant
result.

Thus disputes about the care of children have long been
governed by the 'paramount consideration' of their welfare. (29)   The mother is, or is usually assumed to be,
better placed to supply the children's physical and emotional
needs than is the father.   The law may no longer prescribe
the respective roles of the parties within marriage.   But
when marriage ends, the courts may well reflect traditional
assumptions about those roles when exercising their discretionary powers. (30)   Fathers have sometimes tried to balance
this maternal advantage by urging the 'claims of justice' or
the consideration due to the claims of an 'unimpeachable
parent'.   Both are suggestions that the conduct of the parties towards one another, and in particular the adultery or
desertion of the mother, should influence the custody decision.   The courts have now rejected that argument (Re K.
(minors) (children: care and control) [1977] Fam. 179).
Only conduct which is relevant to the parties' qualities as
parents is relevant.   The welfare of the innocent victims of
the adults' differences cannot be subordinated to, or even
balanced against, the allocation of blame for those differences.

There has also been a radical change in the principles
applicable to housing and finance.   This again was not immediately apparent when the new legislation came into force in
1971. (31)   The courts constructed it from three new
features.   Firstly, their powers now applied equally both for
and against both husband and wife.   This allowed a notional
pooling of the resources and needs of each, rather than a
consideration of how much of what was 'his' a husband should
be made to bestow upon his wife.   Secondly, those powers included not only periodical payments orders but also the
adjustment of the parties' capital and proprietary interests
in whatever way seemed appropriate irrespective of legal
title.   Thirdly, the factors which they were instructed to
take into account included the contributions made by both to
the welfare of the family, home-making and childrearing as
well as breadwinning.

From this three conclusions were drawn. (32)   Firstly,
marriage is to be regarded as an economic partnership to which
each makes a different contribution of equal value.   That
contribution should be recognised in a share of the family's
accumulated assets, at least in so far as this may be realised
without detriment to the housing needs of the parties and
their children. (33)   Secondly, this distribution must be
balanced against future needs, not only for housing but also
for income maintenance.   An equal division of assets should
not be accompanied by an equal division of future joint
income, for this is to have one's cake (dissolving the partnership) and then continue to eat it (making continued demands
upon the resources of a former partner).   Where future income
is necessary, a lesser share of assets is appropriate, hence
the 'starting point' of one-third of each.   Where each partner is free to go his or her separate way, equal division of
assets may be right.   Where the house is needed by wife and
children and the husband has other accommodation, it may be
sensible for her to take a larger share or the whole of the
house while undertaking responsibility for her own income in
future (Hanlon v Hanlon [1978] 1 W.L.R. 592).   The possible
variations are endless.   Thirdly, it follows that matrimonial
conduct is largely irrelevant.   If the partners are equally
to blame, there should be an equal distribution.   Logically,
conduct could only be relevant where one party was demonstrably more to blame than the other.   The courts have expressed
this in the vague term 'obvious and gross'. (34)

These principles involve a radical departure from what had
previously been thought 'just' in the matrimonial context.
They are subject to much attack from many viewpoints.   The
'starting point' of one-third is probably more frequently
departed from than arrived at, but to give one party twice as
much as the other may be criticised for failing to give adequate recompense to the home-making role (e.g. Stone, 1977:
ch. III).   Certainly, the suggestion that the husband will
require twice as much because he will have to hire home-making
services, whereas the wife is expected both to work and to
keep house, must be wrong (Wachtel v Wachtel, supra.).   But
the argument based on the balance between past shares and
future needs is far more convincing.   It is those two concepts which present the difficulties.

Applying the concept of partnership at the end of a relationship yet adhering to the concept of separate property
while the marriage is a going concern presents obvious practical problems as well as confusion for litigants.   These are
exacerbated by the uncertainties inherent in any discretion,
however judicially exercised.   The Law Commission has recommended automatic joint ownership of the matrimonial home, in

which there are already joint occupation rights, but their complex recommendations (35) have yet to be implemented. Thorough-going community of property was considered but rejected. (36)   Both would run counter to the prevailing trends towards non-intervention in the legal affairs of existing relationships and non-discrimination between marital and non-marital cohabitations.

The rationale underlying future income payments is even more confused.   The logic of a partnership approach suggests that these should only be ordered as a means of adjusting losses arising from the relationship - that is, if and for so long as they are necessary to redress the loss of income caused by the division of roles within the marriage.   Even then, there is room for argument about whether support should continue only for as long as the recipient is prevented by the demands of child care from earning her own living or whether recompense should be granted for the permanent damage done to earning potential by preoccupation with home-making tasks in the 'get-ahead' years (Deech, 1977; O'Donovan, 1978).   But at least it should be clear that the old inalienable right of a wife, however able bodied, to be maintained for life has gone.   Unfortunately, the courts' statutory objective in the exercise of its various powers is not to place the parties in the financial positions in which they would have been had the marriage not taken place.   Instead, they are to endeavour, so far as is practicable, to place them where they would have been had the marriage not broken down (Matrimonial Causes Act 1973, s. 25 (1)).   This may, combined with past practice and popular belief, suggest to some courts that a wife who expected to devote most of her life to caring for her husband, home and children is entitled to organise her time in a similar way even though her husband is no longer with her. (37)   Thus while the statutory objective is totally impracticable in the majority of cases, there may still be women who are capable of taking financial responsibility for themselves but look to their former husbands to do so unless and until they remarry. (38)

The retreat from legal regulation of married life has also produced the result that the major areas of discrimination between marital and non-marital relationships are now finance, housing and children.   And as the dependency arising out of a relationship does not differ with the lack of a marriage ceremony, there is a continuing move to extend similar protective and adjustive mechanisms to non-marital unions when they end.

Support obligations between adults, including automatic rights of occupation in the matrimonial home, its proposed automatic co-ownership and the courts' adjustive powers on divorce, are still confined to marriage.   However, the usefulness of periodical payments to many former spouses should

not be exaggerated.   Many men simply cannot afford to keep
two households above the level of supplementary benefit payments.   Any maintenance paid is taken fully into account in
the calculation of means-tested benefits and thus has no
apparent advantage to a recipient claimant.   Even where the
husband can afford to pay more, such payments are notoriously
difficult to enforce.   For every former wife whose claims to
be maintained in the style to which her marriage had accustomed her jeopardise the welfare and comfort of his second
family, there are still more who are effectively condemned to
long-term subsistence on means-tested benefits.   So, of
course, is the unmarried ex-partner.

The courts have already embarked upon the adaptation of
property law devices which were previously used to help wives
in preserving their homes or at least a share in the proceeds
of sale (see Pearl, 1978:252;   Richards, 1976:351).   Legislation giving the courts broad discretion to allocate occupation of the home, designed for protection against domestic
violence but not expressly so limited, has been used to allocate a council tenancy following the non-violent ending of a
non-marital relationship (Spindlow v Spindlow [1979] Fam. 52.
Similarly, automatic claims to the estate of a partner who dies intestate are confined to spouses, but a surviving spouse who is disinherited by the deceased spouse's will
is not automatically entitled to a fixed share.   The courts
have discretionary powers to adjust the dispositions under a
will or an intestacy, and these may be used for the benefit of
adult dependants as well as for spouses and descendants,
although the basis of assessment for spouses is somewhat more
favourable than that for others. (39)   Again, a widow is
automatically entitled to succeed to her late husband's pro-
tected tenancy under the Rent Act, but an unmarried woman may
be able to qualify to succeed as a member of the deceased
tenant's 'family'. (40)

Finally, the status of legitimacy, the automatic legal relationship between father and child, is the very foundation of
marriage.   But the use of marriage for dynastic purposes has
declined both in practicability and in respectability.   It may
not be possible for a father even to ensure that his children
will continue to bear his name. (41)   The succession
rights of illegitimate children have already been substantially improved (Family Law Reform Act 1969, part II), without
noticeable damage to the property holding system.   To a child
law dominated by the concept of welfare, it seems less and
less justifiable to deny the young whatever benefit may be
gained from an automatic relationship with both parents.
Hence the complete abolition of the status of legitimacy is
already under discussion (Law Commission, 1979).

Improvements in the courts' powers to order financial and
housing support for the non-marital child are extremely
likely, and these would confer indirect benefits upon the custodial unmarried parent.

Thus private family law is willing to tolerate and accommodate an ever-increasing variety of personal relationships and
lifestyles.   The insistence on 'Christian' marriage has virtually disappeared.   Curiously, the family lifestyles which
the law finds it most difficult to accommodate are those of
non-Christian ethnic minorities, particularly Asian families.
There is a deep gulf between the principles of modern Western
family law and, for example, arranged marriages, rigid role
demarcation between husband and wife, social and religious
degradation for a divorced wife, polygamy and non-judicial
divorce by unilateral act of the husband.   The many legal
problems which these have raised are too complex for discussion here (see, e.g., Pearl, 1972:120, 1978-9:24).   Generally
speaking, the law has tried to extend to such families the
benefit of its supportive and adjustive mechanisms, for example through the recognition of foreign polygamous marriages
(Matrimonial Proceedings (Polygamous Marriages) Act 1972).
But it is not prepared to revert to the life-long enforceable
union which is what the women in some communities earnestly
desire.   In 1967 an Indian wife who took her decree of restitution of conjugal rights at face value was actually res-
trained by the court from forcing her society upon her husband
in the home which he had established with a new partner
(Nanda v Nanda [1968] p. 351).   And the recognition extended
to the Moslem talaq pronounced abroad (Quazi v Quazi [1980]
A.C. 744 at present denies the wife the benefit of the
adjustive powers of the English divorce court.

Paradoxically, polygamy whether concurrent or serial is
traditionally associated with dynastic marriage systems in
which the woman is of little account.   But the development of
serial polygamy in the West has been closely associated with
the development of equality between the sexes in law and elsewhere.   Serial polygamy presents a challenge to a system of
private law which still assumes the monogamous life-long union
to be the normal arrangement.   Neither its financial nor its
child-related provisions have yet found a coherent answer to
that challenge, but the future will clearly demand one.

THE FUTURE

Major procedural changes, including legal aid and the so-
called special procedure for dissolving marriages without a
court hearing, have been as instrumental as the expansion of

grounds in extending the private law institution of divorce
from a very small section of society to all.   The further
simplification of the ground for divorce may be expected in
the next few years (see, e.g., Family Law Sub-committee of the
Law Society, 1979).   But the assumptions behind that institution are inapplicable to many of the families who are now involved.   The rhetoric of private law insists that a breadwinner must always put the dependants of his first marriage
first, before those of any later union. (42)   The existence
of that obligation is one of the reasons why the contributions
of that breadwinner to compulsory social insurance cannot
finance an automatic, non-means-tested benefit for those
dependants should the marriage fail otherwise than by his
death (another is that one may neither insure against nor
benefit from one's own fault in causing the marriage to end)
(Finer and McGregor, 1974).   Given that the law is no longer
prepared to make any attempt to force couples to stay united,
what is it to do in the usual event that the breadwinner's
resources are quite inadequate to finance two households, let
alone two families?

Private law now admits that it is useless to expect a man
to work to support himself or anyone else, if discharging his
obligations to his former family will reduce his new household below 'subsistence level'.   Although there is some disagreement about how that level should be defined, it is agreed
that the former family can only expect the surplus (Hayes,
1978-9:216).   As the contributory State scheme cannot accommodate them, the balance of what they need to survive must be
made good from the means-tested State system.   The means-
tested scheme treats a couple less favourably than two individuals, for the apparently plausible reason that two can live
together more cheaply than they can live apart.   Further,
public law generally adopts the principle that if marriage
confers a benefit, such as higher income tax reliefs or the
relaxation of immigration controls, this is not to be made
available to unmarried couples.   But if marriage is a disadvantage, as it is if the couple must claim means-tested benefits, then other couples must not be permitted to evade that
disadvantage by non-marital cohabitation.   The result is the
notorious 'cohabitation' rule, which is also applied to otherwise non-means-tested widow's benefits.   It is generally
assumed that the man is supporting the woman, irrespective
both of the lack of any private law obligation to do so and of
other calls upon his resources from obligations which the
private law does recognise.   The resulting dual obligation
may be impossible to meet.   A legal system which pays lip-
service to the prior claims of the first wife and children
while often obliged in practice to accept that the second

family will take precedence produces anomalies which do not command respect.

Somewhat similar ambivalence surrounds the law's approach to the upbringing of children whose parents separate and form new unions. The concept of 'parental rights' has virtually disappeared under the 'paramount consideration' of the child's welfare (Hall, 1972b:248; Eekelaar, 1973:210). But a new right of childhood has been discovered, the right not only to know one's origins but also to maintain, so far as possible, relations with both sides of the family. Access to the absent parent and grandparents is to be encouraged. (43) Adoption into the family of parent and step-parent is to be discouraged. (44) Once again we have the problem that the law's attempts to preserve many aspects of a first marriage 'so long as ye both shall live' may conflict with the reality of new unions which are often trying to look as much like a first marriage as possible. It is not only the law which is ambivalent.

In the next few years private law may be expected to continue the trend which was identified at the beginning of this chapter. Regulation of the conduct of married life will retreat still further if the ground for divorce becomes entirely fault-free. Regulation of the economic and child-related consequences of formal and informal cohabitation will increase if the distinction between legitimacy and illegitimacy is further reduced, if remedies are extended to the unmarried or at least if their contractual arrangements are freed from the taint of immorality, and if a solution is found to the foreign divorce of people living here. (45) These are the obvious directions of family law reform in the relatively near future.

It is less obvious that the law will or can find any solution to the more fundamental problem. It has tried to reconcile an increasing diversity and flexibility in personal relationships with an increasing tenderness to the needs of the more vulnerable members. But that diversity and flexibility has been the product of a pronounced movement away from the collective security of the wider kinship group and towards the exclusive conjugal unit. The association between this 'new marriage' (Clark, 1976:441) and the 'new property' (Reich, 1964:733), in which earnings and substitutes for earnings take the place of heritable property, is plain. Yet when the new marriage fails, the new property is clearly inadequate. The State has then to care, directly or indirectly, for a growing number of stranded individuals. We are only at the beginning of the search for solutions. Some may put their faith in removing the more glaring substantive and procedural anomalies of the present system of family law and in the establishment of family courts (e.g. Finer Report, 1974; Justice, 1975).

Others may accept that families cannot be forced to stay together but advocate far more positive State intervention in counselling and conciliation (Mayo, 1976:409).   Only a few will yet be ready to contemplate the wholesale social, economic and legal revolution implicit in the plea 'once again to turn our thoughts to future generations' (Glendon, 1979).   In the long run, Mr Keynes, we are not *all* dead.

NOTES

1 The law in Scotland differs considerably from that in England and Wales, although its tendencies in this field are broadly similar; see E.M. Clive and J.G. Wilson (1974) and E.M. Clive (1976).
2 The terms are those of J.M. Eekelaar in 'Family Law and Social Policy' (1978).
3 Jewish ceremonies were permitted, but the condition thus entered was the same.
4 See J.F. Stephen, 'A History of the Criminal Law of England' (1883: vol. II, ch. 25); but see J.S. Cockburn (ed.), 'Crime in England 1550-1800' (1977) for evidence of the largely ineffectual efforts of ecclesiastical courts.
5 Lord Penzance in Hyde v Hyde (1866) L.R. 1 P. & D. 130, at p. 133.
6 W. Blackstone, 'Commentaries on the Laws of England' (Oxford: Oxford University Press, 1765), book 1, p. 430; for modern discussions, see G.L. Williams, The Legal Unity of Husband and Wife (1947), 10 'Modern Law Review', 16; Midland Bank Trust Co. v Green (No. 3) [1979] Ch. 496 at 511-26 (Oliver, J.).
7 For an account of divorce by private Act of Parliament, see M. Finer and O.R. McGregor, A History of the Obligation to Maintain, Appendix 5 to the Report of the Committee on One-Parent Families (Chairman: Sir M. Finer) (1974); see also O.R. McGregor, 'Divorce in England: A Centenary Study' (1957).
8 For the development of the concept of the married woman's separate property, see O. Kahn-Freund, Matrimonial Property Law in England, in W. Friedman (ed.), 'Matrimonial Property Law' (1955); for the common form of settlement, see F.R. Crane, Family Settlements and Succession, in Graveson and Crane (1957).
9 Divorce a mensa et thoro from an ecclesiastical court; damages for adultery from a common law court; then petition to parliament for private legislation.
10 E.g. support obligations were imposed upon wider kin; see N.L. Brown, National Assistance and the Liability to Maintain One's Family (1955).

11 Custody of Infants (Talfourd's) Act 1839; Custody of
    Infants Act 1863; Guardianship of Infants Acts 1886 and
    1925, consolidated as Guardianship of Minors Act 1971;
    Guardianship Act 1973.
12 Matrimonial Causes Act 1857, s. 26; Married Women's
    Property Act 1870; Married Women's Property Act (1870)
    Amendment Act 1974; Married Women's Property Act 1882;
    Married Women's Property Act 1893; Law Reform (Married
    Women and Tortfeasors) Act 1935; Married Women (Restraint
    on Anticipation) Act 1949.
13 R. v Jackson [1891] 1 Q.B. 671, C.A.; but see also R.
    v Legatt (1852), 18 Q.B. 781.
14 The decree of restitution of conjugal rights was abolished
    by section 20, Matrimonial Proceedings and Property Act
    1970; see also Nanda v Nanda [1968] P. 351.
15 Matrimonial Homes Act 1967, s. 1(2) as amended by Domestic
    Violence and Matrimonial Proceedings Act 1976, s. 3; see
    also ss. 1 and 4.
16 E.g. Bassett v Bassett [1975] Fam. 76; Walker v Walker
    [1978] 1 W.L.R. 533; Rennick v Rennick [1977] 1 W.L.R.
    1455; for the principles upon which the courts will order
    one spouse to vacate the home in the short term.
17 Domestic Violence and Matrimonial Proceedings Act 1976;
    Domestic Proceedings and Magistrates' Courts Act 1978, ss.
    16 to 18.
18 Direct orders between husband and wife became available in
    the divorce court from 1857; summary remedies in the
    magistrates' courts began in 1878; the principles appli-
    cable in the two jurisdictions were not identical (see
    Finer and McGregor, 1974).
19 It was a decisive but not inevitable step, on the intro-
    duction of judicial divorce in 1857, to permit the court
    to order annual payments in favour of the former wife;
    cf. the law in Scotland until 1964, E.M. Clive and J.G.
    Wilson (1974).
20 The rule that maintenance payments must cease on remar-
    riage was introduced by the Matrimonial Proceedings and
    Property Act 1970.
21 E.g. the approach suggested in Ackerman v Ackerman [1972]
    Fam. 225, of a 'discount' from the wife's maximum entitle-
    ment in proportion to her responsibility for the marriage
    breakdown.
22 Cf. the objectives of a sound divorce law adumbrated by
    the Law Commission in 'Reform of the Grounds of Divorce:
    The Field of Choice' (1966).
23 For a general discussion, see J.M. Eekelaar, The Place of
    Divorce in Family Law's New Role (1975:241).
24 Divorce Reform Act 1969 came into force 1 January 1971;

now consolidated with related legislation in Matrimonial Causes Act 1973.

25 Adultery and intolerability; behaviour such that petitioner cannot reasonably be expected to live with respondent; two years' desertion.

26 For trenchant criticism of this incoherent approach, see B. Mortlock, 'The Inside of Divorce' (1972).

27 See particularly Cleary v Cleary [1974] 1 W.L.R. 73 (adultery not connected with intolerability); Thurlow v Thurlow [1976] Fam. 128 (behaviour resulting from incurable illness).

28 Fuller v Fuller [1973] 1 W.L.R. 730; Naylor v Naylor [1962] P. 253.

29 Guardianship of Infants Act 1925, s. 1; now Guardianship of Minors Act 1971, s. 1; see particularly J. v C. [1970] A.C. 668.

30 Numerous apparently dogmatic statements in reported cases, such as in M. v M. (1978), 9 'Family Law', 92 - 'However good a sort of man he may be he could not perform the functions with a mother performed *by nature* in relation to a little girl' (emphasis supplied) - should be read in the context of the particular facts of the case and of the empirical evidence such as J.M. Eekelaar and E. Clive, 'Custody after Divorce' (1977).

31 Matrimonial Proceedings and Property Act 1970; now consolidated in Matrimonial Causes Act 1973; see particularly ss 22 to 25.

32 Wachtel v Wachtel [1973] Fam. 72; see J.M. Eekelaar, Some Principles of Financial and Property Adjustment on Divorce (1979).

33 Needs before shares, Browne v Pritchard [1975] 1 W.L.R. 1366.

34 Wachtel v Wachtel, supra; e.g. Cuzner v Underdown [1974] 1 W.L.R. 641; West v West [1978] Fam. 1.

35 'Third Report on Family Property: The Matrimonial Home (Co-ownership and Occupation Rights) and Household Goods', Law Com. No. 86 (1978).

36 'First Report on Family Property: A New Approach', Law Com. No. 52 (1973); see also 'Family Property Law', Published Working Paper No. 42 (1971).

37 This view is certainly not denied in one of the leading works for practitioners, J. Jackson, 'Matrimonial Finance and Taxation' (1975 with supplement 1978).

38 The Law Commission has recently recommended the abolition of the statutory objective, together with a greater emphasis on the needs of the children but eventual independence for both spouses; see 'The Financial Consequences of Divorce', Law Com. no. 112 (1982); see also the preceding discussion paper, Law Com. no. 103 (1980).

39 Inheritance (Provision for Family and Dependants) Act
    1975; see Malone v Harrison [1979] 1 W.L.R. 1352;
    Jelley v Iliff [1981] Fam. 128.
40 Hawes v Evenden [1953] 1 W.L.R. 1119; Dyson Holdings v
    Fox [1976] 1 Q.B. 503.
41 E.g., R. v R. (child: surname) [1977] 1 W.L.R. 1256;
    D. v B. (orse D.) (surname: birth registration) []979]
    Fam. 38; cf. W. v A. [1981] Fam. 14.
42 E.g., Tovey v Tovey (1978), 8 'Family Law', 80; Clarke
    v Clarke (]978), 9 'Family Law', 15.
43 M. v M. (child: access) [1973] 2 All E.R. 81; Domestic
    Proceedings and Magistrates' Courts Act 1978, s. 40.
44 Children Act 1975, ss 10(3), 11(4) and, when in force,
    37(2); inspired by the Report of the Departmental Comit-
    tee on the Adoption of Children (Chairman: Sir W.
    Houghton, later Judge F.A. Stockdale) (1972).
45 See Law Commission, 'Financial Relief after Foreign
    Divorce', published Working Paper no. 77 (1980).

Chapter 22

Families and leisure
Michael Collins and Ziona Strelitz

THE LEISURE EXPLOSION

With increased affluence, improved conditions of work and the
stirring of new values appropriate for a 'post-industrial'
era, there has been a literal explosion of leisure activities
especially at home and out of doors.   Served and fuelled by
expanding leisure industries - public and private - there has
been a steady growth in pursuits labelled 'leisure activities'
since the Second World War.   In Britain the basic working
week dropped from 42.1 in 1961 to 40 hours in 1975.   In 1961
97 per cent of the full-time working population received two
weeks or less as annual holiday, whereas in 1973 this percentage had dropped to 6 per cent, with 85 per cent receiving
three weeks or more.   Television became a staple item of
household equipment;   activities involving the use of the
motorcar - going for a drive, taking a trip to the country,
going out for a picnic - increased exponentially.   There was
a similar increase in travel abroad, eating out, use of books
and magazines and entertainments of all kinds (Sillitoe, 1971;
'Social Trends', 1974).
    So great has been the demand to use facilities that Michael
Dower has compared it with some of the earlier social revolutions:
    Three great waves have broken across the face of Britain
    since 1800.   First, the sudden growth of dark industrial
    towns.   Second, the thrusting movement along far-flung
    railways.   Third, the sprawl of car-based suburbs.   Now,
    we see, under the guise of a modest word, the surge of a
    fourth wave which could be more powerful than all the
    others.   The modest word is leisure. (Dower, 1965)
    The trend, which came to an apex in the 1960s and early
1970s has been tempered by economic stringencies in the late
1970s, centred on increases in available cash, free time and

mobility (Patmore, 1970). However, it also related to the escalation of *wants* - for individual satisfaction and self-realisation. These values break definitively with earlier puritanical work-centred values. Accompanied by a commitment of the State to an active role in facilitating them, they were legitimated by the Lords' Select Committee on Sport and Leisure in 1973:

> The state should not opt out of caring for people's leisure, when it accepts the responsibility of caring for most of their needs. The provision of opportunities for the enjoyment of leisure is part of the general fabric of the social services.
>
> Every County Council and Metropolitan District Council and Regional Authority should have a Recreation Committee and a Department of Recreation under its own chief officer.
>
> Each Department of Recreation should be concerned with all forms of sport, physical recreation, the arts, museums and libraries and informal leisure activities. (Lords' Select Committee, 1973)

In the private sector, leisure industries have thrived on the manufacture and marketing of sports clothing and equipment, travel facilities and package holidays especially for the 'mid-teens to mid-20s' market. The growth of public spending to meet the explosive demand for leisure provision has been very rapid, partly by extending existing services - more and bigger sports centres, more and bigger parks, more and bigger libraries and concert halls, and partly by innovations. Departments of sport, leisure and recreation have become part of the local government apparatus.

THEORETICAL PERSPECTIVE ON LEISURE PROVISION

Both amongst professional leisure providers and policy researchers there has been an increased questioning as to whether provision in response to manifest demand is enough. The response of expanded and institutionalised supply has led to forms of provision which are felt in some cases to be inequitable and in others to be remote from people's needs. Thus they are considered to fail in their social mandate (cf. Travis and Hudson, 1979; Dower, Rapoport, Strelitz and Kew, 1981). There is a widespread concern about how to look beyond manifest demand, so as to improve the connection between provision and people's needs.

Working on the premise that providers in all services aim to meet people's needs, a useful approach recognises that people's felt needs in leisure are related to their stage of development in life, to their family situations and

subcultural values and to their roles and involvements in
social institutions such as work, education and community
groups.
   A framework for understanding the interplay of psycho-
biological development and social environment was laid out by
the Rapoports in 1975, and has been developed subsequently
(Dower, Rapoport, Strelitz and Kew, 1981).
Basic are preoccupations; more or less conscious mental
absorptions which arise from psycho-biological development
and interact with people's social conditions.   Developing on
work by developmental psychologists (like Erikson, 1959) and
sociologists (like Reuben Hill, Hill and Rodgers 1964), this
perspective views preoccupations as underpinning *interests*.
Interests are ideas and feelings that people have about what
they want or would like to do, about which they are curious,
through which they feel they might derive satisfaction.
Interests may be chanelled into various *activities*.   These
are spheres of action: driving, dancing, playing tennis.
Activities may have varying appeal and meaning relating to
whichever interests are salient to individuals.   People using
a swimming pool, for example, may do so for fun, to train for
matches, to keep fit and to guard against the risk of a
coronary attack.   Interest in keeping fit may be channelled
equally through swimming, jogging, bicycling or working out in
a gymnasium.   Each strand of life (work, family or leisure)
may be seen to undergo its own evolution, but experiences in
one strand affect those in the others.   Interests may arise
in any strand and either be contained within it or diffuse to
others.   Leisure services can benefit by an appreciation of
this kind of model, in seeking to make available resources
which sensitively articulate people's actual needs.

FAMILY DIVERSITY AND LEISURE PATTERNS

The question of where families fit into the picture of leisure
provision and policy is complex.   One fact is incontrovert-
ible.   Leisure based in the family home forms the most common
cluster of activities.   Its growth has reversed the century-
long trend toward removing functions from the domestic unit.
The development of labour-saving technologies in the home has
not only set free time formerly taken up with household
chores, but through central heating, telephone, radio and TV,
have made homes more attractive places in which to spend free
time.   The growth of second homes, caravans, boats and other
home extensions has also been notable (Downing and Dower,
1973).
   Many observers in different countries, including John Kelly

(1979) and Max Kaplan in the USA (1960), Joffre Dumazedier in France (1967) and Irwin Scheuch in Germany (1960) have noted similar trends in family-centred activities with the growth of leisure. The General Household Survey (1977) shows that home-based activities such as needlework, reading and listening to radio/TV or music are not only the most frequent but that they exhibit the least seasonal variation. Of course, some such as gardening and preserve-making vary.

Family life, as the whole of this book demonstrates, is diverse because of varying composition, how individuals define and enact roles, what values guide their conduct and what resources (material possessions and skills) they have. Though there are many elements which blur the picture, there seem to be differences which affect leisure patterns amongst families of different social classes and of different beliefs and values about sex roles in marriage.

Families respond differently to the external world. Their social networks of kin, friends and associates vary considerably, and hence the interests they develop. Families also differ according to their stage in the family life-cycle in their preoccupations - compare, say, young couples with parents with adolescent children (Rapoport and Rapoport, 1975). Based on a detailed American study, Kelly (1979) writes, 'most adult leisure is thoroughly familial'. Certainly childhood leisure is familial. Family diversity thus has considerable influence on the leisure experiences of individuals, in terms of both constraint and facilitation.

VULNERABLE GROUPS AND VULNERABLE STAGES

Some families suffer particular deprivations which affect their members' needs in leisure. For example Kelly (1979) has directed attention to the loneliness that 'separated people' suffer; Stephen Kew (1979) has indicated the heightened tensions in West Indian families with adolescents; George Brown and his colleagues have documented the high rates of depression suffered by working-class mothers of young children (Brown et al., 1975). People in such 'vulnerable categories' provide focal points for social policy (Strelitz, 1979; Dower, Rapoport, Strelitz and Kew, 1981). Studies in other countries indicate the presence of similar groups, at least in Europe and the USA.

Some forms of family vulnerability are stable, perhaps becoming chronic. For example, a high proportion of poor families remain poor throughout their lives. The reader is referred to Harriet Wilson's chapter in this book. In the wake of a social perspective which points up a leisure

explosion, it is often overlooked that many people do not have
access to personal motor transport (Hillman and Whalley, 1973,
1979).   To the extent that leisure provisions are located on
the assumption that 'we all drive nowadays' people who are
always or for parts of their lives without such transport are
at a disadvantage.

Other states may be transitory, altering in the wake of a
family 'crisis'.   Sillitoe's classic study of British leisure
patterns in the 1960s showed how some family transitions were
accompanied by a diminution of leisure activity (e.g. marriage, having children, divorcing), whilst others were associated with an increase in involvements (e.g. when the children
enter school, retirement from paid work, widowhood).

DIMENSIONS OF FAMILY LEISURE

Families differ from many other kinds of groups in being made
up of people of different ages, of both sexes and of varying
physical capacities, interests and external associations.
The factors that make for cohesion in the face of these diver-
gent tendencies include the familiar ones of sex, economic
dependency, affection and authority.   We can consider family
leisure in four dimensions.

Families at home

Families with young children may come together through children coming into parents' beds, dressing together, sharing bed-
time rituals and relaxing together with play.   But joint
leisure activities at home for the whole family may be very
difficult at this stage, especially if there is more than one
young child.   Different interests, levels of energy, competence and concentration may make many experiences divisive
rather than integrative.   For many families at this stage
doing things separately - e.g. mothers and fathers doing
things alone or with friends, the couple alone, or different
combinations of parents and children may be more fulfilling
(such as father and son swimming, or mother and daughter going
to the shops and the park).   An important issue is keeping
the balance between individual and joint activities, especially when resources including time may be short.   Ritual occasions may be very important for providing cohesion - religious
and secular festivals, birthdays and so on.

To the extent that each can pursue individual or paired
activities, many people seem to find this comforting and relaxing.   'Necessary' activities like gardening and DIY may

also be satisfying if one's family is around, but not preventing the task being completed.   Conversely, having some part
in such activities may arouse interest and enjoyment in children.

As the family ages the balance between being together and
being separate may alter: adolescent children and their
parents feel more need for privacy, but unless occasions are
made for communication and shared experiences, the family may
become very fragmented or discordant.   Leisure activities are
a potential aid in this, but often it is difficult to discover
and sustain common interests.   Adolescents often wish to 'do
their own thing';   and parents often feel that they have had
enough noise and disruption.

For single people loneliness, entrapment and isolation may
be very pressing, even while personal space and privacy is
plentiful.   'Seeing the family' will inevitably involve
travelling or being host.   It seems clear that for many
elderly people living alone the prospect of such visits and
the memory of past ones is substantial or even sufficient fuel
for life's meaning, especially if supplemented by other contacts like telephone calls or letters.   Yet it also seems
clear that many people living alone, both young and old, have
strongly felt needs for sociability and outings beyond their
homes, which carry the opportunity of excitement, change and
novelty.   Not having someone to do these things with can be
very inhibiting.   If such lonely people can become involved
with other individuals and families in 'neighbourliness', perhaps in some helping capacity, they can receive in return
emotional support, companionship and sharing of activity.

Going out: the family together and separately

While most non-work activity may take place in and around the
home, much leisure is taken away from home especially by young
married couples, and people of any age in non-family households.   People whose work takes them away a lot may find comfort and relaxation at home;   for people who are at home most
of the time, the treats tend to be balanced the other way.
This often gives rise to a conflict of needs between husband
and wife in conventional families.   In dual-worker families,
the time needed by both parents to 'unwind' and to get through
home maintenance tasks may conflict with their own felt needs,
and their children's, for stimulation at home and trips out as
a family.

Many familial activities have some element of obligation,
e.g. shopping or visiting friends or relatives.   These may be
undertaken in either a perfunctory or more pleasurable way.

What makes the difference may be who one does it with, or
when.   For example, for a mother with young children it may
be a pleasure to go shopping or visiting alone, or to go 'en
famille', with a husband to help care for the children, but
not with the children only.

Day excursions and holidays are other major forms of
outing.   Not all of these serve to integrate families.
Nevertheless, whether the actual outing is enjoyed or not, one
quality of such experiences is the content they provide for
memories and idealisation (Clawson and Knetsch, 1966).   Certainly people who take holidays away, and who envisage prospective holidays, tend to report higher life satisfactions
(Dower, Rapoport et al., 1981), though partly this may reflect
their standard of living.

Other activities for which families commonly go out
together include religious observance and entertainment.   In
these cases one member may stimulate the rest into activity.

As already suggested how members join or divide for various
activities is numerous.   Members of a family living separately, say, parents with a child at college, or adult children
living in separate neighbourhoods, or middle-aged parents and
their grandchildren may meet outside their respective homes,
and may accompany one another on trips or holidays.

Many families feel a need to go out together, but like to
pursue separate pursuits once out, reconvening afterwards.
Examples of venues where such activities are possible include
parks, libraries, sports centres, clubs and holiday camps.

Families as resource pools

Often the involvements of one member may link a whole family
to a specific activity.   This may result from a commitment,
as in the case of a father who plays football and who takes
along his family to spectate and cheer.   Or it may be a new
role, as when a child enters school and opens for her/his
parents a new world of parents' associations, friends and
acquaintances and volunteer help for playground duty, or baby-
sitting.   Such involvements may quickly become central to a
parent's life.   Hence, through visits and through recounting
news, all the family may benefit from the experiences of any
member.   In such ways, families may be seen as resource
pools, aiding developing of interests among its members.   The
network of the wider family is also a resource, often providing rare opportunities for holidays away from home (Dower,
Rapoport et al., 1981; Strelitz, 1978).   One implication is
that people with no relatives or means of going away may need
help to do so.

Families as inhibiting forces

Families also exercise constraining or inhibiting influences.
For example, in many Asian families teenage girls are not
allowed to attend mixed-sex youth clubs.   In many young
English families fathers may have a passionate desire to play
a sport, but meet resistance from their families who may
resent them spending their Saturday afternoons or Sunday morn-
ings on an activity which excludes the family and takes
fathers out of the home where they may be needed.   Sometimes
restraining influences can be helpful, as when limits are set
to adolescents' roaming about to avoid dangers and to concentrate on their schoolwork.   If this opens doors to further
studies or job opportunities it may have a positive influence on the development of interests in later life.   But this
begs a perennial question in defining provision for leisure.
Are its goals short - or longer - term?   Is it for enjoyment
or for personal development?

PROVIDING LEISURE SERVICES FOR FAMILIES

If we view taking leisure not as consuming a series of custom-
made products, but as a process of enjoying and realising oneself, then providing for it becomes a very diffused and widespread responsibility rather than a narrow 'product-defined'
job.   It becomes part of designing adequate house and garden
space;   part of producing and disseminating suitable books,
records and TV programmes;   part of enabling like-minded and
diverse people, to meet, to work, to travel, to eat and drink,
to exercise and rest.
     Two things follow.   Firstly, leisure provision is the res-
ponsibility of many agencies in the public, private and voluntary sectors.   The range of providers outside the public
sector is enormous.   Table 22.1 suggests the range of agencies involved in very specific provision for certain groups
(e.g. keel boat moorings) to fairly ubiquitous provision which
families can and do enjoy - like the publishing of books,
records and tapes.   Tomlinson (1979) describes the vast range
of voluntary groups who, as a primary or secondary aim, provide from cradle (pre-school play groups) to the grave (day
clubs for the elderly).
     Secondly, 'leisure is so interwoven with the rest of life',
and government intervention in this rest of life is so extensive, that public authorities inevitably become involved in
leisure provision' (Roberts, 1978:156).   Travis (1978a,
1978b, 1979) has set out the scope of this involvement,
through many central government departments and agencies, and

the operation of comprehensive leisure and recreation departments in local governments.   Besides professional leisure
managers, however, there are many other town hall officers
whose actions condition or contribute to people's leisure.
Table 22.1 provides a far from exhaustive list.

TABLE 22.1   Local authority services affecting leisure

Department	Services
Housing	Provision and allocation of house space and garden; associated communal play spaces, community rooms.
Education	School clubs and interest groups; adult education; outdoor pursuits; making space available for hire; parent-teacher associations.
Planning	Ensuring site allocation for leisure functions; protecting public land, historic and natural heritage against loss.
Environmental Health	Preserving amenity (refuse collection; pollution prevention).
Engineers/Transport	Providing footpath, cycleway, road networks; car parks; organising bus services (including family tickets); maintaining street furniture.
Social Services	Adapting housing for the handicapped. Providing transport, skilled services, social support for vulnerable groups (one-parent families, handicapped, elderly). Providing childminders, play groups. Providing social clubs, self-help groups.
Libraries	Books, music, pictures, records, lite-rary schemes. Open University.
Recreation	Providing open space in town and coun-try. Providing sports pitches and build-ings, arts centres, theatres, museums, galleries. Hiring space to other groups

Source: Roberts, 1979.

How much and what sort of leisure then, does the family take together away from home? The evidence available is mainly from public sites which have been surveyed. For many active recreations the proportion of family users appear quite low (Table 22.2) - in sports centres the figure was as little as 24 per cent, even including mixed groups (i.e. family and friends). Similar or lower figures are found for theatres and museums. The figures rise for canoeing and sailing, and more markedly for motor cruising and sea angling which are frequent features of family holidays.

TABLE 22.2 Type of attendance

	(Averages)	% with family or family and friends	% with friends
Sports centres	(7 in England)	14	10
Inland fishing	(5 sites)	20	6
Sea fishing	(2 sites)	42	7
Sailing	(5 sites)	40	18
Motor cruising	(2 sites)	43	32
Canoeing	(2 sites)	25	7
Walking/picnicing	(5 sites)	62	14
Visitor centres in forests, national parks, historic sites	(18 sites)	79	14

Source: Based on Rees and Collins (1979); DART/University of Surrey (1979).

Not until one looks at the activities of a half day or day trip to coast or country - informal sightseeing, picnicing, and walking - do family groups dominate.

Much has been made of the influence of the family car (Elson, 1974), both in encouraging more trips and in bringing the family together, as the charabanc did for earlier genera-tions and the excursion train still does for both family and non-family groups.

Why should there be this emphasis on transport? Regarding sports centres, it was the hope of official committees - Wolfenden in 1960 and Cobham in 1973 - that 'each member of the family can be catered for, including any member who has no particular activity to take part in'. Being catered for,

TABLE 22.3 Trips made by parental age groups

Age group	16-19	20-4	25-9	30-4	35-9	40-4	45-9	50-4	55-9	60-4	65-70
Percentage visiting the countryside with spouse and children	5	12	45	66	61	55	33	17	4	3	1

n = 4341

Source: Fitton, 1978.

however, does not imply playing together even if travelling together, and the virtue of large multiple activity centres for arts, sports and leisure pursuits is that they give choice of activities and opportunities for families to individuate as well as congregate. In fact the main limitations on playing together are work, social and domestic obligations which allow little common free time in many families (Maw, 1969).

Another limitation is that sports and arts or crafts involve learned skills. There are perhaps only two periods when adults and children can directly as opposed to vicariously share their interests: one is with young children in the initial learning phase when parents can act as teachers; the second is the early-mid teenage phase when the children have matured enough (but not too much!) in physique, skill and tactics to play with their parents (Rees and Collins, 1979). Thereafter pressures of further education or apprenticeships, and the search for confirmation of identity in the eyes of their peers often takes young people out of their parents' active leisure life, for other than family holidays and the occasional day trip. Swimming seems to be one sporting exception to this general pattern, with a much higher family participation.

In an attempt to attract families directly some providers have introduced membership schemes usually with a reduced lump sum cost: these can be found in sports centres, arts centres, repertory theatres and concert halls, social clubs, some sports clubs (e.g. golf, badminton, tennis, bowls) and in entry fees to country clubs, safari parks and stately homes. Family tickets are available, especially for off-peak travel, on London Transport, British Rail, most bus companies, some holiday package airline and ferry services and holiday accommodation lettings. Thus for example, 56 per cent of a sample of 131 sports centres offered such memberships in 1977 (Thomasson, 1977). Other organisations - churches for example - would claim to provide for and welcome family participation without the need for a ticket, but with a hope and even an expectation of commitment.

Providing for variants of the two-adult, two-child model family is less frequent. Thus difficulties can range from the trivial, e.g. few families of five or more can get together in some forms of transport or restaurants with fixed four-seat bays to the serious, e.g. many buildings provide relatively poorly for the handicapped, especially the mentally handicapped or elderly people with mobility problems. Some managements look askance on families with members exhibiting 'unsocial' behaviour (e.g. very large families with noisy and unkempt looking children; mentally handicapped members; some hyperactive children). Many clubs demand impeccable

standards of dress and equipment which may pose a social and
an economic barrier - a 'social filter' (Emmett, 1971).
Thomson (1979) relates how in one area of north London with
some 50,000 inhabitants of whom some 7,800 would have some
physical impairment (of mobility, speech, sight or hearing),
there were some 760 public buildings (including 524 shops) of
which only 17 had been adapted to enable easy access (2 municipal offices, all 8 public toilets, 2 of 4 libraries, all 3
swimming pools, 1 sports centre and 1 clinic).   When variant
families are less conspicious, such as the 11 per cent who are
one-parent households or families with unemployed youths whose
lives have no structure and little meaning, not only are the
customers' needs very varied, but they are not obviously different from others of the same age, education, or background.
Yet in a caring society, who would deny that they deserve some
special consideration and some compensatory priority?

ISSUES FOR THE FUTURE

If there are so many sorts of family, and if few people spend
much of their lives in families as leisure-consuming units,
why worry about a policy of providing facilities and services
for families?   Yet provision for families is increasingly a
concern in the provision of leisure services.   We quote a
typical statement, made by a local authority prominent in
leisure provision:
   The philosophy followed by the Centre (and by the Authority
   in general) is known as 'the family formula', namely for
   the Centre not to have a tracksuit image but rather to provide something for all the family;   Centre programmes
   result from policy geared to meeting community need in the
   widest sense. (Torfaen DC, quoted in Cooper and Lybrand,
   1979)
   The fact is 49 per cent of households *are* families with
children, and a further 27 per cent married childless couples
(General Household Survey, 1976).   Marriages may survive for
shorter periods and families be dissolved and reconstituted
more often, but the family will remain the primary means of
socialisation and a prime milieu for achieving personal satisfactions (Parker, 1976).   The early socialisation process, in
which play is an important ingredient, is an essential foundation for whatever schools or youth organisations are able to
do subsequently in further socialisation and development of
personality and resourcefulness (DES, 1979; HMI, 1979).
   Secondly, it is very good business to provide for family
leisure as flourishing hotels and holiday camps on British
and Mediterranean coasts demonstrate.   The high proportion of

family users travelling to splash and swim in the new 'leisure pools' (with their wave machines) provides a public sector example, despite longer travel times and higher entry charges than conventional pools.   Yet aiming to provide for variant families like deprived ethnic groups may mean poorer throughput and income, uncertain bookings and greater leadership effort, at least initially.   This is being accepted by the Manchester Council in their policy for inner city sports centres (reported in Cooper and Lybrand, 1979).   It is a direct result of attempting to reallocate resources to overcome underprivilege (Coventry CDP, 1975).

Thirdly, families *will* provide for themselves in the spirit which has made voluntary groups in leisure a force equal to the public and commercial sectors.   This is an underpinning of mutual support organisations like Gingerbread groups for one-parent families (Streather, 1979), especially where special needs are life long (e.g. mentally handicapped children's societies who provide toy libraries, play groups, outings and sports events from local park to international standard).

In taking provision for diverse families into fuller account in leisure provision there is considerable relevance also to the population at large.   An urgent emphasis is the requirement for smaller-scale provisions within each reach of people's homes.   Many people seem to feel a need for this, whatever relevance large prestige centres may or may not have in their lives.   This includes facilities that individuals cannot provide for themselves, like dark-rooms, and facilities where casual socialising may occur, like play spaces and pocket parks.   Such provision may do much to combat boredom, the isolation of individuals or families from peers of every age, and over-reliance of family members one on another.

Much provision along such lines would benefit people in many types of family situation.   Safety and attractiveness are key issues in people's feelings about local provision. These require collaboration amongst the municipal services as well.   Services such as street cleaning and refuse collection and law and order are involved: mugging and assault in the streets worry, especially the elderly.   Noise and traffic are nuisances, so that planning and traffic regulation are relevant: some parents seek play spaces so that children can cycle or visit neighbours safely.

Dower, Rapoport, Strelitz and Kew suggest that the public sector acquire more *sensitive understanding* of the needs of individuals at the turnstile, and also of the changing kaleidoscope of sub-groups' needs.   SCPR (1979) has set out guidelines for location, transport, publicity, leadership and finance aspects of schemes aimed at other low participant groups in sport (e.g. the elderly, cf. Table 22.4).

TABLE 22.4   Guidelines for choosing venues for recreation for the elderly

---

Main considerations: access and comfort of surroundings.

1   Is there a site close to where the elderly live (e.g. a local hall near old people's flats/bungalows)?   Could the scheme be put on *inside* an old people's home?

2   If not, how good are the public transport links?   Is there a bus stop nearby?

3   Is there safe and easy access to the building?   Is there a dangerous road to cross?   Is there a car-park nearby?

4   Is the area that surrounds the site one where elderly people would be happy to go?   (E.g. one manager decided against holding a scheme for the elderly inside his sports centre because it was considered too rough an area for older people to come to.)

5   Are there other facilities nearby - such as shops, library, etc?   The elderly may like to combine a trip to the sports scheme with a shopping expedition - making it a day's outing.   (E.g. a successful scheme was held in a building in the heart of a city's shopping centre;   its central position and proximity to shops were keys to its success.)

6   If access is difficult, is it possible to set up a lift system or bussing arrangements?

7   How comfortable are the interior surroundings?   A warm sports centre with modern facilities is ideal for this group.   Access to a canteen/restaurant, or at least to cups of tea, is essential.

8   Depending on the type of scheme is there a variety of activities and facilities available?   The opportunity to participate in different sports is very popular with this group.

Leisure provision has implications also, for sharing burdens of family care and enabling some members to go out. Supplementary child care is an obvious need, not just to allow mothers to go out to work, but also so that parents can be themselves - by playing cricket, going to a pottery class, having a hairdo, or just going out as a couple (Rapoport, Rapoport and Strelitz, 1977;   Jackson and Jackson, 1979). There is also the possibility of organising local networks of babysitters - based on mutual parental aid or the help of other generations, teenage or elderly who fulfil their own needs (Emlen and Watson, 1971).   Single parents need even more support (Streather, 1979).

To facilitate more provision of the appropriate scale

within reach of families in local communities, it is important
to take a *broad view* of the community's *collective*, natural,
man-made and human resources and enable them all and not just
the public ones to be used.   For example, in the small town
of Atherton, 350 buildings with potential for recreation
exist, the majority unused (NWSC, 1977).   While for example
some schools are too old or too small for much dual use and
there are real practical problems (Goacher, 1979), there are
still only some 130 joint municipal educational sports
centres.   So many schools are still not used or only by very
narrow spectrum, that Fair Play for Children have launched a
new campaign (1979).

Emphasising the role of people as *their own providers* can
do much to increase people's psychological access to provision
as well as its amount.   Local authorities can do this in a
great variety of ways, from direct to very indirect, as the
Quality of Life studies show (Burton, 1977).

To enable more people to express themselves, especially
poor people, and to prevent financial waste, the notion of resource pools appears very relevant.   This includes equipment
for loan, e.g. for DIY, or for holding celebrations, as well
as communal fixed equipment like swings or climbing frames.
How firmly held are the values of private consumption?   In
inner city areas some shifts towards more communal or neighbourhood leisure have occurred, especially in community
centres, and street or neighbourhood festivals.   In suburban
areas and outlying housing estates many people in the middle
establishment phase of life as well as later years express
needs for more involvement between families (Dower, Rapoport,
Strelitz and Kew, 1980; Gaynor Cohen, 1975).   Perhaps a more
appropriate pattern of material provision will follow.

The challenge is twofold: to provide for families with
children at different stages to have leisure, and to meet the
needs of individual members to do things on their own or in
non-family settings; and secondly, to provide for the leisure
needs of people in other kinds of family situations, including
those who live alone.

Chapter 23

Income maintenance for families with children

Ruth Lister

INTRODUCTION

'Income maintenance' is the rather grand term used to describe
the financial support provided by the State for individuals
and their families. This financial support is not confined
to social security benefits for those out of work. It covers
also a variety of cash benefits paid to people in work plus
the benefit the latter derive from personal tax allowances and
tax reliefs. While income maintenance concerns everyone,
this chapter concentrates on families with children, with some
reference also to the position of families caring for disabled
or infirm relatives at home. The provision of public services, which also help to determine family living standards,
is dealt with in other chapters. I start with a brief outline of how the current provisions have developed and then
assess how far they have been successful in maintaining the
incomes of all families with children relative to other groups
and in preventing poverty. Looking to the future, I raise
some general questions about the role of the State in maintaining family incomes and some specific policy issues which
need to be resolved.

THE DEVELOPMENT OF THE CURRENT INCOME MAINTENANCE SYSTEM

The basic framework for today's income maintenance provisions
was laid down in the Beveridge Report of 1942. The Beveridge
Plan envisaged a comprehensive 'scheme of social insurance
against interruption and destruction of earning power' combined with a 'general system of children's allowances, sufficient to meet the subsistence needs' (para. 267) of children.
Family allowances (for all children but the first) and contributory national insurance benefits (such as unemployment and

Widows' benefits) were introduced after the war.   The Beveridge Plan also included the safety-net of a means-tested national assistance scheme designed to protect the minority who fell through the meshes of the insurance scheme.   It was intended that this safety-net would wither away until it was catering for only a tiny minority.   Instead, because of the failure to pay adequate national insurance benefits, as recommended by Beveridge, the numbers claiming means-tested assistance (renamed supplementary benefit in 1966) trebled from one to three million between 1948 and 1978.   Further, governments have attempted to bolster up inadequate income maintenance provisions for both those in and out of work through the introduction of a range of means-tested benefits, which have been much criticised.   A classic example was the introduction, in 1971, of Family Income Supplement for poor working families, as an alternative to fulfilling an election pledge to increase family allowances.   The failure to pay high enough national insurance benefits and family allowances was one reason for the growing dependence on means-tested benefits.   The other was the exclusion from the Beveridge Plan of people such as the congenitally disabled who could not meet the contribution conditions attached to the insurance benefits.   During the 1970s a number of non-contributory benefits were, therefore, introduced to help the disabled and those at home to care for disabled relatives.   Unfortunately, because these benefits are even lower than the contributory benefits, they have had little impact on the numbers dependent on supplementary benefit.

The overall picture today is, thus, one of a confusing patchwork of contributory, non-contributory and means-tested benefits.   Much of this patchwork has grown up in isolation from the other main element in our income maintenance provisions: the tax system.   I do not intend to dwell here on the extent to which the tax system, through the plethora of tax reliefs, provides a second 'welfare state' for the rich (a theme which has been amply developed elsewhere by Field, Meacher and Pond, 1977).   The tax system also provides an income maintenance function for humbler wage-earning families. The system of personal tax allowances was supposed to ensure that 'there should be no income tax levied upon any income which is insufficient to provide the owner with what he requires for subsistence' (Royal Commission on the Taxation of Profits and Income, para. 158).   I use the past tense advisedly for the personal tax allowances patently no longer perform this function.   The value of the tax allowances has been so eroded since the war that people can now start to pay tax at incomes which are below the poverty line (which is defined below).   And, as Table 23.1 shows, it is families with

children who have fallen furthest behind.   When you take the
growing dependence on means-tested benefits and add to it the
growing numbers of low income working families drawn into the
tax net, the result is one of the more ludicrous aspects of
the income maintenance scheme: 'the poverty trap'.   The
'poverty trap' is a term 'used to describe the situation in
which a family loses more in terms of extra tax paid and reduced benefits received than it gains from a pay increase
which brought them about' (Pond, 1978).   It is families with
children who are most vulnerable to the poverty trap.

The most recent development in income maintenance provision
for families has been the introduction of the child benefit
scheme.   This represented the fusion of two hitherto separate
strands of financial support for children: family allowances
and child tax allowances.   The history of both these allowances helps to explain the position that families find themselves in today and, as I shall argue later, provides a sober
warning for the future.   In the words of the Child Benefit
Now Campaign (1977:8):   'From the very beginning, Government
commitment to adequate financial support for children was
halfhearted and the history of the Family Allowance since then
has been a dismal one of neglect.'   Although child tax allowances did not suffer quite the same degree of neglect, by the
time they were abolished their value relative to the single
personal tax allowance had plummeted.   For example, the 11-15
child tax allowance was worth 89 per cent of the single personal allowance in 1957-8; by 1976-7 it was worth only 46 per
cent (38.5 per cent after 'clawback', a device introduced in
1968 whereby part of the family allowance was 'clawed back'
through a reduction in the child tax allowance).

THE LIVING STANDARDS OF FAMILIES

As a result of this 'dismal' history of neglect, the living
standards of all families with children have fallen relative
to those of the childless.   One indicator of this is the
extent to which families' tax thresholds have fallen over the
last thirty years.   The 'tax threshold' measures the amount
of tax-free income available to a family and Table 23.1 presents this as a proportion of average male earnings.   It
shows that, while all taxpayers have relatively less tax-free
income now than in 1949-50, it is those with children who have
lost out most and, the larger the family, the greater the drop
in the tax threshold.

One measure that has been used to assess the living standards of those with children relative to other groups is what
Margaret Wynn refers to as 'the modest-but-adequate standard'.

TABLE 23.1 Tax threshold (including child benefit) as a percentage of average male manual earnings

Year	Single person	Married couple	Married couple with 1 child under 11	Married couple with 2 children aged 12 and 8	Married couple with 3 children aged 14, 12 and 8	Married couple with 4 children aged 16, 14, 12 and 8
1949–50	39.4	62.8	83.0	99.7	115.4	130.0
1954–55	30.9	52.7	73.1	90.2	106.0	120.7
1959–60	27.4	45.7	63.9	84.3	102.8	124.1
1964–65	30.4	46.7	62.4	79.8	95.9	114.3
1969–70	25.4	37.4	48.0	56.5	67.3	79.6
1974–75	24.2	33.5	42.8	50.5	57.8	66.0
1979–80	24.7	38.5	41.1	43.5	45.7	47.7

Source: 'House of Commons Hansard', 27 July 1979, cols 557–8.

She suggests that this can be defined 'by an income that is
twice the income regarded in any country as being necessary
for minimum subsistence and the avoidance of poverty' (Wynn,
1972).   Using this measure, an analysis of the Family Expenditure Survey by McClements (1976) in the mid-1970s revealed
that 65 per cent of families with children in this country
failed to achieve this standard compared with 38 per cent of
childless non-pensioner households.   One-parent and larger
families were particularly likely to fall below this level of
income.

A similar picture emerges if we use the poverty line itself
as a measure of the well being of families with children.
The amount of money received by those living on supplementary
benefit constitutes a semi-official poverty line.   As the
Supplementary Benefit Commission has observed (1977):

> the supplementary benefit scale rates are the nearest thing
> Britain has to a definition of the minimum standard of
> living which this country is for the moment prepared to
> tolerate.   [It continues] If such a minimum standard is to
> be a defence against poverty, it must enable people to par-
> ticipate in the social system to which their fellow citi-
> zens belong.   That means that the scale rates for a family
> of a given size should not fall too far below the incomes
> of similar families with a breadwinner in low paid work,
> and they should keep pace year by year with changes in the
> average worker's earnings and living standards.

Underlying the SBC's arguments is a 'relative' conception of
poverty which was articulated by Peter Townsend (1978:31) in
the following terms:

> poverty can be defined objectively and applied consistently
> only in terms of the concept of relative deprivation.
> Individuals, families and groups in the population can be
> said to be in poverty when ... their resources are so
> seriously below those commanded by the average individual
> or family that they are, in effect, excluded from ordinary
> living patterns, customs and activities.

The supplementary benefit payment for a couple and two pre-
school children has hovered around 55 to 60 per cent of average male net earnings during the 1970s.   There is a growing
body of evidence which shows that the supplementary benefit
scale rates fail to provide a 'defence against poverty' as
defined by the SBC.   This is particularly the case with respect to the children's scale rates.   Research done in other
countries suggests that they seriously underestimate the costs
of children relative to adults (Lister, 1977, 1979).   More
recently, a study of the costs of children by David Piachaud
(1979) concluded that 'the supplementary benefit scale rates
for children need to be increased by about one half if they

are to provide genuinely for even the minimum requirements for a child'.   Given that these scale rates are used as a bench-mark against which to measure the extent of poverty in the population as a whole, the implication is that official figures could be seriously underestimating the extent of child poverty in this country.

This possibility makes the official estimates of the number of families in poverty even more sobering.   As it is, in 1977 (the latest date for which figures are available) there were nearly half a million children living below the supplementary benefit level and a further million in families on supplemen-tary benefit.   If we include those that can be said to be living on the margins of poverty, i.e. up to 40 per cent above the supplementary benefit level (in line with the measure used by a number of academic researchers), then we are talking about a total of three and a half million children.   Increas-ingly, poverty is casting its shadow over families with child-ren.   Whereas in 1974 about a third of all individuals living below supplementary benefit level were in families with child-ren, three years later the proportion had increased to 38 per cent ('Hansard', 2 November 1979).   Taking the rather broader definition of low incomes used in the Royal Commission on the Distribution of Income and Wealth's Report on lower incomes (i.e. the lowest quarter of the distribution of equivalent net incomes) three-fifths of all individuals on lower incomes were in families with children and about a third of all children were living in low-income families.   In contrast, there has been a slight improvement in the position of the elderly in recent years, though the risk of poverty is still great among the elderly, as it is among the disabled.   What we do not know is the extent of poverty among families caring for dis-abled or elderly relatives.

Income maintenance policies for families with children are concerned with the 'horizontal' distribution of resources. Living standards depend not just on the income coming into a household, they depend also on the demands made on that income.   A family with children requires a larger income than a single person or childless couple to achieve the same stan-dard of living as the latter.   The wages system cannot accom-modate these differences in family needs and therefore it is seen as the role of the State to provide some support for those with children either through the tax or cash benefit systems or both.   It is not, however, always a very popular role, for the attitude 'they choose to have them, they should pay for them' is not uncommon.   (This view often goes hand in hand with the view that benefits for children encourage large families and that it is large families that cause poverty. There is no evidence to support the former view and the latter does not tally with the facts: although it is true that the risk of poverty is greater among large families, half the children living below the poverty line are in families with one or two children ('Hansard', 31 January 1980).)

The case for the community as a whole sharing responsibility for the financial support for children rests on two powerful arguments. The first was put by Sir John Walley (1972: 181) in the following terms: 'A nation's compassion may be shown in its care for the disabled and those past work, but for evidence of its concern for its future (which also includes its capacity to exercise this compassion) we can only look at its care for children.' As Margaret Wynn has pointed out (1972:27), 'most of the time, trouble, and money expended on rearing the next generation falls on the shoulders of a minority of the present generation. Is there not a case therefore for the community as a whole helping to ease the burden slightly from the shoulders of that minority?'

The second argument stems from the fact that, although at any one point in time only a small minority of households are caring for children, many more households have the care of children at some point in their lives. Community financial support for children helps 'to reduce the difference between living standards at different stages of a person's life' (Report of the Committee on Family Policy, 1972) by redistributing resources to the childrearing years when help is needed most. This introduces the concept of the family life-cycle, to which I shall return later. There are also strong economic arguments for providing families with adequate financial support. The alternative for families with inadequate incomes can be the reception of a child into care, which costs the community considerably more money than decent child benefits. The same argument applies to adequate support for those caring for disabled and infirm relatives at home.

SOME POLICY ISSUES

Discussion about income maintenance policies for families has tended in recent years to centre on the question of the overall level of child support. This is not surprising given that the priority has been to raise child support to a more adequate level. But there are many other issues which need to be resolved which concern the structure of that support. In the rest of this chapter I will review briefly the most important of these. They involve two key questions: the changing position and expectations of women and the fluctuations of the family life-cycle.

The changing position and expectations of women

'We have been slow in coming to terms with the greatest social change of the past 40 years - the increase in the proportion of married women at work' (Ennals, 1978).   The extent of this change is documented in Chapter 6.   The implications of it have been recognised by the Supplementary Benefits Commission (1977): 'In more and more families both men and women are combining the role of wage-earner with a share of their joint domestic responsibilities.   There is additionally a greater awareness among both sexes of a married woman's right to the financial independence which she gains through employment.' This has not however yet been recognised in the taxation and social security benefit systems.   With regard to the tax system, which treats a woman's income as belonging to her husband and gives him extra tax relief, the Meade Committee noted (1978:377) that 'the idea that a woman on marriage becomes a dependant of her husband, who is then responsible for her welfare and for that of the family accounts for much of the present treatment of the tax unit', and that this 'notion is less compatible with modern attitudes to the relationship between men and women, and in fact corresponds less and less closely with reality when an increasing number of married women work in paid occupations.'   As the Equal Opportunities Commission commented (1977:4) 'there are few areas where Whitehall has clung so tenaciously to the assumptions of the Victorian era.'   One other such area is the social security system which denies married and cohabiting women a wide range of benefits on the grounds that

It is normal for a married woman, in this country to be primarily supported by her husband, and she looks to him for support when not actually working, rather than to a social security benefit.   Indeed, it continues to be a widespread view that a husband who is capable of work has a duty to society, as well as to his wife, to provide the primary support for his family. (DHSS, 1975)

The growing awareness of women's desire for financial independence has also helped to focus some attention on the question of the distribution of income within the family as well as between families.   Although research is sparce, what evidence there is suggests that it is not valid to assume that the income coming in to a family as a whole necessarily provides an indicator of the standard of living enjoyed by individual members of that family (EOC, 1977).   This is particularly important where the woman is not in paid employment and is dependent on her husband for financial support.   A number of surveys have shown that a husband's pay rise is not always passed on in the housekeeping he gives his wife which, at

times of high inflation, can mean a cut in family living standards.   One of the explicit aims of the transfer from child
tax allowances received by the husband to child benefits paid
to the mother was to transfer resources from 'the wallet to
the purse'.
   The other important social change which our income maintenance system has not yet come to terms with is the growing
number of women who are raising families on their own.   The
question of the effects of marriage break-up is dealt with as
part of the family life-cycle.   But, as Brian Jackson notes,
one point that tends to be overlooked in any discussion of the
'problem' of one-parent families is that a small but growing
minority of women are choosing to raise their children outside
the confines of the conventional two-parent family.

The family life-cycle

Rowntree's research at the turn of the century highlighted
what he called 'the life-cycle of poverty'.   Individuals and
families were most vulnerable to poverty at certain stages in
their lives and the same is true today.   The Royal Commission
on the Distribution of Income and Wealth's Report on Lower
Incomes (1978) pointed out that 'those most at risk of belonging to families with incomes that are low in relation to their
needs are dependent children, the parents of young children
and the elderly.'   The troughs and peaks of the family life-
cycle reflect both the variations in income coming into the
family and the demands placed on that income.   The vulnerable
position of families with children, and in particular those
with young children, stems from the coincidence between a reduced income and higher needs.   The Background Paper to the
Royal Commission Report, which looked at the causes of
poverty, stressed that 'whether a wife works is a crucial
determinant of whether a family is financially-speaking poor'
(Layard et al., 1978).   DHSS figures show that the numbers of
families living below the poverty line would be trebled if it
were not for the contribution of wives' earnings (Hamill,
1976).   But as the Background Paper noted: 'One problem with
women's work is that it is more difficult for her to work just
when she most needs to - that is, when there are children to
be fed.   This explains part of Rowntree's famous "life-cycle
of poverty"' (Layard et al., 1978).   The number of mothers of
pre-school children in paid employment is growing.   But the
1976 'General Household Survey' still found that, whereas 67
per cent of mothers whose youngest child was aged 10 to 15 and
60 per cent of those whose youngest was 5 to 9 were in paid
employment, only 26 per cent of mothers with younger children
were in work.

As children become older, it is easier for both parents to contribute to the family income, but the cost of the children themselves also grows.   One analysis of Family Expenditure Survey data found that families spent nearly twice as much on children aged 11 to 15 as on pre-school children and that older teenagers were another 40 per cent more clostly (McClements, 1976).   And research done in other countries has found that children aged 13 to 15 cost as much as an adult to maintain and older teenagers cost more than an adult.

For a growing number of families, family break-up is a normal part of the life-cycle.   Between 1971 and 1976 the number of one-parent families increased by a third.   The majority are separated or divorced.   They now make up one in eight of all families with children and have the care of over one and a half million children.   A disproportionate number are dependent on supplementary benefit - three out of five of all families with children on supplementary benefit have only one parent - and are living below supplementary benefit level. The Royal Commission's report (1978) showed that 'one half of all one parent families compared with one fifth of two parent families were in the lowest quarter of the distribution of equivalent net family incomes and that there was, therefore, a far greater risk of lower incomes among one parent families than among two parent families.'

Interruption of earnings because of unemployment has also become an increasingly significant factor in the life-cycle of some families - mainly those who are already disadvantaged in terms of ill health or low occupational status.   Growing numbers of families with children are dependent on unemployment or supplementary benefit because of the father's unemployment and married women have also suffered disproportionately from the increase in unemployment during the 1970s.

Finally, although most families can relax in one of the peaks of the life-cycle when their children have grown up, a significant minority have the care of an elderly or disabled relative.   Audrey Hunt's (1968) survey of women's employment in 1965 found that 10 per cent of employed women and 12.5 per cent of non-employed women had the care of an elderly or infirm person.   Her later research into the home help service found that, between the ages of 35 and 64, 'roughly half of all housewives can expect some time or another to give some help to elderly or infirm persons' (Hunt, 1970:424).   A fifth of those aged 35 to 49 and a quarter of those aged 50 to 64 had an elderly or infirm person living in the same household. What her research also revealed was the extent to which it was women who have the responsibility for caring for elderly and infirm relatives at home.   The effect on family income is similar to that when women are unable to go out to work because of the presence of young children.

SOME POLICY OPTIONS

As Melanie Phillips (1978) observed: 'Child Benefit will no
doubt be seen as a watershed when the history of family policy
comes to be written.'   But there are a number of issues concerning child benefits which still need to be resolved and
child benefits are not themselves the be all and end all of
income maintenance for families with children.   With regard
to the child benefit scheme itself, the eventual level of the
benefit still has to be settled.   There appears to be a
fairly wide consensus that the immediate goal should be to
raise the benefit to the same level as the child additions
paid with unemployment and sickness benefit.   After that,
some would argue that the benefit should eventually be high
enough to subsume all the social security additions for children.   Perhaps one of the most crucial requirements is that
child benefit should be index-linked.   In the absence of a
statutory duty to uprate them annually, such as exists for
national insurance benefits, there is a distinct danger that
child benefits will repeat the history of the family allowance
and end up virtually worthless.

Thought also needs to be given to whether the benefit
should continue to be flat rate.   For instance, should larger
families get more help, as in some other European countries?
Some countries also provide more help for older children to
take account of their higher cost.   Certainly it appears
absurd to some people to pay the same for a one-year-old as
a fifteen-year-old.   Moreover cutbacks in the education
budget, which have meant the withdrawal of free school meals
from many children and the abolition of the duty to provide
subsidised school meals suitable as the main meal of the day,
have added to the costs of schoolchildren for parents.   There
is also the question of whether there should be special help
for children who stay on at school after school-leaving age.
At present, such help is only given at the discretion of local
education authorities and is usually totally inadequate.

The only benefits for children that are age-related at
present are the supplementary benefit scale rates.   As I have
already suggested, these are too low to meet even the minimum
cost of maintaining children.   There is a very strong case
for a thorough-going review of the supplementary benefit scale
rates which determine the living standards of over a million
children.   Even the Supplementary Benefits Commission has
been forced to admit that the evidence collected by the DHSS
'strongly suggests that the supplementary benefits scheme provides, particularly for families with children, incomes that
are barely adequate to meet their needs at a level that is
consistent with normal participation in the life of the

relatively wealthy society in which they live' (DHSS/SBC,
1977).   Unfortunately, as the SBC (1979) points out elsewhere, because of a preoccupation with 'work incentives',
'until the incomes of low paid workers with children are improved there will be insurmountable political obstacles to
securing better rates of benefit for families living on supplementary benefit.... Higher child benefits offer the best
means of removing these obstacles.'   This serves to underline
again the importance of the child benefit scheme, even though
improvements in child benefits do not directly help those on
social security.   (This is because an increase in child benefit is offset by a reduction in social security benefits.)

   Preoccupation with the need to improve the child benefit
scheme has helped to divert attention from the question of
whether the community should provide more support for those
with the care of children as well as meet the needs of the
children themselves.   One proposal that has emerged in recent
years has been for a home responsibility payment.   This proposal has taken various forms.   Some have suggested that such
a payment should be made only to those who stay at home to
care for children or other dependants.   The Meade Committee
on the other hand recommended that a home responsibility payment should be paid regardless of whether the parent or carer
stayed at home.   As it would be taxable, it would in any case
be of more value to a family where the person in receipt of
it did not go out to work.   A home responsibility payment
could provide a mechanism for providing extra help for parents
with pre-school children for it could either be confined to
these parents or could be paid at a higher rate to them.   It
could also subsume the invalid care allowance, which currently
is paid only to carers who stay at home to care for severely
disabled people.   Married women are denied entitlement on
the grounds that 'they might be at home in any event' (Social
Security Provision for Chronically Sick and Disabled People,
1974).

   A home responsibility payment that was confined solely to
those who stayed at home to care for dependants would create
a number of practical problems including the creation of a
severe 'poverty trap' when the carer wished to re-enter the
labour market.   More fundamentally, it raises the question of
whether income maintenance policies should be designed to encourage the traditional division of family responsibilities or
whether they should recognise the changes that have been
taking place and facilitate them.   In Sweden, one of the few
countries with a coherent family policy, it has been one of
the explicit aims of this policy to give men and women equal
opportunities for combining gainful employment with the care
of their children.   Under a parental insurance scheme,

parents are allowed nine months leave at 90 per cent of normal earnings after the birth of a child.   This leave can be divided up between the two parents.   In Sweden and also Hungary, Norway, the DDR and the Federal Republic of Germany, parents are allowed paid leave to care for a sick child.   Policies such as these are not even on the political agenda at present in Britain.   Maternity provisions and help with the cost of maternity lag behind those in many other countries.   Child care provision is also important in this context.   As the EOC (p. 24) has pointed out, 'It is clear that the shortage of adequate child care facilities prevents a considerable number of women from making a much-needed contribution to the household income.'   A number of surveys have found that many mothers would return to work sooner if adequate child-care facilities were available.

Adequate child-care facilities (for school-age as well as pre-school children) are particularly crucial for one-parent families.   At present, nearly half of all one-parent families are forced to depend on supplementary benefit.   The Finer Committee on One Parent Families which reported in 1974 concluded that

in terms of families with children ... there can be no other group of this size who are as poor as fatherless families, of whom so many lack any State benefit other than supplementary benefit or family allowance, whose financial position is so uncertain, and whose hope of improvement in their situation is so remote.

And it is doubted whether 'any improvements that could be made would remedy the basic unsuitability of the supplementary benefit scheme as the main source of income for a large proportion of fatherless families.'   There has been no real advance since the Finer Committee reported and its main recommendations are slowly gathering more and more dust.   Although there was little support for Finer's recommendation for a guaranteed maintenance allowance there has been a growing lobby for the introduction of a special social security benefit for lone parents.   The case for such a benefit has been summed up by Paul Lewis (1979) of One Parent Families:

A non means-tested, non-contributory social security benefit at the rate of widowed mothers allowance would lift over 95 per cent of one parent families off supplementary benefit and restore to all one parent families the freedom to work and the dignity and status of an independent income ... it would cut family poverty in half.

The benefit would be taxable but, because there would be no means test, it would not create the kind of poverty trap that the supplementary benefit scheme currently does for lone parents who wish to go out to work.

The case for special help for lone parents is a strong one. But it is important also that lone parents are not treated as a group in isolation from other parents and other mothers in particular. Many of their problems are the problems that all parents face but writ large, and, as the Finer Report itself pointed out, advance for lone working mothers depends on improving the position of all working mothers. Higher child benefit, improved child-care facilities, a home responsibility benefit would benefit one-parent as well as two-parent families. In fact, a home responsibility benefit could provide the framework for a one-parent family benefit as it could be paid at a higher rate to one-parent than two-parent families. In this way, provision for one-parent families could be integrated into provisions made for families in general.

Finally, as pointed out earlier, both the taxation and social security systems have yet to come to terms with the changing position of women. An EEC Directive will require the removal of some of the discriminatory features of the social security scheme but not all of them. Nor will it tackle the principle of aggregation (the treatment of husband and wife as one economic unit) which Lord Houghton argued is 'really what we want to destroy. It will have to be done in taxation. It will have to be done in social security, if women are to have their separate personalities, their separate dignity and their separate economic resources' ('Hansard', 24 January 1978). What is at issue is not just equal rights but women's right to economic independence. In the tax system, the demand is growing for the individual rather than the couple to be treated as the tax unit. Each individual would have his or her own personal tax allowance and the extra tax relief given to married men would be abolished. (This extra tax relief costs the community £3 billion at 1981-2 rates, which, as a number of commentators have pointed out, could be put to much better use in improving financial support for families with children.) In the supplementary benefit scheme, disaggregation would mean giving both husband and wife the right to claim benefit as individuals. Although the prospects for this are probably rather more remote than for individual taxation (because of the cost) the demand is not confined just to the Women's Liberation Movement. A House of Lords Committee came out in favour of an individually based supplementary benefits scheme as it felt that 'the concept of aggregation is in many ways outdated' (Select Committee on the European Communites, 1977).

CONCLUSION

'Income is a means of access to a social system. The significance of low income is that it restricts such access' (DHSS/
SBC, 1977). This observation by the Supplementary Benefits
Commission applies to families and to individuals within families. Income maintenance policies are crucial in determining
the life chances of families and in helping to shape internal
relationships within them. We lack, in Britain, a coherent
income maintenance policy for families, and the living standards of families, and not just low-income families, have
suffered as a result. In this chapter I have tried to argue
the case for a more positive income maintenance policy based
on an acceptance of the changing position of women and of the
community's responsibility towards parents and others with the
care of dependants. Such policies need to be developed in
the context of a wider family policy which embraces in particular employment opportunities and the provision of community
facilities. We are, at present, a long way from such a
family policy.

Chapter 24

Families and personal social services

Bill Jordan

INTRODUCTION

In the past two decades the personal social services have been
an important battleground for rival ideologies in social
policy and a great deal of the conflict has centred on the
family. The diversification of family patterns that has
occurred during this same period has contributed to the conflict; yet the main issues have been about long-standing
problems of the family's relationship with the State; of
their mutual rights and obligations; of the benefits and
costs of intervention. In practice, social services have
been influenced towards greater sensitivity to the diverse
needs of families; but they have also been very heavily influenced by political perceptions of the perils of family
breakdown, the evils of depravity and the dangers of dependence. Thus there has recently been movement in two directions - towards an increased awareness of and responsiveness
towards the new phenomena of the period, but also towards a
paternalistic or authoritarian reaction to old problems, and
away from some of the more promising developments of the post-
war era. Neither change has been universal and both are hard
to quantify, yet they are discernible trends.

In the early 1960s the political debate was low-key, and
centred on the Labour Party's perception of the need to make
local authority personal services less fragmented, and more
focused on families, rather than handicapped individuals; on
prevention rather than patching up; and on community rather
than institutional care. This debate was overtaken by a
much more passionate one about a series of traditional dilemmas of social policy. The 'rediscovery of poverty' posed
questions about the provision of selective and discretionary
benefits and services; rising juvenile crime rates about law
and order; rising divorce rates about family integrity and

financial obligations; and above all, increased publicity for injuries to children about family violence. Every one of these issues had important implications for the shape and style of the unified local authority social services departments which were created in 1971.

In retrospect, the 1970s appear as the decade in which the personal social services overstretched themselves. Social work expanded in response to failures in the major social services, and to new social problems; but it did so precisely at the time when the post-war consensus on social policy was breaking down. Public opinion was hardening against welfare beneficiaries; the political parties were polarising on ideological lines. Even if the major services had pursued far more energetic programmes - new provision for the unemployed and for single-parent families, more generous child benefits, better support for working mothers - and social workers had thus been relieved of heavy responsibilities for propping up the long-term disadvantaged, it is doubtful whether they could have done justice to new powers and increased expectations at the same time as adapting to the demands of far larger organisations. Faced with all these problems simultaneously, and progressively starved of new resources, their failures have become highly visible.

Even so, many new projects have been developed, introducing flexibility, diversity or increased sensitivity into provision for client groups. But these initiatives have tended to be small scale and local.

SOCIAL WORK AND FAMILIES; COERCION OR CO-OPERATION?

The primary aim of those who set up the Seebohm Committee was the creation of a *family* social work service. In the early 1960s many social workers were confident of their ability to improve the quality of life for a wide variety of families under stress, by offers of help in the form of services and counselling. The child-care service in particular enjoyed the patronage of leading Labour politicians and was held in fairly high public esteem. Social workers from all the State services (and the voluntary sector) were united in the belief that support for the family was the major policy goal.

Traditionally, State services had provided substitute care for those deprived of normal family life, and they had only gradually and cautiously moved into 'preventive' work with families, aimed at forestalling the crises that brought vulnerable individuals into public care. All were agreed that too often people of all ages were admitted to long-term institutional care when better services to families could have

avoided this outcome. Institutions were seen as objection-
able on both humanitarian and economic grounds; by deperson-
alising their inmates in sheltered environments, they made
them helpless, and severed their links with the outside community, necessitating years of expensive provision. But it was
recognised that, in the vast majority of cases, the only
viable alternative to institutional care was care by the
family.

Social workers may have underestimated the difficulties of
offering effective help to families caring for handicapped or
disturbed individuals. Moroney (1975), among others, has
shown that the State has always found it much easier to offer
care or support to individuals living outside families than to
those living in them. The ethic of family responsibility is
almost as strong as the work ethic, and is enshrined in the
way in which a great many welfare benefits are given. It is
usually expressed in terms of an expectation of the man as
breadwinner to provide financially for the whole of the family
living under his roof, out of his earnings from work; and for
the woman to look after the home, unaided, doing all the
domestic tasks. Higher rates of unemployment and of marriage
breakdown tend to raise anxiety about these norms and to harde
harden public attitudes to those who depend on State provision. Even when financial assistance is relatively generous,
expectations of role performance may actually become more
rigid.

Although social workers are nominally committed to a much
more flexible approach they are almost certainly more influenced by these stereotypes than they care to recognise.
Michael Power's (   ) research in a seaside town in the west
country suggests, for instance, that social workers offer more
time and more services to old people living alone than to
those living with relatives. Yet he also found that those
living in families were not only much frailer, and thus more
in need of services, but also significantly lonelier. Something about the ethic of privacy, some notion that to need
help is a concession to failure, made it much harder to give
(and also to receive) help in cases where old people were
living with sons or daughters. Only when circumstances
became intolerable and the need was for total, institutional
care, were requests for help unequivocally made and acted
upon. This same ethic also influenced the amount of help
given by volunteers, as well as professionals.

A second difficulty facing the new services was that they
had to deal with both disadvantage and deviance. This raised
an age-old dilemma of social policy - the distinction between
the deserving and the undeserving. The post-war Welfare
State had attempted to banish this issue by defining universal

minimum standards.   The 1948 Children Act was the outstanding piece of legislation that incorporated this spirit into the personal social services.   But it was concerned almost exclusively with removing considerations of 'less eligibility' from substitute care for children.   Since then, attempts to extend a similar attitude to client groups in community (i.e. mainly family) care have been more equivocal.   In the case of the mentally ill and handicapped (Mental Health Act, 1959) and the physically handicapped (Chronically Sick and Disabled Persons Act, 1970), neither the resources nor the planned social work thrust were forthcoming to match the intentions of the legislation.   In fact since 1971 less and less work in the mental health field has been done by area social workers, who have easiest access to families, and more by workers from hospital settings.   But it has been in the field of child care that the spectre of deviance has most haunted social work in recent years.   As problems have come to be defined more in terms of juvenile delinquency or parental inadequacy than in terms of family stress, so interventions have been seen less as help and more as control.   The ideal of a universalistic, preventive service to families, aimed at families with children 'at risk' of court appearances or of coming into care through marital disharmony, has been largely replaced by a service which aims at protecting children perceived as being 'at risk' of abuse by their parents.

The original conception of a family service depended on co-operation between local authorities and parents, a sharing of the problems of bringing up difficult children.   Nothing could be more fatal to such an aim than theories about delinquency or family functioning that defined certain children and parents as bad or destructive and emphasised the need to control them.   Clearly, social workers had always recognised that such children and families existed, and that it was part of their task to identify them and take decisive action;   but this had always been seen as a minor rather than a major aspect of their function.   During the 1970s a number of changes, firstly in the political climate and then in public demands on social workers, fundamentally altered the balance between these aspects of the role.   In the process, they made it much more difficult for social workers to co-operate and share with families over child-care tasks.

Following the reorganisation of local authority services many experienced social workers were absorbed into managerial posts;   others were given caseloads which included clients from specialisms with which they were unfamiliar;   and there were many new and inexperienced workers appointed.   Consequently standards of practice in many fields, including child care, may well have fallen.   However, the outcry which

followed the Maria Colwell scandal and subsequent tragedies
has meant that adaptation to these changes has taken the
direction of more drastic intervention in families, more
willingness to remove children from parents and to use court
orders to keep them in public care.   There is very little
evidence to suggest that 'child abuse' has increased; what
has happened is that its definition has been extended so as to
embrace a wide range of situations in which there is family
conflict.

The Maria Colwell case was crucial in this development.
Her death did not become a public scandal when it occurred, or
even when her stepfather was convicted of causing it; it
attracted the media's attention from the day when Sir Keith
Joseph, as Secretary of State for Health and Social Security,
set up an enquiry into it.   At the time he linked a speech
about the enquiry with his notion of a 'cycle of deprivation'
- the idea that an identifiable group of inadequate parents
were responsible for transferring problems of poverty and mal-
adjustment to the next generation.   The theory encouraged
social workers to seek out such families, and break the cycle
by rescuing children from them.   It was undoubtedly true that
in the Maria Colwell case itself, and in many others, social
workers had been guilty of poor judgment, woolly thinking and
shoddy practice in the question of ties between ambivalent or
rejecting natural parents and their children.   However, it is
equally true that social workers had much to learn about the
delicate tasks of helping well-motivated but over-stressed
parents do better for their children.   An emphasis on rescue
might improve standards in the first kind of situation, but
not in the second.   Sir Keith Joseph (1979) has since
declared that the cycle of deprivation does not exist, and
moved on to other things; but his colleagues still denounce
inadequate parents in still more condemnatory terms.   The
changes in public attitudes heralded by these events have influenced social work practice far beyond the modest changes of
the 1975 Children Act.

The expansion - and elasticity - of official definitions of
child abuse are illustrated by the numbers and variations in
'At Risk' cases on local registers.   East Sussex, with a
population of 660,000 has 1,500 children on its register.
Somerset, with a population of about 410,000 has 30 children
on its register.   Similarly, Olive Stevenson and Christine
Hallett (1977) found no demographic explanations for the fact
that some areas had fewer than ten and others more than 100
case conferences on non-accidental injury in 1976.   Clearly
reactions to the changed climate of opinion vary from area to
area, but there has been a general trend towards a policy of
watchful suspicion of 'known' parents.

Another integral part of the strategy behind a family service was the notion of voluntary agreements between parents
and social workers over plans for helping with difficult situations.   This included voluntary short-term receptions of
children into care.   But with the advent of child abuse as a
major element in child-care work, this voluntary aspect has
waned.   Jean Packman's research (1968) in one city found that
compulsory emergency removals of children from their families
(Place of Safety Orders) were considered in half the cases
where decisions were made about whether or not to receive a
child into care; and that they were used in a third of those
actually received.   Compulsion of this kind was considered
even when children or parents were asking for the reception
into care.   'Child abuse' was mentioned as an issue over the
whole range of children, including adolescents, and even where
such violence as occurred was by child to parent.

It is easy to see how social workers, harried by public
opinion for excessive permissiveness towards bad parents,
should seek to take decisive action and to guard against
changes of mind by parents or children at a future date.
However, compulsory measures, espeically those involving precipitate removal from home without preparation, inevitably
polarise attitudes and jeopardise co-operation, at least in
the short run.   No wonder that Jean Packman found that some
parents referred to the social services staff as 'S.S.' or
'Nazis', and had little trust in them.

Similarly, she found that social workers sought court care
orders on children, even when parents had requested or consen-
ted to care, nominally to allow better control over planning
for the child's future.   However, it is difficult to resist
the conclusion that workers who have frequently been criticised for faulty judgment are not seeking official endorsement
through the court for their decisions to remove children; and
perhaps also insuring against changes of heart by their successors (social workers change jobs about every 18 months)
rather than by parents.   Research suggests that the increased
number of care orders has not reduced the numbers of 'children
who wait' in institutions while plans for alternative family
placements are considered; and Jean Packman's six-month
follow-up on her sample suggested that children received into
care suffered significantly more changes of environment than
those who remained with their families.

Another aim of policy with the creation of a family service
was the reduction of compulsory orders, and especially those
leading to institutional placements, in cases of juvenile
delinquency.   New policies which were to be linked with the
1969 Children and Young Persons Act aimed at providing a more
comprehensive counselling services to families and a wider

range of group activities for young people, as well as more
family placements.   Spencer Millham and his colleagues (1978)
have shown that this philosophy was already being overtaken in
the 1960s by a more punitive one, and that an emphasis on
security for young offenders had ousted the optimistic child-
care approach by the time the new act (in its truncated form)
was implemented.   Certainly fears about a rising tide of
juvenile delinquency contributed towards trends in sentencing
in the 1970s, but social workers did little to counteract
these tendencies, and may well have reinforced them.   Care
orders are now made on younger children with fewer previous
offences;   there are more children under 16 in prisons, borstals and detention centres than ever before, and a whole new
type of secure provision for children has been created, partly
on the insistence of social workers.   Millham et al. show
that the distinguishing feature of children in secure units is
not the degree of family disturbance or the number or seriousness of their previous offences;   it is the number of unsuccessful placements they experienced in their earlier careers
in public care.

     Despite these failures to achieve the aims of those who
sought a family service, social work with families has increased;   indeed the growth of interventions by social workers
in family situations has been one of the most marked features
of the period since the mid-1960s.   It is the focus of interventions that has changed.   As far as can be measured, the
major factor in the expansion of the work seems to have been a
vast increase in the number of contacts concerned with the
provision of practical and material benefits - small amounts
of financial aid, food vouchers, clothes, aids and adaptations, telephones, concessionary bus passes, home helps, play-
group places and so on.   Similarly, increasing numbers of
people refer themselves to social services for advice about
other forms of benefits, or because they are unable to get
satisfaction from other services.   Research indicates that an
increasing proportion of ordinary people see social services
departments as a first point of contact in *all* questions of
material as opposed to relationship) problems.   This trend
was partly anticipated by the Seebohm Committee, and has been
encouraged by many politicians (particularly in the Labour
Party) and by administrators.   It is clear that the provision
of certain services is an integral part of social work and of
effective family work.   What has never been satisfactorily
defined is the range and scope of services best provided by
social workers in a generic department.   For many years
social services have been struggling to deal with the administrative failures of other, larger services - housing, social
security, education, health, even the gas and electricity

boards - and as their responsibilities have become wider and
vaguer, their skills in relationship problems have been dilu-
ted.   The all-embracing welfare role also contributes -
especially in times of economic constraint - to a mutual
stereotyping between clients and social workers that has unfortunate resemblances with relationships between claimants
and staff in social security offices.

I am suggesting, therefore, that local authority social
work with families consists mainly of short-term contacts
about practical matters; but that there is another important
sector of long-term cases, in which a growing number have a
strongly coercive element, concerned with the compulsory removal of children.   Both types of contact are concentrated
disproportionately on families which are already disadvantaged
and the coercive kind particularly on one-parent families and
those where a parent was himself in care.   Poverty or overcrowding often contribute to an initial referral of a family
for practical assistance; in a proportion of cases, these
same factors can play a part in a later decision to remove
children to substitute homes.   It is therefore adversity
rather than diversity that has contributed to this process.

Most of the diversification in family patterns, and changes
in the quality of relationships, that have taken place in the
past two decades have been based on relative affluence and a
degree of geographical and social mobility.   Many writers
have commented on two features of these changes; the fact
that couples are now much more aware of their responsibilities
to each other and to themselves to lead fulfilled and meaningful lives; and the fact that childhoods are now longer and
more embellished by parental attention and concern.   The
family life of the poor has probably changed less than that of
other income groups; disadvantaged families in inner city
districts (whether they are immigrants from the Commonwealth
or the country) are more likely to retain features of the
lifestyles described by Philippe Ariès in his studies of pre-
industrial society.   Young marriage; segregated marital
roles; short, unprotected childhoods; face-to-face relationships in small neighbourhoods, are all characteristic of the
culture of these areas.   When these are found in conjunction
with run-down environments, high unemployment and high rates
of delinquency, hostility to officialdom is also likely.   (In
Jean Packman's sample, most parents of children coming into
care were not people who had drifted into the area, but also
had been born and bred in the city.   Significantly, however,
many had been moved away from their district of origin, and
others were on bad terms with their own family of origin.)

Such families pose for social services departments all the
dilemmas that have faced official policy-makers since the Poor

Law.   It is not surprising that, in an age when politicians
have reverted to the oldest traditions in social policy,
social workers should have become alternately paternalistic in
their provision of assistance, or punitively authoritarian.
However, it is sad that a gulf of suspicion and fear should
have developed between social workers and families in need at
a time when there was promise of real progress towards the
kind of helping through sharing that alone can overcome these
barriers.

The personal social services can never conquer Beveridge's
giants;   indeed, in so far as they try to compensate for the
failures of social security, housing, health, or education
they may sometimes compound the inadequacies of those services, and leave their clients worse off than ever.   As local
authority departments have expanded, a new category of 'welfare cases', discarded by the major agencies, has come into
existence, and is forced to depend on social workers for more
and more of its needs.

The only hope for better services to families lies in the
cultivation of skills and a style which is *more* personal,
rather than more official, as generic welfare provision has
inevitably become.   As Pinker (   ) has pointed out, the
more intimate the problem which requires help, the greater the
stigma.   Stigma can only be overcome in two ways: either the
recipient of State aid identifies strongly with others who
need the same help (something it is very hard for those who
need personal services to do);   or he assimilates the helper
into categories of people from whom he willingly accepts
assistance - family, friends and neighbours, and possibly the
family doctor.   The representative of an impersonal authority, a social worker, is hard to see in this light.

Yet progress has been made in a number of significant
areas.   One of these lies in the recognition of how increased
diversity in the patterns of better-off families can benefit
the children of the most disadvantaged.   Traditionally there
was a rather sharp demarcation between adoption - always seen
as the most satisfactory form of substitute care, but restricted mainly to healthy white babies - and fostering, a more
partial and often temporary substitution, considered suitable
for a far wider range of children living away from their
parents.   With the reduced availability of illegitimate
babies placed for adoption, local authorities and would-be
adopters have co-operated in the placement of an increasing
number of handicapped, coloured and older children - with encouraging results.   At the same time, the 1975 Children Act
has encouraged long-term foster parents to adopt their foster
children, and given them more security in their difficult
task.   Since foster parents have formed an association, their

demands for more recognition of their needs have begun to be heeded.   Gradually both adoption and fostering have come to be perceived in less narrow and restricted terms, doubtless in line with a greater flexibility and self-awareness amongst couples who seek to care for others' children.

Paradoxically, one of the more adventurous developments in fostering has stemmed from one of the greatest failures of the social services departments - the family placement of diffi-cult and delinquent adolescents.   In Kent a pioneering pro-ject has been set up to find placements for young people aged between 14 and 18 who would otherwise have gone to borstals, mental hospitals or secure units.   An entirely new source of foster parents was tapped - families from a variety of social backgrounds, willing to provide a temporary base for disturbed and destructive teenagers, to stick with them through inevit-able troubles and testings-out.   After five years, the suc-cess rates of the Kent project compare very favourably with those of institutions.   Nancy Hazel, who ran the scheme, draws attention to the much greater responsibility and share in decision making given to foster parents by the project, and suggests that it attracted a new breed to the role - articu-late, argumentative people, willing to do battle on behalf of adolescents.   Significantly, nearly all the foster mothers had had full-time jobs and enjoyed them - a contrast with the expectation of home-based foster mothers for younger children.

There have also been some successes in schemes for sharing the care of the handicapped.   In spite of the difficulties mentioned at the start of this chapter, ways have been found to overcome the traditional barriers to effective co-operation between the family and the State - in both social services departments and the health service.   Thus, for instance, in Exeter Dr Brimblecombe's (1974) combination of total care in the first weeks of life of the handicapped child, with subse-quent day care, and short-term admissions (plus groups for parents, volunteers and a home visiting service) has reduced the number of handicapped children in long-term hospital beds in his area to a sixth of the national average.   In Somerset, the social services department has set up a scheme for short-term fostering of mentally handicapped children, where parents make their own arrangements and place the child themselves, although the local authority pays.

It is significant that such innovations are mainly concer-ned with the handicapped.   It seems that social services can more easily share responsibility for a group which is clearly 'deserving';   also, because the families of the handicapped come from the whole social spectrum, their demands for more flexible services are more articulate and their own responses more in tune with social work thinking.   The parents of

children in care, or under consideration for care (whether or
not they are delinquent) are far more likely to raise difficult dilemmas.   By their ambivalence or hostility, by their
neediness in other respects (poverty, housing), by being, in
fact, 'welfare cases', they raise a number of traditional
spectres about deviance and dependence.   Thus at a time when
policy in respect of handicap is moving towards partnership of
an increasingly mutual kind, child-care provision is moving in
just the opposite direction.
   It is instructive to compare the fields of mental illness
and child care.   Madness, has, after all, been traditionally
regarded as a form of deviance rather than as a handicap, and
the insane have been at least as stigmatised as have the
children in our workhouses.   Yet policy has consistently
moved towards making admissions to mental hospital more voluntary and less coercive;   towards involving the family in decisions about admission;   towards community rather than institutional care.   While progress has been slow, it has always
been in this direction.   By contrast, in the past ten years
child-care policy has been the opposite way, with all the
emphasis on court orders and departmental control.   Until
social workers can find ways to build up mutual trust between
themselves and parents, genuine sharing and co-operation
(which has been attempted quite successfully with potentially
violent parents in small-scale projects by the NSPCC) is unlikely to develop.

CONCLUSION

While families have been diversifying, local authority social
services have coalesced.   Neither process has been universal.
Some families have remained stubbornly traditional in their
patterns and in their problems - especially those of the
'rough' working class.   The economic tide has been against
them and the adversity this has brought, together with a
series of administrative changes in the major services, has
driven this group into more frequent contact with social work.
But it was a new style of social work that they met - more
ready to provide material resources, but also applying more
critical and anxious standards to the care of their children.
Crises in such families - whether in the form of marital disharmony between a young couple, or rejection of a difficult
adolescent - are now more likely to be perceived in terms of
a stereotype of 'abuse' and to lead to statutory intervention
and court orders for care.
   Not all departments have become equally heavy handed in
this respect, and not all their work has been conducted in

this spirit.   Some voluntary agencies have opposed these trends and social workers in health services have developed along separate lines.   However, official policy can be seen as an additional factor discriminating against 'rough' poor families, against single parents and against immigrants, tending to standardise and restrict their lives still further, and denying them opportunities available to more fortunate groups.

If the aim of policy has been to extend the spirit of the universalistic Welfare State to provision in the personal social services, it has so far failed.   If anything, the stigma attached to pauperism and delinquency has spilled over into work with deprived children, so that the voluntarism and constructive spirit that characterised child-care services has become tainted with the suspicion and resentment that accompany poor relief, and the control of delinquency and violence.

It may even be that this is part of the price we pay for more freedom and diversity in the family patterns of our more affluent citizens.   Greater interest in family life, higher expectations of child care and parenthood, also raise levels of anxiety.   As middle-class marriages break up more frequently, such anxiety may well be projected onto convenient working-class scapegoats.   As we struggle - often painfully, and with many mistakes - to resolve the conflicts and difficulties of changes in the pattern of family life, we run the risk of exacting a tithe in persecution from already disadvantaged people.

Chapter 25

A family cause? Voluntary bodies, pressure groups and politics

Malcolm Wicks

The major aim of this chapter is to discuss the way in which
changing patterns of family life have been matched by the
activities of different kinds of voluntary organisations and
pressure groups concerned with the family.   Do such organisations illustrate increasing diversity, conflicting needs and
therefore a necessity for a variety of policy responses to the
family or, alternatively, the need for a coherent campaign on
behalf of families and, perhaps, the need for a family movement in Britain?

The concept of a family policy has been discussed by Roy
Parker in Chapter 18.   The likelihood of promoting a family
policy depends on a variety of factors, but a potentially
important one is the extent to which the 1980s will witness
the development of a 'family lobby' or family movement in the
UK, strong enough to exercise some pressure on governments.
There was a development of interest in this idea in the late
1970s, but is a 'family lobby' in Britain viable?   The idea
of a family movement begs a number of important questions
which relate to issues discussed in earlier chapters.   Given
the range of different family types, is there any such thing
as an identifiable 'family interest'?   And do the range of
voluntary bodies, pressure groups and other organisations that
represent families have more common interests than differences?   Can such bodies form the basis for a family movement or
do they simply reflect the plurality of interests and concerns
in contemporary Britain?   In order to consider these questions, it is useful to look at the range of bodies that are
concerned with family life in Britain.

There are certainly a large number of such bodies.   For
example over 100 organisations took the trouble to submit evidence to the Finer Committee on one-parent families. (1)   Six
years earlier some 138 bodies (excluding local authorities)
gave evidence to the Seebohm Committee on Personal Social

Services whose terms of reference charged it 'to consider what changes are desirable to secure an effective family service'. (2)   A recent national conference organised by the National Children's Home in 1978 on Family Life was attended by approximately 300 delegates from a wide range of organisations.   What sorts of bodies are concerned with family issues?

Some are concerned with specific family types; some with women's issues or children's welfare; and some with particular problems affecting families.

FAMILY ORGANISATIONS

There is a diverse range of bodies representing the needs and interests of different family types.   Some of these bodies have membership specifically drawn from the family type in question, some are pressure groups campaigning on their behalf, while others are professional groups.   Some examples can be given.

Today approximately one in eight of all children are in one-parent families.   In 1918 the National Council for the Unmarried Mother and Her Child was established and this became the National Council for One-Parent Families in 1973 reflecting the wider concern about and the changed character of single parenting.   In addition to its work for single mothers and single pregnant women, the National Council assists 'separated and divorced parents, widows and wives or husbands of long standing hospital patients and those serving long prison sentences - anyone in fact, with the problem of caring for a child or children on their own'. (3)

At the grass-roots level, Gingerbread was started ten years ago as a self-help organisation for single parents and there are today nearly 400 groups throughout the country.   Gingerbread aims 'to help parents and children from one parent families who are in need of information and advice and/or who are isolated, lonely and in need of companionship' and 'to educate the public about, and to seek to improve the social and economic circumstances of one-parent families'. (4)

A number of bodies are concerned with children who have no natural family of their own or who are permanently or temporarily separated from their parents.   An example of a professional body in this field is the British Association of Adoption and Fostering Agencies.   There are also a number of voluntary organisations who provide residential care for children and these include Dr Barnardo's and the National Children's Home.

Some are concerned about the position of parents with

children in care and Parents Aid, a self-help group, was
formed in 1979, while the Family Rights Group, made up of
social workers, lawyers and other professionals, aims to
improve the law in this area.

Although many 'family' organisations are concerned primarily with families with children, this is not true of all
bodies.   Thus the National Association of the Childless is a
self-help body 'formed to give support and information to
people undergoing or seeking fertility investigations, to give
advice on alternative ways of parenting such as adoption and
fostering, and helping in finding ways of living a full,
useful and satisfying life without children'. (5)

Further, there are organisations which are primarily concerned with the welfare of the old, and who are consequently
interested in the extended family and its caring role.   Age
Concern is a prime example, as is the National Council for the
Single Woman and her Dependants founded in 1965 to 'help
single women who have or have had the care of elderly or
infirm dependents'.   Its aim is to 'urge greater consideration in social security, health, welfare and fiscal policies
for these women and their dependents', (6) and highlights the
problems of the carers, as well as those being cared for.

Alongside organisations which primarily work for particular
family types, there are a number of bodies which stress the
rights of individual family members.   The Modern Women's
Movement has been particularly involved in issues revolving
around the family.   Locally and nationally, women have campaigned for better policies on health, child care, education,
housing and a variety of issues which are essential for a
better life for families.   Additionally, and in line with the
feminist rejection of the traditional, patriarchal family,
many women have also embraced such causes as better contraceptive and abortion facilities, wider career opportunities and
more realistic maternity leave.   In recent times there has
also been increased recognition of the role of men in family
life.   Families Need Fathers is one organisation which
stresses the importance and rights of fathers within the
family.

The welfare of children is the focus for activities from a
number of other bodies.   Historically a concern to protect
children from exploitative employers, to safeguard children
from parental cruelty and to provide educational and other
welfare services has been a powerful force behind much social
legislation.   Today there is still much activity in this area
and bodies such as the National Society for the Prevention of
Cruelty to Children bring their own, distinctive perspective
to family issues.

Many of the new breed of pressure groups arose from a

concern about one particular issue, such as poverty or homelessness. Such groups therefore seldom have a direct interest in the family per se, but rather campaign around specific
aspects of family life.

There is much activity, for example, on behalf of families
with children under the age of five. The Pre-School Playgroups Association is an example of a voluntary body in this
field and it exists 'to help parents to understand and provide
for the needs of their young children'. (7) A number of such
bodies are members of the Voluntary Organisations Liaison
Council for Under Fives whose membership covers a wide range
of organisations, from large national bodies to small local-
based groups. Several organisations have in common the wish
to promote better relations and understanding between families
and social institutions. The National Association of the
Welfare of Children in Hospital, for example, is concerned
about the harmful effects on children of a stay in hospital
involving separation from parents. NAWCH aims 'to persuade
hospitals that parents have a necessary and practical part to
play in the care of their sick child'. (8)

Other bodies aim to improve the relationship between
schools and families, parents and teachers. School Parent
Teacher Associations are an obvious example. Many of the
special interest, or single issue, groups work on behalf of
children who suffer mental or physical handicap. Over forty
national voluntary bodies with such interests gave evidence to
the Warnock Committee of enquiry into the Education of Handicapped Children and Young People. (9) They included the
Association of All Special Impaired Children, MIND, National
Deaf Children's Society and the Spastics Society.

One of the most important of the 'single issue' groups to
emerge in the 1960s was the Child Poverty Action Group. It
'works to draw attention to the problems of those in poverty
and to advise them on their rights'. (10) It is an example
of one of those pressure groups which, without a large membership or substantial resources, depends to a large extent on
publicising its cause through the mass media and exerting
influence on parliament and government.

DIVERSE NEEDS AND DIFFERENT OBJECTIVES

All the groups mentioned have an interest in 'the family', but
it would be naive to immediately assume that they are all,
somehow, allies, or potential recruits to some hoped-for
'family cause'. In fact the vast majority of the bodies are
concerned with particular aspects of family life, the needs of
women or children within the family, specific moral questions

relating to the family, or with the government services or professions who deliver help to families.   With this range of organisations there is great scope for disagreement about what the family needs, what is 'good' for the family and, indeed, what is meant by 'the family'.

One set of differences of opinion relates to important value questions.   Much of the current interest in the family concerns the impact of a wide range of social, economic, legal and other changes on family life.   Some 'family' organisations, particularly those which are church based, fear that such changes as increasing divorce, growing numbers of one-parent families and even more and more mothers going out to work, are somehow 'bad' for family life.   Others will view such changes as 'inevitable' or desirable developments which institutions, such as government, have to adjust their policies towards.   Given such differences, there will often be disputes between different organisations, particularly at times of proposed law reform.

Earlier we reviewed the range of organisations campaigning on behalf of different family types.   These organisations often have specific objectives relating to the needs of that particular type of family and such bodies will probably be motivated more by their particular concern, than by any general family cause.   In addition, some bodies have interests or objectives that might actually be in conflict with the interests and objectives of other bodies.   Bodies concerned with such diverse matters as fostering, parents rights vis-à-vis their children in care and the position of one-parent families may not all agree on, say, desirable law reforms or social work procedures.   When such bodies do agree, for example on the importance of uprating social security benefits for children, there will be competition for resources with other bodies campaigning for, say, the needs of the elderly.

We noted earlier that several organisations focus on the rights of particular family members - children, women, or fathers.   The needs of children will usually be synonymous with those of families as a whole, but within particular families there may be a conflict of interests.   This may lead to conflict between different organisations.

Concern for the welfare of children has traditionally been a paternalistic one, based on assumptions that children cannot (or should not) act for themselves or exercise their own choices to any substantial extent.   However, in more recent times, a concern for children's rights (rights that the children might exercise in opposition to parents, teachers and others with authority over them) has emerged.   In 1979, for example, the National Council for Civil Liberties published a 'Guide to Legal Rights for Young People' which had a chapter on You and your family. (11)   Recent debates about contraceptive advice for girls under the age of 16 - and whether or not doctors should inform parents in such cases - shows that this is a controversial area.

Another area of conflict concerns the role and status of women in family and society.   Many feminists view the renewed interest in the family with some scepticism.   They feel that it, in part, stems from those who wish to reverse the feminist tide.   Feminists themselves argue that 'the family' can be an oppressive institution and one that awards a low status to women and is often based on an assumption that the male is the family head - an assumption supported by much social policy. Clearly feminists will often take up a different position on many questions than that of bodies concerned with protecting traditional concepts of family.   Abortion, for example, sharply divides those who call for 'a woman's right to choose' from Catholic organisations, or other bodies concerned with the 'rights' of the unborn child.   And whereas some bodies will campaign for more and better facilities for the under-fives in order to allow women to have the choice of working, other groups will talk of the threat to 'family life' posed by employment trends among mothers.

'Family and State' is another controversial area. Although any family movement in Britain would not be concerned exclusively with State action (influencing industry could also be an important aim), persuading government to take full account of family needs will almost certainly be at the heart of any family movement.   Historically, voluntary organisations - and those concerned about enhancing the welfare of the family - have often disagreed about the extent to which government should intervene (through regulations, provision of services, or cash benefits) to aid families.   The introduction of free school meals was opposed by the Charity Organisation Society, for example, on the grounds that it was better to allow 'the sins of the parents to be visited on the children than to impair the principle of the solidarity of the family and run the risk of permanently demoralising large numbers of the population'. (12)

This antipathy to the State finds echoes today with some organisations being deeply suspicious of 'too much' State 'interference' with family life.   Many others argue that support can often be given more effectively (and with less dangerous consequences) by voluntary bodies.   However, the pressure groups that arose in the 1960s and 1970s often have a radically different approach to the State.   They call for *more* State support for families and campaign for adequate cash benefits, better State education and improved local authority housing.   Furthermore, the growth of such pressure groups has been associated with the realisation that the institutions of the Welfare State were not successfully tackling the old problem such as poverty and poor housing; that inequalities in education and other areas have not been eradicated; and that the complexities of the modern Welfare State often presented their own problems for individuals who consequently require organisational support. These groups also often have different styles of campaigning from the more traditional voluntary bodies who fight shy of the political nature of pressure groups. Any 'family movement' could not easily ignore this fundamental question about the State's role and if such a movement were to become effective, it would risk losing support from some quarters.

IS A FAMILY MOVEMENT VIABLE?

There are, then, some formidable obstacles standing in the way of building a family movement in Britain. They may not be insuperable, but certainly any movement would need to plan its strategy carefully.

There are, however, a number of forces that give some support to the idea of a unified family cause and which offer hope to those seeking to promote the idea of a family movement in Britain. Although certainly not the only issue, the financial position of families with children has caused growing concern and it is useful to present in a little detail a review of how this debate has developed in recent years.

INCOME SUPPORT FOR FAMILIES - A BRIEF CASE STUDY

In recent years, the debate about financial support for families with children has become increasingly important and has been a significant element in the wider discussion about 'family policy'. It has also given impetus to those campaigning for some kind of family lobby in Britain.

The Child Poverty Action Group (CPAG) has been a key organisation during this period. As its name makes clear, it is concerned primarily with supporting poor families. Formed in 1965, CPAG spent much of its early years campaigning for schemes such as 'claw-back' (increasing family allowances while simultaneously reducing child tax allowances), which would benefit the poor, rather than all families with children. A wish for selectivity also directed government thinking - witness the introduction of family income supplement in 1971.

During the 1970s, however, the emphasis in thinking and

policy formulation started to shift towards the need to safeguard and enhance the living standards of all families with
children.   In 1972 a Green Paper on tax credits proposed the
unification of family allowances and child tax allowances into
a new child credit. (13)   This raised an important question
concerning the distribution of family income.   Should this
credit be paid to the father (who currently received the benefit of the tax allowance through his pay packet) or to the
mother (who normally collected the family allowance)?

A campaign was mobilised in favour of paying the credit to
the mother and a number of organisations sent in evidence to
the House of Commons Select Committee which was considering
tax credits. (14)   They included the Women's National Commission, the Women's National Advisory Committee of the Conservative Party, CPAG, the British Association of Social Workers
and the Fawcett Society.   It was also significant that the
TUC's evidence was in favour of making the payment to the
mother.

The proposed tax credit scheme fell with the Conservative
administration at the 1974 general election.   However, the
idea of amalgamating family allowances and child tax allowances had gained widespread support and in 1975 the Labour government proposed a unified child benefit which would be paid
to mothers.   Introducing the second reading of the Child
Benefit Bill, Mrs Barbara Castle, then Secretary of State for
Social Services, told the House of Commons that 'It may be
premature to talk of giving the wife and mother her own wage,
but she certainly needs control of her own budget if the
family is to be fed and clothed.' (15)

During the first half of 1976 a not unfamiliar battle raged
in Whitehall between the DHSS and the Treasury about the level
of child benefit. (16)   In the Cabinet discussions on this
question, a new question was introduced, however, which rapidly gained in importance.   This concerned the effect of with-
drawing child tax allowances (therefore reducing fathers' net
pay) on the negotiations that were taking place for a Phase
Three of incomes policy.   For this reason Mr Callaghan had
strong doubts about the scheme.

Despite the fact that the TUC had always supported the
switch from 'wallet to purse' - a switch that was fundamental
to the policy - one factor which strongly influenced the
Cabinet was the reported view of certain TUC leaders.   As the
Cabinet minutes of the time record: 'on being informed of the
reduction in take-home pay, which the child benefit scheme
would involve, the TUC representatives had reacted immediately
and violently against its implementation, irrespective of the
level of benefits which would accompany the reduction in take-
home pay.' (17)   In fact the situation was more complex than

this.   TUC leaders were apparently told by Mr Healey that a
majority of the Cabinet and back-bench opinion was against the
scheme.   This influenced the TUC and its reported reaction
was then used to secure the Cabinet rejection of child benefits!

These anxieties led to the abandonment of the scheme.   As
a 'Sunday Times' story at the time pointed out: 'those most
strongly in favour of the child benefit scheme found themselves not only up against the Treasury in its most penny-
pinching mood; they thought they were up against the Trade
Unions too.   There seemed little choice but to kill the
scheme as quickly as possible.' (18)

There had been some support for child benefits from certain
Cabinet members, back-bench MPs, some trade unionists and a
range of voluntary bodies with an interest in the family, but
it was not enough to save the scheme.   The government's decision provoked opposition, but it was hardly the most burning
issue of the day.   Besides, there was certainly no 'family
movement' to protest.

It took a dramatic article in 'New Society', based very
heavily on, and quoting verbatim from, secret Cabinet minutes
to bring home the full extent of the about-turn on child benefits and the manoeuvrings in Cabinet that led up to it.   The
article, by CPAG's Frank Field, became front-page news and the
pageant that followed included hunts to catch the source of
the Cabinet leak (with policemen roaming the corridors of
power), threatened back-bench revolts, the setting up of a
special TUC-Labour Party Committee to save the scheme and the
mobilisation of a formidable alliance of family groups to campaign for the implementation of child benefits.   Mainly
because of the work of the liaison committee it was eventually
agreed to phase in the child benefit scheme over three years.
However, although its role should not be overestimated, a significant development was the formation of the 'Child Benefits
Now' campaign which included a wide range of organisations -
several of which had campaigned on the issue of who should
draw the child credit.   Its members included the British
Union of Family Organisations, CPAG, FSU, the Fawcett Society,
Gingerbread, Mothers' Union, National Board of Catholic Women,
National Council for One Parent Families, Union of Catholic
Mothers and the Women's Liberation Campaign for Legal and
Financial Independence. (19)

Since the battle over the introduction of child benefits
there seems to have developed a more widespread interest in
the financial circumstances of families with children (and not
just poor families).   Certainly CPAG has felt that the way to
help the poor is through an attempt to utilise what Frank
Field has referred to as the 'sharp elbows of the middle class

in getting the needs of families to the top of the political
agenda'. (20)   At Budget time in recent years many organisations have lobbied the Chancellor for higher child benefits -
Conservative women being an important group in 1980 - and the
new Family Forum has taken up this issue.

The story of child benefits illustrates a number of issues
pertinent to the broader themes of this chapter.   Firstly, it
shows how the specific concern about the position of poor
families has been matched in recent years by a more general
anxiety about the relatively poor financial position of all
families with children.   Secondly, it shows that the question
of the distribution of income within the family is crucial to
the debate.   It is an issue which led many groups to campaign
for child tax credits to go to the mother and later led the
same groups to lobby for child benefits - but its controversial nature was revealed by the anxiety of some trade unionists about the 'wallet to purse' issue.   Finally, this brief
case study shows that, on key issues, a potentially powerful
alliance of voluntary bodies and pressure groups can be built
up and campaign effectively.   This is an important lesson for
those interested in developing an effective family lobby in
Britain.

BUILDING A FAMILY MOVEMENT: PROBLEMS AND OPPORTUNITIES

Earlier in this chapter, it was argued that there were conflicts, existing or potential, among many groups involved with
families and that these presented barriers in the way to forming a family movement in Britain.   However, the child benefit
story shows that, in certain circumstances, alliances can be
formed and they can be successful.   Which issues are likely
to be the unifying ones in the future and which ones will continue to produce divisions?

A common concern of many families, and the bodies that campaign for them, is the way in which government agencies and
bureaucracies relate (or fail to relate) to family needs.
There is a strong sense in which the Welfare State appears to
have grown away from the people whom it should serve: rules
and regulations are made and families have to abide by them;
services are supplied on a 'take it or leave it' basis;   there
is often an absence of choice or 'consumer controls';   the
professional or the official appears to be more important than
the parent, the patient or the client;   there is a failure to
inform, consultation is rare and participation is seldom encouraged;   and benefits grow more complex and more confusing
for families.

These kinds of anxieties have been a developing feature of

British politics in the 1960s and 1970s and they could form a
key theme for any family movement.   For example, might it not
be possible for parents and children to have more say at that
important time when decisions about secondary school allocation are being made?   Should not parents be able to play more
of a part in caring for sick children in hospital?   And
cannot cash benefit provisions be made more intelligible to
families?

Many such issues face families within their communities,
but they also occur at central government level.   Indeed, the
complexity of social security and other benefits is due to the
ad hoc development, by several central government departments,
of different policies over many years.   In principle, then,
there seems to be no reason why a family movement could not
evolve.   But is it likely to in practice?   Enthusiasts point
to the experience of a number of European countries and their
family movements.   However, in Britain there has been an
absence of concern in recent decades about the overall level
of population and arguably many family policies in Europe are
tied up closely with population policies.   Family movements
are also often associated with the overall influence in any
one country of the Roman Catholic church, although this is not
inevitably the case.

It must also be noted that while several issues could unite
families other - more powerful? - factors divide them.   Frank
Field has argued that

British politics have divided on class lines ever since the
early 1920s with the result that it is immensely difficult
for issues which are not class issues to find a place on
the political agenda.   Class issues arise from the vertical distribution of income.   Those who are concerned about
families wish to promote a debate on the horizontal distribution of income - an issue which cuts across classes but
which divides along age lines. (21)

There are interesting parallels to be drawn between the
consumer movement and the embryo family movement.   Many of
the same ideas, and similar slogans, have led individuals to
call for a 'voice for the consumer'.   The National Consumer
Council was formed in 1975 and it now holds an annual congress, has a relatively large staff and a London headquarters
ters.   It is based on the belief that, to take two diverse
examples, the person complaining about a defective colour
television and the tenant of the poorly maintained council
flat are both 'consumers' who need effective representation.
This is a perfectly reasonable argument, but despite much
useful work and a string of reports, there are no signs that
the National Consumer Council has been able to stimulate a
genuine consumer movement.   Is this because the differences

between 'consumers' - differences based on social class and attitudes to housing, education, taxation, profit and trade unions and other matters - are more fundamental, more meaningful, than their common cause as consumers?

Can the family movement be any more effective than the consumer movement? This partly depends on membership. A successful family movement does not just need to recruit into its ranks a reasonable number of interested voluntary bodies, pressure group leaders and concerned academics and politicians, but also, and in the longer term this is probably more critical, it depends on genuine family support for such a campaign. As Michael Fogarty and Barbara Rodgers have noted in Chapter 1: 'in a country as large as Britain the credibility of a family movement, both nationally and internationally, and in particular its ability to impress both local and national government, would depend on strong grass-roots contacts through a network of local family organisations.' There is, as yet, little sign of a development of this kind of grass-roots activity. However, at national level, there is an embryo family movement in the form of the Family Forum.

THE FAMILY FORUM

The Family Forum is the successor to the British Union of Family Organisations. Under the chairmanship of Peter Bottomley, MP, it seeks to bring together organisations and individuals who share a concern for families. To quote from its earlier literature 'the Family Forum provides a focus for consideration of the relationship between families' needs and impact of policies on family life', and is 'the outcome of increasing concern at the lack of a coherent Family Policy in the UK'. (22) It aims to seek to improve understanding of the evolution of family patterns and lifestyles; to provide a focus for the exchange of information between its members at local and national levels, and between policy makers and families. It will pay particular attention to the needs of those who experience social, physical, or financial handicap and aims to be an integral part of the growing family movement with strong links to groups throughout the country.

In practice, much will depend on exactly what kind of body the Family Forum wishes to become. If it is primarily concerned to become literally a forum for the exchange of information and views, this can be a fairly easily implemented strategy and a useful one. However, while useful, this would fall far short of the kind of family movement which others have been seeking and which would be strong enough to impress its claims upon government. However, herein lies the

dilemma, for if the Family Forum is to develop into some kind
of pressure group or 'movement' for all families in Britain,
it will risk losing the support of traditional voluntary
bodies who shy away from 'political action' and will, sooner
or later, require it to spell out the kind of policies which
it is lobbying government to implement.

It is likely that the Family Forum will feel its way cautiously for some time, providing essentially a 'forum' for
individuals and groups, but wherever possible mobilising support around one or two particular issues.   It has already
offered some encouragement to those bodies pressing for higher
child benefits.

CONCLUSION

The late 1970s witnessed a growing interest in 'the family',
and ideas about family policies and family impact statements.
It is too early to say whether this will prove to be a temporary development or whether the interests expressed by politicians and others will develop into moves and policies that
will bring real benefit to families in Britain.   While not
the only factor, the role of voluntary organisations and pressure groups could be a critical factor in deciding which way
it goes.   The idea of developing a 'voice for families' to
match the loud voices that already shout on behalf of big
business, trade unions and many other interests, is an attractive one.   But, behind the rhetoric lie a number of difficult
questions and a number of problems for those seeking to mobilise support for such a campaign.

NOTES

1 DHSS, Report of the Committee on One Parent Families, vol.
   2, Cmnd 5629-1, HMSO, London, 1974, Appendix 1.
2 DHSS, Report of the Committee on Local Authority and
   Allied Personal Social Services, Cmnd 3703, HMSO, London,
   1969, Appendix B.
3 National Council for One Parent Families, leaflet,
4 Ginger, the magazine for one parent families, 'Gingerbread', no. 33, July 1979, p. 24.
5 National Association for the Childless, 'Childless?'
   (leaflet), Birmingham, undated.
6 National Council for the Single Woman and her Dependants,
   leaflet.
7 PPA and its playgroups, Pre-school Playgroups Association,
   1978.

8   National Association for the Welfare of Children in
    Hospital.
9   DES, 'Special Educational Needs', HMSO, London, 1978.
10 Child Poverty Action Group, information and membership
    leaflet.
11 M. Rae, P. Hewitt and B. Hugill, 'First Rights', National
    Council for Civil Liberties, 1979.
12 C.L. Mowat, 'The Charity Organisation Society, 1869-1913',
    Methuen, 1961.
13 Proposals for a Tax Credit System, Cmnd 5116, HMSO,
    London, 1972.
14 Select Committee on Tax-credit, vol. III, Session 1972-73,
    Appendices to Minutes of Evidence and Index, HMSO, London,
    1973.
15 Quoted in Purse or Wallet? How the Cabinet did a Switch-
    Sell, 'Sunday Times', 20 June 1976, p. 17.
16 This account based on Killing a Commitment: the Cabinet v
    the children, 'New Society', 17 June 1976, pp. 630-2 and
    Purse or Wallet?, ibid.
17 Killing a Commitment, op. cit.
18 Purse or Wallet?, op. cit.
19 The Great Child Benefit Robbery, Child Benefits Now
    Campaign, 1977.
20 F. Field, A Lobby for All Children, 'New Society', 29
    September 1977.
21 F. Field, Fair Shares for Families, The Need for a Family
    Impact Statement, Study Commission on the Family, 1980.
22 The Family Forum (draft leaflet).

Part V

Families in transition

Chapter 26

British families in transition
Robert and Rhona Rapoport

Families - intimate domestic groups made up of people related
to one another by bonds of blood, sexual mating or legal tie -
have been our most durable social unit.   From hunting and
gathering bands through the most complex modern State, family
units have been adapting to, and at the same time influencing
the courst of development of other parts of society.   Whereas
the 'technical order' - i.e. technology and its application to
the economy - has advanced step-wise through a series of revolutions from simpler to more complex forms, families have continued to be made up of units of a similar scale.   The
changes in the technical order have allowed for changes in
scale from small societies which were able to harness only
individual members' muscle power and that of domesticated
animals to large modern societies where millions of individuals can harness thousands of times that amount through the
simplest of operations - throwing a light switch, turning on a
television set, driving a motorcar, flying an airplane, blast-
ing a mountainside.   Domestic family units, while benefiting
from this increased power, are still made up of roughly the
same number of men, women and children, relating to one
another with similar mental and emotional capacities.   Families have changed, but perhaps more like kaleidoscopes than
like accumulators.

Each time there is a major transition in the technical
order, families are called upon to make a transition as well
(Aldous, 1978; Hareven, 1978).   In so doing, they do not
merely adapt passively to what is being asked of them.   W.J.
Goode (1963) showed how families in different parts of the
world have responded to the Industrial Revolution in various
ways which at the same time have had some common elements.
Everywhere there is a decline in the authority of elders in
organising the family life of their offspring; everywhere
there is a change in the rights and obligations of the

'extended' network of kin and community ties;   everywhere
there is a decline in the size of the domestic group.   These
are changes *within* the family as an institution, but what
qualitative changes in family relationships may have been involved has been a theme in much of the present debate among
historians like Shorter (1977); Stone (1977);   Laslett (1972)
and Sennett (1970).

THE CURRENT TRANSITION

A case can be made that while the conventional family was an
adaptive solution to the social and economic circumstances of
early industrial society, it is no longer so.   The circumstances have changed.   Young and Willmott (1973) suggest that
under the joint impact of the newer technological changes and
the ideology of feminism, the movement of families is inexorably toward the 'symmetrical family' as a dominant form.   As
Fogarty and Rodgers have pointed out, the Scandinavians and
East Europeans have accepted this as the model for the future.
    Our central argument is that regardless of what situation
prevailed in the remote past, or what situation may prevail in
the long-range future, *families in Britain today are in a
transition from coping in a society in which there was a
single overriding norm of what family life should be like to a
society in which a plurality of norms are recognised as legitimate and, indeed, desirable.*

DIMENSIONS OF DIVERSITY

David Eversley and Lucy Bonnerjea (Chapter 3) leave no doubt
that there has always been diversity in family life in
Britain.   We shall probably never know whether the actual
diversity in past eras was similar or different in amount from
that of today.   Descriptions of family life in 'traditional'
settings imply a relatively high degree of uniformity - e.g.
in the lives of coal miners (Dennis, Henriques and Slaughter,
1956), in Lancashire textile villages (Anderson, 1971) and on
Irish farms (Arensberg and Kimball, 1940).   Arensberg and
Kimball, whose study occurred in the 1930s, wrote that the
pattern was relatively invariable from household to household
in rural Ireland of the era.   The pattern emphasised the separation of the sexes at an early age with boys following the
work of their fathers and girls staying close to home under
their mother's surveillance.   Farming and domestic roles were
unusually sharply segregated, and family authority was strongly patriarchal - though father retained a somewhat distant

position with mother expected to handle emotional tensions
within the family.   Of course variations existed and were
recognised, but they were variations on a single theme.   This
theme was also found in other farming families, but the Irish
situation was a 'classic' case - with its small subsistence
farms, close reliance on horse and plough technology and inheritance pattern which led to a prolongation of dependency,
frequent non-marriage and persistent subservience of women and
older sons.   All this was buttressed in the religion and culture of the region.

In a re-study of this same area in the 1970s, following
intensive modernisation through the introduction of industries
and of more equal opportunities for education, Hannan and
Katsiouni (1977) classified Irish farm families in seven distinct types based on the patterning in the domestic division
of labour.   The transition they analysed was, like Goode's
(1963), from 'traditional' to 'modern' as it occurred in rural
Ireland.   They hypothesised that the new domestic roles were
'negotiated' rather than automatically conformative to traditional norms.   As the west of Ireland moved from a predominantly subsistence farming base, with output limited to what
man and horse could produce, to a society employing power
machinery linked to a market economy and receptive to new
ideas received via schools and the mass media from outside, it
was inevitable that the stable pattern of sex-segregated
patriarchal families would alter.   As there were new variations in wealth, ideas, educational level, etc. it also
followed that couples evolved new variations in their patterns
of domestic relations.

Some of the trends described by Muriel Nissel illustrate
the nature of the recent transition in British family life.
At the heart of the current process is the increased range of
options available.   This does not mean that there have not
also been trends toward homogenisation or standardisation -
e.g. in family size, in overall affluence and access to material goods.   But overall, there is not only a greater range
of recognised patterns, but a greater acceptance of the value
of enhancing personal freedom to choose the desired pattern.
Out of the contemporary diversity, a new norm may emerge (as
in the Scandinavian countries);   or at least a new affirmation
that diversity should not imply infinite flexibility and
family disruption, as Jonathan Brayshaw argues (1980).   A
great deal of the current discussion on the predicament of
families in Britain can be seen to be based on two clusters of
thought: one that considers the emergent diversity of family
patterns an expression of diverse needs and wishes;   the other
that considers the emergent diversity as deviations from some
outside norm - of economic standards, of moral or religious

standards, of biological imperatives.   Our own analysis
favours the first.   We recognise, however, that many families' situations reflect constraints which interact with and
limit the free expression of needs and wishes.   The distinction is, to some extent, one of degree.

We cannot produce a table showing actual household distributions for the mid-nineteenth century to compare with information we now have on some of the contemporary variations, but
Table 26.1 shows some aspects of diversity recognised in official statistics.

TABLE 26.1   Household types (1)

	%
Married couple with children -	
Single breadwinner	20
Two earners	20
Married couple, no children	27
One-parent family household	8
One-person household -	
Over retirement age	15
Under retirement age	6
Two or more people, not a family	3
Two or more families	1
Total	100

1 Based on Central Statistical Office (1978), Tables 2.2 and
   3.4.

Evidence in Anderson's study (1971) suggests that there was
a similar, perhaps even wider diversity of household types in
early Victorian Britain.   But diversity of types does not by
itself mean diversity of *choices*.   Indications are that there
was an accepted standard or norm according to which one sub-
type of household was regarded as most generally desirable.
Smelser describes the Victorian conception of family life
which was widely assumed to represent the highest development
of family life, much as the Church of England was thought to
represent the highest development in religious life, parliament and the British Empire in political life, etc.   Alfred
Lord Tennyson, Victoria's poet laureate, expressed lyrically
the prevalent gender role conceptions:

Man for the field and woman for the hearth;
Man for the sword and for the needle she;
Man with the head and woman with the heart;
Man to command and woman to obey;
All else confusion.

It was also assumed that this pattern brought most 'happiness'. Today it is recognised that the conventional pattern, as we have called it, is one among several and, as Ann Oakley among others has shown, is hardly guaranteed to bring happiness.

On the basis of the chapters in this book - and they are only illustrative - we delineate five types of diversity now recognised.

Organisational

This refers to the diversity of ways in which families organise their internal division of domestic labour and their patterns of linking their families to the external world. Social networks and institutional linkages vary widely and are of immense importance in understanding how families function in today's society. The differences between conventional families, dual-worker families, one-parent families, reconstituted families, illustrate this kind of diversity.

The contributors' analyses also illustrate the transition which we postulate. Ann Oakley (Chapter 5) demonstrates the way in which conventional organisation no longer minimises strain and, indeed, generates distinctive strains of its own; Gowler and Legge (Chapter 6) demonstrate how dual-worker families no longer face so much social criticism but how they present their own characteristic 'mix' of strains and gains; Brian Jackson (Chapter 7) demonstrates the notion that under some circumstances the one-parent family structure may be a favoured option. Burgoyne and Clark (Chapter 14) demonstrate that reconstituted families, for all their particular strains, may also provide a new basis for constructing useful extended family networks or chains of step-relationships. Fostering and adoptive families are also variants with specific associated strains and advantages for all concerned, as Jane Aldgate (Chapter 15) shows. The patterns are perceived as options which may meet some people's needs.

Cultural

This refers to the differences amongst families in their beliefs and values. Though the most striking differences are

seen in the ethnic groups (the three described here - West
Indian, South Asian and Cypriot - are only illustrative) the
contrasts in beliefs and values goes further.   Catholic sub-
groups may differ in significant values from their Protestant
neighbours, both being 'English' families with long-standing
historical roots in Britain.   Contrast may be found *within*
sub-groups - e.g. orthodox Jews vs assimilationist Jews;
middle-class English families who believe passionately in
National Front ideologies, and middle-class English families
who believe passionately in Liberal ideals.   These differences affect not only gender-role conceptions and internal
family division of labour and childrearing, but also attitudes
to work, education, social institutions and other elements in
the social environment.   The ethnic family chapters also suggest the possibility that racial tensions notwithstanding,
there may be more tolerance in contemporary Britain than in
the past for the maintenance of distinctive ethnic lifestyles.
Correspondingly, there is a recognition of their contribution
to British culture.   It is not possible, of course, for a
White English person to *become* a Black West Indian or Brown
South Asian, but it is possible to take a serious interest in
their cultures and to absorb elements selectively.

Class

A family's position in the social class system affects the
availability of resources and access to other institutions in
the environment.
    In general, the literature on family patterns of different
social class groups suggests that working-class families
favour more conventional role relationships between husbands
and wives (what Elizabeth Bott (1971) describes as a more
'segregated' division of labour, as compared with the more
'joint' pattern favoured by many middle-class partners).
However, the Pahls (1971), Young and Willmott (1973) and
Edgell (1980) have shown how in certain middle-class families
a segregated pattern may exist even where jointness is valued
because of the over-riding demands of the husband's career.
The conflict is particularly intense when early career building coincides with the early establishment of the home and
family.   In childrearing orientations, the social class patterns can be summarised as shown in Table 26.2.
    Social class overlaps with but is not identical to 'race'
and 'poverty' as dimensions of diversity.
    There is some evidence that aside from the overall patterns
of individual mobility within the class system, the system
itself seems to be changing in that large sub-groups show a

TABLE 26.2   Some social class differences in marital relations
and childrearing practices (1)

	Middle class	Working class
Marital relations	More emphasis on sharing, equity, communication	More emphasis on 'the place' of men and women, less verbal communication
	More 'joint' division of labour	More 'segregated'
	More 'planful'; instrumental	Less planful
Childrearing practices	High value placed on internalisation of values; reasoning, self-direction, initiative	High value placed on obedience
	Emphasis on ambition	Emphasis on conforming with authority
	Discipline by reasoning and witholding of reward/love	Discipline more physical

1   Sources: Bott, 1971; Goldthorpe et al., 1969; Newson and
    Newson, 1970.

low sense of class consciousness - or 'classness' (Goldthorpe
et al., 1980).   The predictive power of class as a variable
defined by occupational type alone is lessening in many respects and this is part of the transition we are postulating.

Life-course

This refers to the stage in the family life-cycle.   Just as
families with different organisational patterns and different
cultural values develop ways of life characteristic of their
particular circumstances, so do families at specific life-
cycle stages.   They have different expectations from the
marital relationship and different preoccupations.   In some
ways families with dependent children have similar preoccupations regardless of class and sub-culture, contrasting with
families at other stages - e.g. newlyweds, or retired couples
whose children are grown and have left home.   Collins and

Strelitz (Chapter 22) illustrate this for leisure and recreational interests.   The Lords' Select Committee on Recreation
(1973) has legitimated the quest for enjoyment as a human
right in Britain, placing another coffin-nail in the casket of
the Puritan tradition of suffering one's pleasures guiltily.
Leisure provision is, accordingly, an active kind of social
service for all, searching for new ways of reaching recrea-
tionally deprived, and therefore necessarily taking cognizance
of sub-group variation, among them those associated with the
family life-cycle.

Cohort

This refers to the particular historical period in which a
family cycle plays itself out.   Young people before the
Second World War had different characteristics from young
people after the war; children of the depression have different characteristics from children of affluence (Elder, 1974).
Muriel Nissel (Chapter 4) examines the effects of two post-
Second World War British cohorts, comparing families stage by
stage through the family life course.
    The cohort effect is an important issue in at least two
other papers.   The stigmatisation of working couples has
diminished sharply in the past ten years.   A working couple
may expect less criticism and more support now as the legitimacy of the pattern is recognised.   This is mentioned in
Gowler and Legge's account (Chapter 6).   Similarly for
divorce.   The easing of legal and financial constraints on
divorce has made it more possible for a wider range of couples
living unhappily together to break up.   As a consequence, it
too has become somewhat normalised.   This means that the
'hurt' which Jack Dominian describes (Chapter 13) may be less
for younger people today than it was for earlier divorcing
couples - which is not to say that it has become painless;
only that it has become to an extent 'normalised'.   As Jessie
Bernard (1972) pointed out in relation to working mothers, a
statistical trend can lead to an acceptance on normative
grounds after a 'tipping' point is reached.   The Willmotts
indicate how this may work in relation to the impact of new
family forms on children (Chapter 17).
    A decided cohort effect is also likely to be seen amongst
the elderly, with important implications for policy.   Today's
75+ population is unusually biased toward lone females both
because of emigration and wars earlier in the century and the
lower longevity of men.   Their level of education is also
lower than subsequent people in that age group will be.   This
has implications for the development of late-life interests,

the general morale of the elderly and their social care requirements (Abrams, 1978).   The changing ratio of elderly to
younger families in the population has implications for social
care in later life, but the greater resourcefulness of the
elderly will make them less dependent up until they become
physically disabled.

SOCIAL RESEARCH AND SOCIAL POLICY

Michael Fogarty and Barbara Rodgers (Chapter 1) have set a
context for this discussion by indicating six policy issues
which are internationally recognised.   In stating the issues,
it should be kept in mind that they arise amongst people pro-
fessionally concerned with family life, and tend to focus on
current problems.   A statement of policy issues which might
be more universally valid would probably be somewhat different.   This is a challenge for another context.
    In their analysis, Fogarty and Rodgers concentrate on the
question: what does Britain have to learn from the experience
of comparable nations?   In this section we ask: what does
family research in Britain have to contribute to the wider
dialogue on these issues?

Population

In the population field, British research has been of extremely high quality, and the data from demographic analyses reveals characteristic patterns which place Britain within the
same range of social trends as other European countries.   As
in other countries, the size of the family-household has
fallen and the fertility of British families has been compressed into the early years of marriage, which itself has been
occurring earlier.   Whereas in the 1930s, 70 per cent of
women in Britain were married by the time they were thirty,
this percentage rose to 90 per cent in the 1970s.   Whereas
earlier in the century only half of childbearing was completed
by the time wives in Britain were thirty, by the 1970s 80 per
cent of children were born to women under thirty.   These are
convergences rather than increases in diversity, and Eversley
and Bonnerjea (Chapter 3) point out some paradoxical effects -
e.g. that families with three times the national average size
(i.e. six children) are less unusual today than families three
times tha national average size a century ago (i.e. fifteen
children).   Nevertheless, the general drop in family size is
impressive - and note that it was nearing the point where the
population would not be reproducing itself.

Immigration allowed some population growth in categories
which were politically or economically wanted.   But the question of population planning was placed in the hands of the
individuals concerned, expressing a salient British value -
freedom of choice in one's private life.

Recent interest in population issues (other than the small
minority who have a racialist interest in possible displacement of populations with large families of immigrants) has
centred on the issues of finance.   With an aging population
in a Welfare State there must continue to be sufficient active
workers to pay for the pensions and care of the elderly.   If
women work, they pay taxes which help to finance care institutions, but the costs are higher than if they stay at home and
provide home care.   With women seeking jobs and careers
rather than more babies, men may feel themselves pushed out of
their jobs and onto the dole, and the drop in the birthrate
may create problems for planning in education, the social services and the labour force.   Working women also place financial demands on government for child-care facilities.   These
are the sorts of reasons advanced by those who urge women to
return to home and hearth.

Men's and women's roles

Britain has pioneered research on changing roles of men and
women (cf. Fogarty et al., 1971, 1981; Oakley and Mitchell,
1976).   The term 'dual-career families' was coined in Britain
(Rapoport and Rapoport, 1969, 1971, 1976, 1980).   Gowler and
Legge (Chapter 6) review the broad field of research on dual-
worker families in Britain, and in the USA an even more volum-
inous literature has been building up (Pepitone, 1980; Aldous
1981).   The emphasis amongst American dual-working couples
has been on self-realisation; in the USSR on contribution to
the economy as well as on the liberation of women from domestic drudgery and exploitation.   In the Scandinavian countries
the emphasis has been on 'equality' between the sexes.   In
the UK there has evolved an appreciation of the diversity of
motives and rewards in the pattern and an emphasis on 'equity'
rather than equality (Rapoport and Rapoport, 1975).   While
dual-career families tend to be motivated by a mixture of
idealism and the wish for self-realisation, there is usually a
secondary economic motive.   Dual-worker families lower down
in the occupational scale have characteristically given primacy to economic reasons for going out to work.   However,
more recently it has also been recognised that they work for
company and for self-esteem.   The relative lack of communication and confidants in their domestic environments add to this
dimension (Brown and Harris, 1979).

The idea of part-time work for both husbands and wives was originally emphasised in the Scandinavian countries (Gronseth, 1976).   Indeed, it has been resisted in the UK, particularly by the Trade Unions.   But it may find more popular acceptance as a way of saving at least parts of some jobs in the economic recession that is upon us.   In the UK, the idea of the 'right to work' contrasts with the new American emphasis on 'work as a privilege' in a society with such wide usage of microprocessors and service industries.

Also innovative in the context of redefining supports for variant family structures has been the work of Brian and Sonia Jackson (1979) on childminders and some of the points made by Brian Jackson in his on one-parent families (Chapter 7). Being (or staying) a lone parent, like remarrying and reconstituting a new family, are options which can provide new opportunities and satisfactions as well as new strains. Burgoyne and Clark (Chapter 14) convey the duality of response to such situations, as does Jane Aldgate (Chapter 15) in relation to fostering and adoption.   Chapter 5, by Ann Oakley, brings into focus a fresh appreciation of both sides of the conventional family pattern for men as well as for women. Indeed, British research is contributing to the clarification of many ambiguities in usage of the term family.   Roy Parker's chapter (18) points out how such ambiguities can plague the development of a coherent policy.

It is widely appreciated that there should be greater symmetry in the treatment of men and women by the State as well as increased equality in actual participation in the economy by men and women.   Yet the social security system is still based on the assumption that the man is the principal breadwinner, and his wife a dependent (Carter, 1980);   industry is still organised in large part according to the assumption that (male) workers and their families will make conventional accommodations as Nancy Seear describes (Chapter 20).   A recent PSI study (Fogarty et al., 1981) following up the PEP study of Women and Top Jobs ten years ago, has shown increasing acceptance of the *principle* of equal opportunity but has not been effectively matched with measures to insure its implementation in employment practice, particularly as regards the facilitation of a better fit between family and career. Schools are still largely organised with conventional assumptions about their pupils' families, as Daphne Johnson's chapter describes (Chapter 19);   and family law is still in the process of shedding its conventional assumptions about the universality of Christian marriage, as Brenda Hoggett describes (Chapter 21).

So, while Britain is no better than average amongst European countries for her achievement of equality between the sexes, the research available in Britain on this topic is relatively well developed and maps the way for changes still to come.

Family and the external world

Families, as domestic units, are rarely isolated and self-sufficient.   They contain and rely on various kinds of extensions.   When people speak of their families, they may mean a rather vague collection of people extending outward in space and backward in time.   It may never be necessary for them to give an accounting of who is included and who is not, though some occasions require the drawing of boundary lines - e.g. of who should be invited to a party or wedding reception, who should get what by way of inheritance.   But, as Fogarty and Rodgers point out (Chapter 1), policy-makers need to know not only who is included, but who can be counted on - e.g. to feel obligated to provide care for a relative in distress.   The development of policies which involve professionals and government in families relates in part to this sort of assessment.

Part of the discussion about the relationship between the family in society has centred on what might be called their *intimate social networks* - their kin, neighbours and friends. Just as the family is a support system for individuals, social networks are support systems for families and individual members.   This view stresses the importance of kin, friends and neighbours in the informal exchanges of human services which form so much of family life.   These exchanges centre on *personal* involvements in offering help, advice, affection and responsiveness to norms and values.   It is distinguished from the supports given by more formal specialists and organisations based on cash payments or statutory obligations - e.g. doctors, counsellors, schools and governmental agencies.

One view of modern family life emphasises the erosion of *informal* networks as families and individuals have uprooted themselves and moved to new locations in response to job opportunities.   Also with the growth of the Welfare State, with its goal of assuring that no one's needs should go neglected in all these movements, government agencies have taken over more and more responsibility with the effect, some assert, of people becoming less ready to form their own support and exchange networks.

But despite the growth of specialist social institutions, and of welfare services and despite the high degree of social and geographical mobility, families have generally continued to build social networks to meet their needs.   Family social networks have changed - in form and function. But they have usually not disappeared even in the most anonymous urban settings.

The work of the Institute of Community Studies showed some of the ways in which informal social networks continue to function in metropolitan settings; and what some of the difficulties are when these settings are insensitively disturbed. Young and Willmott (1957) showed how mothers and daughters are not only close while the latter reside at home, but also later when they marry and set up a separate household. When the daughters have their babies they often return to their mothers for emotional support and informal instruction in parentcraft, deriving from this 'Demeter' bond a similar kind of emotional solidarity as their men derive from the trade unions. Margaret Stacey and her colleagues report finding in Banbury that this bond is so powerful that it continues to operate even when there is movement of families over great distances and a lessening of routine contacts (1960). Peter Willmott (1963) showed how peer groups of adolescents could function more constructively in the urban environment than many of their elders feared given the semi-delinquent flavour of many street-corner activities. Peter Townsend (1957) showed how old people retained family contacts, even when they lived alone, a finding repeated in other contexts right up to the present. Abrams (1978) found that elderly women living alone are not conspicuously more isolated than those living with others. Men, who are thinner on the ground in the older age groups, are more gregarious when they live alone than are women, until they reach the older, 75+ age groups, following which they become more isolated.

In a study emanating from the Tavistock Institute of Human Relations, Elizabeth Bott (1957) indicated that there were at least two kinds of social networks in the urban setting: one a 'tight knit' type (rather like those studied by anthropologists in tribal settings and found by Raymond Firth and his colleagues (1956, 1969) to persist in London, not only amongst ethnic groups but even in suburban Highgate); and those which are more 'loose knit' - members not being in touch with one another. Whatever the advantages of one or the other in terms of supports to families, each tends to be related to a particular type of internal family structure. The tight-knit network, characteristic of stable traditional working-class areas like Bethnal Green, is associated with an internal division of labour in the family which is highly segregated, men doing traditional men's things and women traditional women's things with relatively little interchangeability. Conversely, families with loose-knit networks tend to be more 'joint' in their internal division of labour, with the issue of 'who

does what' being open for negotiation.   While Bott and subsequent researchers have found the loose-knit network more
associated with modernity, middle classness and mobility, it
is not clear how well either system serves as an informal support structure for families in crises.

What is known is that having a tight-knit network is not an
unalloyed advantage.   Sometimes the social sanctions and controls associated with it are felt to be onerous and behaviour
considered deviant may be punitively attacked and the person
rejected.   Conversely, a loose-knit network does not necessarily mean neglect.   Networks which are so constructed are
more dispersed, but they may in their diverse composition
offer more options.   Friends, rather than kin, are more
likely to be in the intimate zones.   There may be less tendency to include neighbours, and indeed, the avoidance of
friction rather than the search for co-operation may be a
ruling criterion.   What has been stressed in recent research
and policy discussions is the importance of *some kind of informal support network*.   The extreme case of a self-selected,
informal support group is seen in the communal household described by Andrew McCulloch (Chapter 16).   This type of alternative has not flourished in Britain, partly it seems because
it reproduces gender-role inequities, partly because in seeking total autonomy it recreates some of the unmanageable elements of closed systems.   The task of building more co-operation and mutual aid into family groups and their extensions
remains one of the principal challenges of our time (Young and
Rigge, 1979).   What do the chapters indicate?

Conventional families, as Ann Oakley (Chapter 5) shows,
tend in British families today to show a sharp imbalance in
external networks by sex.   Husbands develop work-related networks not open to their wives, who tend to relate locally to
kin and neighbours.   If they live in socially isolated situations such as high-rise housing estates and have few local kin
or developed hobbies or interests, they are at risk of recreational deprivation as Collins and Strelitz indicate (Chapter
22).

Gowler and Legge's analysis (Chapter 6) of dual-worker
families reveals some characteristic patterns for this type of
family.   Here both parents have outside work so that there is
less skewing than in conventional families.   But dual-worker
families need to negotiate a great deal in arranging exactly
which external relationship will take precedence.   Amongst
the many decisions which have to be negotiated in such families are financial, child care, leisure and community involvements.   The higher income made possible by two earners may
provide more financial resources, but there is a tendency in
such families to cut down on external involvements because of

pressures of time and problems of reciprocating hospitality and services.   There is a tendency for individual leisure activities to be pruned sharply, particularly when children are young.

The ethnic chapters indicate different aspects of the issue.   Outside the immediate family household, the world may be polarised into 'English' and 'our people', which can be Black, Asians, Cypriots or others.   Though friends, clients, workmates and even marriage partners may be found amongst them, there is an issue around the question of 'whom can you really turn to or trust?'   As Roger Ballard points out (Chapter 8), the threat to leave home to melt into the English world is a characteristic adolescent rebellion point in Asian families, but as with adolescents generally, the eventual resolution tends to be conservative, with preference expressed for associating with similar kinds of people.   Choices tend to be in favour of 'people like us', so that social bonds and networks continue to be built up along ethnic lines.

There are marked cultural differences amongst the various ethnic groups: it is not enough to think of them all as vaguely patriarchal and 'extended' families in the traditional mould.   Co-operation and corporate loyalty has been a con- spicuous feature in Asian groups, as Roger Ballard notes. This makes for a relatively reliable set of informal supports for families;   a feature also noted for Cypriots.   This kin- based support system is applied not only to the care of child- ren, ill and elderly, but to economic entrepreneurship and co-operation.   In such groups there are also pressures to conform, at which many of the younger generation chafe.   West Indians are less drawn toward traditional family and kin obli- gations;   they have a history of uprooting and transportation from Africa to the New World.   They have, through the experi- ence of slavery and racial deprivation, had to abandon many of their earlier family patterns and evolve new ones to fit their new situations.   In the move from the West Indies to England further adaptations have been made.   The two types of fami- lies presented by Geoffrey Driver (Chapter 9) illustrate this: the Campbells - representing a form of what has sometimes been called the 'matrifocal family', shows heavy reliance on the mother as both economic provider and home-maker;   the Spencers, with the marital partners functioning in the conven- tional family pattern.   West Indians call the first pattern 'English marriage' (despite it being a pattern characteristic of the West Indies) and the latter 'Christian marriage'. 'English marriages' in England are prone to a relatively atrophied network based on the mother's group;   whereas 'Christian marriages' form new links, both through father's work and mother's community availability.   Jocelyn Barrow

(Chapter 10) describes some of the intergenerational problems, particularly with adolescent youth, and how the different types of West Indian families try to cope in the English environment.

Absorption of alien immigrants has provided various strains - on social welfare, health and educational services.   But it has also brought positive elements, such as the demonstration of viability of informal mutual aid and self-help groups in urban settings.   But in evolving, such groups there have sometimes been angry rather than laudatory responses.   Early PEP reports on prejudice in Britain detected this danger (Smith, 1977).   But more recently the other side of the coin is emphasised, i.e. the development of ethnic sub-groups for general cultural enrichment.   Both elements are present. The Notting Hill Carnival expresses the success of the latter view;   the Rastafarian movement might express the former. Roberts (1980) has expressed the anxiety that Black youth drawn into the Rastafarian movement may develop such alienated attitudes to the 'White' world of work that they undermine their own chances for finding useful and satisfying jobs.   A delicate balance, and sensitive inter-group communications are needed if the relationships are to develop in what Rae Sherwood (1980) calls 'benign' rather than 'vicious spirals' between and among the racial groups.   Her analysis of the 'psychodynamics' of prejudice in inter-ethnic relationships exemplifies another point at which British research in these fields is advanced.

Looking at the current state of play in relation to families and formal social institutions, two themes run through the papers in this volume (and would be repeated in chapters on health services, housing and the built environment if we had them).   One theme is that there has been a massive sociocultural lag.   The existing institutions were constructed with one set of assumptions in mind about families – that they were organised and stabilised in the mould of the conventional family;   there is a degree of tension in the relationship because these assumptions are no longer valid.   Schools, employing organisations, social services and other professional providers, all show expectations about what the needs and wants of families are which are less diversified and less dynamic than the actual needs and wants of families.

The second theme is that there must be a new partnership between families and the State.   The State can still rely on the informal motivations of families - loyalty, love, duty - to provide the greatest bulk of human care as Moroney (1976) has shown.   But inevitably some families cope more adequately than others, and in some instances the strains of life tip the balance of family relationships in the direction of disorder

or abuse (Dobash and Dobash, 1980; Pahl, 1978).   In these
instances, intervention and help are needed.   If the State
shifts too much of a burden onto families themselves, it may
produce another kind of erosion of its vast store of popular
care-givers - erosion through overloading.   Muriel Nissel
(1980) warns of this danger, while pointing to the potentials
of family care as yet untapped.   Families need care and servicing themselves if they are to perform the care functions
which they are potentially willing and able to perform.   A
sensitive balance is what is required, and a sense of 'alliance' (Rapoport et al., 1977) or 'partnership' (Parker and
Land, 1978) rather than dependency or antipathy between families and welfare professionals and bureaucracies.   In the
absence of massive governmental support for the development of
such new alliances, the search is on for what the IFER/DART
team call 'small changes that make big differences' in bringing about a better fit between available provision and
people's needs (Dower, Rapoport et al., 1981).

The limits of disruption

Family breakdown, divorce and its aftermath, has become an
international phenomenon of increasing concern.   Earlier,
divorce was regarded as a kind of safety valve, which if it
had to happen in cases of intolerable strain was possibly the
better of two evils, the worse being the perpetuation of a
family which was conflict-ridden, damaging and oppressive.
As pressure on governments to liberalise divorce laws led to
dropping the threshold on constraints in marriage, country
after country, Britain included, has experienced a sharp rise
in divorce rates.   Like working mothers, youthful unrest and
now economic recession - the divorce rate seems to reflect
global tensions as well as those specific to the nation and to
particularly vulnerable families within it.   Robert Chester
(1977), in a collection of national case studies edited for
the 'Groupe pour Recherche sur le Divorce', traces the common
patterns and causal factors: secularisation, changing conceptions of men's and women's roles, increased aspirations for
personal fulfilment, changes in the legal grounds and procedures, increased complexity of family events to be managed and
so on.   Brenda Hoggett's chapter (21) describes some of the
legal issues involved, and Jack Dominian's chapter (13) portrays the process of breakdown and the psychological costs
entailed.   As with other disturbances - unemployment, economic deprivation - some people are more vulnerable than others.
Those with lower educational levels, fewer skills, fewer
social supports, greater strains - are disproportionaly
vulnerable.

If divorce were uniformly liberating as an experience and if there were no problems of public costs, no more attention might be given to the issue of family disruption than to other personal choices such as changes of residence.   But family breakdown may be, and often is, associated with heavy emotional costs to the individuals concerned.   Within families divorce has unequal, sometimes hidden and delayed consequences.   It is tolerated, even encouraged in some quarters because it provides a channel for escape from intolerable problem situations.   But to avoid compounding the problems, intervention in the process of breakdown and reconstitution of family life may be required.   What sort of intervention?

First there is the *financial* issue.   The costs of divorce are high, not only to the individuals concerned but to the State.   Wealthy people may be able to afford alimony, child support and a new reconstituted family.   But there are few who can weather this whole process without feeling the pinch. Typically ex-wives are worse off than ex-husbands unless they remarry.   Their chances of doing so, though improving, are less than their ex-husbands'.   Children are helpless to control their fates, and are often subjected to damaging wrangles over maintenance and custody.

In the USA, the *emotional* as well as financial aspects of the legal wrangles have been studied microscopically by inter-disciplinary teams (e.g. Goldstein, Freud and Solnit, 1973, 1979) or with a multidisciplinary approach (e.g. Weitzman, 1978).   No such multidisciplinary team exists in Britain, though lawyers have worked with social scientists (e.g. Eekelaar and Clive, 1977; MacGregor and Blom-Cooper, 1970) and social scientists concerned with marital breakdown have worked in medical psychological/public health settings (Chester, 1971; Thornes and Collard, 1979).   The tendency has been to propose interventions taking advantage of the special circumstances of the particular professional or institutional setting studied.   Chester points out the advantages in using medical practices, because doctors see patients for general reasons before an intractable problem evolves; MacGregor points to the advantages of the legal setting, because lawyers are advantageously placed to help with such practical matters as financial settlements, custody and access rulings before a resolution is made in court that will rankle subsequently.   Perhaps the most developed British contribution is in the combination of legal and social welfare considerations.   The title of Mervyn Murch's book 'Justice and Welfare in Divorce' (1980) suggests the nexus.   But all admit that it would be better to intervene preventively before these professionals are engaged.   Family life education should prepare young people to take on the strains as well as the joys

of marriage and parenthood. But few generally acceptable
mechanisms for this kind of education exist and it is not easy
to achieve consensus over such issues as how sex education
should be handled.

The fragmentation of care involvement in issues associated
with marital disharmony is a problem. The Department of
Health is concerned with children; marital violence comes
under their general purview. But if the police are involved
it becomes a Home Office matter. Legal issues governing
divorce procedure itself concern the Lord Chancellor's Office.
The Finer Committee on One Parent Families have long advocated
Family Courts, in which the different disciplines could pool
their expertise in the interests of the individuals concerned.
This would help with the handling of emotional, as well as the
material issues surrounding divorce.

With marriage age beginning to rise again and educational
programmes underway to prepare couples for improved management
of stress points immediately following marriage, in association with the arrival of children, and so on - the divorce
rate may stabilise and even fall. Whether this will be
accompanied by a fall in the problems experienced in the
divorce process remains to be seen. The Joint Working Party
of the DHSS and Home Office on Marriage Guidance and their
publication 'Marriage Matters' (1978) recommended the formation of a Central Development Unit to monitor social changes
and apply the knowledge to policy and practice. Jonathan
Brayshaw, in his discussion document published by the Policy
Studies Institute (1980) draws attention to the fact that
though 'Marriage Matters' is both multidisciplinary and multi-
value- orientated in its use of professionals from a broad
spectrum and representatives of the major religions, it concentrates on ways of attaining *individual* well being. In re-
asserting the importance of keeping family well being in the
forefront of people's consciousness, a contribution may be
being made toward redressing the balance which has gone so far
in America and Scandinavian countries toward the preoccupation
with individual self-realisation. There is a revulsion
against the 'narcissistic society' as Christopher Lasch (1978)
calls it, toward something more social, albeit not in the
traditional family mould to be maintained in a rigid form at
all costs. From this may emerge the kind of reversal mentioned by Fogarty and Rodgers (Chapter 1), of the shift toward
marriage counselling from marriage mending recorded in 'Marriage Matters'. Once again, careful and dispassionate research will be required - with a sufficiently long time span
to catch long-term consequences, if hypotheses are to be
tested as to whether this would be a 'good thing' or not in
terms of net life satisfaction.

Economics: family poverty and fiscal policies

Fundamental to the Welfare State concept and the social/human-
istic values underlying it, is the idea that the less fortunate should be helped by the more fortunate. This involves
giving special attention to families with handicap; and it
also involves giving special attention to family poverty in
which many may become entrapped. Though the gap between the
richest and the poorest segments of society has been lessened,
this has been achieved by the trimming of excessive wealth at
the top end (Layard, 1978). Families caught in poverty,
socialising their children to perpetuate the world views and
coping mechanisms of the very poor are to a large extent de-
barred from attaining many of the satisfactions available to
their neighbours as Harriet Wilson describes (Chapter 12).
But getting government to improve benefits and services to
families in poverty is a difficult task. Relentless pressure
from poverty lobby groups like CPAG has helped. But the
obstacles remain formidable. Families do not constitute a
radical threat; if there are many who lack *any* wage-earner,
might it be because they are work-shy, lax, or otherwise undeserving? Is teenage pregnancy to be seen as an acceptable
variant or is it a product of carelessness or selfishness?
Many want a firm line against rewarding people in such situations (e.g. by providing public housing). Paying State benefits to one-parent families seems to some people to be subsi-
dising other people's pleasures or mistakes. But how are
they to be helped? Attitude surveys from the end of the
1950s through the 1970s showed a steady growth of 'Welfare
backlash'. The idea has taken root that pouring public funds
into help for the poor is a bottomless pit of expenditure
which cannot be afforded in present economic circumstances.
The election of a government with this as part of their party-
political platform has set in train a new surge of cutbacks in
expenditure, despite rhetorical support for 'the family',
which will affect many personal social services directed
toward the more disadvantaged families - as Bill Jordan's
chapter (24) outlines. Fogarty and Rodgers (Chapter 1) have
shown that this backlash is widely experienced in Europe, as
indicated in the European Commission Survey. The question
now is at what point and in what way will the reaction set in
against the undesirable consequences of the cutbacks in public
expenditure? As the need for welfare benefits and services
becomes increasingly clear, the question will be where in the
list of priorities for new welfare allotments will a strategy
toward families as units come? Clearly not at the top of the
list with pensioners; but clearly not at the bottom in the
company of students, immigrants and 'welfare scroungers'.

There was a marked swing toward an appreciation of the importance of families' financial problems with the introduction of
child benefit under the last government; and a good deal of
new attention to the needs of families in the DHSS seminars on
The Family and Society in 1977 and 1978.   But the idea of
families, as distinct from men, women and children, remains an
elusive one.

Concern for the damage that might be done to children if
irregular family arrangements are promulgated has been one
source of mobilisation.   Peter and Phyllis Willmott (Chapter
17) show how contemporary family research provides a much more
differentiated picture of the consequences of such irregulari-
ties than was presumed following the Second World War studies
of maternal deprivation.   One-parent families are another
rallying point - for the abandoned (often battered, usually
economically bereft) parents as well as for their children.
But there is the lurking suspicion that some of these lone
parents (particularly the adolescent ones) brought their
plight upon themselves.   Also, there is the new legitimation
of working mothers, which, combined with the research finding
that if they go out to work they lessen the demand for supplementary benefits threefold (McNay and Pond, 1979) reinforces
the emphasis on self-help and mutual aid for this sub-group.
More generally, the sanctioning of working mothers is now more
acceptable in economic terms where it was criticised previously for its supposed damage to children.   Now the encouragement of dual-worker families provides a potential 'second
string' to the family bow in the face of unemployment threats
and a boost to family income in the face of rising inflation.

But, for those in need of economic help to maintain their
families, where is the help to come from?   Ruth Lister (Chapter 23) has reviewed the patchwork of measures current in
Britain and the difficulties entailed in keeping families at
the lower end of the income scale from sinking into poverty.
Two themes seem to run in counterpoint here: the search for
new resource, e.g. by examining the experiences of other countries - parenthood (or even divorce) insurance allowances;
low interest starter mortgages, etc.   On the other hand,
there is an obvious need for simplification.   David Donnison
argues that a key to this problem may be found in aiming for
'middle England' with the social benefits structure, as in the
health services.   This would, incidentally, benefit the poor
but without stigmatising them or attracting a welfare backlash.   Alfred Kahn and Sheila Kammerman have made a similar
argument in their book 'Not for the Poor Alone' (1975).

As Fogarty and Rodgers show (Chapter 1), Britain is not
particularly advanced in developing a modern conceptualisation
of the needs of families, nor of the structure of benefits to

be provided or the source of finance.   Not only is there the
issue of how to apply supports in cash as well as kind, there
is the persisting assumption that wives are dependants and
that their labour can be expected to continue unremunerated.
Recognition that child benefit should be removed from the complexities of marital and divorce arrangements is generally
accepted.   But issues such as the distribution of the economic burden for education, housing, recreation, institutional
health care, pre-school child care, etc., all affecting family
life fairly directly, are highly politicised, with sharp divisions along party lines.   Resolutions may be forced by economic circumstances of the country as a whole, and in the direction of redistributing the burden at grassroots levels, encouraging informal, voluntary activities and pruning the
patchwork thickets of benefits, allowances, services etc.
which have grown up piecemeal over time.   This thrust,
whether or not it is for wrong reasons, may strengthen family
life.

Coherence of family policy

Two impressions emerge from the papers presented.   Firstly,
that whether or not there should be a single organ of government charged with family policy, there is a strong feeling
that there should *not* be a situation in which the fragmentation of policy-making bodies affecting families leads to harmful consequences.   Florence Nightingale said about hospitals
that whatever else they do, they should not make the patients
ill.   If we can assume that government exists partly for families (rather than vice versa) we can argue that whatever else
they do, government policies should not increase family distress.   The Department of Employment and the Department of
Health and Social Security have independent and often uncoordinated responsibilities bearing on working mothers and
their children.   The confusions about whether the provision
for pre-school children belongs with the Department of Health
(who are concerned with child welfare) or the Department of
Education (who are concerned with child development) illustrates the point.   Problems of adolescent youth may be the
concern of the Department of Social Security, unless the problem has to do with the police or with immigrants, in which
case the Home Office is concerned.   If youth recreation is
involved - as in soccer hooliganism, or 'housing vandalism',
the Department of the Environment may be involved.   Stalemate
has often resulted and when these interdepartmental issues
arise the resulting policy is sometimes left implicit.
   Michael Fogarty (1980) has written:

Britain is one of those countries which has not hitherto
had a family policy as that is usually understood, but is
at present discovering the need for one.   Britain does, of
course, have a highly developed welfare state, and this includes many provisions directed specifically to the family
... fiscal and social security systems ... family allowances ... municipal housing programmes geared to family needs
... local authority personal social services ... to provide
a community-based and family-orientated service ... marriage counselling services ... family practitioner services ... and so on.   What has been missing, however, is
the cement binding these individual provisions together.

What do we learn from the chapters presented about where
the binding points may be?   Firstly, is a point about the
need for partnership between families and other social institutions, including the State.   An example, not treated in a
separate paper but mentioned in several, is in relation to the
elderly.   Families, at present, look after their frail elderly members until they can no longer cope, and then hand over
the care completely to the State in its residential or geriatric hospital provision.   It tends to be an 'either-or' situation - the family or the State.   All concerned might benefit by a better coordination of informal voluntary supports
with family care capacities on the one side, and institutional
or professional services on the other.   This kind of partnership requires coordination and resourcefulness, but it avoids
lurching from too much State facilities to too much burden on
families.

Secondly, there is a general consensus that government
should be more sensitive to the needs of families - should
adopt a 'family perspective' in developing its policies generally.   This should also be applied to all major social
institutions whose functioning affects families.

The present volume is an attempt to assemble relevant research information.   The review volumes by Mia Kellmer
Pringle on the needs of children (1974) and Rapoport, Rapoport
and Strelitz (1977) on the needs of parents, had similar
goals.   Britain has not yet provided a level of national
support for family research that matches public expressions
of concern and the wish for information.   We have tried
here to produce a coherent account of what has been accom-
plished in research.   Various disciplines, research institutions and governmental bodies are involved.

Another device for improving the larger sensitivity to
family issues is seen in The Study Commission on the Family.
This Commission is playing a useful role in attempting to
translate these research findings into terms which promote
publicity and media discussion while making them intelligible
to policy-makers.

Finally, there is the formation of the Family Forum, through which groups expressing different family interests can join to channel their views to government. Malcolm Wicks's chapter (25) indicates some of the complexities in bringing together the diverse interests of people and organisations espousing 'the family cause'. But Peter Bottomley, the Member of Parliament who has played a leading role in forming the Forum, has said in a motion introduced to parliament in 1978 ('Hansard', col. 834):

There is a tremendous tradition of voluntary organizations and charities, but voluntary bodies have failed in two ways. They have not got together in an effective forum to present agreed policies to the government and they have not organised families.

Most Hon Members (of Parliament) have in their constituencies ratepayers, residents and tenants' associations, but in only a few areas do these groups get together to represent the interests of families as well as the interests of those who are concerned only with rates, rents or the repairsof pavements. There are associations representing the family on a number of areas ... and they could be taken as models in the vast majority of residential areas, especially in the inner cities, where problems of family life are greatest. I do not intend to criticise any Government. I am trying to learn the lessons of the past, and see how we can raise the level of discussion and ensure more effective public education and political representation for the needs of families.

The Government need a family lobby and movement just as much as families need such a government.

There is, in conclusion, the emergence of a three-pronged approach to improving the quality of family life in Britain.

Research: An approach through strengthening the base of knowledge about family life. The present book is an expression.

Dissemination: The Study Commission on the Family aims to promote public information and debate, presenting research-based information in useable ways in the service of policy-makers and administrators. The present Study Commission is a temporary body; the type of Commission recommended by Jonathan Brayshaw (1980) would provide continuity.

Advocacy: The Family Forum is an expression of this approach, and though a late-starter in Britain compared with other countries with active family unions, a much needed initiative which is likely to succeed.

It is in the fruitful interplay of the three approaches that the distinctive British contribution to family life is likely to emerge, and to the extent that this fruitful interplay is achieved Britain may move from being a country that pays political lipservice to 'the family' to one that understands and supports families and places family life in the valued position its advocates envision.   Results are showing already.   Many bits and pieces are beginning to come together, and a sense of pattern and coherence is emerging.

Bibliography

ABRAMS, M. (1977), 'Profiles of the Elderly', vol. 1, London: Age Concern Publication.

ABRAMS, M. (1978), 'Beyond Three Score and Ten', London: Age Concern Publication.

ABRAMS, P. and McCULLOCH, A. (1976a), Men, Women and Communes, in D.L. Barker and S. Allen (eds), 'Dependence and Exploitation in Work and Marriage', London: Longman.

ABRAMS, P. and McCULLOCH, A. (1976b), 'Communes, Sociology and Society', Cambridge: Cambridge University Press.

ACKERMAN v ACKERMAN (1972) Fam. 225.

ADAMS, B., OKELEY, J., MORGAN, D. and SMITH, D. (1975), 'Gypsies and Government Policy in England', London: Heinemann/Centre for Environmental Studies (CES).

ADAMSON, G. (1970), Foster Parents' Feelings, 'New Society', no. 421, 22 October, pp. 730-1.

ADAMSON, G. (1973), 'The Caretakers', London: Bookstall Services.

AHMED, Shama (1978), Is Racial Matching Sufficient, 'Community Care', 29 November.

AITKEN-SWAN, J. (1977), 'Fertility Control and the Medical Profession', London: Croom Helm.

AKRAM, Mohammed and LEIGH, Sara (1974), 'Where Do You Keep Your String Beds', London: Runnymede Trust.

ALAVI, Hamza, (1972), 'Kinship in West Punjab Villages', Contributions to Indian Sociology (n.s.), 6.

ALDGATE, J. (1976), The Child in Care and his Parents, 'Adoption and Fostering', no. 84, pp. 29-40.

ALDGATE, J. (1977), Identification of Factors Influencing Children's Length of Stay in Care, unpublished PhD thesis, University of Edinburgh.

ALDOUS, J. (1978), 'Family Careers: Developmental Change in Families', New York: Wiley.

ALDOUS, J. (ed.) (1981), 'Dual Earner Families', Special Issue, 'Journal of Family Issues', Sage, vol. 2, no. 2.

500

ANDERSON, M. (ed.) (1966), 'Sociology of the Family', Har-
mondsworth, Penguin.
ANDERSON, M. (1971), 'Family Structure in Nineteenth-Century
Lancashire', Cambridge: Cambridge University Press.
ANDRY, R. (1960), 'Delinquency and Parental Pathology',
London: Methuen.
ANWAR, Mohammed (1979), 'The Myth of Return', London: Heine-
mann.
ARDENER, S. (ed) (1978), 'Defining Females', London: Croom
Helm.
ARENSBERG, C. and KIMBALL, S. (1940), 'Family and Community in
Ireland', Harvard University Press (reissued in 1967).
ARKIN, W. and DOBROFSKY, L.R. (1978), Job Sharing, in R. Rapo-
port and R.N. Rapoport (eds), 'Working Couples', London:
Routledge & Kegan Paul.
ARNOLD, MATTHEW (1869), 'Culture and Anarchy: an essay in poli-
tical and social criticism', London: Smith, Elder & Co.
ARNOLD, MATTHEW (1888), 'Civilization in the United States',
Boston: Cupples & Hurd.
ASCHENBRENNER, Joyce (1975), 'Lifelines: Black Families in
Chicago', New York: Holt, Rinehart & Winston.
ASSOCIATION OF BRITISH ADOPTION AND FOSTERING AGENCIES (1975),
'Ending the Waiting - 1. Which Children and What Plan?',
London: Association of British Adoption and Fostering
Agencies.
ASSOCIATION OF BRITISH ADOPTION AND FOSTERING AGENCIES (1977),
'Child Adoption', London: Association of British Adoption
and Fostering Agencies.
ASSOCIATION OF BRITISH ADOPTION AND FOSTERING AGENCIES (1979),
'Foster Care - Some Questions Answered', London: Association
of British Adoption and Fostering Agencies.
ATKINSON, D., DALLIN, A. and LAPIDUS, G.W. (1978), 'Women in
Russia', Hassocks: Harvester Press.
ATKINSON, P. (1978), Fitness, Femininity and Schooling, in
S. Delamont and L. Duffin (eds), 'The Nineteenth-Century
Woman', London: Croom Helm.
ATTWOOD v ATTWOOD (1968), p. 591.
AURORA, Gurdip Singh (1967), 'The New Frontiersmen', Bombay:
Popular Prakashan.
BABCOCK, C. (1965a), Some Psycho-dynamic Factors in Foster
Parenthood, Part I, 'Child Welfare', vol. 44, no. 9, pp. 485-
93.
BABCOCK, C. (1965b), Some Psycho-dynamic Factors in Foster
Parenthood, Part II, 'Child Welfare', vol. 44, no. 10, pp.
570-7.
BAHR, S.J. (1974), Effects on power and division of labour in
the family, in L.W. Hoffman and F.I. Nye (eds), 'Working
Mothers', San Francisco: Jossey-Bass.

BAILYN, L. (1971), Career and Family orientations of husbands and wives in relation to marital happiness, 'Human Relations', 23, pp. 97-113.
BAKER, J.C. (1976), Company, policies and executive wives abroad, 'Industrial Relations', 15.
BAKER, W.B., EEKELAAR, J.M., GIBSON, C. and RAIKES, S. (1977), 'The Matrimonial Jurisdiction of Registrars', Oxford: Centre for Sociolegal Studies.
BALINT, M., HUNT, J., JOYCE, D., MARINKER, M. and WOODCOCK, J. (1970), 'Treatment or Diagnosis: a study of repeat prescriptions in general practice', London: Tavistock.
BALLARD, C. (1978), Arranged Marriages in a British Context, 'New Community', 6.
BALLARD, C. (1979), Conflict, Continuity and Change: Second Generation South Asians, in V. Saifullah Khan (ed.), 'Minority Families in Britain', London: Macmillan.
BALLARD, R. (1973), Family Organization among the Sikhs in Britain, 'New Community', no. 2.
BALLARD, R. (1979), Ethnic Minorities and the Social Services, in V. Saifullah Khan (ed.), 'Minority Families in Britain', London: Macmillan.
BALLARD, C. and BALLARD, R. (1977), The Sikhs, in J.L. Watson (ed.), 'Between Two Cultures', Oxford: Basil Blackwell.
BALLARD, R. and DRIVER, G. (1977), The ethnic approach, 'New Society', 16 June; reptd in P. Worsely (ed.) (1970), 'Social Problems of Modern Britain', Harmondsworth: Penguin.
BANKS, J.A. (1954), 'Prosperity and Parenthood', London: Routledge & Kegan Paul.
BARBER, D. (ed.) (1975), 'One Parent Families', London: Davis Poynter.
BARKER, D. and ALLEN, S. (eds) (1976), 'Sexual Divisions and Society', London: Tavistock.
BARKER, D. (forthcoming), 'Sex and Generation', London: Tavistock.
BARNES, J. (1980), Kinship Studies: Some Impressions on the Current State of Play, 'Man', 15, 2, pp. 293-303.
BARNSLEY METROPOLITAN BOROUGH COUNCIL, SOCIAL SERVICES DEPARTMENT (1975), 'A Foster Review, July 1974 to January 1975', Barnsley: Metropolitan Borough Council.
BARRETT, M. and ROBERTS, H. (1978), Doctors and Their Patients: the Social Control of Women in General Practice, in C. Smart and B. Smart (eds), 'Women, Sexuality and Social Control', London: Routledge & Kegan Paul.
BARRINGTON BAKER, W. et al. (1977), 'The Matrimonial Jurisdiction of Registrars', Oxford: Centre for Sociolegal Studies, SSRC.
BARRON, R.D. and NORRIS, G.M. (1976), Sexual Divisions and the Dual Labour Market, in D.L. Barker and S. Allen (eds), 'Dependence and Exploitation in Work and Marriage', London: Longman.

BARTH, Frederick (1959), 'Political Leadership among the Swat Pathans', London: Athlone Press.

BEEDEL, C. (1970), 'Residential Life with Children', London: Routledge & Kegan Paul.

BELL, C. (1968), 'Middle Class Families', London: Routledge & Kegan Paul.

BENJAMIN, B. and OVERTON, E. (1981), The Prospects for Mortality Decline in England and Wales, 'Population Trends', Spring, no. 23, pp. 22-8.

BERADU, F.M. (1967), Kinship Interactions and Communication Among Space-Age Migrants, 'Journal of Marriage and the Family', August.

BERGER, B.M., HACKETT, B.M. and MILLAR, R.M. (1972), Child Rearing Practices in the Communal Family, in H.P. Dreitzel (ed.), 'Family, Marriage and the Struggle of the Sexes', New York: Macmillan.

BERGER, M., FOSTER, M. and WALLSTON, B.S. (1978), Finding two jobs, in R. Rapoport and R.N. Rapoport (eds), 'Working Couples', London: Routledge & Kegan Paul.

BERGER, P. (1966), 'Invitation to Sociology', Harmondsworth: Penguin.

BERNARD, J. (1973), 'The Future of Marriage', New York: Bantam Books; London: Souvenir Press.

BERNARD, J. (1975), 'Women, Wives, Mothers', Chicago: Aldine-Atherton.

BEVERIDGE (1942), 'Report on the Social Insurance and Allied Services', Cmnd 6404, London: HMSO.

BIGGS, J.M. (1962), 'The Concept of Matrimonial Cruelty', London: Athlone Press.

BIRD, C., CHESSUM, R., FURLONG, J., JOHNSON, D. (eds) (1981), 'Disaffected Pupils', London: Brunel University.

BLACKSTONE, W. (1765), 'Commentaries on the Laws of England', Oxford: Oxford University Press, book 1, p. 430.

BLAKE, Judith (1961), 'Family Structure in Jamaica', New York: Free Press.

BLOOD, R. and WOLFE, D. (1960), 'Husbands and Wives', New York: Free Press.

BONE, M. (1977), 'Pre-School Children and the Need for Day Care', London: OPCS; HMSO.

BOTT, E. (1957), 'Family and Social Network', London: Tavistock, 2nd edn 1971.

BOTTOMLEY, P. (1978), The Family, 'Hansard', 7 March, col. 832.

BOULDING, E. (1976), Familial constraints on women's work roles, in M. Blaxall and B. Reagan (eds), 'Women and the Workplace', Chicago: University of Chicago Press.

BOWERMAN, C.E. and IRISH, D. (1962), Some reactions of stepchildren to their parents, 'Marriage and Family Living', 24, pp. 113-21.

BOWLBY, J. (1951), 'Maternal Care and Child Health', Geneva, World Health Organization.
BOWLBY, J. (1953), 'Child-care and the Growth of Love', Harmondsworth: Penguin.
BOWLBY, J. (1969), 'Attachment and Loss: I Attachment', London, Hogarth Press.
BRAH, Avtar (1979), South Asian Teenagers in Southall, 'New Community'.
BRANCA, P. (1975), 'Silent Sisterhood', London: Croom Helm.
BRAYSHAW, J. (1980), 'Public Policy and Family Life', London: Policy Studies Institute Discussion Paper No. 3.
BRIDGE, D. (1978), 'Looking at Leisure', London: Epworth Press.
BRIMBLECOMBE, F.S.W. (1974), Exeter Project for Handicapped Children, 'British Medical Journal', 4, pp. 706-9.
BROMLEY, P.M. (1976), 'Family Law', London: Butterworths, 5th edn, p. 15.
BRONFENBRENNER, U. (1971), 'Two Worlds of Childhood: US and USSR', London: George Allen & Unwin.
BROWN, G.W. and HARRIS, T. (1978), 'Social Origins of Depression: a study of psychiatric disorders in women', London: Tavistock.
BROWN, G. et al. (1975), Social class and psychiatric disturbances in an urban population, 'Sociology', 9, pp. 225-54.
BROWN, N.L. (1955), National Assistance and the Liability to Maintain One's Family, '18 Modern Law Review', 110.
BROWNE v PRITCHARD (1975), 1 W.L.R. 1366.
BRYCE, J. (1868-9), 'General Report on the County of Lancashire', Schools Enquiry Commission, vol. ix, London: HMSO.
BRYCE, M.E. and EHLERT, R.C. (1971), 144 Foster Children, 'Child Welfare', vol. 50, no. 9, pp. 446-52.
BULMER, M. (1980), 'Social Research and Royal Commissions', London: Allen & Unwin.
BURCHINAL, L.G. (1963), Research on young marriage: implications for family life education, in M.B. Sussman (ed.), 'Sourcebook of Marriage and the Family', Boston: Houghton-Mifflin.
BURGOYNE, J. and CLARK, D. (1980), Why Get Married Again, 'New Society', 3 April, pp. 12-14.
BURGOYNE, J. and CLARK, D. (forthcoming), 'Making a Go of It: a study of step-parents in Sheffield', London: Routledge & Kegan Paul.
BURMAN, S. (ed.) (1978), 'Fit Work for Females', London: Croom Helm.
BURTON, R. (1977), Leisure and the Social Sciences, in 'Leisure and the Quality of Life', vol. 2, London: HMSO, pp. 409-44.
BUSFIELD, J. and PADDON, M. (1977), 'Thinking About Children', Cambridge: Cambridge University Press.
BYRNE, E. (1978), 'Women and Education', London: Tavistock.

CALLAN, H. (1975), The premiss of dedication: notes towards an ethnography of diplomats' wives, in S. Ardener (ed.), 'Perceiving Women', London: Dent.

CAMPBELL, J.K. (1964), 'Honour, Family and Patronage', Oxford: Clarendon Press.

CARRILINE, M. and SAWBRIDGE, P. (1975), 'Adoption in the Seventies', London: Association of British Adoption and Fostering Agencies.

CARTER, C. (1980), The Purposes of Welfare Services, in C. Carter and T. Wilson (eds), 'Discussing the Welfare State', London: PSI.

CARTWRIGHT, A. (1970), 'Parents and Family Planning Services', London: Routledge & Kegan Paul.

CARTWRIGHT, A. (1976), 'How Many Children?', London: Routledge & Kegan Paul.

CARTWRIGHT, A. et al. (1973), 'Life Before Death', London: Routledge & Kegan Paul.

CENTRAL POLICY REVIEW STAFF (1978), 'Services for Young Children with Working Mothers', London: HMSO.

CENTRAL STATISTICAL OFFICE (1980), 'Social Trends', No. 10, London: HMSO.

CHAMBERLAIN, R., CHAMBERLAIN, S., HOWLETT, B. and CLAIREAUX, A. (1978), 'British Births', 1970 Vol. a, 'The First Week of Life', London: Heinemann.

CHEN, E. and COBB, S. (1960), Family Structure in Relation to Health and Disease, 'Journal of Chronic Diseases', 12, pp. 544-67.

CHESTER, R. (1971a), The Duration of Marriage to Divorce, 'British Journal of Sociology', 22, p. 172.

CHESTER, R. (1971b), Health and marriage breakdown, 'British Journal of Preventive and Social Medicine', 25, pp. 231-5.

CHESTER, R. (1972), Divorce and Legal Aid: a false hypothesis, 'Sociology', 6, p. 205.

CHESTER, R. (ed.) (1977), 'Divorce in Europe, Leiden: Martinus Nijhoff.

CHESTER, R. and PEEL, J. (eds) (1977), 'Equalities and Inequalities in Family Life', London: Academic Press.

CHETWYND, J. and HARTNETT, O. (1978), 'The Sex Role System', London: Routledge & Kegan Paul.

CHILD BENEFIT NOW CAMPAIGN (1977), 'The Great Child Benefit Robbery', London: CBNC.

CHILMAN, C.S. (1968), Families in Development at Mid-Stage of the Family Life Cycle, 'The Family Co-Ordinator', 17, 4 (October), pp. 297-312.

CHODOROW, N. (1978), 'The Reproduction of Mothering', Berkeley, California: University of California Press.

CHRISTENSEN, H.T. (1963), Time of the first pregnancy as a factor in Divorce, 'Eugenic Review', 10, p. 119.

CLARK, H. (1976), The New Marriage, '12 Willamette Law Journal', p. 441.
CLARK, Kenneth (1974), 'Another Part of the Wood: a self portrait', London: John Murray.
CLARKE, A.M. and CLARKE, A.D.B. (1976), 'Early Experience: Myth and Evidence', London: Open Books.
CLARKE v CLARKE (1978), 9 Family Law 15.
CLARKE, Edith (1957), 'My mother who fathered me', London: George Allen & Unwin.
CLEARY v CLEARY (1974), 1 All E.R. 498 (adultery not connected with intolerability).
CLIVE, E.M. (1976), 'The Divorce (Scotland) Act 1976', Edinburgh: Green & Sons.
CLIVE, E.M. and WILSON, J.G. (1974), 'The Law of Husband and Wife in Scotland', Edinburgh: W. Green.
COBBE, F.P. (1863), 'Essays on the pursuits of women', London: Emily Faithfull.
COCKBURN, J.S. (ed.) (1977), 'Crime in England 1550-1800', London: Methuen.
COGSWELL, B.E. and SUSSMAN, M.B. (1972), Changing family marriage forms: complications for human service systems, in M. Sussman (ed.), 'Non-traditional Family Forms in the 1970s', Minneapolis: National Council on Family Relations.
COHEN, C. (1977), Absentee Husbands in Spiralist Families: the Myth of the Symmetrical Family, London: Civil Service College, 'Journal of Marriage and the Family'.
COMMISSION OF THE EUROPEAN COMMUNITIES (1977), 'The Perception of Poverty in Europe: Report on a Public Opinion Survey', Brussels.
COMMISSION OF THE EUROPEAN COMMUNITY (1978), 'Second European Social Budget' (1976-80), Brussels.
COMMISSION ON REFORM OF THE GROUNDS OF DIVORCE (1966), Cmnd 3123, London: HMSO.
COMMUNITY RELATIONS COMMISSION (CRC) (1975), 'Fostering Black Children: a policy document on the needs of ethnic minority children', London: CRC.
CONFEDERATION OF INDIAN ORGANISATIONS (UK) (1980), Observations on 'Marriage Matters'.
CONSTANTINE, L. and CONSTANTINE, J. (1973), 'Group Marriage', New York: Macmillan.
CONSTANTINE, L. and CONSTANTINE, J. (1976), 'Treasures of the Island: children in alternative families', Beverley Hills: Sage Publications.
CONSTANTINIDES, P.M. (1977), The Greek Cypriots: Factors in the Maintenance of Ethnic Identity, in J.L. Watson (ed.), 'Between Two Cultures', Oxford: Basil Blackwell.
CONSTANTINIDES, P.M. (1979), Ethnic Minorities and the National Health Service, London School of Hygiene and Tropical

Medicine, 13 October (paper presented at British Medical
Anthropology Society Conference).
COOPER & LYBRAND ASSOCIATES (1979), 'Providing Sports Facili-
ties: the role of joint and separate provision'.
CORNILLON, S.K. (ed.) (1972), 'Images of Women in Fiction',
Bowling Green, Ohio: Bowling Green University Popular Press.
COSER, L. (1956), 'The Functions of Social Conflict', London:
Routledge & Kegan Paul.
COURT REPORT, 'The Report of the Committee on Child Health
Services', Cmnd 6684, London: HMSO.
COURT, S.M. (1976), 'Fit for the Future', Report of the Com-
mittee on Child Health Services, London: HMSO.
COVENTRY COMMUNITY DEVELOPMENT PROJECT (1975), 'Final Report
Part I, Coventry and Hillfields: prosperity and the persis-
tence of inequality', London.
COWAN, E. and STOUT, E. (1939), A Comparative Study of the
Adjustment made by Foster Children after Complete and Partial
Breaks in Continuity of Home Environment, 'American Journal
of Orthopsychiatry', vol. 9, no. 2, pp. 338-41.
CRAIG, C. and WEDDERBURN, D. (1974), Relative Deprivation in
Work, in D. Wedderburn (ed.), 'Poverty, Inequality and Class
Structure', Cambridge: Cambridge University Press.
CRANE, F.R. Family Settlements and Succession, in R.H. Grave-
son and I.R. Crane (eds), 'A Century of Family Law', London:
Sweet & Maxwell.
CRC (1977), 'Urban Deprivation, Racial Inequality and Social
Policy', London: HMSO.
CRELLIN, E., PRINGLE, M.L.K. and WEST, P. (1971), 'Born
Illegitimate', Slough: NFER.
CRISHNA, Sita (1975), 'Girls of Asian Origin in Britain',
London: YWCA.
CROW, D. (1971), 'The Victorian Woman', London: Allen &
Unwin.
CUNNINGHAM, W. (1897 and 1969), 'Alien Immigrants to England',
London: Kelly.
CUZNER v UNDERDOWN (1974), 2 All E.R. 351.
DAHYA, Badr (1974a), 'Urban Ethnicity', London: Tavistock.
DAHYA, Badr (1974b), The Nature of Pakistani Ethnicity in
Industrial Cities in Britain, in Abner Cohen (ed.), 'Urban
Ethnicity', London: Tavistock.
DANFELD, D. and GORDON, M. (1971), Mate Swapping, in S.A.
Skolnick and J.A. Skolnick (eds), 'Family in Transition',
Boston: Little & Co.
DANIEL, W.W. (1974), 'National Survey of the Unemployed',
London: PEP.
DARTINGTON AMENITY RESEARCH TRUST/DEPARTMENT OF PSYCHOLOGY,
UNIVERSITY OF SURREY (1979), 'Interpretation in Visitor
Centres', CCP. 115, Countryside Commission.

DAVIDOFF, L., L'ESPERANCE, J. and NEWBY, H. (1976), Landscape with Figures: Home and Community in English Society, in J. Mitchell and A. Oakley (eds), 'The Rights and Wrongs of Women', Harmondsworth: Penguin.

DAVIE, R., BUTLER, N. and GOLDSTEIN, H. (1972), 'From Birth to Seven: Second Report of the National Child Development Study (1958 cohort)', London: Longman, for National Children's Bureau.

DAVIS, F. (1963), 'Passage Through Crisis: polio victims and their families', New York: Bobbs-Merrill.

DAVIS, J. (1977), 'People of the Mediterranean: an essay in comparative social anthropology', London: Routledge & Kegan Paul.

DEECH, R. (1977), The Principles of Maintenance, 7 'Family Law', p. 229.

DEFOE, D. (1927), 'A Tour Thro' the Whole Island of Great Britain vol. III', London: G. Strahan

DELAMONT, S. and DUFFIN, L. (eds) (1978), 'The Nineteenth-Century Woman: her cultural and physical world', London: Croom Helm.

DELPHY, C. (1976), Continuities and Discontinuities in Marriage and Divorce, in D. Barker and S. Allen (eds), 'Sexual Divisions and Society', London: Tavistock.

DELPHY, C. (1976), 'The Main Enemy', London: Women's Research and Resources Centre.

DENNIS, N., HENRIQUES, F. and SLAUGHTER, C. (1956), 'Coal is our Life', London: Eyre & Spottiswoode.

DEPARTMENT OF EDUCATION AND SCIENCE (DES) (1972), 'The Health of the School Child', Report of the Chief Medical Officer, London: HMSO.

DES (1977), Education in Schools, a paper for consultation.

DESAI, R. (1963), 'Indian Immigrants in Britain', Oxford: Oxford University Press.

DHONDY, Farrukh (1976), 'East End at Your Feet', London: Macmillan.

DHONDY, Farrukh (1978), 'Come to Mecca', London: Fontana.

DEPARTMENT OF HEALTH AND SOCIAL SECURITY (DHSS) (1976), 'Prevention and Health: everybody's business', London: HMSO.

DHSS (1975), Letter to National Council for Civil Liberties, 28 May.

DHSS (1976), 'A Guide to Fostering Practice', London: HMSO.

DHSS (1977), 'Prevention and Health: Reducing the Risk: Safer Pregnancy and Childbirth', London: HMSO.

DHSS (1978), Comparative Social Security Tables for Member States of the European Communities, cyclostyled.

DHSS/SBC (1977), 'Low Incomes', London: HMSO.

DICKS, H.V. (1967), 'Marital Tensions', London: Routledge & Kegan Paul.

DIRECTORY OF COMMUNES, Commune Movement n.d. (c. 1971).

DIXON, B. (1977), 'Cathing Them Young: sex, race and class in children's fiction', London: Pluto Press.

DOBASH, R.E. and DOBASH, R. (1980), 'Violence Against Wives', London: Open Books.

DODGE, D.L. and MARTIN, W.T. (1970), 'Social Stress and Chronic Illness', Notre Dame, Indiana: University of Notre Dame Press.

DEPARTMENT OF THE ENVIRONMENT (DOE) (1978), 'National Dwelling and Housing Survey', London: HMSO

DOMINIAN, J. (1979a), Marital Therapy, in 'An Introduction to the Psychotherapies', Oxford: S. Bloch.

DOMINIAN, J. (1979b), 'Introduction to Marital Pathology', London: British Medical Association.

DONNISON, D. (1979), Housing the Poorest People, 'Housing Review', March/April, vol. 28, no. 2.

DOUGLAS, J.W.B. (1964), 'The Home and the School', London: MacGibbon & Kee.

DOWER, M. (1965), 'The Challenge of Leisure', Civic Trust.

DOWER, M., RAPOPORT, R., STRELITZ, Z. and KEW, S. (1981), Leisure provision and people's needs, London: HMSO.

DOWNING, M. and DOWER, M. (1973), 'Second Homes in England and Wales', Countryside Commission and Dartington Amenity Research Trust, Publication no. 7.

DRIVER, G. (1977), Ethnicity, Cultural Competence and School Achievement (unpublished PhD thesis, University of Illinois at Urbana-Champaign).

DU BOULAY, J. (1974), 'Portrait of a Greek Mountain Village', Oxford: Clarendon Press.

DUFFIN, L. (1978), The Conspicuous Consumptive: Woman as Invalid, in S. Delamont and L. Duffin (eds) ('The Nineteenth-Century Woman', London: Croom Helm.

DUMAZEDIER, J. (1967), 'Toward a Society of Leisure', London: Collier-Macmillan.

DUNBAR, Janet (1953), 'The Early Victorian Woman: some aspects of her life (1837-59)', London: George Harrap & Co.

DUNCAN, G.J. and MORGAN, J.N. (1976), 'Five Thousand American Families, vol. 4', Ann Arbor: University of Michigan Survey Research Centre.

DUNNELL, K. (1979), 'Family Formation 1976', OPCS, London: HMSO.

DURKHEIM, E. (1969), 'The Division of Labour in Society', Toronto: Collier-Macmillan.

DUVALL, E.M. (1977), 'Marriage and Family Development', Philadelphia: J.B. Lippincott.

DYSON HOLDINGS v FOX (1976), 1 Q.B. 503.

EDGELL, S. (1980), 'Middle Class Couples', London: Allen & Unwin.

EEKELAAR, J.M. (1973), What are Parental Rights?, 89 'Law Quarterly Review', p. 210.

EEKELAAR, J.M. (1975), The Place of Divorce in Family Law's New Role, 38 'Modern Law Review', p. 241.

EEKELAAR, J. and CLIVE, E. (1977), 'Custody After Divorce', Oxford: Centre for Sociolegal Studies, SSRC.

EEKELAAR, J. (1978), 'Family Law and Social Policy', London: Weidenfeld & Nicolson.

EEKELAAR, J.M. (1979), Some Principles of Financial and Property Adjustment on Divorce, 95 'Law Quarterly Review', p. 253.

EGLAR, Zekiye (1960), 'A Punjabi Village in Pakistan', New York: Columbia University Press.

EHRENREICH, B. and ENGLISH, D. (1979), 'For Her Own Good', London: Pluto Press.

ELDER, C. (1974), 'Children of the Great Depression', Chicago: University of Chicago Press.

ELSON, M. (1974), The Family Car, 'New Society', 11 April.

ELSTON, E., FULLER, J. and MARCH, M. (1975), Judicial Hearings of Undefended Divorce Petitions, 38 'Modern Law Review', p. 609.

EMLEN, A.C. and PERRY, J.B. (1974), Child Care Arrangements, in L.W. Hoffman and F.I. Nye (eds), 'Working Mothers', San Francisco: Jossey-Bass.

EMLEN, A.C. and WATSON, E.L. (1971), 'Matchmaking in Neighbourhood Day Care: a descriptive study of the day care neighbour service', Corvallis: DCE Books.

EMMETT, I. (1977), The Social Filter in the Leisure Field, 'Recreation News Supplement' 4.

ENNALS, D. (1978), Mothers and Children: Towards a Reinherited Family, Eleanor Rathbone Memorial Lecture.

EQUAL OPPORTUNITIES COMMISSION (EOC) (1977), 'Income Tax and Sex Discrimination', Manchester: Equal Opportunities Commission.

EOC (1977), 'Women and Low Incomes', Manchester: Equal Opportunities Commission.

EOC (1978), 'I want to work ... but what about the kids?', Manchester: Equal Opportunities Commission.

EQUAL OPPORTUNITIES COMMISSION RESEARCH BULLETIN, vol. 1, no. 1, p. 24.

EPSTEIN, C. (1971), Law Partners and Marital Partners: strains and solutions in the dual-career family enterprise, 'Human Relations', vol. 24, no. 6, pp. 549-64.

ERIKSON, E. (1959), Identity and the life cycle, 'Psychological Issues', 1, 1, 1-171.

ESSEN, J. and LAMBERT, L. (1977), Living in one-parent families: relationships and attitudes of 16-year-olds, 'Child Care, Health and Development', 3, pp. 301-18.

LORD EVERSHED MR (1957), Foreword to R.H. Graveson and F.R. Crane (eds), 'A Century of Family Law', London: Sweet & Maxwell.

EVERSLEY, D. (1979), Regions in Change, Implications for Planning, Proceedings of Annual Conference, RTPI.

EVERSELY, D. and BONNERJEA, L. (1980), 'Changes in the Size and Structure of the Resident Population of Inner Areas', London: SSRC.

FAIR PLAY FOR CHILDREN (1979), 'Why Lock up our Schools?'
FANSHEL, D. (1966), 'Foster Parenthood - A Role Analysis',
Minnesota: University of Minnesota Press.
FANSHEL, D. (1976), Status Changes of Children in Foster Care,
'Child Welfare', vol. 50, no. 3, pp. 143-71.
FARRIS, A. (1978), Commuting, in R. Rapoport and R.N. Rapo-
port (eds), 'Working Couples', London: Routledge & Kegan
Paul; New York: Harper & Row.
FAST, I. and CAIN, A.C. (1960), The Stepparent Role, 'American
Journal of Ortho-psychiatry', 36, pp. 485-91.
FEANDEL, K. (1975), cited in U. Kroll, 'Flesh of My Flesh',
London: Darton, Longman & Tod.
FEE, E. (1976), Science and the Woman Problem, in M.S. Teitel-
baum (ed.), 'Sex Differences', New York: Anchor Books.
FEIN, R.A. (1974), Men and Young Children, in J.H. Pleck and
J. Sawyer (eds), 'Men and Masculinity', New Jersey: Prentice
Hall.
FERGUSON, N. and WILLIAMS, P. (1969), The Identification of
Children Needing Compensatory Education, in 'Children at
Risk', Schools Council Research Project in Compensatory Educa-
tion No. 2.
FERGUSON, T. (1966), 'Children in Care and After', Oxford:
Oxford University Press.
FERRI, E. (1976), 'Growing up in a One-Parent Family', A
National Children's Bureau Report, Slough: National Founda-
tion for Educational Research.
FIELD, F., MEACHER, M. and POND, C. (1977), 'To Him Who Hath',
Harmondsworth: Penguin.
FINER, M. (1974), 'One-Parent Families', Report of the Commit-
tee, London: HMSO.
FINER, M. (1975), Note 16, and Justice, 'Parental Rights and
Duties and Custody Suits', London: Stevens.
FINER, M. and McGREGOR, O.R. (1974), A History of the Obliga-
tion to Maintain, Appendix 5 to the 'Report of the Committee
on One-Parent Families' (Chairman: Sir M. Finer), Cmnd 6269,
London: HMSO.
FIRTH, R. (ed.) (1956), 'Two Studies of Kinship in London',
London: Athlone Press.
FIRTH, R., HUBERT, J. and FORGE, A. (1969), 'Families and
their Relatives', London: Routledge & Kegan Paul.
FISHMAN, W.J. (1976), 'East End Jewish Radicals 1875-1914',
London: Duckworth.
FITTON, A.M.H. (1978), The reality for whom are we actually
providing?, in 'Countryside For All', CRRAG Conference pro-
ceedings, Countryside Commission, Cheltenham/Countryside Com-
mission for Scotland Perth/Sports Council London.
FITZHERBERT, Katrin (1967), 'West Indian Children in London',
London: C. Bell.

FITZHERBERT, K. (1974), The West Indian Background, in R. Oakley (ed.), 'New Backgrounds', Oxford: Oxford University Press.

FLETCHER, R. (1966), 'The Family and Marriage in Britain', Harmondsworth: Penguin.

FOGARTY, M. (1975), '40 to 60', London: Bedford Square Press.

FOGARTY, M.P. (1976), 'The Catholic Marriage Advisory Council and its Clients', London: Centre for Studies in Social Policy (now Policy Studies Institute (PSI)).

FOGARTY, M.P. (1980), How a family policy is born: the case of Britain, Proceedings of the Conference on Family Policy, Centro Internazionale Studi Famiglia, Milan.

FOGARTY, M.P., ALLEN, I. and WALTERS, P. (1981), 'Women in Top Jobs: Twelve Years After', London: Heinemann.

FOGARTY, M.P., RAPOPORT, R. and RAPOPORT, R.N. (1967), Women in Top Jobs: An Interim Report, PEP Report.

FOGARTY, M., RAPOPORT, R. and RAPOPORT, R.N. (1971), 'Sex, Career and Family', London and Beverley Hills: Sage Publications.

FOGELMAN, K. (1976), 'Britain's Sixteen Year Olds', London: National Children's Bureau (NCB).

FONDA, N. and MOSS, P. (eds) (1976), Mothers in Employment, Brunel University Management Programme.

FONER, Nancy (1979), 'Jamaican Farewell', London: Routledge & Kegan Paul.

FORTES, Meyer (1958), Introduction, in J. Goody (ed.), 'The Developmental Cycle in Domestic Groups', Cambridge: Cambridge University Press.

FRANKENBERG, R. (1975), In the Production of Their Lives, Men (?) ... Sex and Gender in British Community Studies, in D. Barker and S. Allen (eds), 'Sexual Divisions and Society', London: Tavistock.

FRENCH MINISTER FOR WOMEN'S AFFAIRS (1980), Comment in 'People'.

FRIEDL, E. (1962), 'Vasilika: a village in modern Greece', New York: Holt, Rinehart & Winston.

FRIEDLAENDER, D. and ROSHIER, R.J. (1966), A Study of Internal Migration in England and Wales, Part I, in 'Population Studies', vol. XIX, pp. 239-79.

FRIEDMAN, L.J. (1971), 'Virgin Wives', London: Tavistock.

FULLER v FULLER (1973), 2 All E.R. 650.

GALBRAITH, J.K. (1973), 'Economics and the Public Purpose', London: Andre Deutsch.

GARLAND, N.T. (1972), The Better Half? The male in the dual profession family, in C. Safilios-Rothschild, 'Toward a Sociology of Women', Xerox College.

GARMARNIKOV, E. (1978), Women and the City, 'Internationa Journal of Urban and Regional Research', vol. 2, no. 3.

GAVRON, H. (1960), 'The Captive Wife', London: Routledge &
Kegan Paul; Harmondsworth: Penguin.
GENERAL HOUSEHOLD SURVEY (1977), London: HMSO.
GENERAL REGISTER OFFICE (1966), Sample Census 1966, England
and Wales, Household Composition Tables.
GEORGE, V. (1970), 'Foster Care - Theory and Practice',
London: Routledge & Kegan Paul.
GEORGE, V. and MILLERSON, G. (1967), The Cypriot Community in
London, 'Race', 8, 3 (January), pp. 277-92.
GEORGE, V. and WILDING, P. (1972), 'Motherless Families',
London: Routledge & Kegan Paul.
GIBSON, C. (1974), The Association between Divorce and Social
Class in England and Wales, 'British Journal of Sociology',
25, p. 79.
GIDDENS, A. (1973), 'The Class Structure of the Advanced
Societies', London: Hutchinson.
GILLESPIE, D. (1971), Who has the power? The Marital Struggle,
'Journal of Marriage and the Family', 33, pp. 445-58.
GINSBERG, S. (1976), Women, Work and Conflict, in N. Fonda and
P. Moss (eds), 'Mothers in Employment', Brunel University
Management Programme.
GLAMPSON, A. and GOLDBERG, E.M. (1976), Post Seebohm Social
Services: the consumer's viewpoint, 'Social Work Today',
9 November.
GLENDON, M.A. (1977), 'State, Law and Family: family law in
transition in the United States and Western Europe', Amster-
dam: North-Holland, p. 1.
GLENDON, M.A. (1980), The New Marriage and the New Property,
in John M. Eekelaar and Sanford M. Katz (eds), 'Marriage and
Cohabitation in Contemporary Societies. Areas of Legal, Social
and Ethical Change: An International and Interdisciplinary
Study, Toronto and London: Butterworths. (Papers presented at
the Third World Conference of the International Society on
Family Law, Uppsala, Sweden, 5-9 June 1979.)
GLICK, P.C. (1957), 'American Families', New York: Wiley.
GLICK, P.C. and NORTON, A.J. (1971), Frequency, Duration and
Probability of Marriage and Divorce, 'Journal of Marriage and
the Family', 33, p. 307.
GLICK, P.C. and NORTON, A.J. (1973), Perspectives on the Recent
Upturn in Divorce and Remarriage, 'Demography', 10, p. 301.
GLICK, P.C. and NORTON, A.J. (1977), Marrying, Divorcing and
Living Together in the US Today, 'Population Bulletin', vol.
32, no. 5, Washington.
GOACHER, D. (1979), 'Use of Opportunities and constraints in
the Community'.
GODBEY, G. and PARKER, S.R. (1976), 'Leisure Studies and Ser-
vice', Philadelphia: W.B. Saunders.
GODDARD, T., POLLOCK, J. and FUDGER, M. (1977), Popular Music,

in J. King and M. Stott (eds), 'Is This Your Life?', London: Virago.

GOFFMAN, I. (1968), 'Stigma: the management of spoiled identity', Harmondsworth: Penguin.

GOFFMAN, I. (1979), 'Gender Advertisements', London: Macmillan.

GOLDSTEIN, J., FREUD, A. and SOLNIT, A.J. (1973), 'Beyond the Best Interests of the Child', New York: Free Press.

GOLDSTEIN, J., FREUD, A. and SOLNIT, J. (1979), 'Before the Best Interests of the Child', New York: Free Press.

GOLDTHORPE, J.A. (1980) (with C. Llewellyn and C. Payne), 'Social Mobility and Class Structure in Modern Britain', Oxford: Clarendon.

GONZALEZ, N. (1969), Toward a Definition of Matrifocality, in Whitten and Szwed (op. cit.).

GOODE, W.J. (1956), 'After Divorce', Chicago: Free Press.

GOODE, W.J. (1963), 'World Revolution and Family Patterns', New York: Free Press.

GOODY, J. (ed.) (1958), 'Development Cycle in Domestic Groups', Cambridge: Cambridge University Press.

GOODY, J. (1958), The Fission of Domestic Groups Among the LoDagaba, in J. Goody (ed.), 'Development Cycle in Domestic Groups', Cambridge: Cambridge University Press.

GORER, G. (1971), 'Sex and Marriage in England Today', London: Nelson.

GORMAN, C. (1975), 'Making Communes', London: Paladin.

GOVE, W.B. (1972), The Relationship Between Sex Roles, Marital Status and Mental Illness, 'Social Forces', 51, September, pp. 33-44.

GOWLER, D. and LEGGE, K. (1975), Stress and External Relationships: the 'hidden contract', in D. Gowler and K. Legge (eds), 'Managerial Stress', Epping: Gower Press.

GOWLER, D. and LEGGE, K. (1979), Cramming and contracting: some reflections on occupational over-commitment in dual-career families, working paper, MRC Social and Applied Psychology Unit, University of Sheffield.

GRAHAM, H. (forthcoming), Preventing and Health: every mother's business: a comment on child health policies in the seventies, in C.C. Harris (ed.), 'The Sociology of the Family', Sociological Review Monograph, University of Keele, Staffordshire.

GRAVESON, R.H. and CRANE, F.R. (eds),(1957), 'A Century of Family Law', London: Sweet & Maxwell.

GRAY, K. (1977), 'Reallocation of Property on Divorce', Abingdon: Professional Books.

GRAY, P.G. and PARR, E.A. (1957), Children in Care and the Recruitment of Foster Parents, 'Social Survey', 249, London: HMSO.

GREBENIK, E.R. and ROWNTREE, G. (1964), Factors Associated
with the Age of Marriage in Britain, 'Proceedings of the Royal
Society', vol. 159.
GREG, W.R. (1869), Why are women redundant?, in W.R. Greg,
'Literary and Social Judgments', 2nd edn, London: N. Trubner.
GRENFELL v GRENFELL (1978), Fam 128.
GRONSETH, E. (1975), Work-sharing families: adaptations of
pioneering families with husband and wife in part-time employ-
ment, 'Acta Sociologica' 18.   Paper for 3rd Biennial ISSBD
Conference, University of Surrey, July, Institute of Socio-
logy, University of Oslo.
GRONSETH, E. (1978), Work-sharing: a Norwegian example, in
R. Rapoport and R.N. Rapoport (eds), 'Working Couples',
London: Routledge & Kegan Paul.
GURIN, G., VEROFF, J. and FELD, S. (1960), 'Americans view
their Mental Health', New York: Basic Books.
HALCOMBE, L. (1973), 'Victorian Ladies at Work: middle-class
working women in England and Wales, 1850-1914', Newton Abbot,
Devon: David & Charles.
HALL, J.C. (1972), The Waning of Parental Rights, 'Cambridge
Law Journal', 248.
HALL, P. (1977), 'Reforming the Welfare', London: Heinemann.
HALLER, J.S. and HALLER, R.M. (1974), 'The Physician and Sex-
uality in Victorian America', New York: W.W. Norton.
HALSEY, A.H., HEATH, A.F. and RIDGE, J.M. (1980), 'Origins and
Destinations: family, class and education in modern Britain',
Oxford: Clarendon.
HAMILL, L. (1976), Wives as Sole and Joint Breadwinners,
mimeo, DHSS.
HANDY, C. (1978), Going against the Grain: working couples and
greedy occupations, in R. Rapoport and R.N. Rapoport (eds),
'Working Couples', London: Routledge & Kegan Paul.
HANLON v HANLON (1978), 1 W.L.R. 592.
HANNAN, D. and KATSIAOUNI, L. (1977), 'Traditional Families?
from culturally prescribed to negotiated roles in farm fami-
lies', Dublin: Economic and Social Research Institute.
HANNAN, D. (1979), 'Displacement and Development', Dublin:
Economic and Social Research Institute.
'HANSARD' (1979), vol. 970 (43), 20 July, col. 2158.
HAREVIN, T. (ed.) (1978), 'Transitions', New York: Academic
Press.
HARRELL-BOND, B.E. (1969), Conjugal Role Behaviour, 'Human
Relations', 22, 1, pp. 77-91.
HARRIS, A. (1968), 'Social Welfare and the Elderly', London:
HMSO.
HARRIS, C.C. (1969), 'The Family', London: Allen & Unwin.
HART, N. (1976), 'When Marriage Ends: a study in status
passage', London: Tavistock.

HARTLEY, J.F. (1978), An investigation of psychological aspects of management unemployment, unpublished PhD thesis, University of Manchester, Institute of Science and Technology.
HARTMAN, M. and BANNER, L.W. (eds) (1974), 'Clio's Consciousness Raised: new perspectives in the history of women', New York: Harper & Row.
HASTRUP, K. (1978), The Semantics of Biology: Virginity, in S. Ardener (ed.), 'Defining Females', London: Croom Helm.
HAWES v EVENDEN (1953),, 1 W.L.R. 1119.
HAWORTH, J.T. (1979), 'Community Involvement and Leisure', London: Lepus Books.
HAYES, M. (1978, 1979), Supplementary Benefit and Financial Provision Orders, 'Journal of Social Welfare Law', 216.
HELMHOLZ, R.H. (1962), 'Marriage Litigation in Medieval England', Cambridge: Cambridge University Press.
HENRIQUES, F. (1953), 'Family and Colour in Jamaica', London: Eyre & Spottiswoode.
HENRY, J. (1963), 'Culture Against Man', New York: Random House.
HERBERT, G.W. and WILSON, H. (1978), 'Parents and Children in the Inner City', London: Routledge & Kegan Paul.
HILL, R. and RODGERS, R.H. (1964), The Developmental Approach, in H.T. Christenson (ed.), 'Handbook of Marriage and the Family', Chicago: Rand McNally.
HILLMAN, M. and WHALLEY, A. (1973), Personal Mobility and Transport Policy, PEP Broadsheet no. 542.
HINCHCLIFFE, M. et al. (1978), 'Melancholy Marriage', Chichester: Wiley.
HM INSPECTORS OF EDUCATION (1979), 'Curriculum 11-16' (Music, outdoor, education, environmental education and physical education), London: DES.
HMSO (1955), 'Boarding Out of Children Regulations (England and Wales)', London: HMSO.
HMSO (1972), Children Act 1975, ss. 10 (3), 11(4) and, when in force, 37(2); inspired by the Report of the Departmental Committee on the Adoption of Children (Chairman: Sir W. Houghton, later Judge F.A. Stockdale), Cmnd 5107, London: HMSO.
HMSO (1973), 'First Report on Family Property: a New Approach', Law Commission no. 52, see also 'Family Property' Law, published working paper no. 42 (1971), London: HMSO.
HMSO (1974), Social Security Provision for Chronically Sick and Disabled People.
HMSO (1977), A Classification of the English Personal Social Services Authorities.
HMSO (1978), Third Report on Family Property: The Matrimonial Home (Co-ownership and Occupation Rights) and Household Goods, Law Commission no. 86, London: HMSO.

HMSO (1978), 'Social Trends', no. 8.

HMSO (1979), 'Social Trends', no. 9.

HMSO (1979), 'Social Trends 1980', no. 10, OPCS.

HMSO (1979), Law Commission P.W.P. no. 74, 'Illegitimacy'.

HOFFMAN, L. and NYE, F.E. (eds) (1974), 'Working Mothers', New York: Jossey-Bass.

HOFFMAN, L.W. (1962), Parental power relations and the division of household tasks, 'Marriage and Family Living', 22, pp. 27-35.

HOFFMAN, L.W. (1974, Effects of Maternal Employment on the child - a review of the research, 'Developmental Psychology', 10.

HOFFMAN, Dallah and WESTWOOD, Sallie (1979), 'Asian Women: education and social change', Leicester: University of Leicester School of Education.

HOGGART, R. (1957), 'The Uses of Literacy', London: Chatto & Windus.

HOLMAN, R. (1966), The Foster Child and Self Knowledge, 'Case Conference', vol. 12, no. 9, pp. 295-8.

HOLMAN, R. (1973), 'Trading in Children', London: Routledge & Kegan Paul.

HOLMAN, R. (1975), The Place of Fostering in Social Work, 'British Journal of Social Work', vol. 5, no. 1, pp. 3-29.

HOLMAN, R. (1970), Unsupported Mothers, 'New Society', 29 October.

HOLMAN, R. (ed.) (1970), 'Socially Deprived Families in Britain', London: NCSS.

HOLMES, C. (ed.) (1978), 'Immigrants and Minorities in British Society', London: Allen & Unwin.

HOLMSTROM, L. (1972), 'The Two-career Family', Cambridge, Mass.: Schenkman.

HOME OFFICE (1979), 'Marriage Matters', London: HMSO.

HONCOMBE, L. (1973), 'Victorian ladies at work', Newton Abbot, Devon: David & Charles.

HOPE, E., KENNEDY, M. and DE WINTER, A. (1976), Homeworkers in North London, in D.L. Barker and S.L. Allen (eds), 'Dependence and Exploitation in Work and Marriage', London: Longman.

HOUGHTON REPORT (1972), Report of the Departmental Committee on the Adoption of Children, Cmnd 5107, London: HMSO.

HOUSE OF COMMONS, 'Hansard', 2 November 1979, 30 March 1979.

HOUSE OF LORDS (1978), 'Hansard', 24 January.

HUBER, J. (1978), 'American Journal of Sociology', 78.

HUMPHREYS, A.J. (1966), 'The New Dubliners', London: Routledge & Kegan Paul.

HUNT, A. (1968), 'A Survey of Women's Employment', London: HMSO.

HUNT, A. (1970a), 'The Home Help Service in England and Wales', London: HMSO.

HUNT, A. (1970b), 'The Elderly at Home', London: HMSO.
HUNT, A. (1973), 'Families and their Needs', London: HMSO.
ILLICH, I. (1975), 'Medical Nemesis', London: Calder & Boyars.
INSTITUTE FOR EDUCATIONAL LEADERSHIP, Interim Report of the Family Impact Seminar (1978), George Washington University (cyclostyled).
INSTITUTE OF PERSONNEL MANAGEMENT (1975), 'Company Nurseries', London: IPM.
INTERNATIONAL PLANNED PARENTHOOD FEDERATION (1980), 'People', special number on Europe's falling birth rates, vol. 7, 1.
IRVINE, J., MILES, I. and EVANS, J. (eds) (1979), 'Demystifying Social Statistics', London: Pluto Press.
R v JACKSON (1891), 1 Q.B. 671, C.A.
JACKSON, B. and JACKSON, S. (1979), 'Childminder', London: Routledge & Kegan Paul.
JACKSON, B. and MARSDEN, D. (1962), 'Education and the Working Class', London: Routledge & Kegan Paul.
JACKSON, B. and GARVEY, A. (1975), 'Chinese Children', National Educational Research and Development Trust!
JACKSON, J. (1969), 'Formation and Annulment of Marriage', London: Butterworths, 2nd edn.
JACKSON, J. (2nd edn 1975 with supplement 1978), 'Matrimonial Finance and Taxation', London: Butterworths.
JAFFE, L. (1965), 'Foster Family Information and Services', Paul Baeruch School of Social Work, Hebrew University of Jerusalem, cited in R. Dinnage and M.L. Kellmer-Pringle (1967), 'Foster Home Care, Facts and Fallacies, London: Longmans.
JAFFEE, B. and FANSHEL, D. (1970), 'How they Fared in Adoption', New York: Columbia University Press.
JAMES, A.G. (1974), 'Sikh Children in Britain', Oxford: Oxford University Press.
JEFFERY, Patricia (1976), 'Migrants and Refugees', Cambridge: Cambridge University Press.
JEHU, D. (1979), 'Sexual Dysfunction', Chichester: Wiley.
JENKINS, R. (1965), The Needs of Foster Parents, 'Case Conference', vol. 11, no. 7, pp. 211-19.
JENKINS, R. (1979), 'The Road to Alto', London: Pluto Press.
JEPHCOTT, P.N.S. and SMITH, H. (1962), 'Married Women Working', London: George Allen & Unwin.
JEROME, J. (1975), 'Families of Eden: communes and the new anarchism', London: Thames & Hudson.
JHABVALA, Ruth Prawer (1955), 'To Whom She Will', London: Allen & Unwin.
JHABVALA, Ruth Prawer (1956), 'The Nature of Passion', London: Allen & Unwin.

JOHNSON, D. (1977), The Key to Keeping Working Families Together, 'The Times', 1 November.

JOHNSON, D. and RANSOM, E. (1980), Parents' Perceptions of Secondary Schools, in M. Craft, J. Raynor and L. Cohen (eds), 'Linking Home and School', 3rd edn, New York: Harper & Row.

JOHNSON, D. et al. (1980), 'Secondary Schools and the Welfare Network', London: Allen & Unwin.

JONES, Caradoc (1945), The Social Problem Group: poverty and subnormality of intelligence, quoted by C.P. Blacker (ed.), in 'Problem Families: five enquiries', London: Eugenics Society, 1952.

JORDAN, W. (1972), 'The Social Worker in the Family', London: Routledge & Kegan Paul.

JOSEPH, Sir Keith (1979), Article on Social Class, 'The Guardian', 18 July.

KADUSHIN, A. (1967), 'Child Welfare Services', New York: Macmillan.

KADUSHIN, A. (1970), 'Adopting Older Children', New York: Columbia University Press.

KAHN-FREUND, O. (1955), Matrimonial Property Law in England, in W. Friedman (ed.), 'Matrimonial Property Law', London: Stevens.

KALISH, R. and JOHNSON, A.I. (1972), Value Similarities and Differences in Three Generations of Women, 'Journal of Marriage and the Family', February.

KAMERMAN, S.B. (1979), Work and Family in Industrialised Societies, 'Signs: Journal of Women in Culture and Society', Summer.

KAMERMAN, S.B. and KAHN. A.J. (eds) (1978), 'Family Policy', New York: Columbia University Press.

KAMERMAN, S.B. and KAHN, A.J. (1979), Who's Taking Care of our Children?, 'Forum', Special Issue, International Year of of the Child.

KANTER, R.M. (ed.), (1973), 'Communes: creating and managing the collective life', New York: Harper & Row.

KANTER, R.M., JAFFE, O. and WEISBERG, D.K. (1975), Coupling, Parenting and the Presence of Others: intimate relationships in communal households, 'The Family Co-ordinator', October.

KAPADIA, K.M. (1966), 'Marriage and Family in India', Bombay: Oxford University Press.

KAPLAN, M. (1960), 'Leisure in America', New York: Wiley.

KARET, T. (1977), Popular Fiction, in J. King and M. Stott (eds), 'Is This Your Life?', London: Virago.

KARN, V. (1977), 'Retiring to the Seaside', Age Concern England Manifesto Series no. 9, London: Routledge & Kegan Paul.

KASL, S. and FRENCH, J. (1962), The Effects of Occupational Status on Physical and Mental Health, 'Journal of Social Issues', 18, 3, pp. 67-89.

KELLY, J. (1979), Leisure adaptation to family variety, in
Z. Strelitz (ed.), 'Leisure Provision and Family Diversity',
LSA Monograph, No. 9.
KENNEDY, W.J. (1863), 'Parliamentary Papers', vol. XLVII.
KERR, M. (1958), 'The People of Ship Street', London: Rout-
ledge & Kegan Paul.
KESSINGER, Tom (1975), 'Vilayatpur 1848-1968: social and eco-
nomic change in a North Indian village', Berkeley: University
of California Press.
KEW, S. (1975), 'Handicap and Family Crisis', London: Pitman.
KEW, S. (1979), West Indian Adolescents, in Z. Strelitz (ed.),
'Leisure Provision and Family Diversity', LSA Monograph,
No. 9.
KHARCHEV, A. and GOLOD, S. (1971), The two roles of Russian
working women in an urban area, in A. Michel (ed.), 'Family
Issues of Employed Women in Europe and America', Leiden:
E.J. Brill.
KING, J. and STOTT, M. (eds) (1977), 'Is This Your Life?,
images of women in the media', London: Virago.
KING, R. (1978), 'All Things Bright and Beautiful: a sociolo-
gical study of infants' classrooms', Chichester: Wiley.
KINSEY, A.C. et al. (1948), 'Sexual Behaviour in the Human
Male', Philadelphia: Saunders.
KITZINGER, S. (1973), 'Giving Brith: the parents' emotions
in childbirth', London: Sphere.
KLEIN, J. (1965), 'Samples from English Cultures', vol. 2,
'Childrearing Practices', London: Routledge & Kegan Paul.
KLEIN, V. (1965), 'Britain's Married Women Workers', London:
Routledge & Kegan Paul.
KLINE, D. and OVERSTREET, H.M.F. (1972), 'Foster Care for
Children: nurture and treatment', New York: Columbia Univer-
sity Press.
KNIGHT, R. and WARREN, M.D. (1978), 'Physically Disabled
People Living at Home: a study of numbers and needs', DHSS
Report on Health and Social Subjects 13, London: HMSO.
KOERBER, C. (1977), Television, in J. King and M. Stott (eds),
'Is This Your Life?', London: Virago.
KOHN, M. and CARROLL, E.E. (1960), Social Class and the allo-
cation of parental responsibilities, 'Sociometry', 23, pp.
372-92.
KOMAROVSKY, M. (1964), 'Blue collar marriage', New York:
Vintage.
KOMAROVSKY, M. (ed.) (1975), 'Sociology and Social Policy:
the case of Presidential Commissions', New York: Elsevier.
KROLL, U. (1975), 'Flesh of My Flesh', London: Darton,
Longman & Tod.

KUPER, L. and COHEN, H. (eds) (1950), 'Living in Town', London: Cresset Press.
LADBURY, S. (1977), The Turkish Cypriots: Ethnic Relations in London and Cyprus, in J.L. Watson (ed.), 'Between Two Cultures', Oxford: Basil Blackwell.
LADBURY, S. (1979), Turkish Cypriots in London: economy, society, culture, change, PhD thesis, University of London.
LADNER, J. (1971), 'Tomorrow's Tomorrow: the Black women', New York: Garden City Press.
LAING, R.D. (1973), 'The Politics of the Family and other essays', London: Tavistock.
LAND, H. (1969), 'Large Families in London', London: G. Bell & Sons.
LAND, H. (1976), Women: supporters or supported?, in D. Barker and S. Allen (eds), 'Sexual Divisions and Society: process and change', London: Tavistock.
LAND, H. (1978), Sex Role Stereotyping in the Social Security and Income Tax Systems, in J. Chetwynd and O. Hartnett (eds), 'The Sex Role System', London: Routledge & Kegan Paul.
LAND, H. and PARKER, R.A. (1978), Family Policy in the United Kingdom, in S.B. Kamerman and A.J. Kahn (eds), 'Family Policy: government and families in fourteen countries', New York: Columbia University Press.
LANDIS, J.T. (1962), Marriages of Mixed and Non-mixed Religious Faith, in 'Selected Studies in Marriage and the Family', New York: Holt, Rinehart & Winston.
LANDIS, J.T. (1963), Some correlates of divorce and non-divorce among the unhappily married, in 'Marriage and Family Living'.
LAPIDUS, G.W. (1978), Sexual Equality and Soviety Policy: a developmental perspective, in Atkinson et al. (eds), 'Women in Russia', Hassocks: Harvester Press.
LASCH, C. (1977), 'Haven in a Heartless World', New York: Basic Books.
LASCH, C. (1978), 'The Culture of Narcissism', New York: Norton.
LASLETT, P. (1971), 'The World we have Lost', London: Methuen.
LASLETT, P. (1972), Mean Household Size in England since the Sixteenth Century, in P. Laslett (ed.), 'Household and Family in Past Time', Cambridge: Cambridge University Press.
LASLETT, P. (1977), 'Family Life and Illicit Love in Earlier Generations', Cambridge: Cambridge University Press.
LASLETT, P. (1972), 'Family and Household in Past Time', Harmondsworth: Penguin.
LAW REFORM (Husband and Wife) Act 1962.

LAW SOCIETY (1979), Family Law Sub-Committee of the Law
Society, 'A Better Way Out', London: Law Society.
LAYARD, R. and PIACHAUD, D. (1978), 'The Causes of Poverty',
Royal Commission on the Distribution of Income and Wealth –
Background Paper no. 5, London: HMSO.
LEACH, E. (1968), The Cereal Packet Norm, 'The Guardian',
29 January.
LEE, B.H. (1974), 'Divorce Law Reform in England', London:
Peter Owen.
LEE, R.M. (1979), Communes as Alternative Families, MPhil
thesis, North East London Polytechnic.
LEESON, J. and GRAY, J. (1978), 'Women and Medicine', London:
Tavistock.
LEETE, R. (1969), Changing Patterns of Family Formation and
Dissolution in England and Wales, 1964-76, 'Studies on Medical
and Population Subjects', No. 39, OPCS.
LEETE, R. (1977), Changing Patterns of Marriage and Remar-
riage, in R. Chester and J. Peel (eds), 'Equalities and In-
equalities in Family Life', London: Academic Press.
LEETE, R. (1978), One-parent families: numbers and character-
istics, 'Population Trends', Autumn, London: HMSO.
LEETE, R. (1979), Changing Patterns of Family Formation and
Dissolution in England and Wales, 1964-76, 'OPCS Studies on
Medical and Population Subjects', no. 39, London: HMSO.
LEETE, R. and ANTHONY, S. (1979), Divorce and Remarriage: a
record linkage study, 'Population Trends', 16, Summer,
London: HMSO.
R v LEGATT (1852), 18 Q.B. 781.
LEONARD, D. (1980), 'Sex and Generation', London: Tavistock.
LEVIN, R.J. (1975), Sexual Pleasure: the surprising preferen-
ces of 100,000 women, in 'Redbook', 52.
LEVINE, J. (1976), 'Who Will Raise the Children? New Options
for Fathers (and Mothers)', Philadelphia: Lippincott.
LEWIS, P. (1979), Cutting Poverty in Half, 'One Parent Times',
Spring.
LIEBOW, E. (1967), 'Tally's Corner', Boston: Little, Brown &
Co.
LISTER, R. (1975), 'Social Security and the Case for Reform',
London: Child Poverty Action Group (Poverty Pamphlet 22).
LISTER, R. (1977), 'Patching up the Safety Net', London: CPAG.
LISTER, R. (1979), 'The No-Cost, No-Benefit Review', London:
CPAG.
LITWAK, E. (1960), Occupational Mobility and Extended Family
Cohesion, 'American Sociological Review', 25.
LOIZOS, P. (1975), 'The Greek Gift: politics in a Cypriot
village', Oxford: Basil Blackwell.
LOMAN, G.B.G. (1973), Census 1971, 'The Coloured Population of
Great Britain', Preliminary Report, London: Runnymede Trust.

LOMAS, P. (ed.) (1967), 'The Predicament of the Family',
London: Hogarth Press.
LOPATA, H.L. (1971), 'Occupation Housewife', New York: Oxford
University Press.
LUNN, J.E. and WRIGHT, C. (1971), Sheffield Problem Families,
'Community Medicine', 26 November.
LUPTON, T. and WILSON, C.S. (1970), The Kinship connections of
'Top Decision Makers', in P. Worsley (ed.), 'Introducing
Sociology', Harmondsworth: Penguin.
MACDONALD, G. (1976), 'Taxation and the Family Unit', Insti-
tute for Fiscal Studies.
McCLEMENTS, L.D. (1976), Equivalence Scales and the Wider
Analytical Framework, DHSS, unpublished.
McCUBBIN, H.I., DAHL, B.B. and HUNTER, E.J. (1976), 'Families
in the Military System', Beverly Hills: Sage.
McGREGOR, O.R. (1957), 'Divorce in England: a centenary
study', London: Heinemann.
McGREGOR, O.R., BLOM-COOPER, L. and GIBSON, C. (1970), 'Sepa-
rated Spouses', London: Duckworth.
McGREGOR, O.R. and ROWNTREE, G. (1962), The Family, in D.V.
Glass et al. (eds), 'Society, Problems and Methods of Study',
London: Routledge & Kegan Paul.
McINTOSH, M. (1978), The State and the Oppression of Women, in
A. Kuhn and A.M. Wolpe (eds), 'Feminism and Materialism: women
and modes of production', London: Routledge & Kegan Paul.
McKINLEY, D. (1964), 'Social Class and Family Life', New York:
Free Press.
McNAY, M. and POND, C. (1980), 'Low Pay and Poverty', London:
Study Commission On the Family.
MacCOBY, E.E. and JACKLIN, C.N. (1975), 'The Psychology of Sex
Differences', Stanford: Stanford University Press.
MACE, D. and MACE, V. (1964), 'The Soviet Family', London:
Hutchinson.
MACINTYRE, S. (1976), To Have or Have Not: Promotion and Pre-
vention in Gynaecological Work, in M. Stacey (ed.), 'The
Sociology of NHS', Keele: University of Keele.
MACKIE, L. and PATTULLO, P. (1977), 'Women at Work', London:
Tavistock.
MACPHERSON, C.B. (1964), 'The Political Theory of Possessive
Individualism: Hobbes to Locke', Oxford: Oxford University
Press.
MADAN, Rrilokinath (1965), 'Family and Kinship: a study of the
Pandits of rural Kashmir', Bombay: Asia Publishing House.
MADDOX, B. (1975), 'The Half-Parent', London: Andre Deutsch.
MALINOWSKI, B. and BRIFFAULT, R. (1956), 'Marriage: Past and
Present', Boston: Porter Sargent.
MALONE v HARRISON (1979), 1. W.L.R. 1352.
MANCHESTER/SALFORD INNER CITY PARTNERSHIP (1979), 'New Life

for the Inner Cities - the inner area programme 1979/80',
London: DoE.
MAPSTONE, E. (1969), Children in Care, 'Concern', vol. 3.
MARSDEN, D. (1968), Autobiographical Note, in R. Goldman
(ed.), 'Breakthrough', London: Routledge & Kegan Paul.
MARSDEN, D. (1969), 'Mothers Alone', London: Allen Lane.
MARSDEN, D. (1979), One Parent Families, in P. Townsend (ed.),
'Poverty in the UK', London: Allen Lane.
MARSH, A. (1979), 'Women and Shiftwork', OPCS, Social Survey
Division, London: HMSO.
MARTIN, R.W., BERRY, K.J. and JACOBSEN, R. (1975), The Impact
of Dual-Career Marriages on Female Professional Careers: an
empirical test of a Parsonian hypothesis, 'Journal of Mar-
riage and the Family', 37, pp. 734-43.
MASSON, J. and BURGOYNE, J. (1979), The English Stepfamily,
paper presented at the Third World Conference of the Inter-
national Society on Family Law, Uppsala, June.
MASTERS, W.J. and JOHNSON, V.E. (1970), 'Human Sexual Inade-
quacy', Boston: Little, Brown & Co.
MATRIMONIAL CAUSES ACT 1957 s. 26.
MARRIED WOMEN'S PROPERTY ACT 1870.
MARRIED WOMEN'S PROPERTY ACT (1870) Amendment Act 1974.
MARRIED WOMEN'S PROPERTY ACT (1882).
MARRIED WOMEN'S PROPERTY ACT 1893.
LAW REFORM (MARRIED WOMEN AND TORTFEASORS) ACT 1935.
MARRIED WOMEN (RESTRAINT ON ANTICIPATION) ACT 1949.
MATTHEWS, B. (1953), 'The Crisis in the West Indian Family',
Port of Spain: University of West Indies Press.
MAW, R. (1969), The construction of a leisure model, 'Official
Architecture and Planning'.
MAYO, M.M. (1976), The Responsibility of the Law in Relation
to Family Stability, 25, 'International and Comparative Law
Quarterly', p. 409.
MEAD, M. (1971), Anomalies in American Post-Divorce Relation-
ships, in P. Bohannan (ed.), 'Divorce and After', New York:
Doubleday.
MEAD, M. (1975), 'Blackberry Winter: my earlier years', New
York: Pocket Books.
MEADE COMMITTEE (1978), 'The Structure and Reform of Direct
Taxation', Institute of Fiscal Studies.
MEADES, M. (1972), 'Taken for a Ride: special residential
homes for confused old people', London: Longman.
MEIR, E.C. (1962), Former Foster Children as Adult Citizens,
PhD thesis, New York School of Social Work, Columbia Univer-
sity, cited in R. Dinnage and M.L. Kellmer-Pringle (1967),
'Foster Home Care, Facts and Fallacies', London: Longman.
MGM MARKETING RESEARCH AND SURVEYS (1978), 'Husbands and Wives
and Shopping for Food', available from MGM Marketing Research
and Surveys, Athene House, 67 Shoe Lane, London EC4.

MIDLAND BANK TRUST CO v GREEN (No. 3) (1979), 2 W.L.R. 594.

MILL, J.S. (1869), 'The Subjection of Women', ch. 2.

MILLER, C. and SWIFT, K. (1976), 'Words and Women', Harmondsworth, Penguin.

MILLER, J.H. (1978), 'Temple and Sewer': childbirth, prudery and Victoria Regina, in A. Wohl (ed.), 'The Victorian Family', London: Croom Helm.

MILLERSON, G. and GEORGE, V. (1967), The Cypriot Community in London, 'Race', 8, 3 (January), pp. 277-92.

MILLHAM, S., BULLOCK, R. and HOSIE, K. (1978), 'Locking Up Children', London: Saxon House.

MILLS, E. (1962), 'Living with Mental Illness', London: Routledge & Kegan Paul.

MILLS, R. (1973), 'Young Outsiders: a study of alternative communities', London: Routledge & Kegan Paul.

MILLUM, T. (1975), 'Images of Women: advertising in women's magazines', London: Chatto & Windus.

MILNE, J.D. (1857), 'Industrial and Social Position of Women in the Middle and Lower Ranks', London: Chapman & Hall.

MILNER, D. (1975), 'Children and Race', Harmondsworth: Penguin.

MITCHELL, J. and OAKLEY, A. (eds) (1976), 'The Rights and Wrongs of Women', Harmondsworth: Penguin.

MOLYNEUX, M. (1979), Beyond the Domestic Labour Debate, 'New Left Review', July/August, no. 111.

MOORE, R. and REX, J. (1967), 'Race, Community and Conflict', London: Oxford University Press.

MORGAN, D.H. (1975), 'Social Theory and the Family', London: Routledge & Kegan Paul.

MORGAN, D.H.J. (1977), Alternatives to the Family, in R. Chester and J. Peel (eds), 'Equalities and Inequalities in Family Life', London: Academic Press.

MORONEY, Robert M. (1975), 'The Family and the State: consideration for social policy', New York: Longmans.

MORTLOCK, B. (1972), 'The Inside of Divorce', London: Constable.

MOSS, P. (1976), The Current Situation, in N. Fonda and P. Moss (eds), 'Mothers in Employment', London: Brunel University Management Programme.

MOSS, P. (1980), Parents at work, in P. Moss and N. Fonda (eds), 'Work and Family', London: Maurice Temple-Smith.

MOSS, P. and FONDA, N. (eds) (1980), 'Work and Family', London: Maurice Temple-Smith.

MOYNIHAN, D. (1965), 'The Negro Family', Washington DC: US Office of Labour.

MURCH, M. (1980), 'Justice and Welfare in Divorce', London: Sweet & Maxwell.

NANDA v NANDA (1968), p. 351.

NAYLOR v NAYLOR (1962), p. 253.

NCSS (1979), 'The Inner Cities Programme Youth Employment and Recreation', London.

NEUGARTEN, B. and WEINSTEIN, K.K. (1969), The Changing American Grandparent, 'Journal of Marriage and the Family', May.

NEWSON, E. and NEWSON, J. (1970), 'Four Years Old in an Urban Community', London: Allen & Unwin (1968); Harmondsworth: Penguin.

NEWSON, E. and NEWSON, J. (1972), 'Infant Care in an Urban Community', Harmondsworth: Penguin.

NEWSON, J. and NEWSON, E. (1976), 'Seven Years Old in the Home Environment', London: Allen & Unwin.

NISSEL, M. (1978), 'Taxes and Benefits: does redistribution help the family?, London: PSI.

NISSEL, M. (1980), A greater place for family responsibility, in M. Nissel et al., 'The Welfare State: Diversity and Decentralization', Policy Studies Institute, Discussion Paper No. 2.

NORTH WEST SPORTS COUNCIL (NWSC) (1977), The Use of Non-purpose Built Facilities, mimeo.

NYE, F.I. (1963), The Adjustment of Adolescent Children, in F.I. Nye and L.W. Hoffman (eds), 'The Employed Mother in America', Chicago: Rand McNally.

OAKLEY, A. (1972), 'Sex, Gender and Society', London: Maurice Temple-Smith; New York: Harper & Row.

OAKLEY, Ann (1974), 'The Sociology of Housework', Oxford: Martin Robertson.

OAKLEY, A. (1979), 'Becoming a Mother', Oxford: Martin Robertson.

OAKLEY, A. and MITCHELL, J. (eds) (1976), 'The Rights and Wrongs of Women', Harmondsworth: Penguin.

OAKLEY, A. and OAKLEY, R. (1979), Sexism in Official Statistics, in Irvine et al. (eds), 'Demystifying Social Statistics', London: Pluto Press.

OAKLEY, R. (1970), The Cypriots in Britain, 'Race Today', 2 (April), pp. 99-102.

OAKLEY, R. (1971), Cypriot Migration to Britain, DPhil thesis, University of Oxford.

OAKLEY, R. (1979), The Cypriot Migration: Family, Kinship and Patronage, in V.S. Khan (ed.), 'Minority Families in Britain: support and stress', London: Macmillan.

OAKLEY, R. (in preparation), 'Cypriots in Britain: a Socio-economic profile'.

O'DONOVAN, K. (1978), The Male Appendage - Legal Definition of Women, in S. Burman (ed.), 'Fit Work for Females', London: Croom Helm.

O'DONOVAN, K. (1978), The Principles of Maintenance: An Alternative View, 8 'Family Law', p. 180.

OPCS (Social Survey Division) (1978), 'The General Household Survey 1976', London: HMSO.

OFFICE OF POPULATION CENSUSES AND SURVEYS (1978), 'Population Trends', no. 13 (August), London: HMSO.

OFFICE OF POPULATION CENSUSES AND SURVEYS (HMSO), 'Population Trends', No. 2 Winter 1975; no. 3 Spring 1976; no. 16 Autumn 1978; no. 17 Autumn 1979.

O'NEILL, N. and O'NEILL, G. (1973), 'Open Marriage: a new life style for couples', New York: Evans.

ONE-PARENT FAMILIES (1979), 'Annual Report', London: National Council for One-Parent Families.

OPCS (1979), 'Population Trends' no. 15 Spring, London: HMSO.

OREN, Laura (1974), The Welfare of Women in Laboring Families: England 1860-1950, in Mary S. Hartman and Louis W. Banner (eds), 'Clio's Consciousness Raised: new perspectives on the history of women', New York: Harper & Row.

PACKMAN, J. (1968), 'Child Care, Needs and Numbers', London: George Allen & Unwin.

PACKMAN, J. (1980), 'The Child's Generation', Oxford: Basil Blackwell.

PAGE, R. and CLARK, G.A. (eds) (1977), 'Who Cares? Young People in Care Speak Out', London: National Children's Bureau.

PAHL, J. (1978), 'A Refuge for Battered Wives', London: HMSO.

PAHL, J.M. and PAHL, R.E. (1971), 'Managers and Their Wives', London: Allen Lane, The Penguin Press.

PAPANEK, H. (1973), Men, Women and Work: reflections on the two-person career, 'American Journal of Sociology', vol. 78, no. 4, January, pp. 852-72.

PARKER, R.A. (1966), 'Decision in Child Care - a Study of Prediction in Fostering', London: George Allen & Unwin.

PARKER, R.A. (1973), Foreword in J. Rowe and L. Lambert, 'Children Who Wait', London: Association of British Adoption Agencies.

PARKER, R.A. (1978), Foster Care in Context, 'Adoption and Fostering', no. 93, pp. 27-32.

PARKER, R.A. (ed.) (1980), 'Caring for Separated Children', London: Macmillan.

PARKER, R. and LAND, H. (1978), in S.B. Kamerman and A.J. Kahn (eds), 'Family Policy', New York: Columbia.

PARKER, S. (1976), 'The Sociology of Leisure'.

PARSONS, Talcott (1961), An Outline of the Social System, in T. Parsons, E. Shils, K.D. Naegele and J.R. Pitts (eds), 'Theories of Society', New York: Free Press.

PATERSON, Alexander (1911), 'Across the Bridges, or Life by the South London River-side', London: Edward Arnold.

PATMORE, J. (1970), 'Land and Leisure', Newton Abbot, Devon: David & Charles; Harmondsworth: Penguin, 1972.
PATTERSON, Sheila (1963), 'Dark Strangers', London: Tavistock.
PEARL, D. (1972), Moslem Marriages in English Law, 'Cambridge Law Journal', 120 and Social Security and the Ethnic Minorities (1978-9), 'Journal of Social Welfare Law', 24.
PEARL, D. (1978), Legal Implications of a Relationship outside Marriage, 'Cambridge Law Journal', 252.
PENZANCE, LORD (1866), Hyde v Hyde, L.R. 1 P. & D. 130, at p. 133.
PEPITONE-ROCKWELL, F. (ed.) (1980), 'Dual Career Families', Beverley Hills: Sage.
PERISTIANY, J.G. (1965a), Honour and Shame in a Cypriot Highland Village, in J.G. Peristiany, 'Honour and Shame: the values of Mediterranean society', London: Weidenfeld & Nicolson.
PERISTIANY, J.G. (1965b), 'Honour and Shame: the values of Mediterranean society', London: Weidenfeld & Nicolson.
PERISTIANY, J.G. (1968), Introduction to a Cyprus Highland Village, in J.G. Peristiany (ed.), 'Contributions to Mediterranean Sociology', The Hague: Mouton.
PETTIGREW, Joyce (1976), 'Robber Noblemen', London: Routledge & Kegan Paul.
PETTITT, P.H. (1957), Parental Control and Guardianship, in R.H. Graveson and F.R. Crane (eds), 'A Century of Family Law', London: Sweet & Maxwell.
PHILLIPS, M. (1978), Family Policy: the Long Years of Neglect, 'New Society', 8 June.
PIACHAUD, D. (1979), 'The Cost of a Child', London: CPAG.
PILLING, D. and PRINGLE, M.L.K. (1978), 'Controversial Issues in Child Development', London: Elek.
PINCHBECK, Ivy (1930), 'Women Workers in the Industrial Revolution', London: Routledge & Kegan Paul.
PIOTROWSKI, J. (1971), The Employment of Married Women and the Changing Sex Roles in Poland', in A. Michel (ed.), 'Family Issues of Employed Women in Europe and America', Leiden: E.J. Brill.
PITT, B. (1973), Maternity Blues, 'British Journal of Psychiatry', 122, no. 669, pp. 431-3.
PITT-RIVERS, J. (1961), 'The People of the Sierra', Chicago: University of Chicago Press.
PITT-RIVERS, J. (ed.) (1963), 'Mediterranean Countrymen', The Hague: Mouton.
PLECK, J. and SAWYER, J. (eds) (1974), 'Men and Masculinity', Englewood Cliffs, NJ: Prentice-Hall.
PLOWDEN, B. (1967), 'Children and their Primary Schools', a report of the Central Advisory Council for Education (England), London: HMSO.

POCOCK, David (1972), 'Kanbi and Patidar: a study of the
Patidar community of Gujerat', Oxford: Clarendon Press.
POHLMAN, E.H. (1969), 'Psychology of Birth Planning',
Cambridge, Mass.: Shenkman.
POLLAK, M. (1972), 'Today's Three-Year-Olds in London',
London: Heinemann.
POLOMA, M. (1972), Role Conflict and the Married Professional
Woman, in C. Safilios-Rothschild (ed.), 'Toward a Sociology
of Women', Xerox College.
POND, C. (1978), 'The Poverty Trap', Milton Keynes: Open
University Press.
POWELL, K.S. (1963), Family variables, in F.I. Nye and
L.W. Hoffman (eds), 'The Employed Mother in America',
Chicago: Rand McNally.
PRADHAN, M.C. (1966), 'The Political Systems of the Jats of
Northern India', Bombay: Oxford University Press.
PRIESTLEY, P. et al. (1977), 'Justice for Juveniles',
London: Routledge & Kegan Paul.
PRINGLE M.L.K. (1974), 'The Needs of Children', London:
Hutchinson.
PROSSER, H. and WEDGE, P. (1973), 'Born to Fail', London:
National Children's Bureau/Arrow Books.
PROSSER, H. (1978), 'Perspectives on Foster Care', Slough:
NFER Publishing Co. Ltd.
PRYCE, K. (1978), 'Endless Pressure', Harmondsworth:
Penguin.
PUBLIC ATTITUDE SURVEYS (1979), 'Leisure Pools', London:
Study 19 Sports Council.
PUGH, E. (1968), 'Social Work in Child Care', London:
Routledge & Kegan Paul.
QUAZI v QUAZI (1979), 3 W.L.R. 402 C.A.
RAINWATER, L. (1966), Curcible of Identity: the Negro lower
class family, 'Daedalus', 95 (2), pp. 172, 216.
RAINWATER, L. (1970), 'Behind Ghetto Walls: Black family life
in a federal slum', Chicago: Aldine.
RAMEY, J. (1976), 'Intimate Friendships', Englewood Cliffs,
NJ: Prentice-Hall.
RAPOPORT, R.N. and RAPOPORT, R. (1975), Men, Women and Equity,
'Family Co-ordination', vol. 24, no. 4.
RAPOPORT, R. (1967), The Study of Marriage as a Critical
Transition for Personality and Family Development, in P.
Lomas (ed.), 'The Predicament of the Family', London:
Hogarth Press.
RAPOPORT, R. and RAPOPORT, R.N. (1971), 'Dual Career
Families', Harmondsworth: Penguin.
RAPOPORT, R. and RAPOPORT, R.N. (1975), with Z. Strelitz,
'Leisure and the Family Life Cycle', London: Routledge &
Kegan Paul.

RAPOPORT, R. (1976-7), On Parenting, 'Concern - Journal of the
National Children's Bureau (NCB)', London, 22, Winter, 13-18.
RAPOPORT, R. and RAPOPORT, R.N. (1976), 'Dual-Career Families
Re-examined', New York: Harper & Row; London: Martin
Robertson.
RAPOPORT, R.N. and RAPOPORT, R. (eds) with J. Bumstead,
'Working Couples', London: Routledge & Kegan Paul;
Australia: University of Queensland Press.
RAPOPORT, R. and OAKLEY, A. (1975), Towards a review of
parent-child relationships in social science, paper given at
working conference, Merrill-Palmer Institute, 10-12 November.
RAPOPORT, R., RAPOPORT, R.N., STRELITZ, Z. with KEW, S.
(1977), 'Fathers, Mothers and Others', London: Routledge &
Kegan Paul; New York: Basic Books and Vintage Books.
RAPOPORT, R. and RAPOPORT, R.N. (1980), The Impact of Work on
the Family, in P. Moss and N. Fonda (eds), 'Work and Family',
London: Maurice Temple-Smith.
RE v BEAUMONT (dec'd) (1979), 3 W.L.R. 818.
REDFORD, A. (1926), 'Labour Migration in England 1800-1850',
London: Kelly.
REES, A.D. (1950), 'Life in a Welsh Countryside', Cardiff:
University of Wales Press.
REES, A.M. (1976), Old People and the Social Services, Univer-
sity of Southampton.
REES, B.J. and COLLINS, M.F. (1979), The Family and Sport: a
review, in Z. Strelitz (ed.), 'Leisure Provision and Family
Diversity', London: Leisure Studies Association.
REGISTRAR GENERAL'S STATISTICAL REVIEW OF ENGLAND AND WALES
(1964).
REICH, C. (1964), The New Property, 72 'Yale Law Journal',
p. 733.
RENVOIZE, J. (1978), 'Web of Violence', London: Routledge &
Kegan Paul.
REPORT OF THE COMMISSION ON THE STATUS OF WOMEN (1972),
Dublin: Stationery Office.
REPORT OF THE COMMITTEE ON FAMILY POLICY, Sweden, 1972.
REPORT OF THE ROYAL COMMISSION ON THE POPULATION (1949), Cmnd
7695.
REPORT OF THE ROYAL COMMISSION ON MARRIAGE AND DIVORCE (1951-
1955), Chairman: Lord Morton of Henryton, Cmnd 9678, London:
HMSO, 1955.
REX, J. (1961), 'Key Problems of Sociological Theory', London:
Routledge & Kegan Paul.
REX, J. and MOORE, R. (1967), 'Race, Community and Conflict',
London: Oxford University Press.
RHEINSTEIN, M. (1972), 'Marriage Stability, Divorce and the
Law', Chicago: University of Chicago Press.

RICHARDS, M. (1976), The Mistress and the Family Home, 40 'Conveyancer' (New Series), 351.
RIGBY, A. (1974a), 'Alternative Realities: a study of communes and their members', London: Routledge & Kegan Paul.
RIGBY, A. (1974b), 'Communes in Britain', London: Routledge & Kegan Paul.
ROBERTS, J. (1979), The Commercial Sector in Leisure, Review for Sports Council/SSRC, London.
ROBERTS, K. (1978), 'Contemporary Society and the Growth of Leisure', especially pp. 93, 108, 126-30, 115-59, London: Longmans.
ROBINSON, J., CONVERSE, P. and SZALAI, A. (1972), Everyday Life in Twelve Countries, in A. Szalai (ed.), 'The Use of Time', The Hague: Mouton.
ROGERS, Susan (1975), Female Forms of Power and the Myth of Male Dominance, 'American Ethnologist'.
ROGERS, S.C. (1978), Women's Place: a critical review of anthropological theory, 'Comparative Studies in Society and History', 20, 1 (January), pp. 123-62.
ROLLINS, B.C. and FELDMAN, H. (1970), Mental Satisfaction Over the Family Life Cycle, 'Journal of Marriage and the Family', vol. XXXII, no. 1, February.
ROSENMAYR, L. (1968), Family Relations of the Elderly, 'Journal of Marriage and the Family', November.
ROSS, Aileen (1961), 'The Hindu Family in its Urban Setting', Toronto: University of Toronto Press.
ROSSER, C. and HARRIS, C.C. (1965), 'The Family and Social Change', London: Routledge & Kegan Paul.
ROSSI, Alice (1968), Transition to Parenthood, 'Journal of Marriage and the Family', vol. 30, no. 1.
ROSSI, A.S. (1972), Family Development in a Changing World, 'American Journal of Psychiatry', 128 (March), pp. 1957-65.
ROWE, J. (1976), 'Adoption in the Seventies', Association of British Adoption and Fostering Agencies.
ROWE, J. (1977), Fostering in the Seventies and Beyond, 'Adoption and Fostering', no. 90, pp. 15-20.
ROWE, J. and LAMBERT, L. (1973), 'Children Who Wait', London: Association of British Adoption and Fostering Agencies.
ROWNTREE, G. and CARRIER, N.H. (1958), The Resort to Divorce in England and Wales 1858-1957, 'Population Studies', vol. 11, pt 3, pp. 188-233.
ROWNTREE, J. (1901), 'Poverty, a Study of Town Life', London: Macmillan.
ROWNTREE, J. (1941), 'Poverty and Progress', London: Longmans, Green.
ROYAL COMMISSION ON THE TAXATION OF PROFITS AND INCOME (1954), Second Report, Cmnd 9105, London: HMSO, para. 158.

RUBIN, L.B. (1976), 'Worlds of Pain: life in the working-class family', New York: Basic Books.

RUNCIMAN, W.G. (1974), Occupational Class and the Assessment of Economic Inequality, in D. Wedderburn (ed.), 'Poverty, Inequality and Class Structure', Cambridge: Cambridge University Press.

RUTTER, M. (1972), 'Maternal Deprivation Reassessed', Harmondsworth: Penguin (reprinted 1974).

RUTTER, M. and MADGE, N. (1976), 'Cycles of Disadvantage: a review of research', London: Heinemann.

RUTTER, M., MAUGHAN, B., MORTIMORE, P. and OUSTON, J. (1979), 'Fifteen Thousand Hours: secondary schools and their effects on children', London: Open Books.

SACKS, M.P. (1977), Unchanging Times: a comparison of the everyday life of Soviet working men and women between 1923 and 1966, 'Journal of Marriage and the Family', November, pp. 793-805.

SAFILIOS-ROTHSCHILD, C. (1978), Handling unconventional asymmetrics, in R.N. Rapoport and R. Rapoport (eds), 'Working Couples', London: Routledge & Kegan Paul.

SAIFULLAH-KHAN, Verity (1976a), Pakistanis in Britain: Perceptions of a Population, 'New Community.

SAIFULLAH-KHAN, Verity (1976b), Purdah in the British Situation, in D.L. Barker and S.A. Allen (eds), 'Dependence and Exploitation in Work and Marriage', London: Longman.

SAIFULLAH-KHAN, Verity (1977), The Pakistanis, in J.L. Watson (ed.), 'Between Two Cultures', Oxford: Basil Blackwell.

SAIFULLAH-KHAN, Verity (1979a), Work and Network: South Asian women in South London, in S. Wallman (ed.), 'Ethnicity at Work', London: Macmillan.

SAIFULLAH-KHAN, Verity (1979b), Migration and Social Stress, in V. Saifullah-Khan (ed.), 'Minority Families in Britain', London: Macmillan.

SCHEUCH, E. (1960), Family Cohesion in Leisure Time, 'Sociological Review', 8, pp. 37-61.

SCHWENDIGER, H. and SCHWENDIGER, J. (1974), 'The Sociologists of the Chair', New York: Basic Books.

SCOTT, J.W. and TILLY, L.A. (1975), Woman's Work and the Family in Nineteenth Century Europe, 'Comparative Studies in Society and History', 17, 1, pp. 36-64.

SOCIAL AND COMMUNITY PLANNING RESEARCH (1979), Sport for all: involving non-participants, Report to Sports Council, London: SCPR.

SEEAR, B.N. (1971), 'Re-entry of women to the labour market after an interruption in employment', Paris: OECD.

SEEBOHM (1968), 'The Report of the Committee on Local Authority and Allied Personal Social Services', Cmnd 3730, London: HMSO.

SELECT (COBHAM) COMMITTEE OF THE HOUSE OF LORDS ON SPORT
AND LEISURE (1973), Report, HLP 193Y, London: HMSO.
SELECT COMMITTEE ON EUROPEAN COMMUNITIES (1977), Social
Security, House of Lords.
SENNET, R. (1970), 'Families against the City', London:
Oxford University Press.
SHAH, Arvind (1973), 'The Household Dimension in the Family in
India', Berkeley: University of California Press.
SHAH, Waris (1973), 'The Adventures of Hir and Ranjah', trans-
lated by F. Usborne, edited by Muntaz Hassan, London: Peter
Owen.
SHAMSHER, Joginder (1972), The Overtime People, in 'South
Asian Review'.
SHANAS, E. et al. (eds) (1968), 'Old People in Three Industri-
al Societies', London: Routledge & Kegan Paul.
SHANKLAND, G., WILLMOTT, P. and JORDON, D. (1977), Inner
London: policies for dispersal and balance, report of the
Lambeth Inner Area Study, London: HMSO.
SHARMA, Ursula (1971), 'Rampal and his family', London:
Collins.
SHAW, M. and LEBENS, K. (1976), Children Between Families,
'Adoption and Fostering', no. 84, pp. 17-28.
SHEARER, A. (1979), Tragedies Revisited 3, 'Social Work
Today', 23 January.
SHIELDS, S.A. (1975), Functionalism, Darwinism and the Psycho-
logy of Women: a study in social myth, 'American Psycholo-
gist' (July), pp. 739-54.
SHERWOOD, R. (1980), 'The Dynamics of Prejudice: Vicious and
Benign Spirals', Hassocks: Harvester.
SHORTER, E. (1977), 'The Making of the Modern Family', London:
Fontana.
SKOLNICK, A. and SKOLNICK, J.H. (1974), 'Intimacy, Family and
Society', Boston: Little, Brown & Co.
SILLITOE, K.K. (1969), 'Planning for Leisure', London: HMSO.
SILLITOE, K. (1979), Ethnic Origin, 1, 2 and 3, OPCS, Occa-
sional Papers Nos 8, 9 and 10, London: HMSO.
SIMEY, T.S. (1946), 'Welfare and Planning in the West Indies',
London: Oxford University Press.
SIMPSON, R. (1978), 'Day Care for School-Age Children',
Manchester: Equal Opportunities Commission.
SINFIELD, A. (1970), Poor and Out of Work in Shields, in P.
Townsend (ed.), 'The Concept of Poverty', London: Heinemann.
SLATER, E. and WOODSIDE, M. (1951), 'Patterns of Marriage',
London: Cassell.
SMART, E. (1978), 'The Assumption of the Rogues and Rascals',
London: Jonathan Cape.
SMART, C. and SMART, B. (eds) (1978), 'Women, Sexuality and
Social Control', London: Routledge & Kegan Paul.

SMITH, D. (1977), 'Racial Disadvantage in Britain' (for PEP, now PSI), Harmondsworth: Penguin.

SMITH, P.K. (1979), How Many People Can a Young Child Feel Secure With?, 'New Society', vol. 48, no. 869.

SMITH, R.T. (1956), 'The Negro Family in British Guiana', London: Routledge & Kegan Paul.

SMITH, D. and WHALLEY, A. (1975), 'Racial Minorities and Public Housing', London: PEP.

SMITH-ROSENBERG, C. (1974), Puberty to Menopause: the cycle of femininity in nineteenth-century America, in M. Hartman and L.W. Banner (eds), 'Clio's Consciousness Raised', New York: Harper & Row.

SOKOLOWSKA, M. (1978), in S.B. Kamerman and A.J. Kahn (eds), 'Family Policy', New York: Columbia.

SPINDLOW v SPINDLOW (1978), 3 W.L.R. 777.

STACEY, Margaret (1960), 'Tradition and Change - a Study of Banbury', London: Oxford University Press.

STACEY, M. (ed.) (1976), 'The Sociology of the NHS', Sociological Review Monograph, 22, Keele: University of Keele.

STACEY, M., BATSTONE, E., BELL, C. and MURCOTT, A. (1975), 'Power, Persistence and Change: a second study of Banbury', London: Routledge & Kegan Paul.

STACK, C. (1970), The Kindred of Viola Jackson, in N. Whitten and J. Szwed (eds), 'Afro-American Anthropology', New York: Free Press.

STEPHEN, J.F. (1883), 'A History of the Criminal Law of England', London: Macmillan, vol. II, ch. 25.

STEVENSON, O. (1968), Reception Into Care - Its Meaning for all Concerned, in R.J.N. Tod (ed.), 'Children in Care', London: Longmans, pp. 8-17.

STEVENSON, O. and HALLETT, C. (1977), 'Case Conferences', Keele: University of Keele.

STIMSON, G.V. (1976), GPs' 'Trouble' and Types of Patients, in M. Stacey (ed.), 'The Sociology of the NHS', Keele: University of Keele.

STIRLING, P. (1965), 'Turkish Village', London: Weidenfeld & Nicolson.

STONE, L. (1977), 'The Family, Sex and Marriage in England 1500-1800', London: Weidenfeld & Nicolson.

STONE, O. (1977), 'Family Law', London: Macmillan, ch. VII.

STREATHER, J. (1979), One parent families and leisure, in Z. Strelitz (ed.), 'Leisure Provision and Family Diversity', London: Leisure Studies Association.

STRELITZ, Z. (ed.) (1979), 'Leisure Provision and Family Diversity', London: Leisure Studies Association, Monograph no. 9.

SULLEROT, E. (1968), 'Histoire et Sociologie du Travail Féminin', Paris, Ganthier.

SUPPLEMENTARY BENEFITS COMMISSION ANNUAL REPORT (1976), para. 1.8, London: HMSO.

SUPPLEMENTARY BENEFITS COMMISSION (SBC) (1979), 'Response of the Supplementary Benefits Commission to Social Assistance', London: HMSO.

SYSON, L. and YOUNG, M. (1975), The Camden Survey, in M. Young (ed.), 'The Poverty Report', London: Maurice Temple-Smith.

SZALAI, Alexander (1972), 'The Use of Time', The Hague: Mouton.

TAINE, H. (1957), 'Notes on England', London: Thames & Hudson.

TALFOURD'S Custody of Infants Act 1839; Custody of Infants Act 1863; Guardianship of Infants Acts 1886 and 1925 consolidated as Guardianship of Minors Act 1971; Guardianship Act 1973.

TAYLOR, J.H. (1976), 'The Half Way Generation', London: NFER.

TEITELBAUM, M.S. (ed.) (1976), 'Sex Differences: social and biological perspectives', New York: Anchor Books.

THOMASSON, H. (1977), 'Charges for Indoor Sports Centres', London: Sports Council.

THOMSON, H. (1967), 'The Successful Stepparent: a practical guide', London: W.H. Allen.

THOMSON, H. (1979), 'The Adaptation of Existing Public Buildings for the Handicapped', London: PCL.

THORNES, B. and COLLARD, J. (1979), 'Who Divorces?', London: Routledge & Kegan Paul.

THORPE, R. (1974), The Social and Psychological Situation of the Long-Term Foster Child with Regard to his Natural Parents, unpublished PhD thesis, University of Nottingham.

THURLOW v THURLOW (1976), Fam. 128 (behaviour resulting from incurable illness).

TINKER, H. (1977), 'The Banyan Tree', London: Oxford University Press.

TITMUSS, R.M. (1962), 'Income Distribution and Social Change', London: Allen & Unwin.

TIZARD, B. (1977), 'Adoption, a Second Chance', London: Open Books.

TIZARD, J. (1976), Effects of day care on young children, in N. Fonda and P. Moss (eds), 'Mothers in Employment', Brunel University Management Programme.

TIZARD, J., MOSS, P. and PERRY, J. (1974), 'All on Children', London: Maurice Temple-Smith.

TOMLINSON, A. (1979), 'Leisure and the Role of Clubs and Voluntary Groups', Review for Sports Council/SSRC, London.

TONGE, W.L., JAMES, D.S. and HILLAM, S. (1975), 'Families without Hope', London: Royal College of Psychiatrists.

TOOMEY, D.M. (1971), Conjugal roles and social networks in an urban working class sample, 'Human Relations', 24, pp. 417-31.

TOVEY v TOVEY (1978), 8 Family Law, 80.

TOWNSEND, Peter (1957), 'Family Life of Old People, London: Routledge & Kegan Paul; Harmondsworth: Penguin (1963).

TOWNSEND, P. (1968), Welfare Services and the Family, in
E. Shanas et al. (eds), 'Old People in Three Industrial Socie-
ties', London: Routledge & Kegan Paul.
TOWNSEND, P. (1979a), 'Poverty in the United Kingdom: a survey
of household resources and standards of living', Harmondsworth:
Penguin.
TOWNSEND, P. (1979b), Reflections, 'Poverty', no. 44,
December.
TRASLER, C. (1960), 'In Place of Parents', London: Routledge
& Kegan Paul.
TRAVIS, A. and HUDSON, S. (1978), The Influence of Local
Authority Structures in Community Leisure and Culture, in
B. Rees and S. Parker (eds), 'Conference Papers, London: LSA.
TRAVIS, A., VEAL, A.J., DUESBURY, K. and WHITE, J. (1978),
'The Role of Central Government in Relation to the Leisure
Services in England and Wales', University of Birmingham:
CURS.
TRAVIS, A. (1979), 'The State and Leisure Provision', Review
for Sports Council/SSRC, London.
TRISELIOTIS, J. (1973), 'In Search of Origins', London: Rout-
ledge & Kegan Paul.
TRISELIOTIS, J. (1978), Growing up Fostered, 'Adoption and
Fostering', no. 94, pp. 11-23.
TUNNARD,J. (1979), 'Uniform Blues', Poverty Pamphlet no. 41,
London: Child Poverty Action Group.
TUNSTALL, J. (1962), 'The Fisherman', London: MacGibbon &
Kee.
TURNER, C. (1969), 'The Family and Kinship in Modern Britain',
London: Routledge & Kegan Paul.
TURNER, C. (1971), Dual Work Households and Marital Dissolu-
tion, 'Human Relations', 24, p. 6.
UNITED NATIONS (1979), 'Demographic Yearbook', Geneva: United
Nations.
VALENTINE, C. (1968), 'Culture and Poverty', Chicago: Univer-
sity of Chicago Press.
VATUK, Sylvai (1972), 'Kinship and Urbanization: white collar
migrants in North India', London: University of California
Press.
VOYSEY, M. (1975), 'A Constant Burden', London: Routledge &
Kegan Paul.
WAKEFORD, J. (1963), Fostering: a Sociological Perspective,
'British Journal of Sociology', vol. 14, no. 4, pp. 335-46.
WALKER, K. and WOODS, M.E. (1976), 'Time Use: a measure of
household production of family goods and services', New York:
American Home Economics Association.
WALLEY, J. (1972), 'Social Security: another British
failure?', London: Charles Knight.

WARD, C. (1979), Children's Leisure Needs in Differing Types of Family, in Z. Strelitz (ed.), 'Leisure Provision and Family Diversity', London: Leisure Studies Association.

WATSON, J.L. (ed.) (1977), 'Between Two Cultures: migrants and minorities in Britain', Oxford: Basil Blackwell.

WEBBER, R. and CRAIG, J. (1976), Which Local Authorities are Alike, 'Population Trends', 5, Autumn, London: OPCS/HMSO.

WEDDERBURN, D. and CRAIG, C. (1974), Relative Deprivation in Work, in D. Wedderburn (ed.), 'Poverty, Inequality and Class Structure', Cambridge: Cambridge University Press.

WEDGE, P. and PROSSER, H. (1973), 'Born to Fail?', London: National Children's Bureau/Arrow Books.

WEINSTEIN, E. (1960), 'The Self Image of the Foster Child', New York: Russell Sage Foundation.

WEISS, R.S. (1975), 'Marital Separation', Basic Books.

WEST v WEST (1978), Fam. 1.

WESTWOOD, Sallie and HOFFMAN, Dallah (1979), 'Asian Women: education and social change', Leicester: University of Leicester School of Education.

WEITZMAN, L. (1978), 'The Marriage Contract', Englewood Cliffs, NJ: Prentice-Hall.

WHITE, C.L. (1970), 'Women's Magazines 1963-1968', London: Michael Joseph.

WHYTE, W.H. (1956), 'The Organization Man', New York: Simon & Schuster.

WILLIAMS, G.L. (1947), The Legal Unity of Husband and Wife, 10 'Modern Law Review', p. 16.

WILLIAMS, P. and FERGUSON, N. (1969), The Identification of Children needing Compensatory Education, in 'Children at Risk', Schools Council Research Project in Compensatory Education no. 2.

WILLIAMS, R. (1958), 'Culture and Society', London: Chatto & Windus.

WILLIAMS, R. (1961), 'The Long Revolution', London: Chatto & Windus.

WILLIAMSON, N. (1976), Sex Preferences, Sex Control and the Status of Women, 'Signs: Journal of Women in Culture and Society', 1, 4, Summer.

WILLMOTT, P. (1963), 'Adolescent Youth in East London', London: Routledge & Kegan Paul.

WILLMOTT, P. and YOUNG, M. (1960), 'Family and Class in a London Suburb', London: Routledge & Kegan Paul.

WILLMOTT, P. and WILLMOTT, P. (1978), The age of family diversity, 'New Society', vol. 46, no. 846/7.

WILLMOTT, P. (1979), 'Growing up in a London Village', London: Peter Owen.

WILLMOTT, P. and MAYNE, S. (1980), 'Case Conference'.

WILSON, Amrit (1978), 'Finding a Voice: Asian women in Britain', London: Virago.

WILSON, E. (1977), 'Women and the Welfare State', London: Tavistock.

WILSON, H. and HERBERT, G.W. (1978), 'Parents and Children in the Inner City', London: Routledge & Kegan Paul.

WILSON v WILSON (1848), 1 H.L. Cas. 538.

THE (WOLFENDEN) COMMITTEE ON SPORT (1960), 'Sport and the Community', London: CCPR.

WOHL, A. (ed.) (1978), 'The Victorian Family', London: Croom Helm.

WOLINS, M. (1963), 'Selecting Foster Parents, the Ideal and the Reality', New York: Columbia University Press.

WOOD, A.D. (1974), 'The Fashionable Diseases': women's complaints and their treatment in nineteenth-century America, in M. Hartman and L.W. Banner (eds), 'Clio's Consciousness Raised', New York: Harper & Row.

WRIGHT, C. and LUNN, J.E. (1971), Sheffield Problem Families, 'Community Medicine', 26 November.

WRIGHT, T. (1857), 'Some Habits and Customs of the Working Classes', London: Tinsley Bros.

WYNN, M. (1972), 'Family Policy', Harmondsworth: Penguin.

YARROW, M.R., CLAUSEN, J.A. and ROBBINS, P.R. (1955), The Psychological Meaning of Mental Illness, 'Journal of Social Issues', 11, 4, pp. 33-48.

YORBURG, Betty (1973), 'The Changing Family', New York: Columbia.

YOUNG, M. (1952), Distribution of Income Within the Family, 'British Journal of Sociology', 3, pp. 305-20.

YOUNG, M. (ed.) (1975), 'The Poverty Report', London: Maurice Temple-Smith.

YOUNG, M. and RIGGE, M. (1979), 'Mutual Aid in a Selfish Society', London: Mutual Aid Press.

YOUNG, M. and WILLMOTT, P. (1957), 'Family Kinship in East London', London: Routledge & Kegan Paul.

YOUNG, M. and WILLMOTT, P. (1973), 'The Symmetrical Family', London: Routledge & Kegan Paul.

YUDKIN, S. and HOLME, A. (1963), 'Working Mothers and Their Children', London: Michael Joseph.

ZARETZKY, Eli (1976), 'Capitalism, the Family and Personal Life', London: Pluto.

ZWEIG, F. (1952), 'The British Worker', London: Gollancz.

Index